READINGS IN CHURCH AUTHORITY

The issues of Authority and Governance in the Roman Catholic Church permeate each and every aspect of the Church's identity, teaching, influence, organisation, moral values and pastoral provision. They have left their mark, in turn, upon its diverse theological and philosophical traditions. The trends of postmodernity, advances in communication, the advent of new ecclesial movements and theologies, and a perceived policy towards increasing institutional centralisation on the part of the Curial authorities of the Church in Rome, have all facilitated a continuous and lively stream of dialogue and disagreement on authority and governance in relation to the place of the Church in our age and the new Millennium.

This comprehensive Reader uniquely gathers together in one volume key writings and documents from the wealth of published literature that has emerged on the issues of authority and governance in the Roman Catholic Church. With guided introductions to each section and to each reading, and end of chapter further reading lists, this Reader offers a balanced range of perspectives, themes, international writings, ecumenical dimensions, and formal church documents and Papal pronouncements on core areas of contemporary study and debate.

Focusing on the modern/post-modern period in the Roman Catholic Church, but grounded in the historical contexts, *Readings in Church Authority* presents an accessible source book and introduction for all those exploring current debates and studying central themes in church authority.

For David Barker

– who has worked tirelessly to promote conversations about authority in the church.

Authority, then, is not an external influence streaming down from heaven like a sunbeam through a cleft in the clouds and with a finger of light singling out God's arbitrarily chosen delegates from the multitude, over and apart from which they are to stand as his vice-regents. Authority is something inherent in, and inalienable from, that multitude itself; it is the moral coerciveness of the Divine Spirit of Truth and Righteousness inherent in the whole, dominant over its several parts and members: it is the imperativeness of the collective conscience. (George Tyrrell, *Through Scylla and Charybdis, or the Old Theology and the New*, London, Longmans, Green, and Co., 1907.)

READINGS IN CHURCH AUTHORITY

Gifts and challenges for contemporary Catholicism

Edited by

GERARD MANNION
RICHARD GAILLARDETZ
JAN KERKHOFS
KENNETH WILSON

ASHGATE

Published by
Ashgate Publishing Limited
Gower House
Croft Road
Aldershot
Hants GU11 3HR
England

Ashgate Publishing Company
Suite 420
101 Cherry Street
Burlington, VT 05401-4405
USA

Ashgate website: http://www.ashgate.com

British Library Cataloguing in Publication Data
Readings in church authority : gifts and challenges for
   contemporary Catholicism
   1. Catholic Church - Government 2. Catholic Church -
   Doctrines 3. Authority - Religious aspects - Catholic Church
   I. Mannion, Gerard
   262'.02

Library of Congress Cataloging-in-Publication Data
Readings in church authority : gifts and challenges for contemporary Catholicism /
edited by Gerard Mannion ... [et al.].
      p. cm.
   Includes bibliographical references and index.
   ISBN 0-7546-0530-2 (alk. paper)
      1. Church--Authority. 2. Catholic Church--Doctrines. I. Mannion, Gerard, 1970-

   BX1746.R39 2002
   262'.02--dc21

                                                                      2002016000

   ISBN 0 7546 0530 2

Printed and bound in Great Britain by MPG Books Ltd, Bodmin, Cornwall

CONTENTS

ACKNOWLEDGEMENTS

The editors wish to express their gratitude to all who engaged in the many conversations which helped to bring this volume into existence. In particular, all the members of the Queen's Foundation Working Party on Authority and Governance in the Roman Catholic Church. Our deep gratitude, also, to Sarah Lloyd and Claire Annals at Ashgate for their continuous advice and support. Many, many thanks, also, to those who assisted with typing and transcribing: Mary Veling, Wendy Lee, Dorothy Knowles, Sylvia Simpson and Kathryn Stenton. We received invaluable help and advice, also, from Mark Chapman, Michael Fahey, Frank Sullivan, Ida Rosa Maria Speranza and Sean Falati.

We have sought, where possible the permission of individual authors but apologise for any omissions. Thanks are also due to the following authors, original publishers or other copyright holders for permission to reproduce the readings included in this book as follows:

Extracts from: Hans Urs von Balthasar: *Who is the Church?* – 1961
From *Spouse of the Word*, vol. II of Explorations in Theology, SanFrancisco, Ignatius Press, 1991. *ET* by A.V. Littledale with Alexander Dru. With kind permission from Ignatius Press.

Extracts from: Leonardo Boff: *The Reinvention of the Church* – 1986
From *Ecclesiogenisis – The Base Communities Reinvent the Church*, London, Collins Flame, 1986 © Leonardo Boff with kind permission of the author.

Extracts from: Avery Dulles: *The Use of Models in Ecclesiology* – 1988
From *Models of the Church – A Critical Assessment of the Church in All Its Aspects*, Dublin, Gill and Macmillan, 2nd edn., 1988, pp. 15–33. Copyright © 1974 by Avery Dulles. Used by permission of Doubleday, a division of Random House, Inc.

Extracts from: Elisabeth Schüssler Fiorenza: *The Ekklēsia of Women* – 1993
From *Discipleship of Equals – The Ethics and Politics of Liberations*, SCM Press Ltd., 1993, pp. 344–52. Used by permission of SCM Press Ltd.

Extracts from: Alvaro Quiroz Magaña: *Ecclesiology in the Theology of Liberation* – 1966
From *Systematic Theology – Perspectives from Liberation Theology*, Jon Sobrino and Ignacio Ellacuria (eds), London, SCM 1996, 178–193. Used by permission of SCM Press Ltd.

Extracts from: *Doctrinal Definition*, 7th General Council, 2nd Council of Nicaea – 787
From Tanner, I, 133. With kind permission by Georgetown University Press.

Extracts from: *First Decree*, Council of Trent – 1546
ET From Tanner, Norman: *Decrees of the Ecumenical Councils*, Oxford, Washington, Georgetown University Press, 1990, II, 808–9. With kind permission by Georgetown University Press.

Extracts from: *Dei Filius* – 1870
ET from Tanner, Norman: *Decrees of the Ecumenical Councils*, Oxford, Washington, Georgetown University Press, 1990, II, pp. 808–9. With kind permission by Georgetown University Press.

Extracts from: Giovanni Colombo: *Obedience to the Ordinary Magisterium* – 1967
From *Seminarium*, new series, year VII, no. 3 July–September, 1967; *ET. Obedience and the Church*, London, Geoffrey Chapman, 1968. With kind permission from Geoffrey Chapman Publishing (Continuum Publishing Ltd).

Extracts from: Francis A. Sullivan: *Weighing and Interpreting the Documents of the Magisterium: What is it? Why do it?* – 1966
From Francis Sullivan: *Creative Fidelity*, London and Dublin, Gill & Macmillan, 1996, pp. 18–25. Used by kind permission of the author and publishers, Gill & Macmillan, Dublin.

Extracts from: Christof Theobald: *The 'Definitive' Discourse of the Magisterium: Why be Afraid of a Creative Reception?* – 1999
From *Unanswered Questions*, Christoph Theobald and Dietmar Mieth (eds), in *Concilium*, (1999), pp. 60–69. With kind permission by T&T Clark (Continuum International Publishing Group Ltd).

Extracts from: John L. McKenzie: *The Tension between Authority and Freedom* – 1966
From *Authority in the Church*, London, Geoffrey Chapman, 1966, chapter 13, pp. 162–74. With kind permission of Geoffrey Chapman (Continuum Publishing Ltd).

Extracts from: Yves Congar: *A brief History of the Forms of the Magisterium and Its Relation with Scholars* – 1982
From C.E. Curran and R.A. McCormack (eds), *The Magisterium and Morality*, New York, Paulist Press, 1982, pp. 322–328. Used with permission of the Director, *Revue des Sciences Philosophiques et Théologiques*.

Extracts from: Karl Rahner: *The Teaching Office of the Church in the Present Day Crisis of Authority* – 1969
From *Theological Investigations*, vol. 12: *Confrontations II*, London, Darton, Longman and Todd, 1974, pp. 23–30 with kind permission of publishers.

Extracts from: John Boyle: *Natural Law and Magisterium – Critical and Constructive Reflections* – 1995
From *Church of Teaching Authority: Historical and Theological Studies*, Notre Dame and London, University of Notre Dame Press, 1995, pp. 53–62. © 1995 University of Notre Dame Press. Used by Permission.

Extracts from: Rudolf Schnakenburg: *Community Co-operation in the New Testament* – 1972
From G. Alberigo and A. Weiler (eds) *Election Consensus, Reception*, in *Concilium*, 7 (1972), 5, pp. 9–19. With kind permission of *Concilium*.

Extracts from: Herwi Rikhof: *Vatican II and the Collegiality of Bishops* – 1994
From J. Provost and K. Walf (eds), *Collegiality put to the Test*, in *Concilium* (1990), 4, pp. 3–17. With kind permission of *Concilium*.

Extracts from: Joseph Ratzinger: *The Pastoral Implications of Episcopal Collegiality* – 1965
From *The Church and Mankind*, in *Concilium* (1965), 1, pp. 39–67. With kind pemission of
Concilium.

Extracts from: Charles M. Murphy: *Collegiality – An Essay toward better Understanding* – 1985
From *Theological Studies*, 46 (1985), pp. 38–49. Used with permission of the editor of
Theological Studies.

Extracts from: Ludwig Kaufmann: *Synods of Bishops: Neither 'concilium' nor 'synodos'* – 1990
From J. Provost and K. Walf (eds), *Collegiality put to the Test*, in *Concilium* (1990), 4, pp.
67–78. With kind permission of *Concilium*.

Extracts from: Karl Lehmann: *On the Dogmatic Justification for a Process of Democratization in
the Church* – 1971
From *Concilium* (1971), 7, pp. 60–86. With kind permission of *Concilium*.

Extracts from: Guiseppe Alberigo: *Ecclesiology and Democracy – Convergences and Divergences*
– 1992
From J. Provost and K. Walf (eds), *The Tabu of Democracy within the Church*, in *Concilium*
(1992), 5, pp. 14–26. With kind permission of *Concilium*.

Extracts from: Peter Huizing: *Subsidiarity* – 1986
From G. Alberigo and J. Provost (eds), *Synod 1985 – An Evaluation*, in *Concilium* (1986),
pp. 118–123. With kind permission of *Concilium*.

Extracts from: Wilhelm de Vries: *The College of Patriarchs* – 1965
From *Concilium – Canon Law* (1965), 8, pp. 35–43. With kind permission of *Concilium*.

Extracts from: *Pastor aeternus* – 1870
ET: Tanner, Norman: *Decrees of the Ecumenical Councils*, Oxford, Washington, Georgetown
University Press, 1990, II: pp. 813–16. With kind permission of Georgetown University
Press.

Extracts from: *Declaration of the German Episcopate* – 1875
From 'Collective Declaration of the German Episcopate on the Circular of the Imperial
German Chancellor concerning the Next Papal Election'. Originally issued in 1875. English
translation is taken from an appendix in Hans Küng, *Council and Reunion*, pp. 284–91, New
York: Sheed & Ward, 1961. With kind permission of Hans Küng.

Extracts from: Karl Rahner: *On the Relation between the Pope and and the College of Bishops* –
1977
From *Theological Investigations*, Volume X, pp. 50–59. New York: Seabury, 1977. Copyright
© 1977. All rights reserved. Used with permission of The Crossroad Publishing Company,
New York.

Extracts from: Yves Congar: *The Pope as Patriarch of the West* – 1991
From *Theology Digest*, 38 (Spring, 1991), pp. 3–7. French original: 'Le Paper comme
patriarche d'Occident', *Istine*, 28 (Oct–Dec., 1983), pp. 374–90.

Extracts from: Patrick Granfield: *The Possibility of Limitation* – 1987
From Granfield, Patrick: *The Limits of the Papacy*, pp. 51–76. New York, Crossroad, 1987. ©
Patrick Granfield. Used with kind permission of the author.

Extracts from: Hermann Pottmeyer: *Papacy in Communion – Perspectives on Vatican II* – 1988
From Pottmeyer, Hermann: *Towards a Papacy in Communion: Perspectives from Vatican
Councils I & II*, pp. 110, 112–17, 129–36, New York, Crossroad, 1998. © 1988. All rights
reserved. Used with kind permission of the author and Crossroad Publishing Company, New
York.

Extracts from: John R. Quinn: *The Exercise of the primacy – Facing the Cost of Christian Unity*
– 1996
From *Commonwealth* (July 12, 1996), pp. 11–20. Used with kind permission of the author.

Extracts from: Avery Dulles: *The Papacy for a Global Church* – 2000
From *America I* (July 15–22, 2000), pp. 6–11. Copyright 2000 by America Press, Inc. All
rights reserved. Used with permission.

Extracts from: Ladislas Orsy: *The Papacy for an Ecumenical Age – A Response to Avery Dulles* –
2000
From *America*, October 21, 2000. Copyright 2000 by America Press, Inc. All rights reserved.
Used with permission.

Extracts from: Christian Duquoc: *An Active Role for the People of God in Defining the Church's
Faith* – 1985
From *The Teaching-authority of the Believers*, J.B. Metz and E. Schillebeeckx (eds), in
Concilium, 180 (1985), 4, pp. 73–81. With kind permission of *Concilium*.

Extracts from: Karl Rahner: *What the Church Officially Teaches and what the People Actually
Believe* – 1981
From *Theological Investigations*, vol. XXII, *Human Society and the Church of Tomorrow*,
London, 1991, pp. 165–175. Used with permission of publishers.

Extracts from: Yves Congar: *Towards a Catholic Synthesis* – 1981
From *Who has the Say in the Church*, J. Moltman and H. Küng (eds), in *Concilium*, 148/8
(1981), pp. 68–80. With kind permission of *Concilium*.

Extracts from: Yves Congar: *Reception as an Ecclesiological Reality* – 1972
From *Election and Consensus in the Church*, G. Alberigo and A. Weiler (eds), in *Concilium*, 77
(1972), pp. 43–68. With kind permission of *Concilium*.

Extracts from: Hermann Pottmeyer: *Reception and Submission* – 1991
From *The Jurist*, 51 (1991), pp. 269–292. With kind permission of the author and *The Jurist*.

Extracts from: Thomas P. Rausch: *Reception Past and Present* – 1986
From *Theological Studies*, 47 (1986), pp. 497–508. With kind permission of the editor,
Theological Studies.

Extracts from: Ladislas Orsy: *Participation and the Nature of the Church* – 1988
From *Priests and People*, vol. 2 (1988), pp. 356–362.

Extracts from: Hans Urs Von Balthasar: *The Place of Theology* – 1960
From *The Word made Flesh*, vol. I of *Explorations in Theology*, San Francisco, Ignatius Press, 1989. With kind permission of Ignatius Press.

Extracts from: Hans Küng: *Who is a Catholic Theologian?* – 1980
From the postscript to the English Edition of *The Church – Maintained in Truth*, London, SCM, 1980, pp. 80–87. Used with permission of SCM Press Ltd.

Extracts from: Francis A. Sullivan: *The Magisterium and the Role of Theologians in the Church* – 1983
From *Magisterium – Teaching Authority in the Roman Catholic Church*, Dublin, Gill & Macmillan, 1983, pp. 190–218. With kind permission of the author and Paulist Press.

Extracts from: Marc Reuver: *Emerging Theologies – Firth Through Resistance* – 1993
From *The Ecumenical Movement Tomorrow*, Marc Reuver, Friedrich Solms and Gerrit Huizer (eds), Kampen, Kok Publishing, 1993, pp. 263–80. Used with kind permission of the author.

Extracts from: Roger Haight: *The Church as the Locus of Theology* – 1994
From *Why Theology?*, in *Concilium*, 1994, 6, pp. 13–22. With kind permission of the author and of *Concilium*.

Extracts from: Linda Hogan: *A Theology for the Future* – 1995
From *From Women's Experience to Feminist Theology*, Sheffield, Sheffield Academic Press, 1995, pp. 163–77. Used with kind permission of the author.

Extracts from: Karl Rahner: *Considerations on the Development of Dogma* – 1957
From *Theological Investigations*, vol. 4, London, DLT, 1966, pp. 3–7; 24–27. Used by permission of the publishers.

Extracts from: Karl Rahner: *The Development of Dogma* – 1961
From *Theological Investigations*, vol. 1, London, DLT, 1961 (2nd ed., 1965), pp. 63–65. Used with permission of the publishers.

Extracts from: Yves Congar: *Tradition and Traditions* – 1966
From Congar, Yves: *Tradition and Traditions – An Historical and Theological Essay*, London, Burns and Oates, 1966, pp. 14–17; 29–36.

Extracts from: Johann Baptist Metz: *Tradition and Memory* – 1980
From Metz, Johann Baptist, *Faith in History and Society*, ET. David Smith, London, Burns and Oates, 1980, pp. 184–5; 189–197. German original, published 1977.

Extracts from: Paul Avis: *Consensus and Criticism* – 1986
From Avis, Paul: *Ecumenical Theology and the Elusiveness of Doctrine*, London, SPCK, 1986, pp. 66–75.

Extracts from: Avery Dulles: *Catholicity at Length – Tradition and Development* – 1985
From Dulles, Avery: *The Catholicity of the Church*, Oxford, Clarendon Press, 1985, pp. 93–103. © Avery Dulles, S.J. 1985. Used by permission of Oxford University Press.

Extracts from: Hans Küng: *The Permanent Necessity of Renewal In The Church* –1961
From *The Council and Reunion*, pp. 14–52. London and New York, Sheed & Ward, 1961. ©
Hans Küng. With kind permission of the author.

Extracts from: Yves Congar: *Renewal of the Spirit and Reform of the Institution* – 1961
From *Ongoing Reform of the Church*, Alois Müller and Norbert Greinacher (eds), in
Concilium, vol. 73, pp. 39–49, New York, Herder and Herder, 1972. With kind permission
from *Concilium*.

Extracts from: John W. O'Malley: *Reform, Historical Consciousness and Vatican II's
Aggiornamento* – 1971
From *Theological Studies*, 32 (1971), pp. 573–601. With kind permission of the author and
the editor of *Theological Studies*.

Extracts from: Avery Dulles: *'Ius Divinum' As An Ecumenical Problem* – 1977
From *Theological Studies*, 38 (Dec. 1977), pp. 681–708. With kind permission of the editor
of *Theological Studies*.

Extracts from: Leonardo Boff: *The Power of the Institutional Church – Can it be Converted?* –
1981
From *Church, Charism and Power – Liberation Theology and the Institutional Church*, New
York, Crossroad, 1985, pp. 47–64. Used with kind permission of the author.

Extracts from: Rosemary Radford Ruether: *The Ecclesiology of Women-Church: Ministry and
Community* – 1985
From *Women-Church – Theology and Practice of Feminist Liturgical Communities*, pp. 75–95,
San Francisco, Harper & Row, 1985. With kind permission by HarperCollins Publishers Inc.

Extracts from: Joseph Ratzinger: *A Company in Constant Renewal* – 1990
From *Called to Communion – Understanding the Church Today*, pp. 133–56, San Francisco,
Ignatius, 1996. With kind permission of Ignatius Press.

LIST OF ABBREVIATIONS

AAS	*Acta Apostolica Sedis*
ASS	*Acta Sanctae Sedis*
CDF	Congregation for the Doctrine of the Faith
CIC	*Codex Iuris Canonici*
CSEL	*Corpus scriptorum ecclesiasticorum latinorum*
D	H. Denzinger, *Enchiridion Symbolorum, Definitionum et Declarationum de Rebus Fidei et Morum*
DH	*Dignitatis Humanae* – Vatican II's *Declaration on Religious Freedom*
DSch/DS	H. Denzinger and A. Schonmetzer, *Enchiridium Symbolorum, Definitionum et Declarationum de Rebus Fidei et Morum*
DV	*Dei Verbum* – Vatican II's *Dogmatic Constitution on Divine Revelation*
EB	*Enchiridion Biblicum*
ET	English translation
GS	*Gaudium et Spes* – Vatican II's *Pastoral Constitution on the Church in the Modern World*
HE	*Historia Ecclesiastica*
LG	*Lumen Gentium* – Vatican II's *Dogmatic Constitution on the Church*
MANSI	J.D. Mansi, *Sacrorum Concilium Nova et Amplissima collectio*, Florence (31 vols), 1759–98
PG	J.-P. Migne (ed.), *Patrologia Graeca*, 161 vols (1857ff)
PL	J.-P. Migne (ed.), *Patrologia Latina*, 217 vols + 4 index vols (1844ff)
Tanner	Tanner, Michael, *Decrees of the Ecumenical Councils* (Oxford, Washington, Georgetown University Press, 1990)
WA	Weimarer Ausgabe (edition)

THE EDITORS

Professor Richard R. Gaillardetz holds the Murray/Bacik Chair of Catholic Studies at the University of Toledo. He has published numerous articles and four books: *Witnesses to the Faith – Community, Infallibility and the Ordinary Magisterium of Bishops* (New York: Paulist, 1992); *Teaching with Authority – a Theology of the Magisterium in the Roman Catholic Church* (Collegeville: Liturgical Press, 1997); *Transforming our Days – Spirituality, Community and Liturgy in a Technological Culture* (New York, Crossroad, 2000); and *A Daring Promise – Toward a Spirituality of Christian Marriage* (New York, Crossroad, 2002). In 2000, he was the recipient of the Sophia Award, an honour offered annually by the faculty of the Washington Theological Union in Washington, DC, in recognition of a theologian's outstanding contributions to the life of the Church.

Professor Jan Kerkhofs, SJ, is a Jesuit and Emeritus Professor of Pastoral Theology in the Catholic University of Louvain in Belgium. He was co-chair of, and the inspiration behind, the European Values Study and founded 'Pro Mundi Vita' (a Vatican II-inspired research, information and co-ordination agency concerned with pastoral issues). His many publications include *Europe without Priests* (ed.) (London, SCM, 1995) and *A Horizon of Kindly Light* (London, SCM, 1998).

Dr Gerard Mannion is Lecturer in Systematic Theology, Ecclesiology and Ethics at Trinity and All Saints University College, Leeds, UK. Educated at King's College, Cambridge and New College, Oxford, he previously taught Philosophy, Doctrine and Ethics at Westminster College, Oxford and was a member of the Queen's Foundation Working Party on Authority and Governance in the Roman Catholic Church. He is the author of *Schopenhauer, Religion and Morality - the Humble Path to Ethics* (Aldershot, Ashgate, 2003) and the forthcoming *Ecclesiology and Postmodernity – a New Paradigm for the Church?*

The Reverend Dr Kenneth Wilson was, until his recent retirement, Director of Research of the Queen's Foundation for Ecumenical Theological Education in Birmingham, UK. He was formerly a lecturer at Wesley College, Bristol, UK, Principal of Westminster College, Oxford, and a member of the Faculty of Theology of the University of Oxford. He was also a member of the Queen's Foundation Working Party on Authority and Governance in the Roman Catholic Church. Amongst his publications is *Making Sense of It* (London, Epworth, 1973) and he is currently working on a book on Theology and Globalization entitled *Accounting for the Future.*

VOLUME FORMAT AND ADVICE TO READERS

The volume is divided into eight parts, each one of which focuses upon a major theme prevalent in the debates today, but which also has served as the basis of significant discussion throughout the history of the Church. Each part is a separate entity in its own right. A certain degree of editorial licence has been permitted in view of the differing natures and complexities of each part's topic. As a rule, footnotes from original sources have been retained where they are referential. Where supportive and/or expansive, it has been mostly left to the individual editor's discretion whether to retain or omit further footnotes. Decisions in this respect have been dictated by the part editor's opinion of the need for detailed footnotes to aid exposition relevant to the nature of the topic or where he has felt that their omission will bring greater clarity to the reader's study of the text.

Each of the thematic parts has its own brief introduction. The purpose of such introductions is to explicate the theme for each part. At the end of the volume, readers will find biographical details for each of the authors whose work is included as well as of those popes under whose name the featured encyclicals were released.

Each part contains a variety of readings from differing perspectives, including excerpts from key church documents and papal pronouncements. The parts are by no means intended to be exhaustive nor even definitive, but *indicative* of the nature of debate upon each topic and of the diversity of opinion which exists in relation to the topics under consideration. An ornament ✿ marks the start of each reading.

Each part concludes with a section containing questions for study, reflection and discussion and recommended further reading. For the church documents recommended in these sections, except where stated otherwise, consult the relevant pages of the Vatican archives at www.vatican.va.

The parts and readings are arranged, primarily, in a *pedagogical* rather than a simple historical or hierarchical fashion.

Each reading is also briefly introduced to indicate the main argument(s) and/or significance of the reading itself. Where deemed necessary, the historical background to a reading is also sketched. In certain cases, extracts have been quoted at greater length. This is on account of either their particular importance (e.g. a seminal church document of relevance to many of our chapter themes such as *Lumen Gentium*, or a highly influential essay), or the desire to make a certain text available to a wider audience (perhaps on account of its being out of print or its particularly original or epitomizing treatment of the themes at hand). In other cases, especially with regard to some church documents, shorter extracts have been included. In some instances, this is because other elements of that document have been included in another chapter of this volume (and so only the most essential sections relevant to the particular chapter are included). In other cases it is to accentuate certain church teachings in particular, or because the readings in that chapter discuss the church documents relevant to that part's primary subject at length in themselves (the latter being particularly the case in Parts 3 and 5, which contain few church documents).

For twentieth-century church documents, it was decided to employ an 'official' translation, as included in the public Vatican archives (made available at www.vatican.va).* This is for reasons of: a) consistency, b) accessibility for readers and the encouragement of technological advances in ecclesiological study, and c) as they represent 'approved' translations of the church's institutional voice, whence these documents originated (e.g. publications such as *Origins* utilize the same translations for recent documents). It is recognized that other editions of translations of certain documents are preferred in many quarters and that some readers might take issue with elements of the language employed in parts of these documents. However, many of these translations represent the language which the institutional church wishes to be employed and the many debates which follow from the implications of these translations cannot be artificially overlooked by the employment of other translations in an educational resource, such as this reader seeks to be. Nonetheless, in certain church documents, we have substituted inclusive terms for 'layman' and 'laymen', as the texts clearly are referring to lay people of both sexes.

All text in [square brackets] is an editorial interpolation, save in official church documents, which have their original section number contained therein, e.g. [4]. All text in the extracts which is in italics or with particular emphasis, has been represented as in the original.

---

* References will be to the relevant *index* in the Vatican archives which provides access to each document via a link under each text's title.

INTRODUCTION: GIFTS AND CHALLENGES FOR THE ROMAN CATHOLIC CHURCH TODAY

Gerard Mannion

Walter Bühlmann concluded his paper on 'The New Ecclesiology of Vatican II', with these words: 'We live in an extraordinarily great Church-time and we probably speak too much of the crisis of the Church and too little of the challenge and chance of the Church.'[1] Undoubtedly, there has been much talk of the 'crisis of authority' in the Roman Catholic church for at least three decades or more. This present volume wishes to contribute to the effort to move the debates forward in a positive fashion. It does so by seeking to provide an educational and reflective resource. Instead of focusing, however, on the negative value-judgmental term of 'crisis' (whoever is deeming it to be a crisis, from whatever ecclesial standpoint), the editors wish to highlight the myriad of issues surrounding the topic of authority in the Roman Catholic church today, and the inseparable topic of governance, as elements of ecclesial life and ecclesiological concern for our times which might best be regarded both as *gifts* and as *challenges*. One may perceive a challenge in a negative light, but one may also see it as an opportunity to inspire or energize one to move on to better things beyond the Status Quo. It is in this light that we see the debates concerning authority today as a challenge – indeed a very positive *set of challenges*. But for any challenge to become positive, it must be met with on positive terms. It must be taken up in a spirit of willingness and determination. It is a task to be confronted, performed. To 'resolutely take the way' initiated by Christ, is to meet the challenges posed to the Christian community/ies today.

The concerns surrounding authority should also be seen as something providential: Christianity bears witness to a providential God, who has not left us alone. It is in this light that the Second Anglican-Roman Catholic Commission spoke of authority:

> The people of God as a whole is the bearer of the living Tradition. In changing situations producing fresh challenges to the Gospel, the discernment, actualisation and communication of the Word of God is the responsibility of the whole people of God. The Holy Spirit works through all members of the community, using the gifts he gives to each for the good of all ... [no. 28]. ... The challenge and responsibility for those with authority within the Church is so to exercise their ministry that they promote the unity of the whole Church in faith and life in a way that enriches rather than diminishes the legitimate diversity of local churches [no. 33].[2]

This reader sets out to explore the implications of such challenges and responsibilities.

---

1. 'The New Ecclesiology of Vatican II', paper given at the SEDOS Seminar, Rome, 3 December, 1996 (see www.sedos.org/english/walbert.htm).
2. ARCIC: *The Gift of Authority – Authority in the Church III*, London, CTS; Toronto, Anglican Book Centre; and New York, Church Publishing, 1999.

THE HERMENEUTICS OF ECCLESIAL AUTHORITY

The issues of Authority and Governance in the Roman Catholic church permeate each and every aspect of that Church's identity, teaching, influence, organization, moral values and pastoral provision. They have left their mark, in turn, upon its diverse theological and philosophical traditions. These issues have always figured prominently in ecclesiological and theological debates, down through the Christian centuries. And, of course, they thereby affect the lives of Roman Catholics wherever they strive to live out the gospel. Following developments in the church's self-understanding at Vatican II and the many subsequent tensions between differing ecclesiologies across the church in the decades which have followed, such issues have been the focal point for many of the key discussions and disputes within the church in recent memory.

Inevitably, the many changes which the world has seen over the last 50 or so years are amongst the most significant explanatory factors as to why this might be so. There have been vast paradigm shifts and developments (by no means to be taken as always being positive) in society, politics, international relations, science and technology, philosophy, culture in general and, of course, in theology itself.

Many of these changes have been bracketed as the characteristic trends and challenges of 'postmodernity', that is to say, the present historical era where all 'grand narratives' or overarching explanatory hypotheses, including religion, are challenged and even the notion of authority itself comes under scrutiny. Absolutist thinking[3] becomes suspect and undermined (and, so too, many aspects of religion with it). The legitimation of particular world-views, value-systems and even individuals in positions of authority all comes under close scrutiny. Related to this is the great 'secularization debate' which particularly preoccupied the Western and so-called 'developed' countries in the 1960s and 1970s, though this phenomenon, once believed to herald a decline in religion in general, has become much more complex in recent years and, of course, was never applicable to many parts of the world, in any case.

In contradistinction to critical postmodernity's championing of the local and particular against the universal, is the phenomenon of 'globalization'. This flies in the face of many critical postmodern predictions and ideals. But it creates as much a challenge to the church today as any reductivistic rejection of religion. The most wealthy and powerful governments, international organizations, multinational corporations and conglomerates are becoming increasingly more, not less dominant in their control over the lives of the world's citizens. There appears to be *less* freedom and scope for expression, both in individual and collective terms.

In contemporary parlance, Roman Catholicism is, of course, a 'global brand' in itself. Nonetheless, it views itself as a challenge to the negative and dehumanizing aspects of globalization, such as global capitalism and mass consumerism: the church sees itself as promoter and defender of community and the place and value of each and every person in each and every community. Yet many sociologists believe that religion is now, also, simply a matter of consumerist choice. People 'pick and mix' their spirituality. Obligation and commitment are replaced by an emphasis upon 'choice' and 'freedom'. Naturally, this raises

---

3. E.g., that there are 'absolute truths' or universally valid ethical principles and norms.

further questions in relation to the continued relevance of and respect for traditions, doctrines and their legitimation. Studies of shifts in values and value-systems bear out some aspects of this, though many interpret such an emphasis as being obsessive and really concerned only with overtly individualistic, i.e., selfish, ends. Indeed, some argue that such choice and freedom are really only illusory and tools of control.

However, such a picture is probably too simplistic and generalizing, helpful and challenging though it may be. Some of those same sociologists interpret religion in the postmodern world in terms of a flight from authority on the one hand and a retreat into fundamentalism or authoritarianism on the other. Yet things are more complicated in reality. Many within and without the Roman Catholic church today agree that it has increasingly resorted to adopting a more authoritarian[4] mindset, as seen in its tactics, structures and official pronouncements. Many see a present disjunction between the rhetoric and reality of the church. The church preaches a gospel of love and communion, the church is the most vociferous defender of human rights on the planet. And yet, critics say, we see within the church's ranks and in its actions and treatment of its own members, particularly those who openly dissent from the perceived 'official' line of teaching, an absence of love, a rupture of communion and a continued violation of fundamental human rights.

All these issues are related to many other developments in recent decades. These developments include the rapid advances in communication, the advent of new ecclesial movements and theologies (to which Vatican II helped provide initial inspiration) and, finally, what many have perceived to be a policy towards ever-increasing institutional centralization on the part of the curial authorities of the church in Rome. All have facilitated a continuous and lively stream of dialogue and disagreement on authority and governance in relation to the place of the church in our age and the new millennium. Perhaps, above all, postmodernity has helped place the question of *context* at the top of many people's agendas. History, locality, self-determination, inculturation, freedom and liberation from oppression and exploitation, and relevance, meaning and fulfilment in human lives – all are themes which have become increasingly important to groups of Roman Catholics across the globe today. The institutional church has sought to apologize for many past wrongs recently, and yet many suggest it seems incapable of apologizing for *recent* wrongs and continued infringements of the 'law' of love and community.

In short, it is no exaggeration to say that the very meaning and continued effectiveness and relevance of the Roman Catholic church, its teaching and tradition are bound up with these and other questions of authority and the related questions concerning how the church is governed. This rings true from the most localized community (for some the family, for others the basic human or Christian community, for others the parish, etc.) to the universal and institutional level.

DEFINING AUTHORITY

What do we actually mean by authority? The word is derived from the Latin for author –

---

4. 'Authoritarianism' is to be contrasted with genuine authority, which involves free assent, as is explained below.

'auctor', hence authority – 'auctoritas'. Thus authority is related to the *source* of something; what brings something into existence. Hence someone who acts with authority or is in a position of authority must gain their entitlement and enablement to do so from some source: they must be 'author-*ized*'. We cannot go into a full debate here concerning the etymology of authority, nor explore the range of interpretations from political theory and philosophy.[5] Suffice to say that political philosophy points to the gaining of true authority through the assent of those over whom such authority is exercised, e.g., one who is elected into a particular office has the power and authority to carry out the duties of that office because those people have *invested* their own 'powers' and interests in that person, hence investing their authority in, authorizing that individual. Authority also relates to that which carries respect and assent – something can be authoritative because general agreement and support is reached concerning its truth, validity or desirability, etc. Indeed, something gains authority in such a manner not simply through such consent, but by being representative of what is 'true', 'good', etc. in itself.

Of course, in the church the matter becomes more complex. God, whom Christians believe to be the 'author' of creation is the supreme authority. Also crucial to the notion of authority in the church is the life and ministry of Christ who (the New Testament teaches us) authorized his disciples and followers to continue that mission. For Christians, the Bible contains sacred and authoritative writings which, it is believed, give witness to the revelation of God's salvific self and truth for humanity and the world. Also authoritative for Christians, are the teachings and witness of Christian communities of the past – including the writings of their leaders – their 'highest' authorities – and the outcome of their discussions and arguments. Roman Catholicism has placed particular value upon such teaching being handed on faithfully from generation to generation, albeit interpreted anew at various times. Thus the importance of *tradition* for Roman Catholicism, as the corporate memory of communities of believers who have striven to live out the gospel in all ages and in all places. Other Christian denominations, albeit to differing extents, prefer to privilege scripture and the teaching of the church fathers (the most influential leaders and teachers from the early centuries of the church), with a lesser role for the teaching and interpretations which follow later.[6] Many believe that such later interpretations and teaching could sometimes deviate from the teachings of the Bible and the definitive preaching and interpretation of the gospels in the first five centuries of Christianity. But the Roman Catholic church believes that the ongoing development of doctrine and witness to the Christian gospel is a living and vibrant entity, from age to age, which inevitably needs to be interpreted anew. The term which it uses to describe the entitlement of the church, its leaders, theologians and, indeed, all baptized believers to do so is 'teaching authority' or, '*magisterium*' (literally, the 'role/authority' of a 'master' in a particular field).

---

5. I have gone into a more detailed exploration of the concept in 'What do we Mean by Authority?' in Bernard Hoose (ed.) *Authority in the Roman Catholic Church*, London, Ashgate, 2002. See also, Gaillardetz, Richard R: *Teaching with Authority*, Collegeville, Liturgical Press, 1997; Raz, Joseph: *Authority*, Oxford, Blackwell, 1990; De George, Richard T: *The Nature and Limits of Authority*, Kansas, University Press of Kansas, 1985; Dominion, Jack: *Authority – a Christian Interpretation of the Psychological Evolution of Authority*, London, DLT, 1976.
6. The Orthodox and (many) Anglican churches have tended towards something in between the 'official' Roman Catholic and Evangelistic protestant understandings in this respect.

Central to the debates with which this book is concerned is the understanding of what actually constitutes the magisterium, who contributes to building it up and what matters of human existence those who exercise this teaching authority are entitled and competent ('authorized') to speak upon. Through the Christian centuries, councils, synods, papal pronouncements and documents emanating from the Roman Curia (the institutional church's 'civil service', so to speak) have all been deemed to carry 'authority' when speaking on matters, in the main, relating to the 'faith' of the church and on matters of ethical concern – morals.[7] In particular the Pope, whose office is understood as continuing that special role entrusted to Saint Peter by Jesus (on a Catholic interpretation), has been seen as exercising a special and universal authority over the entire church. Hence the notion of 'papal primacy'. But all bishops, too, following tradition back to the early church, are seen to exercise special and particular leadership, 'oversight' (i.e., episcopacy) in their own dioceses. When all the bishops 'speak' together, a 'college', as it were, this is seen to be the highest authoritative manner in which the church may teach. A general council has been understood as the most practical way in facilitating the church to speak in such a way. Nonetheless, the church does not understand all this as in any way detracting from the supreme authority of the Papacy, indeed, the authority of the latter can be seen as an exercising of the authority of the college. If that seems to be confusing, then so it is, and we shall encounter complex arguments along the way to try and show either that there is or that there is not something contradictory in such claims. Indeed, the church also speaks of the teaching authority of *all* believers, which alludes most closely to the literal sense of authority as being given through assent. Hence the church speaks of this 'sense of the faithful', the *Sensus Fidelium*, which is a fundamental part (along with related concepts) of the Catholic understanding of tradition, doctrine and their reception. Into all this already crowded equation comes the notion of infallibility and how it pertains to the Papacy, individual popes, their teachings, the magisterium and the church, itself.

As one would expect, the church also pays heed to professional practitioners in the science of theology and so theologians carry a certain authority and make a special contribution to the magisterium, as well. The voice of particular groups and communities, as well as countless individuals of particular holiness, virtue and commitment have also helped build up the body of teaching and contributed to the authoritativeness of the Roman Catholic church's mission and witness in the world. Of course, priests and other ministers of religions also carry a special authority, in line with their calling in the service of the Gospel, the church and its members.

One must never forget, in particular, the role of people who were and are poor, oppressed and marginalized, sometimes at the hands of or through the compliance of members of the institutional aspects of the Roman Catholic church itself.

THE CHALLENGES OF AUTHORITY

Many wrestle with the intricacies of this ecclesial reality and the historical backdrop to it. They

---

7. Although other matters are not beyond their remit, in so far as they are deemed to be connected with revelation and the Christian way of life.

are faced with perplexing questions such as who, then, carries the greatest authority? The Pope, the bishops together, a general council, the entire corpus of the faithful in the church? Christ himself shunned such questions in so far as they are from a competitive perspective. The gospels tell us that he taught a radically new model of authority – one of service, rather than of 'lording it' over people. The greatest must be as the least.

As stated, in recent decades, many within the church have felt that the central 'authorities' and institutional mechanisms of the church have become increasingly more 'authoritarian' in tone, ethos and act. In their view, dissent becomes less tolerated and the centralization of the powers and decisions in the church becomes greater. The notion of the magisterium becomes hardened into something controlled from that centre. To deviate from what the 'official' church teaches or pronounces on a given subject is seen as jeopardizing one's 'full communion' with the church itself. Many believe that individual bishops have less say and hence authority. Theologians are expected to make a profession of faith (of 'orthodoxy' as defined by Rome) and certain methods and styles of interpreting and passing on the faith have become suspect, criticized and sometimes condemned and prohibited. Certain questions must not be disputed, most notably the topic of the ordination of women.

Yet, on the other hand, many of those in such positions of authority and others throughout the church see, instead, a faithful defence of the faith at work in turbulent times. Accordingly, such people would describe the situation in something like the following terms: Vatican II was something very special in the history of the church, but some have interpreted its and other church teachings in too liberal or even an erroneous fashion. One should not speak of an 'institutional' church as if this were separate from the sacramental reality of the communion of all in the Roman Catholic church. The Papacy itself is a special symbol, guarantor and service for the protection of that very unity, that communion. The vision of Vatican II entails a commitment towards enhancing and furthering that worldwide communion, and this requires structures and authoritative teaching. Naturally it is the task of the Pope and the Roman Curia, with the bishops of the church, assisted by the theologians and, where appropriate, other members of the faithful to do so. The scope and limits of the authority of the Magisterium (yes, with a capital 'M') and the Papacy itself must be made clear and adhered to by the faithful. This is the correct response to the ills of a postmodern world rather than any false adopting of inappropriate political models or ideologies for the church or, worse still, allowing the faith to be distorted and diluted by false pluralism and relativism. Truth exists and the church has a duty to preach that God-given truth to the world. The Curia and Papacy exist to safeguard that truth, most definitively made known in the person of Christ, himself. There are distinct limits to how one may interpret, add to or deviate from the official teaching authority of the church. The hierarchical model of church governance has always been understood as being divinely ordained.

Yet the questions and disputes are very real today, just as they have been throughout the entire history of the church. Even in the embryonic church of the gospels and throughout the rest of the new testament, we see that Christians have clashed over whom should have the most authority, whose word counted the most. The 'apostolic' council of Jerusalem, Paul's constant obsession with stressing his authority (as *an* authority) for speaking as he did, the norms which the Pastoral Epistles set down for the organization and leadership of the church

– all illustrate how perennial such concerns are. In a sense, questions of authority and governance are inevitable, indicative of the nature of human communities. Yet many issues pertaining to the authority, governance and leadership of the church have caused much sorrow and disunion through the Christian centuries as well. Every schism in Christianity can be traced, ultimately, to such factors.

EXPLORING THE GIFTS AND MEETING THE CHALLENGES

The challenges which all such questions bring to the church may always be with us but there is no reason why such tensions might not be transformed into a healthy sign of the vitality and openness of the church and hence demonstrative of both its unity and its diversity. For that is indicative of the actuality of Catholicism, indeed of catholicity. As Hans Küng states in one of our readings:

> Catholicity then is gift and task, indicative and imperative, origin and future. It is within this tension that I want to continue the pursuit of theology and as decisively as hitherto to make the message of Jesus Christ intelligible to people of the present time, while being ready to learn and to be corrected whenever it is a question of discussion between equal partners in a fraternal spirit.[8]

Indeed, it is far from Küng, alone, who speaks of such guiding principles for dialogue on these matters in the church. Paul VI's encyclical, *Ecclesiam Suam* proposed love (or charity – *caritas*) as a principle *method* for such. Church teachings and theological writings are littered with such pleas. The task is to put such noble intentions into real practice, to ensure they become reality rather than remain mere rhetoric. In order for these tensions to be healthy rather than detrimental to community in the church, debates need to be held and openly so. The concerns and questions, the grievances and misgivings need to be voiced. The oft-quoted dictum that 'in Rome, we think in centuries', must not be perceived in a solely negative fashion. For it was the emerging historical consciousness of the church, its leading theologians and its people throughout the world, which gave rise both to Vatican II and to much of the more influential aspects of the church's Social Teaching since the Pontificate of John XXIII. The benefit of hindsight is a wonderful thing and Christianity has, indeed, centuries of hindsight upon which to dwell and from which to learn. And, of course, there is a deeper motivating force to see the debates concerning authority and governance as bearing gifts, as well as challenges, and hence in a positive and active light: the inspiration which brings communion into being, perhaps demonstrated most definitively in the fully-inclusive celebration of the Eucharist. As one noteworthy recent work of ecclesiology from a leading Anglican theologian (writing under the influence of Karl Rahner) puts it:

> It seems clear that the present forms of church structure are not absolutely unchangeable, and that many possibilities of convergence between presently separated churches exist. The future of the church is always open to the creative power of the Holy Spirit, so that

---

8. Küng, Hans: *The Church – Maintained in Truth*, London, SCM, 1980, 86–7 (see Chapter 6 of the present volume).

it is unlikely to be constrained by what may turn out to be the social prejudices of the past. So one must not foreclose discussion of the proper forms of hierarchy and governance in the church, forms which must both build up fellowship [i.e. *communion*] in the universal church, and permit the proper freedom into which the Spirit calls the churches.[9]

What should be uppermost in the minds of all concerned with the issues of authority and governance in the Roman Catholic church today is the *ethics of community*. Thus *all* should work towards what enhances community, rather than harms and/or denigrates it. This includes attention to the structures and practices of the official/institutional church, at whatever level. So, also, to the attitudes adopted by many 'progressive' Catholics towards those whose viewpoints may be different or diametrically opposed and/or whose visions for the church of the future moves at a slower pace than their own. Love (charity) must prevail: anything else is contrary to the gospel and radical ethic of Jesus of Nazareth, whom we call the Christ (and so must be opposed).

The many *positive* experiences of the editors and countless others in various conversations and initiatives (some of which are outlined, below) bear witness to the fruits that can flow from engaging with others – listening, putting minds together and jointly working on such issues. This reader marks a small contribution towards bringing together many voices in relation to some of the most pressing issues pertaining to authority and governance in the church of our times.

CONVERSATIONS AND THEOLOGICAL REFLECTION

Our present volume has its origins in the work of the Queen's Foundation Working Party on Authority and Governance in the Roman Catholic Church. This involved a number of Catholics (along with input from other denominations), from a variety of backgrounds, organizations and academic disciplines, engaging in a series of discussions concerning issues of authority, governance, relationships and participation in the Roman Catholic church in Britain today. It sought to engage in and facilitate a sustained series of conversations and reflections concerning such issues, with a view to informing pastoral policy and practice alike. The method of 'conversation' was deliberately chosen so as to avoid the pitfalls that come from more polemical approaches and which lead to stalemate or a breakdown in true communication and community alike. From its work ensued a large number of research ventures and ongoing theological reflection. Many of these 'conversations' investigated the current state and future of the church at parish and diocesan level in Britain. In particular, explorations focused upon issues of pastoral provision and community enhancement, aspects of ministry – including youth, lay, women's and collaborative, and the provision of formation, both clerical and lay.[10] Over 1000 people were involved in this sustained series of lively conversations and two UK conferences were held – in 1997 at Darwen, Lancashire and a follow-up conference at Cambridge in June 2000. One of the values of the method of 'conversation' was that the 1997 conference was allowed to reflect upon the discussions and

---

9. Ward, Keith: *Religion and Community*, Oxford, Oxford University Press, 2000, 178.
10. The project's website can be viewed on: http://www.queensresearch.org/ag/index.html.

material to that date, and to suggest ways forward and topics for further dialogue and research in the years which followed.

Many of these conversations and research projects produced, commissioned, inspired or reflected upon a vast array of papers and literature and, crucially, the personal experiences and testimonies of a great many so-called 'ordinary' Roman Catholics. A number of publications from this project, which are focused upon the current life and possibilities for the future of the church, have recently entered the public domain. They include two volumes of papers;[11] reflections upon the results from in-depth empirical studies across a number of dioceses and parishes;[12] reflections upon national surveys and studies of clerical attitudes and of those who have left the active priesthood and religious life;[13] papers from seminars and studies concerning issues of sexuality and gender in the church;[14] a study of issues of racial justice and the participation of minority groups in the church;[15] as well as a series of other booklets and pamphlets exploring a variety of relevant issues.[16]

The Queen's Foundation project also engaged in discussions with international ventures engaged in similar discussions.[17] It became obvious to me, in the midst of the Queen's project, that there was a wealth of theological literature on these subjects and that further conversations, study and research might be better informed and facilitated if a representative collection of such texts was assembled and published. It was also obvious that such a collection would be greatly enhanced if an internationally diverse team of editors undertook its compilation. Thus we have two members of the laity: one from the USA, the other an Irish Catholic based in England; a Belgian Jesuit, and an English Methodist minister. A good mix, if not as cosmopolitan as some might have preferred!

Hence the origins of the text you now have before you. Just as with all the above mentioned initiatives, its aim is to help fire the conversations of and for the *future* of the church. In the course of our editorial discussions, Kenneth Wilson, commenting from a non-Roman Catholic perspective, has described the present situation in the terms which follow. Given the importance with which Roman Catholicism treats tradition, it is a concern of many in the church, both 'progressive' and 'conservative' alike, that today too many seem to have lost the art of conversation about the faith, and mistrust the intentions of others who wish to

---

11. Timms, Noel and Wilson, Kenneth (eds), *Governance and Authority in the Roman Catholic Church – Beginning a Conversation*, London SPCK, 2000; Hoose, Bernard (ed.), *Authority in the Roman Catholic Church – Theory and Practice*, Aldershot, Ashgate, 2001.

12. Timms, Noel (ed.), *Diocesan Dispositions and Parish Voices in the Roman Catholic Church*, Chelmsford, Matthew James, 2001.

13. Timms, Noel (ed.), *'You Aren't One of the Boys' – Authority in the Catholic Priesthood*, Chelmsford, Matthew James, 2001; Bebb, Andrew and Roper, Anna (eds), *A Painful Process*, Chelmsford, Matthew James, 2001.

14. Selling, Joseph A. (ed.): *Embracing Sexuality – Authority and Experience in the Catholic Church*, Aldershot, Ashgate, 2001.

15. Catholic Association for Racial Justice (CARJ), *Outcaste to Authority*, London, CARJ, 2000.

16. These include the following all published at Chelmsford by Matthew James, 2002: Hoose, Bernard, *Authority in the Roman Catholic Church*; Barker, David, *Change, Communication and Relationships in the Catholic Church*; Barker, Annette, *Leadership, Formation and Participation* and John Mannix's forthcoming work on Laity, Organisation and Management. The Association of Interchurch Families is also preparing the results of its own research for publication on the issue of Eucharistic Sharing.

17. These included the Common Ground Initiative, considering 'Church Authority in American Culture', USA; *Reflexiones Sobre La Autoridad Y Su Ejercico En La Iglesia Catolica*, at the Centro Bellarmino in Santiago, Chile; and the Authority and Governance Seminars at the Jesuit Institute, Boston College, USA.

engage in it seriously. It is apparent from many of his teachings that the present Pope, John Paul II, himself, wishes to engage in serious conversations concerning the future of the church. The concern of many, however, is that others in positions of ecclesial power and authority are less willing and able to do so.

EDITORIAL METHOD

The customary limits of space dictate that this book, alas, must confine itself, for the main part, to the debate *within* Roman Catholicism and particularly in recent decades. The majority of readings also reflect, for the greater part, contributions from theologians in Europe and North America. Although developments in other parts of the world find some treatment as well, the aforementioned limits of space, the contextual situations of the four editors, as well as the need to bring together much of the literature from those parts of the world where the editors live and work (hence with which they are most familiar) dictate such a course of action. This is a short-falling of the present text, but also an opportunity. The respective situations in other parts of the world, i.e., those parts where the greatest numbers of Catholics find themselves today and where our debates are just as pressing, demand that similar volumes are produced which are indicative of the various voices relevant to those contexts, too. Whilst contributions from feminist theologians are included in our text, some will have wished for more. Again, the rich diversity of feminist thought demands at least a representative volume to itself. Indeed, there are already many excellent readers in aspects of feminist theology which also contain discussions of themes relevant to this volume.

As said, a wealth of literature has emerged concerning these subjects, in addition to a solid tradition of relevant material which has been preserved and provides points of reference, for today's church, from earlier centuries. It is our belief that all parties interested in such debates and issues can benefit from this collection. Current literature is usually of a polemical nature – from whatever ecclesial faction or tradition it emanates. It is true that each of the editors might be labelled as 'progressive' in outlook, and no apology is made for a slight majority of the readings being concerned with ways forward, *beyond* difficulties and problematic issues. Nonetheless, this work is an attempt to draw together a balanced range of voices and opinions in as objective a fashion as such qualifications and human limitations may allow. The modus operandi shall be *thematic* – i.e. this volume will focus primarily upon the modern/postmodern period in the church and aims to be indicative of the parameters of key debates rather than historical or fully comprehensive in what is included. It does not seek to be exhaustive but *indicative* of the real concerns and core issues in the present time. No single-volume work could ever claim to be anything more.

In certain sections there is some inevitable overlap but this should be viewed in a complementary fashion e.g., the chapters on the magisterium (Chapter 2) and the role of the theologian (Chapter 6) touch upon similar themes but from different directions: Chapter 2 seeks to explore what the magisterium actually is, as well as its functions and parameters, whilst Chapter 6 seeks to explore what the role of the theologian is and what actually constitutes authoritative theology today.

Of course, hard decisions had to be taken concerning which texts to include and which, reluctantly, to omit. The editors consulted widely in this respect and are particularly grateful to Michael Fahey[18] and Francis Sullivan for their advice and opinions in this regard. To reiterate: it is not because of a *scarcity* of literature on these subjects that we felt this reader was necessary, but because of its plenitude and the universal relevance of the questions involved. However, many important texts had to be excluded – including some which have been omitted because the debates concerning them are still very much in full flow.

Certain prominent theologians could have provided key texts for each and every chapter. Karl Rahner and Yves Congar, in particular, have written influential contributions on nearly every topic upon which the reader touches. So, whilst some authors do have more than one entry in this volume, a further self-limitation which we placed upon ourselves was to avoid relying *too* much upon the most prolific and influential writers. Congar, Rahner and Cardinal Dulles, by the sheer volume and impact of their output on relevant issues, have necessitated some exceptions. We have tried to cover a broader range of opinion and diversity though, for some, this may not prove as broad and diverse as they would like! We hope, at least, that for all who engage with our text, that which *has* been included fires the imagination, study and discussions of all those concerned with the future of the church.

---

18. In particular for making available his private paper: 'Theological Reflection in the 20th Century on "Authority in the Church"', 1999.

Part 1:

Ecclesiology – Envisaging the Church

Gerard Mannion

Any study of questions concerning the nature and scope of church authority presupposes at least some tentative understanding of what the church actually *is*. Further related considerations follow concerning what constitutes church, what it means to be church, what the essence, nature and function of the church are, how the church is to be governed, shaped and facilitated, and how the church is renewed and enhanced from time to time. Then there are further questions about the nature of the church universal, whether in Roman Catholic terms or in relation to Christianity itself, and in relation to particular, regional and local *churches.*

Questions concerning the church embrace many considerations concerning the ways and forms of being community in relation to the love and will of God. For Christians, this was given definitive expression by Jesus of Nazareth and developed by his immediate followers. Through its many centuries, for various historical, political and cultural reasons, the church has grown, changed and taken on various new forms and styles of trying to remain faithful to the original mission given by Christ to his disciples.

Even at the highest level of the 'official' Roman Catholic church itself, history demonstrates that there have been a variety of ways in which those within the church, especially those in positions of authority, have developed a self-understanding of the church itself. So, too, at the grass-roots level, from the communities of the New Testament, to the churches of the fathers, from the radical groups of renewal and reformation, to the rural and far-flung parishes and missions oblivious to the political machinations of the medieval church; from the many denominations and their offspring, to the uniform Roman Catholic identity promoted post-Council of Trent and throughout the nineteenth century onwards. So, too, from the groups of Catholic Action to the base communities of Latin America, from the movement for woman-church, to the local groups of revolutionary and reactionary commitment (in radical, counter-cultural or conservative fashion). And, again, from the indigenous churches who have embraced inculturation, to the parishes of the developed world uncertain of their future, and a legion of other instances, besides. The quest for a vital, energizing and sustainable way of being the community called church has preoccupied, perplexed and fulfilled groups of Christians – those people committed to living the gospel of Jesus Christ, from the time of his own earthly ministry itself.

Hence, whilst 'church' must obviously be understood as one of the central concepts for Christianity, there is no set answer, applicable to all ages and to all places, to the question 'what is church?'. Instead, there is a myriad of attempts to convey and to live some sort of response to a question which is fundamentally, for Christians, a calling long before it can be construed as a sociological, historical or theological exercise.

Thus the self-understanding of the church goes through many transformations, across time and throughout space. Some of the most wonderful images, metaphors and analogies have been employed in an attempt to try and elucidate the nature of church, and many profound theoretical and spiritual treatments have come forth as a result of the efforts of the followers of Christ to understand their lives and discipleship more fully.

Fundamental to the attempts of any part of the Roman Catholic church to understand and direct itself, are a consideration of the church's institutional aspects in relation to its communitarian aspects, as are questions of relations between the hierarchy and the wider church, between clergy and laity, and between universal and local churches. Indeed the dynamics of the relation between '*the* church' and 'the church*es*' reaches far beyond the broad confines of Roman Catholicism itself.

Hence many typologies, images, pictures and templates of what the church is, is about and should/might be have emerged throughout the Christian centuries. Many have become sufficiently influential, successful or even confrontational enough to be labelled 'models' of the church – i.e. as explanatory and exploratory devices for understanding and developing the church alike. The more wide-reaching models, particularly those employed and adapted by elements of the *institutional* church, can be said to have become sufficiently disseminated, sometimes even imposed, throughout the wider church to warrant the title of 'paradigms'.[1] This is because they both help to shape and to capture the essence of a particular self-understanding of the church for a particular era. Some models and paradigms have been restrictive and stifling, some parochial and hierarchical, whilst others have been progressive and dynamic, with some being flexible and egalitarian. Whatever, as the sociologist Max Weber stressed that we must bear in mind when employing typologies, there are no 'ideal types' which exist in reality. Our ventures to understand and direct the church – our ecclesiologies – will always be 'grasping attempts' at trying to capture and shape the fundamental aspects of the Christian community/ies.

But when an understanding of the church, whether it involves spiritual considerations, metaphors, models, paradigms and the like or not, becomes empowering, enabling and results in the enhancement and building up of the community, it can be said to be *visionary*. Here, ecclesiology enters a further dimension, more fully in tune, it might be said (in accordance with the New Testament), with the aims and intentions of Christ and the immediate successors he charged with the building of the kingdom of justice and righteousness.

All Roman Catholic ecclesiology will always be confronted by the twin poles of unity and diversity in its endeavours. Furthermore, it must never shy away from consideration of contextual and cultural considerations. The epistles of the New Testament demonstrate that this has always been the case. So, too, must the 'signs of the times' be given due attention (as John XXIII and Vatican II emphasized). Differing theologies, philosophies and social

---

1. The work of Cardinal Avery Dulles has especially illustrated many such varieties of ecclesiology.

scientific schools, along with differing priorities across the church and the varied manner in which certain groups and individuals connect with often rich and diverse traditions (even just *within* Roman Catholicism), will give birth to differing themes and perspectives in ecclesiology. Nonetheless, given the considerations outlined, but only touched upon in this introduction, that is often no bad thing.

The church's business is as a sacramental presence in the world, striving by its service to bring the message and reality of God's salvific love to humanity, building community and furthering justice and righteousness. These goals help bring us closer both to one another and to God.

Our collection of readings touch upon many of the issues mentioned here, from official church paradigms, to fundamental shifts in the ecclesiological thinking of the hierarchy; from the struggle to articulate and develop a church of the poor and marginalized, to the attempt to theorize a fitting ecclesial 'open-space' for women; from attempts to clarify and/or reverse earlier 'official' ecclesiologies, to pleas that a more diverse, positive and practical vision of the church be cultivated. Alas, the collection is but a small sample of the ecclesiological riches of Roman Catholicism in recent times.

Many of the issues in this part naturally overlap with those which concern other parts, for all of the major themes with which this book is concerned are bound up with the self-understanding and vision of the institutional church, and the understanding of the church held by those in its local settings and at its margins.

1.1 *MYSTICI CORPORIS CHRISTI* – 1943

This encyclical,[2] from the pontificate of Pius XII, sets down a *re*-newed understanding of the church, emphasizing elements of the self-understanding of the community found in the New Testament and the early church. It marks a shift from the 'political society' model of the church, which had prevailed since the seventeenth century. It purports to balance the charismatic and institutional understandings of the church. The encyclical identifies the visible community, i.e., the Roman Catholic church, with the invisible communion as one. Hence being part of the mystical body is seen as conditional upon being a member of and in good standing with the Roman Catholic church authorities. The document contains much symbolic language, (ontological analogies and images, biblical images, communitarian and sacramental language) and does recognize the importance of a diverse range of gifts and roles within the church. However, it clearly emphasizes an institutional and hierarchical model of the church. Thus much of the potential of the symbolic language it employs is thwarted. Many theologians were disappointed by its hierarchical understanding of the church, as well as its exclusivistic tone.

❀

The doctrine of the Mystical Body of Christ, which is the Church,[3] was first taught us by the Redeemer Himself … [1] … If we would define and describe this true Church of Jesus Christ – which is the One, Holy, Catholic, Apostolic and Roman Church – we shall find nothing more noble, more sublime, or more divine than the expression 'the Mystical Body of Christ' – an expression which springs from and is, as it were, the fair flowering of the repeated teaching of the Sacred Scriptures and the Holy Fathers.

That the Church is a body is frequently asserted in the Sacred Scriptures. 'Christ', says the Apostle, 'is the Head of the Body of the Church'.[4] If the Church is a body, it must be an unbroken unity, according to those words of Paul: 'Though many we are one body in Christ.'[5] But it is not enough that the Body of the Church should be an unbroken unity; it must also be something definite and perceptible to the senses… . Hence they err in a matter of divine truth, who imagine the Church to be invisible, intangible, a something merely 'pneumatological' as they say, by which many Christian communities, though they differ from each other in their profession of faith, are united by an invisible bond [14] … .

One must not think, however, that this ordered or 'organic' structure of the body of the Church contains only hierarchical elements and with them is complete; or, as an opposite opinion holds, that it is composed only of those who enjoy charismatic gifts – though members gifted with miraculous powers will never be lacking in the Church. That those who exercise sacred power in this Body are its chief members must be maintained uncompromisingly. It is through them, by commission of the Divine Redeemer Himself, that

---

2. English translation: *The Holy Father, Archives of the Holy See*, www.vatican.va/archive/ holy_father/pius_xii/ encyclicals/.

3. Cf., Col. 24.

4. Cf. Vat. Council, *Constitutio de fide catholica*, c. 1.

5. Rom., 12:5.

Christ's apostolate as Teacher, King and Priest is to endure. At the same time, when the Fathers of the Church sing the praises of this Mystical Body of Christ, with its ministries, its variety of ranks, its officers, its conditions, its orders, its duties, they are thinking not only of those who have received Holy Orders, but of all those too, who, following the evangelical counsels, pass their lives either actively among men, or hidden in the silence of the cloister, or who aim at combining the active and contemplative life according to their Institute; as also of those who, though living in the world, consecrate themselves wholeheartedly to spiritual or corporal works of mercy, and of those in the state of holy matrimony. Indeed, let this be clearly understood, especially in our days, fathers and mothers of families, those who are godparents through Baptism, and in particular those members of the laity who collaborate with the ecclesiastical hierarchy in spreading the Kingdom of the Divine Redeemer occupy an honorable, if often a lowly, place in the Christian community, and even they under the impulse of God and with His help, can reach the heights of supreme holiness, which, Jesus Christ has promised, will never be wanting to the Church [17] … .

Actually only those are to be included as members of the Church who have been baptized and profess the true faith, and who have not been so unfortunate as to separate themselves from the unity of the Body, or been excluded by legitimate authority for grave faults committed. 'For in one spirit' says the Apostle, 'were we all baptized into one Body, whether Jews or Gentiles, whether bond or free'.[6] As therefore in the true Christian community there is only one Body, one Spirit, one Lord, and one Baptism, so there can be only one faith.[7] And therefore, if a man refuses to hear the Church, let him be considered – so the Lord commands – as a heathen and a publican.[8] It follows that those who are divided in faith or government cannot be living in the unity of such a Body, nor can they be living the life of its one Divine Spirit [22].

Nor must one imagine that the Body of the Church, just because it bears the name of Christ, is made up during the days of its earthly pilgrimage only of members conspicuous for their holiness, or that it consists only of those whom God has predestined to eternal happiness. It is owing to the Savior's infinite mercy that place is allowed in His Mystical Body here below for those whom, of old, He did not exclude from the banquet[9] … [23]. Let every one then abhor sin, which defiles the mystical members of our Redeemer; but if anyone unhappily falls and his obstinacy has not made him unworthy of communion with the faithful, let him be received with great love, and let eager charity see in him a weak member of Jesus Christ … [24] … .

Because Christ is so exalted, He alone by every right rules and governs the Church; and herein is yet another reason why He must be likened to a head. As the head is the 'royal citadel' of the body[10] – to use the words of Ambrose – and all the members over whom it is placed for their good[11] are naturally guided by it as being endowed with superior powers, so the Divine Redeemer holds the helm of the universal Christian community and directs its course. And as to govern human society signifies to lead men to the end proposed by means

6. I Cor., 12:13.
7. Cf. Eph., 4:5.
8. Cf. Math., 18:17.
9. Cf. Matt., 9:11; Mark, 2:16; Luke, 15:2.
10. Hexaëmeron, VI, 55: Migne, *PL*, XIV, 265.
11. Cf. August., *De agone Christiano*, XX, 22: Migne, *PL*, XL, 301.

that are expedient, just and helpful,[12] it is easy to see how our Savior, model and ideal of good Shepherds, performs all these functions in a most striking way [37].

While still on earth, He instructed us by precept, counsel and warning in words that shall never pass away, and will be spirit and life to all men of all times. Moreover He conferred a triple power on His Apostles and their successors, to teach, to govern, to lead men to holiness, making this power, defined by special ordinances, rights and obligations, the fundamental law of the whole Church [38] … .

But we must not think that He rules only in a hidden or extraordinary manner. On the contrary, our Redeemer also governs His Mystical Body in a visible and normal way through His Vicar on earth. You know, Venerable Brethren, that after He had ruled the 'little flock'[13] Himself during His mortal pilgrimage, Christ our Lord, when about to leave this world and return to the Father, entrusted to the Chief of the Apostles the visible government of the entire community He had founded. Since He was all wise He could not leave the body of the Church He had founded as a human society without a visible head. Nor against this may one argue that the primacy of jurisdiction established in the Church gives such a Mystical Body two heads. For Peter in view of his primacy is only Christ's Vicar; so that there is only one chief Head of this Body, namely Christ, who never ceases Himself to guide the Church invisibly, though at the same time He rules it visibly, through him who is His representative on earth. After His glorious Ascension into Heaven this Church rested not on Him alone, but on Peter, too, its visible foundation stone. That Christ and His Vicar constitute one only Head is the solemn teaching of Our predecessor of immortal memory Boniface VIII in the Apostolic Letter *Unam Sanctam*;[14] and his successors have never ceased to repeat the same [40].

They, therefore, walk in the path of dangerous error who believe that they can accept Christ as the Head of the Church, while not adhering loyally to His Vicar on earth. They have taken away the visible head, broken the visible bonds of unity and left the Mystical Body of the Redeemer so obscured and so maimed, that those who are seeking the haven of eternal salvation can neither see it nor find it [41].

What we have thus far said of the Universal Church must be understood also of the individual Christian communities, whether Oriental or Latin, which go to makeup the one Catholic Church. For they, too, are ruled by Jesus Christ through the voice of their respective Bishops. Consequently, Bishops must be considered as the more illustrious members of the Universal Church, for they are united by a very special bond to the divine Head of the whole Body and so are rightly called 'principal parts of the members of the Lord';[15] moreover, as far as his own diocese is concerned, each one as a true Shepherd feeds the flock entrusted to him and rules it in the name of Christ.[16] Yet in exercising this office they are not altogether independent, but are subordinate to the lawful authority of the Roman Pontiff, although enjoying the ordinary power of jurisdiction which they receive directly from the same Supreme Pontiff. Therefore, Bishops should be revered by the faithful as divinely appointed successors of the Apostles… .[17] [42] … .

---

12. Cf. St Thos., I, q. 22, a. 1–4.
13. Luke, 12:32.
14. Cf. *Corpus Iuris Canonici*, Extr. Comm., I, 8, 1.
15. Gregory the Great, *Moralia*, XIV, 35, 43: Migne, *PL*, LXXV, 1062.
16. Cf. Vat. Council, *Constitutio de Ecclesia Christi*, Cap. 3.
17. Cf. *Codici Iuris Canonici Fontes*, can. 329, 1.

Christ enlightens His whole Church, as numberless passages from the Sacred Scriptures and the holy Fathers prove … . It is He who imparts the light of faith to believers; it is He who enriches pastors and teachers and above all His Vicar on earth with the supernatural gifts of knowledge, understanding and wisdom, so that they may loyally preserve the treasury of faith, defend it vigorously, and explain it and confirm it with reverence and devotion. Finally, it is He who, though unseen, presides at the Councils of the Church and guides them[18] [50] … .

We desire to make clear why the Body of Christ, which is the Church, should be called mystical. This name, which is used by many early writers, has the sanction of numerous Pontifical documents. There are several reasons why it should be used; for by it we may distinguish the Body of the Church, which is a Society whose Head and Ruler is Christ, from His physical Body, which, born of the Virgin Mother of God, now sits at the right hand of the Father and is hidden under the Eucharistic veils; and, that which is of greater importance in view of modern errors, this name enables us to distinguish it from any other body, whether in the physical or the moral order [60] … .

[T]he Church, a perfect society of its kind, is not made up of merely moral and juridical elements and principles. It is far superior to all other human societies;[19] it surpasses them as grace surpasses nature, as things immortal are above all those that perish.[20] Such human societies, and in the first place civil Society, are by no means to be despised or belittled; but the Church in its entirety is not found within this natural order, any more than the whole man is encompassed within the organism of our mortal body.[21] Although the juridical principles, on which the Church rests and is established, derive from the divine constitution given to it by Christ and contribute to the attaining of its supernatural end, nevertheless that which lifts the Society of Christians far above the whole natural order is the Spirit of our Redeemer who penetrates and fills every part of the Church's being and is active within it until the end of time as the source of every grace and every gift and every miraculous power. Just as our composite mortal body, although it is a marvelous work of the Creator, falls far short of the eminent dignity of our soul, so the social structure of the Christian community, though it proclaims the wisdom of its divine Architect, still remains something inferior when compared to the spiritual gifts which give it beauty and life, and to the divine source whence they flow [63] … .

From what We have thus far written, and explained, Venerable Brethren, it is clear, We think, how grievously they err who arbitrarily claim that the Church is something hidden and invisible, as they also do who look upon her as a mere human institution possessing a certain disciplinary code and external ritual, but lacking power to communicate supernatural life. On the contrary, as Christ, Head and Exemplar of the Church 'is not complete, if only His visible human nature is considered … , or if only His divine, invisible nature … , but He is one through the union of both and one in both … so is it with His Mystical Body'[22] since the Word of God took unto Himself a human nature liable to sufferings, so that He might

---

18. Cf. Cyr. Alex., *Epistula*, 55 *de Symb.*; Migne, *PG*, LXXVII, 293.
19. Cf. Leo XIII, *Sapientiae Christianae*. A.S.S., XXII, 392.
20. Cf. Leo XIII, *Satis Cognitum*. A.S.S., XXVIII, 724.
21. Cf. Ibid., 710.
22. Cf. Ibid., 710.

consecrate in His blood the visible Society founded by Him and 'lead man back to things invisible under a visible rule'.[23] [64].

For this reason We deplore and condemn the pernicious error of those who dream of an imaginary Church, a kind of society that finds its origin and growth in charity, to which, somewhat contemptuously, they oppose another, which they call juridical. But this distinction which they introduce is false: for they fail to understand that the reason which led our Divine Redeemer to give to the community of man He founded the constitution of a Society, perfect of its kind and containing all the juridical and social elements – namely, that He might perpetuate on earth the saving work of Redemption, – was also the reason why He willed it to be enriched with the heavenly gifts of the Paraclet. ... . There can, then, be no real opposition or conflict between the invisible mission of the Holy Spirit and the juridical commission of Ruler and Teacher received from Christ, since they mutually complement and perfect each other – as do the body and soul in man – and proceed from our one Redeemer ... [65].

And if at times there appears in the Church something that indicates the weakness of our human nature, it should not be attributed to her juridical constitution, but rather to that regrettable inclination to evil found in each individual, which its Divine Founder permits even at times in the most exalted members of His Mystical Body, for the purpose of testing the virtue of the Shepherds no less than of the flocks, and that all may increase the merit of their Christian faith. For, as We said above, Christ did not wish to exclude sinners from His Church; hence if some of her members are suffering from spiritual maladies, that is no reason why we should lessen our love for the Church, but rather a reason why we should increase our devotion to her members ... [66].

Likewise, We must earnestly desire that this united prayer may embrace in the same ardent charity both those who, not yet enlightened by the truth of the Gospel, are still outside the fold of the Church, and those who, on account of regrettable schism, are separated from Us, who though unworthy, represent the person of Jesus Christ on earth. Let us then re-echo that divine prayer of our Savior to the heavenly Father: 'That they all may be one, as thou, Father, in me, and I in thee, that they also may be one in us; that the world may believe that thou hast sent me'[24] [102].

As you know, Venerable Brethren, from the very beginning of Our Pontificate, We have committed to the protection and guidance of heaven those who do not belong to the visible Body of the Catholic Church, solemnly declaring that after the example of the Good Shepherd We desire nothing more ardently than that they may have life and have it more abundantly ... . [F]rom a heart overflowing with love We ask each and every one of them to correspond to the interior movements of grace, and to seek to withdraw from that state in which they cannot be sure of their salvation.[25] For even though by an unconscious desire and longing they have a certain relationship with the Mystical Body of the Redeemer, they still remain deprived of those many heavenly gifts and helps which can only be enjoyed in the Catholic Church. Therefore may they enter into Catholic unity and, joined with Us in the one, organic Body of Jesus Christ, may they together with us run on to the one Head in

---

23. St. Thomas, *De Veritate*, q. 29, a. 4, ad 9.
24. John, 17:21.
25. Cf. Pius IX, *Iam Vos Omnes*, 13 Sept. 1868: Acta Conciliorum Vaticana, C.L.VII, 10.

the Society of glorious love.[26] Persevering in prayer to the Spirit of love and truth, We wait for them with open and outstretched arms to come not to a stranger's house, but to their own, their father's home [103].

Though We desire this unceasing prayer to rise to God from the whole Mystical Body in common, that all the straying sheep may hasten to enter the one fold of Jesus Christ, yet We recognize that this must be done of their own free will; for no one believes unless he wills to believe.[27] Hence they are most certainly not genuine Christians[28] who against their belief are forced to go into a church, to approach the altar and to receive the Sacraments; for the 'faith without which it is impossible to please God'[29] is an entirely free 'submission of intellect and will'[30] … [104].

---

26. Cf. Gelas. I, *Epistola*, XIV: Migne, *PL* LIX, 89.
27. Cf. August., *In Ioann. Ev. tract.*, XXVI, 2: Migne, *PL* XXX, 1607.
28. Cf. August., Ibid.
29. Hebr., 11:6.
30. *Constitutio de fide Catholica*, Cap. 3.

1.2 *ECCLESIAM SUAM* – 1964

This, the first encyclical of Paul VI,[31] draws together key concerns for the church as Vatican II was about to embark upon its final session. In it, Paul and his advisers attempt to outline their own 'agenda' for the church of the future. In the encyclical, we see those in positions of ecclesial authority being urged to help the church fulfil its mission both fully and truly. To enable this, the central thrust of the text is a call to the value and necessity of a deeper self-examination for the church. Three principal 'policies' are advocated: first, that the self-awareness of the church be informed by the concerns of the age, leading to an ongoing and transformative self-understanding. A mature faith is seen as the key to this greater awareness, a *sensus Ecclesiae*. Secondly, the importance of renewal and reform for overcoming the church's shortcomings. This is not be understood as reduction or compromise, but rather as a reflective engagement with the world and a *restoration* of the essential features of the church. Thirdly, the importance of *dialogue*, itself, seen here as an all-embracing priority and as a method in itself towards the enhancement of the church and the human family. Dialogue is seen as the practical extending of Christian charity. The document stresses the value and importance of Vatican II towards achieving the aims set out throughout the text. Humanity is seen in terms of a series of concentric circles which incorporate the whole human family, all those of religious faith, all Christians, all Catholics with finally the Roman Catholic church, itself, at the centre. Hence the document sets out an understanding of the church's authority to enter into dialogue – within and without the Roman Catholic church, aimed at furthering the salvation of all humanity.

✿

I SELF-AWARENESS

We believe that it is a duty of the Church at the present time to strive toward a clearer and deeper awareness of itself and its mission in the world, and of the treasury of truth of which it is heir and custodian. Thus before embarking on the study of any particular problem and before considering what attitude to adopt vis-à-vis the world, the Church must here and now reflect on its own nature, the better to appreciate the divine plan which it is the Church's task to implement … [18] … .

The Church itself is being engulfed and shaken by [a] tidal wave of change, for however much men may be committed to the Church, they are deeply affected by the climate of the world. They run the risk of becoming confused, bewildered and alarmed, and this is a state of affairs which strikes at the very roots of the Church. It drives many people to adopt the most outlandish views. They imagine that the Church should abdicate its proper role, and adopt an entirely new and unprecedented mode of existence … . An effective remedy is needed if all these dangers, which are prevalent in many quarters, are to be obviated, and We believe that such a remedy is to be found in an increased self-awareness on the part of the Church. The Church must get a clearer idea of what it really is in the mind of Jesus Christ as recorded and

---

31. Archives of the Holy See, www.vatican.va/holy_father/paul_vi/encyclicals/ also from ET: *The Pope Speaks*, 10 (Summer, 1965), 253–92.

preserved in Sacred Scripture and in Apostolic Tradition, and interpreted and explained by the tradition of the Church under the inspiration and guidance of the Holy Spirit ... [26].

... [E]rrors [are] circulating within the Church itself ... to which people are exposed who have only a partial understanding of the Church and its mission, and who do not pay close enough attention to divine revelation and the Church's Christ-given authority to teach [27] ... .

In this encyclical We are deliberately refraining from making any judgement of Our own on doctrinal issues concerning the Church which are at present under examination by the Council of which We are president. We wish to leave full liberty of investigation and discussion to this important and authoritative assembly. We will express Our own mind at the proper time and in the proper manner, as Our apostolic office of teacher and shepherd and head of the Church demands, and then Our greatest wish will be to have Our own decision in full accord with the judgment of the conciliar Fathers [33] ... .

The mystery of the Church is not a truth to be confined to the realms of speculative theology. It must be lived, so that the faithful may have a kind of intuitive experience of it, even before they come to understand it clearly. And the faithful as a community will indeed recognize that they belong to Christ's Mystical Body when they realize that a part of the ministry of the Church's hierarchy is to initiate men into the Christian way of life, to beget them,[32] teach them, sanctify them, and be their leaders. The hierarchy is a sort of instrument fashioned by Christ, which He Himself uses to communicate to His mystical members the marvelous gifts of truth and grace. He uses it, too, to impart an external, visible structure to the Mystical Body in its pilgrimage through the world, and to give it its sublime unity, its ability to perform its various tasks, its concerted multiplicity of form, and its spiritual beauty.

Images are powerless to convey to the mind an adequate notion of the reality and sublimity of this mystery, but having mentioned the image which St. Paul used, that of the Mystical Body, We should also make mention of the image used by Christ, that of a building, of which He is Himself the architect and builder. Though He founded this building on a man who was naturally weak and frail, Christ transformed him into solid rock, never to be without God's marvelous support: 'Upon this rock I will build my Church.'[33] [37].

If we can only stir up this awareness of the Church in ourselves and foster it in the faithful by the noble and pastoral art of education, many of the apparent difficulties which are today exercising the minds of students of ecclesiology will in fact be overcome. I mean such difficulties as how the Church can be at once both visible and spiritual, free and yet subject to discipline, claiming to be communal in character and yet organized on a sacred, hierarchical basis, already holy and yet still striving for holiness, at once both contemplative and active, and so on. All these matters will become clear through our actually living the Church's life. This is the best illustration and confirmation of its teaching ... [38] ... .

II   THE RENEWAL

... Hence the Church must be gripped with an intense and unfailing desire to learn the ways of the Lord [41] ... . [T]he Church cannot remain indifferent to or unaffected by the changes

---

32. Cf., Gal. 4: 14-16.; 1 Cor. 4, 15.
33. Mt. 16: 18.

which take place in the world around. They influence, modify, and condition its course of action in all sorts of ways. As we know, the Church does not exist in isolation from the world. It lives in the world, and its members are consequently influenced and guided by the world. They imbibe its culture, are subject to its laws and adopt its customs … .

Obviously, there can be no question of reforming the essential nature of the Church or its basic and necessary structure. To use the word reform in that context would be to misuse it completely … [46]. In this context, therefore, when we speak about reform we are not concerned to change things, but to preserve all the more resolutely the characteristic features which Christ has impressed on His Church. Or rather, we are concerned to restore to the Church that ideal of perfection and beauty that corresponds to its original image, and that is at the same time consistent with its necessary, normal and legitimate growth from its original, embryonic form into its present structure … . Some imagine that the only genuine renewal of the Church is one which is born from the ideas of a few, admittedly zealous, people who not infrequently consider themselves divinely inspired. Their vain dreams of the wrong sort of renewal could easily defile the very shape which the Church ought to have … [47] … .

[W]e are also to avoid another danger which the desire for reform can produce, not so much in us pastors, who are restrained by the proper awareness of our sacred duty, as in many of the faithful, who think that the reform of the Church should consist principally in adapting its way of thinking and acting to the customs and temper of the modern secular world. The fascination of worldly life today is very powerful indeed, and many people regard conformity to it as an inescapable and indeed a wise course to take. Hence, those who are not deeply rooted in the faith and in the observance of the Church's laws, readily imagine that the time is ripe to adjust themselves to worldly standards of living, on the assumption that these are the best and only possible ones for a Christian to adopt.

This craving for uniformity is observable even in the realm of philosophy (it is extraordinary how much weight is attached to fashion in a province where the mind ought to be free and independent, anxious only to arrive at the truth, and bowing to the authority of none but proved masters). It is observable also in the realm of ethics, making it more and more perplexing and difficult to define moral rectitude and the right conduct of life [48].

In addition we are confronted with the doctrine of Naturalism, which attempts to undermine the fundamental conception of Christianity. Relativism, too, seeks to justify everything, and treats all things as of equal value. It assails the absolute character of Christian principles. We are also confronted with the growing tendency to prune away from the Christian life everything that requires effort or causes inconvenience. It rejects as vain and futile the practice of Christian asceticism and the contemplation of the things of God. Indeed, sometimes even the apostolic desire for a ready passport into secular society and the determination to make oneself acceptable to men and particularly to the youth of today, prompts certain people to lay aside the principles which characterize our faith and to reject the sort of dignity which gives meaning and force to our determination to make contact with others and makes our teaching effective. Is it not, perhaps, true that some of the younger clergy and religious, in their laudable endeavor to come closer to the masses and to particular groups, aim at becoming like them rather than different from them? By this worthless imitation they forfeit the real value and effectiveness of their endeavors. We must be in the world, but not of it [49] … .

The purpose of this exhortation of Ours is not to lend substance to the belief that perfection consists in rigidly adhering to the methods adopted by the Church in the past and refusing to countenance the practical measures commonly thought to be in accord with the character of our time. These measures can be put to the test. We cannot forget Pope John XXIII's word aggiornamento which We have adopted as expressing the aim and object of Our own pontificate. Besides ratifying it and confirming it as the guiding principle of the Ecumenical Council, We want to bring it to the notice of the whole Church. It should prove a stimulus to the Church to increase its ever growing vitality and its ability to take stock of itself and give careful consideration to the signs of the times, always and everywhere ... [50].

... [T]he Church will rediscover its youthful vitality not so much by changing its external legislation, as by submitting to the obedience of Christ and observing the laws which the Church lays upon itself with the intention of following in Christ's footsteps ... . The Christian way of life as set forth and interpreted by the Church in its prudent legislation, demands a not inconsiderable degree of loyalty, perseverance and self-sacrifice ... . It will not require less of us modern Christians than in the past; it may very well require more. It will require a prompt obedience, no less necessary and difficult now than formerly, but it will be all the more meritorious in that it is inspired more by supernatural motives than by natural ones. Conformity to the spirit of the world, the rejection of the rules of Christian asceticism, indifference in the face of the laxity of contemporary morals, emancipation from the authority of wise and lawful superiors, apathy concerning the contradictory forms of modern thought – these are not the things that can give vigor to the Church and fit it to receive the power and strength of the Holy Spirit's gifts. These are not the things which strengthen the Church in its true following of Christ ... . The only things which can bring these blessings on the Church are the following: the determination to live in accordance with divine grace, faithfulness to the Gospel of Christ, unity in the ranks of the sacred hierarchy and among Christian communities. The follower of Christ is not pliant and cowardly, but loyal and strong [51] ... .

Charity is the key to everything.[34] It sets all to rights. There is nothing which charity cannot achieve and renew. Charity 'beareth all things, believeth all things, hopeth all things, endureth all things'.[35] Who is there among us who does not realize this? And since we realize it, is not this the time to put it into practice? [56] ... .

III   THE DIALOGUE

... Merely to remain true to the faith is not enough. Certainly we must preserve and defend the treasure of truth and grace that we have inherited through Christian tradition. ... But neither the preservation nor the defence of the faith exhausts the duty of the Church in regard to the gifts it has been given. The very nature of the gifts which Christ has given the Church demands that they be extended to others and shared with others. This must be obvious from the words: 'Going, therefore, teach ye all nations',[36] Christ's final command to His apostles.

34. [*Caritas*, love].
35. 1 Cor. 13:7.
36. Matt 28:19.

The word apostle implies a mission from which there is no escaping. To this internal drive of charity which seeks expression in the external gift of charity, We will apply the word 'dialogue' [64].

The Church must enter into dialogue with the world in which it lives. It has something to say, a message to give, a communication to make [65] ... . Here, then, Venerable Brethren, is the noble origin of this dialogue: in the mind of God Himself. Religion of its very nature is a certain relationship between God and man ... [70] ... . The dialogue of salvation was made accessible to all. It applied to everyone without distinction.[37] Hence our dialogue too should be as universal as we can make it. That is to say, it must be catholic, made relevant to everyone, excluding only those who utterly reject it or only pretend to be willing to accept it ... [76].

... To what extent should the Church adapt itself to the historical and local circumstances in which it has to exercise its mission? How is it to guard against the danger of relativism which would make it untrue to its own dogmas and moral principles? And yet how can it fit itself to approach all men and bring salvation to all, becoming on the example of the Apostle Paul 'all things to all men', that all may be saved?[38] ... Furthermore, if we want to be men's pastors, fathers and teachers, we must also behave as their brothers. Dialogue thrives on friendship, and most especially on service. All this we must remember and strive to put into practice on the example and precept of Christ[39] [87] ... . The Church does, however, realize that it is the seed, as it were, the leaven, the salt and the light of the world ... [95].

You may say that in making this assertion we are carried away by an excessive zeal for Our office and are not giving sufficient weight to the true position of the Catholic Church vis-à-vis the world. But that is not so. We see the concrete situation very clearly, and might sum it up in general terms by describing it in a series of concentric circles around the central point at which God has placed us [96].

The first of these circles is immense. Its limits stretch beyond our view into the distant horizon. It comprises the entire human race, the world. We are fully aware of the distance which separates us from the world, but we do not conceive of it as a stranger to us. All things human are our concern. We share with the whole of the human race a common nature, a common life, with all its gifts and all its problems. We are ready to play our part in this primary, universal society, to acknowledge the insistent demands of its fundamental needs, and to applaud the new and often sublime expressions of its genius. But there are moral values of the utmost importance which we have to offer it. These are of advantage to everyone. We root them firmly in the consciences of men. Wherever men are striving to understand themselves and the world, we are able to communicate with them. Wherever the councils of nations come together to establish the rights and duties of man, we are honoured to be permitted to take our place among them. If there is in man a 'soul that is naturally Christian', we wish to respect it, to cherish it, and to communicate with it [97].

In all this, as we remind ourselves and others, our attitude is entirely disinterested, devoid of any temporal or political motive. Our sole purpose is to take what is good in man's life on earth and raise it to a supernatural and Christian level. The Church is not identical with civilization. It does however promote it [98] ... .

---

37. Cf. Col. 3:11.
38. 1 Cor. 9:22.
39. Cf. John 13:14–17.

Then we see another circle around us. This too is vast in extent, yet not so far away from us. It comprises first of all those men who worship the one supreme God, whom we also worship. We would mention first the Jewish people, who still retain the religion of the Old Testament, and who are indeed worthy of our respect and love.

Then we have those worshipers who adhere to other monotheistic systems of religion, especially the Moslem religion. We do well to admire these people for all that is good and true in their worship of God.

And, finally, we have the followers of the great Afro-Asiatic religions.

Obviously we cannot agree with these various forms of religion, nor can we adopt an indifferent or uncritical attitude toward them on the assumption that they are all to be regarded as on an equal footing, and that there is no need for those who profess them to enquire whether or not God has Himself revealed definitively and infallibly how He wishes to be known, loved, and served. Indeed, honesty compels us to declare openly our conviction that the Christian religion is the one and only true religion, and it is our hope that it will be acknowledged as such by all who look for God and worship Him [107].

But we do not wish to turn a blind eye to the spiritual and moral values of the various non-Christian religions, for we desire to join with them in promoting and defending common ideals in the spheres of religious liberty, human brotherhood, education, culture, social welfare, and civic order. Dialogue is possible in all these great projects, which are our concern as much as theirs, and we will not fail to offer opportunities for discussion in the event of such an offer being favorably received in genuine, mutual respect [108].

And so we come to the circle which is nearest to us, and which comprises all those who take their name from Christ … . We readily accept the principle of stressing what we all have in common rather than what divides us. This provides a good and fruitful basis for our dialogue, and we are prepared to engage upon it with a will. We would even go further and declare our readiness to examine how we can meet the legitimate desires of our separated Christian brothers on many points of difference concerning tradition, spirituality, canon law, and worship, for it is Our dearest wish to embrace them in a perfect union of faith and charity.

We must stress however that it is not in Our power to make any concessions regarding the integrity of the faith and the obligations of charity. We realise that this may cause misgiving and opposition in certain quarters, but now that the Catholic Church has on its own initiative taken steps to restore the unity of Christ's fold, it will not cease to exercise the greatest prudence and deliberation. It will continue to insist that the claims it makes for itself – claims which still have the effect of alienating the separated brethren – derive from the will of Christ, not from any spirit of self-aggrandisement based on the record of its past achievements, nor from any unsound theological speculation. Rightly understood, they will be seen to be for the good of all, for the common unity, liberty and fullness of the Christian life. The Catholic Church will never cease to prepare itself by prayer and penance for the longed-for reconciliation [109].

That We, who promote this reconciliation, should be regarded by many of Our separated brothers as an obstacle to it, is a matter of deep distress to Us. The obstacle would seem to be the primacy of honour and jurisdiction which Christ bestowed on the Apostle Peter, and which We have inherited as his Successor.

Are there not those who say that unity between the separated Churches and the Catholic Church would be more easily achieved if the primacy of the Roman pontiff were done away with? We beg our separated brothers to consider the groundlessness of this opinion. Take away the sovereign Pontiff and the Catholic Church would no longer be catholic. Moreover, without the supreme, effective, and authoritative pastoral office of Peter the unity of Christ's Church would collapse. It would be vain to look for other principles of unity in place of the true one established by Christ Himself … . We would add that this cardinal principle of holy Church is not a supremacy of spiritual pride and a desire to dominate mankind, but a primacy of service, ministration, and love. It is no vapid rhetoric which confers on Christ's vicar the title: 'Servant of the servants of God' [110] … .

We address Ourself finally to the sons of God's house, the one, holy, Catholic, and apostolic Church of which the Roman Church is 'mother and head'… [113]. But this desire that the Church's internal relationships should take the form of a dialogue between members of a community founded upon love, does not mean that the virtue of obedience is no longer operative. The right to command and the duty to obey must be present in any properly constituted society, especially in the Church which is structured on a sacred hierarchy. Its authority was established by Christ. It is His representative, the authoritative organ of His Word, the expression of His great pastoral love. Hence obedience has faith as its starting point. It is exercised in the school of evangelical humility. It is a participation in the wisdom, unity, idealism, and charity which are ruling factors in the corporate life of the Church. It confers upon him who commands and upon him who obeys the merit of being like Christ who 'was made obedient even unto death'[40] [114].

Moreover the very exercise of authority becomes, in the context of this dialogue, an exercise of obedience, the obedient performance of a service, a ministry of truth and charity. By obedience We mean the observance of canonical regulations and respect for the government of lawful superiors, but an observance and respect readily and serenely given, as is only to be expected from free and loving children. By contrast, a spirit of independence, bitter criticism, defiance, and arrogance is far removed from that charity which nourishes and preserves the spirit of fellowship, harmony, and peace in the Church. It completely vitiates dialogue, turning it into argument, disagreement and dissension – a sad state of affairs, but by no means uncommon. St. Paul warned us against this when he said: 'Let there be no schisms among you'[41] [115].

---

40. Phil. 2:8.
41. 1 Cor. 1:10.

1.3 *LUMEN GENTIUM* – 1964

Many believe that neither Trent nor Vatican I, the two great post-reformation councils of the Roman Catholic church, satisfactorily dealt with the nature, role and self-understanding of the church itself in any fulsome or systematic fashion. Vatican II's *Dogmatic Constitution on the Church* both reflected key developments in the self-understanding of the church in the 1940s and 1950s, and inspired a further wealth of ecclesiological visions, debates and interpretations. It offered an ecclesiology rich in biblical and everyday imagery and laid a new emphasis upon community and the 'pilgrim' nature of the church in its mission. It marks a further shift from an institutional ecclesiology to one where the church is understood in more open, universal and egalitarian terms. Famously, the second chapter, on the people of God, was placed before the chapter on the hierarchy, reversing the original order. Yet the document is not as anti-hierarchical or quite so radical as many have subsequently believed it to be. Nonetheless, it affirms the priesthood and apostolate of all believers, it focuses upon a model of the hierarchy viewed in terms of its *service* to the church, and it pushes back the boundaries, somewhat, of what constitutes the 'people of God'. It further offers a positive and enabling interpretation of the place and role of the laity. The text[42] betrays the tensions of the council factions, but nonetheless is often masterful in its energizing treatment of fundamental ecclesiological questions. On the whole, its ecclesiology laid the foundations for a more *open* and *dialogical* church,[43] as well as a more *collaborative* and wide-reaching definition of ministry and a *truly* ministerial (as opposed to authoritarian) understanding of leadership and authority.

❋

CHAPTER I   THE MYSTERY OF THE CHURCH

… As all the members of the human body, though they are many, form one body, so also are the faithful in Christ. Also, in the building up of Christ's Body various members and functions have their part to play. There is only one Spirit who, according to His own richness and the needs of the ministries, gives His different gifts for the welfare of the Church. What has a special place among these gifts is the grace of the apostles to whose authority the Spirit Himself subjected even those who were endowed with charisms. Giving the body unity through Himself and through His power and inner joining of the members, this same Spirit produces and urges love among the believers. From all this it follows that if one member endures anything, all the members co-endure it, and if one member is honored, all the members together rejoice. The Head of this Body is Christ … [7].

---

42. *ET* from *Documents of Vatican Council II: Archives of the Holy See*, www.vatican.va/archive/hist_councils/ii_vatican_council/index.htm. Further extracts from *Lumen Gentium* can also be found in Chapters 2, 4 and 8 of the present volume.
43. Reflecting some aspects of *Ecclesiam Suam*.

Christ, the one Mediator, established and continually sustains here on earth His holy Church, the community of faith, hope and charity, as an entity with visible delineation through which He communicated truth and grace to all. But, the society structured with hierarchical organs and the Mystical Body of Christ, are not to be considered as two realities, nor are the visible assembly and the spiritual community, nor the earthly Church and the Church enriched with heavenly things; rather they form one complex reality which coalesces from a divine and a human element. For this reason, by no weak analogy, it is compared to the mystery of the incarnate Word. As the assumed nature inseparably united to Him, serves the divine Word as a living organ of salvation, so, in a similar way, does the visible social structure of the Church serve the Spirit of Christ, who vivifies it, in the building up of the body.

This is the one Church of Christ which in the Creed is professed as one, holy, catholic and apostolic, which our Savior, after His Resurrection, commissioned Peter to shepherd, and him and the other apostles to extend and direct with authority, which He erected for all ages as 'the pillar and mainstay of the truth'.[44] This Church constituted and organized in the world as a society, subsists in the Catholic Church, which is governed by the successor of Peter and by the Bishops in communion with him, although many elements of sanctification and of truth are found outside of its visible structure. These elements, as gifts belonging to the Church of Christ, are forces impelling toward catholic unity.

Just as Christ carried out the work of redemption in poverty and persecution, so the Church is called to follow the same route that it might communicate the fruits of salvation to men. Christ Jesus, 'though He was by nature God ... emptied Himself, taking the nature of a slave',[45] and 'being rich, became poor'[46] for our sakes. Thus, the Church, although it needs human resources to carry out its mission, is not set up to seek earthly glory, but to proclaim, even by its own example, humility and self sacrifice. Christ was sent by the Father 'to bring good news to the poor, to heal the contrite of heart',[47] 'to seek and to save what was lost'.[48] Similarly, the Church encompasses with love all who are afflicted with human suffering and in the poor and afflicted sees the image of its poor and suffering Founder. It does all it can to relieve their need and in them it strives to serve Christ ... [8].

CHAPTER II   ON THE PEOPLE OF GOD

[A]lthough it does not actually include all men, and at times may look like a small flock, [the Church] is nonetheless a lasting and sure seed of unity, hope and salvation for the whole human race. Established by Christ as a communion of life, charity and truth, it is also used by Him as an instrument for the redemption of all, and is sent forth into the whole world as the light of the world and the salt of the earth ... [9].

---

44. 1 Tim. 3:15.
45. Phil. 2:6.
46. 2 Cor. 8;9.
47. Luke 4:18.
48. Luke 19:10.

Though they differ from one another in essence and not only in degree, the common priesthood of the faithful and the ministerial or hierarchical priesthood are nonetheless interrelated: each of them in its own special way is a participation in the one priesthood of Christ.[49] The ministerial priest, by the sacred power he enjoys, teaches and rules the priestly people; acting in the person of Christ, he makes present the eucharistic sacrifice, and offers it to God in the name of all the people. But the faithful, in virtue of their royal priesthood, join in the offering of the Eucharist.[50] They likewise exercise that priesthood in receiving the sacraments, in prayer and thanksgiving, in the witness of a holy life, and by self-denial and active charity … [10].

The holy people of God shares also in Christ's prophetic office; it spreads abroad a living witness to Him, especially by means of a life of faith and charity and by offering to God a sacrifice of praise, the tribute of lips which give praise to His name. The entire body of the faithful, anointed as they are by the Holy One, cannot err in matters of belief. They manifest this special property by means of the whole peoples' supernatural discernment in matters of faith when 'from the Bishops down to the last of the lay faithful'[51] they show universal agreement in matters of faith and morals. That discernment in matters of faith is aroused and sustained by the Spirit of truth. It is exercised under the guidance of the sacred teaching authority, in faithful and respectful obedience to which the people of God accepts that which is not just the word of men but truly the word of God. Through it, the people of God adheres unwaveringly to the faith given once and for all to the saints, penetrates it more deeply with right thinking, and applies it more fully in its life [12].

All men are called to belong to the new people of God. Wherefore this people, while remaining one and only one, is to be spread throughout the whole world and must exist in all ages, so that the decree of God's will may be fulfilled. In the beginning God made human nature one and decreed that all His children, scattered as they were, would finally be gathered together as one … .

It follows that though there are many nations there is but one people of God, which takes its citizens from every race, making them citizens of a kingdom which is of a heavenly rather than of an earthly nature. All the faithful, scattered though they be throughout the world, are in communion with each other in the Holy Spirit, and so, 'he who dwells in Rome knows that the people of India are his members'.[52] Since the kingdom of Christ is not of this world the Church or people of God in establishing that kingdom takes nothing away from the temporal welfare of any people. On the contrary it fosters and takes to itself, insofar as they are good, the ability, riches and customs in which the genius of each people expresses itself. Taking them to itself it purifies, strengthens, elevates and ennobles them … . This characteristic of universality which adorns the people of God is a gift from the Lord Himself. By reason of it, the Catholic Church strives constantly and with due effect to bring all humanity and all its possessions back to its source in Christ, with Him as its head and united in His Spirit.

---

49. Cfr. Pius XII, Allocation *Magnificate Dominum*, 2 Nov. 1954: *AAS*, 46 (1954), 669. Litt. Encyclical *Mediator Dei*, 20 nov. 1947: *AAS*, 39 (1947), 555.

50. Cfr. Pius XI, Litt. Encyclical *Miserentissimus Redemptor*, 8 May 1928: *AAS*, 20 (1928) p. 171 s. Pius XII Allocation *Vous nous avez*, 22 Sept. 1956: *AAS*, 48 (1956), 714.

51. Cfr. S. Augustinus, *D Praedestinatione Sanctorum* 14, 27: *PL*, 44, 980.

52. Cfr. S. Io. Chrysostomus, *In Iohannes Homily* 65, 1: *PG*, 59, 361.

In virtue of this catholicity each individual part contributes through its special gifts to the good of the other parts and of the whole Church. Through the common sharing of gifts and through the common effort to attain fullness in unity, the whole and each of the parts receive increase. Not only, then, is the people of God made up of different peoples but in its inner structure also it is composed of various ranks. This diversity among its members arises either by reason of their duties, as is the case with those who exercise the sacred ministry for the good of their brethren, or by reason of their condition and state of life, as is the case with those many who enter the religious state and, tending toward holiness by a narrower path, stimulate their brethren by their example. Moreover, within the Church particular Churches hold a rightful place; these Churches retain their own traditions, without in any way opposing the primacy of the Chair of Peter, which presides over the whole assembly of charity and protects legitimate differences, while at the same time assuring that such differences do not hinder unity but rather contribute toward it. Between all the parts of the Church there remains a bond of close communion whereby they share spiritual riches, apostolic workers and temporal resources … .

All men are called to be part of this catholic unity of the people of God which in promoting universal peace presages it. And there belong to or are related to it in various ways, the Catholic faithful, all who believe in Christ, and indeed the whole of mankind, for all men are called by the grace of God to salvation [13].

This Sacred Council wishes to turn its attention firstly to the Catholic faithful. Basing itself upon Sacred Scripture and Tradition, it teaches that the Church, now sojourning on earth as an exile, is necessary for salvation. Christ, present to us in His Body, which is the Church, is the one Mediator and the unique way of salvation. In explicit terms He Himself affirmed the necessity of faith and baptism and thereby affirmed also the necessity of the Church, for through baptism as through a door men enter the Church. Whosoever, therefore, knowing that the Catholic Church was made necessary by Christ, would refuse to enter or to remain in it, could not be saved.

They are fully incorporated in the society of the Church who, possessing the Spirit of Christ accept her entire system and all the means of salvation given to her, and are united with her as part of her visible bodily structure and through her with Christ, who rules her through the Supreme Pontiff and the bishops. The bonds which bind men to the Church in a visible way are profession of faith, the sacraments, and ecclesiastical government and communion. He is not saved, however, who, though part of the body of the Church, does not persevere in charity. He remains indeed in the bosom of the Church, but, as it were, only in a 'bodily' manner and not 'in his heart'.[53] All the Church's children should remember that their exalted status is to be attributed not to their own merits but to the special grace of Christ. If they fail moreover to respond to that grace in thought, word and deed, not only shall they not be saved but they will be the more severely judged … [14].

The Church recognizes that in many ways she is linked with those who, being baptized, are honored with the name of Christian, though they do not profess the faith in its entirety or do not preserve unity of communion with the successor of Peter. For there are many who honor Sacred Scripture, taking it as a norm of belief and a pattern of life, and who show a

---

53. Cfr. S. Irenaeus, Adversus Haeresium III, 16, 6; III, 22, 1–3: *PG*, 7, 925 C-926 Aet 955 C-958 A; Harvey 2, 87 s. et 120–23; Sagnard, Ed. Sources Chret., pp. 290–92 et 372 ss.

sincere zeal. They lovingly believe in God the Father Almighty and in Christ, the Son of God and Savior. They are consecrated by baptism, in which they are united with Christ. They also recognize and accept other sacraments within their own Churches or ecclesiastical communities. Many of them rejoice in the episcopate, celebrate the Holy Eucharist and cultivate devotion toward the Virgin Mother of God. They also share with us in prayer and other spiritual benefits. Likewise we can say that in some real way they are joined with us in the Holy Spirit, for to them too He gives His gifts and graces whereby He is operative among them with His sanctifying power. Some indeed He has strengthened to the extent of the shedding of their blood. In all of Christ's disciples the Spirit arouses the desire to be peacefully united, in the manner determined by Christ, as one flock under one shepherd, and He prompts them to pursue this end. Mother Church never ceases to pray, hope and work that this may come about. She exhorts her children to purification and renewal so that the sign of Christ may shine more brightly over the face of the earth [15].

Finally, those who have not yet received the Gospel are related in various ways to the people of God. In the first place we must recall the people to whom the testament and the promises were given and from whom Christ was born according to the flesh. On account of their fathers this people remains most dear to God, for God does not repent of the gifts He makes nor of the calls He issues. But the plan of salvation also includes those who acknowledge the Creator. In the first place amongst these there are the Mohamedans, who, professing to hold the faith of Abraham, along with us adore the one and merciful God, who on the last day will judge mankind. Nor is God far distant from those who in shadows and images seek the unknown God, for it is He who gives to all men life and breath and all things, and as Savior wills that all men be saved. Those also can attain to salvation who through no fault of their own do not know the Gospel of Christ or His Church, yet sincerely seek God and moved by grace strive by their deeds to do His will as it is known to them through the dictates of conscience. Nor does Divine Providence deny the helps necessary for salvation to those who, without blame on their part, have not yet arrived at an explicit knowledge of God and with His grace strive to live a good life. Whatever good or truth is found amongst them is looked upon by the Church as a preparation for the Gospel. She knows that it is given by Him who enlightens all men so that they may finally have life. But often men, deceived by the Evil One, have become vain in their reasonings and have exchanged the truth of God for a lie, serving the creature rather than the Creator. Or some there are who, living and dying in this world without God, are exposed to final despair. Wherefore to promote the glory of God and procure the salvation of all of these ... the Church fosters the missions with care and attention [16] ... .

CHAPTER III   ON THE HIERARCHICAL STRUCTURE OF THE CHURCH AND IN PARTICULAR ON THE EPISCOPATE

This Sacred Council, following closely in the footsteps of the First Vatican Council, with that Council teaches and declares that Jesus Christ, the eternal Shepherd, established His holy Church, having sent forth the apostles as He Himself had been sent by the Father; and He willed that their successors, namely the bishops, should be shepherds in His Church even to the consummation of the world. And in order that the episcopate itself might be one and undivided, He placed Blessed Peter over the other apostles, and instituted in him a permanent and visible source and foundation of unity of faith and communion. And all this teaching about the institution, the perpetuity, the meaning and reason for the sacred primacy of the Roman Pontiff and of his infallible magisterium, this Sacred Council again proposes to be firmly believed by all the faithful. Continuing in that same undertaking, this Council is resolved to declare and proclaim before all men the doctrine concerning bishops, the successors of the apostles, who together with the successor of Peter, the Vicar of Christ, the visible Head of the whole Church, govern the house of the living God [18].

That divine mission, entrusted by Christ to the apostles, will last until the end of the world, since the Gospel they are to teach is for all time the source of all life for the Church. And for this reason the apostles, appointed as rulers in this society, took care to appoint successors ... . Bishops, therefore, with their helpers, the priests and deacons, have taken up the service of the community, presiding in place of God over the flock, whose shepherds they are, as teachers for doctrine, priests for sacred worship, and ministers for governing. And just as the office granted individually to Peter, the first among the apostles, is permanent and is to be transmitted to his successors, so also the apostles' office of nurturing the Church is permanent, and is to be exercised without interruption by the sacred order of bishops. Therefore, the Sacred Council teaches that bishops by divine institution have succeeded to the place of the apostles, as shepherds of the Church, and he who hears them, hears Christ, and he who rejects them, rejects Christ and Him who sent Christ [20] ... .

The supreme power in the universal Church, which this college enjoys, is exercised in a solemn way in an ecumenical council. A council is never ecumenical unless it is confirmed or at least accepted as such by the successor of Peter; and it is prerogative of the Roman Pontiff to convoke these councils, to preside over them and to confirm them. This same collegiate power can be exercised together with the pope by the bishops living in all parts of the world, provided that the head of the college calls them to collegiate action, or at least approves of or freely accepts the united action of the scattered bishops, so that it is thereby made a collegiate act [22].

Bishops, as vicars and ambassadors of Christ, govern the particular churches entrusted to them by their counsel, exhortations, example, and even by their authority and sacred power, which indeed they use only for the edification of their flock in truth and holiness, remembering that he who is greater should become as the lesser and he who is the chief become as the servant. This power, which they personally exercise in Christ's name, is proper, ordinary and immediate, although its exercise is ultimately regulated by the supreme authority of the Church, and can be circumscribed by certain limits, for the advantage of the Church or of the faithful. In virtue of this power, bishops have the sacred right and the duty before the Lord to make laws for their subjects, to pass judgment on them and to moderate everything pertaining to the ordering of worship and the apostolate.

The pastoral office or the habitual and daily care of their sheep is entrusted to them completely; nor are they to be regarded as vicars of the Roman Pontiffs, for they exercise an authority that is proper to them, and are quite correctly called 'prelates', heads of the people whom they govern. Their power, therefore, is not destroyed by the supreme and universal power, but on the contrary it is affirmed, strengthened and vindicated by it, since the Holy

Spirit unfailingly preserves the form of government established by Christ the Lord in His Church [27] ... .

Priests, prudent co-operators with the episcopal order, its aid and instrument, called to serve the people of God, constitute one priesthood with their bishop although bound by a diversity of duties. Associated with their bishop in a spirit of trust and generosity, they make him present in a certain sense in the individual local congregations, and take upon themselves, as far as they are able, his duties and the burden of his care, and discharge them with a daily interest. And as they sanctify and govern under the bishop's authority, that part of the Lord's flock entrusted to them they make the universal Church visible in their own locality and bring an efficacious assistance to the building up of the whole body of Christ. Intent always upon the welfare of God's children, they must strive to lend their effort to the pastoral work of the whole diocese, and even of the entire Church. On account of this sharing in their priesthood and mission, let priests sincerely look upon the bishop as their father and reverently obey him. And let the bishop regard his priests as his co-workers and as sons and friends, just as Christ called His disciples now not servants but friends. All priests, both diocesan and religious, by reason of Orders and ministry, fit into this body of bishops and priests, and serve the good of the whole Church according to their vocation and the grace given to them ... .

Let them, as fathers in Christ, take care of the faithful whom they have begotten by baptism and their teaching. Becoming from the heart a pattern to the flock, let them so lead and serve their local community that it may worthily be called by that name, by which the one and entire people of God is signed, namely, the Church of God. Let them remember that by their daily life and interests they are showing the face of a truly sacredotal and pastoral ministry to the faithful and the infidel, to Catholics and non-Catholics, and that to all they bear witness to the truth and life, and as good shepherds go after those also, who though baptized in the Catholic Church have fallen away from the use of the sacraments, or even from the faith [28] ... .

CHAPTER IV   THE LAITY

Having set forth the functions of the hierarchy, the Sacred Council gladly turns its attention. to the state of those faithful called the laity. Everything that has been said above concerning the People of God is intended for the laity, religious and clergy alike. But there are certain things which pertain in a special way to the laity, both men and women, by reason of their condition and mission. Due to the special circumstances of our time the foundations of this doctrine must be more thoroughly examined. For their pastors know how much the laity contribute to the welfare of the entire Church. They also know that they were not ordained by Christ to take upon themselves alone the entire salvific mission of the Church toward the world. On the contrary they understand that it is their noble duty to shepherd the faithful and to recognize their ministries and charisms, so that all according to their proper roles may cooperate in this common undertaking with one mind ... [30].

... These faithful are by baptism made one body with Christ and are constituted among the People of God; they are in their own way made sharers in the priestly, prophetical, and kingly functions of Christ; and they carry out for their own part the mission of the whole Christian people in the Church and in the world.

What specifically characterizes the laity is their secular nature … . [T]he laity, by their very vocation, seek the kingdom of God by engaging in temporal affairs and by ordering them according to the plan of God. They live in the world, that is, in each and in all of the secular professions and occupations. They live in the ordinary circumstances of family and social life, from which the very web of their existence is woven … [31].

By divine institution Holy Church is ordered and governed with a wonderful diversity. 'For just as in one body we have many members, yet all the members have not the same function, so we, the many, are one body in Christ, but severally members one of another'.[54] Therefore, the chosen People of God is one: 'one Lord, one faith, one baptism';[55] sharing a common dignity as members from their regeneration in Christ, having the same filial grace and the same vocation to perfection; possessing in common one salvation, one hope and one undivided charity. There is, therefore, in Christ and in the Church no inequality on the basis of race or nationality, social condition or sex, because 'there is neither Jew nor Greek: there is neither bond nor free: there is neither male nor female. For you are all "one" in Christ Jesus'.[56]

If therefore in the Church everyone does not proceed by the same path, nevertheless all are called to sanctity and have received an equal privilege of faith through the justice of God. And if by the will of Christ some are made teachers, pastors and dispensers of mysteries on behalf of others, yet all share a true equality with regard to the dignity and to the activity common to all the faithful for the building up of the Body of Christ. For the distinction which the Lord made between sacred ministers and the rest of the People of God bears within it a certain union, since pastors and the other faithful are bound to each other by a mutual need. Pastors of the Church, following the example of the Lord, should minister to one another and to the other faithful. These in their turn should enthusiastically lend their joint assistance to their pastors and teachers. Thus in their diversity all bear witness to the wonderful unity in the Body of Christ. This very diversity of graces, ministries and works gathers the children of God into one, because 'all these things are the work of one and the same Spirit'[57]… [32].

… The lay apostolate, however, is a participation in the salvific mission of the Church itself. Through their baptism and confirmation all are commissioned to that apostolate by the Lord Himself. Moreover, by the sacraments, especially holy Eucharist, that charity toward God and man which is the soul of the apostolate is communicated and nourished. Now the laity are called in a special way to make the Church present and operative in those places and circumstances where only through them can it become the salt of the earth. Thus each member of the laity, in virtue of the very gifts bestowed upon them, is at the same time a witness and a living instrument of the mission of the Church itself 'according to the measure of Christ's bestowal'.[58] Besides this apostolate which certainly pertains to all Christians, the laity can also be called in various ways to a more direct form of co-operation in the apostolate of the Hierarchy. This was the way certain men and women assisted Paul the Apostle in the

---

54. 1 Rom. 12:4–5.
55. cf Eph. 4:5.
56. Gal. 3: 28; cf. Col. 3:11.
57. 1 Cor. 12:11.
58. Eph. 4:7.

Gospel, laboring much in the Lord. Further, they have the capacity to assume from the Hierarchy certain ecclesiastical functions, which are to be performed for a spiritual purpose [33].

    … For besides intimately linking them to His life and His mission, He also gives them a sharing in His priestly function of offering spiritual worship for the glory of God and the salvation of men. For this reason the laity, dedicated to Christ and anointed by the Holy Spirit, are marvelously called and wonderfully prepared so that ever more abundant fruits of the Spirit may be produced in them. For all their works, prayers and apostolic endeavors, their ordinary married and family life, their daily occupations, their physical and mental relaxation, if carried out in the Spirit, and even the hardships of life, if patiently borne – all these become 'spiritual sacrifices acceptable to God through Jesus Christ'.[59] Together with the offering of the Lord's body, they are most fittingly offered in the celebration of the Eucharist. Thus, as those everywhere who adore in holy activity, the laity consecrate the world itself to God … [34].

    … The laity should, as all Christians, promptly accept in Christian obedience decisions of their spiritual shepherds, since they are representatives of Christ as well as teachers and rulers in the Church. Let them follow the example of Christ, who by His obedience even unto death, opened to all men the blessed way of the liberty of the children of God … . Let the spiritual shepherds recognize and promote the dignity as well as the responsibility of the laity in the Church. Let them willingly employ their prudent advice. Let them confidently assign duties to them in the service of the Church, allowing them freedom and room for action. Further, let them encourage lay people so that they may undertake tasks on their own initiative. Attentively in Christ, let them consider with fatherly love the projects, suggestions and desires proposed by the laity. However, let the shepherds respectfully acknowledge that just freedom which belongs to everyone in this earthly city. A great many wonderful things are to be hoped for from this familiar dialogue between the laity and their spiritual leaders: in the laity a strengthened sense of personal responsibility; a renewed enthusiasm; a more ready application of their talents to the projects of their spiritual leaders. The latter, on the other hand, aided by the experience of the laity, can more clearly and more incisively come to decisions regarding both spiritual and temporal matters. In this way, the whole Church, strengthened by each one of its members, may more effectively fulfill its mission for the life of the world … [37].

---

59. Pet. 2:5.

1.4 *COMMUNIONIS NOTIO* – 1992

Issued under the name of Cardinal Joseph Ratzinger, Prefect of the Congregation for the Doctrine of the Faith, this letter[60] seeks to clarify, expand upon and interpret – some would argue reinterpret – the ecclesiology of Vatican II. In 2000, *Dominus Iesus* would further this same task. It espouses an ecclesiology of the church as the sacrament of salvation for humanity and asserts the priority of the authority of the *Universal* church (seen by many interpreters as identified here with the institutional church). The emphasis is upon unity and the *immediate* rather than mediated communion of all individual and local churches with the Universal church (indeed, this being the means whereby they are constitutive of being a 'church' at all). The letter states that it is through a commitment to and participation in the Eucharist and the Episcopacy (with the Pope at its head) that a local/individual church gains full communion with the Universal church. It hence warns against overt claims to autonomy and self-sufficiency in local/individual churches and seeks to set forth a definitive teaching on the respective nature and promotion of unity and diversity in the church (emphasising the former, limiting the latter in certain respects). Some critics saw it as indicative of a *reversal* of the efforts of Vatican II's progressive legacy and a return to the Roman centralizing tendencies more resonant with Vatican I. Such critics see the ecclesiology of communion in the documents of Vatican II as something very different to that espoused in this document. Nonetheless, the document represents a definite 'ecclesiology of communion' which both reflects and has in turn influenced much theologising and teaching in the church in recent decades.

❧

LETTER TO THE BISHOPS OF THE CATHOLIC CHURCH ON SOME ASPECTS OF THE CHURCH UNDERSTOOD AS COMMUNION

INTRODUCTION

The concept of *communion* (*koinonia*), which appears with a certain prominence in the texts of the Second Vatican Council,[61] is very suitable for expressing the core of the Mystery of the Church, and can certainly be a key for the renewal of Catholic ecclesiology … . However, some approaches to ecclesiology suffer from a clearly inadequate awareness of the Church as a *mystery of communion*, especially insofar as they have not sufficiently integrated the concept of *communion* with the concepts of *People of God* and of the *Body of Christ*, and have not given due importance to the relationship between the Church as *communion* and the Church as *sacrament* [1].

---

60. *ET* from *Archives of the Holy See*, www.vatican.va/ roman_curia/congregations/cfaith/index.htm.
61. Cf. *Lumen gentium*, nn. 4, 8, 13-15, 18, 21, 24-25; *Dei Verbum*, n. 10; *Gaudium et spes*, n. 32; Decr. *Unitatis redintegratio*, nn. 2-4, 14-15, 17-19, 22.

Bearing in mind the doctrinal, pastoral and ecumenical importance of the different aspects regarding the Church understood as Communion, the Congregation for the Doctrine of the Faith has considered it opportune, by means of this *Letter*, to recall briefly and to clarify, where necessary, some of the fundamental elements that are to be considered already settled also by those who undertake the hoped-for theological investigation [2].

I   THE CHURCH, A MYSTERY OF COMMUNION

The concept of *communion* lies '*at the heart of the Church's self understanding*',[62] insofar as it is the Mystery of the personal union of each human being with the divine Trinity and with the rest of mankind, initiated with the faith, and, having begun as a reality in the Church on earth, is directed towards its eschatological fulfilment in the heavenly Church.

If the concept of *communion*, which is not a univocal concept, is to serve as a key to ecclesiology, it has to be understood within the teaching of the Bible and the patristic tradition, in which *communion* always involves a double dimension: the *vertical* (communion with God) and the *horizontal* (communion among men). It is essential to the Christian understanding of *communion* that it be recognized above all as a gift from God, as a fruit of God's initiative carried out in the paschal mystery. The new relationship between man and God, that has been established in Christ and is communicated through the sacraments, also extends to a new relationship among human beings. As a result, the concept of *communion* should be such as to express both the sacramental nature of the Church ... and also the particular unity which makes the faithful into members of one and the same Body, the Mystical Body of Christ, an organically structured community, '*a people brought into one by the unity of the Father and of the Son and of the Holy Spirit*'[63] and endowed with suitable means for its visible and social union [3].

Ecclesial communion is at the same time both invisible and visible. As an invisible reality, it is the communion of each human being with the Father through Christ in the Holy Spirit, and with the others who are fellow sharers in the divine nature, in the passion of Christ, in the same faith, in the same spirit. In the Church on earth, there is an intimate relationship between this invisible communion and the visible communion in the teaching of the Apostles, in the sacraments and in the hierarchical order. By means of these divine gifts, which are very visible realities, Christ carries out in different ways in history his prophetical, priestly and kingly *function* for the salvation of mankind. This link between the invisible and visible elements of ecclesial communion constitutes the Church as the *Sacrament* of salvation.

From this sacramentality it follows that the Church is not a reality closed in on herself; rather, she is permanently open to missionary and ecumenical endeavour, for she is sent to the world to announce and witness, to make present and spread the mystery of communion which is essential to her: to gather together all people and all things into Christ; so as to be for all an '*inseparable sacrament of unity*'.[64] [4].

Ecclesial communion, into which each individual is introduced by faith and by Baptism, has its root and centre in the Blessed Eucharist. Indeed, Baptism is an incorporation into a

---

62. John Paul II, *Address to the Bishops of the United Sates of America*, 16-IX-1987, n. 1: 'Insegnamenti di Giovanni Paolo II', X, 3 (1987), 553.
63. St Cyprian, *De Oratione Dominica*, 23: *PL*, 4, 553; cf. *Lumen Gentium*, n. 4/b.
64. St Cyprian, *Epistile ad Magnum*, 6: *PL*, 3, 1142.

body that the risen Lord builds up and keeps alive through the Eucharist, so that this body can truly be called the Body of Christ. The Eucharist is the creative force and source of *communion* among the members of the Church, precisely because it unites each one of them with Christ himself … . Hence, the pauline expression *the Church is the Body of Christ* means that the Eucharist, in which the Lord gives us his Body and transforms us into one Body, is where the Church expresses herself permanently in most essential form. While present everywhere, she is yet only *one*, just as Christ is *one* … [5] … .

II   UNIVERSAL CHURCH AND PARTICULAR CHURCHES

The *Church of Christ*, which we profess in the Creed to be one, holy, catholic and apostolic, is the universal Church, that is, the worldwide community of the disciples of the Lord, which is present and active amid the particular characteristics and the diversity of persons, groups, times and places. Among these manifold particular expressions of the saving presence of the one Church of Christ, there are to be found, from the times of the Apostles on, those entities which are in themselves *Churches*, because, although they are particular, the universal Church becomes present in them with all its essential elements. They are therefore constituted '*after the model of the universal Church*',[65] and each of them is '*a portion of the People of God entrusted to a bishop to be guided by him with the assistance of his clergy*'.[66] [7].

The universal Church is therefore the *Body of the Churches*. Hence it is possible to apply the concept of communion *in analogous fashion* to the union existing among particular Churches, and to see the universal Church as a *Communion of Churches*. Sometimes, however, the idea of a 'communion of particular Churches' is presented in such a way as to weaken the concept of the unity of the Church at the visible and institutional level. Thus it is asserted that every particular Church is a subject complete in itself, and that the universal Church is the result of a *reciprocal recognition* on the part of the particular Churches. This ecclesiological unilateralism, which impoverishes not only the concept of the universal Church but also that of the particular Church, betrays an insufficient understanding of the concept of communion. As history shows, when a particular Church has sought to become self-sufficient, and has weakened its real communion with the universal Church and with its living and visible centre, its internal unity suffers too, and it finds itself in danger of losing its own freedom in the face of the various forces of slavery and exploitation [8].

In order to grasp the true meaning of the analogical application of the term *communion* to the particular Churches taken as a whole, one must bear in mind above all that the particular Churches, insofar as they are '*part of the one Church of Christ*',[67] have a special relationship of '*mutual interiority*'[68] with the whole, that is, with the universal Church, because in every particular Church '*the one, holy, catholic and apostolic Church of Christ is truly present and active*'.[69] For this reason, '*the universal Church cannot be conceived as the sum of the particular Churches, or as a federation of particular Churches*'.[70] It is not the result of the

65. *Lumen Gentium*, n. 23/a; cf. *Ad gentes*, n. 20/a.
66. *Christus Dominus*, n. 11/a.
67. *Christus Dominus*, n. 6/c.
68. John Paul II, *Address to the Roman Curia*, 20-XII-1990, n. 9: 'L'Osservatore Romano', 21-XII-1990, p. 5.
69. *Christus Dominus*, n. 11/a.
70. John Paul II, *Address to the Bishops of the United States of America*, 16-IX-1987, n. 3: as quoted, 555.

communion of the Churches, but, in its essential mystery, it is a reality *ontologically and temporally* prior to every *individual* particular Church.

Indeed, according to the Fathers, *ontologically*, the Church-mystery, the Church that is one and unique, precedes creation, and gives birth to the particular Churches as her daughters. She expresses herself in them; she is the mother and not the product of the particular Churches. Furthermore, the Church is manifested, *temporally*, on the day of Pentecost in the community of the one hundred and twenty gathered around Mary and the twelve Apostles, the representatives of the one unique Church and the founders-to-be of the local Churches, who have a mission directed to the world ... .

From the Church, which in its origins and its first manifestation is universal, have arisen the different local Churches, as particular expressions of the one unique Church of Jesus Christ. Arising *within* and *out of* the universal Church, they have their ecclesiality in it and from it. Hence the formula of the Second Vatican Council: *The Church in and formed out of the Churches (Ecclesia in et ex Ecclesiis)*,[71] is inseparable from this other formula: *The Churches in and formed out of the Church (Ecclesia in et ex Ecclesiis)*.[72] Clearly the relationship between the universal Church and the particular Churches is a mystery, and cannot be compared to that which exists between the whole and the parts in a purely human group or society [9].

Every member of the faithful, through faith and Baptism, is inserted into the one, holy, catholic and apostolic Church. He or she does not belong to the universal Church in a *mediate* way, *through* belonging to a particular Church, but in an *immediate* way, even though entry into and life within the universal Church are necessarily brought about *in* a particular Church. From the point of view of the Church understood as communion, this means therefore that the universal *communion of the faithful* and the *communion of the Churches* are not consequences of one another, but constitute the same reality seen from different viewpoints.

Moreover, one's *belonging* to a particular Church never conflicts with the reality that *in the Church no-one is a stranger*: each member of the faithful, especially in the celebration of the Eucharist, is in *his or her* Church, in the Church of Christ, regardless of whether or not he or she belongs, according to canon law, to the diocese, parish or other particular community where the celebration takes place. In this sense, without impinging on the necessary regulations regarding juridical dependence, whoever belongs to one particular Church belongs to all the Churches; since belonging to the *Communion*, like belonging to the Church, is never simply particular, but by its very nature is always universal [10].

III   COMMUNION OF THE CHURCHES, EUCHARIST AND EPISCOPATE

Unity, or communion, between the particular Churches in the universal Church, is rooted not only in the same faith and in the common Baptism, but above all in the Eucharist and in the Episcopate.

It is rooted in the Eucharist because the eucharistic Sacrifice, while always performed in a particular community, is never a celebration of that community alone. In fact, the community, in receiving the eucharistic presence of the Lord, receives the entire gift of

---

71. *Lumen Gentium*, n. 23/a: *'it is in these and formed out of them that the one and unique Catholic Church exists'* ... .
72. John Paul II, *Address to the Roman Curia*, 20-XII-1990, n. 9: as quoted, 5.

salvation and shows, even in its lasting visible particular form, that it is the image and true presence of the one, holy, catholic and apostolic Church.

The rediscovery of a *eucharistic ecclesiology*, though being of undoubted value, has however sometimes placed unilateral emphasis on the principle of the local Church. It is claimed that, where the Eucharist is celebrated, the totality of the mystery of the Church would be made present in such a way as to render any other principle of unity or universality non-essential. Other conceptions, under different theological influences, present this particular view of the Church in an even more radical form, going as far as to hold that gathering together in the name of Jesus (cf. *Mt* 18, 20) is the same as generating the Church: the assembly which in the name of Christ becomes a community, would hold within itself the powers of the Church, including power as regards the Eucharist. The Church, some say, would arise 'from base level'. These and other similar errors do not take sufficiently into account that it is precisely the Eucharist that renders all self-sufficiency on the part of the particular Churches impossible. Indeed, the unicity and indivisibility of the eucharistic Body of the Lord implies the unicity of his mystical Body, which is the one and indivisible Church. From the eucharistic centre arises the necessary openness of every celebrating community, of every particular Church; by allowing itself to be drawn into the open arms of the Lord, it achieves insertion into his one and undivided Body. For this reason too, the existence of the Petrine ministry, which is a foundation of the unity of the Episcopate and of the universal Church, bears a profound correspondence to the eucharistic character of the Church [11].

In fact, the unity of the Church is also rooted in the unity of the Episcopate. As the very idea of the *Body of the Churches* calls for the existence of a Church that is *Head* of the Churches, which is precisely the Church of Rome, '*foremost in the universal communion of charity*',[73] so too the unity of the Episcopate involves the existence of a Bishop who is Head of the *Body or College of Bishops*, namely the Roman Pontiff. Of the unity of the Episcopate, as also of the unity of the entire Church, '*the Roman Pontiff, as the successor of Peter, is a perpetual and visible source and foundation*'.[74] This unity of the Episcopate is perpetuated through the centuries by means of the *apostolic succession*, and is also the foundation of the identity of the Church of every age with the Church built by Christ upon Peter and upon the other Apostles [12].

The Bishop is a visible source and foundation of the unity of the particular Church entrusted to his pastoral ministry. But for each particular Church to be fully Church, that is, the particular presence of the universal Church with all its essential elements, and hence constituted *after the model of the universal Church*, there must be present in it, as a proper element, the supreme authority of the Church: the Episcopal College '*together with their head, the Supreme Pontiff, and never apart from him*'.[75] The Primacy of the Bishop of Rome and the episcopal College are proper elements of the universal Church that are '*not derived from the particularity of the Churches*',[76] but are nevertheless *interior* to each particular Church. Consequently '*we must see the ministry of the Successor of Peter, not only as a "global" service,*

---

73. St Ignatius of Antioch, *Epist. ad Rom.*, prol.: PG 5, 685; cf. Const. *Lumen gentium*, n. 13/c.

74. *Lumen gentium,* n. 23/a. Cf. *Pastor aeternus*: Denz.-Sch`n. 3051–3057; St Cyprian, *De unitate Ecclesiae*, 4: PL 4, 512–515.

75. *Lumen gentium,* n. 22/b; cf also n. 19.

76. John Paul II, *Address to the Roman Curia*, 20-XII-1990, n. 9: as quoted, p. 5.

reaching each particular Church from "outside", as it were, but as belonging already to the essence of each particular Church from "within".[77] Indeed, the ministry of the Primacy involves, in essence, a truly episcopal power, which is not only supreme, full and universal, but also *immediate*, over everybody, whether Pastors or other faithful. The ministry of the Successor of Peter as something *interior* to each particular Church is a necessary expression of that fundamental *mutual interiority* between universal Church and particular Church [13].

The unity of the Eucharist and the unity of the Episcopate *with Peter and under Peter* are not independent roots of the unity of the Church, since Christ instituted the Eucharist and the Episcopate as essentially interlinked realities. The Episcopate is *one*, just as the Eucharist is *one*: the one Sacrifice of the one Christ, dead and risen. The liturgy expresses this reality in various ways, showing, for example, that every celebration of the Eucharist is performed in union not only with the proper Bishop, but also with the Pope, with the episcopal order, with all the clergy, and with the entire people. Every valid celebration of the Eucharist expresses this universal communion *with Peter* and with the whole Church, or *objectively* calls for it, as in the case of the Christian Churches separated from Rome [14].

IV   UNITY AND DIVERSITY IN ECCLESIAL COMMUNION

'*The universality of the Church involves, on the one hand, a most solid unity, and on the other, a* plurality *and a* diversification, *which do not obstruct unity, but rather confer upon it the character of "communion".*[78] This plurality refers both to the diversity of ministries, charisms, and forms of life and apostolate within each particular Church, and to the diversity of traditions in liturgy and culture among the various particular Churches.

Fostering a unity that does not obstruct diversity, and acknowledging and fostering a diversification that does not obstruct unity but rather enriches it, is a fundamental task of the Roman Pontiff for the whole Church, and without prejudice to the general law of the Church itself, of each Bishop in the particular Church entrusted to his pastoral ministry. But the building up and safeguarding of this unity, on which diversification confers the character of communion, is also a task of everyone in the Church, because all are called to build it up and preserve it each day, above all by means of that charity which is '*the bond of perfection*'[79] [15] ... .

V   ECCLESIAL COMMUNION AND ECUMENISM

... Among the non-Catholic Churches and Christian communities, there are indeed to be found many elements of the Church of Christ, which allow us, amid joy and hope, to acknowledge the existence of a certain communion, albeit imperfect.

This communion exists especially with the Eastern orthodox Churches, which, though separated from the See of Peter, remain united to the Catholic Church by means of very close

---

77. John Paul II, *Address to the Bishops of the United States of America*, 16-IX-1987, n. 4: as quoted, 556.

78. John Paul II, *Address*, General Audience, 27-IX-1989, n. 2: 'Insegnamenti di Giovanni Paolo II' XII, 2 (1989) 679.

79. Col. 3:14. Aquinas, *Exposit. in Symbolum Apostolicum*, a. 9: '*The Church is one ... through the unity of charity, because all are joined in the love of God, and among themselves in mutual love.*'

bonds, such as the apostolic succession and a valid Eucharist, and therefore merit the title of particular Churches. Indeed, '*through the celebration of the Eucharist of the Lord in each of these Churches, the Church of God is built up and grows in stature*',[80] for in every valid celebration of the Eucharist the one, holy, catholic and apostolic Church becomes truly present.

Since, however, communion with the universal Church, represented by Peter's Successor, is not an external complement to the particular Church, but one of its internal constituents, the situation of those venerable Christian communities also means that their existence as particular Churches is *wounded*. The wound is even deeper in those ecclesial communities which have not retained the apostolic succession and a valid Eucharist ... [17].

This situation seriously calls for ecumenical commitment on the part of everyone, with a view to achieving full communion in the unity of the Church; that unity '*which Christ bestowed on his Church from the beginning. This unity, we believe, subsists in the Catholic Church as something she can never lose, and we hope that it will continue to increase until the end of time*'.[81] In this ecumenical commitment, important priorities are prayer, penance, study, dialogue and collaboration, so that, through a new conversion to the Lord, all may be enabled to recognize the continuity of the Primacy of Peter in his successors, the Bishops of Rome, and to see the Petrine ministry fulfilled, in the manner intended by the Lord, as a worldwide apostolic service, which is present in all the Churches *from within*, and which, while preserving its substance as a divine institution, can find expression in various ways according to the different circumstances of time and place, as history has shown [18].

---

80. *Unitatis redintegratio*, n. 15/a.
81. *Unitatis redintegratio*, n. 4/c.

1.5 YVES CONGAR: *POWER AND POVERTY IN THE CHURCH* – 1963

Our extract comes from Congar's masterful attempt to address the key issues of how the church should understand itself in relation to the modern world and how it is currently perceived, as well as to reflect upon how it *should* be perceived.[82] Congar suggests that we re-focus upon biblical images crucial to the formation and work of the church itself, most notable *fellowship, service* and *witness*. He believes the church will be misunderstood if it clings to outdated and now alien forms of representing and implementing its image. Too often the world views the church as being an institution which abuses aspects of its power. The church should rekindle a model based upon the gospel model of a community committed to humility and the ideal of poverty. This will help the church develop a 'new style for her presence in the world'. This new style includes a re-valuation of the place of the clergy and laity in the church. Congar champions the one 'people of God' understanding of the church. The laity are not mere 'clients or beneficiaries' of the clergy. Clericalism and a focus upon the superiority of the ordained to the laity must be replaced with a model of ministry based upon the New Testament ideals of poverty and service alike. Congar's ecclesiology was, of course, highly influential at Vatican II. Though written some decades, ago, Congar's concern that, all too often, the church fails to meet people where they, themselves are at, i.e., on meaningful terms, seems most pertinent for the church of our present times.

❋

Everything that I have said so far shows that several styles have followed one another in the Church's visible presence in the world. No single formula can exhaust the relations of the spiritual with the temporal; none of the forms taken by these relations fully expresses the reality of a Church whose substance escapes time, being of different order from the things of this world. The Church makes full use of the possibilities that history offers her to live and work in the world; but because she is not of the world she reserves the right to lay aside what has served her for a season, and to use other means or give other expression to her life.

Nowadays she is called upon to find a new style for her presence in the world. A presence founded on prestige, exercising an authority whose superiority was acknowledged even on the level of law, may have been acceptable and indeed required in an age of unanimity in religion. When no other voice but the Church's taught men how they should walk, no other arm but hers upheld them, they accepted her not only as the messenger of Jesus Christ but, within the structure of society on this earth and at the very apex of its social organization, as an authority endowed with privileges, splendour, and the means of action that befitted her station. But now men have taken over the ordering of the affairs of the world and become so engrossed by them that they can no longer find interest for anything else. The world has lost the spiritual unity of ancient Christendom; it is divided, and its divisions are in all probability final. Moreover increased production of the means of comfortable living involves men in such

82. 'By Way of Conclusion' from *Power and Poverty in the Church*, *ET*, Jennifer Nicholson (London, Geoffrey Chapman, 1964). French original *Pour une eglise servante et pauvre*, Paris, du cerf, 1963.

relentless competition, intricate organization, and stimulation of appetites and compulsions that even as they become kings they are in danger of losing the health that was theirs in a less affluent and exalted position.

Confronting this world, or rather surrounded by it, the Church finds herself in a situation which must be recognized not only as one historical situation among others, neither better nor worse than others, but also which conforms much more closely with the law of the Gospel; she is called upon to make a clean break with the old forms of her presence in the world, legacies from the days when she controlled the hand that bore the sceptre, and to find a new style of being present to men. Individual initiative and spearhead groups which have made their appearance in every country have already clearly outlined the shape of this new style; now it must be given recognition, some sort of consecration on the scale of the universal Church, and urged in the strongest terms at the next session of the Council.

I was able to say that the present situation of the Church is in closer conformity with the law of Christian life first, because of the distinction and tension between the Church and the world, which was weakened, if not effaced, by the regime of Christendom. And by the same reasoning, because she has been freed from the dangers of an association or symbiosis with temporal society which tempted the clergy to adopt the attitudes of the world, not to be ashamed to speak the language of the world or to wear the world's tawdry livery of tinsel and gilt. In a world that has become, or has become again, purely 'worldly', the Church finds herself forced, if she would still be anything at all, to be simply the Church, witness to the Gospel and the kingdom of God, through Jesus Christ and in view of him. That is what men need, that is what they expect of her. In fact if we listed all their most valid claims on the Church we should find that they amounted to this: that she be less *of* the world and more *in* the world; that she be simply the Church of Jesus Christ, the conscience of men in the light of the Gospel, but that she be this with her whole heart.

The characteristics of this style of her presence in conformity with the Gospel are outlined in the Acts of the Apostles and the writings of the New Testament. They can be reduced to three terms, compact with the greatest possible spiritual meaning: *Koinonia, Diakonia, Marturia* (Fellowship, Service, Witness). The World Council of Churches has made these three terms the foundation, as it were the tripod on which its programme of action stands, and by so doing has gone straight to the heart of truth in its most authentic form. Every initiative inspired by the Gospel leads instinctively in this direction. The ground has been so well prepared, so many appeals are being made to us, that this is the moment for the whole Church to find the new style of her presence in the world by establishing, nourishing and inspiring true communities of brothers, projects and associations for service, and acts of witness.

These three supreme realities could be the starting point of a positive programme of Christian life in the world. The demands they make would not only affect individuals, but the Church herself, *qua* Church, and hence at the ecclesiological level. These three are the sure guides to Christian life; but what part have they in our treatises on the Church? To read them, it seems as if the Church could very well do without Christians and without the life of the Gospel?

A positive programme of this kind entails examination of various forms or attitudes which may in some degree betray the Church. To be honest, we are often more sinned against than sinning in our acceptance of these. We come into an inheritance not lacking in grandeur and titles of respect, but which is now so archaic, rigid and ponderous that we risk being incapable of being *to men* what men themselves and what the Gospel require us to be today. In the outward forms we have inherited from a venerable past we must be ruthless critics of anything that may on the one hand betray the spirit of the Gospel, and on the other, of anything that may isolate us and set up a barrier between us and men. Certain forms of prestige, certain titles or insignia, a certain protocol, certain ways of life and dress, an abstract and pompous vocabulary, are all structures that isolate us, just as there are structures that humiliate or degrade. What was formerly in place in a world much more stable than ours and imbued with respect for established honours is today only a sure way to isolation: a barrier to what we most sincerely desire to express and communicate. Forms designed to inspire respect, to surround us with an aura of mystery, still persist and their effect today is the opposite of what one would wish. Not only do they keep men at a distance from us, they keep us at a distance from men, so that the real world of their life is morally inaccessible to us. This is extremely serious. For it means that we are in fact no longer able to meet men on the ground where they are most themselves, where they express themselves freely, experience their most real sorrows and joys, face their true problems. We are in danger of living in their midst, separated from them by a haze of fiction.

Naturally, our effort should reach down to include spiritual habits or images which themselves depend, at a still deeper level, on the ecclesiology that we profess at least in practice. We are still a long way from reaping the consequences of the rediscovery, which we have all made in principle, of the fact that the whole Church is a single people of God and that she is made up of the faithful as well as the clergy. We have an idea, we feel, implicitly and without admitting it, even unconsciously that the Church is the clergy and that the faithful are only our clients or beneficiaries. This terrible concept has been built into so many of our structures and habits that it seems to be taken for granted and beyond change. It is a betrayal of the truth. A great deal still remains to be done to declericalize our conception of the Church (without, of course, jeopardizing her hierarchical structure), and to put the clergy back where they truly belong, in the place of member-servants. Much remains to be done before we can pass from the simple moral plane where as individuals we act in the spirit of humility and service, albeit within structures of caste and privilege, to the plane of ecclesiological concepts. According to St Paul, ordained ministers in the Church are the joints or nerves on which the whole of the active body relies for its smooth working (cf. Eph. 4: 16); their role is 'the perfecting of the saints' (that is, of the faithful) 'for the work of the ministry' which is laid upon us all, whose end is the building up of the Body of Christ (v. 12).

We are still a long way from the goal!

To help us make the readjustments that are needed, to give us better understanding of what is at stake, to point the way to new forms of expression and presence in the world, nothing can be more useful than frank exchange of views between the Church and the world, between the Church and other Christians, and within the Church between clergy and laity, circumference and centre, parish priests and theologians or specialists in the different disciplines that have something to contribute on this problem. It is in discussion that each finds the truth of his existence, it is the pooling of resources that gives the impetus needed to meet all the demands of one's personal convictions. For the Church, as for every one of us, health consists not only in being herself, but in working out in her life the truth of her relationship with others. A Church thus open to free discussion will be a Church of poverty and service too, a Church which has the word of the Gospel to give to men: less *of* the world and more *for* the world!

1.6 HANS URS VON BALTHASAR: *WHO IS THE CHURCH?* – 1961

In this extract,[83] Balthasar expands upon his famous notion of the 'Marian profile' of the church. Essentially Balthasar believes that the laity, the Christians whom make up the church, should strive to emulate Mary in being as open to God as possible and in being willing to serve God and do his work. This enables Balthasar to expound the notion of the church as the 'bride' of Christ. But there is also another 'profile' to the church and this is compared, in Balthasar's theology, to the person of Peter in the New Testament. This 'Petrine profile' of the church reflects the hierarchical and jurisdictional elements of the church. It helps explain the notion of office in the church, in particular the office of Bishop. However, Balthasar insists that we should not try and view one of these notions of the church over and above the other: the structural and sacramental aspects of the church are also 'mediating and instrumental' in bringing God's grace to those who belong to the church in their quest for salvation. Balthasar sketches a sacramental (indeed ontological) understanding of the church's structures and the functions of office: they exist to bring the believer closer to God. He wishes to present a picture of the church which can resist the (literally) *mundane* ecclesiologies which he believes have come to the fore. Nonetheless, he does not deny that the church, despite its gracious and infallible elements, also contains much that is human and fallible.

In recent decades, Balthasar's ecclesiological thinking has had much influence upon the teaching of the 'official' church, including much of John Paul II's own teaching. He has utilized Balthasar's profiles to suggest ways in which the office of Peter and the episcopacy may serve *all* Christians.

❁

PETER AND MARY

[We exclude] the view prevailing in the late Middle Ages and the Counter-Reformation ... that the hierarchical and sacramental structure of the Church is the Church in the strict or formal sense, while the 'sheep' ruled by the hierarchy and merely receptive of the sacraments belong only to the 'material' element of the Church. On the contrary, the whole structural aspect of the Church is also mediating and instrumental, and even the various modes of divine communication in the Christological graces of the Church are not an end in themselves but are for the sake of those who receive them. The whole purpose of the formal structure and sacramental grace is to reach out to the man as he actually is, to penetrate his being and raise him to the status of member of the mystical Head: only thus is 'the Church' constituted.

The encounter that, at its maximum intensity, merits the name of marriage is personal and takes place between God as person and man as person, though all that gives this encounter an ecclesiological stamp is its prerequisite only and is not the encounter itself. Admittedly, the whole complex of those things instituted by God for salvation is the most sublime, the richest

---

83. From *Spouse of the Word*, vol. II of Explorations in Theology (San Francisco, Ignatius Press, 1991). *ET* by A.V. Littledale with Alexander Dru.

in mystery, the most inaccessible to the human mind, of all that is. Nonetheless, it is there for the sake of the individual creature and fulfills its purpose only when he is reached and brought home to God. Much in these institutions is, in the deepest sense, conditioned by time and disappears when fulfillment is reached in the next world. That is the case with the official, hierarchic structure of the Church and her individual sacraments and also with certain provisional forms of the life of grace they impart: faith and love in their veiled condition, the cardinal virtues as conditioned by time and the necessity of struggle. What never falls away is the nuptial encounter between God and the creature, for whose sake the framework of the structures is now set up and will later be dismantled. This encounter, therefore, must be the real core of the Church. The structure and the graces they impart are what raise the created subjects up to what they should be in God's design: a humanity formed as a bride to the Son, become the Church.

The bride is essentially woman, that is, receptive: one who, through acceptance of the seed but also through all her own female organs and powers is made competent to bring forth and bear fruit. In bringing forth at birth (which, in a broad sense, includes her care of the child and his feeding and upbringing to full independence), woman gives to man the complete, superabundant response. It is to such a Christian womanly role that the creature is educated by the structural, sacramental Church: the office and the Sacrament are forms of communicating the seed; they belong to the male aspect, but their end is to lead the bride to her womanly function and fortify her in it. Part of this indeed, is her ability to receive a supernatural seed, an ability that itself is capable of development from a low to a high potential; and it includes, besides, the power to preserve the seed, to make it bring forth much fruit in the 'good ground', a hundred-, sixty-, and thirtyfold (Mt 15:8-9). In the supernatural sphere of the Church one cannot assume an encounter, on equal terms, between two partners for the imparting of the seed, as one can in the natural order. Here, on the contrary, the preparation of the female partner is, fundamentally, conjoined with the nuptial act of union, and both together are meant by St. Paul with the active verb 'to present' (Eph 5:27). Considered in the terms of Church law, it is true that the representative of the 'office' has the masculine function of the one who gives, and the 'laity' the feminine one of receiving; but it does not follow that the clergy are 'more', the laity 'less', the Church. The reverse is, in fact, the case, since the active communication is instrumental, the passive reception is the end, essentially ordered, to indeed basically one with the female activity of seed bearing, giving birth, and educating.

Admittedly, this distinction between means and end is not of itself sufficient to make clear the genesis of the Church as a subject in her own right, since the structures by which grace is mediated do not exist apart in a sort of space between Christ and the Church; they belong to the latter. In this connection, it is pertinent to take note of the fact that Christ also did not establish them in a void but in the growing faith of his disciples, a faith already come to maturity in Peter's confession … (Jn 6:68–69) … .

[F]or the Fathers, it was precisely in her sacramental action that the Church appeared as a mother's womb giving birth, and as a mother bringing up those born to her. 'The Church lies in anguish', St. Methodius says, 'and bears the *psychike* anew as *pneumatike*, for this reason, she is also a mother. For as the woman receives the man's yet unformed seed, and, in the course of time, brings a complete man to the world, so, we may say, the Church continually receives those who betake themselves to the *Logos*, shapes them into the image and form of Christ, and makes them, in the course of time, citizens of those blessed eternities … . Those whom she gives birth to are the neophytes … and these receive the characteristics, the human mode of Christ, because the image and form of the *Logos* is impressed on them and born in them through perfect *gnosis* and *pistis*, so that in them Christ is born in a spiritual manner. And, therefore, the Church is pregnant and in travail, till Christ is formed and born in us, in order that each one of the saints may be born as Christ through his participation in Christ.' Here the antithesis between office as directed to an end and reception as the end envisaged is resolved in a higher identity, in that the womb of the Church effects prototypically in the individual what the individual himself will have to bring about through his being patterned in this womb. This again supposes that the Church as prototype, if she is to be able to perform the sacramental function, herself possesses not only the 'objectives holiness' of the structures but also the subjective, personal holiness of faith, love, and hope realized in act. Therein she is already, in the fullest sense, the bride who can make to the Bridegroom and his 'word of the Cross' (I Cor I:18) the creaturely, bridal response expected of her – creaturely, because her love is believing and hoping, not seeing and possessing; bridal, because her loving faith and hope are formed supernaturally by Christ's 'word of the Cross'.

All of this can be expressed in a different way: if the content of the ecclesiastical structure is, for the Church herself, 'objective spirit', whose scope and range can only be measured and grasped by the divine subjectivity (for God alone completely 'understands' his own Word, which the disciples proclaim; God alone fully perceives the greatness of the grace that they mediate sacramentally; and God alone knows the divine severity inherent from its foundation in the Church's jurisdiction, when it is applied according to the mind of God), then this 'objective spirit' necessarily presupposes a 'subjective spirit' to receive it. This is Peter's faith. It is obvious, however, that it does not inhere absolutely and exclusively in the subject, Peter. Its existence is only witnessed and represented by Peter at the promise of the office (Mt 16) and its bestowal (Jn 21), as is abundantly clear by the Lord's threefold question before the investiture. What this act brings out above all is that Peter's subjective spirit is not equal to the objective spirit of office and Sacrament, not only because Peter is a sinner and his sinfulness was never more terribly revealed than when he was confronted with the demands inherent in the spirit of the office but even more so because Christ alone can bring unison into the two sides in the uniqueness and singularity of his mission as Redeemer and Sacrifice, one only who can bring together in unison the divine demands of worship and expiation inherent in the priestly office. The identity to which the office points cannot, by any means, exist in the Church, but solely in the Lord, as the Church's Head and Bridegroom.

Yet, and just because of this, this identity must be reproduced in the Church; for the Lord wills to see his Church standing before him, not as a singular, palpable failure but as a glorious bride worthy of him. Here the Marian principle in the Church necessarily comes into play. Mary is the subjectivity that, in its womanly and receptive manner, is enabled fully to correspond to the masculine subjectivity of Christ, through God's grace and the overshadowing of his Spirit. The Church flowing forth from Christ finds her personal center in Mary as well as the full realization of her idea as Church. Her faith, with its love and hope, in its womanly openness to the divine, the Divine-human Bridegroom, is coextensive with the masculine principle, embedded in the Church, of office and Sacrament, even though it is not part of its womanly character to comprehend totally, in the manner of the Bridegroom, the objective spirit therein contained. She is not the Word but the adequate response awaited by God from the created sphere and produced in it by his grace through the Word.

For this, undoubtedly, a special grace is needed, qualitatively different from that of the rest of the faithful, which elevates the Marian response of faith to the status of principle and exemplar of the response of the entire Church. Mary's faith, as the fruitful womb of the Word, is privileged on two counts. In respect of its origin, it is a faith proceeded from her 'immaculate conception'; in respect of its end, it is a faith destined to bear the fruit that is not only Christ's body but also himself as Head. This fruitfulness, therefore, which was previously predicated of the Church as prototype of the fruitfulness of the members, when, from being born, passively, in baptism, they actively bring forth the life of Christ, in themselves and in the Church – this paradigmatic fruitfulness is, in Mary, so far surpassed, raised to such potency, that she not only does what the Church does – bring forth Christ – but also does it archetypally, in that she lets the Head of the Church take flesh in her, him whom the Church will, in turn, deliver from out of herself. The process on the ecclesial level, whereby the soul born of Christ in turn conceives and bears him, in the order of the body, this process is elevated to become an archetypal process in which Mary, preserved from original sin by the grace of Christ's Cross, conceives and bears him in the order of the Head. In the former process, the objective stainlessness of the Church (the 'infallibility of Peter') always effects and supposes a constant purification of the Church by water and the Word, and, therefore, the Church becomes a 'glorious bride' only as she is actually made pure. But in the process on the Marian level there can be no question of a subjective, personal purification as an actual event. Mary, preserved from the outset, has undergone no such purification. In Mary, therefore, the Church is not only infallible in the official Sacramental sphere (though always fallible subjectively and existentially, always defective and hopelessly falling short of the ideal inherent and proclaimed). In her the Church is also personally immaculate and beyond the tension between reality and ideal.

It is on this very account that Mary also stands above and beyond the purely mundane encounter of bridegroom and bride and opens it out into the infinity of the divine Eros insofar as God himself accepts her word of faith and fidelity, and as she is overshadowed not by the *Logos* as such but by the Holy Spirit, who carries the Father's seed into her spiritual and bodily womb, the fruit of this marriage being the Incarnation of the Son, who, in his entire being, is Head and Body, Bridegroom and Bride. There is certainly no question of making a personal distinction, in the union of husband and wife, between the man giving and the seed given, and from this standpoint Mary, as prototype of the Church, is rightly called the bride of the incarnate Word. Nonetheless, what is brought about here is not a repetition of the sex relationship but its prototypal realization between God and man; and God, known and received in this intimate fashion, can only be the God in three Persons. On this account, Mary receives the Son as seed of the Father through the realizing act of the Holy Spirit of Father and Son. And it is for the same reason that, in the sphere of the Church, the actualizing of the sacraments is the work of the Holy Spirit, who places the Father's Word in the womb of the soul for it to generate and give birth. This again does not prevent the Church being the Son's bride, since this entire participation of the created world in the Trinitarian Divinity is the working and prolongation of the incarnate Word. Mary is given to us as prototype so that the

Church may never forget the Trinitarian dimension of her nuptial mystery; just as Christ, too, as he went about on earth, always situated it in relation to an openness to the Trinitarian life.

There is another thing that this reveals, namely, the reason why, according to St. Thomas, the Fiat of the mother of God was spoken *loco totius generis humani* and not, for instance, *loco totius Ecclesiae.* (It could equally be said that, in her, the Church speaks her Fiat to God for the whole human race.) The Word was, in fact, carried into her life of faith in a womb, in order to become flesh. It is part of her mystery and being that the Word became flesh, not only in but also from her, that her self-giving response to God was understood and required as something involving the whole person, something both spiritual and of the body. One cannot divide this response into two parts: one spiritual, her active acceptance of faith; the other bodily, her passive utilization as womb for God becoming man. It is for this very reason that she participated in the formation of the hypostatic union in her own manner, a purely womanly one of surrender. And when the Fathers see the actual *connubium* between God and man realized in Christ himself, in the indissoluble union of the two natures, this is also no purely physical occurrence, with its matrimonial character exclusively derived from the side of God and his intention. It is a real two-sided mystery of love through the bridal consent of Mary acting for all the rest of created flesh. In Mary's flesh is meant 'all' created 'flesh' (Jn 17:2) to which God wills to espouse himself; and since Mary is *caro ex qua*, she is also *fides ex qua.* But the hypostatic union is the carrying out and thus the final indissoluble sealing of the covenant of fidelity, which marks with its sign all future vows of fidelity in the Church: those of baptism, of marriage, and of virginity.

Mary's abiding physical virginity is the bodily aspect of the abiding inner virginity, which means the exclusiveness of her spiritual faith. The glorification of virginity by the Fathers, which they apply both to the Church's virginity and to that of those vowed to it and of each individual member of the Church, even the married, is directed, fundamentally, to a Marian virginity, itself primarily the expression of a personal attitude to the God coming to meet them nuptially. Once again, we can follow out two themes in this glorification: the Church, from her very origin, is virginal (as distinct from the synagogue, so often reproached by God as an adulteress). Also, the Church, as the one 'purified' by Christ, has become 'virginal', and as she is constantly protected by this grace, she must keep herself in the virginity received and not fall away from it again. But both Mary and the Church are fruitful precisely because they are virginal. The exclusive character of love, which virginity involves, is in each the condition for bearing the fruit of God. The themes interlace in the happiest way when the two acts – the 'purification' of the Church and her divine marriage – are seen as one, as in the celebrated Benedictus antiphon of the Epiphany.

Dom Odo Casel has brought out the idea (originally Syrian and subsequently adopted in the West) that the Epiphany is the feast of the marriage between Christ and the Church in that the baptismal water of the Jordan was also understood as the fructifying water of the marriage: 'In the river Jordan has the Church become espoused', sings the Syrian Church during matins of the vigil. The bath of the bridegroom is, at the same time, the marriage bath of the bride, since the bride herself is present prototypically in the flesh of the bridegroom. For this reason, the Epiphany can be, in the East, both the baptismal day of believers and the day of the consecration of virgins; for the sacramental bath is itself the enactment of the nuptial mystery, and the consecration of virgins is done to exemplify the marriage between Christ and the Church, being the explication of what had been begun in the baptismal vows and fulfilled in the conferring of the Sacrament. What essentially demonstrates this for us is that the sacramental baptism received by the individual Christian was originally received by the Church herself, and indeed in the flesh of Christ, which, nuptially united to his Godhead, is the source of the 'Mystical Body'.

The outcome of our study so far is that the first step to answering in a positive way, the question as to the subject of the Church is to relate it to Mary's faith, fruitful because virginal. Alois Müller has rightly shown that the patristic parallel between Mary and the Church, though it contains all the elements for the solution, failed of final elucidation because it was never made sufficiently clear that Mary's faith was what made possible her bodily conception of Christ, and so there was no advance beyond a mere parallel between her bodily bringing forth and the Church's spiritual bringing forth. But once all doubt on the point was overcome, the act of Mary was seen, absolutely, as the basic subjective act of the Church. For Mary's personal act, by reason of its uniqueness and eminence, can be two things at once: the subjective and absolutely complete ground for the subjective act of the Church as such (always qualitatively superior to every act, defective as it is, of the individual); and, since Mary is also an individual believer within the Church community, the subjective and absolutely complete ground of each personal act of faith within the *communia sanctorum*. At the same time, it must always be borne in mind that, as we said before, the subjective act of the Church, even in its perfect fullness in that of Mary, is always one of womanly surrender – an act not of dominance and comprehension (which pertains to the Head) but of humble, handmaidenly following and service. Its character is not one of masculine gnosis, desire for knowledge at all costs; for Mary on earth did not seek after knowledge but was content to keep and contemplate the word in her heart. Even the theological and pastoral knowledge and understanding that the risen Christ laid up in the memory of his Church in opening, for forty days, the Scripture to his apostles was placed deep within this spiritual womb of womanly contemplation. And so, in this respect also, the prophecy was fortified: *femina circumdabit virum.*

Mary, in giving birth spiritually and physically to the Son, becomes the universal Mother of all believers, for the Church as body is born of Christ and is herself Christ. Mary is the prototype of the Church, not only because of her virginal faith but also equally because of her fruitfulness. This is, indeed, not autonomous (as that of the goddesses of fertility) but wholly ancillary, since it is Christ, not Mary, who brought the Church into being by his Passion. All the same, she took part, as an intermediary, in this creation by the universality and unrestrictedness of her Fiat, which the Son is able to use as an infinitely plastic medium to bring forth from it new believers, those born again. Her presence with him at the Cross, her agreement to his abandonment of her to the Church in the midst of his dereliction on the Cross, her eternal role as the woman in labor (Rev 12), show how fully her self-surrender is universalized to become the common source, the productive womb, of all Christian grace.

1.7 LEONARDO BOFF: *THE REINVENTION OF THE CHURCH* – 1977

Here, Boff outlines how the base communities movement seeks to transform the structures of authority, governance and ministry in the church.[84] Boff draws upon social analysis to demonstrate how such ventures as the basic Christian communities allow much greater consultation, collaboration and lay participation in the church. Structures are transformed and new ministries come to the fore. In short, the church is being reformed, reinvented by these groups and their imagination and commitment to a church driven as much by the Holy Spirit as by ecclesiastical structures. Great diversity in ecclesiology results, even throughout the base communities themselves, for each community has its own special identity and structure. Thus such developments help pull the church away from an overt obsession with a *juridical* understanding of church authority. Boff does not reject the need for the hierarchy, but he believes that the self-understanding of the church must be ordered correctly; first the flock, then the shepherds for the sake of the flock. The old hierarchy-centred ecclesiology reverses the natural order. His believes an alternative focus upon the church as being driven by the spirit and presence of the risen Christ leads to a conceptualization of the church 'more from the foundations up than from the steeple down'. This is a vision of the church where all are equal, though people will have different charisms (callings/gifts) and therefore different roles, including the socially-inevitable hierarchical roles, and the role of especial leaders, including the Pope in *the service of* (rather than the presiding over) the *unity* of the whole community. All services come from *within* the community and are *for* the community. Boff calls this a 'more evangelical sense of church' which recognizes diversity. The rigidity of current church structures can be overcome and decision-making processes can become more inclusive of the whole community for the exclusion of the laity from participation in such decisions is a fundamental problem for the church in our times. Hence, the base communities help develop a new non-linear form of church structure where the roles of all, including priests and bishops are transformed. The church is declericalized as the emphasis switches to the whole 'people of God', to whom collegiality now belongs. This all offers not a 'global alternative' for the entire church, but, instead, a 'leaven of renewal' for the church.

✵

WAYS OF BEING CHURCH

The rise of the basic church communities and the praxis of these communities are of matchless value when it comes to questioning the prevailing manner of being church. They are sprung from basic, minimum elements like faith, the reading of the word and meditation on it, and mutual assistance in all human dimensions. As we have seen, they are genuine church. Many functions, genuinely new ministries, appear in them – ministries of community coordination, of catechesis, of organizing the liturgy, of caring for the sick, of teaching people to read and write, of looking after the poor, and the like. All this is done in a deep spirit of communion, with a sense of joint responsibility and with an awareness of building and living actual church. The best conceptualization of this experience is in the frequently heard expression,

---

84. From *ET*, *Ecclesiogenesis – the Base Communities Reinvent the Church* (London, Collins Flame, 1986).

'reinvention of the church'. The church is beginning to be born at the grassroots, beginning to be common fashion of considering oneself to be church. It enables one to discover the true source of the ongoing birth and creation of the church: the Holy Spirit.

The church can be considered from many points of view. Indeed there are as many ecclesiologies as there are basic ecclesial structures. There are those who work out their understanding of the church from its priestly-episcopal-papal structure, although this yields not so much as ecclesiology as a 'parochiology'. There are those whose thinking begins with the word/sacrament structure, so that we have preeminently a prophetico-cultic picture of church. There are those who articulate the church from the figure of the church on a journey, and then we get a preeminently historico-salvific visioin. And there are more. All these ecclesiologies have their sense, their meaning. But each is limited in itself, and must be opened out upon other forms of theoretical totalization of the mystery of church. Otherwise we have an oppressive ideologization of categories against categories, and suffers harm.

The basic church communities are aiding the whole church to overcome an internal obstacle under which it has labored for centuries, and which has prevented it from seeing the more abundant riches of the mystery of church. The church, in the Latin West, has been thought of in terms of a Christ/church polarity, within a juridical vision. The relationships between Christ and the church are formulated on the model of the relationships of a society with its founder. Christ transmits all power to the Twelve, who transmit it to their successors, the bishops and the pope. The latter have been considered as the sole depositaries of all responsibility, and have been seen as amassing for themselves all power in the church, in such wise that they are pictured as in confrontation with the community. Thus the actual community is divided between rulers and governed, between celebrants and onlookers, between producers and consumers of sacraments. In a like systematization, the hierarchy constitutes the sole representative of the universal church and the particular church.

This image suppresses the other one – that of the church as faith community (*communitas fidelium*), globally coresponsible for all the affairs of the church. Further, one begins with the shepherds who are responsible for the flock. But this is to invert the natural order: first comes the flock, and then, for the sake of the flock, the shepherd. *The hierarchical function is essential in the church – but it does not subsist in and for itself.* The hierarchical function must be understood – this is the simple and natural understanding of things – as subsisting within the faith community and in its service, whether by representing all the other churches vis-à-vis this particular church (the authentic face-to-face dimension of any community-and-head), or as principle of unity at the heart of the local church, of which the head is actually a member. The other understanding of church, furthermore, is predicated on a particular Christology which permits it to take Christ only in his sarkical, or fleshly, existence; it does not consider the risen Christ, with the transformations that his resurrection has conferred upon him: his cosmic ubiquity, the spiritual nature of his body (*sōma pneumatikon*, 1 Cor. 15:44), and so on. This consideration would render the institution of the church more flexible, and would reintroduce the 'pneumatic' element as part and parcel of the Christological element. *The church was born not only from the opened side of Christ, but from the Holy Spirit, as well, on the day of Pentecost.* The unity between these two elements is found in Jesus Christ who died and was raised again as the maximum presence of the Holy Spirit in the world, in such wise that we can say: Jesus-according-to-the-flesh constituted the greatest presence of the Holy Spirit in the world; and the Holy Spirit in the church is now the presence-in-history of the risen Christ.[85]

The basic church communities help the whole church to consider itself from the viewpoint of a reality that is more basic, and without which the church does not exist. That reality is faith in the active presence of the risen One and of his Spirit at the heart of every human community, efficaciously enabling it both to live the essential values, without which there is no humanity, and to open out to the Absolute, without whom there is no dignity or salvation. This divine activity acquires a special density in the church. But it excludes no human person. This contemplative view modifies the manner of being church. Now the clergy moves into the midst of the people, towards persons already activated by the Spirit, which, before the arrival of the institutional church, was already shaping an anonymous church by its grace, its forgiveness. This is not a matter, then, of *transplanting* the church deductively, but of *implanting* the church inductively ... .

The church that is implanted explicates, purifies, and prolongs the already existing, latent church. The basic church communities are born of this Spirit manifested and organized in the midst of the People of God. The recognition of the presence of the risen One and of the Spirit in the hearts of human beings leads one to conceptualize the church more from the foundation up than from the steeple down. It means accepting the coresponsibility of all in the upbuilding of the church, not just of a limited conceptualizations of church in the following schemata:

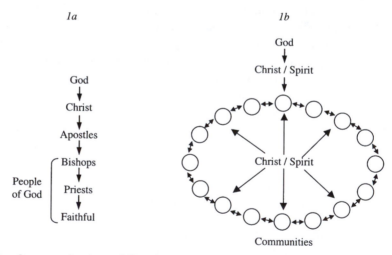

Figure 1   Conceptualizations of Church

In Figure 1a the category 'People of God' arises as the result of a previous organization. The power in this organization is concentrated along the axis of bishop/priest. The laity only receive. They do not produce in terms of organization or structure, but only in terms of reinforcement of the structure. One wonders: Is it really the organization that creates the

85. Cf. Leonardo Boff, 'A Igreja, Sacramento do Espírito Santo', in *O Espírito Santo* (Petrópolis, Brazil: Vozes, 1973).

church? Or does the organization arise, as second act, because the community that is the People of God exists antecedently, as first act? It seems to us that the latter conceptualization is the authentic one. The former would be the ideology of the dominant class, calculated to safeguard the rights and prerogatives of that class. Further, this ecclesiological conception is governed by the category of 'power'. According to this conception, Christ and the Spirit possess no direct immanence. Their only immanence is mediated by the ordained ministry. Hence it is the hierarchy that occupies the center of interest, rather than the risen One, and the Spirit with its charisms. Christ and the Spirit begin, as it were, on the outside, and are brought into the community by means of the representative and sacramental function of the hierarchy. The Christ-Spirit-Church relation is presented not as a vital fabric, an interwoven tissue, but in an exteriority, after the fashion of the relationship of an institution with its founder. This conceptualization is less theological than juridical. The power in question is divine only in its origin. In its exercise it follows the mechanisms of any profane power with its mechanisms of coercion, security, and control.

In Figure 1b the reality that is God's People emerges as primary instance; its organization is seen as secondary, derived, and at the service of the primary. Christ's power (*exousia*) resides not only in certain members, but in the totality of the People of God as vehicle of Christ's triple ministry of witness, oneness, and worship. This power of Christ's is diversified in accordance with specific functions, but it leaves no one out. The laity emerge as creators of ecclesiological values … . Before becoming visible through human mediations – those of bishop, priest, deacon, and so on – the risen Christ and the Spirit already possess a presence in the community. There prevails an ongoing, constant immanence of the Spirit and of the risen Lord in humanity, and in a special way in the community of the faithful. It is these who gather to form the church, who constitute it essentially. *The hierarchy has the sacramental function of organizing and serving a reality that it has not created but discovered, and within which it finds itself.* The theologico-mystical element always has primacy over the juridical. In this understanding it is no longer difficult to grasp the ecclesiality of the basic church communities, and to assign theological value to the various services which arise within the community as manifestations of the Spirit.

As our reflections have shown, the problem of ministries is linked to the model of church on which it is predicated. This model must be submitted to analysis and critique. The basic communities concretize a conception of church as a communion of sisters and brothers, as church-community, church-body-of-Christ, church-People-of-God.

In a *first moment*, a basic equality of all persons is assumed. By faith and baptism all are directly grafted onto Christ. The Spirit becomes present in all, creating a community and a genuine communion of persons, where differences of sex, nation, intelligence, and social position are of no account, since 'all are one in Christ Jesus' (Gal. 3:28). In this community all are sent, not just some; all are responsible for the church, not just a few; all must bear prophetic witness, not just a few persons; all must sanctify, not just some.

In a *second moment*, differences and hierarchy arise within the unity of, and in function of, the community. All are equal, but not all do everything. A great number of needs appear, and these have to be attended to. There are different tasks, functions, and services (cf. Rom. 12:1 Cor. 12) … . The concept of charism is not restricted to extraordinary manifestations of the Spirit. It is concretized in the ordinary everyday, as in love, which is the most excellent of charisms (1 Cor. 12:37). Every baptized member of the community is charismatic, since each has his or her place and function: 'Each one has his gift from God, one this and another that' (1 Cor. 7:7). 'To each person the manifestation of the Spirit is given for the common good' (1 Cor. 12:7; cf. 1 Pet. 4:10). No one is useless or idle. We are 'individually members one of another. We have gifts that differ', and these gifts 'should be used for service' (Rom. 12:5, 7), so that each member may ever be at the disposition of the others.

Charism, therefore, may be understood as each person's own function in the community as a form of manifestation of the Spirit within the community for the community's good ... . Charism, in this sense, is not something incidental and adventitious to church, something that could be wanting to it. It is actually constitutive of church-as-community. Community always appears as organized, however true it be that that organization occurs within the community and is a subdetermination of the community itself – which is antecedent to the organization ... .

This conceptualization of the church as a community of faith, with a variety of functions, services, and tasks, at once occasions a problem. Who will see to the unity of the whole, to the order and harmony of all the charisms, in such wise that all things will work together for the upbuilding of the same body? Here, then, is the need for a specific charism, that of the principle of unity among all the charisms. This will be the charism of assistance, of direction, of administration (cf. 1 Cor. 12:28), the charism of those who preside over and see to the oneness of the whole (1 Thess. 5:12; Rom. 12:8; 1 Tim. 5:17). *The specific formality of this charism does not reside in accumulation and absorption, but in integration and coordination.* This charism is not outside the community, but within it; not over the community, but for the good of the community. The 'monitor' is a basic community, the pastor is a parish, the bishop is a diocese, the pope in the church – all are principles of oneness within a particular local church and, beyond this church, with all the other churches. The service of unity, from monitor to pope, is not an autocratic power *over* the church, but a power at its heart and for its service. As Saint Augustine put it, 'I am a bishop for you, and a Christian with you.' There is no such thing as absolute ordination to the function of direction. There is no such thing as a monitor without a community, a pastor without a parish, a bishop without a diocese. The councils of Nicea (325) and Chalcedon (451) therefore consider absolute ordinations null.[86] And today bishops without an actual diocese must have a 'titular see', a 'defunct see' somewhere in the world, so that they, too, may be bishops of a particular church, and not just a new sort of *episcopi vagants*.

In order to construct this unity, the one presiding in the community is endowed with a special grace. The oneness of the church is not immanent grandeur, but theological grandeur: it is oneness with the various churches, including the Church of Rome, which 'presides over all in charity', as Saint Ignatius of Antioch wrote at the turn of the first century, and it is oneness with the church universal. The nature of the ministry of unity as service therefore implies an ontological character (in the form of a special grace) that is abiding, that is ongoing, for it looks to a permanent need of the community.

We may diagram this model of the church as community of service as follows:

---

86. See the Sixth Canon of the Council of Chalcedon ... .

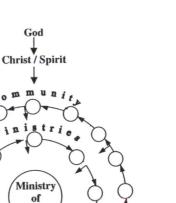

Figure 2   The Church as Community of Services

In Figure 2 (despite all the risks of diagrams) it clearly appears how all services arise within the community and for the community. This diagram is a concrete representation of how basic church communities function, and how they can serve in the recovery of a more evangelical sense of church for our days: for this model corresponds better to the ideals preached and lived by Jesus Christ. The New Testament, of course, offers several models of church. One – in Matthew – is more pyramidal, though with a strong accent on fellowship and communion. Another – in Paul's letters – is more circular, more communitarian-and-charismatic. Another – that of the Catholic epistles – is more explicitly oriented along the lines of the permanent functions of presbyters and bishops. What Jesus had in mind with the Twelve was not just hierarchy but church, for it was from among the community of the disciples that he chose the Twelve … .

This problem raises another. What sort of organization did Jesus want for his church? Here a great diversity of opinion reigns in Catholic and ecumenical theology today … . The Acts of the Apostles (6:1–6) suggests that the church created the ministries of which it had need, within the framework of its essential apostolicity. Basically, the community must be outfitted with 'roles of service' (Eph. 4:12) – with those services, structures, and functions that become necessary in order to render present the risen One, his message, and his Spirit among human persons in such wise as he may be a God-spel, Good News, for them, especially for the poor.

The existence and the functioning of the basic church communities permits us to construct, in simpler and more realistic terms, a whole new state of the question of ministries as subdeterminations of a living and vital model of church: the model of church-community-of-sisters-and-brothers; the model of sacrament of integral liberation in the world, a sacrament endowed with a multitude of charisms. A theological reading enables us to accept as genuine ministries the various services that are rendered in community, some of them permanent and seeing to permanent needs, others transitory and bound up with persons having some special charism. Various services take on different forms as the Spirit becomes present and operative in the community.

GROWING BEYOND CURRENT CHURCH STRUCTURE

The form in which the basic church communities are organized, and the praxis that develops within them, can make a mighty contribution when it comes to overcoming a fundamental obstacle to communitarian life: the current structure of participation in the church. The church is structured, rather, in a schematic and rigid form, as diagrammed in Figure 3.[87]

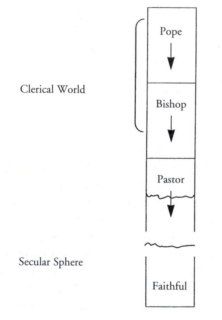

Figure 3   Traditional Church Structure

In terms of decision, the participation of the faithful is totally mutilated. Decision is restricted to the pope-bishop-pastor axis. A community in which the routes of participation are cut off in all directions cannot pretend to the name of community. In a community, as we have stressed, equality must prevail in conjunction with a face-to-face communion of members. And there is a further, aggravating factor: this linear structure has been dogmatically reproduced and consecrated. it has been socialized by theology, and internalized by the ministers themselves, who, in striking their mutual relationships, do so in the framework of the prevailing structure, and thus perpetuated the problem. In this type of relationship the bishop, for example, does not enter into direct contact with the faithful, but only with the priest … .

---

87. Cf. Carlos Alberto de Medina and Pedro A. Ribeiro de Oliveira, *Autoridade e Participaçã: estudo sociológica da Igreja Católica* (Petrópolis, Brazil: CERES/Vozes, 1973).

Carlos Alberto de Medina and Pedro A. Ribeira de Oliveira, sociologists of the Centro de Estatistica Religiosa e Investigações Sociais (CERIS), have analyzed most incisively and with great perception the functioning of this linear, descending line in the Church of Brazil.[88] (Their analysis is valid for the whole church, however, for the church in Brazil reproduces the system uniformly and universally prevailing there.) They find that in the Brazilian church the roles of each agent are defined in such a way that the faithful, in terms of *participation in decisions*, are excluded. The framework of the church may undergo renovation, the laity may be given a share in ecclesial and ecclesiastical activities, but, thanks to the power structure in the church, the damper is put on when it comes to laity influencing decisions. Thus the layman and laywoman at the heart of the particular church are denied their potential for decision-making and creation of religious content. Nothing remains to them but to be creators in the marginal sphere of popular Catholicism.[89]

'The only solution,' admit Medina and Ribeiro, 'lies in an understanding of the layperson as one of the terms of participating structure – one of the terms of the power to make decisions bearing on the specific objectives of that person's church.'... .[90]

Thus it is not a matter of despoiling the bishop and priest of their function in a sham liberation process. It is only that their functions will take on new tasks, with a new arrangement of relationships among bishop, priest, and layperson. The theology of Vatican II, initiated in *Lumen Gentium* and in *Apostolicam Actuositatem* (on the lay apostolate), transcends the linear conception and supplants it with a triangular one, in which each of *three* terms, this time, acquires weight of its own and becomes the vehicle and vessel of ecclesial substance, as Medina and Ribeiro desiderate:

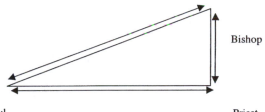

Bishop

Faithful   Priest

Figure 4   A New Church Structure

Here all three terms establish a network of relationships with one another, involving one another in a circularity. As the decree *Ad Gentes* says, 'the Church has not been truly established ... unless there exists a laity worthy of the name'.[91] All three terms are responsible for the entire reality of church. Collegiality is no longer the monopoly of episcopate and clergy. Now it belongs to the whole People of God.

88. Cf. de Medina and Ribeiro, *Autoridade e Participaçã;* Cf. also de Medina, 'A greja Católica no Brasil: uma perspectiva sociológica', *Revista Eclesiástica Brasileira*, 1973, 72–91.
89. de Medina and Ribeiro, *Autoridade e Participaçã*, 59–132.
90. [Cf]. Ibid., 180–8.
91. *Ad Gentes*, no. 21 (in Abbott, *Documents*, 610).

This is the way the basic communities function. Their triangular model has created a new style of priest and bishop. These are now in the midst of the people as principles of animation and inspiration, of unity and universality. At the same time, these communities have caused the laity to emerge as a genuine vehicle of ecclesiological values, whether as coordinators of moderators of the community or in the discharge of other community services. In their own ambit, the laity take up the cause of Christ and share in the decision-making of their local church. The basic church communities are helping the whole church in the process of declericalization, by restoring to the People of God, the faithful, the rights of which they have been deprived in the liner structure. On the level of theory, theology itself has already gone beyond the old pyramid. *But it is not enough to know. A new praxis must be implemented.* This is what the basic communities are saying. They are helping the whole church to 'reinvent itself', right in its foundations. Experiment is gradually confirming theory, and inspiring in the church-as-institution a confidence in the viability of a new way of being church in the world today.

The basic church communities prefigure a new social structuring of the church. Of course, this new structure will include more than just basic communities. These communities constitute a leaven of renewal in the substance of the whole church – not a global alternative for the totality of the church … . Today's basic communities hold a prophecy, a promise that is slowly becoming historical reality. We shall have a new church, a church born of the faith that nourishes God's People.

1.8 AVERY DULLES: *THE USE OF MODELS IN ECCLESIOLOGY – 1988*

From his seminal work in contemporary ecclesiology, this first chapter sets out important methodological considerations for the very business of ecclesiology.[92] In particular, Dulles addresses problems which arise when there is confusion concerning the self-image and/or self-understanding of the church. He suggests that it is inevitable that a variety of images and models will be employed throughout the church in the attempts to understand and direct the work of the church in its mission. Christianity has always employed a plurality of models of the church, some of which have become dominant paradigms for ecclesiology at various points of ecclesiastical history. Dulles argues that we should not see such pluralism as a bad thing, nor feel that differing models must always be viewed as clashing or in opposition. Instead, we should embrace the diversity of the rich ecclesiological imagery which the church possesses. We should seek to allow diverse models to complement each other. Throughout, Dulles succinctly identifies key ecclesiological problems prevalent in the church today. Some feel that, since the publication of this work, Dulles has somewhat tempered the level to which he believes ecclesiological pluralism should be tolerated. Nonetheless, he helps us to appreciate importance of bearing in mind how models and images of the church both reflect *and* shape models of authority (e.g., a predominantly hierarchical understanding of the church naturally leads to a hierarchy in terms of authority).

❋

In May 1972 the New York *Times* carried a typical exchange of views about what is happening in the Catholic Church in the United States. It reported the assessment of an Italian theologian, Battista Mondin, to the effect that the Church in America is falling apart. Two days later the *Times* published a letter to the editor in which the writer conceded, '[Mondin] is right that the traditional Church is near collapse', but then added: 'The disasters he mentions are only such to those churchmen who are so stuck in conservatism and authority that they cannot see the Gospel of Christ for the Code of Canon Law … . My feeling, as a member of an adapting religious community, is that these are the best days of the church.'

Disputes of this type are going on everywhere these days. Christians cannot agree about the measure of progress or decline because they have radically different visions of the Church. They are not agreed about what the Church really is.

When we ask what something is we are normally seeking a definition. The classical way to define a thing is to put it into a category of familiar objects and then to list the distinguishing characteristics that differentiate it from other members of the same category. Thus we say that a snail is a slow-moving gastropod mollusk, or that a chair is a piece of furniture designed for people to sit on. In definitions such as these we are dealing with external realities that we can see and touch, and we are able to pin them down fairly well in terms of familiar categories.

---

92. From *Models of the Church – a Critical Assessment of the Church in All Its Aspects* (Dublin, Gill and Macmillan, 2nd edn., 1988), 15–33.

It used to be thought, at least by many, that the Church and other realities of faith could be defined by a similar process ... . [But t]here is something of a consensus today that the innermost reality of the Church – the most important constituent of its being – is the divine self-gift. The Church is a union or communion of men with one another through the grace of Christ. Although this communion manifests itself in sacramental and juridical structures, at the heart of the Church one finds mystery ... .

Vatican Council II, after rejecting an initial schema on the Church in which the first chapter was entitled 'The Nature of the Church Militant', adopted as the title of its first chapter, 'The Mystery of the Church', and this change of titles is symptomatic of the whole ecclesiology of the Council.

The term mystery, applied to the Church, signifies many things. It implies that the Church is not fully intelligible to the finite mind of man, and that the reason for this lack of intelligibility is not the poverty but the richness of the Church itself. Like other supernatural mysteries, the Church is known by a kind of connaturality (as Thomas Aquinas and the classical theologians called it).[93] We cannot fully objectify the Church because we are involved in it; we know it through a kind of intersubjectivity. Furthermore, the Church pertains to the mystery of Christ; Christ is carrying out in the Church his plan of redemption. He is dynamically at work in the Church through his Spirit ... .

The mysterious character of the Church has important implications for methodology. It rules out the possibility of proceeding from clear and univocal concepts, or from definitions in the usual sense of the word. The concepts abstracted from the realities we observe in the objective world about us are not applicable, at least directly, to the mystery of man's communion with God. Some would therefore conclude that ecclesiology must be apophatic; that we can have only a *theologia negativa* of the Church, affirming not what it is but only what it is not. In a certain sense this may be conceded. In some respects we shall in the end have to accept a reverent silence about the Church, or for that matter about any theological reality. But we should not fall into the negative phase prematurely, until we have exhausted the possibilities of the positive.

Among the positive tools that have been used to illuminate the mysteries of faith we must consider, in the first place, images. This consideration will lead us into some discussion of cognate realities, such as symbols, models, and paradigms tools that have a long theological history, and are returning to their former prominence in the theology of our day ... .[94] Thus there is nothing new in the fact that images play a prominent role in contemporary ecclesiology ... .

Any large and continuing society that depends on the loyalty and commitment of its members requires symbolism to hold it together ... .[95] Religious imagery is both functional and cognitive. In order to win acceptance, the images must resonate with the experience of the faithful. If they do so resonate, this is proof that there is some isomorphism between what the

---

93. Thomas Aquinas, *Summa theologiae*, 2a 2ae, q. 1, art. 4, ad 3; qu. 45, art. 2, *in corp.*

94. See on this subject I.T. Ramsey, *Religious Language* (New York, Macmillan Paperbacks, 1963); I.T. Ramsay, *Models and Mystery* (New York, Oxford University Press, 1964); Max Black, *Models and Metaphors* (Ithaca, Cornell University Press, 1962).

95. On the sociological function of images and symbols sec Kenneth E. Boulding, *The Image* (Ann Arbor, University of Michigan, 1956) and Robert N. Bellah, 'Transcendence in Contemporary Piety', *Beyond Belief* (New York, Harper & Row, 1970), 196–208.

image depicts and the spiritual reality with which the faithful are in existential contact. Religious experience, then, provides a vital key for the evaluation and interpretation of symbols … .

To be fully effective, images must be deeply rooted in the corporate experience of the faithful. In times of rapid cultural change, such as our own, a crisis of images is to be expected. Many traditional images lose their former hold on people, while the new images have not yet had time to gain their full power. The contemporary crisis of faith is, I believe, in very large part a crisis of images. City dwellers in a twentieth-century democracy feel ill at ease with many of the biblical images, since these are drawn from the life of a pastoral and patriarchal people of the ancient Near East. Many of us know very little from direct experience about lambs, wolves, sheep, vines, and grapes, or even about kings and patriarchs as they were in biblical times. There is need therefore to supplement these images with others that speak more directly to our contemporaries. The manufacturing of supplementary images goes on wherever the faith is vital. Today we experience some difficulty, however, since our experience of the world has become, in so many respects, secular and utilitarian. Our day-to-day life provides very few objects having numinous overtones that would make them obvious sources of new religious imagery though there are some brilliant suggestions for new imagery in the writings of theologians such as Paul Tillich, Teilhard de Chardin, and Dietrich Bonhoeffer.

For an image to catch on in a religious community conditions have to be ripe psychologically. As Tillich used to say, images are not created or destroyed by deliberate human effort. They are born or they die. They acquire or lose power by a mysterious process that seems beyond man's control and even beyond his comprehension … .

When an image is employed reflectively and critically to deepen one's theoretical understanding of a reality it becomes what is today called a 'model'. Some models are also images – that is, those that can be readily imagined. Other models are of a more abstract nature, and are not precisely images. In the former class one might put temple, vine, and flock; in the latter, institution, society, community.

The term 'model' has for some time been in use in the physical and social sciences. I.T. Ramsey, among others, has shown its fruitfulness for theology. When a physicist is investigating something that lies beyond his direct experience, he ordinarily uses as a crutch some more familiar object sufficiently similar to provide him with reference points. Billiard balls, for example, may serve as models for probing the phenomena of light … . As Ramsey's analysis shows, the term 'model', as employed in modern physics, is practically synonymous with analogy, if this latter term is shorn of some of the metaphysical implications it has in neo-Scholastic theology.

Having seen a little of the use of models in the physical sciences, let us reflect on the transfer of the method of models to theology … . [O]ne may perhaps divide the uses of models in theology into two types, the one explanatory, the other exploratory.

On the explanatory level, models serve to synthesize what we already know or at least are inclined to believe. A model is accepted if it accounts for a large number of biblical and traditional data and accords with what history and experience tell us about the Christian life. The gospel parables of growth, such as those of the wheat and the tares, the mustard seed, and the leaven, have been valued because they give intelligibility to phenomena encountered in the Christian community since its origins, for example, its capacity for rapid expansion, the opposition it encounters from within and without, the presence of evil even in the midst of the community of grace, and so forth. These images suggest how it is possible for the Church to change its shape and size without losing its individuality. They point to a mysterious life principle within the Church and thus harmonize with the biblical and traditional doctrine of the in-dwelling of the Holy Spirit. These botanical models, however, have obvious limits, since they evidently fail to account for the distinctively interpersonal and historical phenomena characteristic of the Church as a human community that perdures through the generations. Thus societal models, such as that of God's People on pilgrimage, are used to supplement the organic metaphors.

The more applications a given model has, the more it suggests a real isomorphism between the Church and the reality being used as the analogue. The analogy will never be perfect because the Church, as a mystery of grace, has properties not paralleled by anything knowable outside of faith.

By the exploratory, or heuristic, use of models, I mean their capacity to lead to new theological insights. This role is harder to identify, because theology is not an experimental science in the same way that physics, for example, is. Theology has an abiding objective norm in the past – that is, in the revelation that was given once and for all in Jesus Christ. There can be no 'other gospel' (cf. Gal. 1:8). In some fashion every discovery is ultimately validated in terms of what was already given in Scripture and tradition. But even the past would not be revelation to us unless God were still alive and giving himself to mankind in Jesus Christ. Thus the present experience of grace enters intrinsically into the method of theology. Thanks to the ongoing experience of the Christian community, theology can discover aspects of the gospel of which Christians were not previously conscious … .

With respect to the heuristic function of images, there is a particular problem of verification in theology. Because the Church is mystery, there can be no question of deductive or crudely empirical tests. Deduction is ruled out because we have no clear abstract concepts of the Church that could furnish terms for a syllogism. Empirical tests are inadequate because visible results and statistics will never by themselves tell us whether a given decision was right or wrong.

In my own view, theological verification depends upon a kind of corporate discernment of spirits. John Powell, S.J., shows that this type of spiritual perception is closely connected with the 'connaturality' to which we have already referred. Thanks to the interior presence of the Holy Spirit, the whole Church and its members have a new life in Christ.

> As this life of Christ is deepened in us by the Holy Spirit, there is created in the Christian a 'sense of Christ', a taste and instinctual judgment for the things of God, a deeper perception of God's truth, an increased understanding of God's dispositions and love toward us. This is what Christians must strive to attain individually and corporately; theologians call it Christian *connaturality*. It is like a natural instinct or intuition, but it is not natural, since it results from the supernatural realities of the Divine Indwelling and the impulses of grace. No account of dialectical or analytical facility, which is purely human, can provide this connatural instinct. It is increased only by the continual nourishment of the life of God that vivifies the Christian.[96]

---

96. John Powell, *The Mystery of the Church* (Milwaukee, Bruce, 1967), 8.

Thanks to this grace-given dynamism toward the things of God, the faithful, insofar as they are docile to the Spirit, tend to accept whatever in their religious experience leads to an intensification of faith, hope, and charity, or to an increase of what Paul in the fifth chapter of Galatians calls the fruits of the Holy Spirit – love, joy, peace, patience, kindness, and the like (cf. Gal. 522–25). Where the result is inner turbulence, anger, discord, disgust, distraction, and the like, the Church can judge that the Spirit of Christ is not at work. We assess models and theories, therefore, by living out the consequences to which they point … .

In our present context one might say: Because the mystery of the Church is at work in the hearts of committed Christians, as something in which they vitally participate, they can assess the adequacy and limits of various models by consulting their own experience. A recognition of the inner and supernatural dimension of theological epistemology is one of the major breakthroughs of our time. In this type of knowledge, theory and practice are inseparably united. The Church exists only as a dynamic reality achieving itself in history, and only through some kind of sharing in the Church's life can one understand at all sufficiently what the Church is. A person lacking this inner familiarity given by faith could not be a competent judge of the value of the models … .

As already stated, the models used in theology are not scale reproductions. They are what Max Black calls 'analogue models' or what Ian Ramsey calls 'disclosure models'. Because their correspondence with the mystery of the Church is only partial and functional, models are necessarily inadequate. They illumine certain phenomena but not others. Each of them exhibits what can be seen by comparison with some particular reality given in our human experience of the world – e.g., the relationship of a vine to its branches, of a head to a body, or of a bride to a husband. Pursued alone, any single model will lead to distortions. It will misplace the accent, and thus entail consequences that are not valid. For example, the analogy of the head and body would suggest that the members of the Church have no personal freedom and autonomy in relationship to Christ and his Spirit. In order to offset the defects of individual models, the theologian, like the physicist, employs a combination of irreducibly distinct models. Phenomena not intelligible in terms of one model may be readily explicable when another model is used.

Admitting the inevitability of such a pluralism of models, theology usually seeks to reduce this pluralism to a minimum. The human mind, in its quest for explanations, necessarily seeks unity. A unified field theory in theology would be able to account for all the data of Scripture and Tradition, and all the experience of the faithful by reference to some one model. At various times in the history of the Church it has seemed possible to construct a total theology, or at least a total ecclesiology, on the basis of a single model. Such a dominant model is, in the terminology of this book, a paradigm. A model rises to the status of a paradigm when it has proved successful in solving a great variety of problems and is expected to be an appropriate tool for unraveling anomalies as yet unsolved. I am here employing the term 'paradigm' in approximately the meaning given to it by Thomas S. Kuhn. He speaks of paradigms as 'concrete puzzle-solutions which, employed as models or examples, can replace explicit rules as a basis for the solution of the remaining puzzles of normal science'.[97]

---

97. T.S. Kuhn, *The Structure of Scientific Revolutions*, 2nd edn, enlarged (Chicago, University of Chicago Press, 1970), 175.

As a model succeeds in dealing with a number of different problems, it becomes an object of confidence, sometimes to such an extent that theologians almost cease to question its appropriateness for almost any problem that may arise. In the Scholasticism of the Counter Reformation period, the Church was so exclusively presented on the analogy of the secular state that this model became, for practical purposes, the only one in Roman Catholic theological currency. Even today, many middle-aged Catholics are acutely uncomfortable with any other paradigm of the Church than the *societas perfecta*. But actually this societal model has been displaced from the center of Catholic theology since about 1940.

In 1943 Plus XII gave quasicanonical status to the image of the Mystical Body ... . [This] analogy reached its highest peak of popularity between 1940 and 1950. In the late forties theologians became conscious of certain deficiencies in the model and attempted to meet these by appealing to other models, such as People of God and Sacrament of Christ.

Vatican Council II in its Constitution on the Church made ample use of the models of the Body of Christ and the Sacrament, but its dominant model was rather that of the People of God. This paradigm focused attention on the Church as a network of interpersonal relationships, on the Church as community. This is still the dominant model for many Roman Catholics who consider themselves progressives and invoke the teaching of Vatican II as their authority.

In the postconciliar period still another model of the Church has begun to struggle for supremacy: that of the Church as Servant or Healer. This model is already suggested in some of the later documents of Vatican II, notably the Constitution on the Church in the Modern World *(Gaudium et spes)*. This model, with its outgoing thrust, has increased the Catholic Christian's sense of solidarity with the whole human race in its struggles for peace, justice, and prosperity.

As we contemplate the theological history of the Catholic Church over the past thirty years, we cannot but be impressed by the rapidity with which, after a period of long stability, new paradigms have begun to succeed one another. From 1600 to 1940 the juridical or societal model was in peaceful possession, but it was then displaced by that of the Mystical Body, which has been subsequently dislodged by three other models in rapid succession: those of People of God, Sacrament, and Servant. These paradigm shifts closely resemble what Thomas Kuhn has described as 'scientific revolutions'. But the revolutions he describes have occurred in the pursuit of purely scientific goals. The new scientific paradigms have been accepted because, without sacrificing the good results attained by previous paradigms, they were able in addition to solve problems that had proved intractable by means of the earlier models.

With regard to the ecclesiological revolutions we have mentioned, it seems clear that the new paradigms have in fact cleared up certain problems not easily solved under the predecessors. To a great extent, however, the motives for the shift have been practical and pastoral rather than primarily speculative. Changes have been accepted because they help the Church to find its identity in a changing world, or because they motivate men to the kind of loyalty, commitment, and generosity that the Church seeks to elicit. The People of God image, for example, was adopted in part because it harmonized with the general trend toward democratization in Western society since the eighteenth century. Since Vatican II the Servant Model has become popular because it satisfies a certain hunger for involvement in the making of a better world – a hunger that, although specifically Christian in motivation, establishes solidarity between the Church and the whole human family.

Whatever may be said of the relative merits of the various paradigms, one must recognize that the transition from one to another is fraught with difficulties. Each paradigm brings with it its own favorite set of images, its own rhetoric, its own values, certitudes, commitments, and priorities. It even brings with it a particular set of preferred problems. When paradigms shift, people suddenly find the ground cut out from under their feet. They cannot begin to speak the new language without already committing themselves to a whole new set of values that may not be to their taste. Thus they find themselves gravely threatened in their spiritual security. Theologians, who ought to be able to shift their thinking from one key to another, often resist new paradigms because these eliminate problems on which they have built up a considerable expertise, and introduce other problems with regard to which they have no special competence.

It should not be surprising, therefore, that in the contemporary Church, rocked by paradigm shifts, we should find phenomena such as polarization, mutual incomprehension, inability to communicate, frustration, and discouragement. Since the situation is simply a fact of our times, we must learn to live with it. It will greatly help, however, if people can learn to practice tolerance and to accept pluralism. We must recognize that our own favorite paradigms, however excellent, do not solve all questions. Much harm is done by imperialistically seeking to impose some one model as the definitive one.

Because images are derived from the finite realities of experience, they are never adequate to represent the mystery of grace. Each model of the Church has its weaknesses; no one should be canonized as the measure of all the rest. Instead of searching for some absolutely best image, it would be advisable to recognize that the manifold images given to us by Scripture and Tradition are mutually complementary. They should be made to interpenetrate and mutually qualify one another. None, therefore, should be interpreted in an exclusivistic sense, so as to negate what the other approved models have to teach us. The New Testament, for example, combines the images of Temple and Body of Christ in logically incoherent but theologically apposite ways. In 1 Pet. 2:5 we are told that Christians are a Temple built of living stones, whereas Paul in Eph. 4:16 says that the Body of Christ is still under construction. This 'profuse mixing of metaphors', Paul Minear reminds us, 'reflects not logical confusion but theological vitality'[98] … .

---

98. Minear, op. cit., p. 253.

1.9 ELISABETH SCHÜSSLER FIORENZA: *THE EKKLĒSIA OF WOMEN* – 1993

In this work,[99] Fiorenza develops the notion of 'woman-church' into the '*ekklēsia* of women' which she is keen to suggest should function as 'a discursive space and critical site'. She wishes to contribute towards the theoretical bases for the empowerment of women within the church and society alike, by facilitating the wider recognition of the realization that women constitute a 'sociopolitcal category and collectivity'. Ecclesiologically speaking, it thus follows that such a realization and the discussions, studies and collaboration which might follow from this, will further challenge patriarchal and hierarchical models of authority and practices of governance within the church. For it is such as these, Fiorenza believes, which institutionally marginalises women and restrict the fullness of the role which women play in the church. The text is not simply directed at the proponents of the perceived patriarchy in the church, but at the feminist movements themselves: it is a sustained reflection upon the nature of the power relationships within the church and how the collective efforts of women together may give rise to more liberating structures of participation, representation and hence power in the church.

❧

A democratic articulation of the *ekklēsia* of women must be aware of capitalist patriarchy's 'troubled, even antithetical relationship with democracy'. Such an awareness is necessary because only an appeal to political and ethical principles that are already inherent in a society can safeguard its pluralism and difference. Yet democratic principles of freedom and equality are not to be construed as foundational terms but must be seen as signifying practices within Western patriarchal society and Christian religion.

If feminist theology conceptualizes women-church in socio-political terms with radical democracy as its norm,[100] then it can conceptualize the *ekklēsia* of women as a positive theoretical site from which to think about feminist political strategies. Such a theoretical frame could displace the 'otherness' – construct of woman with the democratic construct of the *ekklēsia* of women, which is at one and the same time an ideal vision and a historical reality. It is already present in society and church but not yet accomplished, real but in the process of realization. Historically and politically the image of the *ekklēsia* of women, in the sense of the democratic assembly, the synod or the congress of women is an oxymoron, i.e., a combination of contradictory terms. Its translation by 'women-church' as antonym to patriarchal church identifies Christian community and theology as important sites of feminist political-religious struggles for transforming Western patriarchy.

Situating feminist theorizing and theologizing within the practice and vision of the *ekklēsia* of women allows one to contextualize so-called natural gender arrangements together with those of race, ethnicity, or class. Such a contextualizatoin reveals them as sociopolitical ideological constructions of democratic patriarchy. Women live in societies that are not

---

99. From *Discipleship of Equals – the Ethics and Politics of Liberation* (London, SCM Press, 1993), 344–52.
100. John McGowan, *Postmodernism and its Critics* (Ithaca, Cornell University Press, 1981), 220–80.

simply pluralist. Rather, society is 'stratified, differentiated into social groups with unequal status, power, and access to resources, traversed by pervasive axes of inequality along lines of class, gender, race, ethnicity, and age'.[101] Feminist theory therefore must take care not to reinscribe such patriarchal status *divisions* as positive *diversity* and pluralistic *differences* among women. Rather, a critical feminist theory and theology of liberation must 'denaturalize' patriarchal racial, gender, cultural, and other status inscriptions. It can relativize them by contextualizing sexual differences with the multiplicity of other biological, social, and cultural differences in and among women.

Therefore, it is possible to create the *ekklēsia* of women as a theoretical space where the meaning of women as a sociopolitical category and collectivity can be constructed in practice and theory. In this theoretical space feminist theory can 'denaturalize' social assumptions about gender, sex, or femininity by politicizing them. Such a sociopolitical deconstruction of women and the feminine does not need to repress or deny gender differences. Rather it must first refuse to insert them into an essentializing frame of male–female dualism; then it must refrain from endowing them with ontological symbolic significance; and finally it must take care not to universalize their historically and culturally circumscribed gendered meanings and identity formations … .

Moreover, the *ekklēsia* of women must not be defined in terms of the commonality of women *as women*. Feminist political analyses have shown that assumptions concerning the just political order that surface in feminist texts operate within the parameters established by Plato and Aristotle. Plato's notion of a politically constructed commonality that can bring a heterogeneous population together in a hierarchically organized meritocracy is mirrored in the literal feminist rhetoric concerning negative liberty, equal citizenship, and political participation. Aristotle's conflation of equality and uniformity as the precondition for political membership in an exclusionary *polis* reverberates in the 'dream of separatist' feminist solutions.[102]

The *ekklēsia* of women as a feminist political collectivity must therefore avoid the exclusive alternative of classical philosophy: *either* formal equality among women that does not problematize but reinscribes the patriarchal divisions of race, class, religion, ethnicity, or sexuality among women; *or* essentialist equality that constitutes women's space or feminist space by excluding theoretical and practical differences. In other words, the *ekklēsia* of women must not constitute itself *either* in terms of formal equality based on continuing patriarchal divisions *or* on equality premised on exclusionary homogeneity. Instead, its signifying practice must create a feminist public that seeks equality and citizenship of women by articulating, confronting, and combatting patriarchal divisions. It does so not by declaring itself to be a liberated space of sisterhood, but by engaging feminist theoretical and practical differences as democratic discursive practices … .

Whereas in the 1970s sisterhood was the preferred metaphor for expressing feminist collectivity and solidarity, in the past decade the mother–daughter relationship or relationality as such has been valorized … Recognizing the power differences between women, feminist

---

101. Nancy Fraser, *Unruly Practices: Power, Discourse and Gender in Contemporary Social Theory* (Minneapolis: University of Minnesota Press, 1989), 165.

102. M.E. Hawkesworth, *Beyond Oppression: Feminist Theory and Political Strategy* (New York: Continuum, 1990), 156.

theory in the past decade has problematized and revalorized the mother–daughter relationship. Although the construct of the 'symbolic mother inscribed within the horizon of sexual difference' makes it possible to name inequalities among women and permits both the exchange between women across generations and the sharing of knowledge and desires across differences,[103] it does so by reinscribing the totalizing notion of fundamental gender-difference developed by elite white women. Rather than remaining within the psychoanalytic story of gender system, whose core it is to promote masculinity as separation from the mother and femininity as continuity with the primary bond[104] women-church needs to look for an interpretive frame that neither reinscribes nor denies, but that undercuts the totalizing binary sex-gender system.

In *The Bonds of Love* Jessica Benjamin seeks to explain why we accept and perpetrate relationships of domination and submission in spite of our conscious commitment to equality and freedom. Having demonstrated the complex intertwinement of familial gender and social-political dominance that produces the psychological process of complicity, she proposes *intersubjective theory* as an interpretive frame rather than simply finding a female counterpart to the phallic symbolic mode of representing desire. Intersubjective theory situates gender identity in the relation between self and other with its tension between sameness and difference. It construes this relationship not as a linear movement from oneness to separateness but as mutual recognition sustaining the tensive, paradoxical balance between them. 'Thus a person could alternately experience herself as "I a woman"; "I a genderless subject"; "I like-a-man". A person who can maintain this flexibility can accept all parts of herself and the other.'[105] However, I would insist that such an intersubjective frame must also be spelled out in terms of race, class, culture, and religion. Depending on what is given primacy in terms of identity, the interrelations of these patriarchal structures will define identity differently.

According to Benjamin such an intersubjective frame is best expressed with the metaphor of 'open space'. The notion of 'open space' applies not just to the individual but also suggests a place from which to envision the *ekklēsia* of women as an open rhetorical space bounded by its struggles against multiform oppression. The *ekklēsia* of women metrophrized as 'bounded open space', rather than as sisterhood or daughterhood, can engender historical community and continuity without denying existing differences of experience and power between women and between women and men. In contrast to a single, uniform, oppositional discursive community, it is to be envisioned as a coalition of over-lapping subcommunities or semiautonomous sites that share a common interest in combatting patriarchal relations of oppression. As a feminist counterpublic open space the *ekklēsia* of women as the congress or synod of women is not to be envisioned as a coherent, consistent web but rather as a heterogeneous, polyglot arena of competing discourses. In order to 'denaturalize' and to 'deprivatize' the collectivity of sisterhood and the mother–daughter relationship, feminist theology needs to conceptualize the *ekklēsia* of women as such a political 'open space' in which Divine Presence as mutual recognition and respect of self and others, of identity and difference, of oneness and separation can be experienced.

---

103. See Teresa de Lauretis, 'The Essence of the Triangle', 25 … .
104. Jessica Benjamin, *The Bonds of Love: Psychoanalysis, Feminism, and the Problem of Domination* (New York: Pantheon Books, 1988), 217.
105. Ibid., 113.

THE ETHICS AND POLITICS OF SOLIDARITY

As the intersection of a multiplicity of public feminist discourses and as a site of contested sociopolitical contradictions, feminist alternatives, and unrealized possiblities, the *ekklēsia* of women requires a rhetorical rather than a positivistic scientific conceptualization of feminist theory and theology.[106] In order to constitute *ekklēsia* as a discursive feminist public and democratic polity that defines women as a political-historical category, feminist theological discourses at one and the same time need to engage and to move back and forth between different feminist rhetorical strategies, rather than to construct them as fixed oppositional positions that exclude each other. Such feminist theological strategies are: the rhetoric of liberation, the rhetoric of differences, not just of difference, the rhetoric of equality, and the rhetoric of vision.

Feminist theoretical discourses are then best understood in the classical sense of deliberative rhetoric that seeks to persuade the democratic assembly and to adjudicate arguments in order to make decisions for the sake of the 'common good' of the *ekklēsia*. Feminist theology and strategy need to adjudicate, for instance, between appeals to the universal feminine or to unanimous sisterhood and those to women's historical-political specificity with respect to class, race, gender, ethnicity, sexual preference, and so on. Such a deliberation from within particular struggles and political coalitions acknowledges the multiple discourse locations of feminist voices manifesting themselves in a diversity of intellectual constructs and competing interest groups. If different feminist discursive publics articulate feminist analyses, proposals, and strategies differently, then it becomes necessary to adjudicate between competing feminist definitions of the world and alternative constructions of symbolic universes.

Moreover, such competing feminist analyses of patriarchal reality and divergent articulations of feminist visions are not simply right or wrong. They must not be construed as dogmatic positions but as strategic practices. Feminist theology as rhetorical intervention requires public debate and deliberation if it is not to deteriorate into dogmatic sectarianism. If there is not one 'orthodox' feminist strategy or one single true feminist position, but a multiplicity of feminist positions and discursive practices, then a feminist praxis must be embodied in responsible debate and practical deliberation.

The *ekklēsia* of women can make available polyglot theological discourses through which individual women might shape their own stories in conversation with the stories of either contemporary, historical, or biblical women. Such discourses must render visible again those women who have remained invisible even in feminist discourses. By insisting in its own discourses on the *theoretical* visibility and difference, for instance, of black, poor, colonial, lesbian, or working women, feminist theory and theology make comprehensible that 'women' do not have a unitary essence but represent a historical multiplicity. Many African-American women, e.g., have not just African, but also Native American, diverse European, and Asian ancestry. In addition, feminist discourses must also take care not to portray one group of women, e.g., lesbians, as a monolithic and undifferentiated sisterhood with no competing interests, values, and conflicts.[107]

---

106. See my book *But She Said: The Rhetoric of Feminist Interpretation for Liberation* (Boston: Beacon Press, 1992).
107. E. Frances White, 'Africa on My Mind: Gender, Counter Discourse and African-American Nationalism', *Journal of Women's History* 2, no. 1 (1990): 78.

Such a conceptualization of the *ekklēsia* women as a democratic, public feminist arena for practical deliberation and responsible choice does not repress but invites debates about different theoretical proposals and practical strategies. Rather than simply silence differences as divisive to the movement, it can show that differing feminist positions are related to conflicting needs of different sections of the women's movement in society and church. By constantly engendering critique, dispute, and debate the *ekklēsia* of women must search for more adequate strategies and visions for constructing a different reality and for avoiding orthodox patriarchal divisions. Clarifying and adjudicating contested concepts and proposals, it seeks to engender a long process of moral deliberation and practical solidarity in diverse and often competing struggles for liberation.

The development of an ethics of solidarity is therefore crucial for the dialogic and strategic practices of the *ekklēsia* of women because its diverse subcommunities are differentiated and divided not only by class and race positions but also by institutional locations, professional allegiances, and ecclesial affiliations that draw on a wide range of discursive frameworks.[108] Yet if a feminist discursive rhetorical practice inviting theoretical and strategical differences is not to degenerate into a paralyzing pluralism in which even the most reactionary politics can be labelled 'feminist', an ethics of solidarity must make explicit the patriarchal power relations inscribed in its own discourses and strategies. Moreover, it needs to articulate feminist criteria of assessment and evaluation that privilege the theories and strategies of feminists who speak from within the experience of multiplicative patriarchal oppressions.

If there is not one orthodox feminist position, but a multiplicity of feminist discursive practices, then a feminist ethics of solidarity cannot consist in uncritical assent. Instead, it must be embodied in responsible debate and practical deliberation as a dialogic assessment of the oral significance of practices as it attempts to decide not only what to do next but also what is best in a particular situation and for a particular group of women.

A feminist ethics of solidarity therefore presupposes as sine qua non the democratic agency and self-determination of women. Women must claim the right and power for interpreting their own reality and for defining their own objectives. One group of women cannot speak for all women. Conflicting interests of women must be articulated and adjudicated in public debate so that strategies of solidarity can be forged. Moreover, the *ekklēsia* of women has critically to attend to its own discursive practices in order to enable such self-determination of individual women and subgroups. Which voices are allowed to speak, which are never heard, who is to say, and what stories are still to be told and proposals to be made? In short, the *ekklēsia* of women needs to model how people can work together in complex situations without exploiting one another.

A feminist ethics of solidarity seeks to develop a complex consciousness of liberation that can analyze and challenge the multiplicative interstructuring of patriarchal oppression both in the dominant society and within movements for liberation. It appreciates the ways in which women suffering from multiple oppression have not simply been victims but have also been agents indeveloping strategies of everyday resistance. At the same time it needs to avoid the glorifying 'othering' and stereotyping of women of color or of poor women that is so typical of

---

108. R. Felski, *Beyond Feminist Aesthetics* (Cambridge, Harvard University Press, 1989), 171.

Euro-American middle-class romanticism. As the democratic *ekklēsia* women of diverse groups must be able to interact as individual citizens rather than as representatives of their race, class, or sex if they choose to do so. An ethical discourse of solidarity seeks to foster respect and 'befriending' between women, but it does not presuppose the 'naturalized' solidarity of 'womanhood' or the intimate friendship of 'sisterhood'.

Last but not least: If not gender and biology but historical experiences and struggles against patriarchy are constitutive for a feminist identity formation in the *ekklēsia* of women, we must carefully attend to how we tell or stories and construct women's histories. I began this lecture with a poem by Adrienne Rich in praise of our nineteenth-century foremothers' and foresisters' struggles. Moving with me through the analysis and arguments of this lecture I hope that you have become painfully aware that this story of our heroines and heritage construes feminist struggle as the struggle of elite white Euro-American women in which Native American, African slave, and lower-class European immigrant women are present only as victims. Absent and silent from the record even of such a feminist poet as Adrienne Rich are those feminists who have fought for their equal rights both as women *and* as blacks, immigrants, poor, or indigenous Americans. Into this Euro-American feminist silence the recognition of their struggles and their visions needs to be spoken if feminism is to move out of its gender captivity and complicity. Anna Julia Cooper, I suggest, expresses such a vision that leads into the 'bounded open space' of the *ekklēsia*.

> Now, I think if I could crystallize the sentiment of my constituency, and deliver it as a message to this congress of women, it would be something like this: Let woman's claim be as broad in the concrete as in the abstract. We take our stand on the solidarity of humanity, the oneness of life, and the unnaturalness and injustice of all special favoritisms, whether of sex, race, country, or condition. If one link of the chain is broken, the chain is broken. A bridge is no stronger than its weakest part and a cause is not worthier than its weakest element ... . We want, then, as toilers for the universal triumph of justice and human rights, to go to our homes from this congress, demanding an entrance not through a gateway for ourselves, our race, our sex, our sect, but a grand highway for humanity. The colored women feels that woman's cause is one and universal; and not till the image of God, whether in parian or ebony, is sacred and inviolable; not till race, color, sex, and condition are seen as the accidents and not the substance of life, not till the universal title of humanity to life, liberty, and the pursuit of happiness is conceded to be inalienable to all; not till then is woman's lesson taught and woman's cause won – not the white woman's nor the black woman's, nor the red woman's ... The acquirements of her 'rights' will mean the final triumph of all right over might, the supremacy of the moral forces of reason and justice, and love in the government of the nations of earth.[109]

---

109. Lowenberg and Bogin (eds), *Black Women in Nineteenth-Century America: Their Words*, 330ff.

1.10 ALVARO QUIROZ MAGAÑA: *ECCLESIOLOGY IN THE THEOLOGY OF LIBERATION* – 1996

This is a survey of the key themes and perspectives which liberation theology has brought to ecclesiology.[110] In it, we see how liberation ecclesiology builds upon and moves beyond earlier 'models' (such as those outlined by Dulles) and develops the work of seminal thinkers such as Boff. For liberation ecclesiology, the changing historical and socio-political realities dictate the need for a new self-understanding of church, indeed a renewed way of being church. Such theologians sought to reflect upon existing models of the church and to see how they might form an ecclesiology which would better capture the experience of and serve the needs of the peoples of their continent and, above all, 'incarnate for present history the response of fidelity to the call of the gospel'. In this, they sought to interconnect the core categories of 'church', 'Reign of God' and 'world'. Liberation ecclesiology seeks to show that the church brings the reality of the liberative gospel to the lives of poor, for the church accompanies the poor on the road to socio-historical transformation. Magaña notes the importance of ecclesiological reflection to Liberation Theology on the whole and he recognizes that liberation ecclesiology is a task that is never complete, constantly demanding responses to the ever-changing situation of the people of God. Theologians and church leaders are actually evangelized *by* the poor, who constitute 'the most important agent of … evangelizing liberation'.

The key themes of liberation ecclesiology are identified as the church being understood as the sacrament of historical liberation; the church as sign and servant of the Reign of God; the church as the People of God; the need to recognize and overcome divisions in the church and the importance of new forms of service and ministries in the church, along with new forms of church structure. The church seeks to make God's Reign a reality by proclaiming a gospel in solidarity with exploited classes.

❁

I   AN INESCAPABLE THEOLOGICAL TASK

… [F]or Latin America the current epoch has been one of great ecclesial vitality. We have the impulse of Vatican Council II. We have the challenge, confronted by Medellín, of effecting an ecclesial *aggiornamento* in lands of pillage and inequality, lands of misery, oppression, and injustice. We have the exodus of priests, laity, and religious to the periphery, out to where the poor live. We have the surprising resurgence of the church amid and from among these same poor, who burst upon the historical scene denouncing their unjust suffering and demanding justice and emancipation. We have the conflicts and tensions that arise within a society that resists change, and in a church the majority of whose members are more accustomed to preserving the status quo than to proposing social transformation. We have the dogged

---

110. From *Systematic Theology – Perspectives from Liberation Theology*, Jon Sobrino and Ignacio Ellacuria (eds) (London, SCM Press, 1996), 178–93.

determination of Puebla not to give up, not to forget the poor, not to shut itself off from the grace of making its option for them. We have so much vitality in the church. All of this – truly the gift and power of the Spirit – lived in the midst of the humble and joyful, persevering and sanctified, crucified and suffering effort of men and women, groups and communities, has been the foundation, and is the substance, of this ecclesiological reflection.

This emerging, progressive ecclesial vitality stimulated the need as early as the 1970s, and with a growing urgency, to rethink the church. The classic ecclesiologies which tended to be deductive, ahistorical, clerical, and hierarchical, were deemed insufficient for giving an account of faith and ecclesial life in this situation, amid the waxing, developing Christian praxis. It became essential to narrate the believing life anew, to allow the light of the gospel to shine upon it, to impel it toward a further pledge and commitment.

II   A NEW ECCLESIOLOGY FOR A NEW HISTORICAL SITUATION

In this context, an ecclesiological reflection of a liberative tenor has been taking shape within the vigorous current of Christian thought that is the theology of liberation. It is an ecclesiological reflection that presents itself first and foremost as 'second word' (the first word is praxis), as critical reflection in the light of the gospel on life and on ecclesial Christian practice. It is a theological reflection that faces the question of the meaning of the church from the starting point of believers' growing commitment to the liberation of our peoples, from the liberative practices emerging in the midst of the poor.

1   A 'NEW PRAXIS'

When we speak of a 'new praxis', one demanding new kinds of theological reflection, we find it necessary to say something about the new and the old in the church of the Lord. There has been a great deal of reflection these last decades on the possibility and reality of change in the church. On the one hand, there has been a sense of the need to assert the indefectibility of this church, which is the Lord's, and which receives from him in ongoing fashion nourishment, origin, and life. On the other hand, it has been considered urgent to emphasize the fact that this very life, this very nourishment require that the church, at once holy and in need of purification (*Lumen Gentium*, no. 8), be constantly renewed, reshaped in every age in conformity with the demands of its being and mission. In this sense, new praxis is the same as renewal in fidelity. New praxis is response to a word that constantly summons us to emerge, to take the road to go on a pilgrimage to a new land, to take up the cross and follow Jesus … . [F]or the first time in history, since this is what our epoch requires, the church has addressed the challenge of identifying with the poor and of walking with them along the road to liberation, to sociohistorical transformation. And this is seen as a privileged way of bringing into history the liberation of the gospel of Jesus … .

We are confronted here with a praxis that has come to be shaped by an emerging awareness that the current social situation is unjust and inhumane, that it cannot be willed by God – and likewise by an awareness that liberation is attainable, indeed part and parcel of

God's salvific plan. It is a committed praxis, which seeks to overcome, with lucidity, all forms (so often dissimulated and concealed) of slavery, exploitation, institutionalized violence, and socio-economic marginalization. It is a praxis that consists and can be summed up in the ecclesial option for the poor and their liberation.

In the same fashion this new praxis consists in the poor themselves bursting upon the historical and ecclesial scene. Our eyes have been opened; we cannot continue to overlook the suffering and unjust oppression of the poor who surround us. We went to them to bring them the gospel of liberation, and we discovered that we were being evangelized by them. We came to understand that we could not evangelize without a concrete involvement in the liberation of the poor, and we realized that the poor were the most important agent of this evangelizing liberation – these poor who, with their awareness, their words, and their actions, were proclaiming the gospel in a new way in our lands.

2   NEW ECCLESIAL PRAXIS, NEW UNDERSTANDING OF REALITY

The theses of developmentalism have failed. Instead of diminishing, 'under-development' or socio-economic marginalization has grown tragically and enormously compounded by political oppression and repression. This has obliged Latin Americans to formulate new conceptualizations of the reality of our peoples. Thus it has come to be understood that the situation in question is largely to be explained in terms of dependency; structural inequality; systematic exploitation; and the economic, political, and social transformation – a change in the social system itself … . Does the church have a concrete responsibility regarding the oppression of the poor in Latin America? Is part of the mission of the church to undertake a serious evangelical involvement in the historical liberation of our peoples? Does it pertain to the vital reality of the church to make a contribution to the formation of a historical agent capable of carrying forward this project of liberation? …

III   STAGES OF LIBERATION ECCLESIOLOGY

1   PASTORAL CONCERNS: APPROACH TO LIFE, TO REALITY

In a first stage, we might cite the ecclesiological reflections that have occurred as challenges to forms of pastoral ministry and church life that were no longer felt to correspond either to the reality of the times or to the requirements of change that were making themselves felt in our lands. Ecclesiological reflections were uncovering a certain 'ecclesial malaise' in various groups of Christians, expressed in letters, communiqués, requests, proposals, and pastoral letters … . More critical and analytical reflections, undertaken by theologians involved in this pilgrimage, were yielding the first elements of the theology of liberation. This first stage in Latin American ecclesiology is remarkable for the beginnings of a fertile interaction between church life, theological reflection, and episcopal magisterium. Conflicts between the magisterium of certain bishops and the propositions of certain theologians had not yet appeared. Later there would be talk of a 'parallel magisterium'.

Such reflections called attention to the inadequacy of a pastoral praxis that failed to take account of historical realities understood in the light of more critical analyses. A need was recognised for an understanding of the church in theological forms and models that would permit evolution, change, and adaptation (Juan Luis Segundo, Gustavo Gutiérrez, and others). It came to be seen that the battle for social justice, social commitment, and the transformation of the inhumane conditions of the concrete life of the majority of the inhabitants of Latin America ought to occupy the center of Christian life and the proclamation of the gospel … .

2   REFLECTION ON 'MODELS' OF THE CHURCH

Liberation ecclesiology pointed out the insufficiency of the earlier models – christendom and neo-christendom – to respond to the new situation. The dual-level theologies, and the others that fail to account for the unity of history as authentic salvation history, must give place to theologies that speak more realistically of salvation in history and demonstrate the unity of the human and Christian calling (Gutiérrez, Ignacio Ellacuría, Leonardo Boff). Of course, this had repercussions on a view of the church; on the understanding of its fundamental being; on the way in which its biblical images ought to be understood, especially that of the people of God so dear to the heart of Vatican II; on the way in which the 'notes' of the church, and the services and structures of that church, ought to be understood and projected. This was ecclesiology's 'incarnational' way of accepting the invitation of Vatican II to make the church a church of communion.

All this made it necessary to examine at greater depth the various models of church. The clerical models had to be identified for what they were; more participatory models, which would enflesh an ecclesiology of communion already proclaimed at Vatican II, were proposed. Thus it was useful to characterize the various models, the various ways of being church, that had prevailed in history. These models represented concrete manners of incarnating the ecclesial calling, but not the only such manners. As models, they had their good points, but their limitations as well, and none could pretend to an exclusive validity for our own age.

On one hand, the models in question referred to the internal structure of the church (vertical model, participatory model). On the other, they had to do with its relationship with its broader surroundings, with its place in society as a whole, with its interconnections with the various sectors and classes of society (christendom, neo-christendom, *mysterium salutis*, church of the poor, and so on). This reflection on and discussion of ecclesial models rendered Christian consciousness more flexible, thus permitting the quest for a new model, a model shaped from the starting point of the poor, in the option for them, in the life rising up among them. This new model would respond to concrete situations of oppression and to the steps already beginning to be taken in the direction of liberation. The important thing, it was emphasized, was to find a model of church that would imply an interconnection, adequate for today, of the key categories of church, Reign of God, and world (Leonardo Boff), a model that would incarnate for present history the response of fidelity to the call of the gospel.

3   A REFLECTION AT ONCE CONVERGENT AND DIFFERENTIATED

… While sharing the same perspective, some ecclesiological works have attended more to the life of the church as community of faith and life, while others have emphasized the life of the church in its quality of concrete signification in and to the world. Thus, some have set themselves the task of showing the Christian legitimacy of a new emerging model. They have sought to reinforce the thrust of a church reborn among the poor and making itself a charismatic community of faith and service – becoming a space for participation on the part of the poor, and remodelling its services and forms of authority. Others have insisted especially on the phenomenon of a people of the poor bursting upon the scene of a history built until now behind their backs and on their backs – an irruption that is a denunciation of death and proclamation of life, the presence of the God of life in a new experience of church and evangelization. Here it is that they have located the rebirth of the church … .

Let us repeat: it is a matter of different emphases, not of mutually exclusive approaches. Indeed, if we examine the overall work of the various theologians respectively, we find what they regard as the two aspects of church: the ecclesial *ad intra* and *ad extra*. But this difference of emphasis is enriching for theology and for the life of the community. It calls attention to the reciprocity of a way of being church that, the more churchly it is, the more capable it becomes of plunging evangelically into the history of the poor and thus being a leaven of renewal for the church at large … .

4   THE CRITICAL ACCOMPANIMENT OF THE CHURCH AMONG THE PEOPLE

Beyond a doubt, in gathering up the experiences of the Christian community and handing it back as critical enlightenment and new impulse, this ecclesiological reflection has meant something precious to the pilgrimage of a church reborn with and among the poor – the church of a people, nevertheless, who pursue their course to liberation amidst an ever more evident and prolonged captivity.

Now, it is precisely in this last sense that liberation ecclesiology cannot be a finished whole, a closed system. It is an ongoing task, challenged at every moment by the novelty of history. What does it mean to be church in the midst of the emergence of the people? What is it to be church amidst repression and this obvious historical backsliding? What is it to be church amidst revolutionary struggles? What is it to be church amidst historical transformation, with the powerful seeking to apply a brake to the advance of the poor? And so on. All of these questions … must be addressed by ecclesiology on this continent of hope, as it has been called … . In this sense, then, we must continue to speak of current liberation ecclesiology as an ongoing critical accompaniment of the pilgrimage of a people answering the call of the gospel of liberation.

IV   FUNDAMENTAL THEMES OF THE ECCLESIOLOGY OF LIBERATION

1   THE CHURCH: SACRAMENT OF HISTORICAL LIBERATION

Characteristic of Latin American life and ecclesial consciousness, and of Latin American critical reflection on the church, is the emphasis on the 'mission of the church' in the face of the urgent need of salvation represented by, first, our all but universal misery and oppression, and second, by our longings and struggles for liberation. What we have, then, is an eminently practical consciousness, which keeps before its eyes the question of how to be and how to create church in the face of concrete challenges of this kind. Accordingly, when that consciousness reflects on the church as sacrament of salvation, it underscores the decentralization that this requires. The church is for the world. It exists because there is and must be salvation, and so it asks itself of what salvation it is the sacrament. It is the sacrament not of an individualistic salvation concerned with afterlife and existing outside of history, but rather of a salvation for the individual and for the collectivity. Such a salvation, while greater than history, is nevertheless realized in the form of liberation – must be mediated in the economic, political, and social realities of human existence. Finally, it is a salvation that will be the rising up of the massacred and the eradication of institutionalized violence; a salvation consisting in real, concrete change, in a real community of sisters and brothers, reflected in the very structures of our social life. This is where eschatological salvation will have its starting point.

This is where the church of Latin America is coming to experience its mystery. Here, in the presence of the God of Jesus, this church is coming to discover that it will be a sacrament of salvation to the extent that it becomes a church of the poor and oppressed ... [who thus] come to be the authentic and first subject of ecclesial life and structure.

2   THE CHURCH: SIGN AND SERVANT OF THE REIGN OF GOD

This understanding that the church is a sacrament of salvation has been deepened, in Latin American ecclesiological awareness, by a reflection on the church as sign and servant of the Reign of God. Appealing to Jesus' preaching and history as the foundation of the church, the church discovers itself to be the seed of the Reign, an entity in the service of the Reign. This service will necessarily be performed in the following and discipleship of Jesus – in the adoption of his Messianic practice and his cause ... . There can be no other authentic route for the church, then, than the following of Jesus in the service of the Reign. The ongoing conversion of the church, its words and its deeds, its internal structuring and its manner of presence in society, must be good news – an evangelization opposed to sin and effectively presenting the imminence of the Reign of God.

3   THE CHURCH, PEOPLE OF GOD

... In the wealth of this key biblical image, the theology that reflects from the underside of history, at the side of an oppressed, believing people, has found enlightenment and prophetic strength, a demanding calling and an attitude of thanksgiving, the opportunity to live in the following of Jesus amidst persistent captivity, and an implacable thrust toward liberation.

... In keeping with Vatican II, liberation ecclesiology has underlined the fact that the church, the people of God, is not only structure and organization, but also, and principally, event. The church is the convocation of the people by God, and it is the people's response to God. Liberation ecclesiology has insisted on the primacy of Christian existence in the community over organization and functional differentiation within the same ... . [T]he ecclesiology of liberation has adopted the formula that the building of a church of communion must overcome the vertical, authoritarian, and closed structuring of a pyramidal, hierarchical model of church that fails to adapt to the basic content of the biblical category of people of God … .

When we speak of a church of the poor, then, we mean to testify to the rebirth of the people of God that is taking place on the outskirts of our cities, in rural areas, in native regions, in the places of socio-economic marginalization and helplessness. The expression *church of the poor* connotes a church in which laity and religious, priests and bishops, have experienced a new call and have sought to respond with fidelity in service and solidarity with the poor; a church in which the gospel is announced in solidarity with the exploited classes; a church gathered by the proclamation of the gospel of liberation at the heart of the actual struggles for liberation; a church that is a congregation of all who, accepting Christ, receive the proclamation of his Reign and so serve to make that Reign a living reality … .

4   UNITY AND CONFLICT IN THE CHURCH

Inevitably and from the outset liberation ecclesiology has had to be concerned with the key theme of the unity of the church. In addressing this concern it has emphasized that the most serious breaches of this unity are those that reflect the objective division of society into counterpoised social classes. Here, our ecclesiology insists that the question of church unity cannot be dealt with apart from the sacramental reality of the church and its essential reference to the world. After all, the most profound truth of the unity of the church consists in the communion of believers with God and with one another, in the sharing of the trinitarian love that constitutes the concrete basis of all Christian relationships. The church, then, in our historical conditions, receives the gift of its unity and makes that gift real to the extent that it serves the process of the unification of the world. And in a world radically divided, the unifying function of the church community will be actualized in the struggle with injustice as the cause of division, and in the upbuilding of justice as the incarnation of concrete community … .

Hand in hand with this reflection on unity, another is in progress: one concerning conflict in the church. The great ecclesial vitality to which we have been referring has been accompanied by significant tension in our church … . The key to managing these tensions has been subordination to the Reign of God. Structures, norms, and institutional realities must be submitted to the norm of the Reign, and not vice versa. One must acknowledge one's own sin in this conflict ridden situation; one must understand that it is not easy for the church to adopt this novel, liberative will of God, in the consciousness of which the new ecclesiology has been constructed. A spirituality of conflict, which is not plunged into panic by it but which is capable of discerning the will of God within it, which honestly seeks to transcend conflict in the direction of the Reign of God, and which is capable of undogged perseverance and deathless hope – all of this is the gift of the Spirit. It is a reproduction of the equally conflict-ridden experience of the first Christian communities, that is, their gradual discovery of God's will for the church in circumstances altogether novel and unforeseeable … .

5   NEW SERVICES, STRUCTURES, AND MINISTRIES IN THE CHURCH

Protesting concrete oppression and socio-economic marginalization, and promoting actual participation on the part of Christians in the struggles and striving of liberation, the Latin American church has felt the need for authority and ministry to be exercised in a different way. In the pastoral practice of the church of Latin America, and in the promising experience of the base church communities, a lively impulse of renewal has been at work. Initial successes have been realized in charismatic forms of ministry, service, and participation that are more in accord with the demands of the church's vocation today.

First, we see a growing, theologically sound participation on the part of laity – laity who are poor – in church administration. Everywhere we behold the appearance of new lay ministries. We witness greater autonomy of the laity as they participate as Christians in concrete struggles for liberation. There is an awareness that the praxis of liberation in actual ecclesial experience is a radical response to the Christian calling, and not the implementation of a charge received from the hierarchy. Nonetheless, this still calls for greater reflection and more practice before we arrive at a further clarification of the status of the laity in the church, a status that, on the other hand, must be on guard against an undue 'clericalization' of the new lay ministries.

Second, there are new ways of exercising the priestly and episcopal ministry – more participatory ways, more democratic ways, ways that are more in the spirit of service and solidarity, ways more prophetic and more committed. Many pastors have carried their love to the limit, giving their lives for their brothers and sisters. This has not failed to have a clear impact on Christian awareness, which postulated that the service of Peter in the church universal be performed as that of a pope of the poor … .

V   ASPECTS OF CONFLICT AND POINTS OF DISPUTE

… [I]n Latin America becoming the church of the poor and being committed to the cause of their liberation is experienced not as an alternative, but as a calling of the entire church … .

Precisely here is where a discussion has had to be sustained by the ecclesiology of liberation with other ecclesial sectors on the topic of the meaning of the option for the poor. Christian love cannot be divested of its radicality with adjectives that ignore God's partiality for the poor. Surely God wills that all persons attain salvation and come to the knowledge of the truth … . Once more in the area of liberation ecclesiology, an important investigation pursues the lines of an authentic integration of the political dimension into Christian and ecclesial life … . Liberation ecclesiologists insist that concrete liberation is an intrinsic component of faith. Faith is more than an extrinsic motive for political praxis – as can be seen so clearly in the praxis of Jesus himself. Liberation ecclesiologists endorse a political participation on the part of the poor, a participation even better, ever more lucid. We seek criteria for an adequate participation in this area on the part of priests and religious. We ascribe to politics a broader connotation than that of simple partisan militancy, especially in those countries in which any demand, any quest is considered in and of itself a confrontation with the power of the state … .

VI   THE OUTLOOK FOR LIBERATION ECCLESIOLOGY

As we have indicated, one of the tasks that liberation ecclesiology has taken up is that of a committed, critical accompaniment of a people 'on the way'. In the execution of this task ecclesiology finds that the source of its progress is on the underside of history … . What is important is that the people live, that they have life in abundance, as the God of the Good News would have it … . Another of the tasks of the ecclesiology of liberation is to continue to demonstrate to the greater church the legitimacy of this way of being church … . A greater openness on the part of the church in the difficult times of this winter of faith may be decisive if the people are to have life. The ecclesiology of liberation, with its solid, serious, and believing toil, its radical testimony tendered in communion (albeit at times in conflict as well), can be an important contribution to the maintenance, recovery, and enablement of that openness.[111]

---

111. *ET* by Robert Barr.

QUESTIONS FOR DISCUSSION

1   How might Catholic Christians come to a better understanding of unity and diversity throughout the church, in order to achieve a more harmonious balance between the two?

2   Should the local or the universal church be viewed as having primacy or is the true ecclesiological situation more complex than such terms can express?

3   Are there valid arguments today for 'Continental Patriarchates', where each major region of the world has its own Church Patriarch?

4   How might we, today, best understand and describe the relationship between the *Roman Catholic* church and other Christian denominations?

5   How important are the poor and marginalized in the church? How can their voices be heard and their needs addressed?

6   What structural changes would enable the church to preach the gospel more widely and effectively in the New Millennium?

7   What constitutes 'membership' of the church today? Does this differ from what constitutes 'communion with' the church today?

8   What might be appropriate principles to explain and govern the relationship between the church and the world in our times?

9   What are the most pressing concerns for a global church in an era of 'globalisation'?

10 What is the relation between the gospel and the church?

11 How important is the notion of 'community' for ecclesiology in the new Millennium?

12 There have been many changing images, models and visions employed in ecclesiology in recent decades. What does this say about the nature of the church?

FURTHER READING

CHURCH DOCUMENTS

CDF: *Note on the Expression, 'Sister Churches'*, 30 June 2000.
CDF: *Dominus Iesus*, 2000.
Satis Cognitum, 1896.

DISCUSSION AND DEBATE

Albergio, Giuseppe and Komonchak, Joeph, A., *History of of Vatican II*, 5 vols, New York: Orbis/Peeters, 1995.

Beozzo, José Oscar, and Ruggieri, Giuseppe (eds), *The Ecumenical Constitution of Churches – Concilium*, 2001/3.

Blanchi, Eugene C. and Reuther, Rosemary Radford (eds), *A Democratic Catholic Church: The Reconstruction of Roman Catholicism*, New York: Crossroad, 1992.

Boff, Leonardo, *Church, Charism and Power: Liberation Theology and the Institutional Church*, New York: Crossroad, 1983.

Bühlmann, Walter, *The Church of the Future – A Model for the Year 2001*, Slough, St Paul's, 1986.

Bühlmann, Walter, 'The New Ecclesiology of Vatican II' paper given to SEDOS Seminar, Rome, 3 December, 1996 (see: http://www.sedos.org/english/walbert.htm).

Congar, Yves, *The Mystery of the Church*, 2nd edition, London: Geoffrey Chapman 1965.

DeLubac, Henri, *Catholicism*, London, Burns & Oates, 1958.

DeLubac, Henri, *The Splendour of the Church*, New York, Paulist Press, 1956.

Dubay, William, 'A Church for People', in *The Human Church*, London, Frederick Muller, 1967.

Dulles, Avery, *The Resilient Church: The Necessity and Limits of Adaptation*, Dublin, Gill & Macmillan, 1978.

Dulles, Avery, *The Reshaping of Catholicism: Current Challenges in the Theology of the Church*, New York, Harper & Row, 1988.

Dulles, Avery, 'A Half Century of Ecclesiology' in *Theological Studies*, 50 (1989), 419–42.

Dulles, Avery, *The Theology of the Church – a Bibliography*, New York, Paulist Press, 1999.

Fahey, Michael, 'Continuity in the Church Amid Structural Changes', *Theological Studies*, 35 (1974), 415–40.

Hegy, P., *The Church in the Nineties, Its Legacy, Its Future*, Collegeville, Liturgical Press, 1993.

John Paul II, 'The Church and the Council', in *Crossing the Threshold of Hope*, ed. Vittorio Messori, London, Jonathan Cape, 1994.

Kasper, Walter, *Theology and Church*, London, SCM Press, 1989.

Komonchak, Joseph A., 'The Ecclesiology of Vatican II', speech to The Catholic University of America, 27 March 1999 (see Website for The Catholic University of America, Office of Public Affairs, http://publicaffairs.cua.edu/speeches/ecclesiology99.htm).

Küng, Hans, *The Church*, London, Search, 1968.

McBrien, Richard P., *Catholicism*, London, Geoffrey Chapman, 1994.

McBrien, Richard P., '*Dominus Iesus* – an Ecclesiological Critique', lecture given at the Centro Pro Unione, Thursday, 11 January 2001 (see www.sedos.org/english/McBrien.htm).

McPartlan, Paul, *Sacrament of Salvation: an introduction to Eucharistic Ecclesiology*, Edinburgh, T & T Clark, 1995

Metz, J.B., *The Emergent Church – the Future of Christianity in a Post-Bourgeois World*, London, Burns & Oates, 1980.

Moll, Helmut (ed.), *The Church and Women – a Compendium*, San Francisco, Ignatius Press, 1988.

Montini, Giovanni Battista Cardinal (later Paul VI), 'What the Church is and What the Church is Not', in *The Church*, Montreal, Palm, 1964.

Rahner, Karl, *Writings of 1965–67* (on Ecclesiology, Sacraments, Eschatology and Church and World), in vol. X of *Theological Investigations*, London DLT, 1973.

Rahner, Karl, *The Shape of the Church to Come*, London, SPCK, 1974.

Rahner, Karl, 'On the Structure of the People of the Church Today' and 'Perspectives for the Future of the Church', in *Confrontations II*, vol. XII of *Theological Investigations*, 1974.

Rahner, Karl, *Ecclesiology, Questions in the Church, the Church in the World*, vol. XIV of *Theological Investigations*, London, DLT, 1976.

Rahner, Karl, 'The One Church and the Many Churches' and 'Is Church Union Dogmatically Possible?', in *Jesus, Man and the Church*, vol. XVII of *Theological Investigations*, London, DLT, 1981.

Rahner, Karl, *Concern for the Church*, vol. XX of Theological Investigations, London, DLT, 1981.

Ratzinger, Joseph, 'Introductory Thoughts on the State of the Church', in *Two Say Why – Balthasar and Ratzinger*, London, Search, 1973.

Ratzinger, Joseph, *Church, Ecumenism and Politics*, Slough, St Paul's, 1988.

Ratzinger, Joseph, *Called to Communion. Understanding the Church Today*, San Francisco, Ignatius Press, 1996.

Reuther, Rosemary Radford, *Women-Church: Theology and Practice of Feminist Liturgical Communities*, San Francisco: Harper & Row, 1985.

Sanks, T.H., *Salt, Leaven, Light – The Community Called Church*, New York, Crossroads, 1992.

Schillebeeckx, Edward, *Church – The Human Story of God*, London, SCM Press, 1990.

Schindler, D.C., *Heart of the World, Centre of the Church*, Edinburgh, T & T Clark, 1996.

Segundo, Juan Luis, *The Community Called Church*, vol. 1 of A Theology for Artisans of a New Community, Dublin, Gill and Macmillan, 1971.

Siebel, Wigand, 'The Exercise of Power in Today's Church', in *Power in the Church*, James Provost and Knut Walf (eds), *Concilium*, 197 (1988).

Sullivan, Francis, *The Church We Believe In: One, Holy, Catholic and Apostolic*, Mahwah, Paulist Press, 1988.

Tavard, G., *The Church, Community of Salvation*, Collegeville, Liturgical Press, 1982.

Tillard: J.M.-R., *Church of Churches – the Ecclesiology of Communion*, Collegeville, Liturgical Press, 1992.

Ward, Keith, *Religion and Community*, Oxford, Oxford University Press, 2000.

Willebrands, Cardinal Johannes, 'Vatican II's Ecclesiology of Communion', *Origins*, 17:2 (28 May 1987), 27–33.

Part 2:

The Magisterium – the Church and its Teaching

Kenneth Wilson

In examining the topic of the magisterium, we are exploring the Authority of the Gospel and the Teaching Function of the church. We introduce these topics by focusing upon some of the relevant pronouncements from the creeds and councils. The question of authority is always present. Setting the issue in the context of faith only compounds the problem for faith, which is, paradoxically, beyond mere empirical enquiry, invites the assumption of certainty. In considering the magisterium therefore, the 'teaching function' of the church, we face the question in its starkest form, 'what is to be taught and believed and on whose authority?'. The question is both profoundly stimulating and difficult.

2.1 DOCTRINAL DEFINITION, 7TH GENERAL COUNCIL, 2ND COUNCIL OF NICAEA – 787

One might think that reference to Scripture, the Creeds and Councils of the church would settle matters. The source of all authority is, after all, God in Christ as is made plain, for example, in the doctrinal definition of the Seventh General Council, the Second Council of Nicaea in 787.[1]

The one who granted us the light of recognising him, the one who redeemed us from the darkness of idolatrous insanity, Christ our God, when he took for his bride his holy catholic church, having no blemish or wrinkle, promised he would guard her and assured his holy disciples saying, *I am with you every day until the consummation of the age* (Mt. 28: 20). This promise however he made not only to them but also to us, who thanks to them have come to believe in his name.

---

1. Tanner, I, 133.

2.2 *FIRST DECREE,* COUNCIL OF TRENT – 1546

The Council of Trent, a collaboration of scholars and bishops, faced the question of authority in stark terms given the searing experience of the Protestant Reformation. At its third session on 4 February 1546 the Council confirmed the creed of Nicaea-Constantinople (with the addition of the *filioque* clause first added by the Western church at the Third Council of Toledo in 589) and went on in the fourth session on 8 April 1546 to affirm the acceptance of the sacred books and apostolic traditions in the first decree.[2]

The holy ecumenical and general council of Trent, lawfully assembled in the holy Spirit, with the same three legates of the apostolic see presiding, keeps ever before its eyes this purpose: that the purity of the gospel, purged from all errors, may be preserved in the church. Our Lord Jesus Christ, the Son of God, first proclaimed with his own lips this gospel, which had in the past been promised by the prophets in the sacred scriptures; then he bade it be preached to every creature through his apostles as the source of the whole truth of salvation and rule of conduct. The council clearly perceives that this truth and rule are contained in written books and in unwritten traditions which were received by the apostles from the mouth of Christ himself, or else have come down to us, handed on as it were from the apostles themselves at the inspiration of the holy Spirit. Following the example of the orthodox fathers, the council accepts and venerates with a like feeling of piety and reverence all the books of both the old and the new Testament, since the one God is author of both, as well as the traditions concerning both faith and conduct, as either directly spoken by Christ or dictated by the holy Spirit, which have been preserved in unbroken sequence in the catholic church.

[The text then proceeds, for the avoidance of doubt, to list all the books of the old and new Testaments.]

---

2. Ibid., II, 663.

2.3 *DEI FILIUS* – 1870

The First Vatican Council (1869–1870), like the Council of Trent, met at a moment of crisis for authority in the church, this time brought about by the perceived threat of Modernism. Reason was all very well, and indeed absolutely essential for faith, but things had to be put in order. So in *Dei Filius*,[3] Chapter 4, there is a statement about the relationship of faith and reason.

✻

The perpetual agreement of the catholic church has maintained and maintains this too: that there is a twofold order of knowledge, distinct not only as regards its source, but also as regards its object. With regard to the source, we know at the one level by natural reason, at the other level by divine faith. With regard to the object, besides those things to which the natural reason can attain, there are proposed for our belief mysteries hidden in God which, unless they are divinely revealed, are incapable of being known. Wherefore, when the Apostle, who witnesses that God was known to the gentiles from created things, comes to treat of the grace and truth which came by Jesus Christ, he declares: *We impart a secret and hidden wisdom of God, which God decreed before the ages for our glorification. None of the rulers of this age understood this. God has revealed it to us through the Spirit. For the Spirit searches everything, even the depths of God* (I Cor. 2: 7–8, 10). And the Only-begotten himself, in his confession to the Father, acknowledges that the Father has hidden these things from the wise and the prudent and revealed them to the little ones. Now reason, if it is enlightened by faith, does indeed when it seeks persistently, piously and soberly, achieve by God's gift some understanding, and that most profitable, of the mysteries, whether by analogy from what it knows naturally, or from the connexion of these mysteries with one another and with the final end of humanity; but reason is never rendered capable of penetrating these mysteries in the way in which it penetrates those truths which form its proper object. For the divine mysteries, by their very nature, so far surpass the created understanding that, even when a revelation has been given and accepted by faith, they remain covered by the veil of that same faith and wrapped, as it were, in a certain obscurity, as long as in this mortal life *we are away from the Lord, for we walk by faith, and not by light* (2 Cor. 5: 6–7).

Even though faith is above reason, there can never be any real disagreement between faith and reason, since it is the same God who reveals the mysteries and infuses faith, and who has endowed the human mind with the light of reason. God cannot deny himself, nor can truth ever be in opposition to truth. The appearance of this kind of specious contradiction is chiefly due to the fact that either the dogmas of faith are not understood and explained in accordance with the mind of the church, or unsound views are taken for the conclusions of reason. Therefore we define that every assertion contrary to the truth of enlightened faith is

---

3. Ibid., II, 808–9.

totally false. Furthermore the church which, together with its apostolic office of teaching, has received the charge of preserving the deposit of faith, has by divine appointment the right and duty of condemning what wrongly passes for knowledge, lest anyone be led astray by philosophy and empty deceit. Hence all faithful Christians are forbidden to defend as the legitimate conclusions of science those opinions which are known to be contrary to the doctrine of faith, particularly if they have been condemned by the church; and furthermore they are absolutely bound to hold them to be errors which wear the deceptive appearance of truth.

Not only can faith and reason never be at odds with one another but they mutually support each other, for on the one hand right reason established the foundations of the faith and, illuminated by its light, develops the science of divine things; on the other hand, faith delivers reason from errors and protects it and furnishes it with knowledge of many kinds. Hence, so far is the church from hindering the human arts and studies, that in fact she assists and promotes them in many ways. For she is neither ignorant nor contemptuous of the advantages which derive from this source of human life, rather she acknowledges that those things which flow from God, the lord of sciences, and, if they are properly used, lead to God by the help of his grace. Nor does the church forbid these studies to employ, each within its own area, its own proper principles and method: but while she admits this just freedom, she takes particular care that they do not become infected with errors by conflicting with divine teaching, or, by going beyond their proper limits, intrude upon what belongs to faith and engender confusion. For the doctrine of the faith which God has revealed is put forward not as some philosophical discovery capable of being perfected by human intelligence, but as a divine deposit committed to the spouse of Christ to be faithfully protected and infallibly promulgated. Hence, too, that meaning of the sacred dogmas is ever to be maintained which has been declared by holy mother church, and there must never be any abandonment of this sense under the pretext or in the name of a more profound understanding. May understanding, knowledge and wisdom increase as ages and centuries roll along, and greatly and vigorously flourish, in each and all, in the individual and the whole church: but this only in its own proper kind, that is to say, in the same doctrine, the same sense, and the same understanding.

2.4 *DEI VERBUM* – 1965

The Second Vatican Council (1962–65) was the largest ever assembled and, like Trent, characterized by the involvement of theologians with the bishops, abbots and superiors-general of religious orders in the preparations for, debates at and outcomes of the Council. The purposes of the Council were three: the better ordering of the church, the unity of Christians and the peace of the world. The magisterium is taken very seriously but in what may be referred to as a 'whole' sense: rather than referring to particular doctrines, (although it does), reference is made to the whole gospel as it is known by the whole people of God. Thus, for example, *Dei Verbum*[4] begins:

PREFACE

Hearing the word of God with reverence and proclaiming it with faith, the sacred synod takes its direction from these words of St. John: 'We announce to you the eternal life which dwelt with the Father and was made visible to us. What we have seen and heard we announce to you, so that you may have fellowship with us and our common fellowship be with the Father and His Son Jesus Christ' (1 John 1:2–3). Therefore, following in the footsteps of the Council of Trent and of the First Vatican Council, this present council wishes to set forth authentic doctrine on divine revelation and how it is handed on, so that by hearing the message of salvation the whole world may believe, by believing it may hope, and by hoping it may love[5] [1].

---

4. *ET* from *Documents of Vatican Council II: Archives of the Holy See*, www.vatican.va/archive/hist_councils/ii_vatican_council/index.htm.
5. Cf. St Augustine, *De Catechizandis Rudibus*, C. IV 8: *PL*, 40, 316.

2.5 *AD GENTES DIVINITUS* – 1965

And in the Decree on Missionary Activity:[6]

❀

Let the clergy highly esteem the arduous apostolate of the laity. Let them train the laity to become conscious of the responsibility which they as members of Christ have for all men; let them instruct them deeply in the mystery of Christ, introduce them to practical methods, and be at their side in difficulties, according to the tenor of the Constitution Lumen Gentium and the Decree Apostolicam Actuositatem. While pastors and laymen, then, retain each their own state of life and their own responsibilities, let the whole young church render one firm and vital witness to Christ, and become a shining beacon of the salvation which comes to us in Christ [21].

The seed which is the word of God, watered by divine dew, sprouts from the good ground and draws from thence its moisture, which it transforms and assimilates into itself, and finally bears much fruit. In harmony with the economy of the Incarnation, the young churches, rooted in Christ and built up on the foundation of the Apostles, take to themselves in a wonderful exchange all the riches of the nations which were given to Christ as an inheritance (cf Ps. 2:8). They borrow from the customs and traditions of their people, from their wisdom and their learning, from their arts and disciplines, all those things which can contribute to the glory of their Creator, or enhance the grace of their Savior, or dispose Christian life the way it should be … .

To achieve this goal, it is necessary that in each major socio-cultural area, such theological speculation should be encouraged, in the light of the universal Church's tradition, as may submit to a new scrutiny the words and deeds which God has revealed, and which have been set down in Sacred Scripture and explained by the Fathers and by the magisterium. Thus it will be more clearly seen in what ways faith may seek for understanding, with due regard for the philosophy and wisdom of these peoples; it will be seen in what ways their customs, views on life, and social order, can be reconciled with the manner of living taught by divine revelation. From here the way will be opened to a more profound adaptation in the whole area of Christian life. By this manner of acting, every appearance of syncretism and of false particularism will be excluded, and Christian life will be accommodated to the genius and the dispositions of each culture. Particular traditions, together with the peculiar patrimony of each family of nations, illumined by the light of the Gospel, can then be taken up into Catholic unity. Finally, the young particular churches, adorned with their own traditions, will have their own place in the ecclesiastical communion, saving always the primacy of Peter's See,

---

6. *ET* from *Documents of Vatican Council II: Archives of the Holy See,* www.vatican.va/archive/hist_councils/ii_vatican_council/index.htm.

which presides over the entire assembly of charity. And so, it is to be hoped that episcopal conferences within the limits of each major socio-cultural territory will so coordinate their efforts that they may be able to pursue this proposal of adaptation with one mind and with a common plan [22].

2.6 *GAUDIUM ET SPES* – 1965

And in the Pastoral Constitution on the church:[7]

❁

Secular duties and activities belong properly although not exclusively to the laity. Therefore acting as citizens in the world, whether individually or socially, they will keep the laws proper to each discipline, and labor to equip themselves with a genuine expertise in their various fields. They will gladly work with men seeking the same goals. Acknowledging the demands of faith and endowed with its force, they will unhesitatingly devise new enterprises, there they are appropriate, and put them into action. The laity should also know that it is generally the function of their well-formed Christian conscience to see that the divine law is inscribed in the life of the earthly city; from priests they may look for spiritual light and nourishment. Let them not imagine that their pastors are always such experts, that to every problem which arises, however complicated, they can readily provide a concrete solution, or even that such is their mission. Rather, enlightened by Christian wisdom and giving close attention to the teaching authority of the Church,[8] let the laity take on their own distinctive role.

Often enough the Christian view of things will itself suggest some specific solution in certain circumstances. Yet it happens rather frequently, and legitimately so, that with equal sincerity some of the faithful will disagree with others on a given matter. Even against the intentions of their proponents, however, solutions proposed on one side or another may be easily confused by many people with the Gospel message. Hence it is necessary for people to remember that no one is allowed in the aforementioned situations to appropriate the Church's authority for his opinion. They should always try to enlighten one another through honest discussion, preserving mutual charity and caring above all for the common good.

Since they have an active role to play in the whole life of the Church, the laity are not only bound to penetrate the world with a Christian spirit, but are also called to be witnesses to Christ in all things in the midst of human society [43].

EDITOR'S COMMENT

In considering these church documents, we come to understand that the teaching is thus, it might be said, that which is contained in scripture and tradition confirmed in the Creeds and by the Councils, passed from the apostles to the bishops who declare it and guard its truth. However, the teaching is not all written and it is the task of reason informed by faith in the community of the whole people of God,

---

7. *ET* from *Documents of Vatican Council II: Archives of the Holy See,* www.vatican.va/archive/hist_councils/ii_vatican_council/index.htm.
8. Cf. ... *LG,* ch. I, n. 8: *AAS,* 57 (1965), 12.

the church, to grasp and celebrate the truth of the Gospel in word and action. The theological and moral task is profoundly important if the presence of the Risen Christ is to be really celebrated and the faith of the apostles is to be kept alive and fresh in the minds and hearts of contemporary believers. Moreover, the need for the church to keep thinking these things through led to the emergence of the theological disciplines.

In new situations, as in the case of a missionary church, theological reflection is especially required. This amounts to more than the mere stating of truth in terms in which it has hitherto been expressed, rather it requires careful thought if it is to be intelligible to those to whom the teaching is addressed. The process is complex and demanding; it involves dialogue if the search for incisive translation is to provoke insight and understanding, the ground of the evangelical virtues of faith, hope and love.

Clearly the laity has an essential role in theological reflection. It is they who, on behalf of the whole church, face first the new intellectual, moral and professional worlds of human experience as they emerge in, for example, personal life, economics, science, medicine, technology and politics. To do this successfully the laity require theological expertise *and* professional expertise. This unavoidable process has brought to light many issues on which there is obvious conflict. How does the teaching of the church and the means whereby it is determined and expressed keep pace with the dramatic developments in human understanding of the world and consequent human behaviour? Indeed, there is the important prior question, 'In what way(s), if any, should the Church keep pace with these dramatic developments?' The solution is not obviously already in scripture and tradition, as at present understood, though it is clear that without them there can be no Christian response at all. Reason and faith may not indeed, when properly understood and wisely employed, be in conflict, but their lively interaction can provide rocky as well as inspiring roads on which to travel.

2.7 GIOVANNI COLOMBO: *OBEDIENCE TO THE ORDINARY MAGISTERIUM* – 1967

Cardinal Colombo states the current situation with regard to the ordinary magisterium.[9] All believers are in the same relationship to the ordinary magisterium which he calls the summary of 'the ordinary mind of the Church in a given moment of history'.[10] The ordinary magisterium will contain infallible teaching, but where the teaching is non-infallible, it is the responsibility of every believer to question it, just as he or she would in any human enquiry. The lead will naturally be taken by the theologian whose special task it is to keep the gospel alive in every situation in which the church finds itself. However, it is the duty of the magisterium that is the pope and the bishops, not simply to protect the freedom of the believer to enquire, but also to control the dissemination of the considered results of enquiry when they are held to conflict with the primary purpose of the Gospel, which is to save souls. That these two positions may conflict, and have conflicted, is obvious. Whether now with all the means of communication at our disposal, and in a more educated and curious world, such a 'censorship' of opinion is possible or politic, is doubtful.

Colombo's paper was published two years after the close of the Council in an intriguing collection of essays under the title *Studi sull'obedienza.* The volume consists of 14 essays by a group of pastors and theologians who wanted to take forward, but anchor firmly in the tradition, the implications as they saw them of the Council's perspectives as presented for the most part in the published texts. The volume begins with Karl Rahner SJ on *Christ as the exemplar of clerical obedience*, includes Cardinal Suenens, Archbishop of Malines-Brussels on *Obedience and faithfulness* and ends with a piece on the theological virtue of hope by Cardinal Jachym, Archbishop Coadjutor of Vienna.

❈

The disposition of serene confidence in the teaching of the magisterium should express itself in a correct attitude of assent and obedience, proportioned to the degree of authority and the obligation involved in the various forms in which the teaching authority is exercised.

The *Constitution of the Church* [LG] in the section devoted to the subject (no.25) indicates four forms in which the ordinary magisterium is exercised, to each of which corresponds a particular form of obedience.

a)   We have the teaching of individual bishops in communion with the Roman pontiff. In virtue of his Episcopal consecration and membership of the Episcopal college, each of these is an official witness to divine and catholic truth, and as such must be listened to with reverence by all.

b)   We have, in the second place, the authoritative teaching of the bishop in his own diocese. When he speaks in the name of Christ on matters of faith and morals, the faithful must assent with religious respect to his teaching and his doctrinal decisions.

---

9. In *Seminarium*, new series, year VII, no. 3, July–September, 1967; *ET*: *Obedience and the Church*, London, Geoffrey Chapman, 1968, 91.
10. Ibid.

c) Then we have the authentic teaching of the Roman pontiff when it is manifested without the conditions and guarantees of infallibility proper to his teaching ex cathedra. To this authentic teaching we are bound to give a still deeper religious assent of mind and will, in proportion to the degree of authority involved in the teaching.

d) Lastly, we can have the case of an infallible teaching of the ordinary magisterium, the assent of faith founded on the infallible authority of the teaching church.

The possibility of an infallible ordinary teaching is explicitly taught by the Council, which in this as in everything else reproduces traditional doctrine.

Although the individual bishops do not enjoy the prerogative of infallibility, they can nevertheless teach infallibly. That is so, even when they are dispersed around the world, provided that while maintaining the bond of unity among themselves and with Peter's successor, and while teaching authentically on a matter of faith and morals, they concur in a single viewpoint as the one which must be held conclusively. (*LG* no.25).[11] ...

THE MAGISTERIUM AND THEOLOGICAL RESEARCH

The Catholic theologian does not cease to be a believer when he knows and has to bear in mind that Jesus has appointed a particular class of baptised persons who are endowed with a special supernatural charism to be the teachers and leaders of the Christian people, of all believers. He also knows that this universal magisterium of the Episcopal body or of the Roman pontiff rightfully has the office and authority to transmit the faith integrally and to guard it from error, and to pronounce the final word in the name of Christ in matters of faith and morals.

Thus the Catholic theologian is also aware that he has a duty of religious obedience to the teaching of the magisterium in doctrinal matters. This implies a two-fold dependence. For it belongs to the magisterium to judge the results of theological research, that is, to decide whether they are valid and compatible with revealed doctrine, and it is through the magisterium that the theologian enters into communion with the entire doctrinal tradition of the church and the mind of the present Christian community. His confident union of mind with the authentic magisterium enables him to assimilate the entire spiritual and supernatural heritage of Christian thinking in the Church down through the centuries. Apart from being a certain and accessible source for the acquisition of innumerable truths, this constitutes a magnificent training school for the Christian intellect. If a theologian cuts himself off from the magisterium, he is left to his own resources and is obliged to begin his researches all over again, and he thereby becomes subject to the inevitable dangers of individualism and religious subjectivism. If a Catholic theologian were to withdraw from interior and faithful communion with the magisterium, he would inevitably tend towards a position analogous to that of Protestant theology.

But the theologian is not merely a believer. He is a thinking believer who either by personal vocation or because of his office is called to render to the entire Christian community a most precious service, the service of a faith enlightened to the greatest possible extent,

---

11. Ibid. (English translation), 82–3.

justified, developed and applied to real life. For this reason his work also includes the critical study and justification of the entire teaching of the Church with the aid of an exact theological methodology. In this critical verification, which is an act of theological reason, the proof is not based on the teaching of the magisterium (for this must be verified), but on the validity of method and the force of demonstration. Nothing must be accepted that has not been proved convincingly by a valid and appropriate method.

In the course of research, theology is not obliged to begin from the teaching of the non-infallible authentic magisterium as though it were a certain and definitive datum. It can call this in question, making use of methodical doubt as in any other scientific discussion. Moreover, it is not obliged to reach conclusions always and necessarily in conformity with the expressed tradition of the ordinary magisterium. It may possibly find in this same inadequacies or perhaps even some erroneous interpretation of divine truth. In this case, which does not occur everyday, theology would have the duty and right not merely to withhold the religious assent of the believer but also to propose the reasons which lead it to doubt the truth of the general teaching, in order to help the Church and particularly its teachers to teach a more exact knowledge of the truth.

Religious respect for and confident communion with the magisterium which summarizes the ordinary mind of the Church in a given moment of history; rigorous respect for the demands of reason applied to the theological field – these are the two indispensable components of theological thinking in the course of research. The difficulty of maintaining the right balance between them constitutes the cross and the continual labour of the Catholic theologian, who believes like the ordinary member of the flock but is intellectually exacting as all serious scholars must be.[12] ...

THE MAGISTERIUM AND THE TEACHING AND COMMUNICATION OF THEOLOGY

A more delicate problem arises when we pass from the research phase to the communication of results by teaching and writing. If the theologian is free during the research phase, is he equally free to spread the knowledge of his results?

A theologian can quite easily be led to think that he is equally free, for various reasons. It may be because of the indispensable part which comparison of ideas plays in the progress of theological science, or because of his own part in developing the faith of the community. It cannot be denied that these and other motives have a certain weight, but it is also necessary to take some other considerations into account in order to avoid the danger of a one-sided judgement.

Whereas scientific research carried on in the right place and through the medium of technical publications must enjoy the freedom of discussion necessary for the exchange and assessment of ideas, which is not always easy, the spread of theological ideas constitutes an important and delicate pastoral problem. The way in which these ideas are spread will determine the growth and maturity or the diminution and crisis of faith within the

---

12. Ibid., 89–91.

community. The magisterium, whose duty it is to protect the faith of the Christian community – not only the content of that faith but the spirit and virtue of faith – has therefore an undoubted right to judge and control the pastoral aspect of the spread of ideas.

An analogous consideration applies where teaching is concerned. The first task of the Catholic professor of theology, in any field, is to transmit the teaching of the Church, not his own ideas, and to train his students in an exact methodology of theological thinking. For this reason the faithful teaching of the doctrine of the magisterium, with the precise degree of authority due to each single item, and the education of the student's mind and heart in confident and untroubled union with the mind of the entire Church as expressed by the magisterium, constitute the first and fundamental phase of sound teaching in Catholic theology. Here we have the indispensable and permanent foundation on which the second phase – when critical verification is called for and applied – can by degrees be fruitfully developed.

For this reason and because of the inevitable repercussions of theological training upon the pastoral activity of the clergy and in general upon the life of faith in the Christian community, the magisterium has a duty and a right to control theological teaching. For it must judge whether this teaching is in harmony with the mind of the Church and whether it possesses the pedagogical charity required to foster a right balance between faith and reason in the community.[13]

---

13. Ibid., 91.

2.8 FRANCIS A. SULLIVAN: *WEIGHING AND INTERPRETING THE DOCUMENTS OF THE MAGISTERIUM: WHAT IS IT? WHY DO IT?* – 1996

Cardinal Colombo's paper drew attention to the variety of teaching within the ordinary magisterium and the importance of understanding what the appropriate authority is in each case. Francis A. Sullivan SJ has written extensively in this field. In *Creative Fidelity*,[14] the urbanity and generosity of his writing disguises sharp questions. Not only is the church free to weigh the authoritativeness of each document, it is an implication of faith-relationship with God in Christ through the Holy Spirit that there is a duty to do so. Therefore the question is, in principle, raised for every believer within the community of faith to the extent that he or she is able; which in turn raises the question of theological education and its availability.

Sullivan reviews the variety of doctrinal and moral teaching to be interpreted, focusing particularly upon the new *Catechism of the Catholic Church*[15] in the light of the distinctions provided for in the *Profession of Faith* required of all teachers of the faith.[16] There are first of all the doctrines contained in the Word of God and/or in the deposit of faith committed to the church. Such doctrines are either clearly defined by Ecumenical Council or the pope speaking ex cathedra or are part of the common teaching of the whole college of bishops including the pope. These dogmas require an act of faith on the part of the believer because they are in principle taught by the Church (that is, the whole Church as a community of believers) on the authority of God who has revealed them. Secondly, there are those doctrines concerning faith and morals definitively proposed by the church. These doctrines are not revealed but defined and taught by the church as so intimately connected with revelation as to require an assent of faith. Sullivan points to the statement in the new *Catechism*[17] which requires that they be assented to with an 'irrevocable assent of faith', but claims this is an opinion that would be contested by a great many Catholic theologians. A critical issue arises because of the totally undefined scope of 'necessarily connected truths', especially since the CDF has pointed out, quite rightly, in the *Instruction of the Ecclesial Vocation of the Theologian*: 'It often only becomes possible with the passage of time to distinguish what is necessary and what is contingent.'[18] The third group of doctrines are those over which the pastors of the church 'exercise their authoritative teaching office', namely those relating to faith and morals. The church may here speak with authority but not, Sullivan suggests, with infallibility, especially since on matters of morality the church has wanted to go beyond personal morality and teach on broader matters concerning the ordering of human society.

❀

---

14. Francis A. Sullivan, SJ, *Creative Fidelity*, London and Dublin, Gill and Macmillan, 1996, 18–25.
15. *Catechism of the Catholic Church*, Geoffrey Chapman-Libreria Editrice Vaticana, London, 1994.
16. *Code of Canon Law, 28 January 1983*, para. 1630. The formula was published, together with the test of the oath of fidelity, on 27 February 1989.
17. *Catechism of the Catholic Church*, para. 88.
18. *Instruction on the Ecclesial Vocation of the Theologian*, Dublin and London, Veritas and Catholic Truth Society, 1990, no. 24, 16. [This document is included in Chapter 6 of the present volume.]

The third and last of the brief paragraphs in the Profession of Faith is as follows: '*Furthermore, I adhere with religious submission of will and intellect to the doctrines which either the Roman Pontiff or the College of Bishops propose, when they exercise their authoritative teaching office, even though they do not intend to proclaim those doctrines by a definitive act.*'

What kind of doctrines are involved here? They are the kind of doctrines concerning which the pastors of the church 'exercise their authoritative teaching office': namely, doctrines relating to faith and morals. The Second Vatican Council described bishops as 'teachers endowed with the authority of Christ, who preach to the people committed to them the faith they must believe and put into practice'.[19] Matters of faith and morals embraces whatever pertains to Christian belief and to a Christian way of life.

When the church asserts its claim to speak authoritatively on matters of faith and morals, the latter term includes not only the moral teaching of the gospel, but also the natural moral law. Vatican II expressed this in the following way: 'The church is, by the will of Christ, the teacher of the truth. It is her duty to give utterance to, and authoritatively to teach, that truth which is Christ himself, and also to declare and confirm by her authority those principles of the moral order which have their origin in human nature itself.'[20] In its *Instruction on the Ecclesial Vocation of the Theologian* [*Donum Veritatis*], the Congregation for the Doctrine of the Faith has further spelled out the grounds for this: 'By reason of the connection between the orders of creation and redemption and by reason of the necessity, in view of salvation, of knowing and observing the whole moral law, the competence of the magisterium also extends to that which concerns natural law.'[21] But one must distinguish between competence to speak with authority, and a claim to speak with infallibility. The latter, as we have seen, is limited to truths which are either revealed or are required for the defense or explanation of some revealed truth. The church does not claim to be able to speak with infallibility on all moral questions, regardless of their connection with divine revelation.

The exercise of such authoritative magisterium, especially since the publication of the encyclical *Rerum Novarum* by Pope Leo XIII in 1891, shows that the church does not see its teaching authority in matters of morals as limited to questions of personal morality. It has regularly asserted its competence to pass judgment on the broader issues affecting the order of human society, insofar as these are moral problems, to be determined in accordance with the 'principles of the moral order which have their origin in human nature itself'.

How are these doctrines taught by the pope or bishops? The paragraph we are commenting on answers this question when it says: 'When they exercise their authoritative teaching office, even though they do not intend to proclaim those doctrines by a definitive act.' Here it is a question of what is called the 'ordinary', 'authentic', 'non-definitive', 'non-infallible', 'non-irreformable' exercise of the teaching function by the pope or by the whole college of bishops together with him. It is to be noted that mention is made here only of those who have authority to teach the universal church; no mention is made of the teaching office which bishops exercise either individually in their own diocese, or collectively in particular synods

---

19. *Lumen Gentium*, 25.
20. Declaration on Human Freedom, *Dignitatis Humanae*, no. 14.
21. *Instruction on the Ecclesial Vocation of the Theologian*, Dublin and London, Veritas and Catholic Truth Society, 1990. no. 16, 11 (footnote 16, *Instruction* ... , says; Cf. Paul VI, Encyclical, *Humanae Vitae*, n. 4: *AAS*, 60 [1968], 483).

or in episcopal conferences. Hence, the formula refers only to doctrines which have been authoritatively promulgated by the supreme teaching authority for acceptance by the universal church. Such doctrines are found, for example, in the documents of the Second Vatican Council, which, on the one hand, nowhere expressed its intention to define a doctrine, but, on the other hand, described itself as exercising the supreme teaching authority in the church, and hence calling for the acceptance of its teaching by all the Catholic faithful.[22]

The pope exercises his universal teaching office, without intending to make definitive pronouncements, in his encyclicals, apostolic letters and exhortations, and other documents addressed to the whole Catholic Church. He can also exercise his teaching office by his explicit approval of doctrinal statements which are promulgated for the whole church by the Congregation for the Doctrine of the Faith. In ... [*Donum Veritatis*], this congregation declared: 'The Roman pontiff fulfils his universal mission with the help of the various bodies of the Roman curia, and in particular with that of the Congregation for the Doctrine of the Faith. Consequently, the documents issued by this congregation expressly approved by the pope participate in the ordinary magisterium of the successor of Peter.'[23] However, the pope does not use such documents to proclaim doctrine in a definitive way, nor would any statement issued by the congregation participate in papal infallibility. Indeed, even with papal approval, statements issued by the congregation would be less authoritative than those issued by the pope in his own name.

While the Profession of Faith speaks only of the exercise of magisterium by the pope or the whole college of bishops with him, the Code of Canon Law speaks of the teaching authority which bishops exercise 'whether they teach individually, or in episcopal conferences, or gathered together in particular councils'.[24] Bishops, the code goes on, 'while not infallible in their teaching, are the authentic instructors and teachers of the faith for Christ's faithful entrusted to their care'. Obviously, the authority of the statements made by individual bishops, episcopal conferences, and national or regional councils will be less than that of statements issued by the pope or an ecumenical council for the universal church.

It is obvious, then, that, within the category of the non-definitive magisterium, different degrees of teaching authority will be exercised. Referring to this fact, ... [*Donum Veritatis*], says: 'Here the theologian will need, first of all, to assess accurately the authoritativeness of the interventions which becomes clear from the nature of the documents, the insistence with which a teaching is repeated, and the very way in which it is expressed.'[25] I would say that the very first question to be asked in assessing the authoritativeness of the intervention is: 'Who is speaking?' Non-definitive magisterium can be exercised by an ecumenical council, by a pope, by the Congregation for the Doctrine of the Faith, by a regional council, by an episcopal conference, or by a local bishop. Each of these sources possesses a different level of teaching authority. The second question is: 'To whom is this teaching addressed?' Obviously, it is only those addressed by a teaching who are obliged by its authority. There is an important

---

22. See the Declaration of the Theological Commission, which was the subject of a formal announcement made by the Secretary General to the assembled bishops on 16 Nov. 1964. This Declaration is printed with the documents of the Council, immediately following the text of *Lumen Gentium.*
23. *Instruction on the Ecclesial Vocation of the Theologian*, no. 18.
24. *The Canon Law*, Can. 753.
25. *Instruction ...* , no. 24.

application of this principle with regard to papal teaching. All Catholics are obliged by the authority of the teaching which the pope addresses to the universal church in such documents as encyclicals. But the pope is also bishop of Rome, and when his teaching is directed specifically to the clergy and faithful of his own diocese, only they are obliged by it. Similarly, the teaching which the pope gives to groups of people, either in Rome or in the course of his travels to other countries, even though it is published by the Vatican, does not have the authority of a papal teaching addressed to the universal church.

A third question is: 'What kind of document is issued?' The Second Vatican Council issued two 'dogmatic constitutions', one 'pastoral constitution', one 'constitution', nine 'decrees', and three 'declarations'. There is no doubt about the intention of the council to indicate different levels of authority by these different titles. Similarly, there are different kinds of papal documents with different levels of authoritativeness. One visible sign of this diversity is the kind of seal affixed to the document. The most authoritative documents are sealed with a lead seal (in Latin *bulla*) and on that account are called 'bulls'; lesser documents are sealed with wax, and on others the papal seal is merely stamped in ink. Among the documents thus diversely sealed, the most authoritative are 'apostolic constitutions', 'apostolic letters', and 'apostolic exhortations'. Such documents are usually addressed to the universal church.

A fourth consideration, in assessing the authoritativeness of any non-definitive exercise of magisterium, is suggested by the CDF in … [*Donum Veritatis*], when it distinguished among three different ways in which the magisterium can intervene, without intending to act 'definitively'. The first is that it 'teaches a doctrine to aid a better understanding of revelation and make explicit its contents, or to recall how some teaching is in conformity with the truths of faith, or finally to guard against ideas that are incompatible with those truths' [no. 23]. Secondly: 'the magisterium can intervene in questions under discussion which involve, in addition to solid principles, certain contingent and conjectural elements. It often only becomes possible with the passage of time to distinguish what is necessary and what is contingent' [no. 23]. Thirdly: there are interventions in the prudential order. Of these the CDF says: 'When it comes to the question of interventions in the prudential order, it could happen that some magisterial documents might not be free from all deficiencies. Bishops and their advisers have not always taken into immediate consideration every aspect or the entire complexity of a question' [no. 24]. Here the CDF has explained, more clearly I think than it has ever done officially before, that one rightly distinguishes among many different levels of authority exercised by the 'ordinary' magisterium.

A final question to be asked in assessing the level of authority involved in any exercise of the non-definitive magisterium has to do with the strength of the language which the author of the document chose to use. For instance, popes have sometimes used language, in encyclicals or other letters addressed to the whole church, which has indicated their intention to settle a question that was disputed among Catholics. In his encyclical *Humanae generis* of 1950, Pope Pius XII spoke of this in the following terms: 'If the supreme pontiffs, in their official documents, deliberately pass judgment on a matter hitherto controverted, it is evident to all that, in accordance with the mind and intention of the same pontiffs, that subject can no longer be considered a subject for free debate among theologians.'[26] The language used by

---

26. *AAS*, 42 (1950), 568.

Pope John Paul II in his recent apostolic letter *Ordinatio sacerdotalis* would clearly fulfil, or even surpass, the conditions mentioned by Pius XII. In fact I am not aware of any document of ordinary papal magisterium that uses language quite so strong as the final sentence of this recent letter, which reads: 'Wherefore, in order that all doubt may be removed regarding a matter of great importance, a matter which pertains to the church's divine constitution itself, in virtue of my ministry of confirming the brethren (Lk 22:32) I declare that the church has no authority whatsoever to confer priestly ordination on women and that this judgment is to be definitively held by all the church's faithful.'[27] This language comes very close to that of a solemn definition, but we are assured by Cardinal Ratzinger that it was not the intention of John Paul II to speak *ex cathedra*.[28] In any case, I would say that this statement excluding the ordination of women to the priesthood would have to be put at the very top of any scale measuring the degree of authority that has been exercised by popes in their ordinary magisterium.

What kind of response are the faithful expected to give to the teaching of the ordinary, non-definitive magisterium? The Formula for the Profession of Faith answers this question with the words: 'I adhere with religious submission of will and intellect.' The official Latin text has: *religioso voluntatis et intellectus obsequio adhaereo.* These are the terms that were used by Vatican II in its statement on the matter, and they were repeated in the new Code of Canon Law.[29] In rendering the Latin word *obsequio* 'by submission', I am in agreement with both the Abbott and the Flannery versions of the documents of Vatican II, as well as with the translation of the new code prepared by the Canon Law Society of Great Britain and Ireland. However, the translation of the new code prepared by the Canon Law Society of America translates *obsequium* as 'respect', and versions in other modern languages also vary between 'submission' and 'respect'. In view of the lack of agreement as to the proper translation of the Latin word, I suggest that one should at least not give too strong a meaning to 'submission', or too weak a meaning to 'respect'. In any case, the essential thing, in my view, is to note that *obsequium* should not be translated simply as 'assent'.[30] *Obsequium* denotes an *attitude* towards the teaching authority, which the Congregation for the Doctrine of Faith has described as 'the willingness to submit loyally to the teaching of the magisterium per se not irreformable'.[31] This 'willingness to submit' is said to be 'the rule', but the Congregation recognizes that 'it can happen that a theologian may, according to the case, raise questions regarding the timeliness, the form, or even the contents of magisterial interventions'.[32]

Further light on the meaning of this 'willingness to submit loyally to the teaching of the magisterium' is given in no. 29 of the *Instruction*, which describes what a theologian should do who is said to have 'serious difficulties, for reasons which appear to him well-founded, in accepting a non-irreformable magisterial teaching'. 'In any case', we are told, 'there should never be a diminishment of that fundamental openness loyally to accept the teaching of the

---

27. *Origins*, 24/4 (9 June 1994), 51.
28. *L'Osservatore Romano* (English edition), (19 June 1994), 7.
29. *Lumen Gentium*, 25a; Can. 752.
30. The new version of the documents of Vatican II given in the Tanner edition of the decrees of the ecumenical councils is mistaken, I believe, in translating *obsequium* by 'assent.' See Tanner, II: 869. [The meaning of this term is also discussed in Chapter 7 of this present volume.]
31. *Instruction* ... , no. 24.
32. Ibid.

magisterium.'[33] Here again it is clear that *obsequium* is not to be identified with assent as such, but with a basic respect for the authority of the magisterium, and an openness to its teaching: an attitude that can well persist in people who find that they cannot give a sincere intellectual assent to a particular proposition that has been taught by the same magisterium.

The essential difference between 'assent' and an attitude of willingness to accept the teaching of the magisterium is that assent is an 'either-or' proposition; one either gives one's assent or one does not. On the other hand, an attitude of willingness admits of varying degrees. And these varying degrees appropriately correspond to the varying degrees of authority exercised by the magisterium when it does not teach in a definitive way.

It seems to me that an attitude of basic willingness to accept official teaching will be concretely expressed in the seriousness of one's efforts to overcome any tendency one might have simply to prefer one's own opinion, without giving serious consideration to the official teaching. In other words, an attitude of *obsequium* to the teaching authority will mean making a serious effort, proportionate to the authority which has been exercised in any particular case, to convince oneself of the truth of what has been taught. When people have made such a serious effort to accept a teaching, their attitude of *obsequium* toward the teaching authority can continue to be present, even in the case where they find themselves really unable to achieve intellectual assent to a particular proposition taught by the magisterium. In this case, it is not a lack of willingness to accept the teaching, but the strength of contrary reasons, that makes it impossible for them to give their assent. Assent is an act of the mind by which I really judge a proposition to be true. If my effort to achieve assent has been proportionate to the degree of authority that has been exercised, then I have fulfilled my obligation of *obsequium* toward the magisterium, even though I have not been able to bring myself to agree with some particular point of its teaching.

---

33. Ibid. no. 29.

2.9 CHRISTOF THEOBALD: *THE 'DEFINITIVE' DISCOURSE OF THE MAGISTERIUM: WHY BE AFRAID OF A CREATIVE RECEPTION? – 1999*

We turn to examine the relations between the Magisterium and History. The gospel to be preached is the gospel of Christ; the teaching to be understood and responded to in faith is the revelation of God as found in the teaching of the church which is the present realization of the gospel for faith. However, Sullivan's approach to the interpretation of the ordinary magisterium does raise questions. History is the process in which God's self has been, and continues to be, made known to the world. Human history, however, provides humankind with a huge range of experience of change which at the least poses questions both for the understanding of revelation and the way in which response to it should be lived out personally and in society. It is a theological mistake, of course, to conclude that this raises the question of 'new' revelation for there can be no such thing. However, the question cannot be avoided. How does the revelation of God in Christ remain alive in the teaching of the church, if the magisterium is, by its own terms, precluded from taking account of changing circumstances, new cultures, and a developing awareness of the human 'self' amongst an increasingly educated and knowledgeable humankind? Such a question can cause anxiety because it evokes the memory of 'modernism' which led to Pius X's actions against the Modernists.

Not unnaturally, therefore, a frisson went through the church with the publication of the *Professio fidei* in 1989. What were the implications of this profession? On what assumptions was it based? Is the Magisterium, (printed indeed with a capital 'M', referring perhaps to the official teachers rather than the official teaching of the church), as represented anyway by the Congregation for the Doctrine of Faith, wishing to reinstate a fixed notion of revelation such as was assumed in neo-scholasticism? How can such a position, if now seriously to be taught, be worked out in the light of contemporary understandings of history and the role of a thinking church in the world's history? What has happened to that awareness of the presence of the Spirit bringing new life, new love and new hope, and which is explicitly celebrated in *Lumen Gentium* of Vatican II? In any case, what can be said about the way in which historical circumstances appear to have determined doctrinal statements only to require that they be forgotten or adapted by later generations in the light of changed historical circumstances?

Christoph Theobald seeks to face up to these and other questions.[34]

❊

Clearly 'truths stated definitively' have multiplied over these past years. The recent teaching that priestly ordination is exclusively reserved for males immediately comes to mind, but other examples from the moral sphere remain in our collective memory, like the teaching of the encyclical *Humanae Vitae* (1968) on certain acts of contraception which are 'intrinsically evil' with regard to the natural law. However, a more refined historical analysis will show that since the nineteenth century the pontifical magisterium has issued numerous statements of the same kind: the condemnation of religious freedom in the *Syllabus*, judgments on facts in the Bible,

---

34. From *Unanswered Questions*, Christoph Theobald and Dietmar Mieth (eds), *Concilium* (1999/01), 60–9.

authors, facts considered historical, and so on. These have always been linked to specific cultural situations or a state of research, but have then fallen into disuse before sometimes being discreetly corrected. Who for example still defends the thesis of monogenism to safeguard the dogma of original sin? But in 1950 this was the position of the encyclical *Humanae generis*, and there was no appeal against it.

So in a sense we are facing an ongoing practice. However, recently there has been a shift in the rules of the game relating to this practice, the subtle architecture of the magisterial authorities and the way in which what it presents to the faithful to believe and to hold is described. One can even ask what the priority now is. Is it a particular problem that has to be resolved – contraception, ordination reserved exclusively for males, etc. – and the discernment of the pontifical magisterium on it? Or is it the establishment of a new regulatory system to indicate the obedience due to the official response? If the centre of gravity of the Roman interventions is in fact shifting increasingly from their content to the formal relations between those who hold authority and those who must obey it, must we not see at work here a subtle strategy of immunization aimed at preventing the debate from continuing and disturbing the Christian people, not to mention a way of hiding the weakness of a particular argument? Clearly one would need to examine, case by case, these doctrines proposed 'definitively' and evaluate their arguments in order to confirm or disconfirm what is only a suspicion. However, that is not the object of this article. I want, rather, to reflect on the significance of the actual establishment of a new rule of the game, published for the first time in 1989 and recently introduced in the 1983 Code of Canon Law.[35] Why this change, and what diagnosis of the historical situation of the church by its supreme authorities does it represent?

THREE 'BASKETS' OF CATHOLIC TRUTHS

First of all, let us recall briefly the essential elements in doctrines and questions, the subtlety of which probably escapes the vast majority of Christians. They are in fact addressed to those who exercise a teaching function in the church, to the bishops but also and above all to the theologians, asking them to make a profession of faith before taking up their posts or on certain other occasions (as at the beginning of an ecumenical council).

Since antiquity, the common faith which binds the faithful together and gathers them in communities or churches in communion among themselves and with Peter's successor has been set out in creeds, especially the Niceno-Constantinopolitan creed, the rule of interpreting the Scriptures and tradition, which also includes the new profession of faith (1989). The creed in a way precedes the opening of the three 'baskets', in which all the truths to be believed and held are, or could be, arranged. In the first basket – according to the Latin tradition, this is broader than the simple creed – is the whole content of faith, though the documents do not indicate what this is, being simply content to describe the authorities which determine it or the way in which it is 'arranged': 'all the truths which are contained in the Word of God written or handed down by the tradition *and* put forward by the church to be

---

35. Cf. Congregation for the Doctrine of Faith, 'Profession of Faith and Oath of Fidelity, 9 January 1989', in *AAS*, 81, 1989, 104–16; *Motu proprio Ad tuendam fidem*, in *Osservatore Romano*, 1 July 1998.

believed as having been divinely revealed, whether by virtue of a solemn judgment (conciliar or pontifical) or by the ordinary and universal Magisterium', according to the famous distinction of Vatican I,[36] to which we shall return. We should already keep in mind that it indicates an unfathomable depth in the Word of God received by the tradition, a depth which the defined statements, dogmas deposited on the surface of the awareness of the church, risk hiding. Cardinal Ratzinger's 1998 commentary gives some examples of these dogmatic truths: in addition to the articles of the Creed they are the various christological and Marian dogmas, the doctrine of the institution of the sacraments by Christ and their efficacy in conferring grace, etc.[37]

Then comes a second basket in which are laid out doctrines relating to faith and morals, the specific character of which is that they are 'necessary for keeping and presenting faithfully the deposit of faith'. This is precisely the place where the examples of 'truths put forward definitively', mentioned at the beginning of this article, belong. Furthermore, the commentator from the Congregation for the Doctrine of Faith enumerates them himself,[38] adding that 'their definitive character is implied by their intrinsic connection with revealed truth'.[39] Here he puts his finger on the key point of the system of regulation, the frontier at which revelation touches the history of cultures, with its series of new questions that have haunted the Christian conscience since the beginning of the modern times. Is revelation definitively bound by a pre-modern vision of the historicity of the biblical narratives and what they say about the origins, by the fact that Jesus is not said to have conferred apostolic identity on women, etc.? Must it obey an interpretation of natural law which has hardly been touched, if at all, by the achievements of the human sciences?

If the new profession of faith exempts certain facts bound up with the deposit of faith from historical fluctuations and the meanderings of the public debate between theologians, it is because it presupposes, despite superficial distinctions, that there is a profound link between 'baskets' of truths. The official commentary even suggests 'communicating vessels', since the authorities which regulate the flow from one to another are strictly the same as those which determine the content of the first basket: what constitutes the most common ecclesial awareness of revelation, represented by the ordinary and universal magisterium, can be confirmed or reaffirmed at the moment of a challenge – thus the commentary – as definitive by the Roman Pontiff (second basket), before possibly going into the first basket, where it figures among the defined truths of the deposit of faith. This is a trajectory which was followed, according to the commentary, by the doctrine of papal infallibility and which will be followed – perhaps – by the doctrine that priestly ordination is exclusively reserved to males.[40]

Finally, the third basket, which is furthest from the centre of revelation, contains all the teachings of the bishops and the pope which, without being proclaimed by a definitive act, require of the believer what the text calls 'religious submission of the will and the intellect'.

---

36. *DH* 3011.
37. Doctrinal note 11 (DC 95, 1998, 655).
38. Ibid. Why does the second paragraph of the *Professio fidei* distinguish between *omnia* and *singula* as if the *omnia* did not already contain the *singula*? It is all the more surprising that in the first paragraph 'what is divinely revealed' is simply treated in a global way (*ea omnia quae*).
39. Doctrinal note 6 (DC 95, 1998, 654).
40. Doctrinal note 11 (DC 95, 1998, 655).

The dimensions of this last receptacle are thus immense; however, the texts do not give any example of the content, perhaps because their interest lies elsewhere.

WHAT IS NEW?

To put it brutally: the *Professio fidei* of 1989, recently introduced into the Code of Canon Law, reproduces the broad outline of the *De magisterio* of the preparatory scheme of the church (1962), a text that was rejected not only by the Central Commission but also by the Council itself.[41] Points deliberately left open by Vatican I and Vatican II for further debate are thus decided with reference to a neo-scholastic conception which is little, if at all, affected by the challenge of history or the current plurality of cultures. Already at the time of the Council, the conflict related to the following three points:

1. In the face of an intellectualistic conception which regards revelation as the totality of truths to be believed (the instruction model), the majority of fathers emphasized – in line with John XXIII – the internal unity of the Christian mystery (the communication model). Do not the latest texts of the magisterium again hide this insight that was gained, namely that faith comes from listening to the gospel, which is not primarily passive acceptance of a series of doctrines (even if the regulative aspect – the *regula fidei* – is not in any way excluded)[42] but a definitive encounter with Jesus Christ, interwoven with events and words closely bound together, as a place of God's ultimate communication of himself (cf. *Dei Verbum* 2 and 4)? To criticize the intellectualism of the *Professio fidei* is not to fall into a kerygmatic reduction, but to note with the last Council that a cancerous proliferation of doctrines ultimately risks totally blocking any access to faith, which, according to tradition, never stops at formulae (in the plural) but desires to enter into the very intimacy of God.

2. That is why *Lumen Gentium* 25 makes the preaching of the gospel the principle duty of bishops – something that these latest texts, which base themselves almost exclusively on this passage, pass over in silence – before calling them 'authentic teachers ... endowed with the authority of Christ, to preach the faith to the people assigned to them, the faith which is destined to inform their thinking and direct their conduct'. This duty, not only to preach but also to interpret the gospel with authority in one situation or another, has in fact been fulfilled every day throughout the world since the beginning of Christianity in many ways: this is what Vatican I and Vatican II designate by the technical term 'ordinary and universal magisterium', distinguishing the continuous exercise of it from those few 'extraordinary' occasions when the church adopts a position on the meaning of the gospel, solemnly and always in opposition to a challenge.

But what is the aim of this distinction? First of all to keep open the infinite depth and breadth ... of the practice of faith, that of the pastors who proclaim it and that of the faithful who live it out, together forming the *sensus fidei* of the people of God (*Lumen Gentium* 12).

---

41. The conflict in the Central Preparatory Commission began in November 1961 during the debate on a new profession of faith to be used at the opening of the Council and continued in June 1962 in the discussion of *De magisterio*. In both discussions one finds the same opposition ploy and the same arguments; this confirms the link between the texts, which were both rejected.

42. Cf. e.g. Rom. 10:9 ... .

This can never be reduced to any formula, dogma or sacramental rite.[43] Those who today would like to rely on this secular magisterium to resolve the problems they have in interpreting the gospel in a particular cultural context soon discover that they can only circumscribe its authority after the event and at the cost of intensive historical and theological research, simply by reason of its great 'dispersion' in space and time. But the simple fact that such a doctrine is held to such a practice is accepted by all, everywhere and always – *as self-evident* – is not yet a guarantee of truth. So there is a need to discover what, within history, comes from God and is still binding on us, and to distinguish it carefully from what derives from changing historical and cultural circumstances. This evaluation is at the same time the only way of establishing whether a problem that arises is truly new, so that we must resolve it at our own risk and peril. Can one deduce, for example, from the historical fact that neither Jesus nor the apostles nor any witness of the tradition is said to have admitted women to 'apostolic' identity that it is a 'property of the church, infallibly handed down by its ordinary and universal magisterium', and thus definitively binding on us? Only if one can *prove* that they in fact asked themselves the questions that we ask ourselves today: and that is certainly not the case.

To speak immediately here in 'definitive' terms thus risks short-circuiting, even hiding, the complex process in which communities, theologians and the magisterium engage. This consists in listening both to the conscience of the church – the *sensus fidei* – today and to that of the tradition, in order to establish progressively (in a remarkable *conspiratio*) the exact tenor (old or new) of the question that needs to be resolved. Now on this tricky problem the *Professio fidei* and its commentary simply take up the *De magisterio* of 1962, which in turn quotes the encyclical *Humani generis*:

'Most of the time what is taught and urged (by the encyclicals, etc., as documents of the ordinary magisterium of the church) is already part of Catholic doctrine. If the sovereign pontiffs expressly make a judgment on a matter which was hitherto controversial, everyone will understand that this matter, in the thought and will of the sovereign pontiffs, can no longer be considered to be the object of free discussion between theologians.'[44]

Very strong opposition from the majority within the Central Preparatory Commission[45] and during the Council removed this passage from *Lumen Gentium* 25 and the 1983 Code (canon 750) also ignores it; it was introduced in 1998 in the form in which we now know it. Certainly one can always argue from the fact that 'the successor of Peter is only confirming or reaffirming a doctrine already taught by the ordinary and universal magisterium – which necessarily includes that of the pope'. But can one ignore the fact that the 'universal' in the 'ordinary and universal magisterium' indicates a theological depth and breadth in the historical conscience of the church which can have remarkable surprises in store, particularly in a situation of unprecedented historical acceleration and cultural pluralism? To use a definitive declaration to stop the debate on what at least has the appearance of being a new question is to accredit *one* theology of the magisterium which, in the spirit of Catholic

---

43. This is also the sense of the negative formulation of the rule of 'unanimous consent' at Trent, Vatican I and Vatican II: to accept nothing contrary to that which has always been the sense of the church and its traditions' (cf. *DH*, 1507, 3007 and the regulation of Vatican II, article 40).

44. G. Alberigo and F. Magistretti, *Constitutionis Dogmaticae Lumen Gentium Synopsis Historica*, Bologna, Instituto per la Scienze Religiose, 1975, 95–104; cf. also *DH*, 3885.

45. Cf. in particular the intervention by Cardinal Frings in AP II-II, pars IV, 638.

integralism, risks confusing the always surprising mystery of the Catholic faith with the conceptual transparency of formulae which, because they are necessarily impoverished, can do no more that point to it.

3. The task of interpreting the gospel has become all the more complex today since modernity has made us more aware of the historical roots of the gospel and the diversity of the cultures which are waiting to receive it creatively. So there is no denying the intrinsic link between the 'treasure' (*depositum*) and the creative 'field' in which it is hidden. How else are we to conceive of a revelaton which is not already inculturated or contextualized? Beyond doubt this is the element of truth in talk about the 'connection'.

But once again the *De magisterio* of 1962 casts its shadow on current debates. It is in fact this text which for the first time defines the characteristics of a second basket of Catholic truths: in it there can be 'everything which, without being revealed in an explicit or implicit manner, is nevertheless linked to revealed matters in such a way that it is necessary, in order to safeguard the deposit of faith, to explain it correctly and protect it effectively (*ad tuendam*[46])'; this effectively includes 'the interpretation and the *infallible* declaration of the natural law and judgment on the objective conformity of all human actions with the doctrine of the gospel and the divine law. No field of human actions can be withdrawn, under its ethical and religious aspects, from the authority of the magisterium instituted by Christ'. The text even includes, in relation to historical criticism, the 'authentic judgment on the origin and nature, and above all the doctrinal and moral value, of the sayings and extraordinary facts presented as having their origin in God (miracles)'.[47] Now the last two Councils are not only infinitely more discreet about what this possible specific 'basket' might contain, but above all leave open the question of the status of the connection, namely the form of its link with revelation and the place that is occupied, or could be occupied, in this link, by historical reason, the just autonomy of which cannot be denied (*Gaudium et Spes* 36). It is as if the fathers had felt the latent risk of a historical monophysitism, whereas the magisterium has received the charism of keeping the ultimate character of the gospel of God discernible in the history of humankind.

So it must be understood that the *Professio fidei* is not concerned with a particular problem, nor does it simply substitute a new profession for an older one; it truly introduces a new rule of the game – which was already the intention of the redactors of *De magisterio* in 1962. This action is taking place today in a whole series of measures by which, confronted by globalisation and cultural pluralism, the magisterium of the Church of Rome is trying to reinforce and to specify in law its transcultural and transhistorical competence in matters of faith, at the same time limiting that of diocesan, national (conferences of bishops) and continental synods, and putting the bar in ecumenical dialogue even higher. The issue is its conception of the catholicity of faith and the church.

---

46. This would provide the title for the 1998 *Motu proprio.*
47. *Synopsis* [n. 11], 296, 45–58.

WHAT IS AT STAKE WITH THIS NEW REGULATION?

First of all it can be asked whether such a transformation of the rules of the game by the one who is the guarantor is credible today. Certainly the official commentary on the *Motu proprio* suggests that this is merely an explication of 'the faith in the assistance which the Holy Spirit gives to the Magisterium of the Church and the Catholic doctrine of the infallibility of the magisterium'. But what has preceded this allows one to doubt.

The most serious issue is a hermeneutical one. We have in fact become aware of the diversity of cultures, their multiple interactions and the threat that an abstract and systematic globalization poses to all of them. The gospel cannot simply come to them from outside as a transcultural doctrine or a collection of practices and rites, thought to affect them all in their specific corporeality. It has to be received, in order to fall into the ground there before being recreated in some way by those who have already begun to live by it. This infinitely complex process is turning the church of the nations, which is still too structured by Latinism, into a vast laboratory.

Thus to emphasize the birth of faith and the course which each being and each culture should follow does not mean that the way taken by our fathers has no meaning for us, far less that they took the wrong way. Besides, who would venture to pass judgment on this? But it is certainly important to emphasize today that the necessary recognition of the way taken by others, for example our fathers in the faith,[48] is possible only for those (or more precisely for a particular church) whose faith has already taken, at its risk and peril (i.e., with the assistance of the Holy Spirit), a similar course in its own culture. First of all to emphasize the 'irreformable' character of the dogmatic formulations of our tradition (bound up with the cultural context of ancient Europe without being totally subservient to it), or even to urge the objectivity of a complex of doctrines which is definitively to be held, is an approach which threatens to close the way to the recontextualization of faith and finally to prove contrary to the gospel. Certainly the reception of the gospel is always an act of obedience; but this must liberate a real creativity within each culture. And to use the words of the Gospels: would not each culture love to hear Peter say to it one day what Jesus said, 'My daughter, your faith has saved you'?[49]

---

48. Cf. the rule of Vincent of Lerins, *Commonitorium*, 2: 'In the Catholic Church itself that must be scrupulously observed which has been believed everywhere, always and by all.'
49. *ET* by John Bowden.

2.10 JOHN L. McKENZIE: *THE TENSION BETWEEN AUTHORITY AND FREEDOM – 1966*

We turn to examine the relation between the magisterium, truth and human freedom. The Council stimulated a huge amount of serious theological reflection in the light of the opening of windows on the world. This was particularly the case in respect of the understanding of freedom. Of course, there was no suggestion that a Catholic was now free to believe anything. The question was much more focused upon the freedom that it was the purpose of the gospel to give the human person. What is the nature of that freedom? Who shares in it? Does it have limits and if so who maintains them and how? The magisterium, in the sense of the teaching of the whole church, offers answers to some of these questions. There are the historic creeds, the decisions of the ecumenical councils, the faith as taught by the bishops and the pope and those things defined by the Pope *ex cathedra*. This is all very well, but how is the Magisterium to act responsibly if, as one must presume, their primary reason for teaching the faith that has been revealed is to enhance of the freedom the Gospel offers to every human being? The temptation will always exist to so protect the gift of the Gospel from misinterpretation that its offer of freedom is hidden. An important perspective was offered by John L. McKenzie, SJ, in his judicious reflections on the nature of authority in the church published immediately after the close of the Council in 1966.[50]

❀

In every society there is tension between freedom and authority, a tension which varies with the strength of the two poles. This tension exists in the Church too, and it seems worth saying that the tension ought to exist. In a vital organism tension is a sign of life, and the absence of tension is a sign of death. The metaphor is also valid of a society. Were there no tension between freedom and authority in the Church, it would mean that either freedom or authority had vanished; and neither the defenders of authority nor the defenders of freedom, however devoted they may be to their causes, can really hope for the disappearance of the opposite pole. But not every species of tension is healthy, and it will reward us to consider what the tension ought and ought not to be.

Let the preliminary remark be made that freedom is not given by one man to another. Man is free by nature, not by grant. One man cannot give another freedom; he can only restrain freedom or remove restraint. The ultimate basis for the restraint of freedom is the freedom of the person who restrains, for there is no valid reason for restraining the freedom of one except to preserve the freedom of others. Nor does the abstract freedom which is every man's by his nature add up to an equal portion of freedom for each. In existing reality some need more freedom than others, and the degree of freedom which one has is measured by the degree of responsibility which he has. Parents have greater freedom than children. To meet our problem in this study, those who bear authority in the Church need and have more

---

50. John L. McKenzie SJ, *Authority in the Church*, London, Geoffrey Chapman, 1966, ch. 13, 162–74.

freedom than those who do not bear authority. What is important is to remember that the freedom neither of those in authority nor of those under authority is granted by the other party.

If this principle is retained, it will become clear that the ultimate and most effective protection of authority is not power, but freedom. For authority is freedom and, in this sense, authority is power. But authority cannot endure unless it defends freedom, which means the freedom of those under authority as well as those who bear authority. Privation of the freedom of another deprives me of my own freedom; for I have by the privation put myself under the compulsion of defending a position I have no right to take. I have rendered my authority insecure by abusing it; and I am now hampered in its use. When authority recognizes the freedom of those whom it governs, it has done all it can to secure its own freedom. And authority does not recognize freedom unless it recognizes that freedom in anyone is power. When authority recognizes freedom, authority has that unique security which comes from the free consent of those who are subject to authority; their power is merged with its own.

The recognition of freedom does not remove tension between authority and freedom, but it sustains a healthy tension. For authority and freedom (actually they are both species of freedom) are extremely active principles, each principle tending to realize its own fullness. Hannah Arendt asserts that freedom is not an attribute of the will but of action.[51] Man proves his freedom by what he does rather than by what he wishes, and that freedom which does not issue in action is regarded as purely theoretical at best, as illusory non-freedom at worst. Without restraint, freedom and authority tend to destroy each other. This is the nature of the two principles. The paradox is not resolved by allowing one principle to destroy the other any more than one would choose to get along with either fire or water, but by allowing each principle to exercise that restraint upon the other which no other principle can exercise. There is no restraint of freedom except authority, and no restraint of authority except freedom. This is healthy tension which cannot be removed from society, whether it be the Church or any other society. The presence of this tension is a sign of strength, not of weakness.

Both authority and freedom are vested in men, not angels. The failure of men to act at all times according to their intelligent judgment and sincere good will creates tensions which are not healthy. Both authority and freedom always feel dissatisfied with anything less than total lack of restraint. Where the point of restraint is to be placed is a matter of judgment. It is a vice both of authority and of those who seek freedom to think that this is a unilateral decision. A unilateral decision made by either side will infallibly be wrong. Mutual recognition and respect includes a readiness to accept mistakes as one hopes to have one's own mistakes accepted; but a general and habitual disagreement of judgment takes away mutual recognition and respect and renders the tension unhealthy. What happens is that both those in authority and those under authority become more concerned with their respective power over the other than they are with the ultimate objective of the enterprise in which they are united. Such a society is sick.

The unhealthy tension, then, does not consist merely in the fact that both authority and those under authority think they have less freedom and therefore less power than they ought

51. Hannah Arendt, *Between Past and Future – Eight Exercises in Political Thought*, New York, Penguin Books, 1977, 143–71.

to have; if both authority and freedom are satisfied with their limitations, then they have become weak. The unhealthy tension consists in a loss of rapport, the replacement of mutual respect by mutual suspicion. Ultimately this means that either authority or freedom has overreached itself, and that the other pole is genuinely hampered in its action. Again, this is a matter of judgment, not of mathematical calculation. Unhealthy tension is probably due as much to personalities as to anything else. Weak persons in authority and strong persons under authority almost automatically mean that internecine strife exists. Yet it is also true that strong persons in authority and weak persons under authority lead to the corruption of freedom and responsibility and the relaxation even of healthy tension. Healthy tension demands strength in both poles. Here it seems worth remarking that a bully is not a strong person. When one reflects long enough on the problems involved, one is tempted to the despairing thesis of anarchy that no man is fit to govern another. The thesis is true to this extent, that no man is fit to govern another unless the one governed accepts the governor; and this acceptance is a free act of consent which cannot be compelled. Acceptance must be merited by the governing officer.

It is at this point that I feel I must modify what Joseph A. Fichter calls 'one of the clearest traditions of ecclesiastical administration', the thesis of positional leadership – shared, Fichter points out, with the military and political organizations, but not with the industrial and professional structure.[52] If I read Fichter correctly, I believe he also modifies the thesis more subtly than I am doing it. In the concrete reality of life this distinction between the office and the person is meaningless; and the sustained rationalization which the thesis requires should be imposed on no one. It introduces into the Church that element of depersonalization which may suit the purposes of the military and political organization, but not the purposes of the Church. It means equivalently that the officer call the subjects not friends but servants, inverting John 15:15. Unless superior and subject reach each other as persons and as fellow-Christians, they are not establishing a Christian relationship. There is no built-in protection of authority which protects against the necessity which lies upon all of fulfilling their responsibility. It is a harsh truth, but it is true that those who cannot win the love and respect of subordinates precisely in the fulfilment of the duty of their office should not be appointed to office, and, if by an honest error they should be appointed, they should neither be retained in it nor wish to retain it.

A healthy tension demands that both authority and freedom assert themselves with vigour; in no other way can the equilibrium be maintained. Here we have to ask whether this is the condition of authority and freedom in the Church. One may say that the principle of tension is not valid in the Church. It has been remarked often enough in the preceding pages that the Church is a unique society with unique forms. But we have also observed that the New Testament does not give the Church the kind of dominative or jurisdictional power which exists in secular societies; and the New Testament speaks quite often of freedom. A brief survey of the New Testament idea of freedom will assist us.

The principle of freedom in the New Testament is the Spirit (2 Corinthians 3:17), or the Son (John 8:36), or the truth (John 8:32). All of these signify a freedom which is other than the freedom which is man's by his nature. This freedom comes from revealed knowledge

---

52. Joseph A. Fichter, *Religion as an Occupation*, Notre Dame, University of Notre Dame Press, 1966, 256–74.

and from the indwelling Spirit as a principle of life, of thought, and of action. This is the freedom which is not granted by any authority, even by Church authority; this freedom is the radical reality of the new life in Christ – the freedom which is power. Those who have this freedom live as free men, but as servants of God (1 Peter 2:16). It is freedom to righteousness (Romans 6:21), freedom to fulfil the righteousness which Jesus makes possible. It is freedom from sin (Romans 6:18, 22), for it is the power to overcome sin. For Paul, in particular, Christian freedom is freedom from the Law (1 Corinthians 10:29; Galatians 2:4, 4:22, 26, and 5:1, 13). By a paradox Paul calls the principle which liberates from the law of sin and death the law of the Spirit of Life (Romans 8:2), a phrase similar to the paradox of 'the perfect law of liberty' (1 James 1:25). Paul asserts his freedom as an apostle (1 Corinthians 9:1, 19).

Freedom from the Law is not to be considered as submission to another law. The Spirit and the truth and the Son replace the Law, but they are not law. Everywhere in the New Testament freedom is conceived as life and action; freedom is not defined as a kind of restraint. The only restraint which the New Testament places upon freedom is love, and love, far from being a restraint of freedom, is the fullness of freedom. The Christian does not act from compulsion or coercion or obligation, but because the power of the Spirit within him is a driving principle of action.

This idea of freedom does not suggest an anarchic Church; we have been at pains to show that the Church is structured in authority. But this unique supernatural freedom, while it is subject to restraint, is not subject to that kind of restraint which secular authority employs in secular societies. Christian freedom is restrained by the same principle which confers it, by the Spirit; or, as I have said above, by love. The relations of authority and freedom in the Christian community are determined by love, unless the Christian community wishes to make its decisions on a basis other than the basis which Jesus has established for its decisions. If we are to retain the genuine Christian basis for decision, we cannot think that restraint is imposed only on the freedom of those under authority; authority also is subject to restraint.

Is authority to be restrained only by its own judgment and virtue? Here we face the problems of structure. The Church is open to the temptation which threatens any organization of attributing to structure a sacredness which structure does not have. Structure is a means to an end, and with the passage of time and the change of conditions the means can become inept. The forms of Church authority, we have noticed, have been frozen at the absolute level reached by a combination of Renaissance tradition and a defensive posture against modern attacks on Church authority. The forms of Church offices are the forms of a princely or a ducal court. It is here that tension between the theory of authority and the use of authority exists, for in most modern countries neither the offices of the Church nor its other members are accustomed to these forms. The administration is actually not princely nor ducal, but it is out of harmony with the structure when it is not; and if a crisis comes to pass, authority turns to the absolute measures because it neither knows nor has any other measures – assuming that authority does not turn to absolute measures because authority believes in them.

Belief in absolutism does exist, and the belief affects Church government. We have already noticed that in recent generations the statements of Church officers on obedience and due submission are numerous; one is hard put to it to find an official statement on the nature of responsible Christian freedom. The 1960 Statement of the American Bishops was a splendid exposition of the place which the Catholic ought to fill in the United States as an adult free responsible citizen of a republic whose traditions and institutions repose on personal freedom and which cherishes personal freedom.[53] The statement could easily be adapted to set forth the position of the Catholic Church. I have no way of knowing whether their Excellencies considered their statement applicable to the Church or not. We have noticed that the obedience described in official statements is almost always the obedience paid to an absolute ruler by his subject, and that this obedience is neither in theory nor in practice the obedience given in modern democratic states. There can be no solid reason for denying the possibility of evolution in the theory of obedience toward a more democratic idea. Evolution in this direction appears from our survey of the New Testament texts to permit the restoration of some features of the idea and use of authority in the apostolic Church.

In the contemporary forms of Church authority there are effectively no channels through which the authority which resides in the whole Church can normally affect the authority which resides in the officers of the Church. The freedom of the members of the Church is power, but the power has no outlet. The authoritarian structure of the forms of government, however intelligently and justly it may be administered, reflects the concentration of authority and power in the officers. As such, the structure is a practical denial of the authority and power of the faithful. When this concentrated authority is handled with less than perfect prudence and fairness, the consequences can be most unfortunate. Structurally, there is no way to correct abuses of authority except rebellion, and no one thinks rebellion is a good way to do things. If there were regular channels of communication between authority and members, if the authority of the officers normally took pains to see that it reflected the authority of the members, abuses would be much less likely to arise.

These remarks do not imply that we should think of the Church in terms of a parliamentary form, with the bishop acting as a kind of first minister who should resign on a vote of non-confidence. A bishop should not need a parliamentary vote to resign if he knows that he has lost the confidence of his people. Within modern forms how can he ever learn that this has happened? It would be extremely unrealistic to say that it never happens. Church authority, we know, is not conferred by members of the Church; even when bishops were elected by the faithful of the diocese, the election did not confer authority, but simply designated who should bear it. Of this we are well aware; we are less well aware that Church authority does not confer freedom on the other members of the Church. Modification of the structure would seem to mean at least decentralization of decision, enlarging the scope of action of the individual priest and the individual layman, and broadening considerably the base of policy deliberation. Since the Second Vatican Council opened, there have been numerous suggestions of various councils and commissions which would be channels of expression for the unofficial authority in the Church. These suggestions are at least movements in the right direction, but their success will be very doubtful unless much of the thinking in the Church is changed.

Some recent theological literature deals with the place and authority of the laity in the Church. The major piece in this collection is the massive and carefully reasoned work of Yves Congar.[54] What one misses even in such a study as this is the practical implementation of the

---

53. 'On Individual Responsibility', *The Catholic Mind*, 59 (1961), 557–62.
54. Yves M-J Congar, OP, *Lay People in the Church*, London, Geoffrey Chapman, 1959; ET by Donald Attwater.

function of the layman, admitting that the office of the layman needs a much more thorough theological grounding than it has received. It is my own belief that we shall not know the office and function of the layman until the layman himself, who knows his potentialities and his opportunities better than the clergy do, defines his office and function. When the laity become aware that the decision of what they can do and must do lies with them, they will do it. The lack of real lay leadership is apparent in the very fact that the laity still turn to the clergy for directions on how to lead. Karl Rahner has pointed out three areas in which the laity can make themselves heard now: the Catholic press; Catholic schools; the quality of preaching.[55] In these areas the layman can utter articulate criticism and, once the layman begins to speak, he will find other areas.

Pope Pius XII once spoke of the place of public opinion in the Church. Whatever he may have meant, we have not yet found a way to make public opinion in the Church meaningful. Public opinion in the Church, if it is limited to enthusiastic approval of all hierarchical and pastoral decisions, has as much meaning as an election in Russia. Public opinion is meaningful only when it reviews and, when necessary, criticizes the decisions of authority. Modern democratic processes have shown that public opinion is not a species of insurrection, and that public opinion is quite compatible with a law-abiding and orderly community. Public opinion illustrates a principle which Church officers often forget, that no one ever fights a decision which he thinks he had a part in making. Yet the suggestion that hierarchical and pastoral decisions are subject to review and criticism would seem to many to approach blasphemy. This attitude is as good an example as we can find of the excessive valuation of authority. If authority is not restrained by public opinion, which is the freedom and power of the members of society at work, then what does restrain authority? If we think authority should have no restraint other than self-restraint, then this theoretical position should be clearly stated so that no doubt is left of its meaning. It must be remembered that hierarchical and pastoral decisions have seriously damaged the Church in the past, and we have no guarantee that they will not damage the Church in the future. I cannot say that public opinion would have modified these decisions, but it should have had a chance. One can scarcely find such a decision which was not criticized ineffectively by some contemporary.

It should be apparent without argument that public discussion of issues is preferable by far to private and surreptitious discussion. Public discussion of its very nature is not favourable to manifest unfairness, abusive language, and incautious and undocumented assertions. The person who engages in public discussion sticks his neck out, and, if there were free channels of public opinion in the Church, the number who would be willing to enter the arena of discussion would be small. Public discussion creates a weight of opinion which the private representation does not have. One suspects that this is precisely what is wrong with it. The proposal which issues from public discussion has an excellent chance of being pruned of prejudice, and gossip, and unnecessary verbiage and irrelevancies; such a proposal represents the fruit of mature deliberation. I do not know why this type of discussion is thought to tarnish the image of authority. The image of authority is much more tarnished by the uninhibited private sessions in which authority is so often debased. But the officers are not present at these unauthorized grievance meetings. Presumably they do not know what goes on there or, if they do know, they can afford to ignore these desperate little cells.

---

55. Karl Rahner, SJ, *Free Speech in the Church*, New York, Sheed and Ward, 1959, 9–50.

The absence of regular channels of discussion deprives the Church of a wealth of wisdom and experience in its members. One is sometimes shocked to learn of people who were not consulted in areas in which they had proved themselves masters. Education, carried on under Church auspices, has often been, up to this writing, an outstanding example of failure to consult those who have something to say. Others would adduce other examples. The failure to consult offers no occasion to impute motives; we omit consultation of public opinion because we are not accustomed to consult public opinion. But if the Church is to mobilize its resources for its mission, it must find some way of employing the intelligence and good will of its members other than total control.

It may be unfair to put the question in the form in which I am going to put it, but this risk must be run. Quite simply, the members of the Church are required to show a confidence in the officers of the Church which the officers of the Church do not always reciprocate. The members must assume that they, the members, do not share the dedication of the officers to the Church and that they are not responsible adult Catholics. They must assume not only that they are uninformed on the issues with which authority deals – although it is hard to think of any issue which lies entirely beyond them – but also that they are incapable of grasping these issues even if they were informed. In one word, which we have used before, the members must accept authority as paternal in the sense that the members are children incapable of adult responsibility. There may be better ways of destroying communication with adults than treating adults as children, but I cannot think of what these better ways may be. When adults can be trusted only to obey without questions, they are not being trusted at all. Over-valuation of authority is under-valuation of those who are subject to authority.

Our structural problem can be neatly summarized thus: we must under present forms await the decision of authority for any modification of the structure. The great change initiated by John XXIII is that he invited public discussion of such problems. But if a modification of structure is conceived as a grant of greater freedom and responsibility to the members of the Church, nothing will have been changed. Real change means that authority in the Church recognizes the power and authority which belong to the faithful by the constitution of the Church, not by pontifical largesse. Real change means that the forms and structure reflect the reality of the Church, not the reality of the duchy or The Organization. Real change is real only if it is the work of the whole Church and not exclusively the work of its officers. But the initiative still lies with the officers. We shall know that a change has been made when the initiative no longer lies there. *The Constitution on the Church* [*LG*] provides that the laity should reveal their needs and their desires to their pastors, and under the proper conditions should express their opinions on those things that concern the good of the Church.[56] These expressions should be uttered through the organs erected by the Church for this purpose. Such organs do not yet exist except in a few dioceses in an inchoate stage. Certainly one of the first areas in which the laity can be active is in the erection of such organs. The explicit provision of such organs is an important step away from the princely and the ducal forms.

---

56. B.C. Butler and G. Baum, *The Constitution on the Church of Vatican Council II*, Glen Rock, Deus Books, 1965, ch. 4, no. 37.

2.11 YVES CONGAR: *A BRIEF HISTORY OF THE FORMS OF THE MAGISTERIUM AND ITS RELATION WITH SCHOLARS* – 1982

Turning to explore the relations between faith, the magisterium and theological enquiry, it is important to put the magisterium itself in context. How has it developed? What changes can be observed during its history? How has the church exercised its responsibility to proclaim, preserve and teach the faith? How and when has understanding of the magisterium changed and could such understandings continue to change? Yves Congar published a paper in 1982, originally prepared for the International Commission of Theologians. He shows that, until the Early Modern period, the magisterium was consolidated and papal power grew through the church's witness to the faith, concern for spiritual truth, opposition to heresy, emphasis on sound theological judgement and embroilment with the universities as they emerged with their own strong desire for freedom. The reading concerns the period since the Council of Trent.[57]

The Council of Trent achieved a happy collaboration between theologians and Fathers. First, theologians were admitted to congregations partly composed of bishops; then the congregations of lesser theologians were established, that is to say, not conciliar Fathers, ahead of legates and prelates. The opinion of theologians was considered; then the Fathers drafted a decree and, before publishing it, submitted the text to the theologians. Then, the theologians were allowed to speak in assemblies, which brought the difficulty of limiting their interventions. Among the bishops, several were good theologians. All in all, after a period of resistance by the Fathers, the interventions and importance of theologians have been growing.

With the reactions against the Protestants, the Council of Trent, the Society of Jesus, and then the necessity of meeting the challenges from rationalism and popular and social movements, the four centuries preceding Vatican II developed under the aegis of the affirmation on this authority just as much in its form of 'magisterium'. Let us note, a little schematically, seven points.

1. Faculties of theology remain active until the French Revolution. They continue to condemn theses (Alcala and Salamanca on the subject of Baius; Louvain and Paris against overtolerant morality), but sometimes they intervene in Rome: Louvain about Baius, 1567; on permissiveness, 1677; with the bishop of Ghent on attritionism, 1682ff. Whether invited or not, Rome intervenes in a number of theological questions by censuring propositions: Pius V against Baius, 1567 (DSch 1901ff.), Innocent X against Jansenism, 1633 (2001ff.), against permissiveness, 1665–1666 and 1679 (2021ff., 2351), Alexander VIII against Jansenism,

57. Yves Congar O., 'A Brief History of the Forms of the Magisterium and Its Relations with Scholars', in C.E. Curren and R.A. McCormack (eds), *The Magisterium and Morality*, New York, Paulist Press, 1982, 322–8.

1690 (2291ff.), Clement XI against Quesnel, 1713 (101 propositions: 2400ff.) and finally the rather bland condemnation of the theses of the Jansenist synod of Pistoia. Theology is watched, at least when it bears with consequences for the behavior of clerks and the faithful. But since the days of Paul IV and Pius IV (1564), the Index of prohibited books exists. The papacy disposes of an organism to repress errors.

The situation will change as a result of the suppression of most faculties of theology by the French Revolution and Napoleon – all those in France, thirteen of eighteen in Germany. A restoration of the faculties will take place in the nineteenth century, at Rome first (Roman College, 1824) and in large part under the authority of the papacy and from Rome. The problem of the independence of the 'cathedrae magistales' will not arise again as in the past.

2. The discussions stirred up by Jansenism brought about the emergence of a new category, that of 'dogmatic facts'. Moreover, in the context of the progress of the idea of the infallibility of the papal magisterium, the distinction between the infallibility of the body of the faithful and that of the Pope and pastors is made more precise. This culminated in the distinction between *Ecclesia docens* (the teaching Church) and *Ecclesia credens* or *discens* (the believing or learning Church) (in the middle of the eighteenth century), a distinction which was to become common in the nineteenth, including in catechisms and into our own time, often in debatable formulations such as active and passive infallibility. These are categories and a vocabulary to reconsider.

3. We have sketched out elsewhere the changes in ideas by which, in modern times, we have replaced consideration of the principle of the *quod* by that of the teaching or defining authority, that is, the *quo*. This has been expressed in the categories, valid in themselves, of 'living magisterium' and of 'active tradition' as distinct from 'passive tradition', or again by *regula proxima* as distinct from *regula remota*. Thus there was a tendency to give 'magisterium' an autonomous and absolute value, whereas soundness consists in not separating the form of the apostolic ministry from the content of the tradition. What Luther wrote to Prierias does all the same deserve attention: 'I do not know what you mean by calling the Roman Church the rule of faith, I have always believed that faith was the rule of the Roman Church and of all the Churches' (WA 1, 662). Let us note that many official texts state that the magisterium only guards, proposes and ultimately interprets what is objectively given. Nevertheless, the meaning we have just given was indeed that of a whole train of thought which it is proper to criticize. Of the two classic activities of the magisterium, preserving and defining, the second has been privileged. It seemed under Pius XII that the objective of theology was to prepare 'definitions' and that the purpose of the magisterium was to define. At that time it was forgotten that the essential and first function is to *bear witness to what has been received*. Definition should be handled cautiously, occurring only when required by necessity in order to protect the truth of apostolic witness under threat.[58]

4. The word 'magisterium' appeared in its modern sense, '*the* magisterium'. Our historical and semantic essay expounds and illustrates that. The distinction between ordinary magisterium and extraordinary magisterium is classical. Vatican I introduced the category of 'ordinary and universal magisterium' (DSch 3011) already used by Pius IX to indicate the magisterium of the scattered college of bishops.

---

58. Tradition states that 'definitio' is to be handled cautiously, occurring only when compelled by the necessity of excluding error; cf. A Liégé, article 'Dogme', in *Catholicisme*, 3, 956–7; our *La Foi et La Théologie*, Paris, 1962, 48.

5. Vatican I defined, certainly not, as is said popularly, the infallibility of the Pope, but that of his teaching when, acting in his capacity as pastor and teacher of all Christians, he commits his supreme authority in the universal Church on a question of faith and morals.[59] Vatican I distinguished two powers: order and jurisdiction. It made infallibility an attribute of the primacy (DSch 3065). 'Deducimus ex primatu supremam potestatem docendi tamquam speciem a suo genere' (We deduce from the primacy the supreme power of teaching as a species from its genus), said Gasser on July 11, 1870 (Mansi 52, 1221 A). This approach, as Pottmeyer has shown, is part of the stream of ideas expressed with as much brilliance as sophistry by J. de Maistre, de Bonald, and the first Lamennais, ideas whose roots plunge into the *modern* concept of sovereignty (Bodin, Hobbes). Vatican I took place in a general context of restoration, or opposition to movements of liberation, or affirmation of the highest degree of authority. Such socio-historical conditioning, such unilateralism, call for us to consider Vatican I again, both positively and critically, with good historical studies, even with the questions asked by H. Küng or after him. It will be particularly necessary to define theologically the status of 'magisterium' or what M.J. Scheeben called 'Lehrapostolat' (the teaching apostolate) and to distinguish it from the *genus* 'primatus jurisdictionis' (primacy of jurisdiction). On the other hand the Council speaks (DSch 3072 and 3074) of 'summum pastorale officium' (the highest pastoral office), which is more satisfactory.

6. Vatican I made no precise statement concerning the 'ordinary magisterium' of the bishop of Rome. *In point of fact*, as the 'ordinary magisterium' of Popes had been exercised by excellent Pontiffs in an incredible flow of encyclicals, speeches, and various interjections, this magisterium has assumed preponderant importance and, in the light of an intense 'devotion to the Pope',[60] has been almost assimilated, in current opinion, to the prerogatives of the extraordinary magisterium. Besides, Pius XII, who carried it to its furthest point, expressed in his encyclical *Humani Generis* (August 12, 195) his position on two points of great importance: (1) 'He who listens to you listens to me.' When the Pope has expressed his *sentential* on a point previously controversial, 'quaestionem liberae inter theologos disceptationis iam haberi non posse' (there can no longer be any question of free discussion between theologians) (DSch 3884–3885). (2) The (or a) role of theologians is to justify the declarations of the magisterium: 'eorum est indicare qua ratione ea quae a vivo magisterio docentur, in Sacris Litteris et in divina "traditione" sive explicite, sive implicite inveniantur' (their task is to indicate for what reason those things which are taught by the living magisterium are found in Holy Scripture and divine 'tradition', whether explicitly or implicitly) (DSch 3886). This was already to be found in Pius IX, in the letter *Gravissimas inter* of December 11, 1862 against Frohschammer (ASS 8 [1874] 429). Pius XII saw the theologian teaching only by delegation from the 'magisterium' and doing so strictly in his service and under his control.[61] Is this consonant with what nineteen centuries of the Church's life tell us about the function of 'didascale' or doctor? No, not exactly.

---

59. ... *Pastor Aeternus*, c. 4: DSch 3074.
60. Remarkable documentation on this subject is found in R. Zinnhobler, 'Pius XI in der katholischen Literatur seiner Zeit. Ein Baustein zur Geschichte des Triumphalismus', in *Konzil und Papst. Historische Beiträge zur Frage der höchsten Gewelt in der Kirche*, Munich-Paderborn: Schömingh, 1975, 387–432.
61. Cf. M. Seckler, 'Die Theologie als kirchliche Wissenschaft nach Pius XII und Paul VI', in *Theologishe Quartalschr*, 149 (1969), 209–34.

These positions were all the more serious in that, in their encyclicals (the series begins with *Mirari Vos* of Gregory XVI, 1832), modern Popes have done *theology* – and a determined theology, which the Roman schools have practiced, their personnel being recruited and supervised according to a very definite line. It is not very easy to define the significance of encyclicals in theological terms. On the one hand there are many kinds; on the other they do not fit the classical frameworks of treatises of theological criteriology. Sometimes they simply express a common conviction that has already been reached; at other times they formulate a doctrine that has not yet been accepted. They are intended to be the means, for the Pope, of realizing unity among bishops and, through them, of the body of the faithful around them. There are several books and articles on the value of encyclicals. The present article does not have to deal with this issue itself.

Yet it is necessary, from the historical point of view, to add that if there has been an unfitting inflation of encyclicals' authority, there is now a relativization and criticism of them. People have practically applied to them what Vatican I had said on extraordinary magisterium. Today in contrast we find refusal to accept, at least partially, such documents as *Humanae Vitae*. It is true that we can invoke texts of classical theologians on the right not to assent to a non-infallible teaching.

7. Vatican II has renewed in sufficiently striking fashion collaboration between theologians and conciliar Fathers. 'You are the teaching Church, but we are the informing Church.' The bishops have become aware of the importance of theologians.

The Council itself insists on the necessity of a very frank openness to the questions and resources of our world, and on the vitality and freedom of theological work.[62] Concerning the magisterium, the Council re-established the traditional relationship of subordination of pastoral authority to the given or to the object, in short the primacy of *quod* over *quo*: either by affirming that the magisterium is linked to the Word of God and his service (*Lumen Gentium*, n. 25; *Dei Verbum*, n. 10), or by not taking up (*Dei Verbum*, n. 25) the affirmation that the preparatory schema of 1962 had borrowed from *Humanae Generis* the idea that the magisterium is 'proxima veritatis norma' (the proximate norm of truth). This restoration of *quod* in its traditional sovereignty has allowed recognition of a 'hierarchia veritatum' (hierarchy of truths) (*Unitatis Redintegratio*, n. 11).

Paul VI often spoke of the relations between the magisterium and theologians. At first he spoke along the same lines as Pius XII,[63] still denying all private judgment and insisting on obedient and docile dependence toward the magisterium. Paul VI on several occasions was severe about certain theological researches.[64] In his speech to the International Congress on the theology of Vatican II,[65] he dealt expressly with the relations of theologians and the magisterium. He regarded theology as a function of the Church, taking place in the morphology and physiology of the Church. It mediates in a way between the magisterium and the faithful or the world of men: on the one hand, discerning faith as it is lived by the Christian community, its problems and the resources culture offers, in order to answer men's questions in the light of revelation and tradition, and thus help the magisterium to fulfill its

---

62. ... *Gaudium et Spes*. Nn.44 and 62; Declaration *Gravissimum Educationis*, nn. 10 and 11.
63. Cf. quoted article by M. Seckler, 22ff., 227ff.
64. Cf. opening speech at the Synod (29 September 1967); message to German Catholics (8 September 1968), etc.
65. 1 October 1966: *AAS*, 58 (1966) 892–4.

task more amply; on the other hand, to transmit and explain, by elaborating and justifying it in scholarly fashion, the teaching of the magisterium. For these two meditations there must be an active theology, carried on in a religious climate, fraternally trusting and communicating.

But the period since the Council has been marked by argument, the breaking up of what had represented Catholic unity up to and including Pius XII. With new means of information, men are shaping their ideas by a host of means other than official teaching. This seems insufficient faced with what the critical sciences, philosophy and the social sciences produce as problems and bring as data. The general democratic climate is changing the meaning of authority, which is perceived less as the right to determine the thought and life of subordinates. Former beliefs and practices are no longer effective by virtue of their own weight; people want to do and say other things than they have been taught. People appreciate nevertheless the endeavors of authority and the texts of the magisterium in the light of disciplines such as the sociology of knowledge of K. Mannheim, and notice that affirmation by itself of the magisterium such as it has been practiced is subject to ideological criticism. We cannot not take into account the critical historical study of the magisterium in modern times. Its pretensions seem excessive and unreal. For one thing, the current crisis is to be explained as a reaction against them. Today, theologians are going beyond the ecclesiastical work-category formulated for them by Pius XII and Paul VI; they are living according to a common standard of scholarly research. Obviously it is no longer enough to explain decisions already reached ('Denzinger-theology'); it is a matter of rejoining men in their critical questions with reference to revelation in Jesus Christ. In these conditions the work of theologians is still tied to faith as transmitted and defined, but it cannot be a simple commentary on pontifical teachings. The period since the Council has seen several declarations of the freedom of theological work. Consult also the criticism of that made by *Concilium* in December 1968 by G. Chantraine.[66] Neither these declarations nor his criticism can resolve the real question facing us today.

If we may conclude an historical article with a theological perspective, we will say: the relationship between scholars and the magisterium calls for reconsideration. This supposes that we will first define the status of the 'magisterium' in the Church, and that it will not be isolated from the living reality of the Church. It will be necessary to recognize the fundamental character of the charisma and service of theologians, the necessary specificity of their work within the faith of the Church, to define the conditions for a healthy exercise of their service: an awareness of responsibility, of communion with the concrete life of the faithful, the doxological context and celebration of the mysteries, a mutual criticism actively performed. We cannot define the dependent condition of theologians only with reference to the 'magisterium', even while this retains its truth. In this area as in that of obedience we must not think of the issue just in two terms: authority and theologians. We must think in three terms: above, the truth, the transmitted apostolic faith, confessed, preached and celebrated. Beneath this, at its service, the 'magisterium' of the apostolic ministry, and the work or the teaching of theologians, as well as the faith of the faithful. It is a differentiated service, articulated organically, like all the life of the Church.

---

66. *Vraie et fausse liberté du théologie – Un essaie*, Paris-Bruges, 1969.

2.12 KARL RAHNER: *THE TEACHING OFFICE OF THE CHURCH IN THE PRESENT DAY CRISIS OF AUTHORITY* – 1969

Rahner helps us to explore fundamental questions concerning the magisterium, the church and the churches.

The fact of divisions within the Christian community of faith is a depressing matter of common experience and regret. The celebration of communion within the Roman Catholic Church to which the magisterium bears witness has as its dark side the continuing phenomenon presented by the many Christian communities not in communion with Rome, but whose worship and faithfulness bears more than a little relation to the Catholic faith. It was Yves Congar who, in an article in *Concilium* in 1981, pointed to the many ecumenical conversations (involving then, Protestant, Reformed, Lutheran, Anglican and Orthodox traditions) as ways in which 'being maintained in the truth tends towards a unity of confession of faith'. He went on,

> This is a unity which it is being more and more widely acknowledged will not be uniform either in its expression or even in the internal structure and emphases of the component parts. It seems to me that the major ecumenical question for us today is precisely this question as to how much diversity is compatible with communion. *Truth is symphonic.* The conductor is the Spirit of truth. Who better to speak in the Church and to bring us into or keep us in the truth?[67]

The desire for unity was central to the purposes of Vatican II; that the desire remains alive and fresh is witnessed to by Pope John-Paul II's Encyclical *Ut Unum Sint* (25 May 1995) in which he invites all other Christians traditions to say how the Office of the Papacy might become the sign of unity for all Christians. It was a bold and important move to focus at this stage on the office around which the most anger and misunderstanding centres.

In March 1969, Karl Rahner lectured at the 30th Conference of the Ecumenical Study Circle of Protestant and Catholic Theologians on the theme, Authority in Crisis.[68] After an introduction in which he points to the magisterium, ordinary and extraordinary, as a conscientious attempt to protect the essential and proper substance of the faith, he explores ways in which it may be better understood and more widely accepted. He carefully examines the possibility of democratic decisions, what this might offer as a means whereby the magisterium would be more widely understood in the Catholic Church and accepted by the churches. The possibility is rejected as both false and impracticable: it would not achieve the object of unity. The second part explores the relationship between the legal authority of the Church and the content of faith, a major matter of ecumenical concern.

---

67. Yves Congar 'Towards a Catholic Synthesis' in *Concilium*, 148 (1981), 78 (see Chapter 5 of this present volume). Since this date these conversations have continued, and other traditions (e.g. Methodist) have begun to talk with Rome. *Dominus Iesus*, published by the Congregation for the Divine Faith on 6 August, 2000, makes it clear that there is a very long way to go.
68. Karl Rahner, 'The Teaching Office of the Church in the Present-Day Crisis of Authority', in *Theological Investigations*, vol. 12: *Confrontations II*, London, Darton, Longman and Todd, 1974, 23–30.

So far we have been attempting to consider the teaching office of the Church in its relationship to the Church as a whole. We must now consider the question of the teaching office from yet another point of view. In our introductory remarks we have already drawn attention to the fact that in the usual theology of seminaries, by reason of the formal and juridical categories in which the nature and power of the teaching office are conceived of, the formal authority to be attached to the teaching office is thought of almost independently of the actual *truth content* which it attests. In this seminary theology the content of the faith on the one hand and the formal authority of the teaching office on the other are presented as two separate entities almost without connection. It is true that it is stated clearly that the teaching office is obviously constituted under divine revelation, that it must be subordinate and obedient to it, and that through the power of the Spirit that has been promised to the Church it will also be preserved in this obedience. But this is in itself not enough really to make clear the precise relationship which exists between the formal authority of the teaching office and the *fides quae* which is intended to mediate it to the *fides qua* of the individual believer. We shall enquire into this relationship in respect both of its essential constitution and of the forms which it inevitably assumes today.

With regard to the basic relationship which constantly exists between the formal authority of the teaching office and the content of the faith which that teaching office is designed to present it must first be stated simply and unambiguously that according to fundamental theology and the interpretation of the faith of the Catholic Church the formal authority of the teaching office is not the first and most fundamental *datum* in the content of the faith such that all other elements in it are based upon this one as their necessary foundation. There is a well-known saying of Augustine[69] (which unfortunately is quoted all too often and in a sense that is misleading) to the effect that he would not give the allegiance of his faith to the gospels unless the authority of the Church had moved him to do so. Now taken in a strict and absolute sense, and as a universal principle applicable to the faith as such this statement is simply false. Of course it is true as a matter of history that the gospel has come down to me, the individual, historically separated as I am from Christ, through the mediation of the Church. It has come down to me in this sense as that which at once commands and makes possible my belief, as the grace given power of the Kyrios and as containing the fundamental truths of the Christian faith. But this is still very far from saying that the *formal* authority precisely of the *teaching office* of the Church is in the specifically theological sense the first and most fundamental datum for a Catholic Christian in his faith. Ultimately speaking he believes in the formal authority of the Church's teaching office because prior to this he already believes in God, his grace, in Jesus Christ the crucified and risen Lord, and not e converso. In the hierarchy of truths referred to by the Second Vatican Council the fact that there is in truth and in reality a teaching office of the Church is not in fact a first and foremost datum, but a relatively secondary one, though this is not for one moment to deny that this truth does belong, albeit in its due and proper place, to this hierarchy of truths.

Both in reality and also as recognized in the subjective conscience of the believer, the doctrine of the teaching office is itself based upon certain more radical truths of faith and is

---

69. *PL*, 42, 176.

not either logically or ontologically speaking the basis on which all else rests. Precisely in order to be Catholic in our belief we must turn Augustine's axiom 'the other way round' by saying 'I would not believe in the authority of the Church if I were not moved to do so by the gospel'. This is not to deny that in the unity of the whole structured hierarchy of the Catholic faith there is also, in a certain sense, a *mutual* relationship of interdependence between the Church, her institutional structures, and her officialdom on the one hand, and the true substance of the faith on the other as recognized in the individual conscience of the individual believer. Nor do we deny that Christian faith is always the faith of the Church as well.

But in this unity and in this wholly *mutual* relationship, in which each of the individual elements in the faith conditions and modifies the others, there is still an overriding order. From this point of view belief in the Church's teaching office is both objectively and subjectively sustained by a reality of the faith which is prior to this teaching office and to faith in it. Hence too in any book on Catholic fundamental theology even of the traditional kind it is taken for granted – indeed we might almost say too much taken for granted – that the section dealing with the existence and authority of the teaching office in the Church as vested in the pope and bishops is included only at a very late stage. A further point is that the truth that in founding his Church Christ gave it an official authority to teach in this sense in virtue of his own authority and promise is obviously no easier to recognize than any other truths of the Christian faith which subjectively and objectively speaking are of more fundamental character. Since the Second Vatican Council and in the age of a sincere ecumenism a Catholic should not hesitate to concede that the more fundamental realities of faith common to all Christians, and at the same time more vital to their salvation (whether logically speaking or at least under God's saving providence as it de facto exists) are actually *easier* to apprehend in faith than the specifically Catholic truth of the teaching office of the Church. Now these facts, however self-evident, have certain consequences for the teaching office of the Church as applied in practice which, as I feel, are not always recognized and observed.

When the teaching office of the Church arrives at decisions (whether definitorial or merely provisional, albeit authentic ones) if in doing so it relies simply and exclusively on its own formal authority it is in a real sense acting against the obvious truths mentioned above. It is true that within the theoretical system of the Catholic faith this formal authority is itself an obvious factor. But it is not so in the subjective conscience of the individual Catholic believer to which such a decision is addressed. Here his authority is no primary datum, but rather a dependent function, a truth based upon other truths, indeed a truth which is more assailable and more easily imperilled than the fundamental truths of the Christian faith. Hence in taking such a decision the teaching office of the Church has the duty of showing that the content of this decision does not rest merely on its own formal authority. Rather it must show as clearly and convincingly as possible that it is intrinsically connected with the original basis of the Christian faith in general. In doing this it will at the same time have again and again to enable believers to understand afresh that this authority of the teaching office derives from this basic essence of the Christian faith which the subject to whom this particular decision of the teaching office is addressed must already have apprehended prior to any assent on his part to the formal authority of the teaching office.

If, and to the extent that, the Christian faith is ultimately one and all elements in it *mutually* condition one another it can uncompromisingly be asserted that there is a mutual interdependence here too. It is just as true to say that the formal authority of the teaching office depends upon the power of the truth of faith as proclaimed to command the allegiance of our faith as to say that the latter depends upon the former. This relationship in which either factor influences the other is distorted, however, if we rely exclusively upon the formal authority of the teaching office. It can be stated absolutely as a matter of principle that in its individual decisions and the preliminary proposals leading up to these the teaching office of the Church acts best and most correctly when it allows the truth which is sustained by grace and inherent in the reality itself which it is treating of and seeking to teach to make its own impact, and allows its own formal authority almost to be completely effaced by giving pride of place to this truth. As we have said this is the right approach to adopt simply because the truth that the teaching office has this formal authority is in any instance supported and kept alive by faith in the fundamental truths of Christianity. Hence in the concrete exercise of its functions the teaching office must again and again re-establish its connections with these truths.

The urgency of the point which we are making here becomes still clearer when we reflect upon the way in which the teaching office of the Church exercises its functions in the situation which prevails *in the present day*. Very many authorities whom we encounter in the world and in the course of human living have a certain power regardless of whether or not the legitimacy of their formal claims to power are recognized by the individual in his own conscience. For the most part these various kinds of authority (that of parents, of groups in secular society, of teachers or experts, or of the state) are reinforced with a certain degree of *power*, whether explicit or implicit, consciously adverted to or unconsciously taken for granted. So far as the conscious awareness of the individual is concerned moral authority and the power accompanying this are far from being clearly distinguishable from one another. When we recognize authority we are very largely, without actually noticing it, submitting ourselves to the power (which itself in turn may take many forms), and when authority is claimed by those in whom it is vested these likewise are aware of and rely upon this power which they take for granted without explicitly reflecting upon the fact. This is particularly true in those cases in which the parties involved take it for granted that their authority is accompanied by such power. In such cases authority imposes itself in virtue of the power attached to it and not in virtue of itself. Now right down to these present times in which we live the authority of the Church and of the churches has had power of this kind which extends to their teaching function as well. They have had this power in virtue of public opinion, many institutional factors, the extremely close connection which they have had with secular society, and all the opportunities they have enjoyed of influencing public awareness in general.

This is not the place to enquire how far such power should be attached to the formal authority of the Church's teaching office as of right, what historical factors and situations have caused this supplementary power to be attached to the teaching office in society and in the awareness of the individual, or what reasons, whether regrettable or providential, have led to a situation in which it has to a large extent lost this power. At any rate the situation which prevails today and which will come to prevail still more in the future is that the power which in earlier times was ascribed to the teaching office in addition to the authority which it was recognized as having in itself has to a large extent disappeared and is in process of disappearing more and more. The teaching office has less and less 'authority' in itself in virtue of this power which was formally attached to it prior to and independent of the assent of faith in which the individual recognized its existence as legitimate. In other words what it lacks now is any effective influence upon the individual prior to his assent of faith precisely to this teaching office. The only real significance which it still has depends almost exclusively, and in increasing measure today, upon the question of whether and how far it succeeds in making its own spiritual authority credible on the basis of the gospel itself. Today less than ever before can it assume *a priori* that its own formal validity as a teaching office has already been acknowledged as *de fide* in the conscience of the individual Catholic Christian, and so rely simply and exclusively upon this as a justification of the specific doctrine which it promulgates. Every time a specific doctrine of this kind is promulgated without its own intrinsic claim to truth being made clear (this does not necessarily have to mean rationally comprehensible in itself, but it surely does mean intrinsically intelligible and following logically from the Christian faith as a single whole) it always entails a threat to the formal authority of the teaching office as a whole such that there is a real danger that it will not be acknowledged. The reason is that, as we have already said, this authority does not of itself command any greater degree of credibility in terms of fundamental theology than other truths of the faith. And since today all kinds of purely formal authority are under attack it follows *a fortiori* that this particular kind of authority cannot constitute the fixed and unquestionable point of departure for considering questions of truth in the subjective conscience of the individual with regard to truth. Hence any appeal merely to the formal authority of the teaching office as a factor which is given and can be assumed as obvious and beyond all dispute will to a large extent be ineffective even though in itself it may, from one specific point of view, be perfectly legitimate as following logically from the faith.

Again in the situation which prevails precisely today every time the teaching office proclaims a specific doctrine of the faith it must justify its own formal authority in doing so, and it must of course do this not merely by speaking in abstract terms about its own formal authority, but by establishing the connection between the content of the individual doctrine which it promulgates and the totality of the Christian faith and the Christian interpretation of existence. It must do this in order that it may, to some extent, lighten the burden which is placed upon its own formal authority, and at the same time state the basis on which it itself rests.[70]

In other words: when an individual doctrine is promulgated by the teaching office the actual content of the truth that is proclaimed should impart credibility to the formal authority of the body which proclaims it. It should do this in virtue of the conviction which it carries of its own nature, and which is immanent within itself, and in virtue of the clear connection which it has with the totality of the faith. Moreover it must do this in a manner which is in conformity with the contemporary situation as well as the actual truth which is involved. This does not render the significance of the formal authority of the teaching office superfluous. On the contrary what we are requiring here is, as we have already said, justified on the grounds that the formal teaching authority is based on a truth which is prior to itself, and on the fact that the individual truth which is being taught can never be a truth of the faith as an isolated

---

70. It may be doubted whether all the more recent pronouncements of the Church's teaching office have in fact met this requirement.

doctrine, but must always be so only in virtue of its connection with the totality of the Christian faith in general.

If these two factors are borne in mind then the requirement which we have stated above is in a real sense self-evident; the requirement, namely, that the teaching office itself must so act as to render itself in a certain sense, and speaking approximately, more and more superfluous. This requirement is further strengthened by the fact that it would be quite untrue to say that the progressive development of the Christian faith has ever found its anchor-holds or its turning-points first and last in the teaching office as one particular institution within the totality of the Church. This is of course not to exclude the fact that in the life of the individual believer and of the Church as a whole particular situations have arisen, can arise, and will arise in the concrete in which the assurance that a specific doctrine is a genuine explicitation of the faith as a single whole is provided by the pronouncements of the teaching office.

It is not possible here to develop these considerations any further so as to show, by means of individual examples of the practice of the Church's teaching office, that in the life of the Church in the concrete it has consistently been taken for granted right from the first that these requirements must be fulfilled. Still less should our readers be left with the impression that in what has been said here everything is covered or at least touched upon which it is necessary to demand if in the contemporary crisis of authority the teaching office is to achieve what it is capable of in order to survive this crisis. The present-day situation is such that many further consequences arise from it in addition to those mentioned here which have a bearing on the continuing function of the teaching office. Thus for instance a situation has arisen today in the development of ideas in which it is necessary and inevitable that there should be a pluralism of theologies even within the one Church and in spite of the unity of her creed. This again implies a quite new situation for the exercise of the Church's teaching office, because precisely in its pronouncements and critical judgments it is quite impossible any longer to assume, that there is any one theology common to all with a single uniform language. It would even be possible to raise the further question of whether the future development of dogma in the Catholic Church, and so too the further functioning of the teaching office can or will lead to further dogmatic explicitations of individual points of doctrine which, as it were, are still waiting to be developed over and above the existing hierarchy of truths, or whether alternatively the future task of the teaching office will consist simply in preserving the basic substance of the Christian message in a far more radical and concentrated way than hitherto.

If we hold the second opinion then it will become still clearer that in the present and future situation of crisis the best and most effective way for the Church's teaching office to defend its own formal authority is for it to present itself as the official body which bears witness with the uncompromising courage and hope that arises from faith itself to that basic substance of the faith which is common to all Christians. Perhaps we ought to express this more cautiously by saying that this is what ought to be the case. If the teaching office of the Catholic Church bears witness with unwavering faithfulness to faith in God and Jesus Christ, and again and again gives fresh life to this faith, then even it has its greatest opportunity for achieving advances in the ecumenical field.

2.13 JOHN BOYLE: *NATURAL LAW AND MAGISTERIUM: CRITICAL AND CONSTRUCTIVE REFLECTIONS* – 1995

Finally, we turn to debates concerning ethics, natural law and the magisterium Nowhere has the authority of the magisterium been more publicly questioned than on matters of ethical judgement and on no topic has the discussion been more divisive than that of artifical birth control. Pope Paul VI issued the encyclical Humanae Vitae on 25 July 1968. The encyclical condemned all methods of birth control except the 'rhythm method'. Notwithstanding the fact that, it is believed, the majority of the commission which he had appointed to consider the matter, favoured acceptance of the morality of artificial contraception, Paul VI declared against it on the grounds of the sanctity of natural law. Many questions are raised by this decision, not least the understanding of natural law itself. How in this context are we to understand the ordinary magisterium? Are the Pope and the bishops alone the authentic teachers of the church or is it rather that (especially in matters of moral concern), the whole Christian community shares in the responsibility for sound moral judgement as opposed to mere obedience? There are huge issues raised for the traditional position by the results of human enquiry and the status of human knowledge in regard to moral teaching when that is assumed to be *de fide* and even a matter of revelation. The fact is that even granted that some of the natural law is revealed, the question remains how the Pope and the bishops can know with absolute certainty those parts of the natural law which are not revealed but which are accessible to human reason. Medicine, economics and politics in their influential dimensions constitute crucial areas of concern.

John P. Boyle argues that the living of a life of faith in the Spirit can be shown to have an impact upon the way in which individuals and the Christian community as a whole approach the matter of moral judgement.[71] However, he suggests, in many contexts if not all, there is need for dialogue within the Church because the function of the wider Christian community is not simply receptive but crucially participative in the making of and carrying through of the implications of moral judgement. The matter is one critically of ecclesiology which is why the shift in perception at Vatican II from a juridical to a communion model for the Church is of such vital importance for the life of the Church in itself and for its influence in the world.

THEOLOGICAL ANTHROPOLOGY

Reflecting on the scriptures, Catholic theology has described the indwelling Holy Spirit as 'uncreated grace.' Karl Rahner has written of the indwelling Spirit as a quasi-formal cause and the primary meaning of grace in human beings and their world to which God has determined to communicate himself.

---

71. John Boyle, *Church Teaching Authority: Historical and Theological Studies*, Notre Dame and London, University of Notre Dame Press, 1995, 53–62.

[T]he First Vatican Council taught that natural law was accessible to reason without the aid of grace and faith – at least in principle. However, much contemporary Catholic theology agrees with Rahner's criticism of the traditional conception of the relation of nature and grace. In Rahner's view there is in fact no nature apart from grace. God's decision to communicate himself to human beings constitutes a 'supernatural existential', i.e., a component of concrete human existence prior to any human action. Therefore the only world, the only human nature there is, is graced. Suarez's 'pure nature' is only an abstraction, a 'remainder concept' arrived at by peeling away the effects of grace by careful theological analysis. Whatever may be the possibilities of human nature in principle, the fact is we have no experience of nature apart from grace.[72]

It is the work of the Holy Spirit that produces the effects of grace ('created grace') in those who have accepted the offer of God's self-communication. The question we must address now is whether this grace affects a person's ability to know, and in particular one's ability to know what is morally right and wrong.

In an earlier study[73] I reviewed the work of Rahner and Bernard Lonergan and concluded that in their view Christian faith does indeed affect the believer's moral perception, judgment, and action. When Rahner speaks of faith and Lonergan of conversion, both are talking about a transformation of subjectivity by grace which produces an opening out of the subject's world of meaning and the transvaluation of his or her values. Such is the transformation worked by faith that the believer and the unbeliever perceive the world, meanings, and values differently. Even if their words are the same at times, their meanings are different nonetheless, since they are defined by different horizons of meaning.

This work of transformation is, of course, most conspicuous in those whose faith is explicit and who have associated themselves with the community of believers. But it should be noted here that both Rahner and Lonergan insist that God's grace is offered to every human being and that some accept the offer of grace, if only implicitly, as they follow their consciences enlightened by God's grace. Whether or not the term 'anonymous Christian' is apt, the point to be made is that the sort of transformed subject described here can surely be found outside the institution of the church.

This brief description of the transformation worked by grace in the believer also suggests a response to the questions raised earlier about the perception of things which are not said to be revealed or of things which are revealed but are not in principle inaccessible to human reason. These meanings and values, even if not revealed, are perceived more fully by one who has experienced the shift of horizon and transvaluation of values that Rahner and Lonergan describe. There is, moreover, the effect of a *gratia sanans* which heals, at least in part, the effects of sin on the understanding and the will. It follows that the effects of grace decribed here will affect not only the ability to perceive divine revelation but also the ability to perceive what is genuinely good and thus to be done or genuinely evil and to be avoided. Thus the perception of natural law, even if not revealed, is assisted by the work of grace. But a question remains whether this assistance is confined to the ordained or must be available in principle to all as conversion and grace are open to all. Moreover, it is not clear how even an appeal to

---

72. See Karl Rahner, 'Concerning the Relationship between Nature and Grace', in *Theological Investigations*, London, Darton, Longman and Todd, 1961, vol. 1, 292–317; and 'Nature and Grace' in *Nature and Grace: Dilemmas in the Modern Church*, trans. Dinah Wharton, New York: Sheed and Ward, 1964, 114–49.
73. J. Boyle, 'Faith and Christian Ethics in Rahner and Lonergan', *Thought*, 50 (1975), 247–65.

the sacramental *gratiae gratis datae* of Holy Orders could define a bishop's unique ability to know the natural law.

ETHICS

Our discussion so far has centered on the knowing subject, the community of moral discernment, and the action of the Holy Spirit upon that community's perceptions and judgments. Now we must touch on several ethical issues pertinent to our question.

We turn first to the natural law. I have reviewed elsewhere a range of views among contemporary Catholic theologians about the natural law and the appropriate method to be followed in knowing it.[74] It is neither possible nor necessary to adjudicate here disputes between those who argue for a transcendental method in defining human nature and those who follow the more traditional view that human beings can know the good to which human nature inclines and by reflecting on those inclinations can come to know moral obligation based on the dictates of reason.

Other contemporary Catholic thinkers ground moral obligation on human relationships or on objective values, especially the value of the person. The influence of Max Scheler and Dietrich von Hildebrand on these latter writers is often explicit.[75]

Any of these approaches seems consonant with the definition of Vatican I that in *principle* the natural law is accessible to human reason without the aid of grace or faith. The council's definition was aimed at traditionalism: it did not address itself to the question of fact.

Contemporary theology is also marked by a consciousness that nature is not simply a 'given' which has come just as it now is from the hand of the Creator. The historicity of the world and everything in it, human beings included, is more apparent to us than to generations past. This explains in part why the contemporary discussion of natural law has taken a transcendental turn. It seeks to locate a constant or at least a reference point in the flux of history.

In any event, many contemporary theologians insist that the natural law and the law of Christ ought not to be envisioned as two juxtaposed fields, but as two points of a continuum on which faith is the ultimate and all-encompassing degree. Other theologians see the relationship as one of sublation, with nature being taken up into the order of grace as a condition is taken up by the conditioned.

---

74. See J. Boyle, *The Sterilization Controversy*, NY, Pauplist, 1977, 30–50. See also Bruno Schuller, 'La théologie moral peut-elle se passer du droit naturel?', *La nouvelle revue théologique*, 88 (1966), 449–75, and 'Zur theologischen Diskussion über die lex naturalis', *Theologie und Philosophie*, 41 (1966), 481–503. Much attention has been given for more than two decades to the proposals of Germain Grisez for a new understanding of Thomistic natural law, conveniently summarized in the context of fundamental moral theology in his *The Way of the Lord Jesus*, vol. 1, *Christian Moral Principle*, Chicago, Franciscan Herald Press, 1983.

75. On human relationships see Hans Rotter, 'Zum Erkenntnis problem in der Moraltheologie', in *Neue Erkenntnisprobleme in Philosophie und Theologie*, J. Lotz, Freiburg, Herder, 1968, 226–47. Value theory appears in both Rahner and Lonergan; see J. Boyle, 'Faith and Christian Ethics'. On Lonergan see also F.E. Crowe, 'An Exploration of Lonergan's New Notion of Value', *Science et esprit*, 29 (1977), 123–43, and Walter E. Conn, 'Bernard Lonergan on Value', *The Thomist*, 40 (1976), 4–22.

As a logical construct, a 'natural law' is still a possibility, but in the real order there is no 'natural' morality, there is only an order of grace in which the law of Christ is the law – at least for believers.

Contemporary theologians in large part agree with Suarez and the older tradition that the 'law of Christ' adds no new material norms to the natural law. What is specific to Christian ethics must therefore lie at another level.[76]

Two points can be made at once. The first is that it is a mistake to conceive of the natural law as something which the church knows by reason alone. 'Natural Law' is the product of extended theological reflection. The second is that the authority of pronouncements by those who hold the teaching office must admit of degrees, ranging from those definitive utterances in matters of faith and morals for which the assent of faith is claimed and which are kept free of error by the charism of infallibility to those pronouncements setting out teaching based in the natural moral law which is not revealed and which demand assent short of an act of faith. Such pronouncements are held with a lesser degree of certitude.[77]

Both of these points cohere with a view of the church as a community of moral discernment and with the view of the work of the Holy Spirit in the church which transforms the knowing subject, and with [an] eschatological 'not yet'.… . It coheres too with the role we have suggested for authorized teachers in the church in dialogue with the community of faith. Their authority is grounded in the Spirit's work; it is not simply juridical.

There is one further point. Moral decisions must be made about specific concrete matters. In making such decisions a moral agent must consider all the relevant factors, including conflicting values and principles. For a member of the church community, the moral insights and convictions of that community, its view of the world, of human beings and their relationship with God will be important factors. Yet it is essential to the notion of moral agency that the agent ultimately assumes the burden and responsibility of moral decisions.

If that is true, it suggests a limit to the knowledge of the church and its authorized teachers in the field of morals, for whatever the competence of the church with respect to the natural law, the nature of moral decision would seem to exclude a notion of official teaching which can claim authority to descend to such particulars as to effectively substitute itself for the moral agency of the believer.[78]

There are other limits. Karl Rahner has written of an existential ethic, or moral commands given by God to the individual person precisely as such. Such commands are not in conflict with general moral principles, but neither are they derivable from them. Existential ethical obligations have a personal and individual character which puts them outside the limits of church authority without putting them in conflict with general moral law. Each person's conscience has the function of discerning these personal moral obligations. For our purposes the point is that there exists a field of moral obligation in harmony with general moral principles but not derived directly from them and which cannot be discerned, much less imposed, by church authority.

---

76. See, for example, Joseph Fuchs, SJ, 'Gibt es eine spezifische christliche Moral?', *Stimmen der Zeit*, 185 (1970), 99–112; English translation, 'Is There a Specifically Christian Morality?', in *Readings in Moral Theology*, no. 2, Charles E. Curran and Richard A. McCormick (eds) New York: Paulist Press, 1980, 3–19.

77. This view of the teaching authority is in contrast to an older one which drew a very hard distinction between infallible teaching and that which is only authoritative … .

78. See Elizabeth Anscombe, 'Authority in Morals', in *Problems of Authority*, John M. Todd (ed.), London and Baltimore, Darton, Longman and Todd, and Helicon, 1962, 179–88.

An ethics which looks to an adequate anthropology must also take note of what Rahner, Lonergan, and others have said about the horizon of knowledge which is transformed by grace and about the relationship between our global unthematic knowledge of moral values and the arguments we offer in defense of our moral choices. Rahner has explicated this latter aspect of our moral knowledge in his writings on moral instinct and its implications for a method of moral argument.

Rahner is interested not only in his contention that moral argument often seems to assume what it is attempting to prove, but also in the fact that moral arguments so often seem unpersuasive. These issues are akin to those treated by Bernard Lonergan in his chapter on 'dialectic' in *Method in Theology,* in which he offers an account of similar problems and proposes to deal with them in terms of differing horizons grounded in the presence or absence of his multiple conversions and also in terms of what Lonergan calls 'differentiation of consciousness'.[79]

I cannot pursue these matters here. I draw attention to them only to indicate the multiplicity of factors which affect the ability of the knowing moral agent to perceive moral values and make judgments and decisions about them. Since believers and officeholders in the church are such agents, these facets of moral knowledge affect them too.

SUMMARY: EPISTEMOLOGICAL ISSUES

We began by asking epistemological questions raised by the moral teaching of the hierarchical magisterium based on the natural law. *Humanae Vitae* is the most discussed example, but the corpus of modern Catholic social teaching is important as well. We conclude by addressing a series of epistemological issues.

1. What is it that authoritative teachers know when they know the 'natural law'?

Bruno Schuller[80] has suggested that 'natural law' be understood as the whole of those moral norms which human beings can know in a way at least logically independent of divine revelation. Moreover, the Catholic tradition asserts that moral obligation for human beings is grounded in human existence, although that is not essential to Schuller's definition of natural law.

I have pointed out that Catholic theologians today understand the natural law and the roots of moral obligation in a variety of ways. For our present interests, it is enough to hold that authoritative teachers in the church can know the moral obligations of the Christian life which are not derivable, certainly not directly, from divine revelation. I can point to the

---

79. See Boyle, 'Faith and Christian Ethics'. See also Karl Rahner, 'On Bad Arguments in Moral Theology', *Theological Investigations*, 18, New York, Crossroad, 1981; London, Darton, Longman and Todd, 1984, 74–85. In this article Rahner has further explored the role of unthematized, global moral knowledge in making moral arguments convincing or not. He again points out that the church may know moral right and wrong better than it can formulate arguments for its point of view, but he now argues that the reverse can also be true: the church may be offering arguments convincing only to those whose prethematic knowledge disposes them to accept the arguments. If that knowledge is incomplete, the arguments may in fact be bad ones. Rahner concludes to a critical – and thankless – role for moral theology vis-a-vis the moral pronouncements of the magisterium.
80. See Schuller, 'La théologie morale', and 'Zur theologischen Diskussion'.

corpus of Catholic social teaching in the nineteenth and twentieth centuries as an example, together with much Catholic sexual ethical teaching. For the most part the warrant for this teaching is explicitly the natural law, not revelation as transmitted by scripture or tradition.

It is not necessary to hold exclusively to one of the several theories of the origin and nature of natural law obligations, the ontological status of moral values, and the like to hold at least this much. What is basic is the objective, given character of moral value.[81]

I would hold further that knowledge of the natural law is a prerequisite to insight into the implications of the Christian life as this is defined by the Christian proclamation (*kerygma*). If such insights are logically independent of revelation, it remains to be explained to what extent the moral insights of bishops differ from and are more authoritative than those of others. The 1990 Instruction of the CDF at n. 16 states that the magisterium must be competent in matters of natural law 'by reason of the connection between the orders of creation and redemption' and *ratione salutis*, its necessity for salvation, so to speak. The connection between the order of creation and the order of redemption could be understood as Schuller understands it, but the Instruction does not go beyond the statement cited. Max Seckler shows that Pius XII argued for the authority of the magisterium in moral matters from the promises made by Christ to the church, while Paul VI understood the authority as having its roots in the sacrament of Holy Orders, which relates better to an argument from the relation of morals to salvation than a purely extrinsic divine command.[82] The nature and extent of the knowledge which underlies the moral teaching of the magisterium (i.e., the pope and bishops as authoritative teachers) derived from the natural law remains in urgent need of clarification.

2. Who can know about the natural law?

First, it is basic to the Catholic position on the natural law that it is accessible, at least in its general principles, to every human person. I have suggested above the problem of accounting for the influence of grace in the lives of those who are not explicitly Christians, but it is enough to define our problem to note that even unbelievers can and do know of the natural law.

Second, everyone who has received the gift of grace and faith and therefore has experienced the horizon shift effected by faith also can know the natural law – but within a quite different horizon of meanings and values. The moral perceptions of the Christian are informed moreover by his faith in Jesus Christ and acceptance of his commandments, by his experience of the demands of the kingdom of God announced by Jesus, and by the presence and power of the Holy Spirit.[83]

These are the believers whose global perception of moral values may or may not be in harmony with their enunciation of reasons for their moral judgments, as Rahner has pointed out. It is the community of these believers, with their experience of the Christian life and its demands in a changing world, which provides one side of the dialogue with church officeholders.

81. The objective nature of moral obligation is a major theme of the encyclical *Veritatis Splendor* published by Pope John Paul II, 6 August 1993. Text in *Origines*, 23 (1993), 297–334, London, Catholic Truth Society, 1993.
82. Seckler, 'Die Theologie als kerchliche Wissenschaft'.
83. See Raymond Collins, 'Scriptures and the Christian Ethic', in *Proceedings of the Catholic Theological Society*, 29 (1974), 215–41.

Third, it seems possible to speak of a kind of 'collective consciousness', a sedimentation of moral experience within the community of belief which is something larger than the experience of numerous individuals.[84] This collective or corporate consciousness extends, I would argue, not only to matters of belief and matters of practice clearly related to belief, but also to moral knowledge which is logically independent of revelation but often presupposed by it.

Fourth, the natural law is known by those who are authoritative teachers in the church. I pointed out above that these officeholders are first of all believers and members of the church community. Their knowledge is not therefore the result of personal revelation, and it is distinguished from the inspiration of the writers of scripture. Like other believers who are morally and religiously converted, officeholders have experienced a transformation of consciousness.

But in addition the officeholders who are bishops have experienced the further action of the Spirit in Holy Orders which further transforms their consciousness. In virtue of this action of the Spirit, and in dialogue with the community of believers they serve, officeholders have insights into the moral demands of the Christian life correlative to the historical situation of the world in which the community finds itself.[85]

These insights are related to their office of apostolic preaching (*kerygma*) but extend, as the example of the New Testament itself shows, to a continuation of the apostolic instruction (*didache*) as well. There is an element of mystagogy in this instruction which clearly relates to the priestly office of bishops as stewards and celebrants of the Christian mysteries. However, a purely kerygmatic notion of the authoritative teaching office of bishops does not seem adequate either to a notion of the teaching office precisely as authoritative, nor to the practice of the church, which certainly has not limited the authoritative teaching of the bishops to the apostolic kerygma.[86]

Two observations are in order. One is that the traditional distinction of the three offices of the church, prophetic, priestly, and pastoral, cannot be pressed; clearly the roles of preaching/teaching, liturgical and other priestly acting, and the pastoral direction are closely linked. The second is that both the sources and the authority of the practical pastoral directives of teachers and pastors in the church have not been adequately clarified. Karl Rahner has suggested in his essays on the pastoral constitution of Vatican II that such directives are a kind of existential ethic for the church community, recognized as representing the binding will of God by the charismatic action of the Spirit in the church. Especially those directives in the fields of politics, economics, and the like, in which the church possesses no special competence, are the church's response to the binding will of God in a particular time and place but are not conclusions drawn from general principles. Because they are God's will and are known as such, they are indeed obligatory, yet they are known only through the charismatic action of the Spirit, and therefore are not general principles binding on everyone.

---

84. H. Mühlen, *Una Persona Mystica: Eine Person in Vielen Personen*, 3rd edn, Munich, Schonigh, 1968, 74–88, discusses the problems of the notion of 'corporate personality'. Notions of the church as the Body of Christ and the People of God suggest that some such notion is widely accepted in Catholic theology.

85. Ibid., 342–58; on sacramental character, *Dei Verbum*, ch. 2, and *Lumen Gentium*, es chs. 1–3.

86. See Cardinal William W. Baum, 'Magisterium and the Life of Faith', *Origines*, 8 (1979), 76–80. The address was given to the Fellowship of Christian Scholars, 28 April 1978.

Thus they do not meet the definition of 'natural law' despite the fact that much modern church social teaching has offered the natural law as its warrant.[87]

The role of authoritative teachers in this process of formulating pastoral directives is clearly one of discernment and articulation, a function fully in harmony with the gifts of the Spirit given to bishops by their ordination … .

CONCLUSION

The very complexity of the issues of theological anthropology, ecclesiology, and ethics which arise in a study of epistemological problems assures us that no simple solution to these problems is available.

Nonetheless the inadequacy of a purely juridical approach to the magisterium and its exercise in the area of the natural law is apparent. The multiple actions and gifts of the Spirit in the church (and outside it) suggest rather that a dialogic model of magisterium is needed. In such a model the bishops' proposition of Christian belief and practice guided and protected by the Spirit is received by a community which has also received the gifts of the Spirit. It is scarcely an accident that Vatican II could teach with such confidence that the consent of the church will never be lacking to infallible teaching because of the work of the Holy Spirit.

But the function of the community is not purely receptive. The community is the bearer of revelation and it is through the experience of the community that the implications of this revelation develop in the church. Therefore the moral experience of the community is of profound religious significance, precisely because it is the experience of a community gifted by the Spirit.

This experience includes that of the natural law, however it may be precisely defined, at least as the presupposition of grace and revelation. Since this knowledge is available to the community of believers, and indeed to human beings generally, it is impossible to claim for the church community or for its authoritative teachers exclusive knowledge of natural law. That alone is reason to be cautious in claiming for church teaching based on natural law peremptory authority to silence further discussion of an issue… .

But because its knowledge is not exclusive, the church can and must appeal to the moral perceptions of its own community and of humanity generally. What our study suggests is not exclusive knowledge, but gifts of the Spirit that can enable believing individuals, the community of belief, and its authoritative teachers to have an insight into the demands of the moral life at a given time and place that may be absent in the larger community. Thus the role of the church will often be a prophetic one, calling attention to dimensions of the moral life that are neglected – as it has done in its appeals on behalf of human rights, especially of the

---

87. I have dealt with this theology of pastoral directives in *Faith and Community in the Ethical Theory of Karl Rahner and Bernard Lonergan*, Ann Arbor, University Microfilms, 1972, 97–103. The importance of this issue appeared in the drafting of the American bishops' pastoral *The Challenge of Peace* Washington: USCC, 1983, and resulted in useful distinctions being made in the text between enduring principles and their allocation to complex concrete problems. Similar distinctions appeared in the later pastoral letter on the American economy. Rahner wishes to avoid a kind of deductive approach to pastoral directives, in the conviction that the church does not have competence outside the religious sphere. Yet he recognizes that the church cannot be silent on the moral aspects of such matters as nuclear war … .

poor; of life, including that of the unborn; and of peace. Since the notion of a natural law affirms a communality of moral experience and moral judgment among human beings, that prophetic role of the church can hope to elicit a response in the larger human community.

Karl Rahner has written of the 'liberating modesty' of an attitude of the church to the world which respects its legitimate autonomy.[88] It is my judgment that a teaching authority which recognizes its own function and its own limits in the field of natural law morality will find itself both liberated from pretensions to omniscience false to the historical experience of the church and at the same time freed for a perhaps more modest but indispensable prophetic role in modern society.

---

88. Karl Rahner, 'Church and World', in *Sacramentum Mundi*, 1, 346–57.

QUESTIONS FOR DISCUSSION

The questions that require attention can be divided into three groups:

1   Those that are doctrinal. In this category one would include, those that concern revelation and the nature of the gospel itself. Given the lively purpose of the gospel to liberate and make free, any formulation of doctrine to be true must stimulate reflection and action.

2   Those that are ecclesiological. In what essential form will the lively force of the Gospel of Christ be effectively celebrated and enjoyed by all?

3   Those which arise as a result of past or present misjudgement. How do we best cope with the matter of correcting past error?

Of course, each question that we consider is likely to impinge upon the three areas which have been alluded to; no theological question is likely to be discrete in its implications or assumptions, unless it is defined so to be, or treated as a question of another kind, e.g,. historical, legal or sociological. The key affirmation which is confirmed by the readings in this section is that there are essential theological questions which involve all members of the community of faith, and which are not merely to be considered the province of those 'in authority'.

Naturally, we do not begin without guidance, neither are we left without authority; where we are is where we always have been – faithful persons seeking to make sense of their experience in the light of the revelation of God in Christ, to which we have witnesses. It is as witnesses to the gospel, that the Magisterium can be authoritative, and as the script of faith that the magisterium should be read. Thus, in reflecting upon such considerations, we consider the following questions:

1   How can the believer faithfully learn how to give appropriate weight to the teachings of the Church?

2   What can a believer be commanded to 'believe'?

3   What are the moral limits to ecclesiastical authority?

4   How can the Church teach so that the world may learn?

5   How far does true obedience depend upon genuine understanding?

6   What are the major matters on which the authority of the church is challenged by the world? Do you think they are moral, doctrinal, spiritual or intellectual?

7   What does it mean to 'share' the faith?

FURTHER READING

Curran, Charles E. and McCormick, Richard A. (eds), *The Magisterium and Morality*, New York, Paulist Press, 1982.

Curran, Charles and McCormick, Richard A. (eds), *Natural Law and Theology*, vol. 7 of Readings in Moral Theology, New York, Paulist Press, 1991.

Daly, Gabriel, 'Which Magisterium is Authentic?', in *Who Has the Say in the Church?* (eds) Jürgen Moltmann and Hans Küng, *Concilium*, 148 (1981).

Dulles, Avery, *The Survival of Dogma – Faith, Authority and Dogma in a Changing World*, New York, Crossroad, 1982.

Fries, Heinrich, 'Is there a *Magisterium* of the Faithful?', in *The Teaching Authority of the Believers*, Johann Baptist Metz and Edward Schillebeeckx (eds), *Concilium*, 180 (1985).

Gaillardetz, Richard A., *Teaching with Authority*, Collegeville, Liturgical Press, 1997.

Hogan, Linda, *Confronting the Truth – Conscience in the Catholic Tradition*, New York, Paulist Press, 2000, and London, DLT, 2001.

Lash, Nicholas, *Voices of Authority*, London, Sheed & Ward, 1976.

Lefébure, Marcus, Metz, Johann Baptist, Schillebeeckx, Edward (eds), *The Teaching Authority of Believers*, *Concilium*, Edinburgh, T & T Clark, 1985.

MacRéamoinn, Sean, *Authority in the Church*, Blackrock, Columba, 1995.

McClelland, V.A., *By Whose Authority? Newman, Manning and Magisterium*, Bath, Downside Abbey, 1996.

Moltmann, Jürgen and Küng, Hans (eds), *Who Has the Say in the Church?*, *Concilium*, 148 (1981).

Orsy, Ladislas, 'Teaching Authority' and 'Assent and Dissent', in *The Church – Learning and Teaching – Magisterium, Assent, Dissent, Academic Freedom*, Wilmington, Glazier, 1987.

Rahner, Karl, 'What is a Dogmatic Statement?', in *Later Writings*, vol. 5 of Theological *Investigations*, London, DLT, 1966.

Rahner, Karl, 'Basic Observations on the Subject of Changeable and Unchangeable Factors in the Church', 'The Faith of the Christian and the Doctrine of the Church' and 'The Dispute Concerning the Church's Teaching Office', in *Ecclesiology, Questions in the Church, the Church and the World*, vol. 14 of *Theological Investigations*, London, DLT, 1976.

Rahner, Karl, 'The Church's Responsibility for the Freedom of the Individual', in *Concern for the Church*, vol. 20 of *Theological Investigations*, London, DLT, 1981.

Ratzinger, Joseph, 'Freedom and Constraint in the Church', ch. 10 of *Church, Ecumenism and Politics*, Slough, St Paul's, 1987.

Sanks, T. Howland, *Authority in the Church – A Study in Changing Paradigms*, Missoula, Scholars, 1974.

Sullivan, Francis A., *Magisterium – Teaching Authority in the Roman Catholic Church*, Dublin, Gill & Macmillan, 1983 (esp. ch. 2, 'Magisterium').

Part 3:

Synodality and Collegiality – the Dynamics of Authority

Jan Kerkhofs

Christians cannot forget that, according to John, Jesus called his disciples not 'servants' but 'friends'. When friends meet, they talk, they listen to one another, particularly when they have to take decisions. This attitude has characterized the early church and lasted for several centuries. The first communities were very small; at the end of the first century experts count not more than 7500 Christians around the Mediterranean. However, when the number of Christians increased and the church became more linked with secular powers, the relationships amongst Christians copied the feudal ones. The original model did continue, more or less successfully, in the religious orders where the members considered one another as 'brothers' and 'sisters'. St Benedict stated in his rule that even the opinion of the youngest member in the community had to be taken into account.

'Synodos' means that people are 'together on the road' and 'concilium' implies an open exchange of views in order to promote the life of the entire community. According to the Acts of the Apostles the community had its say in the co-optation of Matthias by the Eleven (1:21–6), as also in the choice of Stephen and his six colleagues (6:5–6), and further when Barnabas had to be sent to Antioch (11:22). In his Letter to the Corinthians (around 96) Clement of Rome writes that the apostles 'and other prominent men' appointed the leaders of the community 'with the agreement of the whole Church'. This model became a tradition. The Didachè (end of the first century) invites the Christians as follows: 'You should choose bishops and deacons worthy of Lord.' The Apostolic Tradition of Hippolyte of Rome (around 230) states 'that the one elected by the whole people should be consecrated bishop', a formula repeated in the fourth century in the Apostolic Constitutions. At the beginning of the fifth century Pope Celestine I declares as a general rule: 'One should not impose upon the people a bishop it doesn't want' (Ep. 4:5). Afterwards Pope Leo I (the Great) said the same: 'He who has to preside over all, should be elected by all' (Ep. 10:4). Paulinus of Nola (d. 431) uses a strong argument: 'We have to take into account every believer, that in everyone it is the Spirit who inspires.' Even authoritarian popes such as Innocent III (1198–1216) and Boniface VIII (1294–1303) have kept the old principle: 'What concerns all, should be discussed and approved by all' ('Quod omnes tangit, ab omnibus tractari et approbari debet'). It is only in the fourteenth century, with Boniface VIII, that the idea of an absolute pontifical monarchy is imposed, so unilaterally expressed by Pius IX.

But still the tradition of chapters and councils was not lost. In particular, Vatican II reaffirmed the importance of dialogue in the church, as well as the dialogue of the Roman Catholic church with the other Churches and with the world. It appears symbolic that in the doctrinal constitution *Lumen Gentium* the chapter on the 'People of God' was put before the one on the hierarchy. Most important is also that the Council mentioned in many places the presence of the Spirit in the life of the church, a Spirit at work in all its members. In this context one has to interpret the many places where the Council stresses the role of consultative bodies, such as priestly senates, parish councils, and diocesan pastoral councils for implementing the synodality of the church. The *motu proprio, Apostolica sollicitudo* (1965), of Pope Paul VI introduced the Roman Episcopal Synods, mainly as a tool meant to strengthen the mutual listening of the leaders of the church with the aim of continuing the spirit of the Council. After Vatican II several countries did organize national Synods (as in Denmark, Germany, Switzerland, Austria), diocesan Synods (as in France, Italy, Spain, Poland, etc.) or other interdiocesan pastoral encounters (as in the Netherlands, USA, England, Flanders and Wallonia in Belgium). Through them a large number of Catholics became involved in the application of the decisions of the Council. Until the mid-1970s this movement towards a more open dialogue has raised enthusiasm and hope for many.

However, soon caution and polarization reappeared. Theologians as well as church leaders had to struggle with the challenge of combining the letter and the spirit of Vatican I with those of Vatican II. Many became afraid of a too great demand for democratization in the church, while other groups went too far in their promotion of participation. Some were concerned about the rights of minorities, even proclaiming that often the minority is right and the majority wrong. At every level, certain groups wanted a return to Vatican I, while others, aware of the acceleration of history, supported the convoking of a Vatican III. In many local churches the dialogue came to a standstill. Many, in Europe at least, were so disappointed that they left the church.

One has to admit that, for a church, 'participation' is not a simple task. History teaches us that no initiative promoting 'conciliarism' has succeeded. The church cannot simply copy the democratic procedures of secular states. It will always try to obtain a certain unanimity, as has been the case at Vatican II (as opposed to Vatican I). It has to avoid what happened in France which, in 1875, became a Republic by 353 votes in the *Assemblée Nationale* in favour with 352 opposed, or in Canada, where it was decided in 1995 not to split with Quebec by a difference of only 1 per cent of the votes. The church is faced with the obligation to foster participation as well as to protect the unity of the flock. The difficulty of combining both, and the tensions involved in so doing have been developed in many theological publications.

3.1 PIUS X: *VEHEMENTER NOS* – 1906

Pius, a saint and a very committed pastor, feared any renewal in the church, and thus those biblical scholars (such as Lagrange) and church historians (e.g., Duchesne) who tried to open the atmosphere and enter into dialogue with modern sciences. This explains his concern for a strong hierarchical structure. Read after Vatican II, the following excerpt from his encyclical[1] reveals a fundamental change in the ecclesiological climate.

❀

… It follows that the Church is essentially an *unequal* society, that is, a society comprising two categories of persons, the Pastors and the flock, those who occupy a rank in the different degrees of the hierarchy and the multitude of the faithful. So distinct are these categories that with the pastoral body only rests the necessary right and authority for promoting the end of the society and directing all its members towards that end; the one duty of the multitude is to allow themselves to be led, and, like a docile flock, to follow the Pastors … [8].

---

1. ET from *The Holy Father, Archives of the Holy See*, www.vatican.va/archive/holy_father/pius_x/encyclicals.

3.2 RUDOLF SCHNACKENBURG: COMMUNITY CO-OPERATION IN THE NEW TESTAMENT – 1972

Here[2] we see the nature of service and leadership in the early church outlined, with the hope of contributing to debates in recent decades. In particular, Schnackenburg wishes to show how co-operation and co-responsibility were fundamental features of life in the earliest Christian communities, along with the importance of the notion of 'brotherhood' to continuous ecclesial reform.

❀

How can lay people (the majority of the people of God) share, in full co-responsibility, in the decisions of the Church? This is one of the most urgent questions confronting Christians today; any attempt to answer it in the light of the New Testament must be based on examination of the special relationships prevailing when the Church was founded.

The risen Lord had given full power to the apostles to proclaim the Gospel, and they were the first to call the Christian communities into being. Their own call gave them a very special position in the early communities, although, being active in missionary work, they did not live permanently in those local communities, and so did not act as leaders in the way that others were able to do later in the history of the Church. The early communities had to evolve their own way of life and to create their own structures for this purpose. The communities were differently structured and organised. There was relatively little contact between them, and so considerable pluriformity. In some, those with charismatic gifts provided the necessary services. In others, those who would 'labour' among their brothers (see I Thess. 5:12) had to be found to devote their time and strength to local problems. Because each community was so distinctive, it is difficult to find a common denominator for the life and attitude of them all.

Our knowledge is very incomplete. Paul's letters offer only an imperfect insight into the relationship with the communities he established, and our main source of information concerning the community of Jerusalem is open to suspicion because – imperceptibly – the author of the Acts of the Apostles included in his account the relationships prevailing in his own times. All the other written material is early post-apostolic and therefore cannot give us satisfactory answers. But we can venture a few comments which may help us to draw some cautious conclusions with a bearing on the present problem. Although we should really begin with the letters of Paul, which are earlier in date and more reliable, I have decided to consider first the evidence in Acts, because of the importance of the 'primitive community of Jerusalem' for the present question.

---

2. 'Community Co-operation in the New Testament', in G. Alberigo and A. Weiler (eds), *Election, Consensus, Reception, Concilium*, 7 (1972), 5, 9–19.

Before Pentecost, Matthias was elected as one of the twelve to replace Judas at a meeting in the community. He was not freely chosen by the members of the community, but, by 'casting lots', was elected by the Lord (Acts 1:15–26). Several aspects of this account, which was shaped by the author (Peter's address), but not freely devised by him (the two candidates named), are, however, worth noting. Peter assembles not only the other members of the circle of twelve, but also all the 'brethren ... about a hundred and twenty', so that all the believers, including women (see 1:14), take part. They are told why the election is held, nominate two candidates (or at least consent to the nomination) and acknowledge the result as the Lord's decision. The whole unique process can hardly have been invented by the author. Memory of Jesus' having chosen from his disciples 'twelve, whom he named apostles' (Luke 6:13) undoubtedly played a part here, but choice by casting lots, which was a common Jewish practice in the temple cult, points, together with the names, to a Jewish-Christian tradition.

The sharing of the whole community in the appointment of the seven in Acts 6:1–6 is even more clearly revealed. The 'seven' were certainly not simply chosen to look after the poor, but, like the 'apostles', had the task of proclaiming the word as independent leaders of the Jewish-Hellenistic group in the community of Jerusalem. The author seems to place these seven men under the authority of the apostles (6:6) but in his report attempts to reconcile any possible tensions. He also states explicitly that the 'twelve' summoned an assembly of all the brothers (6:2) and proposed that the seven should be nominated (6:3). The whole community consented to the appointment and chose the seven, who were then named (6:5). This is a clear case of co-operation by consensus and choice.

The 'Council of Jerusalem' (Acts 15) followed a somewhat different course. The delegates from the predominantly gentile community at Antioch, Paul and Barnabas (15:3), were welcomed by the community and 'the apostles and elders' in Jerusalem, but some converts from Judaism demanded that the gentile Christians should be circumcised (15:5). This was, of course, a question of the utmost importance for the future of the mission. The council was composed of 'apostles and elders' (15:6, 22, 23). Is the author simply recording his own views here, or are we to give credence to what he says, especially from the historical point of view?

It is not clear what part the 'apostles' played in the community of Jerusalem: only Peter and James spoke at the council. The 'elders' or 'presbyters', however, are especially interesting. Although Luke says that such presbyters were appointed in Paul's communities (14:23), this statement cannot be historically correct, at least as a title for the office these men occupied, because Paul does not tell us about 'presbyters'; it is therefore possible that the author of *Acts* used a word current in his own period and environment for an office in the community of Jerusalem.

There are, however, serious counter-arguments. The office of 'elder' was a very old Jewish institution. The elders were representatives of the 'community of the Lord', which had, the Jews believed, to regulate its own affairs. It is possible, then, that the 'Hebrews' in the community of Jerusalem also chose representatives on the model of the 'Hellenists'. Certainly these 'elders' do not feature very prominently in *Acts*. Although they are only mentioned once later with James (21:18), they have the important task of persuading Paul to dissipate the growing mistrust of his teaching by accepting the four Nazarites (21:20–26). It appears that the 'elders' supported James here, acting as an authoritative consultative body with the power of taking joint decisions. It is possible, therefore, that the author mentioned the 'apostles' summarily in Acts 15, but that the circle of the twelve was already in the course of breaking up, while a new structure with James as leader and the elders as representatives of the community was already being formed in Jerusalem.

The decision not to insist on the circumcision of the gentile converts was taken by the whole assembly after James's important vote. The author says: 'It seemed good to the apostles and elders, with the whole church, to choose men from among them and send them to Antioch … ' (15:22), but the decree reads simply: 'The brethren, both the apostles and the elders, to the brethren … in Antioch … greetings.' The second statement is more exact, because the elders were the representatives of the whole community. In any case, there can be no doubt that the whole community gave its consent, even if we refer to the passage in Gal. 2, where Paul speaks of those 'who were of repute' (*hoi dokountes*) or of the 'pillars', James, Cephas and John, who had given their consent to the decision not to impose circumcision on the gentile converts (2:6; see also 2:9). In the course of his argument, however, Paul stresses how important it is for his apostolate to be independent of that of the earlier apostles (*pro emou apostolous*, 1:17; see also 1:19). The community could be included in *autois* (2:2a) because Paul laid down his gospel before 'those who were of repute' (*kat' idian*, 2:2b). Although the Pauline text is in many ways not clear, we cannot conclude that the community of Jerusalem was not asked to give its consent. In the Acts of the Apostles, this consensus was confirmed by sending Judas (Barsabas) and Silas, 'leading men among the brethren', to Antioch (15:22) … .

[Schnackenburg describes then, more briefly, the co-operation in the Pauline communities, in the communities in the Gospel of Matthew and later developments, before concluding]:

In the struggle against false teaching, however, those who held office and were committed to the sound teaching of the apostolic tradition were bound to gain in significance. This led to a development in which, from the second century onwards, the communities tended more and more to become separated into 'shepherds and flocks', with an increasing stress on the 'monarchical' episcopate. None the less, the co-operation and co-responsibility of the whole community, so prominent in New Testament times, were indispensable elements in the life of the Church, which must be taken even more seriously into account today. The fundamental idea of 'brotherhood' has to be seen as a constant call to renewal in the Church.

3.3 HERWI RIKHOF: *VATICAN II AND THE COLLEGIALITY OF BISHOPS* – 1994

Our extract[3] deals with the ambiguity of *Lumen Gentium* nos 22 and 23, particularly in relation to the very concept of collegiality. The constitution's salvation-historical framework places the issue in the context of ecclesiology on the one hand. Yet, on the other, it also contains much obscurity and indicates much tension concerning the notion of collegiality, itself. Perhaps, Rikhof suggests, such tensions have been with the church throughout history. Nonetheless, the time has come for them to be resolved in reality, as much as principle, so that collegiality may be given that greater importance in the church which contemporary ecclesial considerations demand.

❀

If we look in the documents of Vatican II for texts in which the collegiality of bishops is discussed, two documents seem to be relevant: the dogmatic Constitution on the Church, *Lumen gentium* (1964) and the Decree on the Pastoral Office of the Bishops in the Church, *Christus Dominus* (1965). Of these two documents the former has a more important status. Moreover on the issue of collegiality there are no great differences between *Christus Dominus* and *Lumen gentium; Lumen gentium* is cited explicitly and with approval in *Christus Dominus.* Therefore in what follows we concentrate on a reading of *Lumen gentium*, paragraphs 22 and 23 … .

Both paragraphs, which deal with the collegiality of bishops, are in the third chapter of the Constitution, after three paragraphs which deal with the origin of the episcopate and before the paragraphs on the threefold task of the bishops and those on priests and deacons. This means that the theme of collegiality occupies a prominent place: what is held in common comes before the individual elements (task) or the distinguishing features (priests, deacons). This structure reflects the structure of *Lumen gentium* as a whole. In other words, the constitution's view of the Church generally, the characteristic of which is that what is held in common has priority over marks of differentiation, is expressed in reflection on the ministry.

But the parallels with this view of the Church and its influence go even further. In the Constitution, that which is held in common is set within a theological or salvation-historical approach to the Church. This approach is called theological or salvation-historical because a link with the saving actions of God, Father, Son and Spirit, in history has a central place in it.

Characteristic of this approach is attention on the one hand to the 'inner dimension', to grace and salvation, and on the other to its historical manifestation. This new view, which may in fact claim to be the oldest and most important within the history of the Church, can also be described as a view of *communio*. It is logical that when an important question is discussed

---

3. 'Vatican II and the Collegiality of Bishops', in J. Provost and K. Walf (eds), *Collegiality put to the Test*, in *Concilium* (1990/4), 3–17.

within the framework of such a view, this view should make itself felt in the presentation and the argument. In other words, the salvation-historical framework determines which aspects are noted and given attention, and also what is accepted as an argument.

Now in the first paragraphs, the origin of the episcopate is described in terms both of its historical roots and of its sacramental character, and in this way the broad theological framework of the *communio* view is taken up. And this framework returns when there is express mention of the college of bishops: the first part of 22 is a repetition and summary of 19–21. The structure of the whole of *Lumen gentium* and its far-reaching theological consequences thus define not only the point at which the episcopate is spoken of (after the people of God) but also what is said about the episcopate itself. In this way great weight is attached to collegiality and it is given an extra foundation: the collegiality of the bishops is not primarily (or, to put it less strongly, not just) a question of bishops or a view of the ministry, but primarily (or also) a question of the Church or a view of the Church. The collegiality of bishops belongs in a Church as community, or, to put it even more strongly: the two cannot be separated.

The paragraph about the college of bishops and its head (22) can be divided into three sections: one on origins, one on power and the relationship of authority within the college, and one on the exercising of power by the college. In the section on origins, a connection is made between the college of bishops and the college of apostles, and a number of historical facts in the practice of the Church are recalled. The ecumenical councils are said to be the clearest evidence. Membership of the college is located in consecration and communion with the head and members of the college. In the section on authority it is said of both college and pope that they have supreme and complete power within the Church. On relationships, it is ruled that the college has no authority without the pope, who can always exercise his power freely. In the last section it is stated that the college expresses both difference and unity and exercises its power in the ecumenical council, though other forms of collegial action are possible.

The paragraph on relationships within the college (23) can also be divided into three sections. The first section deals with the link between the bishop and the local Church, in which the bishop is the foundation of the unity of the local Church and represents it: the one Catholic Church exists through and in the local Churches, and the college of bishops with the pope represents the whole Church. The second section discusses the care of all bishops, as members of the college, for the whole Church, this care being extended to both those who are members of the Church and to those who are not. In the third section attention is paid to the difference in traditions which has developed through history and to contemporary possibilities of collegiality. These three sections are connected with what has gone before by the observation that the solidarity of the college is also expressed in the mutual relationships of the bishops. …

[Rikhof describes further how the Constitution tries to combine this view with Vatican I, where the power of the pope is so strongly stressed, and he continues]:

The tension emerges most clearly in the part about the authority of the college of bishops. The course of the argument and the way in which it is put are revealing. This part begins with a sentence in which the use of 'however' (*autem*) suggests a contrast with what has gone before.

In the preceding section the existence and importance of the college is indicated with reference to scripture and tradition. Moreover a negative phrase is used in the main sentence: the college has no authority (*auctoritatem non habet*). The subordinate clause which indicates the conditions on which authority is spoken of is dominated by 'the pope of Rome', who is said to be Peter's successor and head of the college; it is also said that this primacy over leaders and believers remains unassailed. In this first sentence it is also striking that the verbs of the main clause and the subordinate clause do not match: 'have authority' and 'understand'. In the subordinate clause one would expect a verb like 'function', or in the main clause a formula which has something to do with 'understanding' rather than 'have no authority' … .

[Rikhof concludes his analysis by stating]:

So this reading discloses a text full of obscurities, contrary movements and unresolved tensions. Central to it is the framework within which the collegiality is expressed. Is this observation the last word, or can and must not more be said, if prehistory and intention are also involved in the reading? …

[He tries then to dig deeper in the history of the drafting of *Lumen Gentium* and in the intention of its writers. His conclusion is somehow disturbing]:

It emerges from a reading of *Lumen gentium* 22–23 that the text does not give a clear and unambiguous view of the place and content of collegiality. It emerges from the analysis of the prehistory that the tension was always there and has deep roots. From an analysis of the intention it emerges that in principle the opposed movements need to be resolved in the direction of a view in which the central place of collegiality is given full weight. It must emerge from history subsequent to the council whether this solution in principle has also become reality.

3.4 JOSEPH RATZINGER: *THE PASTORAL IMPLICATIONS OF EPISCOPAL COLLEGIALITY* – 1965

In 1965, Ratzinger, at the time still teaching theology at the university of Münster, wrote this long article in *The Church and Mankind*, the first issue of *Concilium* (pp. 39–67).[4] Later he qualified and, in my opinion, changed his position, as we will see by comparing the following excerpts with the 'Motu proprio' *Apostolos suos* of John-Paul II, a text basically inspired by Ratzinger himself.

❁

… At the very outset, it must be stated that the doctrine of the collegiality of bishops is based on two historical facts.

1   THE COLLEGIALITY OF THE APOSTLES

The first is the collegial character of the apostolic office which first appeared as the office of 'the twelve' even before it became, as a result of the events of Pentecost, an office involving a mission, an 'apostolate' in the strict sense of the word. Today exegetical research has brought forth two concepts: 'the twelve' and 'the apostles', of which the first is older and the latter must be regarded as originating after Pentecost … .

Let us dwell briefly on the original task: the eschatological sign of the number twelve. We deduced from this that the first 'office' in the growth of the nascent Church was to signify the new community since the office was connected with the number. The office existed only in the communal union of the group, each individual member had his significance only in union with the others of the group. Two more notes will have to be added since the symbolic meaning of 'the twelve' is the symbolic anticipation of the final restoration of Israel after the pattern of the symbolic actions of the Old Testament prophets.

If this is true, then these men represent not only the future bishops and officials but also, indeed primarily, the 'new people' that will be called the 'Church'. This no doubt presents certain difficulties for theologians because without further investigation they will not be able to determine whether any tasks assigned by Jesus to the apostles were meant only for the future officials or were addressed to 'the twelve' as the representatives of the faithful.

It is a principle of Protestant exegesis to accept the latter explanation and to see in it an important support of their doctrine of the universal priesthood of all believers. It overlooks the fact, however, that 'the twelve', even during the life of Christ, were a group apart and clearly showed thereby the special position of the office. On the other hand, Catholic exegesis

---

4. 'The Pastoral Implications of Episcopal Collegiality', in *The Church and Mankind, Concilium* (1965/1), 39–67.

is in danger of forgetting that in another respect 'the twelve' stand for the whole Church and represent the unity between office and community, which we may conceive to be a new note of the office instituted by Christ. This is closely connected with the last mark to be discussed here: the eschatological character of the office … .

The declaration in which Vatican II, following the tradition of the Church, designates the apostles as a *collegium* may be considered an interpretation of the community character that was proper to the original office of 'the twelve' as shown above. The interpretation here means a transfer to a new set of concepts. The situation of Israel at the time of Christ was unknown to the Christians from the gentile world. An attempt was made to express the original community of the apostolic office in the juridical concept of *collegium*. Vatican II has taken this thought of the patristic age, which – to be rightly understood – must be seen against the background of its biblical origin, since the term *collegium* alone fails to convey the fullness of its meaning.

2 THE COLLEGIAL CHARACTER OF THE ECCLESIASTICAL OFFICE IN THE ANCIENT CHURCH

We come to the second historical basis for the doctrine of collegiality. The first, we repeat, is the collegial character of the original office of the twelve apostles who only together are what they are supposed to be, namely, a sign of the eschatological Israel of God. One might be tempted to construct the following syllogism: Since the office of the apostles is collegial and the bishops are the successors of the apostles, the bishops are also collegial insofar as their *collegium* has taken the place of the *collegium* of the apostles. And just as each apostle has his function by belonging to the others who together with him formed the apostolic community, so each bishop has his office only by belonging to the *collegium* which is the post-apostolic continuation of the apostles.

This syllogism is indeed a summary of the whole doctrine of the collegiality of bishops. But by itself it is insufficient to support the doctrine because the decisive realities of the Church are not a matter of conclusions but of historical facts. This syllogism has value only insofar as it is an explanation of the historical development of the ecclesiastical office in the ancient Church.

This process is the second pillar of the concept of collegiality.

A rough sketch may again suffice. While in the books of the New Testament we find the ecclesiastical offices still in the fluid state of formation, we see them at the threshold of the post-apostolic era in St. Ignatius (d. not later than 117) fully developed in the form which, for the Catholic Church, has remained the basic structure: bishop – presbyter – deacon; the office of the priest and deacon being collegial, while the bishop represents the community of the faithful. As St. Ignatius states in his letter to the Philadelphians: 'Be zealous, then, in the observance of the one Eucharist. For there is one flesh of our Lord, Jesus Christ, and one chalice that brings union in his blood. There is one altar, as there is one bishop with the priests and deacons, who are my fellow workers … .'[5]

---

5. [4:1].

To understand this situation correctly one must not forget that this threefold office, terminating in the bishop as its unifying summit, describes the structure of the individual local Churches. This is significant for two reasons. It shows that for the early Christians the word *ecclesia* meant first of all and most conspicuously the local Church. In other words, the Church is realised immediately and primarily in the individual local churches which are not separate parts of a larger administrative organisation but rather embody the totality of the reality which is 'the Church'.

The local Churches are not administrative units of a huge apparatus but living cells, each of which contains the whole living mystery of the one body of the Church: each one may rightly be called *ecclesia*. We may then conclude that the one Church of God consists of the individual Churches, each of which represents the whole Church ... .

The individual Church is indeed a closed totality that embraces the full essence of the Church of God, but it is at the same time open in all directions through the bond of communion. It is only through this openness, by being caught up in this network of communion, that it can maintain its reality as a Church. The closed and complete character of the local Church must not mean separation; its integrity involves openness, unity through mutual communication. We might also say that unity in the ancient Church is characterised by the two elements of 'catholicity', the communion of all the Churches among themselves, and 'apostolicity', *i.e.*, the episcopal principle. Here the intimate connection of the two principles becomes immediately evident, for the bishop is bishop only by being in communion with the other bishops. Catholicity is impossible without apostolicity and vice versa ... .

In line with our argument, the episcopal office in the ancient Church is related to the community of bishops, and the individual bishop can have his episcopacy in no other way than in his communion with the other bishops. The discussions of Vatican II and the wholesome necessity resulting therefrom of considering the data of tradition have developed many proofs for this thesis. A few examples may suffice. In assuming his office the individual bishop must ascertain his *koinonia* with the other bishops, without which he cannot exercise his episcopal office. The very fact that he must be consecrated by at least three bishops signifies that he is being received by the community into the community.

Above all, it can be shown that the bishops of the ancient Church were intensely conscious of their responsibility for the whole Church. This led to the many forms of their common care for the whole Church ... . We must mention also the early custom of bishops' synods in which all the more important matters were treated 'collegially'.

As a matter of fact, the word *collegium* itself appears in the 3rd century as a designation for all the bishops as well as of partial communities within the episcopate, although such other expressions as *ordo, corpus* and *fraternitas* are also in use. This variety of concepts is significant because it shows the insufficiency of the categories offered by Roman law and contemporary philosophy to express adequately the reality of the communal character of the episcopal office. Hence, various concepts were used which, by approaching the subject from various sides, sought to approximate and clarify its meaning. The same search is also of importance for our discussion today ...

The objection that the concept *collegium* cannot be taken in a juridical and consequently binding sense for the Church, only goes to show the inner limitation of this notion. In fact, it is only one among several definitions, none of which alone adequately describes what is meant. The use of this word in the history of the Church plainly shows this. It reveals, moreover, that the very rise of the idea of collegiality marks a shrinking of a spiritual understanding originally much richer and wider. A mere indication of the problem must suffice.

In the first two centuries all classes of Christians addressed one another as brothers and sisters in view of the word of the Lord: 'Do not you be called 'Rabbi', for one is your Master, and all you are brothers. And call no one on earth your father; for one is your Father who is in heaven' (Matt. 23:8f.). Accordingly, the individual Church communities called themselves *adelphotês*, i.e., community of brothers. This usage became frequent in the 3rd century … .

A second contraction or change takes place when the word 'brother', which breathes the simplicity of the Gospel and its disregard of officialdom, is gradually replaced by the formal title of *collega* taken over from Roman law. Simultaneously the word *fraternitas* is discarded in favour of the word *collegium* which we find in the 4th and 5th centuries as the current designation for the community of bishops. Also, the other terms that are now in use, such as *ordo* and *corpus*, are taken from the language of the law and indicate the same development.

Considering these facts one might be tempted to say that the rediscovery of the concept of collegiality by the theologians and the Church assembled in the Council is a great gain because in it the basic structure of the undivided Church of the patristic age has become visible. There is, however, the danger of stopping short at the already somewhat hardened structure of the 5th century, instead of going all the way so as to discover behind the closed and juridically fixed *collegium episcoporum*, the brother-relationship pervading the whole Church as its sustaining foundation. Collegiality can unfold its full fruitfulness only when it is related back to the fundamental reality of those who through 'the First-born of the Father' became brothers.

3 COLLEGIALITY OF THE BISHOPS AND PRIMACY OF THE POPE

Before taking up the question of the pastoral fruitfulness of the doctrine of collegiality, we must first deal with another question which no doubt has come in the reader's mind, namely, does this conception of the structure of the Church not disregard for all practical purposes the Catholic doctrine of the primacy of the Roman bishop or, at least, largely empty it of its meaning? What function can the primacy have here? At Vatican II similar questions were the main reason for the vehement opposition to the doctrine of the collegiality of the episcopal office. As a result of the controversy over this objection, the problems inherent in collegiality, its connection with the brother-relationship of the whole Church and similar problems were not sufficiently considered. After all the theological work already done in the discussions of this question, our answer may be brief.

The doctrine of the collegiality of the bishops will bring some modifications, by no means unimportant, of certain presentations of the doctrine of the primacy, but it will not nullify it. Instead, it will point up its central theological significance. This may make it more understandable to our Orthodox brethren. The primacy cannot be patterned on the model of an absolute monarchy as if the pope were the unrestricted monarch of a centrally constituted, supernatural State called Church; but it means that within the network of the Churches communicating and thus forming the Church of God there is one official point, the *Sedes Romana*, by which the unity of faith and communion must be orientated.

This official centre of the collegiality of bishops is not the result of a human need or purpose (although it might be suggested also by such reflection); but exists because the Lord himself established, beside and together with the office of 'the twelve', also the special office of the Rock. To the eschatological sign of 'the twelve' is added the sign of the Rock which is likewise taken from the eschatological symbolism of Israel. From these resulted, after the resurrection of Christ, the twofold office: the office of the witnesses and the office of the first witness in which St. Peter figures in the resurrection accounts and in the lists of the apostles. Through the theology of St. Irenaeus (which, unfortunately, was later largely forgotten) this view became the theological conception the early Catholic Church had of itself. This view contains the foundation of a fully consistent doctrine of the primacy, altogether consonant with its biblical origin.

We cannot develop these thoughts more fully here. For our purposes it may be enough to state that the primacy of the bishop of Rome in its original meaning is not opposed to the collegial character of the Church but is a primacy of communion in the midst of the Church living as a community and understanding itself as such. It means, we repeat, the faculty and the right to decide authoritatively, within the network of communication, where the Word of the Lord is witnessed correctly, and consequently, where there is true communion. It presupposes the *communio ecclesiarum* and can be understood correctly only in reference to it.

4   THE PASTORAL IMPLICATIONS OF THE DOGMATIC STATEMENT

We come at last to the question of the pastoral implications of the doctrine of collegiality. We purposely say 'implications', not practical application or some similar phrase. The pastoral concerns are not merely a pious gloss added to the dogma, but dogma itself implies pastoral problems. In other words, the doctrine of collegiality of the episcopal office and, with it, of the Church itself is not just a theory for specialists but a dogmatic statement and one immediately related to men and to the realities of life in the Church ... .

1   'I' AND 'WE' IN THE CHURCH

One becomes a bishop, as we have seen by entering in the community of bishops. In other words, the episcopal office exists essentially always in plural, a 'We', which gives significance to the individual 'I'. To enter upon a spiritual office, to which is entrusted the orderly function of the Church of God, means to fit oneself into a 'We', which as a whole carries on the apostolic heritage. Community – being united with one another, having respect for one another, working with one another – these are essential to the structure of his office in the Church.

It seems to me that something very important emerges here, a situation of very general and far-reaching significance that enlightens the whole structure of Christian realities. Although the Christian faith has pointed up the importance of the individual who is called to eternal life, yet the 'I' is in all things fitted into a more comprehensive 'We' from which and for which it lives. We may perhaps say that this pluralistic structure of Christian life and the spiritual office in its ultimate depth is related to the triune God in whom the eternal God, without injury to his indivisible unity and oneness, comprises the 'We' of the Father, the Son and the Holy Spirit; a God who is one not in the formless unity of a rigid monad but in the plentiful reality of infinite love … .

It seems to me that putting the declarations of Vatican II into ecclesiastical practice ushers in an important task. The proper appreciation of this will depend on whether or not the renewal of the doctrine of collegiality will result in a reform of the Church. For, against this doctrine, fears have already been voiced on the part of Protestants lest it lead to a yet greater clericalism in the Church and thus deepens the chasm between separated Christians. It is feared that the increased importance of the episcopacy may lead to a further lessening of the importance of the priesthood and especially of the laity in the Church.

This danger will be effectively obviated only if the increased importance of the bishops is understood as giving increased importance to the Churches entrusted to them; if the individual bishop, enmeshed in the college of bishops who are guiding the Church of God, in his turn knows himself obligated to a brotherly union with his presbyters and community. In other words, collegiality of the bishops fulfils its meaning only if the individual bishop really and truthfully represents his individual Church and thus, through him, a part of the Church's plenitude is inserted into the totality of the Church's unity.

Thus, it will be an important obligation to insure that the increased importance of the episcopal office does not result in making individual bishops little popes, as it were, by increasing and strengthening their monarchical powers; rather, they must be placed more clearly in the multiple relationship with their brethren with whom they govern the Church of God. Against this background the character of service and the ultimately pastoral meaning of the bishop's office will be seen. The bishop is related on the one hand to his brethren in the same office, but also to his brothers and sisters in the same race who are, like himself, baptised in the name of Christ. He can meet his episcopal brethren in the right way only if he always comes to them from the brotherly union of those who have the same faith … .

2   THE MYSTICAL AND EUCHARISTIC BODY OF CHRIST

From about the 12th century on, a distinction is made in the episcopal office between the *ordo* and *jurisdictio*, i.e. between the power of ordination and the power of governing. The power of ordination is then, particularly related to the 'true Body of Christ' in the holy Eucharist in which the priest, by virtue of his *ordo*, consecrates the bread in the holy mass, while the power of jurisdiction is said to be related to 'the Mystical Body of Christ'.

It should be noted that because of this view medieval theology denied that episcopal consecration was a separate degree of the sacrament of holy orders, since in the ordination of the priest the full power of eucharistic consecration was conferred, to which nothing could be added. Today, in the light of biblical and patristic studies, we consider the distinction, if not insignificant, at least insufficient. Mentioned several times in our discussion of collegiality, its clarification from this point of view entails far-reaching consequences ... .

It would seem that the thesis that the *ordo* is related only to the *corpus eucharisticum* and has nothing to do with 'collegiality' will have to be turned around so as to read: if and because the *ordo* is related to the eucharist its whole function is related to *koinonia* which is the contents of the eucharist and the original concept of 'collegiality' in one. This can be proved even by the very usage of the terms inasmuch as the word *ordo* originally was an alternate for *collegium*. In pagan Rome the word *ordo* designated the estates of classes of the people where the *ordo amplissimus* of the senate was placed over against the *populus Romanus, ordo et plebs, ordo et populus* were current expressions where *ordo* signifies those who govern the city.

In the formula *nos et plebs tua sancta* of the canon of the Roman mass we have an echo of this conception in the spirit of which was coined the expression *ordo episcoporum* which declares that the bishops are an estate, a community, a *collegium*. The very idea of sacrament contains the idea of community. The sacrament is not a physical entity to which is ordered a separate power of jurisdiction; it is itself the builder of a new community and is meant to serve the community ... .

UNITY IN PLURALITY

'Collegiality' applies not only to the episcopal office but to the structure of the whole Church. It means that the one Church is built up through the communion of the many Churches and that, consequently, unity of the Church essentially comprises the element of plurality and plenitude. This has always been known as a principle but has not always been sufficiently respected in practice. A Protestant theologian in Germany some years ago coined the formula: the unitary Church prevents the unity of the Church. Though this statement is extreme, it cannot be denied all justification. The unity of the spirit can be preserved only where there remains room for many charisms ... .

... These reflections applied to the whole Church would mean that there should also be initiatives from the various parts of the church; initiatives that indeed would have to be co-ordinated, clarified and supervised by the centre, but should not simply be substituted by uniform directions. Why is it that today there are no such things as the letter of St. Ignatius of Antioch, of St. Polycarp, of St. Dionysius of Corinth? Why should it not be possible that bishops' conferences address themselves to each other with words of thanks or encouragement or even correction of false ways if such have been followed?

Let us dwell for a moment on the bishops' conferences that seem to offer themselves today as the best means of concrete plurality in unity. They have their prototype in the synodal activity of the regionally different 'colleges' of the ancient Church. One not infrequently hears the opinion that the bishops' conferences lack all theological basis and could therefore not act in a way that would oblige the individual bishop. The concept of collegiality, so it is said, could be applied only to the common action of the entire episcopate. Here again we have a case where a one-sided and unhistorical systematisation breaks down ... .

... We should rather say that the concept of collegiality, besides the office of unity which pertains to the pope, signifies an element of variety and adaptability that basically belongs to the structure of the Church, but may be actuated in many different ways. The collegiality of bishops signifies that there should be in the Church (under and in the unity guaranteed by the primacy) an ordered plurality. The bishops' conferences are, then, one of the possible forms of collegiality that is here partially realised but with a view to the totality.

After what has been said it appears important that the bishops' conferences do not exist side by side but in a kind of *perichoresis*, lest the movement toward plurality lead to a splintering. Mutual exchange will be more important the more the individual areas of the Church unfold their particular characteristics. In comparison to the tasks of former times, the primacy will face quite new tasks in aiding and initiating such exchanges ... .

3.5 CHARLES M. MURPHY: *COLLEGIALITY: AN ESSAY TOWARD BETTER UNDERSTANDING* – 1985

An attempt to offer some clarifications on the very notion and nature of collegiality itself. Murphy examines seminal church documents and a variety of interpretations from church leaders.[6] He believes that any solution must avoid the polemics which ignore both the multitude of competencies in the church, and the very nature of ecclesial communion, itself. The issue must be approached with an open mind, aside from preconceived ideas and solutions. In seeking a resolution and in shaping new ecclesial structures, the trilogy of 'communion-collegiality-synodality' is vital.

❈

Lying behind the continuing theological discussion about the meaning and extent of the principle of collegiality in the Church are the vigorous debates in the Second Vatican Council that preceded the issuance of its dogmatic constitution on the Church *Lumen gentium*. The serious concern about the implications of collegiality led Paul VI, it will be recalled, to annex the famous 'explanatory note' after the conclusion of the constitution itself. Twenty years later the debates continue. Some have shifted their positions, as we will see, as attention is focused upon the theological bases and practical consequences of the national conferences of bishops already mentioned and endorsed in *Lumen gentium* and the world synod of bishops created by the *motu proprio* of 1965 *Apostolica sollicitudo*, in time for inclusion of the synod in the council's decree on the pastoral office of bishops, *Christus Dominus*.

Is collegiality to be limited to the two pillars of the Church which are *de jure divino*, the primacy and the episcopate, or does it extend to institutions which are *de jure ecclesiastico*? Can there be, strictly speaking, collegial acts which are other than the two instances specifically mentioned by *Lumen gentium*, namely, the acts of an ecumenical council and the acts of the entire college dispersed throughout the world in union with the pope? Can the personal charism of the bishop given him through sacramental consecration in any sense be said to be capable of being delegated to a 'representative' assembly? Is the primacy of the Roman Pontiff potentially undermined by these new assembles of bishops? Is the unity of the Church endangered if one or more national hierarchies issue teachings potentially at variance with those of other nations? These are some of the issues that need further clarification and which I will address in some way.

Bishops by virtue of their assumption of the episcopal office by sacramental means and in hierarchical communion with the pope, become members of the college of bishops and assume a care not only for their own particular Churches but for the whole Church … .

---

6. 'Collegiality: An Essay toward better Understanding', *Theological Studies*, 46 (1985), 38–49.

The phrase 'instruments of collegiality' belongs to Pope John Paul II, who in the programmatic address of the start of his pontificate stated:

> Collegiality certainly means the adequate development of organisms, some of which will be entirely new, others updated, to ensure a better union of minds, intentions, and initiatives in the work of building up the Body of Christ which is the Church. In this regard I mention above all the synod of bishops ... .[7]

The synod of bishops and the national conferences of bishops, to which the synod corresponds to an important degree as its base, are two new instruments of collegiality which have already had a great impact upon the Church ... .

However restricted juridically (namely in Canon Law) may be the roles of the synod and national episcopal conferences, their existence and continued life and activity are new historical facts and sources of further development of their theological significance and of the concept of collegiality itself. This is the major point of an early and much-cited reflection by Joseph Ratzinger upon the national conferences of bishops (namely in *Concilium* 1 (1965), 39–67). *Sacrosanctum concilium*, the first document passed by Vatican II, conceded regulation of the liturgy within certain limits to competent territorial bodies of bishops, i.e. national conferences. Ratzinger states that 'this small paragraph, which for the first time assigns to the conferences of bishops the canonical authority, has more significance for the theology of the episcopacy and for the long-desired strengthening of episcopal power than anything in the *Constitution on the Church* itself'. Ratzinger continues:

> One not infrequently hears the opinion that the bishops' conferences lack all theological basis and could therefore not act in a way that would oblige the individual bishop. The concept of collegiality, so it is said, could be applied only to the common action of he entire episcopate. Here again we have a case where a one-sided and un-historical systematisation breaks down. The *suprema potestas in universa ecclesia* ... applies of course only to the college of bishops as a whole in union with the bishop of Rome. But is it always a question of *suprema potestas*? We should rather say that the concept of collegiality, besides the office of unity which pertains to the pope, signifies an element of variety and adaptability that basically belongs to the structure of the Church, but may be activated in many different ways. The collegiality of bishops signifies that there should be in the Church (under and in the unity guaranteed by the primacy) an ordered plurality. The bishops' conferences are, then, one of the possible forms of collegiality that is here partially realised but with a view to the totality.[8]

Ratzinger cites an article by Jérôme Hamer, O.P., which claims that limited and partial expressions of the collegiality of the Church have a theological basis which goes beyond mere pragmatism, for 'there are not two episcopal collegialities, a universal one and a regional one. There is only one – that of the entire episcopate and the pope. The conference is a legitimate historical and practical expression of the collegiality which is of divine right' ... . In very recent times Ratzinger, now prefect of the Sacred Congregation for the Doctrine of the Faith, and

---

7. In *Osservatore Romano*, 17–18 September 1979.
8. Ratzinger, Joseph, 'The Pastoral Implications of Episcopal Collegiality', *Concilium*, 1 (1964), 63–4.

Hamer, presently prefect of the Sacred Congregation for Religious, have reflected upon these issues and produced new refinements and precisions.

[After summarizing the much discussed work of Henri de Lubac, SJ, *Eglises particulières et église universelle* (1971) Murphy continues]:

Hamer writes that 'collegiality' has come to be used in a far too loose a way. In a manner very similar to de Lubac, Hamer distinguishes a collegial act, which is always of the college as such, never of individuals or even groups of individuals, from a collegial spirit and collegial activities, which pertain to a synod or national conference of bishops. Synods and conferences are representative bodies, but bishops cannot delegate to representatives what belongs to them as individual members of the episcopal order by virtue of sacramental ordination and hierarchical communion: 'The members of the college do not personally dispose of the collegial power which constitutes a unique reality; it is capable neither of transmission nor of delegation.'[9]

If according to Hamer, the synod lacks the authority to take decisions that *ipso facto* engage the whole Church, it can do much to prepare for such decisions by its discussions and recommendations. He is positive about the present process of the synod, which he regards as unique, preserving without confusion the various competencies involved. He concludes with a warning that the collegiality espoused by Vatican II should not be played off against the residency requirement for bishops stressed by the Council of Trent. The primary responsibility of bishops, according to Trent, is the *cura animarum*, which cannot be done at a distance. Hamer joins de Lubac in seeing the danger of multiplying collective activities in the name of collegiality.

Ratzinger, who in his article of 20 years ago saw the emphasis of Vatican II on the particular churches as a needed counterweight to a 'monolithic universalism', urges in a significant recent writing as a private theologian upon the final report of the Anglican-Roman Catholic dialogues that the relation of the universal Church and the particular churches must be carefully worked out:

> Apostolic succession is the sacramental form of the unifying presence of tradition. For this reason the universal Church is not a mere external amplification, contributing nothing to the essential nature of Church in the local churches, but it extends it into that very nature itself. Here it is necessary to contradict the ARCIC Report where it says: 'The Second Vatican Council allows it to be said that a church out of communion with the Roman See may lack nothing from the viewpoint of the Roman Catholic Church except that it does not belong to the visible manifestation of full Christian communion.' With such an assertion wrongly claiming the support of Vatican II, church unity is debased to an unnecessary, if desirable, externality, and the character of the universal Church is reduced to mere outward representation, of little significance in constituting what is ecclesial. This romantic idea of provincial churches which is supposed to restore the structures of the early Church as well as the concrete experiences of history, to which one must certainly not turn a blind eye in considerations of this sort. The early Church did

---

9. Hamer Jérôme, 'Les conférences épiscopales, exercice de la collégialité', *Nouvelle Revue Théologique*, 85 (1963), 966–9.

indeed know nothing of Roman primacy in practice, in the sense of Roman Catholic theology of the second millennium, but was well acquainted with living forms of unity in the universal Church which were constitutive of the essence of provincial churches. Understood in this sense, the priority of the universal Church always preceded that of particular churches.[10]

Ratzinger thus underscores the principle of the unity of the universal Church embodied in the primatial office; he also emphasises that individual bishops even in their own dioceses articulate the voice of the universal Church. Such theological principles must be kept in mind when we evaluate the effectiveness of bodies like the synod in expressing the meaning of collegiality.

An analysis of the procedures and results of the 1980 synod on the role of the family published two years ago (namely: Jan Grootaers and Joseph A. Selling, *The 1980 Synod of Bishops on 'The Role of the Family': An Exposition of the Event and an Analysis of its Texts*, Leuven University Press, 1983) highlights the issues involved in the attempt to clarify the meaning of collegiality provided above. As in the synods since the one held in 1971, the 1980 assembly produced no formal document of its own apart from a brief 'message' at its conclusion. Instead, it remitted certain 'propositions' to the pope from which he issued his own apostolic exhortation *Familiaris consortio* on November 22, 1981. The authors, Jan Grootaers and Joseph Selling, lament that the wide and comprehensive discussions of issues in the particular churches which were part of the synod's preparatory phase and the rich exchange of experiences which took place among the bishops during the synod sessions themselves became funnelled through a process which resulted in secret propositions transmitted to the pope. 'One searches desperately for something in *Familiaris consortio*' they write, 'that emanated specifically form the synod and was not already part of pre-synodal teaching and practice'. They fault the exhortation because they find in it 'no spirit of inquiry, no initiation of further study or willingness to rethink fundamental presuppositions'.[11]

Even the critics, however, would have to concede that the synod represents a substantial advancement in the practice of collegiality. It provides the pope, his curia, and the bishops with access to one another on a continuing basis. Given the fact that there are now 3000 bishops in the Church, such regular assemblies would seem to be essential even if only 300 of them can attend a synod at any one time. The diversity of cultures and theologies becomes more apparent with each synod, underscoring the necessity of developing fraternal relations and interaction. As Grootaers himself has noted, a certain practical collegiality of a very effective kind is already evident through the mutual influence provided by the synods: *Gaudium et spes* of the council influenced *Populorum progressio* of Paul VI, which carried great weight with the bishops of CELAM meeting at Medellin, who in turn made some contribution to the thinking that went into *Octogesima adveniens* of Paul VI, which provided the framework for the document on *Justice in the World* issued by the synod 1971. The synod of 1974 resulted in *Evangelii nuntiandi*, which made so powerful an impact on the Puebla meeting of CELAM.

---

10. Ratzinger, Joseph, 'Anglican-Catholic Dialogue: Its Problems and Hopes', *Insight*, l, 3 (March 1983), 5.
11. Pp. 337–8.

Whether one calls the results of the synod or national conference merely 'collective acts' or 'collegial activity' with de Lubac and Hamer, or distinguishes with Tomko true collegial acts of various grades from acts of the college itself, such instruments do recapture for the Church a way of thinking and acting with concern for every part of it in view. This is collegiality in the larger sense and it may be of greater importance.

A host of theological issues are involved when one proposes, as Grootaers, Selling and Alberigo do, to make substantive changes in synodal practice and procedures. They usually cite the early works of Ratzinger on the local church and Hamer on the Church as a *communio* without taking into account the later reflections and refinements to which I have alluded. Then there is the unique role of the primacy and the nature of the episcopate, which comprise not only a *collegium* but also a body of witnesses to, and authoritative teachers of, the divinely-given deposit of faith. It is certainly helpful that there be wide consultation in the Church before a synod convenes and that there be a frank exchange of experiences by all the synod participants, but given the charismatic basis of the Church's *communio* and the nature of divine revelation given once for all, purely inductive approaches of doctrine and concerns about whether the synods are deliberative or merely consultative do not strictly apply.

On this subtle but essential point the reflections of Karol Wojtyla, writing as archbishop of Krakow in 1972, are illuminating. The doctrinal and pastoral character of the powers of the episcopate in the Church are given expression at the synod, he writes, through a common action and a collegial vote on issues of significance to the Church today. The importance of such a vote is that it is taken within the episcopal college collegially acting, rather than its formal aspect, that is, as a consultation for the head of the college. A vote of this special kind is 'a testimony of the faith and life of all the churches, the express witness given by the bishops who have responsibility for these churches, a demonstration of the concern for the entire Church'. Such a vote, therefore, does not fit categories of deliberative or consultative, he maintains, for it has a 'weight of ecclesial quality'.[12] A pope obviously could not be opposed to such an expression of the churches' faith and love.

The present methods of the synod remain the subject of continual review and discussion, but in its present form it achieves its purpose reasonably well within the severe limitations of time (four weeks) and the size and diversity of its membership. New issues for theological reflection and pastoral action do emerge, but their resolution often must await a quiet living with them by the whole Church until a consensus upon them can be achieved. A polemical resolution of such issues or one that does not respect differing competencies would not be in keeping with the nature of the Church. The problems attendant upon 'doctrine by committee' have been well described by Paul Ramsey in his book about the 1966 Geneva Conference on Church and Society, *Who Speaks for the Church?* (Nashville: Abingdon, 1967) in which he explains the difference between a group or body that simply speaks *to* the Church and one that truly speaks *for* the Church.

The principal danger to be avoided in discussing the forms of interaction in the Church is to approach these questions with preconceived models and then try to fit the realities of the Church's ongoing life into them. The trilogy, communion-collegiality-synodality, emerges as a truer theological basis of these new instruments – the synodal practice reflecting the collegial

---

12. Wojtyla, Karol, *E il sinodo dei vescovi*, Vatican City, Liberia Editrice Vaticana, 1980.

nature of the Church as a communion. The preparations for the synods, the work of the national conferences, the pastoral letters and theological exchanges, the expressions of mutual charity, the atmosphere of respect for one another, and fidelity to the faith are all part of this process which should always be going forward in the Church. Apart from such a trilogy, Tomko believes, collegiality would appear to be in a state of 'suspension' between collegial acts.

It is vastly more complicated to accomplish this task in the world today, but with the leadership of a dynamic primacy and the help of an episcopate renewed by the collegial principle new modalities can be developed and older ones improved to bring this about. Continual communication is the key, as Cardinal Woityla said at the synod of 1969, communication of personal gifts and insights, and, more than external structures, the internal participation of persons themselves.

3.6 LÉON-JOZEF SUENENS: *CORESPONSIBILITY IN THE CHURCH* – 1968

Cardinal Suenens's passionate promotion of the participation of the laity in the life of the Church was demonstrated, in a practical sense, by his establishment of an 'interdiocesan pastoral council' in Flanders and, here, in our extract, we see it in a theological sense.[13] The following excerpts deal with the episcopal coreponsibility: first, in relation to the Roman Synods and how these can become more effective; secondly, with 'democracy' in the church and the laity's coresponsibility – addressing concerns about the governance of the church today and how bishops together may enable the laity to play their full part in the church today and tomorrow.

✿

CORESPONSIBILITY AND THE SYNOD OF BISHOPS

Coresponsibility pertains to the very structure of the church, but its actual practice in regard to the hierarchy can assume many forms according to historical circumstances. We are not treating here of the divinely conferred aspects of the episcopacy or those things which pertain to the very essence of the church, but rather of their concrete applications. And this is subject to development and revision.

The council gave existence to a new organism pertaining to this realm of contingent concretisation: the world synod of bishops. Before the convocation of the council, the central preparatory commission had already expressed the idea of establishing within the church a sort of 'limited permanent council'. At the council itself several of the fathers asked for an institution within the ordinary governing body of the church which would facilitate collaboration between the bishops and the pope, under his authority.

As we know, Pope Paul VI took the initiative in establishing the world synod of bishops. He announced his intention at the beginning of the fourth session of Vatican II. As defined by the motu proprio of September 15, 1965, the synod is conceived as a permanent institution in the church. That is to say, it is permanent as an institution: its members are chosen principally by the episcopal conferences for a limited time, according to various needs, and with a view to specific problems.

The synod, as we have it, is conceived as a purely consultative body, and in this it differs from the concept held by its promoters at the council. It responds to matters put before it, and only to those. There is no question of a 'miniature council' – an ambiguous expression at

---

13. From *Coresponsibility in the Church*, New York, Herder & Herder, 1968, 79–85, 187–200.

best – because at a council all the bishops of the world are convoked, and they are there with the full right of deliberative vote. These differences are essential.

Some theologians saw in the synod a collegial reality which, even though not conciliar, could exercise power over the universal church. Others contested this view, saying that there is question here only of an assistance asked by the pope in the exercise of his primacy of power. It seems to me that this second opinion is the true one, but that a development is not only possible but desirable. At the present moment the synod is a place where the pope can 'go and think', and it does not have a deliberative power. This synod has nothing in common with those synods known to the Eastern church. It is not specifically an expression of collegiality even though 'existentially' it is such an expression by the very act that it arises out of Vatican II, the council of collegiality. It seems best, then, to restrict ourselves to the definition given by Cardinal Marella: 'The synod could be defined not as an expression of actual collegiality in a doctrinal sense as is, for example, an ecumenical council.'

These juridical distinctions have their importance, but the decisive value of the world synod of bishops lies in the possibility that it opens for a fuller collaboration between the pope and the bishops present at the synod representing the episcopacy of the world. Life itself is richer and more fruitful than law.

The first world synod of bishops took place in Rome from the 29th of September through the 29th of October 1967. In opening the synod the pope said that he awaited from the bishops there present 'the help, support and counsel which we hope to receive in greater measure from the bishops in the apostolic ministry'.

A backward glance at the synod will allow us to draw up a balance sheet, indicating both its assets and its deficiencies. First and foremost, the existence of the synod, something unthinkable before the council, marks a significant point in the development of the church. To use the expression of Cardinal Conway, co-president of the synod, 'We have made a test flight, the plane has taken off and landed again without difficulty. Now we must improve the performance'. This will meaning tuning the motor more delicately, improving the capacity for acceleration, and more clearly defining the route of the flight.

The composition of the synod and the interventions made there constantly highlighted the importance of the role of the episcopal conferences. The bishops who were at the synod were not, as at a council, there as individual persons, but as delegates, elected by their peers in a secret vote. They were there incarnating that special type of full responsibility implied in every episcopal conference. This is a very significant fact. The members of the synod were not forbidden to speak in their own name, but they were asked to indicate this explicitly when they made personal interventions. Such interventions were the exception, and each bishop was presumed to be the representative of the bishops of his country and region.

It was agreed that general laws are most valuable for the whole church whether it be a question of canon law, priestly education, liturgy or catechetical directorate. But is was also stressed that these laws should be more of the nature of general principles, sufficiently broad and supple to admit diversity of context and particular traditions, and to allow the local and regional bishops greater latitude in applying them. This is a good example of the principle of subsidiarity, so often invoked at the council, according to which each authority should assume full responsibility at its own level for those things which pertain to its competence.

The synod strongly accentuated the pluralism in the church. For nearly every question highlighted two contributions, that of the head and that of the rest of the body there present, and these were brought to a meeting in order to find harmony. It seemed that regional or even continental pluralism was a very solid reality determining certain options common to the nations as a whole. This reality will most probably be called upon to play a greater role in the further development of the synod.

If the synod of 1967 shows many important assets on its balance sheet, it is also true that it was the object of some criticism, both from within and from without. From without, Christian opinion reproached the synod for not having considered the burning questions of our day which affect both people and clergy: birth control, optional celibacy and the great problems of the world which weigh on men, such as the underdevelopment of two-thirds of the world. The synod seemed to be concerned only with the internal order of the church, and did not really appear as relevant to a church open to the world. Then too, the synod was criticised by the world press which felt frustrated by the lack of communication and information.

To these reactions from without, which we recount here in the name of objectivity, one could add a certain number of observations made from those who lived the synod. These latter were asked to make their own ideas known in order to aid in the direction and development of the institution.

It seems to us that the success of similar meetings in Rome will depend to a large degree upon the work which prepares for them. A preliminary consultation in writing on the themes which are to be studied, with a classification of the responses, and a synthesis elaborated by experts, would permit a more fruitful exchange of ideas and more profitable debates.

There was too long a succession of monologues, an absence of theologians representing diverse tendencies in the church, and the matter to be considered was divided into workshops; all of this must be reviewed and better organised. If collaboration is to be effective, then all must be able to profit by the experience of collaboration. Without doubt, this will be the task of a permanent secretariat working during the interval between synods to gather and organise the various suggestions. It will also be necessary to avoid too rigid a structure. Even at the council, the structure was modified after the experience of the first session. Such adaptation should be easier at the synod since it is not as large a body as the council.

It is perfectly normal that an institution as new as this one should require some time to adjust all its moving parts and should need periodical overhauling. It will be up to sociologists and pastoral specialists to indicate how similar meetings in the world of today can be held in such a way that we avoid a feeling of frustration among the men of our time, and among our fellow Christians, while still according to those participating in the synod the right of dedicating time and study to the internal problems of the church. The mass media have to find, in common accord with authority, a means of respecting both the legitimate demands of information and the right to privacy required by certain deliberations. No one, for example, demands a complete account of what takes place at a cabinet meeting or at a meeting of heads of state. There has to be some balance found between a necessary discretion and the desire for openness characteristic of the church and the world today; something like the formula found in Vatican II beginning with the second session. Such a balance is all the more necessary now that the people of God are consciously concerned with the problems of the church. This growing awareness on their part brings with it the right not to be deceived insofar as this depends on us.

Theologians must discover the relationship between the synod and that collegiality which is of divine institution, drawing from this latter some of its practical applications. Canonically speaking, the synod as it is now conceived does not derive from episcopal collegiality. Nevertheless, collegiality remains an immanent factor in the structure of the church. Life itself must find the balance between these two realities: integral respect for a divinely conferred primacy within the church, and a full realisation of an authentically exercised collegiality ... .

THE CORESPONSIBILITY OF LAYMEN

THE COUNCIL AND THE LAITY

History will render glory to the council for having beautifully defined the nature of the church, the people of God, and for having boldly sketched the place and the role of the laity in the church. History will no doubt also accuse us of not having sufficiently put into practice that which is so well defined – the coresponsibility of the laity.

Admittedly, during the course of the consultations which preceded the council, some lay experts exercised, within certain commissions, an influence which was not negligible. Then too, during the different sessions, some laymen and later on some laywomen were admitted as auditors, these latter not without some difficulty. Nevertheless, we must admit that neither before the council nor during its progress was there, between fathers of the council and the lay people, a true dialogue.

It is not that lay people should form a sort of pressure group and act as though it were a session of congress. Neither is there question of establishing them as judges in matters of faith; this is the role reserved to the magisterium. Nevertheless, they should have been invited to assume real complementary functions.

The formula which describes the deliberations of the Council of Jerusalem, the first in the Church's history, contains some lessons for us: 'the apostles, the presbyters, and the whole church decided ... ' (Acts 15:22). The implication is obvious: it was the whole people of God who were engaged in making the decision.

Vatican II met at the time when the theology of the laity was still largely a thing of the future, and it suffered from this lack. The extreme reticence of canon law in its section on the laity is well known. Though the code has something to say about lay people, the faithful and associations of the faithful, the sum total of what it says is rather meagre, and no complete image of the layman emerges from the text.

Since 1917, the year when the code was published, there has been some real progress, but there are many stages yet to be achieved before the life of the layman in the church receives adequate juridical expression.

As is usually the case, life is ahead of law. Since the council, we witness daily the greater part played by the Christian community in the liturgy, we see to what degree pastoral renewal accents and animates the community dimension of the sacraments. Institutions have arisen which actualise the coresponsibility of lay people: there is the parish council, and at the diocesan level the pastoral council, which was established by Vatican II itself.

IS THE CHURCH A DEMOCRACY?

The renewal of community in the church, which ultimately derives from faith, naturally finds its place within the progress of a world moving more and more in the direction of democracy. It could seem that as we accentuate the role of the laity we deny the hierarchical character of the church. But this is not true, provided that we understand how the church accepts democracy within herself, and the historical context in which, not authority itself, but its way of being exercised has come about.

The incarnation of the Word took place at a given point in space and time. Christ's personality bears the mark of his place and time of birth. The church carries the same marks; as a human society it bears the imprints of the time in which it lives.

History shows us how, through the course of ages, the concrete way of exercising authority in the church at all its levels has developed. There is an undeniable process of osmosis and imitation between the manner of ruling in the secular world and in the church, and this is to be expected. The church has seen rule of the type of Constantine, feudal lords and enlightened despots. Today most developed countries have adopted a democratic form of government. All of this pertains to the realm of contingency.

It is precisely in this realm that we find a real uneasiness in the church. There is a crisis of confidence, not in authority as such, but in the government of the church as a human system and structure. We meet in books and magazines criticism of the ecclesiastical regime as such independent of any particular personalities. These criticisms are special in that they often come from priests and lay people, devoted children of the church, whose fidelity cannot be doubted, and who suffer from the situation they deplore. The directing bodies, they say, have a way of functioning which is no longer conformed to the atmosphere of our time, as expressed by the spirit and customs with which we are all familiar in the civil life of democratic regimes. Expressed in this way, such criticism is ambiguous and requires greater clarification.

But let us say right away: our temporal categories are never adequate to express, much less to enclose, the profound mystery of the church. To wish to catalogue the church under the label of monarchy, oligarchy or democracy is a futile task. The church's reality is too rich and too complex to fit within human categories and analogies.

There are within the church elements which are monarchical, others which are oligarchical, and still others which are democratic. The papacy, the bishops and the laity could be invoked as illustrative of these elements. Within the church there is at one and the same time one principle of unity (monarchy), a pluralism of hierarchical responsibilities (oligarchy), and a fundamental equality of all in the communion of the people of God (democracy). All of these must mutually integrate one another since they are all essential to the truth of the church. The church can admit of no exclusive reliance on any one facet, whether it be papism, episcopalism or conciliarism. The papal primacy has aspects about it which are monarchical. But the papacy is unintelligible except as integrated within a universal episcopate, and in living connection with the whole body. The episcopacy for its part is not a self-sufficient oligarchy, but reaches out in both directions in a twofold living relationship: one, with its leader the pope, and the other with the whole presbyterate and laity.

The vocabulary of a given time must be constantly corrected so that it does not prove false to the reality for which it stands. Having made this reservation, we can now say that the Second Vatican Council certainly was moved in the direction of 'democratisation' because of the accent it placed on the people of God, by the stress it placed on the hierarchy as a service, and by its creation of certain organisms within the church which favour democratic methods of government.

History teaches us that, while the structure of the church is hierarchical by the very will of its founder, the ways of exercising authority in the church have varied throughout the centuries. It is possible to trace a long history of these variations occasioned by a thousand temporal and contingent factors, whether it be an election of a pope, the appointment of bishops or practically anything else. All of this was expressed from age to age according to the conditions in which the church found itself. It is normal, then, that our age, characterized by democracy, would also tend, and rightfully so, to influence the human and variable factors of the church, rendering them more apt in governing men of today.

We cannot apply the same norms, as is obvious, to doctrines which pertain to the faith: a credo is not established by a majority vote. The divinity of Jesus Christ, his resurrection from the dead and his presence in the eucharist are not things decided by ballot. The Lord confided to the apostles the mission of expressing and passing on the content of faith, and it is to their successors, the bishops united with Peter and under his authority, that the Lord has assigned the continuance of his task, and has promised the special assistance of the Holy Spirit. The problem, then, is not to know what men desire to hear today, but rather what the Lord wishes to reveal to them.

Every bishop accomplishes his mission in coresponsibility with the whole episcopal body united to its head. Doubtless, the magisterium must take account of the common belief of the faithful before pronouncing itself. But the episcopal college has not only the mission of recording this faith as it is lived, it must also discern the elements of this faith and pass judgement on them. And this judgement is binding on the consciences of the bishops as well as upon the faithful.

In the context of these clarifications, the question of a greater or less democratization of the church's government remains a valid one. The solution to the question cannot but influence the status of the layman in the church of tomorrow.

[Quoting a list of texts from Vatican II, the cardinal develops the different aspects of the common responsibility of the faithful. All belong to the same community and, as faithful, all are primarily brothers and sisters. He adds]:

But this fundamental equality is not a mass-produced identity. To the degree that grace is accepted, in the measure of each individual's holiness, there is a scale of spiritual values at the top of which there are those who are the most holy in the eyes of the Lord. There is a spiritual hierarchy, so to speak, still invisible on this earth. But this is the primordial hierarchy because it establishes forever differences in eternal life. This is the fundamental and primary perspective of the church.

3.7 LUDWIG KAUFMANN SJ: *SYNODS OF BISHOPS: NEITHER 'CONCILIUM' NOR 'SYNODOS'* – 1990

Kaufmann's remarks are complementary to the judgement of Cardinal Suenens. He covers the historical emergence of the synod, following Vatican II, as well as exploring parallels between local synods and the world synod. The article[14] offers a reflection upon structure and method. Problems of consultation, communication, preparation and organization are explored. The examination leads Kaufmann to suggest that the reality of this ecclesial body falls short of its intended function. Neither the term concilium nor synodos truly represents it as it stands. Hence, in reality, the body is found wanting, leaving many hopes raised at Vatican II unfulfilled.

❀

These reminiscences of a journalist have to begin with a mention of the fear of publicity. In 1967, when the synod of bishops met for the first time, everything that had laboriously been brought out into the open in the course of the four sessions of the council seemed to have been forgotten again. The walls of secrecy surrounding what went on in the Vatican clouds of 'broken heads' (*teste rotte*) was such a deterrent that the city press of Rome went on strike over the synod for two days. While things may subsequently have improved over the years, so that the members of the synod have been invited to give a summary of the interventions in the plenary session to the press, things have also got worse, to such a degree that even the results or preliminary results have fallen victim to official secrecy. At the most recent synod (1987), fourteen newspaper editors therefore presented a petition for better information. The overall impression since the first synod is one of non-communication. The bishops want to keep themselves to themselves.

The first step in this direction was the limitation of the role of theologians, who could not be excluded from the council, to a very few experts or special secretaries appointed by the Curia. Moreover, observers from other churches have been excluded. In 1967 Paul VI at least expressed regret that they had not been invited. Finally, there was an opportunity for this same first synod to be open for a few days to the 'Third International Congress for the Lay Apostolate' scheduled by the pope for some days of the same month of October. However, the meeting was limited to a service and a reception, and as the congress wanted to present to the synod two petitions arising from a consensus (one on mixed marriages and one on birth control), there was not even a question-and-answer session, let alone an official presentation and acceptance.

---

14. 'Synods of Bishops: Neither "concilium" nor "synodos"', in J. Provost and K. Walf (eds), *Collegiality Put to the Test, Concilium* (1990/4), 67–78.

If the task of a journalist is to arouse interest in a matter, he or she is not least dependent on the expectations attached to this matter, just as these expectations are what drives history forward. Expectation initially fed on the still vivid recollection of the council as a symbol of change (which is nowadays called 'Perestroika') in an institution the monarchical constitution of which had previously been thought to be unchangeable: that it was put in question by a gathering which as such could refer to the earliest tradition (the Eastern churches, the early church, the gospel) and at the same time corresponded to modern democratic and parliamentarian views of government. The interesting question was: 'what will happen after the council?'

The authentic synodical movement which the council sparked off in the first decade after its conclusion and which we journalists could share in and pass on as a process of communication at the local and regional levels of the church proved that the synodical tradition of the early church could still be realised. Indeed at the opening of the council Pope John XXIII had pointed out how history taught him that all the councils, not just the great 'ecumenical' councils but also the provincial and regional councils, bore witness to the life of the church. Some bishops, like those of Hildesheim, Meissen (East Germany) and Vienna in the German speaking-area, then immediately announced a diocesan synod. In legal terms this only needs the support of the 1917 Canon Law, which in the canons 356–62 and 283 prescribed that a diocesan synod should be held at least every ten years and a provincial synod at least every twenty years. In fact these regulations were a relic from 'better' times and had long been ceased to be urged. Thus in 1966 the Coadjutor Archbishop of Vienna, Franz Jachym, could also draw the negative lesson of history of what not holding synods had meant for the church's life of faith. At all events, since the foundation of the Archdiocese of Vienna in 1469 only one diocesan synod had taken place. That the 'democratic element' (Jachym) was now being renewed was evidently a result not of regulations but of the need for dialogue (among the representatives of various spheres of pastoral care and between these and the bishop) and for dialogical structures. At the same time people were aware that laity also had to have a say in implementing the council and taking it further; there was a reference to *Lumen gentium* 35 (the prophetic ministry and its *sensus fidei*) and an equal balance was achieved between priests and laity. Beginnings were also made, in Vienna and in Switzerland, on a very successful questioning of the grass roots: numerous faithful took part in it or wrote their 'letter to the bishop'.

The Swiss synod of 1972–75 was an original federalistic combination of diocesan synods and the work of interdiocesan national experts and negotiators. Chronologically it preceded the Dutch Pastoral Council. In order to make it easier for laity to be included the Dutch church province invented this name, whereupon Paul VI (in his letter to Cardinal Alfrink of 23 November 1966) spoke of an 'attractive and delicate enterprise', indeed of something 'quite new and unique'. Here the decisions lay completely with the bishops. Nevertheless mistrust arose in Rome: there was fear that tabus like celibacy, the ordination of women and so on might be touched on here. In Switzerland, too, the bishops stated that there would be 'no tabus' in the Synod and the Swiss even ventured further than others: they sent a carefully worked-out proposal for the reform for the procedure for examining doctrine to the pope and in so doing learnt that the great majority of all the wishes and proposals sent to Rome did not meet with any positive response (this was also to be found out by the General Synod of West German dioceses in Würzburg which was held at the same time, in 1972–75). The fact that in the Swiss case in addition a subsequent institution resolved on by the synod – an interdiocesan pastoral council – was expressly forbidden by Rome ended the experience of dialogue, no less positive for the bishops than for the other members of the synod, was just as frustrating. The frustration can also be measured by the fact that in none of the three countries mentioned – and to this may be added the 'synodical process' in Austria which was carried through at little expense – was there a return to a plan to start a new synodical enterprise after an interval of ten years.

So if the blossoming of the synodical movement was short-lived, during the first decade in the regions concerned it kept alive awareness and hope that something of the spirit and praxis of the council would continue. No wonder that the same expectation was raised by the committed circles in the Roman synod of bishops as well, and that they were measured by it. Indeed it may conceivably be said 'in itself' that lessons for the implementation of these synods of bishops could have been learned from the enterprises, especially as an international (European) exchange of experience had been carried on by the leading authorities of the synods mentioned, in which a Roman representative (the congregation of bishops) was also able to take part. One might have expected even more that an efficient, historical gathering of the bishops of a whole continent, like that of Medellin 1968, which was in fact opened by the pope in person, could have been the experiential basis for the communications structure of the synod of bishops, not least because of its inductive methods of understanding the situation.

The dialogue structure of Puebla (1979) could again have been a valuable impetus towards a reform of the mode of working of synods of bishops, had there been any interest on the part of the authorities that counted – specifically the pope, who was then newly elected. In reality the modest dynamic for the development of the power of expression of this world forum of bishops, in so far any of it could be detected by us 'outsiders' in the tension of a horizon of expectation that was still in some way open, was already at an end after the 1974 synod. But on what were these expectations based that were still alive in the first decade? What structural conceptions were at odds with one another?

There was no tradition in church law for synods at a world level, nor was there any model except in the 'ecumenical' councils which we know from the history of the imperial 'Reich councils' and the mediaeval papal councils. Karl Rahner was not the first to stress that the Second Vatican Council was the first Catholic 'world council'; the point had already been made by Pope John XXIII a month before it began. Since its preparation the question had arisen how in concrete terms it could develop into a more frequent, less enormous and less expensive, and above all into a permanent yet not rigid representation of the church 'from all the ends of the earth'. The first experience of such a numerically limited representation which worked under the pope alongside the Curia was the central preparatory commission of the council, a body of about one hundred people. Moreover, with reference to this experience, on 21 February 1962 (in the fourth session of this commission) Cardinal Alfrink announced the project of a *concilium in forma contracta* which since December 1959 he had been presenting as a 'crown council' (i.e. a council of chosen bishops with legislative competence). But how was this election to be made from the 'episcopal college', scattered all over the world and becoming increasingly numerous?

A first pointer at the council itself was the 'self-structuring' which the plenary of initially around 2500 and later around 2300 fathers undertook in the first General Congregation on

13 October 1962. With a view to elections to the commissions, a postponement was decided on, so that, beginning from existing groupings or groupings to be formed (national conferences of bishops and possible larger groups) lists could be drawn up and the possibility of combinations of lists could be investigated. This self-structuring developed its own dynamic alongside the official groups of the council (plenary and commissions) in a great many meetings, which were sometimes very discreet and sometimes relatively open, not even excluding journalists. Here I am thinking of the meetings of the French- or English-speaking Africans, to which a variety of theologians and even council fathers like Cardinal Suenens gave lectures, helping them to develop a common view and awareness. All this contributed to the emergence from the amorphous ranks not only of distinctive individual personalities but also of an increasing number of groups. So the day could come when a council father could say in the plenary, 'I speak in the name of all the bishops of Africa'. At this moment as it were a continent was born in the sphere of the church, or better, it had achieved a face, a voice and as such had be taken into account.

This phenomenon of growing continental solidarity, for which an episcopal umbrella-organisation had been created first in Latin America in 1956 with the foundation of CELAM, and for which, alongside the European Symposium of Bishops (Noordwijkerhout, 1965) or Council of Bishops (since 1971), there is also an Asian federation of conferences of bishops. The continental structure became tangible in the composition of the so-called 'standing council' of the synod of bishops, for which three representatives each were chosen for four continents: Africa, the two Americas, Asia and Europe. It was then expressed on a large scale when in the permanent continental bodies there was shared preparation of the synod of bishops and at any rate an agreement about concentrating supplementary *vota*. At the most recent synods this has been learned, for example, from the Asian federations.

The 'panorama' report read out at each opening of the synods during the 1970s was also divided up by continents. It was based on a survey by the conferences of bishops of current developments and problems in the three years previous. This was expected to produce stimuli for the choice of the theme of the next synod. The climax of a 'continentality', which also emerged in the focal points of the content of the *vota*, came with the statements about experiences in missions at the 1974 synod. The focal points were inculturation (Africa), non-Christian religions (Asia), liberation (Latin America) and secularization (Europe and North America). At this synod, moreover, the Third World had its greatest weight, after the accent of 'liberation' had already been introduced above all by Latin America (and especially by the Peruvian episcopate) with the theme of 'Justice' in 1971, and when for the first time in 1969 both the numerical strength of the Third World episcopate and its quite unanimous criticism of a certain Eurocentric or 'Western' superiority had become manifest.

All this has to do with a 'horizontal' catholicity or collegiality involving partnership, and in its encouragement by the synod of bishops I see by far the greatest and most productive significance of this institution — however little the legal structures may say about it. It is connected with the reality of life and the reality of the world and takes place almost automatically: it could be even more effective were not the remarkable idea of consultation for (not with) the pope, who himself neither asks questions nor gives answers, but listens in the plenary, a determining factor both in the legal framework and in the specific course of events.

In fact the question of the subordination of the synod to the pope and the Curia also occupied a good deal of space in the reporting on the synod. In practice, in all the years the issue was still what Pope Paul VI had made of the suggestions put forward at the council, how he took them into his own rule and reshaped them accordingly: the synod of bishops might not grow out of the council, might not come into being by a resolve of the council and thus by a collegial act *par excellence*, but must one-sidedly be derived from the *motu proprio* of the power of the papal primacy. Thus there was neither conception nor birth, but the womb of the council was good enough to note, in *Christus Dominus* (On the Pastoral Office of Bishops in the Church, no. 5), that here was something *called* the synod of bishops, though this was simply a 'council' in which 'chosen bishops' gave 'the Supreme Pastor' 'more effective service'. More effective than what? One might ask. More effective, perhaps, than the Curia? The context does not satisfy our curiosity. But at all events here, without an experience, there is the assumption of a 'should' and not an 'is'. And the one, five-line, Latin sentence that the council squandered on the structure 'auxiliary council/synod of bishops' goes on in the same style. In addition it can be said that this also means, or expresses (*significat*), something 'as the representative of the whole Catholic episcopate' – does that mean 'at the same time'? Is it fact or theory that 'all the bishops participate in hierarchical communion in the care of the universal church'? So here tortuous language reflects the unsolved problem of a double function: on the one hand with a *consilium* we have 'operative' help for the pope, and on the other hand with a synod we have a 'significant' (symbolic?) representation of the whole episcopate. How the symbolic function relates to the instrumental function is left open by the text, but whereas there is reference to *Lumen gentium* 23 for the former, this depends for the way in which it is exercised on what the pope 'has already defined or has still to define'. Only the note with the date of the *motu proprio*, 15 September 1965, indicates that even before the passing of the decree it was the pope who had ordained the name and form for a dreamchild of the council which previously had been seen more along the lines of a (permanent?) 'Council' (*coetus vel consilium*). In other words, the pope intervened without allowing the process of opinion-forming among the fathers to come to a clear conclusion.

This process had begun in the plenary session, in the context of the debate about the schema on bishops during the second session of the council (5–15 November 1963). The schema contained only a minimalist account of the suggestions which had already been made by the end of 1962, and the *relatio* by bishop Carli – known in any case of being no friend of innovations – was no better. The general criticism related both to the ignoring of the 'collegiality' which was already developing as a doctrine and also the lack of inductive stress on particular needs, so that the scheme was not even any use as a catalogue of problems. The attempt to get round this by proposing a special chapter on the 'Council of Bishops' and the formation of a petitionary commission in this connection, and indeed an immediate vote, was squashed. Cardinal Liénart, who proposed this on the very first day of the debate, did not win through, although he was one of the twelve presidents of the council. Was it that procedural motions or motions on the agenda were not provided for at Vatican II, just as this right is still lacking in synods of bishops today?

Among the various *vota* for a 'council' or 'senate' of bishops, that by the Syrian Melchite Patriarch Maximus IV Saigh went the furthest. In his view, which made a great impression because of its historical and theological competence, a representative body of the patriarchates and the conferences of bishops should replace the college of cardinals (originally conceived in Roman terms) as a true 'holy college'. Further (on the model of the permanent synod in the Eastern churches), there should be a 'Supreme Council of the Church', which stood alongside the pope and to which all the offices of the Curia were to be subordinate. The mediaeval Western tradition of the consistory was also brought out (Lercaro, Bologna); but in that first round, which was also concerned with reform of the Curia, there was as yet no clarification of the various functions. Since no special sub-commission on this question was formed – though it could have worked out two alternative proposals – a petition to the pope was resolved on, and this collected 500 signatures. After the third session had passed without anything happening, Paul VI surprised the plenary at the beginning of the fourth session by announcing in person what was read out the next day, on 15 September 1965, as a fixed and finished statue. The council fathers applauded because there was mention of elected representatives of the conferences of bishops, but at the same time they gave up the opportunity (which was psychologically now past) to convey further wishes or insist on those which already had been presented.

It was soon clear to the attentive reader of the *motu proprio* that the new institution brought no effective exercise of collegiality in the sense of legislative and executive co-responsibility and involvement. But Paul VI saw a possible development 'on the basis of experience', while at the same time left it to the papal pleasure to give the synod the right to make a resolution on a particular theme.

In the full sense of legal validity, as at the council, so far there has not yet been such a resolution; i.e., in legal terms this has still remained a 'council' for the pope. But even as a *consilium*, the synod has only rarely arrived at a clear expression of opinion. The climax for the public in this respect was the 1971 synod: on the one hand through the document on 'Justice in the world' passed as a synod document, and on the other hand by the voting on the theme of celibacy, which was followed with interest all over the world. This was in reality a decision against the freedom of the conferences of bishops to decide on the admission of (married) *viri probati* to the priesthood. The expectation that the 1974 synod would also publish a document on evangelisation was not fulfilled.

But the synod did show a degree of independence when it rejected a mixed work made up of two drafts, one conceived of inductively and the other deductively. Behind the mixed work was a jungle of obscure and complicated proceedings on the part of a variety of bodies, some of which were in turn mixed. Two things could be concluded from this: first, the double track of a 'theological (doctrinal) part' and an 'empirical part' (which was already followed over the 'question of priests' at the 1971 synod) was carried *ad absurdum*; secondly, hardly anyone could any longer overlook the defective nature of the whole procedure, especially in its closing phase.

Now there had been criticism of the agenda from the beginning. Its first version of 8 December 1966 had been worked out one-sidedly by the Curia (Cardinal Felici?), and after that the bishops were able to make their own insertions and suggestions at the synod (1967). One of the problems was how the synod could be given a degree of permanency. Initially the papacy appointed merely 'a general secretary', and in essence the secretariat of the synod is still its only permanent institution. On the wishes of the (extraordinary) synod of 1969, Paul VI then allowed the election of the 'council' mentioned above at (or for) the secretariat of the synod. This election was the most autonomous action of the synod. But the council is in office only between the gatherings of the synod. It has some say on the choice of the themes and also on the preparation of documents which are described as consultation papers or questionnaires (*lineamenta*) and – after the inclusion of the answers from the conferences of bishops – as *instrumentum laboris* (a working basis). It is obvious that how the questions and problems are raised is a matter of some importance, but I have been told by a member of the council who has been re-elected on several occasions that the influence of the council is small, and that when it meets, most of those involved are already prejudiced.

The greatest handicap is probably that the council cannot itself present and explain its work before each new plenary session and that it is not to give any account of it. As soon as the plenary meets, it disappears. So the synod council is not something like a 'lesser synod' for the constant advising of the pope alongside or even above the Curia. In practice it exhausts its 'co-responsibility' in the preparation for each new synod, though then above all it is the 'special secretaries' nominated on each occasion by the pope who seem to have the say. Since the abolition of the 'panorama report' (see above), despite clearly formulated proposals for reform, the course has hardly changed at the synods of the second decade, between 1977 and 1987: broad statements, i.e. 1. the reading of the *vota* of the conferences of bishops or their delegates on the theme as set out in the 'working document'; 2. summary in a number of points by the special secretariat; 3. discussion in the *circuli minores* divided by languages and the working out of 'propositions'; 4. report of the *circuli* in plenary; 5. combination of the propositions of the *circuli* into an overall series of propositions by the special secretary (ies) with the spokesmen of the *circuli*; 6. voting on the final propositions.

As I recall, process 5 has been most subject to criticism because it (a) is obscure and open to manipulation and (b) leads to a neutralisation of what is said and proposed by the groups, so that often nothing significant is left. But the criticism sometimes already begins with the lack of freedom and/or boldness within the *circuli* and a general climate of 'censorship'. I had to note such spontaneous criticism at the 1980 synod on the 'family' over affirming or developing *Humanae vitae*. 'There is no freedom of expression here' said a by no means insignificant bishop, who had just come from a group. Where there is such freedom and a group makes a distinctive statement; this certainly does not find its way into the final propositions. These no longer represent a challenge for the pope and Curia with which they would have to struggle.

In reality, the whole process is an empty one, which begins with the unreal and curially directed way in which the questions are raised or not raised. Therefore the name synod is misleading if it is supposed to mean that both delegate bishops and the pope and his staff are involved, in a partnership with equal rights, in finding the way to truth and forming opinion. But the body cannot perform a real advisory function either, because the procedure is hardly aimed at leading to a decision between alternatives. The malaise which repeatedly develops time and again, that the 'mountain brings forth a mouse', also has a paralysing and disillusioning effect on other bodies within the church. Unfortunately I can see no sign of the pope and the curial apparatus wanting to change anything in it.

3.8 KARL LEHMANN: *ON THE DOGMATIC JUSTIFICATION FOR A PROCESS OF DEMOCRATIZATION IN THE CHURCH – 1971*

In agreement with the votes of the famous German national synod (1972–75), Lehmann tried to combine the drive for more participation with the tradition of a hierarchical church along with the task of keeping his faithful together and in communion with the whole church. This led to a qualified approach of a certain 'democratization' in the church. Indeed, applied to the church, any form of participation needs discernment. After having reflected upon the secular meanings of 'democratization' Lehmann opens horizons for the life of the Church.[15]

❄

... To the extent that the Church lives in the context of the modern and democratic world, the greatest possible 'democratisation' of her organisation is admittedly necessary, though this does certainly not mean that from the theological point of view she must undergo any fundamental change of structure or any radical loss of identity. It is in this that the 'problem' of the democratisation of 'the' Church, or alternatively *in* the Church, consists.

1 'COMMUNIO' AND 'BROTHERHOOD' AS SUBSTRUCTURES

Here too we should take as our starting-point the idea of democracy as 'a form of life' in the sense defined above, and, on the basis of this presentation of the question, seek for analogies, above all for the anthropological and ethical presuppositions to it. In fact the correspondence we are seeking for here can be attained to methodologically on historical and systematic grounds. The initial impulse which led to the development of certain elements in democracy was provided by the Christian stock of ideas, however mistaken the attitude of individual Christians may have been in history to these 'runaway children' of Christianity itself. In effect the very fact that the Christian Churches represent a union of members who have come together of their own free decision is in itself sufficient to constitute an intrinsic approximation to democracy.

The very fact that the radically free and personal act of faith by which the membership of the Church is primarily constituted (for the moment we are abstracting from the question of infant baptism) means that there are certain sustaining elements in the basic nature of the church which exhibit points of contact with the ethos of democracy as a form of life. The

---

15. 'On the Dogmatic Justification for a Process of Democratization *in the Church*', in *Concilium* (1971/7), 60–86.

freedom of the children of God, the universal priesthood, the imparting of the Spirit to all (charismata), the conscious holding of faith in common on the part of the believers, the basic equality of Christians, the equality of dignity attached to the name of Christian and other elements provide the basis for the fundamental structure. Additional strength is imparted to this factor by the fundamental reality that all are there for one another and with one another, working from the life-principle of brotherhood and brotherly love. The specific concepts of community (*koinonia, communio*), of collegiality and of solidarity are only the outward forms of this fundamental characteristic of the Church.

2   THE CHRISTIAN ETHOS AND DEMOCRATIC STRUCTURES

In connection with this it is certain, first of all, that a basic spiritual demand is expressed in Holy Scripture: solicitude for one another in an intense degree, a radical concern for the interests of one's neighbour, a surrender of one's personal life on behalf of one's brother, an understanding for those who are differently constituted, mutual forgiveness, 'vicariousness' (taking another's life upon one's self), etc. On no account must this be reduced to a mere 'spiritualising'.

But it is also undeniable that this fundamental reality, this demand which is made upon Christian living in Scripture and in the early Church still does not, in itself, represent a directly *juridical and institutional* basic constitution. It is the form of life lived in the existing circumstances in the concrete, and also the effective basis for it, and these two factors taken together determine all human relationships in the concrete in the community. Now 'prior to' all juridically and institutionally assured procedures the intrinsic depths of an invisible substructure of this kind to the Christian life as lived in the concrete implies a fundamental ethos. Nowhere are freedom, partnership, brotherhood and mutual service, considered as the necessary prior conditions for any co-existence of this kind, more plainly evident than in a Church brought together by God's sovereign grace into a 'communion of saints'. The common state of being-in-Christ ('*Christus totus*') is the basis in life for this 'democratic' existence.

It is true that this does not provide any institutional pattern for the common life of the Church. But at the same time we must in principle guard against relegating these structures exclusively to the realm of an unworldly 'mental attitude'. There is no need to do this either from considerations of a falsely spiritualising interiorisation. Certainly there is a kind of 'brotherliness' at the spiritual and pastoral level which actually does the greatest possible harm to this fundamental brotherhood. It is here that we come to the critical point: the sort of 'brotherliness' which remains only at the level of a moralising slogan and appeal, usually applied to one's neighbour, but which never finds expression in new forms, remains, in the deepest sense, ambiguous.

The Christian community can only succeed as a brotherhood when this goal is also given real embodiment in the systems and social relationships in which we live. The spiritual dimension of Christian brotherliness should not prevent us from entering wholeheartedly into these practical and down-to-earth ways of giving it reality. If the spiritual dimensions do not carry enough spiritual power and real conviction to make their impact and to imprint themselves deeply upon these present forms of human co-existence, then they are indeed unlikely to be effective in any sense. For this reason it must not be made impossible for these basic elements in a Christian community to express themselves in those forms of fulfilment found in the contemporary world which have a stronger element of rationality in them as a result of having been thought out in common.

The interconnection and interplay of 'interior' and 'exterior' elements can become a real touchstone by which to prove the concrete truth of fine words and 'attitudes' which are constantly invoked. For instance there would have been no founding of orders if the charisms had not been able to break out and to transcend the constitutional structures in all their spontaneity and explosive force. If the institutional elements allowing for this had not already been in existence, then they would have had to be created at the time. Why should this not be possible, within certain limits, for other forms of living in the church as well?

3   THE OPPORTUNITIES FOR AND THE LIMITS TO AN INSTITUTIONALISATION OF DEMOCRACY AS A 'WAY OF LIFE'

Nevertheless the devising of forms for this does not *ipso facto* or necessarily have to imply a juridical or 'political' system. It would be the worst possible pattern which could be devised on the basis of a formalistic understanding of democracy if we were to lay the emphasis exclusively upon the constituent elements, e.g., the assigning of jurisdiction, the division of power, the factor of majority decision, etc. 'Brotherhood', for instance, is a more comprehensive *principle* of life. We can attain to a greater possibility of discussion and agreement, for example, by way of *counsel* (so long as we are aware of the effectiveness of really good counsel) than by defining the limits of specific 'rights'. The personal example of a good official of the government in word and behaviour, for instance, can lead to a 'democratisation' of the whole style of social, constitutional or even ecclesiastical procedures, which can hardly, if at all, be achieved through legal enactments.

It is not always the institutions, therefore, that need to be perfected. But anyone who reacts against the transformation of many forms which have hitherto existed as powers to instruct into forms of counsel and common resolution, or who seeks only to establish the 'spirit', for instance, of brotherliness, almost necessarily loses credibility today. Many forms of authoritative behaviour can and should be abolished. In all hierarchies forms of communication between the 'rulers' and 'ruled' have been traditionalised. Today they are anachronistic, and therefore in the process of disappearing. Every official representative today must recognise which particular ways of performing his function can be adopted so as to produce a state of corporate participation, partnership and co-operation.

Precisely in those cases where the enticements of power have become common and habitual, and are characterised by modes of behaving which are autocratic, that kind of authority which is genuinely ready to accept reform can commit itself to the obligations of concrete forms of partnership or mutual respect for the views of different parties through institutional 'safeguards' and common ways of procedure.

Moreover, those who are ready wholeheartedly to give themselves to the service of others should not be afraid to commit themselves by an unambiguous assent to accepting ways in which others can play a responsible part in the taking of decisions. This is still not to exclude the exercise of a veto in decisions of principle when there are good reasons for this.

The hesitations of many hierarchical authorities (not only in the Church) to agree to such procedures, and their practice of appealing again and again merely to established attitudes in response to all those who demand 'democratisation' tempts these to regard all exhortations of this kind merely as attempts to inculcate the 'spirit' of submissiveness, and to this end all the more resolutely to suppress (even by political means of oppression and with admonitions to obedience) the demands for structural and technical changes to be introduced. These again are misinterpreted by the 'opponents' as so many 'external' and organisational superficialities. In practice both the upholders of the demand for democratisation and the groups who oppose it very often regard it without taking into account the fact that it is rooted in the context of the more basic demands for democracy as a 'way of life', and for this reason it not infrequently becomes a barren object of strife between the two opposing fronts. Only when the substructures and sustaining forces of 'democracy' are taken into consideration is it possible to arrive at any meaningful plan for democracy. This also applies to the ecclesiastical and theological sphere....

[Lehmann then discusses 'the existence of constitutional elements which cannot be altered']:

There are various ways of achieving an approximation to the central problem in the relationship of a concept of democracy to ecclesiastical structures. For instance, we may examine various analogies between the two (for example, synodal elements, the charismatic principle, the common awareness of faith held by the people of God as a whole, etc.). Elements from the secular form of democracy as a constitutional reality which are capable of finding a corresponding application in the contemporary Church might also be found, for instance, the strengthening of constitutional principles (above all a greater possibility of what is just, developing means of protecting the rights of the individual), certain aspects of the division of authority, the development of constitutional jurisdiction, collaboration in the appointment of officials, the most important committees conducting their business as far as possible in public, etc.

Even when these indispensable concrete applications have been achieved the factor which is basic to the whole system still remains indeterminate and ambiguous, and when this is treated of it is not infrequently designated as the 'sovereignty of the people', something which, in the last analysis, is totally unacceptable so far as the Church is concerned, since here the only dominion which can be in question is that of Jesus Christ. But though this distinction is in itself correct, it does not contribute any greater clarity since even in the conception proper to the new age and actually entertained since the time of Rousseau the element of *direct* sovereignty of the people has in any case been realised only to a limited extent ... .

[Lehmann explains thereupon that democracies are also limited by their Constitutions, which, of course, can be changed by the people. Applied to the church the analogy is limited]:

Admittedly – and in point of fact this constitutes a fundamental point of difference – the control over the 'basic substance' of the constitutional reality is still narrower in the Church. Precisely in the concept of self-determination in the full sense, which is something more than a power to give counsel or a right to *contribute* to decisions on the part of the governed, a postulate which has been included in principle since the seventeenth century is that of *total* dependence of the rulers on the confidence of those who, as the 'people', remain the ultimate subject of the decisions taken. In the Church, on the other hand, the *basic* elements – namely the revelation of Jesus Christ as expressed in the dimension of a truth to be accepted by faith and, arising from this, the ethical principles and the basic institutional form of the Church – are, to a large extent, set apart from the area which the members of the Church have power to control for themselves.

This does not exclude the fact that God has bestowed upon the Church a right understanding of the Gospel both as a gift and as a task which she has to perform in the world maturely and responsibly, and that this in turn gives her the right to a certain scope of freedom in order that she may interpret and apply the basic truth which has thus been bestowed upon her in the sphere of history. But even here the fact still remains that all the activities designed to achieve an effective application of the Gospel in concrete history in this sense continue to be primarily and radically subject to a right hearing of the 'word of God'. Here a duty of obedience arises from the very fact of revelation, which, in fact, we need not shrink from subjecting to any kind of rational examination, but yet at the same time which recognises no autonomous power of control over that which has been entrusted to it.

Christian faith does indeed demand that the recipient of it shall in every respect act as a partner, free and subject to no compulsion whatever. But it cannot eliminate from its nature an acknowledged dependence of man upon God. If God is, in Jesus Christ, the *Kyrios* of the world, then *this particular* 'dominion' can never be totally reconstituted in a democratic form.

If we sought to work out in more precise detail what this 'basic substance' in the life of the Church which is not subject to our control consists in, we would have to give an account of the 'essence of Christianity' in all its fundamental aspects. In doing this we would have to adopt a more cautious approach today with regard to the dogmatic statements of faith and the institutional elements which go to make up the Church as it has evolved in history to establish what really is 'unalterable' in Christianity.

Far too much of that which has grown up from quite specific situations and circumstances belonging to particular epochs in the way of views and characteristic forms has been pronounced 'unalterable' or 'eternal' by theologians and canon lawyers. In any case a precise delimitation cannot be achieved for all areas of the Church's life or on a global scale.

The distinctions can only be worked out in the actual experience of the Church's life in the concrete. This is a task which does not belong to the more limited scope of this article. It is sufficient for our present purposes that the *actual fact* has been made clear in principle *that* there are in the Church expressions of faith and of law which man has indeed been charged with the duty of giving historical form, yet which in fact derive from the task and the testament bequeathed by Christ and as such are not subject to man's control … .

[Lehmann deals further with 'the official organisation of the Church and the concept of democracy', a theme touching directly upon the problem of ministry in the Church]:

… The distinctive characteristic of an office in the Church consists in the act that in itself it recognises no *independent* authority. Power in the Church is nothing else than the power of Jesus himself. In the light of the New Testament we can only speak of this 'office' in any meaningful way so long as it remains subordinated to the ministry and power of Jesus Christ. It is the authorisation of the crucified Lord, which is complemented by a readiness for unreserved service and for 'lowliness' which this 'official' activity entails. Of itself alone and in isolation this 'office' is nothing.

Its justification and its 'unique quality' is to be found only in a radical abandonment of all positions of power and an attitude in which the subject sets himself free for that which this 'office' guarantees. It is only because he, the Lord, lives on in the ministry of his servant that there is any 'authority' attached to this office. Hence, too, theological tradition tells us that it is Jesus Christ himself who baptises, preaches and celebrates the Eucharist … . Primitive Christianity, therefore, was perfectly right in regarding the official positions in the ecclesiastical community, which were only fully developed in the post-Easter Church, not primarily as mere functional or organisational entities, designed to facilitate the activities of the community, but *primarily* as a gift of the glorified Lord to his Church … .

… In many respects it is certain that traditional theology has been too hasty in ascribing certain elements, forms of expression and modes of manifestation in this official ministry to the dimension of its immutable origin, i.e., to 'divine right' (*jus divinum*), and thereby has mistakenly pronounced many elements in it inviolate and beyond criticism. The critico-historical approach to exegesis and Church history has shown that although there is a level in these official positions in the church which is ordained by God as inviolate in this sense, and so not for man to alter, still it needs to be far more narrowly circumscribed. But at the same time it has also become clear through these findings that the *existence* and 'nature' of the 'official ministry' understood precisely in *this* sense do in fact belong to these 'primary factors' which cannot be set aside in any process of 'democratising' the Church.

This does not mean that we are seeking to bar the way to a far-reaching reform, or to those changes in the form of the Church's official ministry which go with this, by imposing limits which could have the effect of acting as apologetic, or even ideological props to support certain cravings for authority. On the contrary, it is only by isolating and defining the irreducible minimum of content which admittedly cannot be removed in the official ministry that scope can be provided, and thereby a surprising degree of freedom assured, in the re-shaping of the Church's official ministry.

It must be conceded that it is only when we view this ministry in its character as being ultimately christological in origin that we can understand that *for this very reason* an inalienable responsibility is attributed to it *uniquely*, one which, while it cannot be separated from the community, is not to be seen either as deriving from it alone; one which, in virtue of the will of Jesus Christ as founder of the Church, belongs to the 'immutable constitutional rights' of the Church.

It is self-evident that this does not exclude some form of participation by the community, for instance in the appointment of an individual to an office in the Church … .

[In a concluding discussion Lehmann deals thereupon with 'the Freedom of the Christian and the Church's official Authority']:

There is no room in the Church for that kind of authoritarianism which amounts to a demand for an attitude of unconditional submissiveness and an uncritical recognition of the claims of authority or its unrestricted exercise. True authority is that quality which exists in virtue of a fully thought-out *assent* to an offering of guidance or a claim upon the individual's active collaboration, and achieves recognition on this basis.

In the Church every kind of basic qualification to hold office ultimately derives from the authority of Jesus Christ. Now if this is true, then it follows, with regard to the question of what the basis for this authority is, that it can never *formally as such* be transmitted *wholly* 'from below'. This is perfectly reconcilable with the principle that every exercise of official authority must remain constantly rooted in the soil of a community conceived in terms of brotherhood and collegiality.

The fact that 'officialdom' and authority in the Church are first and foremost 'christocratic' in their basis and structure means that in practice they should never lead to man dominating man… .

In the light of the content of faith there is no room for any discrimination between the 'rulers' and 'ruled', because all together belong first and foremost to their one Lord. The community will also be thankful when a brother in the faith preaches the Gospel of Jesus Christ to them in the spirit of service and dedication which is appropriate to a minister in the fullest possible sense (i.e., to a 'supreme official'), and acts 'in Christ's place' (2 Cor. 5:20) to make actual in the present the reality of his salvation. The 'holder of office' himself will be conscious of belonging primarily to the community of the believers. In many respects he must constantly be searching for the word of truth in company of his fellow believers. Nor does he in any sense 'possess' salvation – least of all for himself … .

The holder of office must himself develop a 'mode of presentation' which conveys to the rest of his fellow believers the fact that in his official activities it is only their own essential 'heritage' that he is engaged upon and striving to promote. When the community as a whole realises and accepts this as their common conviction, seeing it as part of their call to accept the love of Jesus Christ that frees them, and when they give it reality in their faith, their worship and their brotherly love for one another, then the very meaning of the Christian community is such as to leave no further room for playing off the freedom against authority, the official ministry against the charismatic elements, official direction against 'democratisation', 'authority' against 'guidance by the Spirit' … .

The assigning of relative positions such as 'superior' and 'inferior' does not, in any case, represent categories which have any objective justification. That view in which official authority on the one hand and the community on the other are seen as two opposite poles, or in which a positive 'opposition' between the two is postulated, does not, in any case, represent the normal relationship between them. A community which has a genuine spirit of obedience to Jesus Christ will not even wish its leader to be in a position of *total* dependence upon the community, and only able to 'reproduce' that which is already a living force in itself. Certainly the official minister is the spokesman for men with God. But however true this may be, still he also continues to be the prophetic messenger and agent of God who constantly has to contend and remonstrate with man in order to bring him back to heeding the word of God in its pristine and undistorted form … .

It must be remembered, however, that what the message demands first and foremost is the practical application of an attitude of fellowship, understanding and mutual love. And because of this the first fruits in the relationship between community and official ministry must be an intercourse that is conducted with mutual respect for one another's views, a renunciation of any vain clinging to one's own opinions, and selfless collaboration for the same aims. The more this community effectively binds itself to what is central to its own 'basic substance', the more it will liberate itself so as to give an increasing place to working out the problems of living together by means of dialogue and by the removal of all inequalities, provided only that they are such as can be avoided.

If we fully think out this basic attitude, then truly we can only wonder why there should be so few 'democratic structures' in the Church in the sense that has been explained. Why do we not already take it completely for granted that much in the style and forms of the Church should be 'democratic'? Only in those cases in which no effective and basic agreement in the sense described above has been arrived at, and no continuous and open dialogue has been achieved in conditions of freedom and trust, does the phenomenon arise of insatiable demands being made for a 'democratisation' of the Church's official ministry. And the motives for these are often merely at the level of a formal legalism or of ecclesiastical politics. The bitterness with which this demand is often pursued and the uncompromising obstinacy with which, not infrequently, it is rejected, betray something of the almost pathological state of affairs in the attitude towards the question of official ministries in the Church, and, moreover, an attitude that is found on all sides … .

Christianity has been unable to adopt any 'blueprint' from the historical environment of any particular epoch for the forms of its own institutions without profoundly altering them so as to make them correspond to its own specific intentions. For this reason it is not surprising that the same principle applies to the recipe constituted by democracy. At the same time, however, it would be less than candid to suppress the fact that in giving concrete form to the elements in her own constitution, the Church has all along taken advantage to a very considerable extent of secular models and ideas of official administration. It must be admitted that any rigid adherence to the concept of 'democratisation' is not very meaningful here, for the very reason that no distinctions are drawn within the concept, and also that as a general recipe it is useless.

Nothing is more urgently needed than a *concretisation* of the discussion. In order to estimate how far those who seek to promote the *reality* of 'democratisation in the Church' are contributing to the *real* well-being of the community in doing so, two criteria have to be applied which have received little attention in the literature on the subject until now:

1   The demand for democratisation in general must be translated into specific and practicable models in which strong priority must be given to the problems of how the areas affected of the Church's life can be organised and made functionally efficient and effective.

2   Anyone who voices the demand for 'democratisation in the Church' and does not at the same time strive actively to ensure that Christians shall be really and effectively equipped to play an active part in the life and decisions of the community to which they belong in effect brings discredit on his own cause. Unless all members of the particular section of the society involved achieve a greater degree of readiness to share in the responsibilities, the term 'democratisation' comes all too easily to signify merely the overthrow of 'government' … .

A Church which is intended to have relevance for the men of this age cannot close itself to justifiable demands, and these not merely with regard to subjective states of mind (attitudes, modes of behaviour, etc.), but also with regard to factors which are juridically or institutionally binding. This is especially true in view of the fact that the Church either already has, or else can acquire, in many elements an intrinsic affinity with the basic values of democracy.

3.9 GIUSEPPE ALBERIGO: *ECCLESIOLOGY AND DEMOCRACY: CONVERGENCES AND DIVERGENCES* – 1992

Here,[16] Alberigo develops similar ideas to Karl Lehmann and further explores the question of democracy in the Church. In particular, he confronts the arguments of those who resist any elements of 'democracy' in the church, particularly with an appeal to history and praxis. He believes synodality is a fundamental issue in addressing the whole question of democracy in the church. The church is not identical to a democratic society, not least of all because of its foundation in Christ and sacramental character. Nonetheless, this does not exclude aspects of democratic *method* from being employed in the church. He explains 'there are important and significant analogies between Christianity and democracy ...'.

❊

Any reply has to be largely empirical. In fact on the one hand 'democracy' in contemporary cultures has differing meanings: what we see is not so much a single system, far less a *Weltanschauung*, but rather a group of methods for regulating political life which commands a consensus above all in the societies of the northern hemisphere of the planet. On the other hand, it has been clearly recognised that the Christian church is in origin a 'convocation' regulated by a covenant between God and human beings, 'from Abel to the last of the righteous'. Here is a metahistorical element – a call responded by a faith – which makes the church unique, at the institutional level as well. Every time that a political model is applied too mechanically to the Christian church there is a risk of polluting, destroying or changing this basic nucleus of its nature.

In the various historical cycles so far it has been the experience of the church that it constitutes a 'model' for political societies, though sometimes the opposite has proved the case (and today a number of people are in fact asking whether the church should not adapt itself to the democratic model). However, the most fruitful elements of this relationship have always been characterised by indirect transpositions and analogies, whether from the church to society or vice versa.

Up to the beginning of this century, structurally the Catholic Church appeared to be organised according to a pyramidal scheme, the result of a sedimentation extending over many centuries, emphasised in more recent decades by an accelerated radicalisation. The ecclesiastical pyramid seemed to be headed by the pope, who was the apex and the source of legitimation. Then came the bishops – often seen as representatives of the pope in the various provinces of the church (dioceses); with the pope they formed the 'ecclesiastical hierarchy'. Further down the pyramid came the clergy – both the secular clergy and those in orders – and

---

16. 'Ecclesiology and Democracy: Convergences and Divergences', in J. Provost and K. Walf (eds), *The Tabu of Democracy within the Church, Concilium* (1992/5), 14–26.

the mass of the faithful. These formed the massive base of the pyramid and were the principal and essentially passive recipients of the activity, decisions and teaching of the authorities (sacraments, preaching, internal discipline, ethical behaviour).

The ecclesiastical pyramid had been given a doctrinal dimension which put the emphasis above all on the pope and his faithful. The pope was presented as the 'vicar of Christ', endowed with singular powers and privileges not shared by others (*plenitudo potestatis*). All other authority in the church derived from him, and he was the sole source of it: the bishops themselves, even when solemnly gathered in council, did not have any authority than that attributed to them by the pope. Alongside the ecclesiastical pole, the faithful formed the second firm pole of the church, but had an essentially passive role (the 'learning' church), and only small qualified groups (Catholic Action) were accepted for work – as subordinates – with the ecclesiastical class. The ordinary faithful *qua* laity (i.e. not as members of the clergy) were in a condition of subjection, with no positive connotations nor any significant way of expressing themselves, so that it could be said that the whole Catholic church was one great parish of universal dimensions of which the pope was the parish priest. In this context the hypothesis of a relationship between the church and democracy appeared subversive.

Today the problems in this relationship have been eased by the way in which Vatican II has developed the aspect of the church as communion (*koinonia*), brought into being by the Spirit and structured by the sacraments, above all baptism. According to this ecclesiology, the church is the people of God travelling in history between the incarnation and the second coming of Christ. These constitutive and immutable data, in due course referred to as *status ecclesiae*, divine law, the essence of Christianity, are relatively circumscribed and have not prevented the church or its parts in the course of their historical experience from adopting very different institutional forms (*statuta ecclesiae*), depending on the impulse of the Spirit or cultural circumstances.

The people of God – 'a chosen race, a royal priesthood, a holy nation' (1 Peter 2:9) – and each of his members participate in the prophetic, kingly and priestly qualities of Christ himself. That makes all the faithful equal, apart from the different measure of faith of each one of them, and it equips all for the many services necessary for the life of the ecclesial community. Further sacramental sanctions (holy orders, episcopal consecration, marriage) ratify and specify the diversity of destinations and responsibilities.

The substantial and original equality is the basis for the choice of persons to exercise ecclesial or electoral responsibilities (deacons, priests, bishops, etc.). That has been the case for a long time and can be the case again on the basis of electoral procedures in the democratic usage of this word, i.e. with the participation of all. The democratic sense of 'election' moreover fits well with its 'theological' meaning, implying divine calling guaranteed and expressed in the sacraments. The democratic method could also be followed for appointments to service or responsibility for whole ecclesial communities, and not just individuals.

The use of the democratic method in the church not only as a determination which respects the majority but also the habitual involvement of the *universitas fidelium* can affect many aspects of church structure in a variety of ways.

SERVICES IN THE CHURCH AND THE DEMOCRATIC METHOD

The sacrament of baptism makes any individual a member of the church by incorporating them fully into what is essentially a social reality, albeit one which is *sui generis*. This is a reality which from the New Testament onwards is called the 'body of Christ' or people of God, emphasising the communal nature of Christianity. Christianity has never been a matter of an individual act but a sharing, communion. Such a characteristic puts the Christian church in a historical perspective which converges with many aspects of democracy, in so far as democracy is a set of rules aimed at allowing a number of subjects who are equal under the law to live together in society.

If they are considered from this perspective, the fundamental dimensions of the life of the church fit in with and back this convergence.

The liturgy as the characteristic act of the people of God is the act of many people, which by its very nature needs to be structured in such a way as to require the active involvement of all (*actuosa participatio*, as Vatican II puts it), though in different and complementary ways. Each time that this basic requirement is neglected, the church itself is disfigured and the liturgical act becomes fossilised, losing its clarity as a testimony to communion with the Father of the ecclesial communities and among the faithful themselves and therefore potentially with all humanity. The exclusion of the people of the faithful from the creativity of celebrations, which has now happened in the name of the 'purity' and 'regularity' of the rites, imposing a uniform culture from on high, has had the effect of marginalising popular piety, but also of evacuating the liturgy, giving place to a division between official 'rituality' and popular 'devotions'. In different historical periods the confraternities and the movements have often been the reaction to this expropriation of the faithful.

In this context also belong the problems relating to the recognition of the exemplary nature of the life of some Christians, the 'saints'. The preoccupation with guaranteeing the correctness of such recognition has led to the formulation of complex procedures of 'canonisation', which have removed responsibility from the Christian community, relegating it to a passive position which is exclusively that of the 'consumer'. It is well known what distortions arise from this at the doctrinal level as well, to the degree that for centuries what has been recognised has been almost exclusively a sanctity of the highest classes (sovereigns, 'lords', etc.) or at any rate one that is alien to the condition of ordinary Christians (in that it comprises only popes, bishops, priests and brethren, monarchs, etc.).

Paradoxically one of the arguments used most frequently in favour of these expropriations lies in the affirmation that in this way the faithful are defended from the abuses of particular groups, since otherwise they would be deceived and exploited. This is an argument which is always used when there is a desire to impose a discipline from on high, without popular participation or consent. All attacks on democratic regimes tend to have something of this kind about them, going so far as the burning of 'dangerous' books (and even persons). This has an undercurrent which is not only politically unacceptable because it denies the capacity for discernment of the ordinary citizen, but is also aberrant from the ecclesiological point of view because it at least implies the rejection of the *sensus fidei* of the community.

The *sensus fidei* of the people of God in all its complexity above all constitutes a crucial link which has still not been analysed sufficiently, particularly in connection with the emphasis put on the *magisterium*. In ecclesial physiology it is the *sensus fidei* above all which plays a decisive and creative role, whereas the *magisterium* has to be limited to the responsibility for authentication, for confirmation in the faith. The profession lived out in faith by some of the faithful, their orthopraxis which constitutes the 'concrete catechism', is the constant and irreplaceable testimony to and representation of the gospel for all humanity. In more recent centuries the scope of the *sensus fidelium* has been increasingly circumscribed, to the point that it has almost become an abstraction. Too many people accept its importance only in terms of 'reception', i.e. of consent which is given after the event (and often passively, as a matter of duty) to conclusions arrived at previously by the authorities. The scholastic model of bourgeois society, entirely dominated by an exclusively 'descending' sense, has profoundly influenced the tendency to reverse the roles between the *sensus fidelium* and the *magisterium*. It is significant that these forms prove to be alien above all to less educated cultures.

At this level we find one of the most tenacious instances of resistance to the ecclesial use of aspects of the democratic method. It is countered that determining whether something is in conformity with revelation cannot be entrusted to the dialectic between majority and minority. But it should be noted that on the one hand this is a classical argument used in resisting democracy and, above all, on the other that it ignores the ineradicable qualitative difference between the church and civil society in that the *sensus fidelium* is rooted in the faith and is strengthened by the inspiration of the Spirit. If this were not the case, how would the great Christian tradition have been able to accept the approval of the majority in conciliar decisions, from that of the council of Jerusalem (Acts 15:1–29) onwards? It is correct, but also too easy, to stress the difficulties inherent in the criteria for accepting the consensus of the majority; it remains true that on the historical occasions on which it has been necessary, the discernment of the church has been effective. This does not mean abandoning oneself to providentialism, but affirming the conviction that the problem is not insoluble, as the past itself shows … .

THE KEY ISSUE OF SYNODALITY

The fundamental criterion is that of synodality, which significantly is shared by all the great Christian traditions, though with different emphases and at different stages. This criterion was taken up by Vatican II, both in the very holding of the council and in the ecclesiological pointers which prevailed at it; in turn the World Council of Churches has adopted the criterion with deep commitment. Here too the analogy with a fundamental dimension of democracy is evident, though this should not lead us to ignore the limits and the contradictions which the method of holding assemblies has thrown up in almost all democratic experience. At a general level, as is already beginning to happen – albeit very timidly with the Synod of Bishops and with some consistories dedicated to specific matters – it will be important for there to be experiences of effective co-responsibility in shaping major and complex orientations avoiding the temptation to be content with formal and ultimately triumphalistic choruses. The local experiments which are going on – at a continental, national, regional and diocesan level – of holding synods to achieve an increasingly wide involvement that can help the whole community to profit from the riches of the diversity of charisms are equally important.

The growing imbalance between the number of priests and the number of territorial communities seems to be an urgent indication of the need for more elastic forms of ministry and availability than those which were tried out in past centuries through the presidency of Christian communities (which were essentially 'monarchical' or 'lordly'). In the long term it will be at this basic level that it will be possible to bring about a reappropriation of effective co-responsibility. It is here that the Christian community can also acquire and consolidate the habit of transparency, from the economic sphere to that of reading the signs of the time. 'Give a reason for the faith which is in us' (1 Peter 3:15) is not an impalpable spiritual authority but a specific commitment from which no one is exempt and which is above all binding on those in positions of responsibility. Above all within modern Roman Catholicism people have become used to control being exercised from above (whether they exercise it or contest it), whereas in a healthy ecclesiology of communion the control has to be 'circular', as is implied by the ancient practice of *correctio fraterna*, which is structurally reciprocal.

So the perception which is widespread in so many Christian spheres of the parallelisms and convergences between Christianity and democracy is not a forced one, even if the central Roman authorities are showing doctrinal mistrust and active resistance. However, the sphere and the limits of these relationships need to be made more precise, particularly if they are to be translated into modifications of mentalities and structures.

The point of maximum contact, which is also that of most marked divergence, is over the equivalence of all Christians in the church to that of all members within a democratic society. In fact, while it is undeniable that baptism constitutes a person a member of the ecclesial community with an even greater radicalism and definiteness than the effects of the attribution of citizenship in a democratic state, on the other hand it is clear that whereas in democracy the people is the prime holder and ultimate repository of power, in the church the sources of all responsibility and all mandates to service lie in Christ, and that these can be participated only by means of a sacramental act.

On that basis it would not make sense to affirm that 'the church is a democracy', just as it never made sense to argue that 'the church is a monarchy' or 'the church is an aristocracy'.

However, the introduction into the church of aspects of the democratic method is a different matter. In truth, in this connection Christians are in the presence of a characteristic 'sign of the time', constituted by the request for participation and co-responsibility which characterises the majority of contemporary cultures. In fact this demand, so often made by groups which are economically and culturally marginalised, clearly bears the hallmark of the gospel in that it leads us to rediscover important aspects of the primitive Christian proclamation which successive centuries have disguised, and have even banished them to the world of utopias. The brotherhood which makes all – both individual Christians and individual churches – equal in dignity and in responsibility, the complementarity of the charisms which form the precious and inalienable treasure of each community, the chorality in the important actions of each church, are widespread and constant characteristics in primitive Christianity, despite their rugged diversity.

That is important, not as a sustenance for an erudite or nostalgic archaeologism, but because it bears cogent testimony to an origin which, over and above practices adopted spontaneously in very different spheres (Jewish, Hellenistic, Roman, Persian, etc.), indicates an inspiration that goes back to the apostolic community and to Jesus' own preaching.

In the light of this, there is no question of schematically coming down in favour of a complete identity (or division) between democracy and Christianity. Rather, we must understand how the democratic authority demanded by Christians is a richer and fuller development of features of the gospel which have been obscuring for too long. There are important and significant analogies between Christianity and democracy, the full scope of which deserve further investigation and development.

ANALOGICAL RELATIONS

The relationship between Christianity and democracy is not an ontological and static given, but depends on historical and cultural contexts which are by definition changeable. It therefore involves analogies which have to be rethought and sometimes put in different social situations, as for example those which at present characterise the northern and southern hemispheres of our planet respectively. In any situation these analogies are partial and necessarily approximate. If, for example, it is quite evident that democracy implies and nourishes a social dynamism of individual and groups, in turn the centrality in Christianity of the trinitarian reference generates an ecclesial dynamism which is not only expressed in the inner universe of the believer or in the metahistorical mystery of the communion of saints but can and should also manifest itself in the historical order of the church.

From it derives the legitimacy of creating situations, occasions and institutions which allow and favour – or at least do not get in the way of – the expressions of such dynamism. There is a vital need for dynamism between laity and clergy, between women and men, between uneducated and educated; also between committed communities at one of the poles of the gospel (word, charity, mission, prayer, Eucharist), and finally, between small communities, historical traditions (Roman Catholic, Orthodox, Anglican, Protestant) and the great church. Outside this dynamic it is impossible, or a matter of sheer nominalism, to understand the Christian church as communion – far less as the people of God.

It seems to me that in this case an analogy can be recognised between ecclesial dynamism and democratic dynamism, though we must also be aware that the original trinitarian dynamism is much more radical and much more complex than that of the democratic matrix. In the present state of the life of the church why not recognise that the dynamism of democracy can offer valid stimuli and points of references for extending ecclesial dynamism and making it more effective (rather than evanescent and abstract)?

The analogy between democracy and Christianity is a very different one when it comes to guarantees. The democratic regimes entrust the guarantee that social rules will be respected first of all to a constitutional pact and secondarily to a distinction between powers. Recently, attempts have been made in the Catholic Church to adopt the same course with the formulation in the 1960s of a project of 'fundamental law' (*Lex Ecclesiae fundamentalis*). The confrontation which developed as a result brought out the impracticability of this. Opposition came essentially in the name of the profound nature of the church which, unlike democratic regimes, does not have its own foundation in itself (and moreover, in the latter the authority of the constitutions is diminishing). It has to be seen that the guarantees of the ecclesial communion, while being no less important than those needed in democratic systems, are essentially rooted in the conscience of the *universitas fidelium* with modest and partial institutional projections.

Similar considerations relate to the significance of the principle of subsidiarity, according to which the more complex authorities can only take over the responsibilities of the basic social realities in emergencies or as a supplement to them. In fact this principle has an important function in the social and political sphere, given that in democratic orders the point of reference is the state. However, in the church the real point of reference is above all the eucharistic community, i.e. the local church, and not just the universal church. Moreover, the eucharistic community is an essential factor in Christian ecclesiology, and therefore an abuse of subsidiarity on the part of the wider authorities is not only a functional *vulnus*, a wound, but also disrupts the fundamental economy of the church.

So the relations between Christianity and democracy are effective and significant, provided that it is recognised that they are both analogical and imperfect. To reject a naive mechanical concealment of the structures of the church on the basis of the democratic method also guarantees that the church will not run the risk of repeating in our age the experience of the forms of Christianity ('Christendom') which conditioned and burdened much of the mediaeval period. If in fact Christendom is seen as the name for a relationship of tendentious and reciprocal identification and reciprocal support between society and church, we must remember that today a parallelism between the democratic system and ecclesial regimes could produce equivalent effects. That would imprison the church in a historical and transitory system and prevent it from discharging a function of criticism and stimulus in the face of social systems. At all events, the most authentic support the church can give to a democratic order of society remains that of an effective and increasingly profound praxis of communion within itself.

The older Christian tradition identifies, characterises and describes the church in terms of notes of unity, holiness, catholicity and apostolicity. That is also important in connection with 'democratisation'. The church is not a formless entity which can be shaped in unlimited ways; its essential physiognomy is a given. The 'notes' express it adequately, above all in their circularity and complementarity. The analogy with democracy cannot ignore them, far less harm or damage them.

Can the dynamic consonance between the *lex orandi* and the *lex credendi* express creatively and in a coherent way a *lex communionis*, that is, rules and institutions, and above all a style and a mentality suitable for serving the fundamental values of Christian life?

3.10 *APOSTOLOS SUOS* – 1998

Meanwhile, introducing a 'democratic style' in the Church remains a very difficult task. Even at the level of bishops' conferences, the evolution towards more participation remains a very slow one. The Holy See is afraid of anarchy and, at the basis of the church, many groups, fearing change, prefer to stick to what they consider as an immutable tradition, while other groups tend to become quasi-autonomous free churches. But even at the highest level, that of the bishops' conferences and the Holy See, tensions are on the increase.

In this 'motu proprio',[17] Pope John Paul II expresses his concern about the role of the bishops' conferences. He refers to Paul VI: 'In 1966, Pope Paul VI by the "motu proprio" *Ecclesiae Sanctae*, called for episcopal conferences to be established wherever they did not yet exist; those already existing were to draw up proper statutes; and in cases where it was not possible to establish a conference, the bishops in question were to join already existing episcopal conferences; episcopal conferences comprising several nations or even international episcopal conferences could be established'.[18] The 'motu proprio' which follows is believed to have been heavily influenced by Cardinal Ratzinger. Along with several of his statements in recent years, it indicates, at least in part, a change in Ratzinger's opinion concerning the bishops' conferences. John Paul II states:

❉

… Without prejudice to the power which each bishop enjoys by divine institution in his own particular church, the consciousness of being part of an undivided body has caused bishops throughout the church's history to employ in the fulfilment of their mission means, structures and ways of communicating which express their communion and solicitude for all the churches, and prolong the very life of the college of the apostles: pastoral co-operation, consultation, mutual assistance, etc.

From the first centuries on, the reality of this communion has found an outstanding and typical expression in the holding of councils … The practice of holding particular councils continued throughout the Middle Ages. Following the Council of Trent (1545–1563), however, they became less frequent. Nevertheless, the 1917 Code of Canon Law, seeking to revitalise so venerable an institution, included provisions for the celebration of particular councils … The new Code of Canon Law of 1983 retains a considerable body of laws governing particular councils, both plenary and provincial. [3].

Alongside the tradition of particular councils and in harmony with it, starting in the last century, for historical, cultural and sociological reasons, conferences of bishops began to be established in different countries. These conferences were set up for specific pastoral purposes as a means of responding to different pastoral questions of common interest and finding appropriate solutions to them. Unlike councils, they had a stable and permanent character.

---

17. *ET* from *The Holy Father, Archives of the Holy See*, www.vatican.va/holy_father/john_paul_ii/motu_proprio/index.htm (also, in *Origins*, 28 (1998), 152–8).
18. No. 5, cf. Paul VI, Motu Proprio *Ecclesiae Sanctae* (6 August 1966), I. *Normae ad exsequenda Decreta SS. Concilii Vaticani II* 'Christus Dominus' *et* 'Presbyterorum Ordinis', no. 41: *AAS*, 58 (1966), 773–4.

The instruction of the Sacred Congregation of Bishops and Regulars issued on Aug. 24, 1889, mentions them expressly by the name *episcopal conferences*.

The Second Vatican Council, in the decree *Christus Dominus*, not only expressed the hope that the venerable institution of particular councils would be revitalised (cf. No. 36), but also dealt explicitly with episcopal conferences, acknowledging the fact that they had been established in many countries and laying down particular norms regarding them (cf. Nos 37–38). Indeed, the council recognised the usefulness and the potential of these structures, and judged that 'it would be in the highest degree helpful if in all parts of the world the bishops in each country or region would meet regularly, so that by sharing their wisdom and experience and exchanging views they may jointly formulate a program for the common good of the church' … [4].

Following the Second Vatican Council, episcopal conferences have developed significantly and have been the preferred means for the bishops of a country or a specific territory to exchange views, consult with one another and co-operate in promoting the common good of the church: 'In recent years they have become a concrete, living and efficient reality throughout the world.' Their importance is seen in the fact that they contribute effectively to the unity between the bishops and thus to the unity of the church, since they are a more helpful means of strengthening ecclesial communion. Even so, the growing extent of their activities has raised some questions of a theological and pastoral nature, especially with regard to the relationship to the individual diocesan bishops. [6].

Twenty years after the close of the Second Vatican Council, the Extraordinary Assembly of the Synod of Bishops held in 1985 acknowledged the pastoral usefulness, indeed the need, in the present circumstances of episcopal conferences. It also observed that 'in their manner of proceeding, episcopal conferences must keep in mind the good of the church, that is, the service of unity and the inalienable responsibility of each bishop in relation to the universal church and to his particular church'.[19] The synod therefore called for a fuller and more profound study of the theological and consequently the juridical status of episcopal conferences, and above all of the issue of their doctrinal authority in the light of No. 38 of the conciliar decree *Christus Dominus* and Canons 447 and 753 of the Code of Canon Law.

The present document also is a fruit of that study. In strict fidelity to the documents of the Second Vatican Council, its aim is to set out the basic theological and juridical principles regarding episcopal conferences, and to offer the juridical synthesis indispensable for helping to establish a theologically well grounded and juridically sound praxis for the conferences … [7].

The supreme power which the body of bishops possesses over the whole church cannot be exercised by them except collegially, either in a solemn way when they gather together in ecumenical council or spread throughout the world, provided that the Roman pontiff calls them to act collegially or at least freely accepts their joint action. In such collegial acts the bishops exercise a power which is proper to them for the good of the faithful and of the whole church, and although conscientiously respecting the primacy and pre-eminence of the Roman pontiff, head of the college of bishops, they are not acting as his vicars or delegates. There it is clear that they are acting as bishops of the Catholic Church, for the benefit of the whole church, and as such they are recognised and respected by the faithful … [9].

---

19. *Final Report*, II, C), 5: *L'Osservatore Romano*, 10 December 1985, 7.

Equivalent collegial actions cannot be carried out at the level of individual particular churches or of gatherings of such churches called together by their respective bishops. At the level of an individual church, it is in the name of the Lord that the diocesan bishop leads the flock entrusted to him, and he does so as the proper, ordinary and immediate pastor. His action is strictly personal, not collegial, even when he has a sense of being in communion. Moreover, although he has the fullness of the power of the sacrament of orders, he does not exercise the supreme power which belongs to the Roman pontiff and to the college of bishops as elements proper to the universal church, elements present within each particular church, that is, a particular presence of the universal church with all the essential elements pertaining thereto.

At the level of particular churches grouped together by geographic areas (by countries, regions, etc.), the bishops in charge do not exercise pastoral care jointly with collegial acts equal to those of the college of bishops [10].

To provide a correct framework for correct understanding how collegial union is manifested in the joint pastoral action of the bishops of a geographic area, it is useful to recall – even briefly – how individual bishops in their ordinary pastoral ministry are related to the universal church. It is necessary, in fact, to remember that the membership of individual bishops in the college of bishops is expressed, relative to the entire church, not only in so-called collegial acts, but also in the care for the whole church which, although not exercised by acts of jurisdiction, nonetheless contributes greatly to the good of the universal church. All bishops, in fact, must promote and defend the unity of faith and the discipline which is common to the whole church, especially in efforts to increase faith and to make the light of the truth shine on all people. 'For the rest, it is true that by governing well their own church as a portion of the universal church, they themselves are effectively contributing to the welfare of the whole mystical body, which is also the body of the churches.'[20]

Bishops contribute to the good of the universal church not only by the exercise of the *munus regendi* in their particular churches, but also by the exercise of the offices of teaching and sanctifying ... [11].

When the bishops of a territory jointly exercise certain pastoral functions for the good of their faithful, such joint exercise of the episcopal ministry is a concrete application of collegial spirit (*affectus collegialis*), which 'is the soul of the collaboration between the bishops at the regional, national and international levels'.[21] Nonetheless, this territorially based exercise of the episcopal ministry never takes on the collegial nature proper to the actions of the order of bishops as such, which alone holds the supreme power over the whole church. In fact, the relationship between individual bishops and the college of bishops is quite different from their relationship to the bodies set up for the above-mentioned joint exercise of certain pastoral tasks.

The collegiality of the actions of the body of bishops is linked to the fact 'that the universal church cannot be conceived as the sum of the particular churches or as a federation of particular churches'.[22] 'It is not the result of the communion of the churches, but is a reality

---

20. Cf., Lumen Gentium, 23.
21. Synod of Bishops of 1985, *Final Report*, II, C), 4: *L'Osservatore Romano*, 10 December 1985, p. 7.
22. Ibid.

ontologically and temporally prior to every individual particular church.'[23] Likewise the college of bishops is not to be understood as the aggregate of the bishops who govern the particular churches nor as the result of their communion; rather, as an essential element of the universal church it is a reality which precedes the office of being the head of a particular church. In fact, the power of the college of bishops over the whole church is not the result of the sum of the powers of the individual bishops over their particular churches; it is a pre-existing reality in which individual bishops participate. They have no competence to act over the whole church except collegially. Only the Roman pontiff, head of the college, can individually exercise supreme power over the church. In other words, 'episcopal collegiality in the strict and proper sense belongs only to the entire college of bishops, which as a theological subject is indivisible'.[24] And this is the express will of the Lord … [12].

Groupings of particular churches are related to the churches of which they are composed, because of the fact that those groupings are based on ties of common tradition of Christian life and because the church is rooted in human communities united by language, culture and history. These relationships are very different from the relationship of mutual interiority of the universal church with respect to the particular churches.

Likewise, the organisations formed by the bishops of a certain territory (country, region, etc.) and the bishops who are members of them share a relationship which, although presenting a certain similarity, is really quite different from that which exists between the college of bishops and the individual bishops. The binding effect of the acts of the episcopal ministry jointly exercised within conferences of bishops and in communion with the Apostolic See derives from the fact that the latter has constituted the former and has entrusted to them, on the basis of the power of the individual bishops, specific areas of competence … [13].

Episcopal conferences constitute a concrete application of the collegial spirit. Basing itself on the prescriptions of the Second Vatican Council, the Code of Canon Law gives a precise description: 'The conference of bishops, a permanent institution, is a grouping of bishops of a given country or territory whereby, according to the norm of the law, they jointly exercise certain pastoral functions on behalf of the Christian faithful of the territory in view of promoting the greater good which the church offers humankind, especially through forms and programs of the apostolate which are fittingly adapted to the circumstances of the time and the place' … [14].[25]

Episcopal conferences are as a rule national, that is, they bring together the bishops of one country only, since the links of culture, tradition and common history as well as the interconnection of social relations among citizens of the same nation require more constant collaboration among the members of the episcopate of that territory than the ecclesial circumstances of another territorial entity might require. Nevertheless, canonical legislation makes provision for an episcopal conference to 'be erected for a smaller or larger territory so that it includes either the bishops of some particular churches constituted in a given territory or those presiding over particular churches belonging to different countries'.[26] It follows that

23. John Paul II, *Speech to the Bishops of the United States of America* (16 September 1987), 3: *Insegnamenti*, X, 3 (1987), 555.
24. John Paul II, *Address to the Roman Curia* (20 December 1990), 6: *AAS*, 83 (1991), 744.
25. *Code of Canon Law*, Canon 447; Cf. Second Vatican Ecumenical Council, Decree on the Pastoral Office of Bishops in the Church *Christus Dominus*, 38, 1.
26. *Code of Canon Law*, Canon 448, 2.

there can be episcopal conferences of varying territorial extension or of a supernational extension. The judgement on the circumstances relative to persons or things which suggest a greater or lesser extension of the territory of a conference is reserved to the Holy See. In fact, 'after hearing the bishops involved, it pertains to the supreme church authority alone to erect, suppress or change the conferences of bishops'[27] ... [16].

In the episcopal conference the bishops jointly exercise the episcopal ministry for the good of the faithful of the territory of the conference; but for the exercise to be legitimate and binding on the individual bishops there is needed the intervention of the supreme authority of the church which, through universal law or particular mandates, entrusts determined questions to the deliberation of the episcopal conference. Bishops, whether individually or united in conference, cannot autonomously limit their own sacred power in favour of the episcopal conference, and even less can they do so in favour of one of its parts, whether the permanent council or a commission or the president. This logic is quite explicit in the canonical norm concerning the exercise of the legislative power of the bishops assembled in the episcopal conference: 'The conference of bishops can issue general decrees only in those cases in which the common law prescribes it or a special mandate of the Apostolic See, given either *motu proprio* or at the request of the conference, determines it.' In other cases 'the competence of the individual bishop remains intact; and neither the conference nor its president may act in the name of all the bishops unless each and every bishop has given his consent' ... [20].

[At the end of the *motu proprio* four 'complementary norms', regarding the conferences of bishops are added]:

Article 1. In order that the doctrinal declarations of the conference of bishops referred to in No. 22 of the present letter may constitute authentic magisterium and be published in the name of the conference itself, they must be unanimously approved by the bishops who are members or receive the *recognitio* of the Apostolic See if approved in plenary assembly by at least two-thirds of the bishops belonging to the conference and having a deliberative vote.

Article 2. No body of the episcopal conference outside of the plenary assembly has the power to carry out acts of authentic magisterium. The episcopal conference cannot grant such power to its commissions or other bodies set up by it.

Article 3. For statements of a different kind, different from those mentioned in Article 2, the doctrinal commission of the conference of bishops must be authorised explicitly by the permanent council of the conference.

Article 4. The episcopal conferences are to review their statutes in order that they may be consistent with the clarifications and norms of the present document as well as the Code of Canon Law, and they should send them subsequently to the Apostolic See for *recognitio*, in accordance with Canon 431 of the Code of Canon Law.

[Cautiously, footnote no. 1 of the *motu proprio* states]:

---

27. *Code of Canon Law*, Canon 449, 1.

The Oriental churches headed by Patriarchs and Major Archbishops are governed by their respective Synods of Bishops, endowed with legislative, judicial and in certain cases, administrative power … : The present document does not deal with these. Hence no analogy may be drawn between such synods and episcopal conferences … .

3.11 PETER HUIZING SJ: *SUBSIDIARITY* – 1986

Of course, we should here add, it is possible that in the future, the universal church may further develop theologically the role of the episcopal conferences, in particular when they cover a whole continent or a vast region with a particular culture. Yves Congar opened some perspectives in this direction in the first chapter of his *Eglise et Papauté* (Cerf, Paris, 1994), entitled: *Le pape, patriarche d'Occident. Approche d'une réalité trop négligée*, (pp. 11–30).[28] He proposes the possibility of introducing in the Latin church the model of the ancient patriarchates, enjoying a large relative autonomy in liturgy and discipline. All this has to do with the application of the principle of subsidiarity to the church. In the following contribution,[29] Huizing reflects on a principle which, applied to the church, adds an important dimension to the relationship between the individual bishop, the bishops' conferences and the primacy.

❋

The final report of the Extraordinary Synod of Bishops in 1985 contained in Section C 'The Church as a Community' (*Communio*), n. 8, c, the following remarkable 'recommendation': 'It is recommended that an investigation should be conducted into the question as to whether the principle of subsidiarity that applies to human society is also applicable within the church and, if so, to what extent and in what sense it can be applied and is possibly necessary' (see Pius XII, ASS 38, 1946, p.144).

This recommendation is above all remarkable because it is *in complete contradiction to the text of Pius XII to which it refers.* In other words, it is diametrically opposed to what the pope said to the recently appointed members of the College of Cardinals on 20 February 1946 on the occasion of the internationalisation of the College. The pope took as his point of departure Paul's outline to the Christian community at Ephesus of the building up of the Church on the basis of different gifts given by the Lord to the faithful to equip the 'saints' for their work of service, building up 'the body of Christ' (Eph 4:11–16). He then quoted from the Encyclical *Quadragesimo anno* promulgated by Pius XI on 15 May 1931, in which it is stated that it is in conflict with God's law to withdraw from man what he can achieve individually with his own efforts and his own plans and hand it over to the community. Pius XII applied this directly to the relationships between smaller and lower and bigger and higher communities. He then continued with the quotation from *Quadragesimo anno*: 'All the activity of the community is by virtue of its being and conception subsidiary. It has the task of supporting the members of the community, but should not annihilate it or swallow it up.' Finally Pius XII himself explained that this principle applied to all branches of social life, including the life of the Church, without injury to its hierarchical structure.

---

28. See Congar, Yves. 'The Pope as Patriarch of the West', *Theology Digest*, 38 (Spring, 1991), in Chapter 4 of this present volume.
29. 'Subsidiarity', in G. Alberigo and J. Provost (eds), *Synod 1985 – an Evaluation, Concilium* (1986), 118–23.

It is clear from the pope's address to the Second World Congress on the Lay Apostolate on 5 October 1957 that he did not intend this addition to be interpreted as a restriction in the sense of 'on condition that it does not harm its hierarchical structure'. In that address, he explained that the authority of the Church has to apply the principle of subsidiarity with regard to the lay apostolate, in other words, that the laity has to be entrusted with the tasks that it can carry out as well or even better than the priests. Lay people must be able to act freely and accept responsibility within the limits of their particular task and that which is placed before them by the universal importance of the Church. This principle of subsidiarity was, for Pius XII, *a fundamental norm of justice both for the hierarchical authority of the Church and for the order that had to be maintained by that authority.*

But there are further reasons for regarding the recommendation of the 1985 Synod as very remarkable. One reason is that it does not agree at all with the *judgement of the First Universal Assembly of the Synod of Bishops* that was held in 1967 shortly after the Second Vatican Council with regard to the principle of subsidiarity in the government of the Church. A number of principles were submitted to that Synod for the bishops to assess in connection with the revision of the Code of Canon Law. These principles had been suggested by the Papal Commission that had been appointed to revise the Code and composed with the explicit intention of establishing *general guidelines* so that the principles themselves and the spirit of the Council would be felt in the revised Code.

Principle No. 4 was entitled: 'The Inclusion of Special Powers in the Code', but it implied more than this. Until then, the diocesan bishops had asked Rome about all kinds of matters – some of them quite senseless – or received special powers from Rome for them. The conciliar decision concerning the pastoral task of the bishops (No. 8) laid down that diocesan bishops, as the successors of the apostles (!), would in future have, by virtue of their office, direct authority in their own dioceses to be exercised on their own responsibility. That competence would include the authority that was required for the exercise of their pastoral office, but it would not include the authority of the popes to reserve certain clearly defined cases for themselves or for other authoritative bodies. The diocesan bishops also obtained the authority to exempt believers for whom they had direct care in exceptional cases from having to observe the universal law of the Church, if they regarded that as something that was in the interest of their spiritual well-being. This power was given to the bishops also with the exception of certain clearly defined cases that were reserved to Rome … .

In the First Extraordinary Assembly of the 1969 Synod of Bishops, Paul VI referred to the principle of subsidiarity, which, even when the Synod was being prepared, many bishops had presented as an important norm in the relationship between the people and those bearing office in the Church and between the pope and the bishops. Pope Paul VI stressed in his address that this principle should be applied carefully without jeopardising the general well-being of the Church through the existence of too widely different and too far-reaching forms of autonomy in local churches. But even in that Synod, there was no doubt at all that the principle had to be applied … .

[Huizing shows then that in the Extraordinary Synod of 1985, J. Hamer raised a series of arguments against subsidiarity. Huizing regrets that this had prevented any further development of the principle of subsidiarity. As a conclusion we may say that the tension between primacy, the Roman curia, bishops' conferences, individual bishops and particular churches has not yet reached a satisfying equilibrium. One should not forget that the curia had opposed the foundation of the *Federation of Asian Bishops'* *Conferences* (FABC) and seriously tried to reduce the influence of the 1979 Puebla general assembly of the Latin American bishops' conference CELAM, after its assembly in Medellin (1968). Meanwhile the Council of European Episcopal Conferences (CCEE) is still not entitled to use the name 'Conference'. It is also widely known that the main proposals of the national Synods (as in Germany and Switzerland in 1972–75) were not accepted by Rome. Many bishops complain that, since 1985, the Roman Ordinary Synods of Bishops were far from satisfying. The debate on the content of the 'synodality' of the Church continues.]

3.12 WILHELM DE VRIES SJ: *THE 'COLLEGE OF PATRIARCHS' – 1965*

Because, all too often, the experience of the Eastern Churches is not well known in the West and, as Catholicity implies more than the Latin church, the essay which follows[30] can be informative to the debates concerned with rethinking the concept of collegiality. Some excerpts serve well as a conclusion to our chapter on synodality and collegiality. It is clear that the tradition of the Eastern Catholic churches, linked with Rome and enjoying a particular kind of autonomy, is very important for the future evolution of the dialogue with the Orthodox and other non Roman Catholic Oriental churches. In a Roman Catholic church with more than one billion members, it seems urgent to look for a real decentralisation at the highest level. Collegiality as well as ecumenical councils will have to adapt to this formidable quantitative change, particularly when we take into account, as is said, that at the end of the first century the total number of Christians around the Mediterranean was limited to about 7500.

�֎

The college of bishops headed by the pope as heir to St. Peter's office, is the successor of the college of the apostles. The first one thousand years, during which East and West were still organically united in the universal Church, and to which this article is confined, show that there was a certain classification within the body of bishops, particularly in the patriarchates. At the head of each patriarchate stands a bishop who embodies the fullness of episcopal powers and in whose favour the other bishops have renounced part of their rights for the sake of better government in the Church. The question is whether these higher bishops or patriarchs constitute by themselves a distinct 'college', again under the leadership of Peter's successor, and whether this body is entitled to some supreme collegial authority over the whole Church. The answer is 'no' if we mean by 'college' a corporate body, such as a supreme Senate in the Church, which would meet regularly or at least rather frequently and which would have certain definite and canonically determined rights in the government of the universal Church. In fact, this situation has never existed; whether in Rome or in Constantinople. Even the *synodos endemousa* which played an important part in Constantinople in the government of the whole Eastern Church, did not, as we shall see, represent the patriarchate, nor was it a Senate of Patriarchs.

Nevertheless, the patriarchs form a unity, a whole, to which apostolic succession belongs in a very special way. This 'whole' or 'college' has decisive importance for the 'communion' of all bishops among themselves and with their head, the successor of Peter, and a certain supreme collegial authority is attributed to it in ecumenical councils and other special functions. We can therefore rightly speak of 'college of patriarchs' although not in a strict juridical sense. This college will, of course, look different according to whether we approach it from the point of view of Rome or from that of the East.

---

30. The 'College of Patriarchs', in *Concilium* – Canon Law, (1965/8), 35–43.

THE 'COLLEGE OF PATRIARCHS' FROM THE POINT OF VIEW OF ROME

In reality, Rome recognised only three patriarchal Sees as 'units' in the strict sense of the word. They are the so-called Petrine Sees of Rome, Alexandria and Antioch, which are identified by their common apostolic, or even Petrine, origin. The popes had certain reservations about the claims of Constantinople and Jerusalem because they were based on the law laid down by the Council of Chalcedon which Leo the Great already considered contrary to the inspired and therefore inviolable Canon of Nicaea. Nicholas I still recognised the bishops of Constantinople and Jerusalem as patriarchs in name only. In practice, however, the popes recognised the patriarchates of Constantinople and Jerusalem, albeit reluctantly. In 591 Gregory the Great informed the patriarchs of Constantinople, Alexandria, Antioch and Jerusalem together of his election. Here the order, usual in the East, is already accepted *de facto*. This order was incorporated in canon 21 of the fourth Council of Constantinople (869), and one can take it that Pope Hadrian II recognised this order when he officially approved the Council's decisions.

The popes, however, do not recognise a pentarchy of five patriarchs, as usually accepted in the East. In their view, only the three Sees which were derived from Peter had a real patriarchal function. The classic text clearly underlining the unity of the three Petrine Sees stands in the letter sent by Gregory the Great to Eulogius of Alexandria in November, 597:

> Although, then, there are many apostles, supreme authority belongs only to the See of the prince of apostles, and this See is one and the same (Peter's) though it exists in three places. For he himself enhanced the See where he entered upon his rest and ended his earthly life; he also honoured the See to which he sent his disciple, the Evangelist (Mark), and he consolidated the See which he occupied for seven years although he left it afterward. Since, therefore, only one See is concerned, belonging to one person, but now occupied by three bishops by divine right, I count as mine all the good I hear from you; and when you hear something good about me, you must attribute it to your own merit because we are one in him who said, 'That all may be one, even as thou, Father, in me and I in thee, that they also may be one in us' (John 17:21).[31]

The point here is not to examine the historical and theological contents of this teaching about the three Petrine Sees, which was held by such popes as Damasus, Leo the Great, Nicholas I and Leo IX, but simply to state the fact that in the mind of these popes these three patriarchal Sees constituted a strict unity, with a special function in the government of the universal Church … .

… The communion of all patriarchs among themselves and of all with their head, the successor of Peter, is particularly evident at the election of a new patriarch who notifies Rome and his colleagues of his election and receives the ecclesiastical 'communio' from Rome and the others. Thus the community of the college of bishops, the highest body of Church government, comes about through its highest members who are in direct communion with each other. The main function of the college of patriarchs is precisely to link all the bishops

---

31. *Acta Romanorum Pontificum*, 498, n. 268; cf. *Monumenta Germania e Historica*, VII/37, 485–6.

together who are linked thereby with the head and with each other through the juridical and sacramental bond of the 'communio' … .

… A confession of faith is an essential part of all these notifications of patriarchal election. They are usually styled *Litterae synodales* or *Inthronistica*, and regularly contain such a confession. In the same way the popes usually informed the other patriarchs and included in this document a confession of faith. The communion of the patriarchs with each other and with their head was therefore rooted in the unity in faith.

The other bishops are in communion with Rome and so with the universal Church through their patriarchs. *Only* the patriarch notified Rome of their election and received a reply from the pope. This assured them of belonging to this communion but was not equivalent to either an appointment or a transmission of jurisdiction, as I have pointed out elsewhere. That the other bishops are in communion with the head of the Church through their patriarchs is occasionally mentioned explicitly. Pope Damasus sent Paulinus of Antioch a confession of faith to be signed by his suffragan bishops, and he added:

> We have sent you a confession of faith; for you should not hesitate and when it is a matter of receiving into the Church caution should not lead to dilatoriness. The confession of faith is not so much destined for yourself since you are already associated with us in the communion of the same faith, but rather for those who, by signing (this confession) wish to be in communion with you, and through you, dear brother, with us… .[32]

… Hence in the eyes of Rome the main function of the college of patriarchs is to secure the communion of all the bishops with the centre of the Church. On the other hand, Rome admits that the patriarchs together have, at least on occasion and in a certain measure, a collegial authority in the universal Church. Rome, too, accepts the importance of the patriarchs' participation in ecumenical councils in the matter of their universal validity, even though this idea is not so clearly expressed in the West as in the East. For example, Nicholas I, in a letter written in 865 to Emperor Michael, compared the Council of Nicaea (325) with the synod which deposed Patriarch Ignatius. The Council of Nicaea had this advantage over the synod that there were not only many bishops present from many regions, but that the patriarchs presided over it: 'But it is also reported that the patriarchs presided over it', while there was not one patriarch present at the synod which deposed Ignatius … .[33]

… There is no doubt that this bishop of Rome (Agapetus) considers himself head of the college of patriarchs. When he grants *communio*, this is unquestionably decisive. Whoever is received in this *communio*, belongs to the Church and is the legitimate patriarch; this cannot be said when this *communio* fails. Within the college of patriarchs the Bishop of Rome is not merely a *primus inter pares* (first among equals), but he holds a leading position that is decisive. This can be proved by numerous texts, too many for the scope of this article. I can give only a few instances.

Pope Leo IX, whose ghost-writer was the aggressive Cardinal Humbert of Silva Candida, uncompromisingly expressed the necessity of communion with Rome in a letter to Emperor Michael, of January 1054:

---

32. Pope Damasus: AD 375, *Acta Romanorum Pontificum*, 71–2, n. 15; cf. *PL*, 13, col. 356.
33. Letter of July 9, 514 (*Acta Romanorum Pontificum*, 413, n. 214); cf. *PL*, 63, cols 455f.

The Roman Church is so little alone, or as you seem to think, but one among many that any nation anywhere on earth which arrogantly breaks off relations with her, can no longer be called 'Church' and considered as such, but is rather nothing at all or perhaps a false council of heretics or a gathering of schismatics and a synagogue of Satan.[34]

This text presupposes of course, as is clear from the word *superbe* (arrogantly), that the here-mentioned schismatics and heretics act with malicious intent. An irenic attitude was still absent from the mentality of those days.

But long before this time the Holy See used to demand that anyone who wanted to be in communion with Rome should not be in communion with those to whom the successor of Peter refused this communion. An illustration of this is provided by the letter of pope Felix III to Thalasios, an archimandrite in the city of Constantinople, whom the pope strictly forbade to get in touch with Acacius before Rome had granted him her *communio*.

As true head of the college of patriarchs, the Bishop of Rome claimed the authority to decide against his colleagues if necessary. Thus, for instance, Pope Sergius rejected the Acta of the Trullan Synod (692), although they had been signed by three Eastern patriarchs. Nicholas I referred to the case of the 'Robbers' Council' of Ephesus, in 449, which was rejected by Rome although accepted by patriarchs.

THE COLLEGE OF PATRIARCHS FROM THE POINT OF VIEW OF THE EAST

Lack of space allows only a very brief survey. I have been mainly concerned to show that Rome, too, recognised a certain collegiality of patriarchs. That this collegiality operated in the East has been known for a long time, and I shall refer only to some of the most important evidence.

The five patriarchs in the East were compared to the five senses of Christ's Mystical Body. Anastasius the librarian, who was really a Westerner but was trained by Greek monks in Rome, developed this point in his introductory speech at the fourth Council of Constantinople (869), which was essentially an Eastern council. In his Body, which is the Church, Christ has instituted five senses, just as any mortal body has five senses. These are the five patriarchs. The See of Rome is more in communion with all than any other. The five patriarchs therefore constitute a strict unity, a supreme government body, of which Rome is the head. They are closely linked together and must be concerned for each other … .

… According to the Easterns there are a number of cases where this college of five patriarchs has a definite collegial authority. With the exception of Rome each of these patriarchs can be judged by the other four if he deviates from the true faith or commits some other grave wrong. Thus the priest Elias, representing the Patriarch of Jerusalem at the fourth Council of Constantinople, declared that Photius had been condemned by Rome and the three other (patriarchal) Sees. The case had therefore been decided. What had been decided in common with Rome and the other Sees was final … .

---

34. *Acta Romanorum Pontificum*, 781, n. 371; cf. *PL*, 143, col. 776.

... I have already pointed out that the theory of the pentarchy, as held by the Greeks while they were still in communion with Rome (and also by Anastasius the librarian who was secretary to Pope Nicholas I), in no way excluded the primacy. It is true that later on this theory developed in the sense of complete equality of all the patriarchs, including Rome, away from the primacy. I cannot deal in the brief space of this article with the complicated question in what sense the Greek Church held the primacy of the pope during the first millennium. I can refer only to one or two instances to show that this teaching was in any case accepted somehow. In fact, however, the Eastern patriarchates of Alexandria, Antioch and Jerusalem gravitated around Constantinople rather than Rome.

For Theodore of Studios, Rome is the first See, to which one turns in cases of conflict, as is the matter of the veneration of icons, and where one looks for certainty in matters of faith. The same Theodore admits that, according to ancient custom, orthodox synods cannot be convoked without informing the pope. Canon 21 of the fourth Council of Constantinople expresses quite clearly the preeminence of Rome. Many Easterns address the Bishop of Rome in their letters as 'Universal Patriarch'. The papal primacy is fully recognised in a letter of the 'highest priests of the East', i.e., the patriarchs of Antioch, Jerusalem and Alexandria, to Tarasius of Constantinople, in which they explain that the Arab occupation prevents them from being present at the forthcoming synod of Constantinople. If necessary the synod could proceed without them, since this had also happened at the sixth synod (third Council of Constantinople, 680), which in spite of absences had rightly proclaimed the doctrine of the faith, the more so as the most holy and apostolic Pope of Rome had agreed and had been represented by his envoys.

Yet, as has been said, for the Eastern patriarchates the most important centre was, in fact, not Rome but Constantinople. The notification of patriarchal elections was much more frequently addressed to this centre than to Rome, although even the exchange of information with Constantinople was not regular because it was frequently prevented by adverse political situations. We still have, by way of illustration, the letter of Patriarch Tarasius of Constantinople (785) to the patriarchs of Alexandria, Antioch and Jerusalem. He asked them to support him as fathers in his lack of courage with the power of their episcopal staff and their fatherly teaching, and to help him as brothers. 'According to the holy and apostolic custom' he sent them a confession of faith to convince them of his orthodoxy.

The Eastern patriarchs were represented by envoys in Constantinople if the political situation allowed. There is evidence for this already in the 6th century. The name of the Patriarch of Constantinople was mentioned in the liturgy. Since Chalcedon (451) Constantinople began to exercise a definite influence on these patriarchates. Even before that time many interventions have been recorded. Before 451 Anatolius of Constantinople ordained a bishop for Antioch, contrary to the canons. Canons 9 and 17 of Chalcedon were interpreted, perhaps from the start, but certainly later on, as implying a right of appeal to Constantinople, also from other Eastern patriarchates. E. Herman has shown in detail how the primacy of Constantinople developed after the Council of Chalcedon.[35]

A decisive factor in this was the so-called *synodos endemousa*. It was composed of bishops who were resident in Constantinople or happened to be there at the time. Only now and then

---

35. Herman, E., Grillmeier, A. and Bacht, H., *Das Konzil von Chalkedon. Geschichte urad Gegenwart*, vol. 2, Würzburg, Echter, 1953, 459–90.

were bishops from the Eastern patriarchates or even patriarchs themselves present. The *synodos endemousa* became a powerful instrument of centralisation throughout the East. Through it Constantinople exercised its function of 'ecumenical patriarchate' the authority of which extended beyond the boundaries of its own territory into that of the other patriarchates. According to J. Hajjar[36] the disciplinary measures of the synod were limited to the patriarchate of Constantinople, while the dogmatic decisions had an ecumenical bearing. From the beginning of the 9th century the *synodos endemousa* took on also administrative functions in the general movement toward centralisation which spread throughout Christendom, and these extended beyond the territory of Constantinople. Thus the synod became more and more an organ of central government for the whole Eastern Church, but it never became a kind of Senate of patriarchs.

Constantinople, then, was the centre for the three Eastern patriarchates. Nevertheless, this did not mean that, apart from unfortunately frequent tensions, Rome's dominant leadership was put aside during these ten centuries. In 1024 Patriarch Eusthatius still sent a message to Pope John XIX, with gifts, to request that Rome recognise the Church of Constantinople as universal within its limits while Constantinople was prepared to recognise the preeminence of the Church of Rome throughout the world.

Finally a brief word about what the Syrians who were separated from Rome, thought about the college of patriarchs. The Syrian Monophysites recognised four patriarchs – those of Rome, Alexandria, Constantinople and Antioch, which were all instituted by apostles. If a patriarch erred in matters of faith 'the other three should meet and judge him'. Of these four, two (Rome and Constantinople) had fallen away from the true faith. The Church is therefore limited to the patriarchates of Alexandria and Antioch.

Among the Nestorians, the theory of the pentarchy is very similar to that of the Greeks. The five patriarchates are: one in the East, that of Seleucia-Ctesiphon, and four in the West, Rome, Alexandria, Antioch and Constantinople. About this Timothy I (728–823) wrote: 'One and the same Spirit perfects the Catholic Church which exists in all the heavenly regions, through these five Sees as through the five senses of body and soul … .'[37]

We are therefore entitled to speak of 'College of Patriarchs', though not, as above, in the strict juridical sense of the words. In the East the idea of collegial authority of the patriarchs was strongly developed, but in Rome, too, it was not unknown. There are, however, between Rome and the East many differences in detail and emphasis.

---

36. Hajjar, F., *Le Synode Permanent daps l'Eglise Byzantine des origines au XIe siecle*, Rome, Orientalia Christiana Analecta, 164, 1962, 191.
37. See de Vries, W., *Der Kirchenbegriff der von Rome getrennten Syrer*, Rome, Orientalia Christiana Analecta, 145, 1955, 46.

QUESTIONS FOR DISCUSSION

1 Notwithstanding the fact that according to an old tradition the 'people' must be heard in the appointment of bishops, the reality is generally very different. Even the bishops in the country of the candidates are often not consulted in any full or proper manner. What can be done to change this situation?

2 Catholic universities and, particularly, Catholic Faculties of Theology can be an important element in the shaping of a renewed collegiality. In reality, they are very rarely consulted on important matters, as if their 'magisterium' is non-existent or a hindrance. Why might this be so?

3 The Roman Episcopal Synods are more and more criticized even by the participating bishops. Is it possible to redefine effectively the role of the Roman Curia in such a way that the weight of these Synods becomes a more real expression of collegiality?

4 In a church with more than a billion members and great historical and cultural differences it seems urgent, as Congar suggests, to decentralize much more. For example, why do African, Indian and Chinese local churches still have to 'belong' to the Latin one?

5 Can the Latin church not learn more from the experience of the Catholic churches of Eastern rites, keeping more of their synodal traditions?

6 Why are women totally absent from the power in the church? It is difficult to understand that at the 1994 Roman Episcopal Synod on religious life not a single female religious superior had the right to vote, even though two-thirds of the religious are women. Is it, at least, not possible to split the *potestas jurisdictionis* from the *potestas ordinis*?

FURTHER READING

DISCUSSION AND DEBATE

Black, Antony, 'The Government in the Church', in *The Church Today*, John Cumming and Paul Burns (eds), Dublin, Gill & Macmillan, 1980.

Broucker, José de, *The Suenens Dossier – a Case for Collegiality*, Dublin, Gill & Macmillan, 1970.

Buckley, M.J., *Papal Primacy and the Episcopate*, New York, Crossroad, 1998.

Delooz, Pierre, 'Participation in the Catholic Church', *Pro Mundi Vita – Bulletin*, nr. 84 (1981).

Gaudemet, Jean, 'Bishops – From Election to Nomination', in *Electing Our Own Bishops*, Peter Huizing and Knut Walf (eds), in *Concilium*, 137 (1980).

Granfield, Patrick, 'The Senus Fidelium in Episcopal Selection', in *Electing Our Own Bishops*, Peter Huizing and Knut Walf (eds), in *Concilium*, 137 (1980).

Grootaers, Jan, 'The Collegiality of the Synod of Bishops – an Unresolved Problem', in *Collegiality Put to the Test* (eds) James Provost and Knut Walf, in *Concilium* (1990/4).

Hastings, Adrian, 'The Authority of the Church, Universal and Local', in *The Theology of a Protestant Catholic*, London, SCM, 1990.

Kerkhofs, Jan, 'Episcopal Leadership', *Pro Mundi Vita – Bulletin*, 65 (1977).

Kerkhofs, Jan, 'Church Leadership in the Roman Catholic Church. Some Contemporary Challenges', in P.H. Hanson (ed.), *Church Leadership*, Uppsala, Tro and Hanke, 1997.

McSorley, Harry, 'Some Forgotten Truths about the Petrine Ministry', *Journal of Ecumenical Studies*, 11 (1974), 208–37.

Pailler, A., 'Considerations on the Authority of the Church', in *Problems of Authority*, John Murray Todd (ed.), Baltimore, Helicon Press, 1962 (the 1961 Bec symposium).

Rahner, Karl, 'On Bishops' Conferences' and 'Pastoral-Theological Observations on Episcopacy in the Teaching of Vatican II', in *Concerning Vatican II*, vol. 6 of *Theological Investigations*, London, DLT, 1969.

Rahner, Karl, 'On the Relationship between the Pope and the College of Bishops', *Theological Investigations*, 10 (1973).

Ratzinger, Joseph, 'The Structure and Tasks of the Synod of Bishops', in *Church, Ecumenism and Politics*, Slough, St Paul's, 1988.

Reese, Thomas, 'The selection of Bishops', *America*, 25/8 (1984).

Rudge, Peter, *Management in the Church*, London, Mc Graw-Hill, 1976.

Schatz, Klaus, 'After 1870 – Is there a Future?', in *Papal Primacy: From its Origin to the Present*, London, Michael Glazier, 1996.

Schedler, G., 'A Theory of Collective Responsibility', *Heythrop Journal*, 23, 4 (1982).

Swidler, Leo and Fransen, Peter (eds), *Authority in the Church and the Schillebeeckx Case*, New York, Crossroad, 1982.

Tillard, Jean M.R., 'The Servant of Communion', in *The Bishop of Rome*, London, SPCK, 1983.

Tillard, Jean M.R., 'The Bishop of the Church of Rome', in *Church of Churches – The Ecclesiology of Communion*, Collegeville, Liturgical Press, 1992.

Part 4:

The Papacy – Supreme Authority?

Richard R. Gaillardetz

Roman Catholics hold that the papacy is an indispensable gift to the church, yet popes from Paul VI to John Paul II have admitted that the papacy has become a significant obstacle in ecumenical dialogue. Clearly, many of our non-Catholic dialogue partners are not yet persuaded of the virtues of this 'gift'. Pope John Paul II acknowledges this in his encyclical *Ut unum sint* and reminds us that in assessing the papacy one must distinguish the indispensable doctrinal core of papal authority from its many historical forms subject to revision. There can be no denying the fact that the papacy has, over almost two millennia, assumed dramatically different forms. The bishops of Rome during the first five centuries, with only a few exceptions, had no role in the appointment of bishops. They had no exclusive authority to canonize saints. They neither convoked nor presided over ecumenical councils. They had no curia. They wrote no encyclicals. The titles of 'pope', 'vicar of Christ' and 'sovereign pontiff' were not uniquely theirs, if they were employed at all. Individual bishops and synods generally granted the bishop of Rome's unique authority and they frequently appealed to him in disputed matters, but failure to secure such approval did not automatically separate them from the Catholic Christian communion. While the selection of readings included in this chapter will not directly attend to the history of the papacy, this sense of the papacy as a vital, living institution taking different forms in different ecclesiastical settings will serve as an important presupposition for discussion.

In many ways, the modern papacy was born with the pontificate of Pope Pius IX and the teaching of Vatican I. As the longest reigning pope in history, Pius IX responded to the encouragement of 'ultramontanists' (those who claimed that in church matters one must look 'beyond the mountains' to Rome for leadership) to expand and solidify the scope of the spiritual authority of the papacy even as he ultimately lost the battle to preserve temporal authority over the Papal States. The teachings of Vatican I, often interpreted in a rather one-sided manner, gave rise to a line of thinking about the church which was quite papo-centric. The Second Vatican Council embraced the teachings of Vatican I but by placing these teachings within the context of a broad ecclesiological renewal, opened the door to new lines of theological reflection on the Petrine ministry today. The selections included in this chapter offer several examples of how this reflection on the Petrine ministry has developed in contemporary Catholic thought.

It is important to note the self-imposed editorial restraints that have been placed on the selection of texts. We have tried to choose important seminal texts by respected theological figures that have each in their own way addressed the question of the Petrine ministry today.

While important contributions have been made by theologians and church leaders outside of the Roman Catholic communion, doing justice to the diverse approaches offered by non-Catholic Christian authors would be impossible under the constraints of a single volume reader. Moreover, within the larger theme of papal authority one could identify at least two important sub-issues that could not be addressed in detail: 1) the specific scope, limits and character of papal infallibility and 2) how one might speak of the institution of the papacy in relation to divine providence and divine law. In spite of these limitations, we hope that these selections will give the reader a greater appreciation for the quality and character of contemporary Catholic theological conversation on the papacy and its place in the life of the church.

4.1 *PASTOR AETERNUS* – 1870

The First Vatican Council (1869–70) was a council of reaction. In the eyes of many Catholic bishops, Pius IX was the victim of unjust persecution at the hands of the secular leaders of Europe. Thus when the Pope convened Vatican I, largely to further his cause against the liberal forces of modernity, there was a great deal of personal sympathy extended towards him. The council members at Vatican I had intended to promulgate a comprehensive constitution on the church. The first draft of that constitution consisted of fifteen chapters, only one of which dealt with the papacy. After brief consideration all but the material on the papacy was returned to committee for revision. Unfortunately, the council was interrupted when the Italian troops entered Rome during the Franco-Prussian war, and the rest of the constitution was never considered. Only the material on the papacy would be promulgated, in expanded form, as *Pastor aeternus*.[1]

❀

That which our lord Jesus Christ, the prince of shepherds and great shepherd of the sheep, established in the blessed apostle Peter, for the continual salvation and permanent benefit of the church, must of necessity remain for ever, by Christ's authority, in the church which, founded as it is upon a rock, will stand firm until the end of time … . Therefore whoever succeeds to the chair of Peter obtains, by the institution of Christ himself, the primacy of Peter over the whole church … . For this reason it has always been necessary for every church – that is to say the faithful throughout the world – to be in agreement with the Roman church because of its more effective leadership [ch. Two].

And so, supported by the clear witness of holy scripture, and adhering to the manifest and explicit decrees both of our predecessors the Roman pontiffs and of general councils, we promulgate anew the definition of the ecumenical council of Florence, which must be believed by all faithful Christians, namely, that the apostolic see and the Roman pontiff hold a world-wide primacy, and that the Roman pontiff is the successor of blessed Peter, the prince of the apostles, true vicar of Christ, head of the whole church and father and teacher of all christian people … . Wherefore we teach and declare that, by divine ordinance, the Roman church possesses a pre-eminence of ordinary power over every other church, and that this jurisdictional power of the Roman pontiff is both episcopal and immediate … . This power of the supreme pontiff by no means detracts from that ordinary and immediate power of episcopal jurisdiction, by which bishops, who have succeeded to the place of the apostles by appointment of the holy Spirit, tend and govern individually the particular flocks which have been assigned to them. On the contrary, this power of theirs is asserted, supported and defended by the supreme and universal pastor … . Since the Roman pontiff, by the divine right of the apostolic primacy, governs the whole church, we likewise teach and declare that he is the supreme judge of the faithful, and that in all cases which fall under ecclesiastical

---

1. *ET*, Tanner, II, 813–16.

jurisdiction recourse may be had to his judgment. The sentence of the apostolic see (than which there is no higher authority) is not subject to revision by anyone, nor may anyone lawfully pass judgment thereupon [ch. Three].

That apostolic primacy which the Roman pontiff possesses as successor of Peter, the prince of the apostles, includes also the supreme power of teaching … . For the Holy Spirit was promised to the successors of Peter not so that they might, by his revelation, make known some new doctrine, but that, by his assistance, they might religiously guard and faithfully expound the revelation or deposit of faith transmitted by the apostles … . Therefore … we teach and define as a divinely revealed dogma that when the Roman pontiff speaks *ex cathedra*, that is, when, in the exercise of his office as shepherd and teacher of all Christians, in virtue of his supreme apostolic authority, he defines a doctrine concerning faith or morals to be held by the whole church, he possesses, by the divine assistance promised to him in blessed Peter, that infallibility which the divine Redeemer willed his church to enjoy in defining doctrine concerning faith or morals. Therefore, such definitions of the Roman pontiff are of themselves, and not by the consent of the church, irreformable [ch. Four].

4.2 DECLARATION OF THE GERMAN EPISCOPATE – 1875

Shortly after the abortive ending of Vatican I, the German Chancellor Bismark published a letter in which he offered a skewed reading of Vatican I's teaching on the relationship between pope and bishops. In Bismark's view papal authority had, by conciliar decree, essentially absorbed any and all legitimate authority of the local bishops. The German bishops felt compelled to offer a forceful response to Bismark, rejecting his interpretation and offering what amounted to an important commentary and even development of the council's teaching. In 1875 Pope Pius IX explicitly made his own the teaching of the German bishops.[2]

❋

Each of these statements [those of Bismark] is without foundation, and is in flat contradiction to the decisions of the Vatican Council ... According to these decisions [those of Vatican I] the ecclesiastical authority of the Pope is indeed a 'potestas suprema, ordinaria et immediata' ... but this is not a new doctrine; it is a truth of the Catholic faith which has always been recognized ... . According to this doctrine of the Catholic Church the Pope is Bishop of Rome, not bishop of any other city or diocese, not Bishop of Cologne or Breslau or anywhere else. But as Bishop of Rome he is, at the same time, Pope, i.e., shepherd and head of the whole Church, head of all the bishops and all the faithful, and his papal authority does not simply come to life in certain exceptional cases but has power and validity always and everywhere. Being in this position, the Pope has to see to it that each bishop carries out the whole of the duties of his office, and where a bishop is prevented from doing so, or any other necessity demands it, the Pope has the right and duty, not as bishop of the diocese in question but as Pope, to order everything in it which appertains to its administration.

... Nor do the decisions of the Vatican Council give any shadow of ground for stating that they have made the Pope an absolute sovereign, more totally absolute, by virtue of his infallibility, than any absolute monarch in the world. In the first place, the field in which the Pope's ecclesiastical authority operates is essentially different from that in which the secular sovereignty of a monarch operates ... . But quite apart from this, the description of absolute monarch even with reference to the church's affairs, cannot be applied to the Pope, because he stands under the divine law and is bound by the provisions made by Christ for his Church. He cannot change the constitution given to the Church by her divine founder, as a secular legislator can alter the constitution of a state ... . It is in virtue of the same divine institution upon which the Papacy rests that the episcopate also exists; it, too, has its rights and duties, because of the ordinance of God himself, and the Pope has neither the right nor the power to change them.

---

2. 'Collective Declaration of the German Episcopate on the Circular of the Imperial German Chancellor concerning the Next Papal Election'. Originally issued in 1875. English translation is taken from an appendix in Hans Küng, *Council and Reunion*, New York: Sheed & Ward, 1961, 284–91.

4.3 *LUMEN GENTIUM* – 1964

The bishops at the Second Vatican Council (1962–65) knew that the teaching of Vatican I on the papacy needed to be complemented by a more developed exposition of a theology of the episcopate. The third chapter of *Lumen Gentium,*[3] Vatican II's Dogmatic Constitution on the church, was entitled, 'The Hierarchy: With Special Emphasis on the Episcopate'. Without in any way repudiating the teaching of Vatican I, the Second Vatican Council nevertheless placed papal primacy in a new context. At one level the council situated the ministry of the bishop of Rome within the framework of the council's development of episcopal collegiality. At a second level, the papacy is presented within the council's larger reappropriation of the theological foundations of the church as sacrament, body of Christ, people of God, temple of the Holy Spirit, messianic people and pilgrim church.

❁

Just as in the Gospel, the Lord so disposing, St. Peter and the other apostles constitute one apostolic college, so in a similar way the Roman Pontiff, the successor of Peter, and the bishops, the successors of the apostles, are joined together. Indeed, the very ancient practice whereby bishops duly established in all parts of the world were in communion with one another and with the Bishop of Rome in a bond of unity, charity and peace, … . But the college or body of bishops has no authority unless it is understood together with the Roman Pontiff, the successor of Peter as its head. The pope's power of primacy over all, both pastors and faithful, remains whole and intact. In virtue of his office, that is as Vicar of Christ and pastor of the whole Church, the Roman Pontiff has full, supreme and universal power over the Church. And he is always free to exercise this power. The order of bishops, which succeeds to the college of apostles and gives this apostolic body continued existence, is also the subject of supreme and full power over the universal Church, provided we understand this body together with its head the Roman Pontiff and never without this head. This power can be exercised only with the consent of the Roman Pontiff. For our Lord placed Simon alone as the rock and the bearer of the keys of the Church, and made him shepherd of the whole flock; it is evident, however, that the power of binding and loosing, which was given to Peter, was granted also to the college of apostles, joined with their head. This college, insofar as it is composed of many, expresses the variety and universality of the People of God, but insofar as it is assembled under one head, it expresses the unity of the flock of Christ. In it, the bishops, faithfully recognizing the primacy and pre-eminence of their head, exercise their own authority for the good of their own faithful, and indeed of the whole Church, the Holy Spirit supporting its organic structure and harmony with moderation [22].

The Roman Pontiff, as the successor of Peter, is the perpetual and visible principle and foundation of unity of both the bishops and of the faithful. The individual bishops, however,

---

3. *Lumen Gentium*, Ch. 3. Vatican II's Dogmatic Constitution on the Church. *ET, Documents of Second Vatican Council, Archives of the Holy See*, www.vatican.va/archive/histcouncils/ii_vatican_council/index.htm.

are the visible principle and foundation of unity in their particular churches, fashioned after the model of the universal Church, in and from which churches comes into being the one and only Catholic Church. For this reason the individual bishops represent each his own church, but all of them together and with the Pope represent the entire Church in the bond of peace, love and unity ... [23].

And this is the infallibility which the Roman Pontiff, the head of the college of bishops, enjoys in virtue of his office, when, as the supreme shepherd and teacher of all the faithful, who confirms his brethren in their faith, by a definitive act he proclaims a doctrine of faith or morals. And therefore his definitions, of themselves, and not from the consent of the Church, are justly styled irreformable, since they are pronounced with the assistance of the Holy Spirit, promised to him in blessed Peter, and therefore they need no approval of others, nor do they allow an appeal to any other judgment. For then the Roman Pontiff is not pronouncing judgment as a private person, but as the supreme teacher of the universal Church, in whom the charism of infallibility of the Church itself is individually present, he is expounding or defending a doctrine of Catholic faith ... . To these definitions the assent of the Church can never be wanting, on account of the activity of that same Holy Spirit, by which the whole flock of Christ is preserved and progresses in unity of faith ... . The Roman Pontiff and the bishops, in view of their office and the importance of the matter, by fitting means diligently strive to inquire properly into that revelation and to give apt expression to its contents; but a new public revelation they do not accept as pertaining to the divine deposit of faith [25].

4.4 *UT UNUM SINT* – 1995

Amidst an impressive collection of papal encyclicals, Pope John Paul II's encyclical on ecumenism, *Ut unum sint*,[4] may well prove to be his most significant. In this 1995 encyclical the pope offered a positive assessment of the real gains made in Christian ecumenism in the years since the council. The work of Christian ecumenism is important, first because it corresponds to Christ's prayer that his disciples be one, second because it was a specific mandate of Vatican II, and third because of the evangelical importance of a common Christian witness. In this encyclical, the pope also forthrightly acknowledges the way in which the papacy has itself become an obstacle in ecumenical conversation. He offers a bold invitation to non-Catholic church leaders and theologians to engage in dialogue about the precise manner of exercising papal primacy most appropriate to the contemporary situation.

❋

Among all the churches and Ecclesial Communities, the Catholic Church is conscious that she has preserved the ministry of the successor of the Apostle Peter, the Bishop of Rome, whom God established as her 'perpetual and visible principle and foundation of unity' and whom the Spirit sustains in order that he may enable all the others to share in the essential good. In the beautiful expression of Pope Saint Gregory the Great, my ministry is that of *servus servorum Dei*. This designation is the best possible safeguard against the risk of separating power (and in particular the primacy) from ministry. Such a separation would contradict the very meaning of power according to the Gospel: 'I am among you as one who serves' (Lk. 22:27), says our Lord Jesus Christ, the Head of the Church. On the other hand ... the Catholic church's conviction that in the ministry of the Bishop of Rome she has preserved, in fidelity to the Apostolic Tradition and the faith of the Fathers, the visible sign and guarantor of unity, constitutes a difficulty for most other Christians, whose memory is marked by certain painful recollections. To the extent that we are responsible for these, I join my Predecessor Paul VI in asking forgiveness ... [88].

The Bishop of Rome is the Bishop of the Church which preserves the mark of the martyrdom of Peter and Paul: 'By a mysterious design of Providence it is at Rome that [Peter] concludes his journey in following Jesus, and it is at Rome that he gives his greatest proof of love and fidelity. Likewise Paul, the Apostle of the Gentiles, gives his supreme witness at Rome. In this way the Church of Rome became the Church of Peter and of Paul'[5] ... [90].

As the heir to the mission of Peter in the Church, which has been made fruitful by the blood of the Princes of the Apostles, the Bishop of Rome exercises a ministry originating in the manifold mercy of God. This mercy converts hearts and pours forth the power of grace where the disciple experiences the bitter taste of his personal weakness and helplessness. The authority proper to this ministry is completely at the service of God's merciful plan and it must always be seen in this perspective. Its power is explained from this perspective ... [92].

---

4. *ET, The Holy Father, Archives of the Holy See*, www.vatican.va/holy_father/john_paul_ii/encyclicals.
5. Address to the Cardinals and the Roman Curia (28 June 1985), 3: *AAS*, 77 (1985), 1150.

This service of unity, rooted in the action of divine mercy, is entrusted within the College of Bishops to one among those who have received from the Spirit the task, not of exercising power over the people – as the rulers of the Gentiles and their great men do – but of leading them towards peaceful pastures … . The mission of the Bishop of Rome within the College of all the Pastors consists precisely in 'keeping watch' (*episkopein*), like a sentinel, so that, through the efforts of the Pastors, the true voice of Christ the Shepherd may be heard in all the particular Churches. In this way, in each of the particular Churches entrusted to those Pastors, the *una, sancta, catholica et apostolica Ecclesia* is made present. All the Churches are in full and visible communion, because all the Pastors are in communion with Peter and therefore united in Christ. With the power and the authority without which such an office would be illusory, the Bishop of Rome must ensure the communion of all the Churches. For this reason, he is the first servant of unity. This primacy is exercised on various levels, including vigilance over the handing down of the Word, the celebration of the Liturgy and the Sacraments, the Church's mission, discipline and the Christian life. It is the responsibility of the Successor of Peter to recall the requirements of the common good of the Church, should anyone be tempted to overlook it in the pursuit of personal interests. He has the duty to admonish, to caution and to declare at times that this or that opinion being circulated is irreconcilable with the unity of faith. When circumstances require it, he speaks in the name of all the Pastors in communion with him. He can also – under very specific conditions clearly laid down by the First Vatican Council – declare *ex cathedra* that a certain doctrine belongs to the deposit of faith. By thus bearing witness to the truth he serves unity [94].

All this however must always be done in communion. When the Catholic Church affirms that the office of the Bishop of Rome corresponds to the will of Christ, she does not separate this office from the mission entrusted to the whole body of Bishops, who are also 'vicars and ambassadors of Christ'.[6] The Bishop of Rome is a member of the 'College', and the Bishops are his brothers in the ministry. Whatever relates to the unity of all Christian Communities clearly forms part of the concerns of the primacy. As Bishop of Rome I am fully aware as I have reaffirmed in the present Encyclical Letter, that Christ ardently desires the full and visible communion of all those Communities in which, by virtue of God's faithfulness, his Spirit dwells. I am convinced that I have a particular responsibility in this regard, above all in acknowledging the ecumenical aspirations of the majority of the Christian Communities and in heeding the request made of me to find a way of exercising the primacy which, while in no way renouncing what is essential to its mission, is nonetheless open to a new situation. For a whole millennium Christians were united in 'a brotherly fraternal communion of faith and sacramental life … . If disagreements in belief and discipline arose among them, the Roman See acted by common consent as moderator'.[7] In this way the primacy exercised its office of unity. When addressing the Ecumenical Patriarch his Holiness Dimitrios I, I acknowledged my awareness that 'for a great variety of reasons, and against the will of all concerned, what should have been a service sometimes manifested itself in a very different light. But … it is out of a desire to obey the will of Christ truly that I recognize that as Bishop of Rome I am called to exercise that ministry … I insistently pray the Holy spirit to shine his

---

6. *Lumen Gentium*, no. 27.
7. Vatican II *Decree on Ecumenism Unitatis Redintegratio*, no. 14.

light upon us, enlightening all the Pastors and theologians of our Churches, that we may see – together, of course – the forms in which this ministry may accomplish a service of love recognized by all concerned'[8] [95].

This is an immense task, which we cannot refuse and which I cannot carry out by myself. Could not the real but imperfect communion existing between us persuade Church leaders and their theologians to engage with me in a patient and fraternal dialogue on this subject, a dialogue in which, leaving useless controversies behind, we could listen to one another, keeping before us only the will of Christ for his Church and allowing ourselves to be deeply moved by his plea 'that they may all be one ... so that the world may believe that you have sent me' (Jn. 17: 21)? [96].

---

8. Homily in the Vatican Basilica in the presence of Dimitrios I, Archbishop of Constantinople and Ecumenical Patriarch (6 December, 1987), 3: *AAS*, 80 (1988), 714.

4.5 KARL RAHNER: *ON THE RELATIONSHIP BETWEEN THE POPE AND THE COLLEGE OF BISHOPS* – 1977

The essay[9] included here was written soon after the close of Vatican II. It represents an important trajectory in post-conciliar thought on the papacy and papal authority. This trajectory focuses on the universal church and the proper relationship between the college of bishops and the pope. For Rahner, papal primacy is to be comprehended within an understanding of the college of bishops as a kind of 'executive board' over the universal church.

❋

I

In the Dogmatic Constitution *Lumen gentium* concerning the relationship between the papacy and the episcopacy the Council itself does not make any exhaustive pronouncement in the sense indicated because it leaves specific questions open to further discussion among theologians. It lays down that in accordance with the defined doctrine of the First Vatican Council the pope possesses '*plena et suprema potestas*' in the Church, and that he can exercise this plenary power even without any collegiate act in the true sense on the part of the united bishops. In this he is not bound by any juridical guidance which these bishops have to offer. It states further that the united episcopate as such, i.e. considered as a collegiate entity, is likewise the bearer of the same full and supreme power in the Church, though of course only to the extent that it is not simply the sum total of all the individual bishops, but a *corpus, ordo, collegium* that is constituted with and under the pope as its indispensable head and to the extent that it is only capable of a 'collegiate act' with the free agreement of the pope himself. This remains true even though in concrete fact and in the actual circumstances of history this may take place in very different ways.

In the defining relationship between the pope and the universal episcopate the Council does not go beyond this formulation. This means that the statement in question contains nothing else than what all along had been held clearly and explicitly as a matter of faith by the Church both before and after the First Vatican Council. For what is said here about the united episcopate and its relationship to the pope and the plenary power he enjoys as primate is precisely the same as what has all along been said about the relationship between an Oecumenical Council and the pope, vested as he is with this plenary power as primate. In this it is in fact obvious that it is not merely as a result of being summoned to assemble at a particular point that the Council acquires this *plena et suprema potestas* in the Church. Rather

---

9. Rahner, Karl. 'On the Relationship between the Pope and the College of Bishops', in *Theological Investigations*, Vol. 10, New York, Seabury, 1977, 50–59.

the united episcopate must already possess this power in order that they can hold a Council. If the bishops were in possession of such power neither as individuals nor as a body, then the mere act of coming together in a particular place could never bring it about that they suddenly acquired this power. This could never be the case even if we were willing to assume that they could only actually *exercise* this power (whatever their reasons for doing so) when they were actually assembled together in a particular place. If it were sought to suggest that the bishops as locally assembled only acquire this power belonging to an Oecumenical Council precisely as a result of being called together by the *pope*, then (and this is a point we shall have to return to in greater detail at a later stage) we should have to say that the prior supposition on which this theory is based was false, because a power that is *transmitted* within the Church herself (as opposed to one that is imparted by Christ) cannot, by definition, be the *supreme* power, since the power of him who imparts it must in fact be higher than itself.

In the light of this it becomes self-evident that the teaching of the Second Vatican Council with regard to the united episcopate as the upholder of supreme and plenary power in the Church and with regard to the relationship between this united episcopate and the pope is simply a repetition of the classic doctrine concerning the power of a Council (and in fact with regard to that of the united episcopate) which has always been in force, and which was explicitly put forward at the First Vatican Council by Gasser, Zinelli etc. But precisely because of this it is also clear that those questions about the relationship between pope and Council (= united episcopate) which have been matters of theological controversy up to now were not touched upon, and therefore that they still remain matters of controversy today. The only increase in clarity that has been achieved is that the hitherto disputed question regarding the relationship between pope and Council is now presented in a better and more realistic form as the question of the precise relationship between the pope and the united episcopate.

Scholastic theology is accustomed to give precision to the form in which the question with which we are here concerned is presented by asking whether there are two 'incompletely distinct subjects' vested with full and supreme power in the Church or only one. Those who chose the *second* of these two alternatives as their answer to this question obviously presuppose that the *one* subject involved can only be the pope. Those who choose the *first* alternative as their answer equally obviously imply thereby that there cannot be two 'completely distinct subjects' vested with one and the same supreme power in the Church. For the purposes of the considerations offered here let it be explicitly acknowledged and taken as read that the two presuppositions here involved are valid, even though in themselves they are not sufficient to answer the question. For (and this is relevant to the first presupposition) let us suppose that the pope is not vested with this power in virtue of his own personal office, but instead of this that he derives this power of his (even though verbally acknowledged as supreme and plenary) from the united episcopate (= Council). For, in the scholastic controversy referred to, the power of the Council is commonly held to be derived from the pope in just this way. But on this hypothesis it is no longer possible to see in what sense this power could be the supreme power, and how it could ever be exercised by the pope even *seorsim*, apart from the Council and the united episcopate. There is something more to be said also which touches upon the second presupposition. If it were possible to conceive of two distinct subjects existing in the

Church both vested with the supreme power, then it would cease to be comprehensible how the unity of the Church would not be, in essence, radically broken. Furthermore this would be tantamount to denying the truth that the united episcopate exists as a college only with and under the pope. In view of all this, therefore, let us take as read the validity of both the two presuppositions involved in the two answers given by the scholastics to the question which has been put. Even so, however, with regard to these presuppositions we still have a few further remarks to make, which are not unimportant for the further considerations which we have to offer.

With regard to that theory of the scholastics which maintains the absolute unity of the subject vested with supreme power in the Church the first presupposition is not so obvious as it appears. For in fact this position presupposes that there can be *one* subject such that it can be vested with supreme and plenary authority in the Church, although this power belonging to it is derived from another source (still *within* the Church), likewise vested with authority. For what is being asserted on this view is in fact that the Council is vested with such authority in virtue of being given a share of, or allowed to participate in the supreme plenary power of the pope. But if this does not involve any intrinsic contradiction then it would in fact be just as valid to hold the opinion that the pope was vested with plenary and supreme power in the Church even though he possessed this power as a result of having 'derived it' from the united episcopate or Council either by participation or by having it conferred upon him, or in some other way. Precisely according to the principles presupposed by this first scholastic opinion therefore the statement that the pope is the possessor of this supreme power in the Church could not, taken by itself, enable us to draw the conclusion with compelling force that he does not possess this power through having derived it from the united episcopate. This consideration is enough of itself to show what a dangerous presupposition precisely for the *papacy* itself underlies the opinion that the supreme power of the united episcopate or Council can be derived from the power of the pope.

With regard to the *second* principle mentioned above as presupposed in the doctrine of the two *incompletely* distinct subjects, this does, in fact, indisputably have some foundation in virtue of the incontestable truth that the pope himself is supreme and indispensable precisely as member and head of the college of bishops. But the other ground on which it is based, which is likewise not unimportant – is indeed in reality more fundamental – nevertheless does entail certain problems. The argument here is as follows:

The unity of a society is such as of its essence to exclude the possibility of two *completely distinct* bearers of supreme power over it. Purely from the juridical point of view this may in fact be wholly enlightening. But it is possible to hold the view that in the *Church* precisely as such this difficulty with regard to the unity of the society is removed through the power of the *Spirit* within her. In other words that the unity of the Church is sufficiently guaranteed by the Spirit in spite of power in her being vested in two completely distinct subjects. In support of this view it could be pointed out that precisely according to the Second Vatican Council it is the *Spirit* which preserves the 'organic structure' of the Church in spite of the heterogeneous character of this structure, and that this in turn is neither caused nor guaranteed by any formal juridical norm.

The least that can be concluded from this consideration is that when it is a question of how two different functions can exist side by side in the Church without mutually cancelling each other out or themselves in turn needing to be reconciled through the human application of some common juridical principle, caution is needed. We need not always, or from every aspect, demand a principle unequivocally applicable at the *juridical* level, in virtue of which we can test the Church's unity juridically. At the same time this is not intended to imply that the attempt we are about to make will lead to a 'spiritualisation' of relationships which necessarily are juridical, or that its primary aims lie in the sphere of Church politics. Against such objections we shall be *thinking out,* in what follows, the problem of juridical law involved in the relationship concerning which this question has to be raised. The only points which will concern us, therefore, in discussing opposed positions will be the actual arguments put forward and their power to throw light upon the problem.

II

With regard to this question an attempt will here be made to justify the following thesis:

The bearer of the highest and supreme power in the Church is the united episcopate with and under the pope as its head. This single bearer can exercise its plenary power either in a 'collegiate act' in the true sense, or through an act of its head, the pope, who even in this case acts precisely *as* head of the college, without having been commissioned for this by the rest of the bishops (the mere fact that they are such does not in itself constitute them as a college) by means of a juridical act on the part of these other bishops. *Thus there is only one subject endowed with supreme power in the Church: the college of bishops assembled under the pope as its head. But there are two modes in which this supreme college may act: a 'collegiate act' properly so-called, and the act of the pope as head of the college.*

The first point to be made with regard to this thesis is that in no sense does it derogate from the significance and dignity of the primacy of the pope. In fact the Council explicitly declares that the pope is in possession of his plenary powers not as a private person but as head of the entire Church. In this statement, then, the position of the pope is not underestimated by the fact that his office and the significance attached to this in general can be understood only in relationship to the Church, though this certainly does not mean that it is given to him by the Church. Now if this be the case then we cannot in any way be derogating from the dignity and uniqueness of his office either by saying that he possesses this plenary power precisely *as* head of the college of bishops. In no sense is there any implication in this thesis of the idea that his office and the plentitude of power which goes with it is handed over to him by the college of bishops. It is given to him by Christ. But it is given to him together with all that is included in it inasmuch as he is the appointed head of this college, which apart from him would not exist at all. For this college is constituted as such in virtue of the unity it achieves through the presidency of the pope (Peter), and by being one with him. Without the pope it itself is nothing, and he is the pope in virtue of the fact that, and to the extent that he is its head together with all the rights which precisely belong to this headship. In virtue of these rights he can also act *seorsim* i.e. by a separate act of his own as distinct from a collegiate one. But even so he is still acting precisely *as* head of the college. Of course the fullness of his power cannot be derived from any *abstract* concept of what 'head of a college' means. The pope is head of the college in precisely *that* manner which has been worked out in concrete fact as the faith of the Church throughout a progressive development of dogma, and which has been defined in the First Vatican Council. But the plenary power vested in him in this sense is precisely that of one who holds the prerogatives pertaining to the college of bishops as it actually exists in the concrete, so that however he acts he is still acting precisely *as* head of this college. This does not mean, however, that he has to be specially commissioned for the purpose by the rest of the bishops. When, therefore, we say that the pope holds his office as visible head of the Church, and only in union with her, this does not derogate from the importance and uniqueness of his primacy as bishop of Rome. Rather it is only in this way that we can arrive at an understanding of its true nature. And if this is the case, then we cannot be in any sense belittling the primacy either by saying that the pope holds his official position precisely *as* head of the college of bishops. A further point constantly to be borne in mind is that the Church of which he is head is a socially structured entity, and the papacy is not the sole factor in determining what this structure shall be. On the contrary the episcopate too is numbered among those elements in it which are *juris divini.* If, therefore, the pope is pope precisely because he is head of the Church and only in virtue of this, then it follows that he is head of a Church which is also episcopal in its constitution, and this too is *juris divini,* as a matter of divine right. It is, therefore, quite impossible for the pope to be head of the Church without at the same time and in virtue of this also being head of the united episcopate. If, therefore, the bishop of Rome enjoys his plenary powers precisely *as* head of the Church, then it necessarily follows that he also enjoys them in virtue of being head of the united episcopate. It is true of both these facts that the one implies the other in the *same* sense, and with *equal* validity: the fact that the office of the pope relates to the universal Church implies that it relates in the same sense to the united episcopate and vice versa.

That this interpretation cannot simply be false from the outset is also shown by the following fact: the pre-Conciliar version of the Constitution on the Church, even though it was composed primarily by Roman theologians, had stated unreservedly that the pope is endowed with infallibility precisely *as* head of the Church *and* of the college of bishops (No. 30 in this schema): '*Tamquam universalis ecclesiae pastor et doctor, et collegii episcoporum caput.*' It is true that in the final definitive text of *Lumen gentium* (Nos. 22, 25) this passage was omitted, or rather the term '*collegii episcoporum caput*' was transferred to another place in such a way that the two phrases were no longer explicitly presented as interchangeable. But the reason for this alteration was not that the statement contained in the pre-conciliar text is false, but rather that it was felt that this question should be left open.

Even from what has been said up to this point it will be clear that the teaching of the First and Second Vatican Councils does not exclude the thesis we have put forward at least in any positive sense. This also applies to the term *seorsim* in the *Nota Praevia Explicativa.* Having regard to the total context in which it is used this term 'by himself' only serves to rule out any necessity for a 'collegiate act' on the part of the united episcopate. What is sought to be conveyed by it is that even when the pope makes use of supreme power invested in him 'by himself', he is acting validly and in a manner which is binding upon the Church. He is not bound in this to seek any special agreement on the part of the rest of the bishops in such a way that this agreement would be prior to the act of the pope himself and its binding force, and that it would only have full validity in this sense in virtue of this prior agreement. A further and separate question is what the nature of such an act is considered *ontologically*. Is it *ipso facto* and of its very nature the act of the head of the united episcopate, or rather the act of an individual who is indeed also (*qui*) the head of the college, but precisely in this act is not acting as (*qua*) such a head? On this point the term *seorsim* as used in the Declaration remains indeterminate. The opinion that this question was not affected by the *Nota Praevia* is also shared by e.g. Y. Congar, O. Semmelroth, A. Grillmeier, who were members of the theological commission of the Council.

A further objection to our thesis which is raised is that the pope holds supreme power in the Church 'alone' and 'in person'. To this it must simply be said that the term 'alone' has exactly the same force as that of *seorsim*, so that this difficulty is to be met with the same answer as that given above. Even if it is true that 'the pope in person' possesses this plenary power, still we cannot see what consequences can be drawn from this which run counter to our thesis. In this context the phrase 'in person' can only mean 'as a concrete physical individual', since in fact 'in person' cannot mean 'as a private person'. When it is said that the pope 'alone' receives this supreme power from Christ, the word 'alone' here can only mean that he is given this power actually as a physical individual. But it cannot mean that the united episcopate does not have this power, since it does in fact undoubtedly possess it. 'Alone' and 'in person', therefore, mean simply that he possesses his power as a physical individual in the concrete, and that as such he is also the 'bearer' (certainly not merely the 'exerciser') of this power.

But in all this nothing whatever has been said in reply to a *further* question which might be asked: How can we find more precise terms in which to define what is distinctive in the position of the pope, if we are asked in what *official* (as opposed to private) capacity he 'alone' and 'in person' is the bearer of supreme power in the Church? If it is suggested that according to our version the pope exercises this power not 'in person' but 'in the name of the college of bishops', this latter being the unique bearer of this power, then we must reply that to formulate our position in these terms is most misleading. For this phrase 'in the name of the college' insinuates that in order to exercise his power the pope would need to be commissioned for the purpose by the rest of the bishops. But of course that is not the case, and is in no sense asserted by the terms of our thesis either. On the contrary what this states is: The act of the pope, which he exercises in virtue of the commission given to him directly by Christ, is *ipso facto and in itself* an act of the college (*not* a collegiate act), because this power conferred upon him 'in person' and on 'him alone' by Christ of itself makes him the 'mandatory' of the college. If it is stated that the pope possess his primatial not only independently of the individual bishops but also independently of 'all of them together' (DS 3060) this is, of course, correct. But it proves nothing against our thesis. The mere fact that this phrase is *Simul omnes* of the First Vatican Council is, as applied to the united episcopate, precisely *not* equivalent to the term 'college' is in itself enough to establish this point. For the pope himself belongs to the college as such as a constitutive member of it and indeed the supreme member of the college itself. If, therefore, he were to hold this primatial power of his independently of the actual college as such, and not merely independently of the sum total of all the rest of the bishops, then he would hold it independently of himself also – a position which is meaningless. In the strictest and most precise sense the pope has a supreme power not as a figure over and against the college or above it, for this college is in fact itself indisputably vested with this same supreme power. The position is, rather, that the pope exercises this same power as an individual also, and this is precisely why in his possession of this power he is set apart from every other individual bishop and also from the sum total of all the bishops (though these are not identical with the college of bishops as such).

4.6 JEAN-MARIE R. TILLARD: *THE SERVANT OF COMMUNION* – 1987

The following selection[10] is taken from Tillard's book, *Church of Churches – the Ecclesiology of Communion*. Tillard's treatment of the papacy in this excerpt is both a distillation and development of the theology of the papacy he first developed in his earlier work, *The Bishop of Rome*. As such, it represents a second trajectory in post-conciliar thought on the papacy in so far as it attempts to re-situate papal authority within a patristic ecclesiology of communion. Unlike Rahner, Tillard views the college of the bishops as a concentrated manifestation of the communion of the local churches. The pope functions as the servant of that communion.

THE VISIBLE COMMUNION OF THE CHURCHES

The profound *communion* which the Eucharist – and it alone – accomplishes emerges in a visible way only when those who preside at the Eucharistic celebration today everywhere in the world and who have presided at it since Pentecost as an image of Christ 'gathering together in unity' the people of God, are themselves united in one single ministerial body. They form in this way, in the multitude that they are, one single instrument of ecclesial gathering together. Tradition says that they are a college having for their core the ministry of unity of one among them. It sees there a requirement of *communion*.

When the Catholic Church affirms that it is the community in which the Church of God subsists (*subsistit in*) in all its force and with the fullness of the means of Salvation, it puts among the guarantees of this fullness the presence in it of the ministry of unity confided to the Bishop of Rome. More than that, it holds that it alone possesses such a ministry. Whereas for the totality of faith and sacramental life – even in what concerns the apostolic origin and the significance of the episcopal ministry – it is recognized with the Eastern Churches (which it calls for that reason, since Paul VI, its sister Churches) in a basic *communion,* this point forbids it to solidify this unity in a full *communion* of life and structure. In fact, the ecclesiology which we have presented can – at least for what is essential – be accepted by these churches. But from the time that the chapter on Roman primacy is opened up, everything is spoiled. It is evident that the problem is complicated because of the groups which were born of the Reformation or its spirit.

---

10. *ET*, Tillard, J.M.R., 'The Servant of Communion', in his *Church of churches – the ecclesiology of Communion*, Callegentle, Liturgical Press, 1992, pp. 256ff. French edition, *Eglise d'eglises*, du cerf, Paris, 1987.

THE SERVANT OF THE SERVANTS OF GOD

In order to get rid of any ambiguities, it is important to begin by clearing all the underbrush from the terrain. When, rereading Vatican I in light of an episcopal theology which ties together with that found in the great Tradition, Vatican II presents the ministry of the Bishop of Rome, it is careful to inscribe in it the ministry which is confided to the entire episcopal body. It does not make him a bishop above this body but on the contrary it makes him one bishop among the bishops. The papacy is not a sacrament, nor even a degree in the fullness of the sacrament of orders. It is a particular way of putting into operation the episcopal, sacramental, common grace. For a tradition which maintains the absolute priority of the sacramental over all the rest and even affirms that the Church has only a sacramental source, this remark is of capital importance. The Church, born of the Spirit and growing through him, gets its life from baptism, which seals the acceptance of the Word of Salvation, and of the Eucharist around which radiate other rites. It celebrates these sacraments in the local Churches whose preservation in the heart of apostolic tradition is guaranteed by the ministry of the bishop conferred in the sacrament of ordination. The papacy would not be in harmony with the economy of God for his Church if it would not insert itself in this sacramental circle.

It is, therefore, in the mission of the episcopate *as such* that it is necessary to understand the function of the Bishop of Rome. And everything depends on what we have said at length about the why of the collegial nature of the episcopal ministry and the link of each bishop with his Church. On the one hand, the Church is one in the unity proper to a *communion*. It is neither an addition of parts, nor entirely shared: it is a *communion* of local Churches, *Church of Churches*. On the other hand, in his local Church, each bishop, especially by the teaching of the faith and presiding at the Eucharist, has a mission to preserve the total fidelity of the community to what has been transmitted and lived since the time of the apostles and in total harmony with what is taught and lived *hic et nunc* in the other communities of the same apostolic tradition, guaranteeing in this way its insertion into *communion*. Bishops and communion in the *catholica*, episcopal thrones and ecclesial *koinonia* are on this point united that a break in episcopal unity implies a break in ecclesial communion. The schism of a bishop leads to the schism of his community because he can no longer preside at the Eucharist (where his local Church 'manifests' itself) in communion with the other bishops and their Churches. It is necessary, therefore, to have an unbreakable communion of the bishops – in faith, witness and service – if one wishes both to assure and intimate the communion of local Churches. It is the local Church which creates the unity of the Church of God on this earth.

Besides, the local Churches are different in their customs, traditions, problems, soul, often even in their organization … . However, pluralism ceases to be in harmony with the very nature of the Church of God when it is no longer founded on a unity of faith, sacramental life and mission. It is then transformed into division. Inculturation cannot turn into the process of making differences absolute or the claim that in either one of the communities alone can the valid essence of the Church of God be carried out. It belongs to the identity of the local Church to be a group which does not take refuge behind its special qualities which it would consider absolutes. It is the one which, so inculturated with Christianity, confesses and celebrates the faith which is also lived *hic et nunc* elsewhere, which was lived in the past since the time of Pentecost, and which will be lived in the future until the coming of the Lord.

The local Church finds its identity only in this totality: elsewhere, since the apostles, until the Coming. That is also why every local Church must convey in its very life concern for other local Churches … .

Also the Bishop of every local Church has among the central components of his responsibility, by his ordination for the service of this local Church, the responsibility of seeing to the opening up of his local Church to *all* Churches. He accepts the *sollicitudo omnium Ecclesiarum*. He exercises it in communion with the other bishops, in a dialog which creates harmony between one and the multitude.

The function of the Bishop of Rome is none other than a very special form of this *sollicitudo omniun Ecclesiarum* given with the episcopal grace, hence a particular form of exercising the common sacrament of the episcopate. It is a service within the all-encompassing mission of the episcopal college, the function of the 'servant of the servants of God' according to the ideal which Gregory the Great put forth and which is expressed in the title of every conciliar document of Vatican II. It does not support this mode of a sacramental hierarchy which would make him a 'super bishop'. But, a bishop like all other members of the episcopal college, it is he, on the *cathedra* of the local Church of Rome, whom his link with Peter and Paul invests us with a special responsibility (a *sollicitudo*) for the communion with all the Churches within the faith, witness and service. It is from this primacy of *his* local Church in the midst of *all* the local Churches that the Bishop of Rome has his primacy in the college of bishops. In this college, which possesses *in globo* the full and supreme responsibility over the whole Church he guarantees a particular and necessary function which affects precisely the cohesion of the bishops and their unity in the faith which Peter and Paul sealed by their martyrdom. The constitution *Pastor aeternus* of Vatican I, and *Lumen gentium* of Vatican II which reiterates the former, do not say anything different … .

As far as what concerns the opening up of each local Church to the needs of others, the task of the Bishop of Rome is still 'to be on the watch'. The *sollicitudo omnium Ecclesiarum* could very well be buried, even refused, because of the urgency of local problems. It could also be put into practice by a scattering of things around but ignoring those things which are urgent. By his place in the episcopal college, the Bishop of Rome has the responsibility to promote and harmonize the eccelesial solidarity which – as Paul's preoccupation already shows at the time of the collection for the Church of Jerusalem – belongs to the soul of the Church.

One cannot imagine, therefore, this function of the Bishop of Rome as that of the 'universal bishop'. And if Paul VI adds to his signature on the actions of Vatican II the title of *episcopus Ecclesiae catholicae*, it is in the old sense of 'bishop of the local Church of Rome who has remained faithful to the apostolic faith'. A person is bishop of a local Church, and it is necessary at any price – with the danger of confusing everything – to respect the link between bishop and local *cathedra*. It is precisely because their mission, in large part intransmissible, precedes every local Church that the apostles cannot be called the 'first bishops' … .

Bishop among bishops, but Bishop of Rome and for that reason charged with the *singular* power attached to the seat of the *potentior principalitatis*; such is the episcopal status of the Primate in the episcopal college and in regard to the *communion* of the Churches confided to him. Nothing in his function, and the power which corresponds to it, escapes the episcopal grace. But this grace – which in every bishop is always given for *communion* – is proportionate to the place of *his* Church in the heart of this *communion*. His relationship to Christ and to the Church is situated there, inside the relationship of the episcopal college *as such*, a college which bears in itself as a principle of unity the singular 'service' of one of its members, charged with going back continually to the witness of Peter and Paul. This *singularity* is episcopal; it remains in the control of the episcopal grace *as such*. However, it is proper to this bishop and makes him not a super-bishop but certainly *the first* in responsibility … .

The charge confided to the Bishop of Rome is a service of the Church accomplished not by short-circuiting that of the bishop of each local Church but, on the contrary, as even the text of Vatican I states, by 'affirming it, strengthening it and defending it'.[11] This service consists in preserving with the uneasiness about the universal (of the *catholica*) the ministry of each bishop and maintaining it at any price within the demands of the unbreakable solidarity of *communion*. It is the ministry of *this* local bishop which is at the heart of the life of this local Church. The role of the Bishop of Rome does not consist in an intervention which is added over and above, as that of the Prime Minister compared to the mayor of the city. It is the question of a presence making itself felt inside even the involvement of this bishop, 'evangelizing it' so that it will be what it is supposed to be … .

Wherever the local bishop acts in *communion* and in function of it, and wherever the Bishop of Rome is faithful to not going beyond the specifics of his function, then there are not two authorities in the diocese (the local Church). There is that of a bishop in whom are transmitted faith, witness, concerns, objectives, teaching, and mission which are those of the entire episcopal college and that he 'receives' in his *communion* with the one who has the responsibility of seeing to the cohesion of this college in fidelity to the apostolic deposit of faith. It happens, obviously, that a bishop may slip out of *communion* or that the Bishop of Rome may act as if he were the only bishop. Reading history is enough to be convinced of it. Then the osmosis is broken; two authorities superimpose themselves. But then also the nature of the Church is falsified.

It is true that in what the code of canon law continues to call the Latin Church, relations between the Bishop of Rome and other bishops are complicated by the fact that the limits of the patriarchate of the West (whose patriarch is the Bishop of Rome) and those of the totality of Churches in communion with the Roman See are clouded over. One of the consequences of the break with the East has been this narrowing of the ecclesial space where bishops preside in communion with the Bishop of Rome, and the quasi-identification of this space with the patriarchate of the West. The exercise of primacy and that of the patriarchal authority have almost become one and the same. But the patriarchal authority is by nature administrative and centralized. It implies making decisions for the churches in his jurisdiction and a vast right of inspection. Very attentive to the choice of bishops, it exercises in their regard a particular 'surveillance' judging their offences, exempting certain groups from their authority, sometimes nibbling away at their influence, receiving appeals, intervening in major problems. Since the exercise of the primacy assumes several of these characteristics of the exercise of the patriarchate, it can no longer be seen in all its purity. It appears under a disguise which no longer permits an adequate perception of its identity.

11. DS, 3061.

Certainly, it must be recognized that even in what concerns its relations with other patriarchates before the break, the Roman See was tempted to add prerogatives which came from the primacy of claims which exceeded the nature of it. It will hint, then affirm that the authority of the other primates and other patriarchs – like that of the metropolitans and bishops of these churches – comes from a concession of privileges and powers which come from it. The famous theory of the three chairs of Peter – in Antioch, Alexandria and Rome – will often serve to justify this 'patriarchal' meddling of the vicar of Peter beyond the West, provoking in way a meshing of primatial authority over patriarchal rights. The East, although it saw in Rome the center of doctrinal reference and even under certain circumstances resorted to mediation from the bishop of this seat, obviously resisted a similar infringement. It was not a stranger to a climate ending in schism. Besides, even in the West, important areas vigorously affirmed their right to a relative autonomy … .

These reactions must be taken seriously. They show that in the undivided Church, for reasons that it would be thoughtless to identify solely or without fine distinctions in regard to their political aspirations – although desire for power and prestige are not absent from them – the compenetration of various types of authority with which the bishop of Rome is invested has not gone on by itself. In particular the quasi-confusion of his authority as primate of all the Churches and his function as patriarch of the West, inducing him to act with the bishops of other patriarchates in the way which his title as patriarch authorized him to do in the West, has caused a problem … .

Within these perspectives, it becomes possible to get to the core of the authority which Catholic tradition recognizes in the Roman primate and to measure with greater clarity the 'power' that its exercise requires. In a negative way, it is necessary, first of all, to restate that it is not a question formally of a power of *dominion* but of a 'power' which is pastoral and oriented toward service. It is regulated by the authority which others (the other bishops) have received and which it must strengthen and guarantee. Besides, *by himself*, it is not up to the primate 'to make bishops'. We have seen that down through the centuries the churches have chosen their pastors, according to their own customs, all the while remaining in communion with the Bishop of Rome. And in nothing did he contest this right of each local Church to take one of its own whose faith it knew and whose uprightness it was aware of, in communion with the neighboring Churches, then to have him ordained. Therefore, he does not take control or wield a heavy hand over the episcopate. It is not even, in the political sense, a power of government but a 'power' of leadership. The nuance is important. To govern, is to rule (sometimes by giving in to the temptation to dominate or coerce); to exercise leadership is to win over, to guide, to lead each one towards what the Spirit wants him to become … .

One is closer here to the choir director who, for the harmony of all parties, 'sees to' the accuracy, the tone, the volume of each voice by putting it in its place within the context of the whole choir, like the power of an army general. And the quality of the choir depends on its director, on the experience which he transmits.

Positively, the 'power' of the primate is that of intervening, in certain cases, in the life of a local church, when the good of the *communion* demands it. In fact, it happens that through a lack of resources or simply because it does not have the means to make by itself the decisions which are imposed, a Church slips into a situation which compromises its quality, perhaps even its fidelity to the gospel. Certainly, the primate must first of all urge the local bishop to act by himself, to alert the neighboring Churches. But a direct intervention can be imposed: an explicit request for help made to another Church, a convocation of a local synod or of a provincial council, the sending of the necessary men, or an official expression of his disagreement … .

Here we are on the level of subsidiarity. This implies that in regard to a community over which it has a real power, but which is confided to a special authority, the 'superior' entreaty seeks to reduce the interventions as much as possible. It refuses to meddle with the affairs of this group as long as it has not put its own means into operation, and mobilized all of its resources. In other words, it does not seek to take the place of those who are in positions of responsibility, to substitute for them. Its primary attitude is to awaken their attention, to recall to them (vigorously perhaps) the task which is incumbent on them. But, when it ascertains that alone they cannot overcome the crisis, it owes it to itself to intervene. Without that, in fact, this group will let itself deteriorate or vegetate in a way which threatens its identity. In this sense, the Bishop of Rome has the power, and the duty, to act for the good of the whole Church (at stake in each local church, since this is where it is realized) when a local Church compromises the good of *communion* … .

The primatial 'power' is exercised also on another level. It would be foolish to pretend that only the Bishop of Rome has the 'power' to convoke a council. That would be tantamount to denying history. But it is impossible to refuse him this 'power,' even in the hypothesis of an authentic ecumenical council of the Church finally gathered together in unity. It is clear then the methods and conditions of exercising this 'power' would be determined carefully. Yet in a world where the Christian notion of the emperor is no more than a memory, one can hardly see how the decision to hold a council could be taken without the bishop of the Roman see intervening. The idea of such a council can be proposed to him. But the convoking must at least involve his *placet*, just as the promulgation of the *acta*, 'una cum patribus'.

This necessity comes from the very nature of every ecumenical council and of its crucial importance for *communion*. Authority of the Bishop of Rome and authority of the council are in a process of osmosis, even if sometimes there are conflicts and tensions. In the exercise of his function, the primate should not forget the principle '*quod omnes tangit ab omnibus tractari et approbari debet*'. On their part, however, the bishops of the other Churches cannot forget that the unity of the Church demands a common point of view and a unanimous doctrinal vision on the serious questions which are asked about the faith. But the council is precisely the moment in which all the churches – by those who represent them – treat together what concerns all of them … .

Declaring *ex cathedra*, as the primary one responsible for the *communication* of faith, a solemn infallible *judgment* on a point touching at the heart of the Christian content of faith and under very precise conditions is more complex. Let us note very well that it is a question of an infallibility of *judgment*. This signifies formally that *such an* affirmation, declaring 'what is', in the area of what is necessary to believe or reject for salvation, is guaranteed by the judgment of the one who made it. He has spoken infallibly. It is neither a revealed word nor an inspired word but a word spoken with the help of the Spirit preventing *at that time* the one who speaks from falling into error. His declaration, or proposition, is undoubtedly true … .

It may be that its formulation is not the best, that it does not express the entire content of the truth in question, that it may be closely linked to the categories of an era or a culture. It is, in fact, a declaration espousing the laws of the human language, therefore limited, and by that fact subject to corrections. But it expresses a truth which will always be true, even if one day the need for formulating it otherwise is felt. It even may be that in other circumstances, while he did not intend to declare himself *ex cathedra*, the same Bishop of Rome has stated debatable words. But infallibility is guaranteed only in certain judgments, declared under very precise conditions, surrounded with numerous precautions, because it is a question of rare and easily discernible cases where the Bishop of Rome decides to convey by himself the judgment which an ecumenical council normally would have conveyed. And this judgment does not have to be submitted to the verdict of a higher tribunal. The 'power' in question is, therefore, plain and clear-cut … .

In brief, the proper 'power' of the Roman primate, perceived as we have just done so in his specific acts, is from all its angles united with that of the other bishops, in *synergy* with it. And this is true all the way to the proceedings which at first glance seem to be the most solitary ones, that of definitions *ex cathedra*. It is a service 'power' of the episcopate, not the power to supplant the authority of the episcopal college over the totality of the Churches and that of each bishop over his local Church. It is, according to the intuition of Gregory the Great, a 'power' of confirmation of the other bishops in their own service of the ecclesial *communion* of faith, of witness and of mission, not the power to absorb their ministry in a 'sovereign' way. It is a 'power' of promotion and support of the ministry of his brother bishops, not the power of holding everything in his hands. In one word, it is a power *in* the episcopal college and *for* the episcopal college. It is this episcopal college which is the first beneficiary of it.

4.7 YVES CONGAR: *THE POPE AS PATRIARCH OF THE WEST* – 1991

Our extract[12] is a short essay on the pope as patriarch of the West. Congar contends that the recognition that the pope wears many ecclesiastical 'hats' (e.g., bishop of Rome, primate of Italy, and patriarch of the West) can remind us that not all exercises of papal authority have been exercises of the pope acting as universal pastor of the church. The ecclesiological significance of the pope's role as patriarch of the West lies in the recognition that many exercises of papal authority are patriarchal and might not have a bearing on churches not belonging to the patriarchate of the West.

❉

From the 6th century, patriarchates grew from the combination of Church organization conforming to structures of civil administration and the recognition given to churches of sees governed by the Apostles. Early councils gave special recognition to the sees of Alexandria, Rome, and Antioch, and Constantinople was acknowledged to have primacy of honor after Rome since it was the New Rome. These with Jerusalem formed the Pentarchy whose participation in a council was considered a condition and criterion of ecumenicity. Maximus the Confessor (mid-7th century) and Theodore of Studios (beginning of the 9th century) systematized this Pentarchy theory, although they also appealed to Rome in struggles against monothelitism and in the Iconoclastic Controversy.

Each church had its bishop, but a metropolitan with jurisdiction over a province had authority over several churches and sees. The patriarch with jurisdiction over a civil diocese began to absorb some prerogatives of the metropolitan. Names of the patriarchs were pronounced in the liturgy as a sign of communion.

The bishop of Rome had his local church, but he was also metropolitan of suburbicarian Italy. The Latin west included more than the metropolitan structure. Because of the way the Empire was divided, the patriarchate of the bishop of Rome extended to Greek speaking areas: Illyrium and Greek areas of southern Italy and Sicily. The metropolitan structure as it existed in the West limited the exercise of patriarchal power. This power was strengthened in Africa by the primacy of the bishop of Carthage and a tradition of independence (whence the forbidding by the Council of Carthage of appeals to Rome). From other areas of the West, however, the pope received appeals and acted as arbitrator, and so had a judicial authority.

The East had its own patriarchs. It often appealed to the authority of the pope, but was also convinced of its autonomy. The popes did not intervene in the West as patriarchs, but intervened with judicial authority to insist on orthodoxy, respect for canons, or regularity of elections, even going against a council to depose or re-establish a bishop. They saw themselves

---

12. Congar, Yves, 'The Pope as Patriarch of the West', in *Theology Digest*, 38 (Spring, 1991), 3–7. French original: 'Le Pape comme patriarche d'Occident', *Istina*, 28 (Oct.–Dec., 1983), 374–90.

as exercising the authority and responsibility of Peter of whom they were 'vicars' or representatives. The East shows little awareness of this view.

PATRIARCHAL POWER ABSORBED

Even in enacting decrees for the West alone, for Italy, or only for Rome, the popes never appealed to their patriarchal rights as distinct from their rights as supreme pastors: they appealed, rather, to the rights of the Chair of Peter. Papal interventions in Gaul in the 9th century were not in the name of patriarchal power, but as head of the church (Imbart de la Tour). The two powers were merged in the person of the pope, and it was his power as pope that prevailed.

The False Decretals used texts claiming to be from early popes to attribute to the primacy privileges that actually belonged to the pope as metropolitan. Rome did not manage to separate the apostolic responsibility from the essentially administrative patriarchal idea, wrote J. Ratzinger (1964). The East could not acknowledge Rome's claim presented in this form. The image of the church as a centralized state does not come simply from the responsibility of Peter but from the amalgam of this responsibility with the patriarchal task that fell to the bishop of Rome for all of Latin Christianity. Ratzinger's thought is consistent with that of J.J. von Allmen: in the Carolingian era, clinging to the form of the local church of Rome became a way of maintaining unity for the Empire. Gradually the whole West adopted the Roman liturgy, and all local churches became incorporated into the Roman church. Into its *urbs* Rome integrated the whole Latin *orbis*. The West became one local community and lost its early structure of unity in plurality.

The Orthodox East escaped this process, but the Eastern rite churches in union with Rome did not. The notion of the patriarchate was hardly understood, and so not honored by Rome. Any reference to it was connected with Peter through the theory of the three Petrine sees, Rome, Antioch, and Alexandria. The creation of a Latin patriarchate following the fourth crusade led to the idea that patriarchal privileges were a concession from the papacy, an idea expressed fully in the (spurious) profession of faith read at Lyons (1274):

The Roman church admits other Churches to a share in its responsibility ... especially the patriarchal churches, the ... Roman Church has honored with various privileges.

DISTINCTION OF PAPAL TITLES

What relation is there among papal titles such as Bishop of Rome, Vicar of Christ, Successor of Prince of the Apostles, Sovereign Pontiff of the Universal Church, Patriarch of the West, Primate of Italy, Metropolitan of the Roman Province? Vicar of Christ is not independent from Successor of Peter, but is Successor of Peter the same as Bishop of Rome? Peter was not a bishop at or of Rome. We can't call the apostles bishops (an Orthodox argument against Roman theses). The earliest lists do not do so (cf. Irenaeus III, 3, 3), but early texts do speak of the Chair of Peter. The term *cathedra* (and *thronos*), on the basis of biblical use, was the equivalent of episcopate as early as the 2nd century (Hermas, Muratorian canon, Tertullian,

Hippolytus). It referred especially to teaching. St Cyprian used 'cathedra Petri' to indicate the catholic episcopate grounded in Peter, or the episcopal chair of Rome (E 59, 14). Texts from the 3rd to the 5th century assert the office of the episcopate began in Peter. In the earliest witnesses the Roman church has the primacy because it is the church where Peter and Paul taught, were martyred, where their bodies rest, and where they are ever present. The bishops who received the episcopal charge from this church have the primacy.

Paul VI confirmed this understanding when he spoke of care of the eternal city 'confided to the Roman Pontiff, successor of the holy apostle Peter over the See of this city and – precisely as such – supreme pastor and visible head of the church' (1977). In effect, the successor of Peter at Rome is the bishop of the Roman church.

This is the point at which we must evaluate the title Vicar of Christ. It is not independent from the title Successor of Peter as occupying his cathedra. From the time of his election as pope, said Agostino Trionfo of Ancone (d. 1328), he possesses the title 'Vicar of Christ', for he receives universal jurisdiction in its fullness – this even if he is not a bishop. Such appalling theology shows the ambiguity of the title Vicar of Christ. Fortunately the 1975 Apostolic Constitution regulating election of the pope stipulates that if he is not already a bishop, the one elected pope is to be ordained immediately, before receiving tribute from the cardinals and before the election is to be announced.

The Orthodox recognized the pope as Bishop of Rome and as first of the bishops. The Catholic view implies more. The pope is a member of the college of bishops, but he is its head. Peter was one of the Twelve but he received a special designation. Innocent III pointed out that Christ first gave to Peter alone what he then gave to the Twelve, including Peter. So while all the apostles are the foundation (Eph. 2:20), Peter is the first rock (Mt. 16:18); all are pastors (Acts 20:28), but Peter is universal pastor (Jn 21:15–17).

Peter, then, embodies two values: as one of the Twelve, he is and has what the others are and have. But he personally receives these gifts in a way that sets him apart. He not only believes and witnesses to faith, but will confirm it. In the Gospels and Acts he speaks for all, answers for all, and takes initiatives that involve the church. These two aspects will be found in Peter's successor. It is part of the apostolic structure of the church, but of a church involved in history. Whatever there is of divine right in the church exists concretely only in relative human conditions which have changed and still can change. To maintain nuncios to states, for example, or to be Sovereign of a State, comes from history, not divine law.

When we consider the origins of the Roman church and its primacy we must consider not only Peter's charism, but Paul's. In solemn acts such as convening councils, canonizing, or in dogmatic definitions, the popes appeal to 'the authority of the Apostles Peter and Paul'. Paul represents care of all the churches, teaching, pursuit of communion of the Gentile churches with that of Jerusalem by means of the collection. Theologians have attributed doctrine to Paul and governing authority to Peter. We must honor the plan of Providence which has chosen to add Paul, 'the first after the unique one' (E.B. Allo) to the Rock which is Peter.

Within the college the bishop of Rome, as successor of Peter, receives a special charism of office which makes him heir of the privileges of Peter in the college and in the universal church. What name is to be given to this office? 'Vicar of Christ' needs explanation and risks being excessive. The Bishop of Rome is not bishop of the whole church as one is bishop of a see; he is not 'universal bishop'. But other titles would serve – Head of the College, Head of the Church, Universal Pastor. 'Universal Pastor' could replace 'jurisdiction' without eliminating it. It would highlight the aim of papal power – which is to unite all in the fervent profession of the faith and love of the Lord. Indeed, it is the service of communion of the churches through the communion of Christians. 'Universal Pastor' is consistent with equivalents used in Vatican II.

Vatican I guides our understanding of pontifical primacy when in the prologue to *Pastor aeternus* it states, Christ:

> Placed St Peter at the head of the other apostles that the episcopate might be one and undivided, and that … the whole multitude of believers might be preserved in unity of faith and communion by means of a well-organized priesthood. He made Peter a perpetual principle of this twofold unity … . (DS, 3050)

Although this ecclesiology is static and oriented toward the hierarchy, it is important from the perspective of communion among the churches. It legitimates the primacy with its aim of maintaining communion among the churches and of maintaining all in unity of the apostolic faith. This end is the basis for the powers needed to carry it out. History shows these powers can be overvalued and abused (cf. the theory of the two swords). But in general when popes have exercised primacy outside of their patriarchate (in the East), the facts fit rather well with the principle of using that power for unity. Peter's successor is neither universal bishop nor a 'super bishop'. He is more than first of the bishops in the sense of 'first among equals'. He has the office and therefore the power and charism as guardian of peace, as promoter and harmonizer of communion in the apostolic faith. Indeed, it is through this communion in faith that plurality is bought back to unity. The church was founded on Peter's *faith* in Christ the Son of the living God.

APPLICATION TODAY

What are we to make of a Latin patriarch that includes the U.S., Asia, Australia, the Pacific Isles, and even Japan? Are the episcopates of Latin America, Africa and Madagascar, and Asia not organs of possible patriarchates that have no patriarchs? What would it mean today to say the ecumenicity of a council is assured by participation of (the five) patriarchs?

In the 15th century Nicholas of Cusa, exploring meanings of the expression *ecclesia Romana*, spoke of the pope as patriarch and spoke of the Roman church as a patriarchate. This church, he said, has greater assurance than the others of not erring in the faith. The fact that the pope or his legate presides over a council does not thereby make the council 'universal'; it may simply be a patriarchal council. The Roman patriarchal council enjoys an inerrancy in faith. Unfortunately, he wrote, today 'there is just one council of the universal church and of the Roman patriarchal see, since the whole church has been reduced to the single patriarchate'.

John Stoykovic (1438) spoke of the Roman church in the sense of patriarchate of the west and as a church that enjoyed infallibility. Normally, he said, a council assembled the five patriarchs, but when the East fell into error, the church was reduced to the Roman patriarchate.

These 15th century theologians could be relevant for the problem of councils held without the Greeks. Paul VI did not refer to the Council of Lyons (1274) as ecumenical as had been done since Bellarmine, but rather as the 'sixth general council held in the West'. (The previous five were the four Lateran councils and Lyons, 1245.) Could we not speak of councils of the patriarchate of the West? The case is different for Florence, Trent, and Vatican I and II. But this designation is worth considering for the medieval councils of Vienne and Lateran V.

Prelates of the curia have expressed similar views. Cardinal Benelli (1973) has noted that the pope's real jurisdiction over the whole church is one thing, but centralization of power is another. His jurisdiction is of divine law, but centralization of power comes from human circumstances. J. Ratzinger pointed out that the patriarchates largely carry out administrative tasks in their respective areas. On this level, he said, 'Rome has no more right than do the other patriarchates'. Rome's primacy does not include being entrusted with central administration.

Although the pope's primacy and patriarchy are barely distinguishable today, there are still things the pope does not or should not do in those Eastern churches in communion with his See: nomination of bishops, calling patriarchal synods, judging pending matters and everyday decisions – those things which, if he does in the rest of the church are done as patriarch. To recognize this distinction will probably not change anything in the concrete life of the 'rest' of the church – unless other patriarchates are set up; but such recognition has great ecumenical value – because it is ecclesiologically sound and historically accurate.

Historically and theologically, then, it is questionable if one can say the right to appoint bishops belongs by nature to the Roman Pontiff. We must distinguish. A pontiff may use his primacy in naming bishops, but primacy does not require that he do so. For centuries bishops were chosen and some sees were even set up with no papal intervention, though the pope had exercised primacy if the need arose.

Can we imagine a church as a collegiality of patriarchates that would include the Pentarchy; those of Moscow, Rumania, Serbia, Bulgaria; and of others that could be set up (Canterbury, Africa, Latin America, India)? Is it unreasonable? Unrealistic? Utopian? Not if we consider ecclesiological notions of an old tradition.

4.8 PATRICK GRANFIELD: *THE POSSIBILITY OF LIMITATION* – 1987

The following selection[13] is taken from Granfield's book, *The Limits of the Papacy*. In this volume he addresses a number of the contemporary controversies associated with the exercise of papal authority. He explores the balance between the legitimate rights of the papacy and the real limits to the exercise of papal authority that can be found in the Catholic tradition.

THE POSSIBILITY OF LIMITATION

The Pope may determine his own competence, define the scope of his power, and judge all cases, even those in which he is involved. The history of the Church reveals, as Gustave Thils has noted, 'the imperturbable movement towards the same point – the concentration of everything in the papacy'.[14] The expansion of papal power may be understandable in view of historical circumstances, but to many it seems far removed from the scriptural idea of authority as humble service within and for the people of God. Catholics and non-Catholics inevitably ask about the limits of papal authority. What are the boundaries that determine the legitimate exercise of papal authority? This chapter attempts to address this issue... .

THE OFFICIAL LIMITS

By official limits we mean those that emerge from the office of the papacy itself. Catholic tradition has constantly taught that the mandate or purpose of the primatial office provides the most fundamental limitation of the Pope. Since the papacy exists within the Church, and the Pope is a member of the Church, to understand the purpose of the Papacy and its possible limits it is necessary first to understand the purpose of the Church ... .

The purpose of the papacy functions as a principle of limitation. The Pope should use all necessary or useful means to achieve the purpose of his office and avoid anything that hinders it. The Pope tries to make the directing idea of the Christ event a living reality. 'The institution,' according to Eric Voegelin, 'is successfully perfected when the ruler has become subordinate to the idea ... . The power of a ruler has authority insofar as he is able to make his factual power representative of an idea.'[15] Papal authority has its specific purpose or mission that, in an overarching sense, determines and delineates all its actions.

13. From Granfield, Patrick, *The Limits of the Papacy*, New York, Crossroad, 1987, 51–76.
14. 'The Theology of Primacy: Towards a Revision', *One in Christ*, 10 (1974), 24.
15. *The New Science of Politics*, Chicago, University of Chicago, 1952, 48.

What is the mission and purpose of the papacy? According to Vatican I, the Pope is the 'perpetual principle' and 'visible foundation' of the unity of the Church (DS 3051). His mission is to preserve all believers in the unity of the faith and communion (DS 3051, 3060), to maintain the perpetual welfare and lasting good of the Church (DS 3056), and to ensure that the episcopate is one and undivided (DS 3051). By fulfilling this mandate, the Pope strengthens the bonds of communion with the Church of Rome and enables the members of the Church to form a united body (DS 3057).

The mandate of the Bishop of Rome, therefore, is to maintain and safeguard the visible unity of the Church and to show solicitude for all the local Churches that belong to the *communio*. The idea of the *sollicitudo omnium ecclesiarum* has a long tradition going back to St. Paul who referred to 'my daily pressing anxiety, the care of all the churches' (2 Cor. 11:28). Many of the early Popes also used the idea of solicitude to describe their mission as successors of Peter: Siricius (384–399); Innocent I (401–417); Celestine I (422–432); and Leo I (440–461).

The Pope is the symbol of ecclesial unity. He expresses the unity of all Churches as he functions uniquely as the universal authority. He should vigorously promote peace and justice in the world. By facilitating communication, mutual help, and solicitude, the Pope is less a lawgiver than a focal point of inspiration and support. 'The basic function of the Pope in the Church,' writes Ludwig Hertling, 'is not his performance of certain official duties, but simply that he be present.'[16] This does not mean that the Pope is simply 'a lifeless rock or an abstract principle',[17] but rather that he plays a sacramental and symbolic role as a center of the *communio* of the Churches. The Pope is an effective and juridically empowered symbol.

Another aspect of the mandate of the papacy that relates to limitation is the traditional idea that the papal authority should build and not destroy the Church (*ad aedificationem et non ad destructionem*). It is taken from St. Paul: 'Maybe I do boast rather too much about our authority, but the Lord gave it to me for building you up and not for pulling you down, and I shall not be ashamed of it (2 Cor. 10:8)'... .

This principle, because of its generality, is admittedly vague. It is difficult, if not impossible, to establish specific norms that apply to every concrete situation. The principle, however, is still important as an objective norm of limitation. It serves as a constant reminder to the Pope that in sanctifying, teaching, and governing his flock he is accountable for his actions. The papacy exists in order to strengthen the Church, to ensure the salvation of humanity, and to allow the Spirit to animate its members. Any action that violates these goals is blameworthy and may even be invalid.

THE LEGAL LIMITS

In the past, theologians have sought to compare Church government to civil government. Although they recognized that the Church is unique and that any comparison to forms of civil authority is analogous, many argued that the Church is a monarchy. Robert Bellarmine (d.

---

16. *Communio: Church and Papacy in Early Christianity*, Chicago, Loyola University, 1972, 71.
17. Ibid., 72.

1621), for example, felt that a pure monarchy was the ideal form of government, but 'because of the corruption of human nature' a form of government that has elements of monarchy, aristocracy, and democracy is preferable.[18]

Vatican I did not use the term 'monarchy', but, in fact, it did give a monarchical description of the papal office. There are sound theological reasons to avoid calling the Church a monarchy: the idea seems to foster unilateralism in decision-making, triumphalism in style, and excessive centralization in government. Papal monarchism tends to stress the juridical at the expense of the spiritual, isolate the Pope from the rest of the Church, and neglect the charismatic gifts in the Church at large.

But if the Church is called a monarchy, then it is a unique one. It is not hereditary nor absolute but constitutional. At Vatican I, Gregory II, Youssef, the Melkite Patriarch of Antioch, recommended unsuccessfully that *Pastor aeternus* state clearly that the Church is not an absolute monarchy. Bishop Joseph Papp-Szilagyi of Hungary said that Orthodox Christians considered heretical the idea of an absolute and unrestricted monarchy of the Pope. The Pope is not an absolute monarch because he does not have unlimited authority. He is bound by the constitution of the Church and by certain doctrinal and structural restraints. The German episcopate, responding to Bismarck in 1875, clearly stated this position: 'The title of the absolute monarch cannot be rightly applied to the Pope even in purely ecclesiastical affairs, for he is subject to divine law and bound by the dispositions made by Christ for his Church.'[19]

Two important texts emphasize this point and in doing so give us the starting point for our discussion of the legal limitations of the papal primacy. The first text is from Vatican I. Bishop Zinelli of the Deputation of the Faith declared:

> From all the sources of revelation it is clear that full and supreme power in the Church was conferred upon Peter and his successors, full in the sense that it cannot be limited by any greater human power but only by the natural and divine law.[20]

The second text is from Vatican II. In the discussion of the papacy in chapter three of *Lumen gentium*, Paul VI suggested that the phrase 'accountable to the Lord alone' ('*uni Domino devi*[n]*ctus*') be added to the text describing the exercise of papal primacy. The Theological Commission rejected this amendment for the following reasons:

> It is an oversimplified formula. The Roman Pontiff is also bound to revelation itself, to the fundamental structure of the Church, to the sacraments, to the definitions of earlier councils, and other obligations too numerous to mention. Since such a formula would also require long and complicated explanations, the Commission has decided that it is better not to use it. There is also a psychological reason, lest in appeasing some we cause anxiety among others, especially in our relations with the East, as is clear in the history of another formula '*ex sese et non ex consensu ecclesiae*'.[21]

---

18. *Opera omnia, De controversiis christianae fidei. De summo pontifice*, ed. J. Fèvre, Paris, L. Vivés, 1870, liber I, cap. 1, 461. Also liber I, cap. 5, 469.

19. DS, 3114.

20. *MANSI*, 52: 1108 D-1109 A.

21. Text in *Acta synodalia sacrosancti concilii oecumenici Vaticani II*, Vatican City, Typis Polyglottis. 1973, vol. III, part 1, 247.

These two texts, even though they do not possess formal conciliar authority, are significant. They clearly indicate that it was the mind of the two Vatican Councils that the Pope does not have absolute power but is limited by the very constitution of the Church. It is necessary, then, for us to examine the limitations on papal actions dictated by natural, divine, and ecclesiastical law.

NATURAL LAW

Popes, like the rest of humanity, are bound by fundamental norms of conduct, which have their source in human reason. God makes possible this natural wisdom by giving human beings the ability to ask and answer questions. These answers lead to more and more perfect generalizations binding on all men and women. The Pope, for example, must act according to the precepts of the natural law, such as to do and pursue good and avoid evil, to give to each his own, to use his faculties reasonably, and to avoid such sins as idolatry, murder, lying, and theft … .

Because he is not God, he cannot alter the structure and laws of the physical universe, control the weather, heal the sick, or confer immortality. Yet the medieval canonist Panormitanus (Nicolas de Tudeschis), who died in 1453, said: 'Whatever God can do, the Pope can do.'[22] A more realistic view, long before Ignatius or Bellarmine, was given by Guilemus De Auduno (d. 1343) who held that not even the Pope can turn black into white.

DIVINE LAW

The Pope is also limited by the divine positive law, which is a law not derived from natural law but from revelation. The meaning and application of divine law is a complex theological problem and admits of many interpretations. It is difficult to delineate precisely what is *ius divinum* in the sacraments and structures of the Church and what is simply *ius humanum*. Piet Fransen noted that the term '*ius divinum*' has a potential for misinterpretation. It becomes, he said, 'the atom bomb of the reactionary', when it is extended to 'matters where no such evidence is to be found'.[23] My purpose here is not to unravel the complexities of the meaning of divine law, but to indicate how it relates to the papacy as a factor of limitation.

Magisterial documents use the terms 'divine law' ('*ius divinum*') or similar terms (e.g., 'divine institution') most often in relationship to something instituted by Christ himself, thus connoting permanence and irreversibility. The Council of Trent, for example, declared that all the seven sacraments were instituted by our Lord Jesus Christ (DS 1601) and that sacramental confession was instituted by divine law and is necessary for salvation according to the same law (DS 1706). Trent also taught that it is necessary by divine law to confess each and every mortal sin we remember, even secret sins, and to confess the circumstances that change the species of a sin (DS 1707).

---

22. *Commentaria decretalium librum* (Venice: Iuntas, 1588), lvi, 34.
23. 'Criticism of Some Basic Theological Notions in Matters of Church Authority', *Journal of Ecumenical Studies* (1982), 67.

The Pope can approve or define elements related to the validity of the sacraments, but he cannot abolish them because they are divinely established. Not even the Pope, for example, can dispense from marriage impediments that come from the divine positive law, such as consanguinity in the direct line or in the second degree of the collateral line (can. 1078, 3) … .

ECCLESIASTICAL LAW

This limitation is not as stringent as the other legal limitations we have considered, but it is still an important factor. The Pope is expected to observe the positive laws of the Church and its established customs. Even though he is the supreme legislator and free to change any law, it does not mean that he need not follow the laws of the Church. He may not be bound legally to do so or risk having his 'illegal' acts invalidated but, according to the mission and purpose of his office, he is per se morally obliged, though he may make prudent exceptions. The harmony, unity, and good of the Church require – unless there is a sufficient reason to the contrary – that he observe the procedures and practices instituted by custom or ecclesiastical law.

Bishop Zinelli at Vatican I responded to those who feared that supreme papal power would have no limits. He rejected the view that the Pope could annul 'all canonical decisions enacted with wisdom and piety by the Apostles and the Church.' His principal reason was that 'moral theology teaches that the legislator is subject to his own laws if not by coercive power at least in the manner of a directive'.[24] He also noted that precepts that are unjust, null, and harmful do not require obedience except for the sake of avoiding scandal … . Many papal prerogatives, which are now part of the Church's law or custom, originally belonged to the local Church. Dispensations, benefices, reservations, appeals, and other rights were progressively reserved to the Bishop of Rome. In the future, the Pope may wish to return many of these rights to diocesan bishops or to episcopal conferences. The nomination of bishops is a good example … .

THE DOGMATIC LIMITS

In exercising his teaching ministry, the Pope is limited by revelation. He cannot reject the 'deposit of faith' and repudiate everything in Scripture and tradition. Nor can the Pope define something that is in no way related to revelation. Papal definitions of doctrine are, according to Vatican I, consonant with the Holy Scripture and apostolic tradition (DS 3069). They are not new revelations, but rather articulations of what has already been revealed (DS 3070). Vatican II taught that the magisterium has the exclusive right of authentically interpreting the Word of God, but it added that 'the magisterium is not above the Word of God, but serves it, teaching only what has been handed on' (*Dei verbum*, art. 10).

---

24. *MANSI*, 52: 1109A.

Vatican I clearly indicated that even infallibility is subject to specific limits and conditions. A passage from the official *relatio* of Bishop Gasser of Brixen on infallibility is worth repeating:

> Absolute infallibility belongs only to God, the first and essential truth who can never deceive or be deceived in any way. All other infallibility, by the fact that it is communicated for a certain end, has limits and conditions by which it is judged to be present. This is also true of the infallibility of the Roman Pontiff.[25]

An obvious general condition for a legitimate *ex cathedra* definition is that the Pope act freely without violence, fear, or coercion. In addition, severe mental illness would be an obstacle to authentic teaching, since the Pope would be incapable of making a genuine and free human act. Vatican I gave more formal conditions (DS 3074). The Pope who intends to define something *ex cathedra* must act according to the following four conditions:

a)   The Pope must speak as the supreme pastor and teacher of all Christians. He is not infallible as a private theologian or even as Bishop of Rome, but only when he acts as a universal pastor of the Church.
b)   He must act in virtue of his supreme apostolic authority as a successor of Peter.
c)   He must teach in the area of faith or morals.
d)   He must propose the defined doctrine as something to be held by the universal Church.

The Code of Canon Law adds one more requirement: 'No doctrine is understood to be infallibly defined unless it is clearly established as such' (can. 749, 3).... .

Popes are also limited by previous doctrinal decisions. The Catholic Church has always exhibited a reverence for the past. The early creeds, the *regulae fidei*, and the professions of faith show the Roman concern with fidelity to apostolic teaching. Popes have frequently expressed their acceptance of the binding force of the councils and canons. Leo I (440–461), for example, recognized the councils as established by the Holy Spirit and hence inviolable. Martin 1 (649–655) expressed a typical sentiment among early Popes: 'We cannot transgress the ecclesiastical canons; on the contrary, we are their defender and protector, not their violator.'[26] Likewise, Gregory I (590–604) declared: 'I confess that I accept and honor the four councils as I do the four books of the Holy Gospel.'[27]

Every Pope, then, is obliged to adhere to the dogmatic canons of the councils and to all previous dogmatic articulations of faith. He is not free to reject them or declare them as nonbinding; he may neglect them, but he cannot deny them. This norm, however, must not be understood simplistically. When the Church or a council defines a truth of faith, it is doing so through the assistance of the Holy Spirit. Dogmas are irrevocably true, but they give only limited insights into the mystery of divine truth; deeper understanding and development are possible and necessary.

Dogmas must be interpreted; they are not isolated, ahistorical events. Piet Fransen, in his discussion of the authority of ecumenical councils,[28] gives three fundamental norms of

25. *MANSI*, 52: 1214 A.
26. Ep. 9, *MANSI*, 10: 823.
27. A synodal letter of February 591. *Monumenta germaniae historica*, Epp. 1, 36.
28. 'The Authority of the Councils', in *Problems of Authority*, ed. John M. Todd, Baltimore, Helicon, 1962, 60–72.

interpretation: (a) Only the central assertion in a dogmatic decree or canon is defined. The reasons, arguments, or illustrations used to support a particular dogma do not have the same authority as the decree or the canon. (b) One must distinguish between teachings that are addressed to the universal Church and those that are addressed to one or several local Churches. Dogmatic definitions bind the entire Church, but some disciplinary norms or ecclesiastical laws may apply only to certain Churches. A particular law does not automatically have universal application. (c) The text must be read in the spirit in which it was written ... .

What happens if a Pope unambiguously and publicly denies a truth of faith, repudiates Scripture and tradition, rejects the sacraments, attempts to suppress the very office of the papacy and episcopate, or dismisses the dogmatic teachings of previous popes and councils? John of Torquemada answered this question: 'Were the Pope to command anything against Holy Scripture, or the articles of faith, or the truth of the sacraments, or the commands of the natural or divine law, he ought not to be obeyed, and in such commands he is to be disregarded'[29] ... .

Medieval canonists argued that the Pope, unless he is a heretic, can be judged by no one. Some suggested that the concept of heresy also included schism and other crimes, such as fornication or simony, since they were then considered equivalent to heresy. Later canonists took a narrower view: only notorious or manifest heresy or schism deprives a Pope of his jurisdictional power. They also applied this norm to a Pope who was clearly insane, since mental illness may render a person incapable of acting in a free, human way. What procedures are used to dispose a heretical Pope?

Two main solutions have been proposed. Some theologians (John Torquemada and Robert Bellarmine) said that a Pope who denies the faith cuts himself off from the Church; he is no longer a Christian and no longer the Pope. He does not have to be formally deposed by the church, since he is already deposed by divine law, that is, by God himself. If a Church council does judge the case, it simply makes a declaratory judgment of what in fact has already taken place. Others (Cardinal Cajetan, Francis Suarez, and John of St. Thomas) said that a disposition by the Church is necessary. A heretical pope, they argued, does not automatically cease to be Pope until some judicial body in the Church – the cardinals or an ecumenical council – establishes his guilt and declares him a heretic.

Vatican I discussed the possibility of an incorrigibly heretical Pope or one who is habitually insane. Bishop Zinelli referred to these as 'hypothetical cases' that, in all probability, would never happen. But if God would permit such evils to occur, he would give sufficient means to deal with them. In any event, he continued, these hypothetical possibilities do not weaken the doctrine of the universal power of the Roman Pontiff.

The present Code of Canon Law has no articles of impeachment or procedures for dealing with an heretical Pope. But, as Patrick J. Burns has noted, prophetic protest rather than judicial process has been the primary Catholic response to abuses of the papacy. He suggests that public criticism within the Church is 'ultimately a much more effective protection against the abuse of papal power than any conceivable juridical system'.[30] In the

---

29. *Summa de ecclesia,* Venice: M. Tramezimun, 1561, lib. II, c. 49, p. 163B.
30. 'Communion, Councils and Collegiality: Some Catholic Reflections', in Paul C. Empie and T. Austin Murphy (eds), *Papal Primacy and the Universal Church: Lutherans and Catholics in Dialogue V*, Minneapolis, Augsburg, 1974, 170.

unhappy event that a future Pope would fall into heresy, the Church, under the guidance of the Spirit, would have to deal with the situation in a manner that is most beneficial to ecclesial unity and good order … .

CONCLUSION

The office of the papacy, granting its extensive prerogatives, is not a pure example of unfettered or absolute power. The pope's actions are limited by the purpose of his ministry, the natural, divine, and ecclesiastical law; revelation, defined doctrine; and practical circumstances. The examples of limitation described above give us only broad norms; they must be seen in detail.

4.9 HERMANN J. POTTMEYER: *PAPACY IN COMMUNION: PERSPECTIVES ON VATICAN II* – 1998

Our selection is taken from his book, *Towards a Papacy in Communion: Perspectives from Vatican Councils I and II*.[31] In this concluding chapter Pottmeyer carefully analyses many of the theological approaches to papal authority already encountered in earlier selections in this reader. He then offers a set of conclusions regarding the issue of papal authority in the light of his perceptive and historically informed reading of the teaching of Vatican Councils I and II.

❀

REBELLION AGAINST CENTRALIZATION AND EMERGENCE FROM A GHETTO

The Second Vatican Council has left us a building site. It resembles the building site of St. Peter's in the sixteenth century: Alongside the ancient Roman basilica there towered into the heavens the four monumental supporting columns that were later to carry the most beautiful dome in the world, the one that today arches over the tomb of Peter the Apostle.

Like Vatican I, Vatican II was unable to complete its work. While Vatican I was hindered by a war, Vatican II was unable to complete the reform of the church and ecclesiology because the maximalist interpretation of Vatican I, combined with pragmatic concerns, stood in the way. The work of Vatican II has remained a building site. Alongside the old edifice of nineteenth- and twentieth-century Vatican centralization arise the four mighty supporting columns of a renewed church and a renewed ecclesiology: the church as people of God; the church as sacrament of the kingdom of God in the world; the college of bishops; and ecumenism. While the building erected by centralization awaits demolition, as the old St. Peter's Basilica did in its day, the four supporting pillars of a renewed church and a renewed ecclesiology wait to be crowned by the dome that draws them into unity … .

THE NIGHTMARE OF SHARED GOVERNANCE

Proof that the constitution *Lumen gentium* contains little that is new can be found especially in its third chapter, on the hierarchical church. This chapter also deals with the office of the pope. It is in chapter three that the continuity with Vatican I is most conspicuous. The discussion of the papal office makes use, almost exclusively, of citations from Vatican I: the

---

31. From Pottmeyer, Hermann, *Towards a Papacy in Communion: Perspectives from Vatican Councils I & II*, New York, Crossroad, 1998, 110, 112–17, 129–36.

doctrine on the college of bishops likewise appeared at Vatican I, although the council did not have time to define it. The fact that this doctrine is celebrated as a great accomplishment of Vatican II shows how effectively the maximalist interpretation of Vatican I had suppressed this teaching. It is reported that when a great controversy over the doctrine of collegiality arose, Paul VI had to persuade himself by means of study night after night that the doctrine is not opposed to tradition and Vatican I.

The majority at Vatican II was not successful in its attempt to end Vatican centralization by means of its teaching on collegiality. The history of Vatican I is important because it shows how and why the doctrine on collegiality can very well coexist with a concept of the papacy that promotes centralization. At that earlier council the majority had prevented the introduction of the normal appropriateness of cooperation between pope and bishops in important decisions affecting the universal church. The only concern of those bishops was the independence and freedom of action of the pope. From this silence of Vatican I the maximalist interpretation drew the conclusion that centralization was the norm.

Now, at Vatican II, the minority was motivated by the same concern. They objected to saying that the bishops already share in the supreme and universal power of jurisdiction of the episcopal college only by reason of their episcopal consecration. For then, they objected, the bishops would have their power of jurisdiction directly from Christ, and the pope would be obliged to let them take part in the government of the universal church. However, they said, such a shared governance contradicts Vatican I, which condemned the teaching of Bishop Maret, namely, that the pope 'possesses merely the principal part, and not all the fullness of this supreme power'. Moreover, to avoid this error and its consequences, it is not enough to say that the college of bishops possesses supreme jurisdiction only habitually, while its exercise always depends on the pope. For a jurisdiction that cannot be exercised is useless and empty. The minority, therefore, demanded that, as at Vatican I, the question be left open whether the bishops have their collegial jurisdiction directly from Christ or from Christ through the pope. The doctrine that the bishops obtain their entire jurisdiction from the pope had been described by Maret as the key principle of the 'absolutist school'.

At Vatican II, the criticism of the minority was directed at this sentence: 'One is constituted a member of the episcopal body in virtue of the sacramental consecration and by the communion with the head and members of the college' (LG 22). The spokesman for the Doctrinal Commission explained that fear of a shared governance was unfounded, because the next sentence reads: 'The college or body of bishops has, for all that, no authority unless united with the Roman Pontiff, Peter's successor, as its head, whose primatial authority, let it be added, over all, whether pastors or faithful, remains in its integrity.' However, in order to accommodate the minority, the word 'communion' in the objectionable sentence was changed to 'hierarchical communion' – an unfortunate addition, since it weakens the idea of communion without actually saying anything new. In addition, it is pointedly said that 'together with its head, the Supreme Pontiff, and never apart from him [the order of bishops] has supreme and full authority over the universal church; but this power cannot be exercised without the agreement of the Roman Pontiff' (LG 22).

In order to allay the misgivings of the minority at Vatican II, a further sentence expressly emphasizes the pope's freedom of action: 'For the Roman Pontiff, by reason of his office as

Vicar of Christ, namely, and as pastor of the entire Church has full, supreme and universal power, over the whole Church, a power which he can always exercise unhindered.'

Since the minority at Vatican II still saw a contradiction with Vatican I, Paul VI found himself obliged to intervene directly in order to win the agreement of the minority, which included many members of the Roman Curia. After the council, the pope said, there should be no victors and vanquished.

By the famous 'Preliminary Explanatory Note'[32] the Doctrinal Commission had to notify the following clarification of chapter three to the council fathers: 'The word *College* ... does not imply *equality* between the head and members of the college, but only a proportion between the two relationships: Peter – apostles and pope – bishops.' The special place of the pope in the college of bishops was underscored by this clarification and by the expression 'hierarchical communion'. Two further remarks brought out the pope's freedom of action: 'The Roman Pontiff undertakes the regulation, encouragement, and approval of the exercise of collegiality as he sees fit for the well being of the church'; and: 'The Pope, as supreme pastor of the church, may exercise his power at any time, as he sees fit, by reason of the demands of his office.' The spokesman for the Doctrinal Commission explained that the 'Preliminary Note' was not an integral part of the constitution but 'that it is according to the mind and sense of this note that the teaching contained in chapter three is to be explained and understood'.

In the constitution and the note, the minority succeeded in having the pope's independence and freedom of action stressed in a way that these had not been emphasized even in the Vatican I definition. Analysis of Vatican I has shown that this earlier council had avoided every reference to a collegial collaboration of the episcopate in the governing of the universal church; it had done so for strategic reasons, namely, out of fear that such references could be misunderstood along Gallican lines. This fear had become groundless by the time of Vatican II. Why, then, was this action taken now, and for what reasons?

The reasons can be gathered from the already cited arguments of the Vatican II minority. The first reason was the maximalist interpretation of Vatican I and especially of the statement in the canon directed against Maret. The second reason was the fear that the pope would no longer be free to govern the church if the bishops had a right to share in the government. Since the leading members of the minority of Vatican II were also members of the Roman Curia, the pragmatic character of this argument is obvious. These men were afraid of losing their own shared governance with the pope... .

The conception of the primacy of jurisdiction as sovereignty was also present and active in the texts of Vatican II with their one-sided emphasis on the pope's freedom of action. This concept could exist alongside the teaching on the college of bishops, because the exercise of collegial jurisdiction depends entirely on the pope. At the very least, it is striking that nothing is said with comparable clarity about the obligation of the pope to involve the bishops in decisions affecting the universal church. We cannot help but think of such an obligation, when it comes, for example, to the passing of laws for the universal church. Is not such legislation a matter also of the collegial co-responsibility of the bishops for the universal

---

32. 'Preliminary Explanatory Note', in Austin Flannery (ed.), *Vatican Council II: The Conciliar and Post Conciliar Documents*, Dublin, Dominican Publications, 1988, 424–6.

church, and does it not interfere with their ordinary and immediate jurisdiction over the particular churches, and this to such a degree that it should not occur without the participation of the bishops? But for the minority at Vatican II such an obligation would have been an instance precisely of the shared governance it feared, for they understood such shared government as a division of the primacy of jurisdiction, as the maximalist interpretation of Vatican I saw it.

In contrast, the ideas of the majority of Vatican II moved in the direction of some form of permanent participation of the bishops in the leadership of the church. The council decreed the establishment of a synod of bishops. 'This council, as it will be representative of the whole Catholic episcopate, will bear testimony to the participation of all bishops in hierarchical communion in the care of the universal church.'[33] The rights of bishops to collaborate fell far short of the original ideas of the majority when Paul VI, in 1965, formally established the synod of bishops and published the norms for its operation; many council fathers expressed disappointment. Those original ideas, too, had fallen victim to the nightmare of shared governance ... .

TOWARDS A MINISTRY OF COMMUNION WITHIN THE UNIVERSAL CHURCH

We have reached a double conclusion: It is not Vatican I itself but only the maximalist interpretation of its definitions that hinders the development of a papacy in communion; the desire for an ecclesiology of communion was present at Vatican I in the persons of the minority, and this prevented the definition of an absolute and separate papal infallibility.

In the documents of Vatican II the maximalist interpretation (the primacy as sovereignty) is still operative and has prevented a more consistent development of structures that promote communion. Nevertheless, Vatican II does provide the theological foundations for an ecclesiology of communion.

This result explains the persistence of a centralizing structure and practice after Vatican II. The majority of the council fathers intended to overcome centralization; in this regard they failed. The council did not, however, fail in its purpose of bringing the faithful to an awareness that all of us are the church. In many particular churches and regional churches this consciousness has led to structures and a practice of communion and participation.

It is especially in the question of the papacy and its concrete form that Vatican II has left behind what is simply a building site. The Petrine office will acquire its true dimensions only when it becomes a ministry of communion for all churches and Christians. In paving the way to this future for the Petrine office, the following tasks arise on the level of theology.

First, there must be agreement on an ecumenical ecclesiology of communion in all the churches and in the ecumenical dialogue. Only from this perspective will the Petrine office be understood as a ministry of communion – for the community of churches and its unity. The Petrine office and its mission must be defined in terms of the church instead of the church being defined in terms of the papacy.

---

33. Decree on the Pastoral Office of Bishops in the Church, *Christus Dominus*, no. 5.

Second, there is the task of reaching an agreement on the commission given to Peter in the Bible and on its significance for an ecumenical community of churches at the present time and in the future. To this end we must acknowledge the developments and changes of form which the Petrine office has undergone in the course of many centuries. Of special interest should be the understanding, form, and practice of the Petrine office in the first centuries when the church was still undivided and understood itself to be an ecumenical community of churches. Even though there can be no return to the early church, we can certainly learn from it. Knowledge of the historical changes in the form of the Petrine office gives us the freedom to shape this office according to the unique needs of the present and the future. If this second task is to be successful, there must also be agreement on a common method of interpreting the scriptures, tradition and history, and the signs of the times.

Third, on the basis of an ecclesiology of communion, the Catholic Church, with the help of the other churches, must renew and develop, more consistently than hitherto, its own form as a community of churches. Only if the church takes the form of a communion will the Petrine office take a communal form.

In all three of these tasks we do not start at point zero today. In the area of theology many studies and proposals have already been published that lead us farther along the way. Vatican II and postconciliar reforms have taken the first steps. In the ecumenical realm, the dialogue between Lutherans and Catholics in the United States on the church and the Petrine office has thus far been the most productive. In conclusion, let me offer, in regard to the third task, concerning church structures, some comments that emerge from current observations.

Frequently we come up against the view that communion has nothing to do with juridical or organizational structures – that it describes only a way of thinking, the spirit of communion, and corresponding personal behavior. It is true, of course, that forms of participation are, in fact, empty, dead structures if they are not animated by the spirit of communion. On the other hand, like all of life, a living communion cannot develop if it is not given scope, forms, and structures.

It is an illusion to think that communion means total harmony. The people who think this way believe they can appeal to a good many formulations of Vatican II, in which communion is presented as an ideal and is described as a gift from the Holy Spirit. However, the language of the council is meant to be taken as normative and not simply idealistic; when the council speaks of trusting in the Holy Spirit, it does not by any means intend to exclude structures of communion. Nevertheless, those who are critical or call for structures of participation are often accused of disturbing harmony and being mistrustful of the action of the Holy Spirit. However, accusations of this sort confuse communion with harmony.

The recommendation of the *spirit* of communion instead of *structures* of participation, and the confusion of *communion* with the total *harmony* are sometimes used to support persisting monopolies of responsibilities and powers, as well as centralization. Communion here is interpreted as the duty to practice a subordination that is called for in the name of the spirit of communion.

Structures of communion are also needed so conflicts, which are unavoidable in a living church, may not be suppressed but can be dealt with and resolved in a Christian and orderly way. The central conflict that determined the course of the debates at Vatican I and II may serve as an example. It was the conflict between the paradigms of the church in the first and second millennia. Each one of the paradigms represented a basic function of the church; the conflict between them expressed a vital process of deepening awareness and growth. The communion of witnesses to a tradition that must be preserved (the first millennium paradigm) had to become a communion of all those who actively shape this tradition in order to keep it alive (the second millennium paradigm). However, for the time being that vital process of deepening awareness has achieved only a partial expression. In the course of the second millennium, a monopoly on decision-making turned the pope increasingly into the sole agent in the active shaping of the church and tradition.

The conflict at Vatican I and II arose because the bishops, as official witnesses to the tradition, were now also demanding to participate in the active shaping of the church and tradition; they were, therefore, calling for structures of collegial participation. Another expression of deepening consciousness and growth is the conflict now going on, after Vatican II, under the false and misleading name of 'democratization' of the church. Appealing to the teaching of the council on the people of God, active believers are demanding, as laypersons, to be included in the shaping of the church's life. However, structures of communion and participation are not only the object of demands; these participatory structures also make it possible to resolve the conflicts.

The development of structures of communion needs to be guided by three principles. The first is the principle of *catholicity*. These structures must make it possible for a multiplicity of agents and the many-sidedness of life to find space in the church to replace existing centralization and uniformity. The second is the principle of *collegiality* and *cooperation*. These structures must make it possible for decision-making to take a collegial form and for the determination of decisions to be made to involve the cooperation of all the faithful. The third is the principle of *subsidiarity*. These structures must make it possible for decisions that do not threaten the unity and communion of the universal church to be made within limited regions of the church. The application of these three principles does not weaken the papacy; on the contrary, it presupposes a center of unity and a ministry of communion acknowledged by all.

The full application of the three principles of catholicity, collegiality, and subsidiarity is not possible, however, without the restoration of the original three-membered, or triadic, form of church structure. In the early church this form was the most important principle at work in the organization of the universal church: the particular church with its bishop; the regional ecclesiastical units, especially the patriarchal churches with their patriarchs; and for the universal church, the pope. In a passage of Vatican II that was cited earlier (LG 23), the development of the intermediate level is ascribed to divine providence; on this issue, the council gives first place to 'the ancient patriarchal churches'.

Vatican II gave us a very specific description of the function of these regional structures of communion. Such structures make it possible for the particular churches, 'while safeguarding the unity of faith … , to have their own discipline, enjoy their own liturgical usage and inherit a theological and spiritual patrimony'. They also allow the churches of a region to be linked among themselves 'by bonds of a more intimate charity in what pertains to the sacramental life and in a mutual respect for rights and obligations' (LG 23). In fact, in the early church these regional structures had a twofold function. They made it possible for the churches of a region to enjoy a more concrete and closer kind of communication and communion than is possible over the expanse of the universal church; and in their common faith, and through the patriarchal church, they were linked to the universal church. Furthermore, the regional structures made it possible for these churches to acquire a distinctive form that was independent, yet rooted in the surrounding cultural world; together with the other churches of the same region, they could preserve and develop this form. In other words, they made inculturation possible.

The patriarchal churches were governed by the patriarchs, together with the synod of bishops. In the first millennium the papacy recognized their administrative autonomy and special heritages. It intervened only rarely, especially in important questions of faith, and then only when it was called upon as a court of appeal. In the West there was the Latin patriarchate of the bishop of Rome. Only when the patriarchal structure of the West came to be understood as the structure for the universal church did the two-membered, or dual, structural form replace the triadic. Only then did the church of the West lose its character as a communion of churches and replace this with uniformity and centralization. On the other hand, the Eastern church, now lacking the center of unity and the ministry of communion, saw its unity disintegrate into a multiplicity of autocephalous or autonomous churches, which have not found their way to a workable communion among themselves.

The renewal and further development of the triadic form of church structure is, then, an essential condition for the church to regain its original distinctive form as a communion of churches. Only within this triadic form can the collegiality of the episcopate and the participation of the entire people of God become active forces without having their claims lead immediately and inevitably to a polarization between pope, episcopate, and local churches. Joseph Ratzinger was, therefore, one of the first to call, even during the council, for the 'building up of patriarchal spaces' in which 'the consciousness of reciprocal interconnections at the horizontal level' can develop.[34] The establishment of continental episcopal conferences and the holding of continental synods can be the first step in this direction.

Closely connected with this proposal is another that refers to the pope and results from the renewal of the triadic division: the separation of the Petrine and the patriarchal functions of the bishop of Rome. Soon after the council, Ratzinger described this as a 'task for the future: to separate more clearly the office proper to the successor of Peter from the patriarchal office and, where necessary, to create new patriarchates and separate them from the Latin church'. For 'a uniform canon law, a uniform liturgy, a uniform filling of episcopal sees by the Roman central administration – all of these are things that do not necessarily accompany the primacy as such, but result only from this union of two offices'.[35] The primacy by its nature, according to Ratzinger, 'does not necessarily entail the position of Rome as an administrative center (centralization), but entails only the spiritual and juridical power that goes with responsibility for the word and for communion'.[36] This distinctive form of the papal office in which the functions of the patriarch of the West have become a part of the apostolic primacy was described by Ratzinger as a 'universal patriarchate'.[37]

---

34. Joseph Ratzinger, 'Konkrete Formen bischöflicher Kollegialität', in Johann Chr. Hampe (ed.), *Ende der Gegenreformation? Das Konzil, Dokumente und Deutung*, Stuttgart, Kreuz, 1964, 159, 161.
35. Joseph Ratzinger, *Das neue Volk Gottes*, Düsseldorf, Patmos, 1969, 142.
36. Joseph Ratzinger, 'Primat', in *Lexikon für Theologie und Kirche*, Freiburg, Herder, 1963, 8:763.
37. Ratzinger, 'Konkrete Formen', 157.

The separation of the patriarchal and the Petrine functions of the pope must be matched by a breaking-up of the functions of the Roman Curia. Since the patriarchal responsibilities of the pope are a matter of ecclesiastical and not divine law, the corresponding functions of the Curia, says Ratzinger, can 'definitely be shared by the episcopate throughout the world – in fact, the situation of the church undoubtedly demands such a sharing'.[38] In this respect, 'the college of bishops as such, together with the pope, could regard itself as superior to curia and could cooperate in shaping it'.[39] It is obvious that these suggestions are extremely important not only for the reform of the church and for the form of the Petrine office, but also for a truly ecumenical future.

For this reason the ecumenical Community of Dombes (Groupe des Dombes) took these proposals into its document on the ministry of communion within the universal church. In the context of their own suggestions for a conversion of the confessions, the group sees it as the task of the Catholic Church to establish a balance between the communal, collegial, and personal dimensions of the Petrine ministry of communion ... .

'To set the others free for service in their special mission': that is precisely the service to be rendered by the structures of communion; this is the perspective of Vatican II. Consequently, the renewal and further development of these structures does not signify a limitation or weakening of the Petrine office; rather it is an essential part of the Petrine commission. The more the universal church becomes once again a communion of churches, the more clearly the structures of communion recover their distinctive form, and the more the church gains in catholicity: the more the church will need the Petrine ministry of communion and be able to understand the Petrine ministry as a gift of God to the church.

---

38. Joseph Ratzinger, 'Ekklesiologische Bemerkungen zum Schema 'De Episcopis', in *do-c* no. 135 (1964), 5.
39. Ratzinger, 'Konkrete Formen', 158.

4.10 JOHN R. QUINN: *THE EXERCISE OF THE PRIMACY – FACING THE COST OF CHRISTIAN UNITY – 1996*

Our selection[40] is the text of a lecture Quinn gave on 29 June, 1996 in Oxford on the occasion of Campion Hall's centennial. In the lecture Archbishop Quinn responds to the invitation of Pope John Paul II, in his encyclical on ecumenism, *Ut unum sint,* to undertake a new dialogue on the manner of exercising papal primacy today. He has since expanded many of the ideas introduced here in his new book, *The Reform of the Papacy.*[41]

❁

THE CHALLENGE OF JOHN PAUL II

… The pope himself, in apostolic discernment, sees that there must be new forms of exercising the primacy as the Church approaches the threshold of a new millennium. He calls the Christian family to look at how the gift which is the papacy can become more credible and speak more effectively to the contemporary world.

Those, of course, who respond to the request of the pope, must bear in mind the paradoxical nature of the project they are undertaking. The Holy Father asks for public consideration of new forms in which the Petrine ministry can be embodied and exercised. But one can only advance the need for new forms if the past or current forms are evaluated as inadequate. To consider inadequacy seriously is to embark upon careful criticism. This obviously must be done if one is to give attentive and loyal response to the papal request. But that very response, which issues out of an obediential hearing, can be misread as carping negatively, a distancing of oneself from the Holy See. Exactly the opposite is true. The pope has asked us for an honest and serious critique. He has every right to expect this call will be heard and that this response will be especially forthcoming from those who recognize the primacy of the Roman Pontiff – as the Church searches out the will of God in the new millennium that is before us.

The 'new situation' is shaped by the shattering of the Berlin Wall and the collapse of the Communist dictatorships, by the awakening of China and her movement into the political and economic world of the twentieth century, by the movement toward unification in Europe, by a new and spreading consciousness of the dignity of woman, by the arrival of an immense cultural diversity in the Church, by the insistent thirst for unity among Christians. This new situation is not only political, economic, cultural, and technological. It is marked as

---

40. Quinn, John R. 'The Exercise of the Primacy – Facing the Cost of Christian Unity', *Commonweal* (12 July 1996), 11–20.
41. New York, Crossroad, 1999.

well by a new psychology. People think differently, react differently, have new aspirations, a new sense of what is possible, new hopes and new dreams. In the Church there is a new consciousness of the dignity conferred by Baptism and the responsibility for the mission of the Church rooted in Baptism.

The 'new situation' is also one in which the Church confronts great challenges. It is estimated that by the year 2000 there will be more than fifty million internally displaced persons and refugees in the world. The gap between the wealthy and poor nations is growing. There is real danger that Africa may become a marginalized continent. Large numbers of Catholics are turning to sects or non-Christian religions.

The 'new situation' for the primacy is indeed comparable to the situation which confronted the primitive Church when it abandoned the requirements of the Mosaic Law and embraced the mission to the gentiles. This action required immense courage, vision and sacrifice. It was an uncharted path, a major change. There were grave reasons for keeping the Mosaic Law, not least of which was the fact that Our Lord himself had observed it. Yet trusting in the Holy Spirit, the Apostles made that momentous decision. There was intense and bitter opposition to it, so much so that some scholars believe that there is founded evidence to show that it was ultraconservative members of the Christian community at Rome, opposed to the changes Peter and Paul had introduced, who denounced them to the Roman authorities and bought about their arrest and execution.[42] Similarly today, there are strong divisions within the church and accompanying pressures pulling in conflicting directions. The decisions required by the 'new situation' will be exacting and costly.

The Church and the papacy in particular have to respond to this 'new situation' and Pope John Paul II courageously asks the question of how the primacy can be exercised in a way that is open to this great cosmic drama … .

MORAL VERSUS STRUCTURAL REFORM

To ask the question about new ways of exercising the primacy 'open to a new situation' is to raise the issue of the reform of the papacy. Yves Congar, the distinguished theologian, named cardinal later in life, has pointed out the inadequacy of a purely 'moral' reform. He believes that any true and effective reform must touch structures. He goes on to observe the lesson of history that personal holiness of itself is not sufficient to bring about a change and that great holiness has existed in the very midst of situations that cried out for change.

But he comes to a fundamental and inescapable challenge when he raises the question of why reform-minded men and women of the Middle Ages in fact missed the rendezvous with opportunity. Why did so little happen when there was such a general thirst for reform? Among other things, he cites their penchant for focusing on this or that specific abuse such as concubinage, failure of canons to fulfill their obligations in singing the office in choir, the notorious failure of bishops to live in or even visit their dioceses.

Most of those who wanted reform, he said, were prisoners of the system, incapable of reforming the structures themselves through a recovery of the original vision, incapable of

---

42. See Raymond E. Brown, *Antioch and Rome*, New York, Paulist Press, c. VII, 124–5; c. IX, 168–9.

asking the new questions raised by a new situation. Reform meant to them simply putting the existing structures in order. The further, deeper, long-term questions were never asked.[43] Their vision stopped at the water's edge. The moment passed, and a wounded Church suffered an incomparable tragedy.

It is these deeper, more incomprehensive issues in regard to the exercise of the primacy that must be raised in the search for unity: What does a realistic desire for unity demand in terms of changes in curial structure, policy, and procedures? What do the signs of the times, the desire for unity, the doctrine of the episcopal collegiality, the cultural diversity of the Church, the new technological age call for in curial reform and adaptation to what the Pope calls 'a new situation'? What does all this demand of the Pope himself? …

THE ROMAN CURIA AND THE SEARCH FOR UNITY

The curial system was not created by Pope John Paul II. Though the curia existed in some form since the time of Gregory I in the sixth century, it goes back, as we know it, to Pope Sixtus V in 1588. And so if we are to search for new ways of exercising the papal ministry we must go beyond the personal style of the pope and consider the curial system itself. The question of new forms or new ways of exercising the primacy is not only personal. It is also systemic. The curia and the pope cannot be completely separated.

It is self-evident that the pope could not fulfill his responsibilities of communion and communication with more than three thousand bishops and dioceses in a wide diversity of cultures and languages without the curia. At the same time it must be admitted that any reformulation or change the pope may personally decide to pursue can be retarded or diminished, even thwarted, by segments of the curia which may not agree with him or may have a different vision. It is a matter of record, for instance, that powerful segments of the curia strongly opposed the convocation of the Second Vatican Council.[44] Paul VI touched on this in his 1963 address to the curia telling the members of the curia that if there had been resistance and disagreement before, now was the time for the curia to give public witness to its solidarity with the pope and the aims of the council.[45] The pope is necessarily dependent to some degree on his curia for the effectiveness of his relationship with the college of bishops and of his ministry … .

Yet it must be honestly acknowledged that many Orthodox and other Christians are hesitant about full communion with the Holy See not so much because they see some doctrinal issues as unsolvable, not because of unfortunate and reprehensible historical events, but precisely because of the way issues are dealt with by the curia.[46] It must also be said that this is a concern all over the world. Recent events in Switzerland, Austria, Germany and France, in Brazil, Africa, and the United States are only one indication of how widespread this

---

43. See Y. Congar, *Vraie et Fausse Reforme dans l'eglise*, Paris, Editions du Cerf, 1950; cc. 2 and 3.
44. See Giuseppe Alberigo and Joseph A. Komonchak, *History of Vatican II*, vol. 1, Orbis/Peeters 1995; c. 2, part V, n. 1, 133–5.
45. Pope Paul VI, ibid., 795–6.
46. *See,* Cardinal Yves Congar, *Eglise et Papaute*, Les Editions du Cerf, Paris, 1994; c. II, n. 3, pp. 59–64; *see* also, Emmanuel Ghikas, *Comment 'redresser' les definitions du premier concile du Vatican, Part II, La Primaute de Juridiction, Irenikon*, vol. 68, n. 2, 1995, pp. 182–204.

concern is. The concern has to do with the appointment of bishops, the approval of documents such as *The Catechism of the Catholic Church*, the grave decline in the number of priests and the consequent decline in the availability of Mass for the people, the cognate issue of the celibacy of the clergy, the role of the episcopal conferences, the role of women and the issue of the ordination of women. Two things are involved in these issues: the decision of the Holy See on a specific issue and the way in which these decisions are reached and implemented. For instance, are such decisions imposed without consultation with the episcopate and without appropriate dialogue? Are bishops appointed against an overwhelming objection of people and priests in a given diocese? Where the answer to these and other such questions is affirmative there are serious difficulties for Christian unity.

The importance of a major structural reform of the curia cannot be underestimated. After the internationalization effected by Paul VI and the rearrangement of some competencies, the reforms have taken place since have been relatively minor and have been designed by members of the curia itself. The major change of outlook and structural reform which 'the new situation' requires would ideally be the work of a broader constituency. A commission, for example, could be created with three presidents. One, a representative of an episcopal conference, one, a representative of the curia and the third, a lay person.

Under this three-member presidency, there could be a working commission which would include bishops, priests, religious and lay persons. The commission should be given a time line of not more than three years and should have authority to consult experts in management, government, theology, canon law, and other useful disciplines and professions. The pope and the episcopal conferences should be kept informed of the progress of the work. When it is completed and in a state which the pope indicates he could accept, the plan should be presented for a vote to the presidents of episcopal conferences in a meeting held for this purpose and finally presented to the pope for approval and implementation. At this time the pope in consultation with the episcopal conferences could create an implementation commission to oversee the carrying out of the restructuring and with the mandate to report to the pope periodically. The work of the commission should be public and its conclusions should be public … .

THE CURIAL SYSTEM AND THE EPISCOPATE

The doctrine of episcopal collegiality is firmly in possession in the Church, explicitly affirmed by the Second Vatican Council, and frequently invoked by Pope John Paul II. In any realistic dialogue about the primacy, there has to be some consideration of how collegiality is lived, and how, not merely in theory, but in actual fact, the Papal Curia – an administrative structure – relates to and fosters collegiality – a doctrine of faith.

The curia is the arm of the pope. But the curia always runs the real risk of seeing itself as a *tertium quid*. When this happens, in place of the dogmatic structure comprised of the pope and the rest of the episcopate, there emerges a new and threefold structure: the pope, the curia, and the episcopate. This makes it possible for the curia to see itself as exercising oversight and authority over the College of Bishops, to see itself as subordinate to the pope but superior to the College of Bishops. To the degree that this is so and is reflected in the policies and actions of the curia obscures and diminishes both the doctrine and the reality of episcopal collegiality.

Yet the Vatican Council points out explicitly that the curia is in the service of the bishops. 'These [the departments of the Roman curia], therefore perform their duties in his name and with his authority [i.e., the name and authority of the pope] for the good of the churches and in the service of the sacred pastors.'[47]

The same risk exists also in regard to papal nuncios who can easily assume too great a directive power in regard to the episcopate of a nation, weakening the authentic collegiality of that episcopate. Nuncios, of course, can also be a source of great strength to episcopates under duress, encouraging them and backing them up when they take public positions denouncing injustice or oppression in a nation. And nuncios can play an effective role of reconciliation in countries where an episcopate is divided[48] ... .

COLLEGIALITY AND THE TEACHING OFFICE

I begin with the first of the threefold offices of Christ in which the bishops participate, the office of teaching. It is significant that it was Pope Pius IX, who defended the dogma of papal primacy and infallibility, who also vigorously upheld the public statement of the German bishops that bishops are not mere legates of the pope.[49] This doctrine was more amply articulated in the Second Vatican Council.[50] Such a doctrine cannot be affirmed in theory and denied in practice. Yet there are practical instances which are tantamount to making bishops managers who only work under instructions rather than true witnesses of faith who teach – in communion with the pope – in the name of Christ.

There comes to mind, for instance, the English version of *The Catechism of the Catholic Church*. On the positive side, bishops from various parts of the world were involved in preparing the *Catechism* and did in fact complete their work. An English translation was prepared which was agreed on by the English-speaking task force charged with its preparation. But objections to the translation were raised. Because of these objections, the Congregation for the Doctrine of Faith halted publication, rejected the proposed translation, and called for a completely new translation. The majority of the active English-speaking cardinals of the world supported the original translation and vigorously opposed any new translation. Yet they were overruled.

This suggests that the English-speaking cardinals, and the bishops of English-speaking countries, were not competent as teachers of the faith to judge the appropriateness or accuracy of an ecclesiastical document in their own language. This is certainly a diminishment of what it means to say that bishops share in the teaching office of Christ, and a diminishment of true collegiality.

---

47. Second Vatican Council, *Degree on the Bishops' Pastoral Office in the Church*, c. I:9. [Author's square brackets.]
48. See ibid., n. 10.
49. See *Declaratio Collectiva Episcoporum Germaniae*, February 1875; Denzinger–Schonmetzer (DS), Editio XXXVI, Herder 1976, N. 3113 and 3115; Pius IX, Letter to the German Bishops, *Mirabilis illa constantia*, 4 March 1875, ibid., n. 3117.
50. Second Vatican Council, *Dogmatic Constitution on the Church*, n. 27.

In addition, a collegiality which consists largely in embracing decisions which have been made by higher authority is a very attenuated collegiality and the question must be asked how such limited collegiality truly responds to the will of Christ and how it responds 'to the new situation'. For instance bishops and episcopal conferences feel that such grave questions as contraception, the ordination of women, general absolution, and the celibacy of the clergy are closed to discussion.

The pope is not just a member of the Episcopal College. He is member and head. No one who understands this denies the pope the right to teach on his own initiative as he judges it necessary or appropriate. Granting that he has such a right, the real issue is when and under what circumstances he should prudently exercise such a right. Often discussion of these questions in the Church becomes frustrated because when they are raised it is said that one does not have sufficient loyalty to the pope or that there is a defect in one's faith. But faith and loyalty are not at question. It is the question of prudence and appropriateness. Far from signaling a lack of loyalty or defect in faith, raising such questions respectfully and honestly is in reality an expression of both faith and loyalty … .

Since it is the constant teaching of the Church that bishops are judges and teachers of the faith,[51] it would be more in keeping with this truth of faith if bishops were seriously consulted, not only individually but also in episcopal conferences, before doctrinal declarations are issued or binding decisions are made of a disciplinary or liturgical nature. In this way there would be a true, active collegiality and not a merely passive collegiality … .

The bishops, if routinely and widely consulted on doctrinal and other important pronouncements could be a better support to the pope, could help in bringing to bear the mind of the whole Church on a given issue and in formulating a teaching so that the pope would not have to bear the burden all alone. The evident participation of bishops in these major decisions would also dispose larger numbers of people to accept them more readily. In other words, even in doctrinal matters, there should be an effort to prepare and dispose people to accept teaching. The ancient canonical principle, 'What touches everyone must be approved by everyone',[52] bespeaks not only prudence but an understanding of human nature … .

The international Synod of Bishops is another exercise of the collegial teaching office of bishops. But the synod has not met the original expectations of its establishment. The synod was envisioned as being a way for the bishops of the world with the pope to deal with major issues touching the Church. At the present time, however, the topic of the synod is identified by a small commission of approximately fifteen cardinals and bishops, elected by the synod, who present their proposal to the pope. Ultimately the pope chooses the topic. An approach more expressive of episcopal collegiality would be to charge the presidents of episcopal conferences to get input from their national conferences and then to meet together and vote on three topics in order of priority. The topic receiving a majority of votes would be presented to the pope for confirmation and approval for the next synod.

Many bishops feel that issues which they would like to discuss responsibly cannot come up, such as those mentioned above, as well as others, such as divorce, remarriage, and the

---

51. Second Vatican Council, *Dogmatic Constitution on the Church*, n. 25.

52. '*Quod autem omnes uti singulos tangit, ab omnibus approbari debet*' See, *Code of Canon Law*, 1983, canon 119, n. 3. *Code of Canon Law*, 1917, canon 101, I, n. 2; see also, Cardinal Yves Congar, *Eglise et Papaute*, c. 2, 42–3.

reception of the sacraments. I am not here taking a personal position on any of these issues. My point is simply to underline that issues of major concern in the Church are not really open to a free and collegial evaluation and discussion by bishops, whose office includes being judges in matters of faith. A free discussion is one in which loyalty to the pope and the orthodoxy of the faith of those who discuss these issues are not called into question. In subtle ways and sometimes in very direct ways, the position of the curia on these issues is communicated to bishops at synods and intimidates them. In addition it is made clear that certain recommendations should not be made to the pope at the conclusion of a synod.

Responsible for unity, bishops do not want to create an appearance of rebellion and so, perplexed, they keep silence. The bishops also have great faith and a personal reverence for the pope and do not wish to embarrass him by the appearance of conflict.

The procedures of the synod are outdated and not conducive to collegiality in its fuller sense. They would, in fact, prove alien to many of those seeking unity who are used to parliamentary procedures and more free exchange and debate on issues. A new way of structuring and holding these synods could have a significant effect on the search for unity and the exercise of true collegiality.

It would make the synod more truly a collegial act if the synod had a deliberative vote and not merely a consultative one. And this, too, would be a greater incentive to unity and a more authentic embodiment of collegiality … .

COLLEGIALITY AND THE SANCTIFYING OFFICE

The second of the threefold offices is sanctifying. A number of bishops in various parts of the world believe that general absolution has beneficial effects in some instances and desire to authorize this practice. Certainly there are some obvious points against general absolution. For example, since the penitent does not have the opportunity for spiritual and pastoral direction in this circumstance, he can be left with a troubled conscience. But it would be a fitting work of collegiality if bishops themselves could face the various problems connected with general absolution in a full and free discussion of its doctrinal and pastoral aspects.

Inculturation of the liturgy is another source of tension in many epsiscopates. Here the fundamental question must be raised and discussed: the principle that the Roman Rite must serve as *the* Rite in the Latin Church. When this principle was adopted in the Second Vatican Council, there was not yet a sufficient appreciation or consciousness of the great cultural diversity in the Church. The Roman Rite with its hieratic, measured gravity greatly appeals to many people and rightly so. But there are other cultures which are not well-suited to this approach. Bishops as judges of the faith and those who preside over the liturgy and prayer of their Churches should have the opportunity in synod or council to address this question more openly and in light of their experience. Difference in culture is, however, not the only consideration. We also have to keep in mind that there is a basic, common humanity shared by all peoples and which recognizes the need for reverence, adoration, the acknowledgment of the transcendence of God. There is as well the need for some common signs and practices in the Church which express her universality and communion.

COLLEGIALITY AND THE OFFICE OF GOVERNING

The third office of Christ is governing. Here I would instance the policies regarding the appointment of bishops. The process as we have in the United States, begins when a bishop presents names of candidates to be discussed at a meeting of the bishops of a particular region called a provincial meeting.

At the provincial meeting, the names and qualifications of the candidates are discussed in strict confidence and a vote taken. The names, with accompanying information, are sent to the nuncio in Washington, who forwards the list and the assembled information to Rome to the Congregation for Bishops. The nuncio's judgment is generally thought to have the greatest weight, more than that of the local episcopate. The material is then presented to a meeting of some fifteen cardinals and a few bishops who are called 'members' of the Congregation for Bishops. This body discusses the candidates and votes on them. They usually, but not always, endorse the candidates as proposed by the nuncio. When the voting is completed the cardinal prefect of the Congregation for Bishops brings the results to the pope and the pope personally makes the final selection.

It is not uncommon for bishops of a province to discover that no candidate they proposed has been accepted for approval. On the other hand, it may happen that candidates whom bishops do not approve at all may be appointed. There have been instances of priests of religious orders being named bishops without the knowledge of their own provincial superior and of diocesan priests appointed bishops when their own bishop was not consulted. Under the existing policy, collegiality in the appointment of bishops consists largely in offering bishops an opportunity to make suggestions. But the real decisions are made at other levels: the nuncio, the Congregation for Bishops, the Secretariat of State.

There are, indeed, certain things to recommend the existing procedure. It distances the appointment of bishops from local factions and pressures. It prevents the development of pressure groups favoring one candidate and rejecting another. In some instances it also removes the possibility of the State becoming involved in the appointment of bishops. Yet honest, fraternal dialogue compels me to raise the question whether the time has not come to make some modifications in this procedure so that the local churches really have a significant and truly substantive role in the appointment of bishops. In light of the decrees of the Vatican Council itself, the participation of the local churches in this process cannot properly be confined merely to the participation of bishops but must include a meaningful and responsible role for priest, lay persons and religious ... .

COLLEGIALITY AND SUBSIDIARITY

Clearly linked, then, with the doctrinal truth of collegiality is the principle of subsidiarity. John Mahoney, SJ, has made the point that the word 'subsidiarity' derives from the Latin word *subsidium* which means 'help' or 'support'.[53] Hence the principle of subsidiarity means that a larger social body with more resources does not routinely absorb the role or functions

---

53. John Mahoney, SJ, 'Subsidiarity in the Church', *The Month* (Nov. 1988).

of smaller or less powerful bodies. But it does help and support the smaller bodies to be able to fulfill their own role … .

Subsidiarity in the Church has been a growing concern … . This concern has been expressed now over a period of thirty years. The Synod of 1967 voted to apply subsidiarity in the revision of the Code of Canon Law. The Synod of 1969 voted in favor of applying it to episcopal conferences. And in the preface to the 1983 Code of Canon Law, we read that one of the important principles which underlies the new law is 'the principle of subsidiarity which must all the more be applied in the Church since the office of the bishops and their powers are of divine law'.[54] Notice that the reason given for subsidiarity is not because it is a sign of the times but for dogmatic reasons.

In order to do justice to this declaration of Pius XII, to the Vatican Council, and subsequent documents, not to mention that aspirations of Catholics and other Christians who hope for unity, many of the existing procedures and policies involved in the 'way of exercising the primacy', as well as of the papal curia need to undergo a major and thorough revision. This should recognize the true authority given to bishops by Christ and proclaimed by both the First and Second Vatican Councils and the popes who presided over them. Large segments of the Catholic Church as well as many Orthodox and other Christians do not believe that collegiality and subsidiarity are being practiced in the Catholic Church in a sufficiently meaningful way. The seriousness of our obligation to seek Christian unity sincerely means that this obstacle to unity cannot be overlooked or dismissed as if it were the quirk of malcontents or the scheme of those who want to undermine the papacy. On more than one occasion, Pope John Paul II has said, 'We must take every care to meet the legitimate desires and expectations of our Christian brethren, coming to know their way of thinking and their sensibilities'.[55]

… But in the end, the real question is not about the style, or 'forms' or the 'ways of exercising' the papal office, important and critical as these are. For in the encyclical on Christian unity, *Ut Unum Sint*, there is the unspoken question driving everything else. The ultimate question which the pope – and all of us who seek the unity of Christians – must ask first and last is: 'What is the will of God?' The question we must address is in the last analyses not a question of management, it is not how to reconcile differences or resolve disputes. The question is: 'What is God's will for Peter?' This is the courageous question Pope John Paul II has raised, the question he admits he struggles with and cannot answer alone.

Newman, who was treated very badly by bishops and by Rome over a period of many years, stands as an example of the search for God's will in the face of great personal suffering at the hands of the Church and the undeniable human defects of her ministers. When asked whether he had found what he hoped for in the Catholic Church, he replied:

> 'Have I found,' you ask of me, 'in the Catholic Church, what I hoped and longed for?' … I did not hope or long for any 'peace or satisfaction', as you express it, for any illumination or success. I did not hope or long for anything except to do God's will … .[56]

---

54. *Codex Iuris Canonici*, Libreria Editrice Vaticana, 1983; Preface, p. xxii, n. 5, Latin text.
55. Pope John Paul II, *Ut Unun Sint*, n. 87.
56. Page, John R., *What Will Dr. Newman Do?*, Collegeville, Liturgical Press, 1994, c. 2, 122.

The challenge of John Paul II to search out as brothers and sisters a new way of shaping the papacy as we approach the dawn of a new millennium is a sign of Christ, the Conqueror of sin and death and division. It is a sign of Him who is the Beginning and End of all human history and who says, 'Behold, I make all things new'.[57] Christ as Lord makes everything new, a new heaven, a new earth, a new humanity. He is drawing us all forward into the future by the Spirit of the new covenant of love. We and the whole of creation are straining toward that future which God has prepared for those who love Him and do His will.

I am conscious that what I have said here today in Newman's Oxford has potential for distorted reporting and distorted appropriation by various extremes with their own agendas. These agendas are not mine. I speak completely in fidelity to the Church, One and Catholic. Indeed in the Second Vatican Council many cardinals and bishops said much of what I have said here today.

My reflections, then, are offered as a response to the pope by one who wishes to walk with him in an unbreakable communion of faith and love on the costly journey of discovery as together we search for the Will of God. It is the response of one who reverences the papal office and the person of the pope, who loves the Church, who was born of her womb in Baptism, who received the name of Christ from her lips.

Most importantly, it is the response of one who prays to Christ each day as Newman did, '... that I may receive the gift of perseverance, and die, as I desire to live, in Thy faith, in Thy Church, in Thy service, and in Thy love'.[58]

---

57. Rev. 21:5.
58. J.H. Newman, *Meditations and Devotions*, Maryland, Christian Classics Inc., 1975, 289–90; *Prayer for a Happy Death*.

4.11 AVERY DULLES: *THE PAPACY FOR A GLOBAL CHURCH* – 2000

Our selection is a revised version of the text of Dulles's McGinley Lecture given on 22 March 2000[59] and is responding to a number of recent theological publications calling for a reform of the papacy. Dulles believes that, contrary to much opinion, two of our most recent popes have done much to consult widely and broaden the horizons of the church through their exercise of the papal office. He warns that, in our present 'global' era, some cries for reform might well lead to structures which are *less* conducive to communion and vitality in the church.

❋

THE PAPACY FOR A GLOBAL CHURCH

Conscious of his pastoral responsibility for the whole flock of Christ, Pope John Paul II in his 1995 encyclical letter *Ut Unum Sint* (No. 96) invited leaders and theologians of other churches to suggest ways in which the papal office, without prejudice to its essential features, could be exercised in ways more conducive to Christian unity. Some of the early responses seemed to say that the very existence of the primacy as it had been defined at Vatican I and Vatican II was ecumenically unacceptable. But more recently the Anglican/Roman Catholic International Commission indicated a remarkable openness on the part of Anglicans to the idea of a universal papal primacy.

Individual Protestant theologians such as Wolfhart Pannenberg have seen the desirability of having a pope for all Christians. The views of others can be found in the interesting volume of essays, *A Pope for All Christians? An Inquiry Into the Role of Peter in the Modern Church,* ed. Peter J. McCord (New York: Paulist, 1976), with contributions by distinguished theologians representing the Lutheran, Roman Catholic, Baptist, Reformed, Orthodox, Methodist and Anglican perspectives.

A number of Catholic theologians have taken the pope's invitation as an occasion for expressing their own views on how the papal office might advantageously be restructured. Not surprisingly, the proposals have come principally from authors who are dissatisfied with current procedures. Essentially their complaint is that the papacy has become too active and powerful. Before accessing the proposals, it will be helpful to reflect on recent trends.

---

59. Dulles, Avery, 'The Papacy for a Global Church', *America* (15–22 July 2000), 6–11.

GLOBALIZATION OF THE PAPACY

During the past two centuries the popes have become increasingly aware of their planetary responsibilities and have transformed the papacy into a more potent symbol of Catholic unity. The First Vatican Council (1869–70), followed by the *Code of Canon Law* of 1917, attributed new powers to the pope as vicar of Christ for the universal church. He received practically unlimited authority over the development of doctrine and ecclesiastical legislation. Through its expanding diplomatic corps, the Holy See came to be morally present in many nations, overseeing the affairs of the church and interacting with secular governments. With the help of nuncios and apostolic delegates, Rome controlled the appointment of bishops everywhere.

At the Second Vatican Council (1962–65) bishops from Western Europe (France, Belgium, Holland and Germany), together with their theological advisers, spearheaded a program of reform that sought to restore the dignity and rights of individual bishops and give real though limited autonomy to regional churches. Missionary bishops of Asia and Africa, anxious to insert the Catholic faith more deeply into the lives of their people, welcomed the program. Without reversing the teaching of Vatican I on papal primacy, Vatican II promoted inculturation; it rehabilitated local and regional churches; it upgraded the episcopate by redefining the bishop as a priest who enjoys the fullness of the sacrament of order. It formulated the doctrine of collegiality, teaching that all bishops in communion with Rome are fellow members of the supreme directorate of the universal church.

To implement these principles Vatican II initiated several structural changes. It called for the internationalization of the Roman Curia, which up to then had been almost exclusively Italian. It erected a system of episcopal conferences, one for each major nation or territory in the world. In concert with Paul VI, the council also set up a totally new institution: the Synod of Bishops, which meets periodically in Rome to deal with matters of concern to the universal church.

Pope Paul VI, faithfully implementing the council's program, made the papacy truly a global institution. He internationalized the Roman Curia and supervised the establishment of the episcopal conferences and the Synod of Bishops. Following a suggestion of this synod, he established the International Theological Commission to advise the Holy See … .

John Paul II is, like Paul VI, preeminently a pope of Vatican II. As a young bishop he participated in all four sessions of the council. Enthusiastically supporting its teaching, he assiduously applied it to his archdiocese of Kraków in Poland. Throughout the decade from 1967 to 1977 he was a leading figure in the Synod of Bishops. His election as the first non-Italian pope since the 16th century dramatically underlined the international character of the contemporary papacy.

Like Paul VI, John Paul II sees himself as a 'pilgrim pope'. He has made more than 100 trips outside of Italy in the 22 years of his pontificate thus far. He has spoken at UNESCO in Paris and has twice addressed the General Assembly of the United Nations in New York. He has frequently met with leaders of other Christian churches and has engaged in interreligious events at Assisi and elsewhere. In the name of social justice he has denounced oppressive regimes and supported participatory forms of government as more consonant with the dignity and freedom of the human person. The success of the bloodless revolutions in Central and Eastern Europe in 1989 has been attributed in great part to his moral influence.

Although he abstains from partisan politics, no pope since the Middle Ages – or perhaps in all history – has been such a major actor on the world stage.

As did Paul VI, John Paul II works collegially with the bishops of the world. He has held regular sessions of the Synod of Bishops approximately every three years. In 1985 he called an extraordinary meeting of the synod to celebrate the 20th anniversary of the conclusion of Vatican II. He has convoked special sessions of the synod for national and regional groups of bishops, including the four great assemblies for Africa, America, Asia and Europe, leading up to the Great Jubilee of 2000 … .

John Paul II also believes strongly in inculturation. The faith, he believes, must be successfully incarnated in the many cultures of the world. This task, however, is a delicate one. Cultures are not morally and religiously neutral. They need to be evangelized so as to be hospitable to, and supportive of, authentic Christianity. Lest cultures become self-enclosed and divisive, John Paul II insists that they must respect universal human values. In the church, believers of different cultural regions must be able to recognize one another as fellow members of the same body, sharing the same apostolic heritage. If these conditions are met, the plurality of cultures in the church can be a positive asset. It can bring the riches of the nations to Christ the Lord, to whom they were given as an inheritance … .

PROPOSED PRINCIPLES OF REFORM

Many of the recent reform proposals may be seen as reactions against the global papacy of the post-Vatican II era. Seeking greater autonomy for individual bishops and local churches, Catholic reformers frequently invoke the principle of subsidiarity. John Paul II has concisely explained the meaning of this principle in his encyclical *Centesimus Annus* (1991): 'A community of a higher order should not interfere in the internal life of a community of a lower order, depriving the later of its functions, but rather should support it in case of need and help to coordinate its activity with the activities of the rest of society, always with a view to the common good' (No. 48) … .

It is debated to what extent, or exactly how, subsidiarity applies to the church. Unlike the state, the church was established from above, so to speak, by God's action in Christ, who gave special powers to Peter and the Twelve. The church began to pulse with life when the Holy Spirit descended upon the church as a whole at Pentecost. Only subsequently, as the faith spread to Antioch, Rome, Alexandria and other cities, was it necessary to set up local authorities in charge of particular churches. These particular churches were, as Vatican II puts it, 'fashioned after the model of the universal church', which is therefore antecedent to them, even though it in certain respects depends on them ('Dogmatic Constitution on the Church', No. 23). They can be called churches inasmuch as 'the Church of Christ is truly present in all legitimate local congregations' ('Dogmatic Constitution on the Church', No. 26).

Because the principle of subsidiarity has been formulated with reference to secular societies, its applicability to the church is debatable. Whatever the outcome of the debate, common sense requires that merely local problems should, if possible, be handled locally. In today's world, however, local questions often have ramifications for the universal church, and therefore require the involvement of higher authority … .

I am not suggesting that the church should go back to the pre-Vatican II situation. The conciliar reforms have enabled the church to enter into the globalized universe of our day. The council quite properly called for inculturation, collegiality and a renewed emphasis on the local church as a center of pastoral life and worship. The structures erected since the council have served well, though further experience and adjustments will be needed for them to function as smoothly as might be desired.

There should be no question of choosing between centralization and decentralization. Decentralization could be disruptive and centralization oppressive unless the centrifugal and centripetal tendencies were held in balance. The process of growth at the extremities places more burdens than ever on the Roman center. In the words of Vatican II, the chair of Peter 'presides over the whole assembly of charity and protects legitimate differences, while at the same time it sees that such differences do not hinder unity but rather contribute to it' ('Dogmatic Constitution on the Church', No. 13).

SPECIFIC PROPOSALS FOR STRUCTURAL REFORM

In the light of the principles already stated, we may turn our attention to some specific proposals for reform frequently found in recent theological literature. Five recurrent suggestions seem to merit special mention.

First of all, there is the issue of the nomination of bishops. Since the mid-19th century, the selection of bishops by secular princes and by cathedral chapters has all but vanished. No Catholic wants to go back to the old system in which civil governments practically chose most of the bishops. Under the present system, the papal nuncio or delegate has major responsibility for gathering names from his personal knowledge and from consultation with appropriate persons. The appointments are then discussed in the Vatican's Congregation of Bishops, which includes bishops from different regions, who make their own suggestions. The Pope receives all the recommendations and makes the final choice.

Many reform-minded theologians would like a more open and 'democratic' process in which names are submitted by the local church, filtered through the national or regional conference of bishops, and eventually proposed to Rome for approval or disapproval. Since the process of appointment is always subject to approval, suggestions of this kind should not be rejected out of hand. But the proposals I have seen are not free from weaknesses. By erecting representative committees they would unleash factionalism and political power struggles within the local churches. By considering only names surfaced within the diocese, they would also create a risk of excessive inbreeding. A church with an eccentric tradition would perpetuate its own eccentricity rather than correct it … .

Although mistakes are occasionally made, the existing procedure, in my opinion, has given us a generally excellent body of bishops who can be trusted to serve as faithful pastors of their flocks. They compare favorably with the elected bishops of other churches.

POWER OF THE SYNOD OF BISHOPS

A second issue has to do with the powers of the Synod of Bishops. As presently constituted, it consists primarily of bishops elected by their respective episcopal conferences, which are represented according to their relative size. Plenary sessions are held about once every three years and are relatively brief – not more than a month in length. The bishops could hardly afford to be absent from their sees for longer or more frequent periods. The synod is not a legislative body but a forum for the bishops to express their views on the theme of the meeting and ascertain the degree of consensus among them. The synod assemblies often make useful suggestions to the pope and the Curia. The apostolic exhortations that issue from these assemblies have demonstrated the value of the synodal process.

There are voices in the church that would like to see the synod transformed into a body that could enact laws and issue binding doctrinal pronouncements. Given the ad hoc make-up of the assemblies and the relatively brief time of the meetings, I am inclined to disagree. I doubt that the Catholic faithful would wish to be bound by the decrees of such an assembly. The pope can, of course, give the synod power to decide some issue by majority vote, but he has thus far preferred to seek recommendations from the synod and let the Roman congregations follow-up with the necessary actions.

The assembly of 1985, for example, made four major recommendations: the early completion of the Code of Canon Law for Eastern Catholic churches, the preparation of a universal catechism or compendium of Catholic doctrine, a study of the nature and authority of episcopal conferences and a study of the applicability of the principle of subsidiarity to the internal life of the church. In his closing speech the pope accepted the first three suggestions, all of which have been carried out in subsequent years. As for the principle of subsidiarity, it seems well to allow the question to mature in theological literature before the magisterium makes a formal announcement.

A third issue under discussion is the role of the episcopal conferences such as, in the United States, the National Conference of Catholic Bishops. As constituted by Vatican II, they are primarily consultative in nature. They permit the bishops of a nation or region to benefit from one another's wisdom and coordinate their polices as they govern in their own dioceses. The conferences do not normally make binding legislation, but they can do so on occasion either by unanimous vote or by a two-thirds majority together with formal approval (*recognitio*) from Rome.

In the summer of 1998, the pope published a letter in which he clarified the nature and doctrinal authority of episcopal conferences, such as the Synod of Bishops of 1985 had requested. He ruled that the conferences could not teach obligatory doctrine without a two-thirds majority followed by Roman recognition. Some critics contend that this ruling showed excessive distrust of the conferences. But Vatican II did not establish the conferences as doctrinal organs. How could the Catholic people in the United States be bound by a vote of their bishops to profess some belief that was not taught throughout the church? Do the diocesan bishops and the Catholic people really want to be bound in matters of doctrine by the majority vote of their bishops' conference – especially if it be a small conference that might have less than a dozen members?

A fourth point under discussion is the power of the Roman Curia. The pope can not effectively govern the universal church without a kind of cabinet consisting of the Roman congregations, tribunals and councils. The heads of these organs are normally bishops, and, in the case of congregations, cardinals. Diocesan bishops often complain that Rome is interfering too much in the affairs of the local churches. But Rome rarely intervenes on its own initiative. It is usually responding to complaints from the local church against some questionable proceeding … .

In doctrinal matters, Rome's policy has generally been to encourage the diocesan bishops and the bishops' conferences to take greater responsibility for overseeing the orthodoxy of what is preached and taught in their respective areas. But the bishops usually rely upon Rome to assure them that they are teaching in communion with the universal church since doctrines are by their very nature universal. The Congregation for the Doctrine of Faith cannot avoid being drawn into discussions where questions of orthodoxy are raised.

A fifth and final question has to do with papal teaching authority. The present pope, like Paul VI, has thus far refrained from issuing ex cathedra dogmatic definitions, but he has several times made conclusive doctrinal determinations without any formal vote by the college of bishops. In these cases he has used his own authority as universal primate to 'confirm the brethren' (Lk. 22:32), authoritatively gathering up the general consensus of bishops, past and present. Some theologians apparently hold that the pope ought to conduct a poll or call for a vote before issuing such pronouncements. But it may be answered that even if a few bishops disagree, the voice of the pope together with a solid majority of bishops over a long period of time obviates the need for a head count. Such cumbersome processes could easily prevent a timely and effective response to critical situations.

A PAPACY IN DIALOGUE

Since Vatican II the principal drama in the Catholic Church has been the dialectical tension between centralizing and decentralizing tendencies. The decentralizers tend to see themselves as progressives and to depict their adversaries as restorationists, but the opposite case can equally well be made. Those who want to reinstate the conditions of patristic Christianity tend to be nostalgic and anachronistic.

In the end, the question should not be posed as an either/or. Precisely because of the increased activity of particular churches and conferences, Rome is required to exercise greater vigilance than ever, less the unity of the church be jeopardized. The global character of the Catholic Church today, together with the rapidity of modern communications, makes ineluctable new demands on the papal office. It will be for members of other churches to judge whether a strong and energetic papacy is ecumenically acceptable. More than a few, I suspect, are looking toward Rome to provide effective leadership for the entire *oikoumene* (the whole inhabited world). The contemporary world situation, as I understand it, demands a successor of Peter who, with the divine assistance, can teach and direct the entire people of God. The Petrine office, as it has developed since Vatican II, has a unique capacity to hold all local and regional churches in dialogue while reaching out in loving service to all. Paul VI and John Paul II are to be praised for having discharged this mission with loyalty, strength and openness to the Spirit of God.

4.12 LADISLAS ORSY: *THE PAPACY FOR AN ECUMENICAL AGE – A RESPONSE TO AVERY DULLES – 2000*

The following essay[60] was written as a response to Dulles' McGinley Lecture. It challenges many of the presuppositions in Dulles' text. Orsy believes that many of the reforms dismissed or misrepresented by Dulles are urgently needed in the church today, particularly in the light of the new ecumenical situation concerning the relation between the Roman Catholic church and other Christian denominations.

❋

Ever since the Second Vatican Council, the Roman Catholic Church has committed itself irrevocably to the task of restoring the unity of the church of Christ. Then, as it entered into dialogue with sister churches and ecclesial communities, they, one after the other, voiced their common concern: there is a need to find new ways of exercising the papal ministry. Since all baptized persons are incorporated into Christ and they, too, have the Holy Spirit, their virtually unanimous demand should give us pause.

It has given pause to Pope John Paul II. The result is his extraordinary encyclical *Ut Unum Sint* ('That They Be One', 1995). In it he charts new ways. He accepts that the Roman Catholic Church is in need of perpetual conversion, *metanoia* (No. 15). Then he pointedly recalls 'how the Master concerned himself with Peter's conversion' (No. 91) and adds that his own ministry is 'open to a new situation' (No. 95). He goes on to conclude, 'I insistently pray the Holy Spirit to shine his light upon us, enlightening all the Pastors as theologians of our churches, that we may seek – together, of course – the forms in which this ministry may accomplish a service of love recognized by all concerned'.

The pope, the teacher, wants to be a learner. To make sure that his point is not missed, he insists, 'This is an immense task, which we cannot refuse and which I cannot carry out by myself' (No. 96).

Theologians and leaders of churches were taken by surprise and were at first slow in responding to the pope's request. Then they began to understand the invitation and take up the challenge. Some scholars and members of the hierarchy held symposia (two in Rome, one in Innsbruck); others published articles and books; and now, a healthy 'disputation' is spreading and expanding among Catholic and non-Catholic Christians – that is, within the entire church of Christ.

Avery Dulles, SJ, a professor at Fordham University, made a contribution to this exchange [included in this chapter as 'The Papacy for a Global Church']. His approach is clear but puzzling. The information he provides is partial. He reports the activities

---

60. Orsy, Ladislas: 'The Papacy for an Ecumenical Age – A Response to Avery Dulles', *America* (21 October 2000).

of the center faithfully, but he does not speak of the weaknesses in the provinces. Then, on the basis of incomplete data, he reaches the conclusion that no significant change is needed. As for the ecumenical outcome, here is his position: 'It will be for members of other churches to judge whether a strong and energetic papacy is ecumenically acceptable.' In other words, the contemporary way of exercising the papacy is not open to a new situation.

A puzzling response, indeed, to the pope's demand. Surely, John Paul II meant what he wrote: he wants to preserve the substance of his office intact but does not want to cling to unnecessary historical accretions that can impede the union of the churches. To achieve that goal, he asks for fresh ideas and creative insights. Among theologians, an honest 'disputation' is in process. Learned, wise and responsible scholars from the world over are joining it. (One of the first meetings was sponsored by the Congregation for the Doctrine of the Faith!)

ALL IS NOT WELL

All should welcome Father Dulles's contribution. His opinion must be respected – and subjected to careful scrutiny. This has been the rule for 'disputations' ever since the Middle Ages. In this spirit, I intend to examine his positions but do not wish to get entangled in 'useless controversies' (John Paul's words in *Ut Unum Sint*, No. 96). In a positive fashion, I wish to move beyond what divides us into a broader field of vision and show Catholics and non-Catholics alike that our tradition is rich enough to be the source of inspiration for new ways of exercising the papal ministry without losing any of its substance. For this reason the title of my article is 'The Papacy for an Ecumenical Age'. Ecumenism, not globalism, is John Paul's concern.

Father Dulles's point of departure offers an overview of the achievements of a 'strong and energetic' central government. In recent times, the Roman Catholic Church has become more visible in the entire world than ever before; it is enough to think of the two million young people celebrating the jubilee in Rome. Its administration is well ordered and efficient. Should trouble arise at any place, it is able to intervene with speed. Those entrusted to speak in the name of the church are loyal in words and deeds. The secular principalities and powers admire us as never before; they are sending their ambassadors to the strongest moral power on earth. And the church stands in the forefront of the struggle for human rights. For these things we must be grateful.

No sensible person would contest the overall truth of such an assessment; no wise person wants to weaken the church in its service to the human family. Yet in accessing the state of the church, we have a duty to search for the full truth, no matter how disturbing facts and events may be – an inquiry that Father Dulles did not undertake … .

… [Dulles] fails to perceive the immense energies of the Holy Spirit in the bishops' assemblies – energies unused. He does not mention the supernatural instincts of the faithful that can guard and infallibly recognize the truth – an instinct that hardly ever is allowed to play a role. In failing to contemplate such invisible realities, the unduly restrictive nature of several legal provisions (to be named as this article progresses) escapes him.

Yet the purpose of canon law is precisely to create a friendly climate for the operation of the Spirit.

To be sure that we follow the right paths in our reflections, let us return to the request of John Paul II and search for its meaning to the fullest extent. Surely, his demand is not (and cannot be) an invitation to produce just cleverly conceived norms and guidelines (a kind of blueprint) for the exercise of his office. Propositions, good as they may be, are without life. New ways must grow out of the living church; they must be the organic product of the body that is the church.

It follows that if we want (if John Paul wants) a new understanding and fresh ecumenical practice of his office, the whole church must be involved. It must become strong and energetic not only in the center but everywhere in searching for and finding new ways to exercise the papacy. The movement toward an ecumenical primacy must begin by strengthening the Roman Catholic communion in the provinces, where the weaknesses are. When the whole body, in each and every part, is functioning fairly and fully, other churches and communities will notice it. They will be attracted by the strength and harmony manifest in the community. Of course, the road to unity will still be long, but we would be marching with increased hope.

Here is our central suggestion: *The new manner of exercising the Petrine office should begin by strengthening the Roman Catholic communion in all its parts.* The words of the Lord to Peter come to mind, 'Strengthen your brethren' (Lk. 22:34). After all, what else can a future ecumenical primacy be than the ongoing strengthening of the whole body of Christ in all its members, in their unity and in their immense diversities?

Before we turn to particular issues, some general principles must be clarified.

THE UNIVERSAL CHURCHES AND THE PARTICULAR CHURCHES

Father Dulles's theology of the church (as it is displayed in his article) rests on a principle for which he invokes the authority of Vatican II. He writes, 'The particular churches were, as Vatican II puts it, "fashioned after the model of the universal church", which is therefore antecedent to them even though it in certain respects depends on them' (see 'Dogmatic Constitution on the Church', No. 23). From this 'principle of antecedency', he argues for a highly centralized administration and then concludes that the principle of subsidiarity is 'debatable'. The council, however, never used the term 'antecedent'. Father Dulles's translation of the Latin original (*ad imaginum ecclesiae universalis formatis*) is questionable, if not misleading. In Tanner's edition of the council documents, Clarence Gallagher of Oxford, who is well practiced in interpreting conciliar texts, is closer to the original: 'particular churches [are] formed in the likeness of the universal church' (*Decrees*, vol. 2, 867). A scrutiny of the Latin text and of the surrounding debates suggests the meaning (my paraphrase): 'the internal form of a particular church reflects the image of the universal church', that is, particular churches are one, holy, Catholic and apostolic as the universal church is. But what is the universal church? The council gives a straightforward answer in a balancing clause that Father Dulles does not quote: it exists 'in and from' (*in quibus et ex quibus*) the particular churches; in other terms there in no universal church (not even conceptually) apart from the particular churches. (All this is technical but indispensable. The principle on which we build must be sound and clear.)

In truth, the question *Which is prior, the universal church or the particular church?* Is a misconceived question, a trap for the unwary. Anyone who walks into it must choose either the one or the other. It is like asking *Which is prior, the body or its members?* A body without members is no body; members that do not form a body are not members.

In the post-apostolic Catholic tradition, there has never been, and there could not be, a universal church without particular churches. Such an 'abstract' church could not even have a head, since Peter's successor is the bishop of Rome! And in the apostolic times, the Spirit descended on the church of Jerusalem; 'in it and from it' the universal church then and there arose.

SUBSIDIARITY

Once the 'antecedency' principle is discarded, the principle of subsidiarity appears in a new light. It is not a luxury; it is not an option. It is the intrinsic law of any organic body. For the body to operate well, each of its members must function to its normal capacity. If the brain unduly interferes with the heart, the harmony of the body is lost. Now Father Dulles is correct in noting that the principle was first articulated 'with reference to secular societies', but he fails to see that it was the discovery of an operational law applicable to every human community. The grace that pervades the church does not take away its humanity. (Perhaps a better name for the same principle would be 'principle of integrity', in the sense that the operational integrity of every single organ is essential for the health of the whole body.)

COLLEGIALITY

It would have made no sense for Vatican II to affirm collegiality, nor for opponents of the doctrine to resist it so fiercely and for so long, if by *collegiality* the council fathers meant mere consultation. Nor would it have made much sense to proclaim collegiality at length if it can be operational at an ecumenical council or through a universal consensus of the bishops only. For centuries no one doubted that in such cases the bishops acted collegially. The action of the council makes sense only if the fathers perceived a need for the practice of effective collegiality in the ordinary, day to day, operations of the church. After vigorous debates, the council proclaimed the doctrine. It left, however, the creation of appropriate norms and structures to the legislator. As yet these do not exist.

Father Dulles fails to perceive the distinction between consultation and collegiality. He represents the celebration of synods, the meeting of the pope with various groups of bishops as collegial acts. They are consultations. Collegiality means participation in the act of a decision, as it happens precisely at an ecumenical council.

So much for general principles: we are in position to turn to particular issues.

THE APPOINTMENT OF BISHOPS

The internal well-being of the church depends to a high degree on the laws and ordinances for the selection of the bishops, which have varied a great deal in the course of history. There is not, and there cannot be, any secular model for such procedures, because they are meant for a unique ecclesial act. Father Dulles is right in saying that the selection should not be left to any civil authority, but he is wrong in insinuating that the only alternative is the system presently in place. Our tradition is much richer than that. There is enough wisdom in the church to find alternative ways without going to the secular power … .

Since the 19th century, the Holy See increasingly has asserted its own exclusive right to appoint bishops the world over. When a see falls vacant, the pontifical legate (nuncio, apostolic delegate) plays the central role. He is duty bound to consult widely among the local bishops and the clergy, and he may consult lay persons 'eminent in wisdom'. At the end his recommendations are paramount; he proposes the *terna*. It is a method that has done much to extinguish provincialism and exclude politics. Still, the question remains: could a way be found to let the wisdom of the episcopate and of the laity play a more significant role? Why should we fear them?

The system in place is not wrong; it just lacks equilibrium. Any highly centralized government is tempted (and often tends) to favor unity over diversity, to reward unquestioning loyalty and to distrust creativity. If that happens, there will be weakness in the limbs and the whole body will suffer from it. In the church no administration can be *catholic* unless it promotes with equal force unity and diversity. Let us recall that if the pope is the principle of unity, the local bishops, each one of them, are principles of diversity … .

EPISCOPAL CONFERENCES

The inspiration for handling the business of the church through the assemblies of the bishops comes from the Acts of the Apostles. When the conflict … erupted about the imposition of the Mosaic laws, 'the apostles and the elders held a meeting to look into this matter' (Acts 15:6). No small matter: the first issue of planting the Gospel in 'another' culture. An assembly was needed to resolve it.

Ever since, when a crisis emerged in the community, or when a pressing need demanded attention, bishops gathered, prayed, deliberated and then decided with an amazing authority: 'It pleased the Holy Spirit and us … .' The people listened, and with that 'supernatural sense' ('Dogmatic Constitution on the Church', No. 12) that faith alone can give, they recognized the voice of their authentic pastors. Undoubtedly, the Apostles, the elders and the people remembered the promise of the Lord: 'For where two or three are gathered in my name, there am I in the midst of them' (Mt. 18:20). If that is true of a gathering of the faithful, how much more it must be true when the shepherds come together!

From early times the community distinguished the 'great synods' (Nicea, Constantinople, Ephesus, Chalcedon and so forth) from assemblies of lesser significance. Yet as far as we know, it never occurred to them that a regional meeting of bishops would be deprived of a *special* assistance of the Spirit. For this reason, while the church recognized the 'great synods' as the decisive witnesses of our tradition, it also respected lesser assemblies as having authority 'in the Spirit'.

Out of this old tradition grew the institution of the episcopal conferences. The same energy of the Spirit is welling up in them (they are bishops!) that animated the particular synods through centuries. They are not infallible, they do not possess the highest degree of prudence. Some of their doctrinal statements may eventually demand completion or even correction; some of their practical actions may need adjustment or even reversal, but that is not the point. They gather in the name of the Lord.

Moreover, the conferences are needed because within the great cultural regions of our world, the voice of a lonely bishop is hardly heard, his action scarcely noticed. The bishops must join forces to proclaim the Gospel forcefully. Together, they must plant the seeds of the Kingdom into the soil of their culture. In order for these things to happen, the conferences need fair freedom and well-measured autonomy.

Suffice it to say here that today the canonical regulations for episcopal conferences are such that the bishops have little freedom, if any at all, 'to cast fire upon the earth' (Lk. 12:49). Yes, there is need to announce with one voice the good news, but there is the crippling rule of unanimity for any doctrinal statement – and what preaching is not a doctrinal statement? Yes, there is the need for creative initiatives but no action can be effective unless 'reviewed' by Rome – and by the time the answer comes a precious opportunity may be lost. In the practical order, episcopal conferences exist and operate at the good pleasure of the Holy See.

THE ROMAN SYNOD OF BISHOPS

Paul VI instituted the Roman Synod (the periodical meetings of the representatives of the episcopal conferences with the pope) to build a closer link with the world wide episcopate. He may have intended it to develop into an effective practice of collegiality. No such development has taken place; the synod has remained a consultative body. Its members are invited to discuss the issues laid down before them. They are called to inquire about the general well-being of the church. They are not allowed to make any decisions. They are entitled only to make recommendations to the pope.

Such synods are of great benefit to the universal church, not so much for what they are doing but for the potential they are hiding. Always presided over by the pope, they could be guided to a higher status; they could become organs of effective collegiality and be part of decision-making processes at the highest level. The power of Peter's vicar would not be diminished since without him the synod could not exist; rather, he would be helped by the collective wisdom of the representatives. This would be a development especially welcomed by the Orthodox Churches: They would recognize in it an affinity with their tradition of synodal government.

PAPAL TEACHING

Concerning papal teaching, I wish to focus on the one issue that Father Dulles mentions, that of 'definitive' declarations. My aim is not to argue but to report briefly their history and to signal the problems (mostly unresolved) that they have created.

Ever since the publication of the encyclical *Humanae Vitae* in 1968, the Holy See has been searching for ways and means to enforce acceptance of some of its doctrinal declarations that did not amount to papal definitions but were seen as 'definitive', that is, 'irreformable'. Ways and means to do it were found, and they were introduced one by one.

In 1989 the Holy See published an 'extended' profession of faith, required from all candidates for ordination or for an ecclesial office. They must be willing 'to embrace firmly and to hold all and each [point of doctrine] definitively proposed by the church'.

Also in 1989 the Congregation for the Doctrine of the Faith imposed a new Oath of Fidelity to be taken by the same persons, an oath that regards the present and the future: 'I shall follow with Christian obedience what the sacred pastors, as authentic doctors and teachers of faith, declare.' Obedience to 'definitive' declarations is clearly included.

Finally, in 1998 a new canonical penalty at the discretion of the ecclesiastical superior was inserted into the Code of Canon Law applicable to dissenters from 'definitive' doctrine.

These provisions coalesce into a tightly knit pattern that excludes anyone who is not willing to embrace a definitive teaching from functioning 'in the name of the church'. ...

The negative impact of these new regulations on the ecumenical movement is far reaching – known to those Catholics who are 'out in the field' quietly working for the union of the churches. Their partners in the dialogue do not fail to communicate discretely but firmly their concern.

THE ROMAN CURIA

During Vatican II the complaints against the Roman Curia reached a high level. On Nov. 8, 1963, Cardinal Joseph Frings of Cologne voiced the frustration of many Fathers. Focusing in particular on the (then) Holy Office, he remarked: 'Its procedures are out of harmony with modern times, are a source of harm to the faithful and of scandal to those outside the church.'

In our own days complaints abound again. Are the reported grievances unjust allegations? Or, is the *sensus fidelium* at work alerting the community that something is not well in the body of Christ?

To handle this problem, two principles should be invoked. One is that the pope must have a staff of intelligent and prudent persons who can expedite the business of the Holy See. Another is that such a staff must never encroach on the legitimate freedom of the local episcopate and the people. Can such a delicate balance ever be achieved?

Cardinal Frings thought yes. Here are some of his suggestions:
There should be a clear distinction between administrative and judicial procedures.
No Roman congregation should have the authority to accuse, judge and condemn an individual who has no opportunity to defend himself.
No one should be consecrated a bishop just in order to honor him or the office he holds.
Efforts should be made to use fewer bishops, fewer priests and more laymen (cf. *Council Daybook*, NCWC, 1965, 247).

Nearly four decades later, here are some additional thoughts:

We learned that diverse citizenships at the Curia do not necessarily result in an international outlook. A person from the provinces can bring his own narrow horizons into the center and impose it on the world wide church. But how could the horizons of persons working in the center be broadened – especially when such persons think they are already broad enough? Perhaps those in charge of higher offices should from time to time visit far away churches and just listen – yes, just listen – to women and men, priests and bishops, Catholics and non-Catholics. Is this suggestion an impossible dream?

The following is certainly possible: The term of years for major offices should be strictly enforced. It is not to the benefit of the church that a person in an administrative-executive position should impose his personality on the whole church for a long time.

Over the decades after the council we learned that good suggestions are not enough – Cardinal Frings made very good ones. Implementation is the real problem.

In the practical order, a permanent mechanism is needed that could watch over the delicate balance described above. Could a 'papal committee' be created, in imitation of the institution of the 'ombudsman?' Complaints could be brought before it, and it would have the power to bring to the attention of the pope undesirable attitudes and administrative excesses. The very existence of such an institution would improve the Curia's performance.

IN PLACE OF A CONCLUSION

Let me propose a thought experiment to the theologians. (We should use thought experiments much more than we do.) Let us assume that someone with the power of healing the wounds of the church of Christ raises a wand of peace and restores our lost unity.

The result is that Christian communities from one end of the earth to the other are one in all necessary beliefs, free in all matters doubtful, bound to one another in charity. They have unity *and* they display immense diversities. Let us assume further that the One who healed the church installs the successor of Peter as 'the bishop of this one, holy, catholic, and apostolic church'.

Here is the question: could he govern that church in the same manner as he governs the Roman Catholic community today?

If not what changes would be needed?

This is a different methodology. The search for new ways is not limited by the horizons of the Roman Catholic communion. It looks even beyond the divided and dispersed Christian communities. It contemplates the wholesome image of the church of Christ intact. There cannot be a better source of inspiration. We heard the pope's request; we have his mandate. Our task is spelled out for some time to come. Will Father Dulles join us in this holy enterprise?

QUESTIONS FOR DISCUSSION

1 Do you agree with the traditional Roman Catholic assertion that papal primacy has an *essential* role in the life of the church?
2 Which view of the pope's relationship to the college of bishops seems to have a more firm ecclesiological foundation, that of Rahner, or Tillard? Why?
3 Which vision of the papacy for the third millennium do you find more compelling, that of Dulles or Orsy? Why?
4 Of the various limits on the papacy proposed by Granfield, which do you find most frequently overlooked?
5 Which aspect of the papacy, as it is exercised today, do you think presents the biggest obstacle to ecumenical agreement on a universal ministry of primacy?

FURTHER READING

CHURCH DOCUMENTS

Aeterna Dei Sapientia – On Saint Leo the Great, 1961, esp. nos 42ff.
Humani Generis – 1950.

DISCUSSION AND DEBATE

Alberigo, Giuseppe, 'The Authority of the Church in the Documents of Vatican I and Vatican II', in *Authority in the Church*, Piet F. Fransen, Leuven, Peeters (eds), University Press, 1983.

Balthasar, Hans Urs von, *The Office of Peter and the Structure of the Church*, San Francisco, Ignatius Press, 1986.

Bermejó, Luis M., *Infallibility on Trial*, Westminster, Christian Classics, 1992.

Buckley, M.J. *Papal Primacy and the Episcopate*, New York, Crossroad, 1998.

Burgess, Joseph A., Empie, C. Paul and Murphy, T. Austin, *Teaching Authority and Infallibility in the Church*, Minneapolis, Augsburg, 1980.

Collins, P., *Papal Power – Proposals for Change in the Earth's Third Millennium*, London, Fount, 1997.

Cooke, Bernard (ed.), *The Papacy and the Church in the United States*, New York, Paulist Press, 1989.

Dionne, J. Robert, *The Papacy and the Church – a Study of Praxis and Reception in Ecumenical Perspective*, New York, Philosophical Library, 1987.

Duffy, Eamon, *Saints and Sinners – a History of the Popes*, New Haven, Yale University Press, 1997.

Eno, Robert, *The Rise of the Papacy*, Wilmington, Michael Glazier, 1990.

Farmer, William, and Roch Keszty, *Peter and Paul in the Church of Rome – The Ecumenical Potential of a Forgotten Perspective*, New York, Paulist, 1990.

Gaillardetz, Richard R., *Teaching with Authority*, Collegeville, Liturgical Press, 1997.

Granfield, Patrick, *The Papacy in Transition*, Garden City, Doubleday, 1980.

Jalland, Trevor, *The Church and the Papacy*, London, SPCK, 1944.

Küng, Hans (ed.), *Papal Ministry in the Church*, in *Concilium*, 64, New York, Herder and Herder, 1971.

Küng, Hans, *Infallible?*, London, SCM, 1994.

LaDue, William, *The Chair of St. Peter – A History of the Papacy*, Maryknoll, Orbis, 1999.

MacEoin, Gary, *The Papacy and the People of God*, New York, Orbis, 1998.

McBrien, Richard, *Lives of the Popes*, San Francisco, HarperCollins, 1997.

McCord, P., *A Pope for All Christians*, New York, Paulist Press, 1976.

Miller, J. Michael, *What are They Saying About Papal Primacy?*, New York, Paulist Press, 1983.

Miller, J. Michael, *The Shepherd and the Rock: Origins, Development, and Mission of the Papacy*, Our Sunday Visitor, 1995.

Rahner, Karl, 'The Episcopate and the Primacy', Part IV of *Studies in Modern Theology*, London, Burns & Oates, 1964, 303–94.

Roberts, Thomas D'Esterre, *Black Popes – Authority, Its Use and Abuse*, New York, Sheed & Ward, 1954.

Schatz, K., *Papal Primacy from its Origins to the Present*, Collegeville, Liturgical Press, 1996.

Tillard, J.M., *The Bishop of Rome*, London, Michael Glazier, 1983.

Torquemada, J. de, *Disputation on the Authority of the Pope and Council*, Oxford, Blackfriars, 1988.

Zagano, P. and Tilley, T.W. (eds), *The Exercise of the Primacy*, New York, Crossroad, 1998.

Part 5:

The Sensus Fidelium and Reception of Teaching

Jan Kerkhofs

After Vatican II and probably more so in continental Europe than elsewhere, Catholic laity and priests have been promoting greater participation in the church, not only in liturgy but also in matters pertaining to the reinterpretation of the faith. This phenomenon can easily be explained: the Council had raised great interest in all the layers of the church. More Catholics than ever before were better trained in religious studies. After the horrible experiences with communism and Nazism, the general climate strongly supported democracy, not only in politics, but also in the field of education, in health care and particularly in socio-economic affairs (e.g. through membership of trade unions).

The dogmatic Constitution *Lumen Gentium* placed chapter two, on the 'people of God', before the one on the hierarchy. In no. 12 we read: 'The body of the faithful as a whole, anointed as they are by the Holy One (cf. John. 2:20, 27), cannot err in matters of belief. Thanks to a supernatural sense of the faith which characterizes the people as a whole, it manifests this unerring quality when, "from the bishops down to the last member of the laity", it shows universal agreement in matters of faith and morals. For, by this sense of faith which is aroused and sustained by the Spirit of truth, God's people accepts not the word of men but the very Word of God (cf. 1 Thessalonians 2:13)'. In the fourth chapter on the laity we read in no. 35:

> Christ, the great Prophet, who proclaimed the kingdom of His father by the testimony of His life and the power of His words, continually fulfils His prophetic office until His full glory is revealed. He does this not only through the hierarchy who teach in His name and with His authority, but also through the laity. For that very purpose He made them His witnesses and gave them understanding of the faith and the grace of speech … .

And we read in no. 37: 'Laity, by reason of the knowledge, competence, or outstanding ability which they may enjoy, are permitted and sometimes even obliged to express their opinion on things which concern the good of the Church.' Which sentence is integrated in the Code of Canon Law (can. 212: 2 and 3). Of course, the church is neither a democracy nor a monarchy. It is a structured movement of believers, inspired by the Gospel, by tradition and most of all by the in-dwelling spirit of the Lord. Even if in the course of history the church has embraced secular political models (a pope as monarch of pontifical states, or prince-bishops), influencing liturgy, canon law and even dogmatics, the church nonetheless remained an institution with peculiar features.

From the early beginning the 'people' has been very important in shaping its identity and in influencing her evolution. Indeed this has even been true for the Gospel itself. The four gospels have developed from catechetics and liturgies in small local communities. Which is also true for the tradition, which has always been plural, based on specific mentalities in particular churches, as in the Eastern and Western ones. And this remained the case throughout history, as is shown in the great number of different 'spiritualities', emanating from below.

In the main, two expressions reveal the lasting influence of the people: the 'sensus fidelium' and the 'reception'. The 'sense of the faithful' has to be distinguished from the 'sensus fidei' (sense of the faith) and still more from the 'consensus fidelium', though all three terms have in common that they stress the input of the faithful in expressing the faith. The 'sense of the faith' means that a believer or a group of believers live spontaneously in accordance with the great tradition of the church. It is seen as a spiritual 'instinct'. 'Sensus fidelium' is more or less the same, but expresses the fact that most faithful feel that a doctrine or a behaviour is inspired by the Gospel, even when a new situation demands new answers. 'Consensus fidelium' means that all or most agree with truths, belonging to the core of the faith.

'Receptio' is an aspect of the 'sensus fidelium'. It means that statements and decisions coming from the hierarchy, as those of Councils, are 'received' by the faithful, while 'non receptio' shows that the majority disagrees. In many Eastern churches dogmatic statements are only really such at the moment they are received. The history of the Councils learns that sometimes conciliar statements are first received, later on qualified and sometimes even no longer received, which is then confirmed by other Councils (cf. G.-Y. Congar).

All this shows that the church is a living body on pilgrimage through history, searching for the truth in particular cultural settings and often progressing through trial and error. One easily understands that this dynamic interpretation in the course of centuries creates specific challenges, as in today's period of accelerated ecumenism. What to do when one church 'receives' something, while another church does not? By way of illustration, some state that only the first eight Councils are definitely dogmatic, the church not yet having been split. Others disagree with this view. Great scholars, such as Cardinal A. Grillmeier, argue that even these eight Councils need a reinterpretation. Whatever the case may be, all Christians accept that the Spirit guides the church through history and that thanks to this lasting presence the church remains indefectible in basics. Development of doctrine is a never-ending process. And this development is nourished by the research of theologians, by the living faith of the believers and by the decisions of the hierarchy. Some lay more emphasis upon one of these sources. Catholic faith takes all three together. Everyone accepts that the development is greatly influenced by changes in secular philosophy, by the socio-cultural surroundings and by new and previously unforeseen scientific discoveries.

5.1 JOHN HENRY CARDINAL NEWMAN: ON CONSULTING THE FAITHFUL IN MATTERS OF DOCTRINE – 1871

Newman was well aware of the work of the Spirit in the church and of the many changes which occurred in the course of history. One impressive example is given in his *Essay on the Development of Christian Doctrine* which he published in 1845 (London and New York, 1960). Several years later he deepened this approach in our extract – originally an article in the *Rambler* (July 1859). A part of it, with some additions and amendments, was reprinted in 1871 as an appendix to the third edition of *The Arians of the Fourth Century*. Many years later John Coulson edited this text again (London, 1961). In his introduction Coulson writes: 'This work is fundamental not only to a fuller understanding of Newman's theory on doctrinal development, but to an appreciation of the importance he attaches to the laity in theology.' Newman particularly focuses upon the meaning of the 'sensus fidelium'. The following quotations need no further explanation. Newman first addresses the question concerning the importance of the 'sensus fidelium':[1]

❀

Why? And the answer is plain, viz. because the body of the faithful is one of the witnesses to the fact of the tradition of revealed doctrine, and because their *consensus* through Christendom is the voice of the Infallible Church.

I think I am right in saying that the tradition of the Apostles, committed to the whole Church in its various constituents and functions *per modum unius*, manifests itself variously at various times: sometimes by the mouth of the episcopacy, sometimes by the doctors, sometimes by the people, sometimes by liturgies, rites, ceremonies, and customs, by events, disputes, movements, and all those other phenomena which are comprised under the name of history. It follows that none of these channels of tradition may be treated with disrespect; granting at the same time fully, that the gift of discerning, discriminating, defining, promulgating, and enforcing any portion of that tradition resides solely in the *Ecclesia docens*.

One may lay more stress on one aspect of doctrine, another on another; for myself, I am accustomed to lay great stress on the *consensus fidelium* … .

[Newman continues by referring to a meeting he had in Rome in 1847 with Fathers Perrone and Passaglia. For him both were most illuminating concerning the historical tradition of the 'sensus fidelium'. Whereupon he writes]:

It seems, then, as striking an instance as I could take in fulfilment of Father Perrone's statement, that the voice of tradition may in certain cases express itself, not by Councils, nor Fathers, nor Bishops, but by the 'communis fidelium sensus'.

---

1. *On Consulting the Faithful in Matters of Doctrine*, John Coulson (ed.), London, Collins Liturgical, 1986, originally published by Chapman, 1961, esp. 63, 77, 86, 103, 104, 106.

I shall set down some authorities for the two points successively, which I have to enforce, viz. that the Nicene dogma was maintained during the greater part of the 4th century, not by the unswerving firmness of the Holy See, Councils, or Bishops, but by the 'consensus fidelium'.

On the one hand, then, I say, that there was a temporary suspense of the functions of the 'Ecclesia docens'. The body of Bishops failed in their confession of the faith. They spoke variously, one against another; there was nothing, after Nicaea, of firm, unvarying, consistent testimony, for nearly sixty years. There were untrustworthy Councils, unfaithful Bishops; there was weakness, fear of consequences, misguidance, delusion, hallucination, endless, hopeless, extending itself into nearly every corner of the Catholic Church. The comparatively few who remained faithful were discredited and driven into exile; the rest were either deceivers or were deceived … .

[After having given 22 examples, Newman develops the second point)].

Now we come secondly to the proofs of the fidelity of the laity, and the effectiveness of that fidelity, during that domination of imperial heresy to which the foregoing passages have related … .

[Again he mentions 21 examples. Newman concludes the excerpts taken from history as follow]:

As to the particular doctrine I have here been directing my view, and the passages in history by which I have been illustrating it, I am not supposing that such times as the Arian will ever come again. As to the present, certainly, if there was ever an age which might dispense with the testimony of the faithful, and leave the maintenance of the truths to the pastors of the Church, it is the age in which we live. Never was the Episcopate of Christendom so devoted to the Holy See, so religious, so earnest in the discharge of its special duties, so little disposed to innovate, so superior to the temptation of theological sophistry. And this perhaps is the reason why the 'consensus fidelium' has, in the minds of many, fallen into the background. Yet each constituent portion of the Church has its proper functions, and no portion can safely be neglected. Though the laity be but the reflection or the echo of the clergy in matters of faith, yet here is something in the 'pastorum et fidelium *conspiratio*', which is not in the pastors alone. The history of the definition of the Immaculate Conception shows us this; and it will be one among the blessings which the Holy Mother, who is the subject of it, will gain for us, in repayment of the definition, that by that very definition we are all reminded of the part the laity have had in the preliminaries of its promulgation. Pope Pius has given us a pattern, in his manner of defining, of the duty of considering the sentiments of the laity upon a point of tradition, in spite of whatever fullness of evidence the Bishops had already thrown upon it … .

[Later, during Vatican I, Newman would not always agree with Pius IX. He ends his *On Consulting* … with a very important sentence]:

I think certainly that the *Ecclesia docens* is more happy when she has such enthusiastic partisans about her as are here represented, than when she cuts off the faithful from the study of her divine doctrines and the sympathy of her divine contemplations, and requires from them a *fides implicita* in her word, which in the educated classes will terminate in indifference, and in the poorer in superstition.

5.2 *FAMILIARIS CONSORTIO – APOSTOLIC EXHORTATION ON THE FAMILY – 1981*

After the publication of the encyclical *Humanae vitae* (1968), in the countries where reliable statistics are available, even the majority of practising Catholics did not 'receive' the passage of the encyclical dealing with the use of artificial contraceptives. This appears clearly from the facts that, according to the surveys of the *European Values Study* (1992),[2] these Catholics see 2.5 children as the ideal number in a family, and that in no European country, as with the white, Anglo-Saxon Protestant (WASP) population in the USA, do women under the age of 45 have an average of two children.[3] Several bishops' conferences, though accepting the encyclical, did stress, as had been stated in the pastoral Constitution *Gaudium et Spes*, the respect for everyone's individual conscience. When in 1980 the Roman Synod of bishops had to discuss the family, many participating Fathers did express their uneasiness. In an Apostolic Exhortation, released on 15 December 1981, Pope John Paul II made some critical remarks on the public opinion, stating it was not identifiable with a sane 'sensus fidelium'. The text[4] appears as a classical example of how difficult it is to relate sociology with ecclesiology, to discern amidst a climate of serious polarization and to keep the dialogue open. No. 5 of the Exhortation deals with the 'evangelical discernment'.

❀

The discernment effected by the Church becomes the offering of an orientation in order that the entire truth and the full dignity of marriage and the family may be preserved and realised. This discernment is accomplished through the sense of faith, which is a gift that the Spirit gives to all the faithful, and is therefore the work of the whole Church according to the diversity of the various gifts and charisms that, together with and according to the responsibility proper to each one, work together for a more profound understanding and activation of the word of God. The Church, therefore, does not accomplish this discernment only through the pastors, who teach in the name and with the power of Christ, but also through the laity: Christ 'made them his witnesses and gave them understanding of the faith and the grace of speech' (Acts 2:17–18; Rev. 19:10), so that the power of the Gospel might shine forth in their daily social and family life. The laity, moreover, by reason of their particular vocation have the specific role of interpreting the history of the world in the light of Christ, inasmuch as they are called to illuminate and organise temporal realities according to the plan of God, creator and redeemer.

The 'supernatural sense of faith', however, does not consist solely or necessarily in the consensus of the faithful. Following Christ, the Church seeks the truth, which is not always

---

2. Cf., D. Barker, L. Halman and A. Vloet, *The European Values Study 1981–1990 – Summary Report*, The Gordon Cook Foundation, Aberdeen 1992.

3. 2.1 children is the average necessary to keep the European population stable. Hence a large majority, including of Roman Catholics, must use contraception.

4. *ET* from *The Holy Father, Archives of the Holy See*, www.vatican.va/holy_father/john_paul_ii/index.htm (also in *Origins*, 11 [1981], 44).

the same as the majority opinion. She listens to conscience and not to power, and in this way she defends the poor and the downtrodden. The Church values sociological and statistical research when it proves helpful in understanding the historical context in which pastoral action has to be developed and when it leads to a better understanding of the truth. Such research alone, however, is not to be considered in itself an expression of the sense of faith.

Because it is the task of the apostolic ministry to ensure that the Church remains in the truth of Christ and to lead her ever more deeply into that truth, the pastors must promote the sense of faith in all the faithful, examine and authoritatively judge the genuineness of its expressions and educate the faithful in an ever more mature evangelical discernment.

Christian spouses and parents can and should offer their unique and irreplaceable contribution to the elaboration of an authentic evangelical discernment in the various situations and cultures in which men and women live their marriage and their family life. They are qualified for this role by their charism of specific gift, the gift of the sacrament of matrimony.

5.3 CHRISTIAN DUQUOC: *AN ACTIVE ROLE FOR THE PEOPLE OF GOD IN DEFINING THE CHURCH'S FAITH* – 1985

Our extract[5] discusses the non-reception of the encyclical *Humanae vitae* – when so many throughout the church challenged and, for many, eventually rejected or simply ignored the teaching of the official church as expressed in this papal encyclical. Duquoc structures his response around three questions: (a) the challenge to hierarchy; (b) the theological and juridical status of the notion of 'people'; and (c) forms of believers' authority. He believes the evidence suggests that in matters pertaining to morals and ministry, we see the greatest disjunction between the intentions proclaimed at Vatican II and the present reality, as experienced by the people, who continue to have no real share in the teaching of the faith. A way needs to be found to recognize, in practice, Vatican II's pronouncement that the church *is* the people of God and the hierarchical offices are there to serve them.

❁

... Today the traditional method of operation of the Roman Church is being challenged. Many Roman Catholics no longer accept that only the Catholic hierarchy has the real right to pronounce authoritatively on the fundamentals of their relations with Christ and God or their moral attitudes. Many, in other words, are pressing for a restoration to the faithful of real authority in the discernment and teaching of the faith. What theologians call the *sensus fidei*, the intuition of believers about the internal coherence of the propositions of the faith, is inadequate to define the institutional or political scope of a reciprocal and responsible relationship between base and hierarchy, since it is still interpreted as passive. Accordingly, many people believe that the internal *sensus* or intuition should have an institutional correlate which would allow the faithful to have an active role, to exercise adult responsibility in the definition of the faith proclaimed by the Catholic Church ... .

1   THE CHALLENGE TO THE HIERARCHY

The history of the Catholic Church since Vatican II has demonstrated the unsuitability of an ecclesial model produced by the struggles against the Reformation. One of the demands of the Reformation had been the restoration to the people of the interpretation of scripture. Since everyone receives the Spirit, it was argued, it is intolerable that a few should reserve to themselves the authorised interpretation of scripture. In this form the scriptural principle has a democratising effect: it makes hierarchy empty or reduces it to a subordinate, managerial

5. 'An Active Role for the People of God in Defining the Church's Faith', in *The Teaching Authority of the Believers*, J.B. Metz and E. Schillebeeckx (eds), *Concilium*, 180 (1985/4), 73–81.

role. In the face of this threat to dismantle its organisation, the Catholic Church over the last three centuries and in particular in the nineteenth century, developed a more elaborate theory of the place of the hierarchy, based on the sacrament of order. As a result hierarchical power can no longer be shared.

The practical difficulties experienced in the operation of the hierarchical system as a result of the increasingly democratic environment in Europe led to questions about its theoretical correctness. Despite the efforts of the Roman administration to make the idea of infallibility into a symbol of papal primacy, shifts of power took place as a result of the need to interest every Catholic in the survival of their Church in a hostile and indifferent world. The appeal to the laity to share in the hierarchical apostolate could not be put into practice without a silent revolution in the exercise of power. If the people are asked to be active in witnessing, if they are invited to be militant and no longer simply to apply as individuals the individual and social ethic decided by the top officials, it becomes more and more difficult to deny them the right to express their opinions on the policy of the Church (in the sense of the external and internal management of the Church's action). The challenge arises out of the latent contradiction between the appeal to militancy and the hierarchical rigidity of the institution. Vatican II resulted from the increasingly intolerable discrepancy between the expressed intentions of the institution and its operation. The Constitution *Lumen Gentium*, in reversing the relationship between hierarchy and people, is a good example of this need for a break with the model which emerged from the Counter-Reformation, in which the people were more or less nothing and the hierarchy took decisions unchecked.

A Constitution and a law are only as important as their application, and application, since Vatican II, has not matched the fine words spoken. Despite some modifications, such as the consultative pastoral council, the people still have no real share in power and therefore in the teaching of faith. The gaps between the intentions proclaimed at Vatican II and the current opinion among the people has appeared most clearly over ethical matters and the organisation of ministry.

In ethics the promulgation of the encyclical *Humanae vitae* (1968) was perceived as a statement made without real consultation and so as an intolerable interference in an area in which everyone could express a view. The documents on priestly celibacy and the exclusion of women from the priesthood were also seen as the result of arbitrary decisions because they were not the result of wide consultations. The recent condemnations of theologians have reinforced this feeling. People now talk quite openly about the hierarchy operating like a bureaucracy, in a way which either provokes opposition or leads to indifference. The laity no longer feel involved since their status as witnesses is not taken into account. Despite the decisions to the contrary of Vatican II, the hierarchical system of government remains dominant, and the people are still confined to a passive role in the doctrinal expression of the faith. How are we to get out of this situation of subordination and recognise that the people also have an active role to play in the doctrinal expression of the faith? A firm answer to this question requires a clarification of the idea of 'people of God'. This will be the subject of the next section.

2 THE THEOLOGICAL AND JURIDICAL SCOPE OF THE NOTION OF 'PEOPLE'

Despite inadequacies in its implementation, the work of Vatican II, and in particular that of the Constitution *Lumen gentium*, was not in vain. The reversal of the relationship between the people of God and the hierarchy is a gain which will have a long-term influence on the law and practice. The Constitution recognises that the Church as it exists is not a flock led by shepherds who alone know the destination; it is a conscious people which appoints leaders for the mission entrusted to it. The people, in other words, has its witness to bear to the Gospel. It is true that that witness belongs primarily to the practical sphere – attitudes, morals, spirituality, social and political questions – but that does not mean that it can be separated from its considered formulation, which is the basis of teaching. This takes us to the heart of the matter, which can be summed up in a question: Is the reversal of the people–hierarchy relationship in the Constitution *Lumen gentium* purely formal or does it lead to a recognition of lay authority in the doctrinal expression of the faith?

The planners of this volume of *Concilium* [1985/4] have distinguished between *teaching office or function* and *authority in teaching*. The offices are part of the structure of the people; within the people all do not have the same function. In the Church functions are ministries; and ministries are services designed to make the people act effectively in accordance with the Gospel. It is the witness it bears to Christ which makes the people specifically the people of God, provided that its witness is not separated from its situational correctness in relation to God. All do not have the same ministry: it would be an abuse of language to say that the people have the office of teacher, pastor and so on. There are believers among the people to perform these functions with greater or lesser authority according to the legal definition of their task.

Accordingly, the idea of the teaching authority of the people is not concerned with office. Office is a matter of ministries and their definition. If the people have authority it is a regulatory role, analogous to that of public opinion in a democracy. By this I mean that the people's evangelical interests cannot be imposed on it by those who hold office within it. The offices interact with the opinions of the people; those opinions are the authority. But while it is easy to define the juridical limits, and so the authority, of a specific ministry, it is correspondingly difficult to pinpoint the authority of public opinion. It is certainly the framework of all offices, but in what sense does this framework have authority? How does it define in law the aims and the approaches of office?

An example from the area we are dealing with, teaching, will illustrate the complexity of the juridical treatment of the problem. Paul VI, in *Humanae vitae*, decided that the use of contraceptives was not in accordance with the demands of morality. He justifies this decision by appealing to his pastoral and doctrinal responsibilities. It is well known that this decision was badly received. Resistance operated at two levels. First, in the practical level the decision had little effect, since many Catholics did not feel themselves bound by it. Secondly, on the theological level it had little resonance, since many bishops and theologians judged it to be based on inadequate premises.

In the first case, what value should be attributed to this resistance? Does it indicate moral weakness, and does it therefore have no doctrinal authority, or, on the contrary, is it a sign of the emergence of a different teaching from the allegedly traditional teaching promulgated by Paul VI? The doctrinal authority of a practice remains to be assessed since, *ex hypothesi*, opinion has no official representation. Or is it in fact represented through believers who have no recognised juridical status but are recognised as having real authority because of their competence or their services, as in the case of certain intellectuals or activists? If this is so, such people could be said to express in a considered way the spontaneous reactions of the people. For example, if the people refuse to follow certain decisions, they would indicate that this refusal was not perverse but expressed a desire for a more open definition. In recent years theologians have often claimed for themselves the role of spokespersons for the people in dealings with the hierarchy. In this way their works have come to seem signs of opposition.

Opposition, whether spontaneous or considered, proves at least this, that we have left behind the hierarchical model. Of course, in that model hierarchical decisions might not have been any more consistently followed, but departures from them did not claim evangelical support; they were accepted as weaknesses. If the majority practice which contradicted *Humanae vitae* was supported by considered theories, the reason is that it was not expressed in the first place as a fault, but as a challenge to what was felt to be the encyclical's inadequate basis in Christian tradition. The practice of the churches in the Reformed tradition inevitably led to this reaction. The majority of Catholics found it hard to see how, if churches profess allegiance to the same Gospel and maintaining relations of more than courtesy had such plainly opposed opinions on the subject, the Catholic position could not by that very fact, be relativised. But noting the fact does not clarify the law. How can this popular resistance to hierarchical decisions be justified in a context in which the people does not want a breach in the Church? The question of the authority of public opinion in the Church rests in this paradox, to remain faithfully in the Church while maintaining a degree of liberty in relation to its authorities.

The popular authority in question here, as noted above, is not related to a juridically defined function, as would be the case with a hierarchy or recognised ministries. This authority cannot therefore be defined in terms of a precise field of operation; it is expressed in a more fluid way. In this sense, it corresponds to what is represented by public opinion in democracies.

I say 'in democracies'. Dictatorships attempt to suppress public opinion which differs from the opinion of the leadership. This is one of the reasons why dictatorships in practice suppress the freedom of press, one of the possible forms of public opinion.

The authority which public opinion is recognised in democracies is based on a consensus, the desire to live together while accepting differences. This desire implies that no group should impose its private views. This wish to live together implies tolerance, and in this sense public opinion plays a regulatory role. It no longer operates if its shifts towards a refusal to live together: various types of racism and other totalitarian positions seem to breach the consensus necessary for democracy, while democracy, because of its principles, cannot exclude them by violence. At present many movements are based on the authority of public opinion, and make use of its power – Amnesty International is one example.

Can this model be transposed in the Roman Church? This is what we have to clarify if we wish to assert that the people have authority in the doctrinal expression of the faith.

We saw that public opinion has authority when it is based on a prior consensus. In the case of democracies I defined this consensus as a desire to live together while respecting differences. In the case of the Church it is perhaps possible to define this desire as the effort made to establish Gospel relationships among human beings on the basis of a radical trust in the God of Jesus Christ by virtue of the gift of the Spirit. It is therefore for the believing people to act in such a way that the promise of the kingdom is anticipated in relationships among human beings and in this way an account is given of 'the hope which is in us'. The propositions of the faith express this aim as it is rooted in remembrance of Jesus the Christ.

Between this consensus and the various doctrinal or ethical productions of the hierarchy there is no obvious link, except that declared by the recognised authority or competence of the leaders.

In the hierarchical system, in which the competence of leaders is taken for granted, there is little concern about the gap between the consensus and the inflation of propositions: the individual makes the best of it. However, once the people want to test the validity of the propositions, it is obliged to measure them against the underlying consensus. The people may feel that the propositions threaten the consensus under the pretext of defending it. In this situation the conditions for a regulatory public opinion exist.

Our next task is to work out the form in which this Christian public opinion might exercise this regulatory function, and to establish its legitimacy. This will be the aim of the last section.

3   THE FORMS OF THE BELIEVERS' AUTHORITY

The movement from a hierarchical society to a community of the people of God does not eliminate a role of leadership; it places it in a different setting, the one created by the new power of public opinion. This term comes from the vocabulary of democratic control. Its use in the Church derives from the new place accorded to the believing people. If it is accepted that the people have a non-official authority in relation to the doctrinal expression of the faith, the way this authority is exercised has to be determined. The pressure exerted by public opinion on political leaders seems to me a good analogy for what is emerging in the Church, the legitimacy of which remains to be established.

In fact, though the role of Catholic public opinion may be recognised, it remains difficult to see precisely how it would work. In an attempt to do this, I shall review the various possibilities, institutional and non-institutional.

At the non-institutional level, Catholic opinion is expressed negatively by indifference or lack of interest, and positively in resistance.

To take the negative side first, the Christian people perform a selection among what is handed down to them. They ignore a certain number of elements proposed by the leadership or carried along by tradition. The people feel spontaneously that these elements are not important to the authenticity of moral action, faith in Christ and the hope connected with it. There is a break between scholarly Christianity which examines tradition and the Christianity lived by the majority of the Catholic population. The transmission of the faith is not identical with the contents of the official catechisms (which themselves select considerably among the elements of tradition), but is shaped by an imponderable, what appears to the majority important for access to God in Christ's truth.

This selection does not operate by rejecting the input of the tradition, but by lack of interest in some of its elements. This lack of interest applies to areas as different as ethics, liturgical practice and dogmatics. It is sometimes so clear that no-one dares to confront it: I am thinking of the allergy to certain exaggerated forms of retribution, the notion of expiatory sacrifice, the detailed distinction between grave and venial sin, and so on. This lack of interest effects an almost spontaneous scrutiny of the alleged coherences between faith and its historical expressions and abandons what does not lead to conversion. Public opinion in this negative form of lack of interest shows us the people of God sitting loose to traditional teachings in a way which stimulates leaders to redefine the main themes of their preaching.

The positive side is represented by resistance. The question here is more delicate, because resistance pushes for a conscious choice. It is of a different order from lack of interest. Lack of interest gradually surrounds the leader because it gives no basis for a quarrel. Resistance drives the leader to a strategy of defence, or even of repression. As a result it sometimes becomes difficult to identify the moment when this choice slides over into illegitimacy because it dismantles the community. Nonetheless resistance is necessary to ensure that the people can exercise their regulatory function.

Resistance, however, presupposes effective expression; it has to be sustained by organised groups. We need think no further than the way opposition before and after Vatican II was expressed. A variety of groups, with their books, articles and journals, succeeded in making certain procedures used by the authorities in the Catholic Church seem abnormal, and certain ethical or dogmatic formulations archaic. More recently, basis communities are often mentioned as sources of this resistance. This seems to me true: their action had brought about a relativisation of hierarchical power and reoriented Christian faith towards the fundamental issues of our societies. We know the result: the hierarchy now listens to the base. The discussions about liberation theology are much more about more democratic procedures in the Catholic Church than about borrowings from Marxist ideologies.

This non-institutional regulation of the doctrinal expression of the faith goes hand in hand with measures taken by the institution, the recognition of certain groups or the appointment of certain Christians to sit on the bishop's pastoral council.

The recognised groups are numerous. They cover a wide area, from Catholic Action to charities. They each have their own way of approaching doctrine according to their objectives: a catechetical group does not necessarily have the same approach to the faith as a prayer group, a Catholic Action group or a charity. These groups have a diffuse influence on the doctrinal management of the Church, an influence which is all the more difficult to measure in that it depends on the many possible ways of defining the relationship between doctrine and practice.

Pastoral councils were established by Vatican II with the aim of reducing the influence of organised groups by allowing individual Christians to have delegates on the bishop's council through direct elections. The intuition is remarkable, even if not easy to put into practice. The Swiss, German and Dutch synods, even though their results may not have lived up to expectations, were the fruit of this idea.

As a result, by means of recognised groups and pastoral councils, public opinion not only exercises regulatory authority negatively through inertia or positively through resistance; it also enjoys institutional rights. The effective exercise of these rights requires a degree of pressure from the base. Without this the delegates or the officials would have an advantage, and could become manipulators of public opinion.

This form of institutionalised regulation is more closely involved in a dialectical interplay with institutional authority than the more intangible form of lack of interest or the more aggressive one of resistance. We must now try to define the legitimacy of these forms of Catholic public opinion.

The ideas which support the view that the laity have authority in the doctrinal expression of the faith are very simple. They derive from the gift of the Spirit in baptism, a gift which confers on every believer a share in the prophetic office of Jesus Christ. All have received the Spirit, as the Pentecost story shows, and this reception by all creates the distinctive character of the Church. True, it does not destroy office, but office has no status except in relation to this primary gift. The authority of believers is thus linked with baptism as the sacrament which confers the Spirit and incorporates in the Church. It follows that what has to be worked out in relation to this primary gift is the role of the hierarchy, not the other way round. There is one mediator, Christ who gives the Spirit. The hierarchy is not a mediator in the sense of determining the gift of the Spirit.

The thrust of this argument, if it were to be pursued, would lead us to re-examine the relationship between the hierarchical offices in the Church and the acknowledged authority enjoyed by the Christian people through baptism. This would take us beyond the subject set. It will suffice to say the following: The classical theology of the Catholic Church since the Counter-Reformation has been engaged in a reflection on the role of the hierarchy and its regulatory function in relation to the faith. In reaction to the ecclesial democratisation resulting from the Reformation, it has ignored an indispensable element in the doctrinal expression of the faith, regulation by the believing people. No doubt this element does not operate in the same way as the regulatory function exercised by the leaders but, since it derives from the same Spirit, it is entitled to be recognised as legitimate and to be one of the structural elements of doctrinal authority. This recognition would do justice to the reversal carried out by Vatican II in the Constitution on the Church: the Church is the People of God and the hierarchical offices are at its service.

5.4 KARL RAHNER: *WHAT THE CHURCH OFFICIALLY TEACHES AND WHAT THE PEOPLE ACTUALLY BELIEVE* – 1981

Well aware of the tensions existing between what ordinary people believe and what the official Church teaches, Rahner is not, here,[6] explicitly dealing with the *sensus fidelium*. However, his critical approach is a warning: the opinions of believers need serious discernment in order to separate the chaff from the wheat. This is, not least of all, because the 'gap' between official church teaching on the faith, and the actual faith of people, is something very different from previous times. In its official teaching, the church should not continue to address the people as if they constitute a relatively homogeneous group that fundamentally respects the magisterium. Indeed, the magisterium should continue to learn from the actual faith of the people of God. The following extracts may assist in improving the discernment Rahner deems to be necessary.

❀

If we consider the material content of the faith, nobody can deny that there exists a considerable difference between that which is explicitly and officially taught as part of the content of the faith and that which the average Christian in the Church knows about the faith and believes. Most Christians believe explicitly much less than what is explicitly present in the doctrine of the magisterium. This actual faith is to a considerable extent ridden with misunderstandings. Many things are held as belonging to this faith that in reality do not belong to it.

As matters stand it is not so easy to avoid the difficulty by insisting that, despite its weakness, the actual faith of these Christians includes the absolute assent of faith, whereby people believe, at least implicitly, all that the Church tells them to believe. For in their actual faith many Christians not only do not affirm this or that truth of the faith with absolute assent, they do not even affirm the absolute authority of the Church's magisterium (even in its definitive decisions) with an absolute assent of faith. Therefore it is not as easy as it might appear to avoid the difficulty by appealing to the implicit faith of the average believer … .

The difference between what the Church officially believes and what the average Christian actually believes has always existed. We might safely say that the pluralism of New Testament theologies is already a proof of it. One can distinguish, for instance, several levels of Origen's understanding of faith, and one is pressed to make theological heads and tails out of that. We hear of Christians who, as they were dying, professed their full assent to the faith of the Church. This implies that a material identity between the official faith of the Church and their personal faith is not to be taken for granted and that eventually they wanted to make sure of that identity by this profession. Moral theology has inquired what truths of the faith

---

6. 'What the Church Officially Teaches and what the People Actually Believe', *Theological Investigations*, vol. 22, *Humane Society and the Church of Tomorrow*, London, DCT, 1991, 165–75.

have to be known and professed explicitly by all Christians. This question takes for granted therefore that there is a considerable difference between the official faith of the Church and the actual faith of many Christians. Attempts have been made, by the way, to narrow this difference by means of the doctrine that, in the long run, a positive atheism is not possible without serious subjective guilt. But it looks as if Vatican II has quietly dropped this doctrine.

So although the situation we are discussing has always been recognised to some extent, theological reflection has never probed it very intensively. Today it has assumed an important new aspect. Among average Christians of former times, those who could barely read or write ('the unlearned'), the awareness of the content of the faith might have been fragmentary and incomplete. But it was not opposed to other opinions, to other *Weltanschauungen*, because they did not exist in the consciousness of such people. A 'primitive' awareness of the faith was, roughly speaking, matched only with ignorance. That is why in a feudal society, in which authorities decided on the faith of their subjects, one could suppose that everybody naturally shared the same faith and that there really existed Christian and Catholic peoples. This is no longer true today.

A fragmentary and imperfect faith coexists today with countless other ideas, many of which – at least as they are actually understood – stand in logical contradiction to the content of faith, whether people are clearly aware of it or not. It follows that the material defectiveness of actual faith is quite different from what it used to be. This explains why, as mentioned above, even the formal principle of faith, the formal authority of the Church, is threatened. Today's faith is not like the fragmentary faith through simple ignorance of former times, but coexists with positively contradictory elements in some kind of mostly unconscious schizoid state. Even if we suppose that no objective contradictions exist among the particulars in an individual's consciousness (statements of faith included), these contents are incredibly complex and almost impossible to harmonise. It is practically impossible for individuals to harmonise all the data of consciousness with the contents of faith, although it is a tenet of that faith that such harmonisation is theoretically possible. This is one more reason why the gap between the official faith of the Church and the actual faith of the people differs essentially today from what it used to be … .

In our official jargon, we continue to speak of 'Christians' or 'Catholics', wherever such people have not explicitly left a Christian Church or the Catholic Church or have not in some other way explicitly made known their total dissent from Christianity.

Thus 'Catholics' are opposed to the new laws on abortion. Some 'central committee' speaks in the name of 'German Catholics'. With the use of colours on maps, religious statisticians continue to designate regions that are more than 50 percent 'Catholic'. There is, of course, nothing wrong in this way of speaking, but the statistics have nothing to do with the inner faith of the people. They misrepresent the fact that the percentage of 'practising' Christians is quite low. Spain is a Catholic country, even though on Sundays only 10 percent of the people of Madrid attend Sunday mass. In theological discussions (for instance, with Hans Küng) official reports anxiously refrain from asking what percentage of Catholics might agree with the official position and what percentage might agree with the condemned opinion.

As a rule official announcements simply presuppose that those who read them have no doubts about the formal authority of the magisterium. That is why they generally do not take the trouble to explain to these 'Catholics' the intrinsic reason for their decisions. (A theologian who used to be influential in Rome told me once that this custom is quite legitimate, since it derives from the very nature of the magisterium. Defending the decision with rational arguments should be the task of theologians, not of the magisterium.)

This mentality takes for granted that Catholics are well informed. As a rule it does not try to address non-Catholics and the many very poorly educated Catholics. As a result, in their properly theological parts, important Roman documents of the Church use an esoteric theological language. They presuppose that their readers admit many things which these readers do not. They ignore fundamental theology and continue to use Scripture in the old way by quoting *dicta probantia*. In a word, the official Church and its magisterium presuppose, without ever saying so, that, when they address Catholics, they have to do with a relatively homogeneous group of people whose *Weltanschauung* contains, in fact, nothing but a clearly articulated Christian faith, together with a more or less absolute respect for the authority of the Church's magisterium.

While this situation, naturally, is not explicitly affirmed and many statements and actions presuppose the opposite, yet, roughly speaking, what we have said is true. In theory and practice, hardly any notice is taken of the extraordinary difference between the official faith of the Church and the actual faith of a large percentage of Catholics. This might open up to fundamental, dogmatic, and pastoral theology a wide field for reflection. I would like to add a couple of simple remarks, although I am afraid that they do not reach the heart of the matter… .

[Rahner then tries to give 'a positive theological evaluation of the difference']:

First, it seems to me that this difference does not have a merely negative value, but a theologically positive aspect as well. The fact that the *index systematicus* of *Denzinger* can rarely be found in the heads of ordinary Christians is not as deplorable as it may seem to many people who are tempted to identify saving faith with theological formation. Sophisticated knowledge of something may be even a great obstacle to its personal assimilation. I suspect that today's catechisms, however modern they claim to be, still contain too many things and that they do not present the heart of the Christian message, that which must by all means be said in a striking, really intelligible way. Moreover, it is the faith in the Church that actually exists in heads and hearts, and not properly official Church doctrine, that immediately and in itself is *the faith* that constitutes the Church … .

We may not judge this faith by its objective verbal contents. Even when its objectification in words and concepts is very poor and deficient, it is still God's action in us, constituted by the self-communication of God in the Holy Spirit. As such it infinitely transcends the most sublime theological objectification of the faith. The *depositum fidei* is not first and foremost the sum of statements formulated in human language. It is God's Spirit, irrevocably communicated to humankind, activating in persons the salutary faith that they really possess. Of course, the same Spirit also brings forth in this way the community of the faithful, in which the unity and fullness of Christian faith are objectified and brought to consciousness in what we perceive as the official faith of the institutional Church. Nevertheless, what matters above all is the faith that really lives in the ordinary Christian. That is the faith that actually saves, in which God communicates himself to humanity, however pitiful and fragmentary its conceptualisation may be … .

[Rahner thereupon tries then to develop 'the normative significance of popular faith for the magisterium']:

These considerations allow us to say that the actual faith of the faithful in the Church has a normative significance for the official faith of the Church. The latter, of course, has a normative significance for the former, a point that is rightly emphasised by the teaching of the Church. Certainly we may not say that the faith of the magisterium should be directed by that of the faithful, as discovered by an opinion poll. That would be false, not only because of the very nature of the faith but also because it is impossible to discover, by the usual canvassing methods, what the faithful believe.

The official faith of the Church contains data that derive from the history of the Church's faith, data that have become irreversible and normative for the faith of the present-day Church. The Church possesses an authoritative magisterium that is, in principle, normative for the faith of the individual, although this magisterium, while remaining essentially the same, is itself affected by historical change in its existence and its praxis. But this does not exclude the fact that the actual faith of Christians has a normative influence on the magisterium and on the official faith of the Church. However, this 'normativeness' is essentially different from the one we attribute to the magisterium and its faith. These two influences *mutually* condition each other, although we must add that mutual does not mean equal.

First, it is obvious that, considered historically, the official faith of the Church depends for its growth and differentiation on the growth and differentiation of the actual faith of the faithful. Among them are theologians with their work even though this work, just like the faith of others in the Church, operates in constant dialogue with the Church's official doctrine. To put it with a bit of malice: *before* the doctrine of the Council of Florence on the Trinity, theologians held a similar doctrine that had not yet received the blessing of the magisterium. The doctrine of the seven sacraments or of transubstantiation were theologumena *before* the Church's magisterium declared them defined propositions.

We should keep this in mind in looking at the last two centuries, when some popes have spoken as if the task of theologians consisted merely in defending and explaining the statements of the magisterum. If we do not want to make of theologians a special group in the Church, like that of the bishops, we must say that theologians belong to the People of God. To be sure, their concern is also the traditional faith that has already been officially approved. But it is broader than that. And whatever they work at, they do as members of the People of God with its concrete 'theology'. That is why their theologumena belong to the actual faith of the People of God, especially since they too may be called to order by the magisterium.

It is from these elements of the actual faith of the People of God that the Church's magisterium learns and should continue to learn. While it does keep learning, the magisterium declares that the doctrine discovered this way is binding because it belongs to the actual faith of the Church and shares therefore in the infallibility of the believing Church. It follows that the actual faith of the Church has not only an actual but also a normative influence on the Church's official faith. Distinguishing what merely happens to be present in the consciousness of the people of God from what is binding in faith may, in the final analysis, be a prerogative of the magisterium of the Church. The magisterium is then considered an indispensable component of the Church, as a community of faith. Yet it remains true that the faith of the People of God, as actually existing and not merely as officially approved, is a source of, and to some extent a norm for, the official faith of the Church. Nor does it follow that there would have originally existed a believing church without a magisterium (the first apostolic 'witnesses') or that there would have been a time in which these two realities would not have mutually, although differently, influenced each other … .

The official faith of the Church is a norm for the actual faith of the Church. The faithful should be clearly aware of this. On the other hand, in its preaching, the magisterium should also pay attention to the actual faith of the faithful as it has always unconsciously done to some extent. It praised the devotion to the Sacred Heart after this devotion had already been promoted by the faithful in the Church. Countless such examples might be mentioned. However, in our age when people have become more aware of such things even in the church, the question may be raised whether this influence on the magisterium by the actual faith of the people might not to some extent occur in a more conscious way, by means of surveys, adapted for this special purpose and different from other opinion polls.

This would not amount simply to a yielding to modern trends in the actual faith of the people. It might be possible that the official teaching from above is already being influenced by the faith from below, without noticing it, and that this would become clear only if this faith from below were better known. For instance, has the preaching of the possibility of eternal rejection of a person, that is, of hell, not become considerably more subdued during the last few decades, under the influence of today's general mentality? Whether this is a legitimate development is, of course, quite a different question and does not have to be decided here. It is not clear what form such 'feedback' of actual faith upon the magisterium and its teaching should take. But it is certain that there can be no question in Catholic theology of withdrawing a defined doctrine because a considerable part of the faithful have refused to accept it.

However, this does not answer a further question: should this widespread non-reception not induce the magisterium to give more thought to its doctrine (even if defined), to formulate it in a wider and newer context, and to remove accretions that do not really belong to the faith and that may unconsciously adhere to a defined doctrine? Time and again, in the Church's awareness of the faith the accent has shifted. The history of dogma shows this very clearly. Would it not be possible today, prudently and discreetly, and with an eye on the actual faith of the people in the church, to make such shifts consciously?

Let us take an example. The Church continues to give the impression that she makes known moral alternatives between which people must choose for their salvation or their perdition. That is the prevailing impression, while teachings about God's saving activity have a slighter impact. At the same time, compared with former times, people worry much less about their eternal salvation. Rather than feeling guilty in the presence of God they ask God to answer for the dreadful world he has created. Might not such remarks lead to a very important shift of emphasis in official teachings, without the need for the Church to deny any dogma that she has already proclaimed?

Even if we did not touch the real core of the question, it is easy to see that such considerations are important for ecumenical endeavours. Between the actual faith of devout Protestants and that of practising Catholics (we are not speaking of their church organisation or of liturgy) there is today hardly any difference. In our ecumenical efforts should we not attach to this simple fact the importance it deserves? To be sure, in the eventuality of the unification of the Catholic Church with the Reformed churches, the Catholic Church would not withdraw the dogmas which the other side challenges. But does she necessarily have to insist that, when the churches have united, these dogmas be expressly taught by the magisterium as absolutely binding? This is really a valid question, when we see how the Catholic Church keeps very quiet about the fact that her own members do not accept quite a number of dogmas. It is a question when we see that the *filioque* does not have to be expressly mentioned everywhere in the profession of faith, when we may doubt that the procession of the Spirit 'from the Son' and the procession 'through the Son' mean absolutely the same thing. It is a question when we keep in mind the diversity of the material mediations of the one salvific faith in all stages of the history of salvation.

Our mentality today is not the same as it used to be. In earlier times people thought along simple either-or lines, or according to propositions to which an absolute assent was at least presumed. Today they rather presume that a simple either-or is a priori false. And propositions are as a rule affirmed conditionally until, as is always possible, the opposite is demonstrated. It would be wrong to attach an absolute value to today's mentality. That would contradict its own nature. But even if we attach only a relative value to it, we may still wonder whether the differences between Christian churches must be formulated in the same way in which they were and had to be formulated under a different mentality.

Can we still seriously think, as in the time of the Reformation, of an either-or with regard to the number of sacraments? If we take the modern mentality into account, might we not iron out differences concerning Vatican I, for instance, by explaining more clearly how the pope's decision is connected with the faith of the whole Church, by emphasising more simply and clearly the fact that even a papal definition is historically conditioned, and so on? If the great regional churches in the Catholic Church have a certain autonomy, and if that also implies an autonomy of their theologies which do not simply echo Roman theology, something similar should also be true for the churches of the Reformation if they are again united with Rome. What this means more precisely should, of course, first be explained. And that would undoubtedly also involve some reflection on the actual faith of the people in the churches.

A last consequence of our reflections deserves to be explicitly mentioned. All salutary Christian faith must contain a moment of absolute assent. This assent, even as absolute with regard to the salvific and saving incomprehensibility of God, contains an empirical moment of mediation. But as pointed out above, this empirical moment of mediation has been incredibly varied in the course of salvation history. On the evidence of empirical facts, this moment in the Catholic Church has not always and everywhere been the infallible authority of the Church's magisterium. That authority is often questioned and ignored, and believers have in mind quite different mediations for their absolute assent to God's saving self-communication, for instance the Christ event or an unconditional hope.

That is why the Church's teaching should try the most efficient and obvious moment of such a mediation *in our time*. We should not preach indiscriminately everything that belongs to the fullness of the faith of the official Church. Judicious emphasis is needed. And it should be put where the actual faith, or a real possibility of faith, for humanity today exists. From this point of view too, the actual faith of the people would have a (correctly understood) 'normative' significance for the Church's official faith and teaching. This actual faith must certainly not be the whole of what is taught, but it should serve as a starting point. That may be a platitude, but is a very important one, and one that is too often forgotten.

5.5 YVES CONGAR: *TOWARDS A CATHOLIC SYNTHESIS* – 1981

Out extract was, in part, inspired by and develops Congar's reflections on *Tradition and traditions: an historical and theological essay* (London, 1966).[7] Congar examines the dynamics of the relation between the people of God and catholic tradition and teaching. What follows is an informative historical survey, followed by incisive theological analysis and judgement.[8]

'TEACHING CHURCH', 'CHURCH TAUGHT'?

(A)   DIFFERENTIATION

The whole people of God preserves the *Tradition*, celebrates and lives the truth received from the apostles. The whole Church is apostolic. The whole body is given life by the Spirit which distributes its charisms throughout it, that is to say, talents and gifts of grace (see Rom. 12:6). But the body has a structure, it is organised. Christ established apostles, prophets, evangelists in it and the Letter to the Ephesians adds that pastors and teachers are for 'the equipment of the saints, for the work of the ministry, for building up the body of Christ' (4:12). From the time of the apostles the community, alive as a whole, has been internally differentiated: if there are pastors, there is a flock or 'the brethren'. This differentiation within the 'brotherhood' in due course developed into:

(i)   a distinction between clergy and laity, a distinction which was clear from the third century onwards but which came to take the proportion of a fundamental juridical structure for those who disregarded it: 'Ordo ex Christi institutione clericos a laicis in Ecclesia distinguit' ('By Christ's institution order distinguishes the clergy from the laity in the Church');

(ii)   the massive and often repeated affirmation, especially from the time of Gregory XVI onwards, of the fact that the Church is a 'societas inequalis, hierarchica'. From then on, until Vatican II, this assertion became fundamental;

(iii)   the distinction, expressed in various analogical ways, between 'teaching Church' and 'Church taught'. Apart from certain anticipations on the part of anti-Protestant controversialists, the initial context of this distinction seems to have been a reaction to Jansenist ecclesiology and to the refusal of the bull *Unigenitus*. It was current towards 1750 and in the catechisms at the beginning of the nineteenth century. It was generally

---

7. Chapter 7 of this present volume.
8. Congar, Yves, 'Towards a Catholic Synthesis', in *Who has the Say in the Church*, J. Moltmann and H. Küng (eds), *Concilium*, 148/8 (1981), 68–80.

tied to a distinction between the 'infallibilitas in docendo' ascribed to the body of bishops united with the pope and the 'infallibilitas in credendo' attributed to the faithful. It is clear that this distinction needs to be carefully understood.

(B)   WITHOUT OPPOSITION

The bias of these distinctions, their heavily juridical form and the importance they came to have derived from the necessity, in itself salutary, of allowing the Church an autonomous law and of ensuring its existence effectively against the claims of the princes. This was the inspiration of the reform of the eleventh century (Leo IX and Gregory VII). This brought a reinforcement of the law of celibacy for priests in its wake. We should like to think that the fact the East did not experience this struggle and that the imperial power continued to take responsibility, 'symbolically', for large areas of the social life of the Church, has something to do with the particular genius the East has for uniting clergy and layfolk together in a vital way that is its particular pride. Not that I wish by these remarks to belittle the depth of the anthropological and ecclesiological doctrine of 'Sobornost'.

We go along with the criticism Leonardo Boff makes of the distinction, at least when it becomes an opposition, between 'teaching Church' and 'Church taught'. His dialectical approach is very interesting. Should we, by way of a foil, cite some of the strictly monstrous but significant expressions of an attitude which used to be widely held? Here are two examples: 'The passive infallibility of the faithful thus consists in listening as one should to the *magisterium*.'[9] 'Are not the parish priest the Church taught in regard to the bishop and the bishop in regard to the pope, like the faithful?'[10]

It was ideas like this that drew Tyrell's fire against the Church that was infallible 'because she possesses an infallible Pope – much as a flock of sheep in union with its shepherd might be called intelligent'.[11] But let us leave caricatures aside. We can avoid them if we think of a single Church which as a whole listens, celebrates, loves, confesses, and in which each member is challenged to exercise his or her function. *It is the whole Church that learns, it is the whole Church that teaches, but in different ways.* The Fathers testify to this verity in abundance. The secret of a balanced position is expressed in the formula which St Augustine often repeated in different guises: 'Vobis sum episcopus, vobiscum Christianus', 'I am a bishop for you, a Christian with you.'[12] Before H. Schell Dom Gréa showed that the model of this life of the Church lay in the Trinity.[13] The Persons exist for each other, with one another, within each other. Between them they as it were form a council, realise a 'concelebration', said Gréa.

It follows that in the Church each and everyone has the say. But under what conditions, in what way? This is what we must now go on to see; although we shall have to do it bit by bit, with the consequent risk that we shall in the very process of analysis and noting differences lose sight of the organic unity which we have just stressed.

---

9. Goupil, A.A.: *Le Règle de foi*, n. 17, 2nd ed., Paris, 1941, 48 … .
10. *Le Rôle dans laics l'Eglise* Carrefour, Montreal, 1952, 9.
11. *Medievalism*, London, 1908, 86.
12. *Sermo*, 340, 1, PL, 38, 1485 et very often. Or else 'condiscipulus.'
13. Schell, *Kathische Dogmatick*, III/I, 382–5; A. Gréa *De L'Eglise et de sa divine constitution*, Book I, ch. 8, §4.

THE CHURCH SPEAKS THOUGH ITS INSTITUTIONS, THROUGH ITS HISTORY

(a) *The liturgy is no doubt the most important way in which the Church speaks.* Here the Church lives at full stretch and in its purest form. Edmund Schlink once pointed out that dogmatic formulations in the Bible are often found in the context of doxologies. The Church celebrates its mysteries and expresses its faith through this celebration. St Thomas characterises worship as a 'protestatio fidei', a proclamation of the faith. If I celebrate Easter I cannot doubt either the redemption or the resurrection. If I celebrate the annunciation, I cannot doubt the incarnation. St Cyril of Alexandria sent Nestorius the Nicene creed and wrote: 'here is the faith of the Catholic and Apostolic Church which the orthodox bishops of East and West unanimously confess in their praise'.[14] The Marian feasts in effect constitute that 'Christological auxiliary' of which K. Barth spoke. The feasts of the saints express the truth of the mystical Body and faith in everlasting life. They also give the Church an atmosphere of warmth that no merely theoretical word can achieve. The eucharistic anaphoras are great doxologies and anamneses. In 1978 the bishops of France were able to publish a great profession of faith by way of a commentary on the fourth eucharistic prayer. As for the sacraments, they are actions, but also word – not only because they include words but because they are celebrations. Just think what the celebration of the Eucharist *says*, what the rites of marriage and ordination *say* … . To take the example of the funeral of Paul VI, what an expressive gesture the arrangements and ceremonial were!

(b) *Institutions also speak.* Schools, hospitals, for example, or the property of the Church. The world sees all this and assesses the Church accordingly. The internal institutions and structures speak within the Church independently of what they may actually be saying, even as institutions or structures of a certain sort. Think of the episcopal function, of episcopal conferences, of synods. The bishop of Rome alone speaks more loudly than other bishops, and that by his mere existence and style independently of what he may say. He has a symbolic function, he personifies Catholic unity and identity. Disposed round him the curia, the secretariats, the central organisations also speak. Their style, their methods of work say something by themselves. What interested the public in the affairs of Küng and Schillebeeckx was the procedures rather than the doctrinal issues, even though the former were sometimes ill enough understood. Reactions to *Opus Dei* show the same thing. The ways in which human rights are exercised, religious use money, forgiveness and reconciliation are concretely practised, women are treated – and so on – are all examples of how the manner in which things are done and seen to be done is in practice more important than what is said about them. *Facts* may even clash with words. *They have their own eloquence.*

---

14. *Acta Conc. Oec*, I, 1, 34; PG 77, 109.

THE FAITHFUL SPEAK. 'SENSUS FIDEI', 'SENSUS FIDELIUM'

(A)   THE LAY COMMITMENT

The way we dealt with this question in 1953 [ch. VI of *Jalons pour une théologie du laicat*] is now outdated. We did so under the light of a division between what belongs to the clergy as teachers – the public domain – and the private domain. Today we are all concerned with the construction of the Church, with testifying to the gospel. The faithful do more than just express themselves in informal groups: there they find it possible to speak freely and so make their Christian word or the expression of their prayer coincide with what they really are and do. Apart from the very radical groups, such groups want to be Christian and do not deny that they belong to the Church. Many of the faithful are active in domains which are formally, and even officially the Church: catechesis, including a share in the creation of the forms thereof, the animation of parishes and Sunday assemblies without a priest, pastoral councils … .

The fact that many of the faithful study theology, although still rarely teach and particularly produce it, is new and promising … .

At the bottom of all this is the sentiment of being the People of God which is concerned to serve the cause of the gospel as one whole: 'nostra res agitur', 'we're in this together'. It is no longer the business of the clergy with their little circle. We are all called to serve, though clearly in different ways. In this connection people sometimes talk of the democratisation of the Church (in France this term has too political a flavour to be much used). It would be better to speak of brotherhood. At the same time it cannot be denied that the general climate does have an impact on the way we live in the Church. Human beings today want to take an active part in the decisions that concern them. Underlying is a new sense of truth, akin to the feeling for authenticity: we commit ourselves where we feel we are recognised; truth is what enables us to place ourselves in the world in relation to others and to ourselves.

(B)   PUBLIC OPINION IN THE CHURCH

This is what explains so many manifestations of opinion or protest. Public opinion, at least that of defined groups, is expressing itself in a new fashion in the Church and in Church matters. There are numerous studies or articles on this subject or on 'free speech in the Church', to which reference may be made. Opinion has long been a factor. It has been observed that certain decisions of the popes over the temporal authority of the kings – for example, the power to depose them – vanished as soon as they lost popular support. Daily opinion conditions the exercise of the most authoritarian powers and can prevent the application of certain laws. Public opinion really came to its own during the nineteenth century. In regard to Church matters, pastors reacted, as Monsignor Dupanloup did, for example, against Louis Veuillot. But Emile Ollivier, head of the liberal government, came back at him:

> The pamphleteering prelate loses no opportunity to rebuke journalists and complains that, layfolk as they are, they do not leave delicate questions, most intimate, serious and inside questions to the bishops. This is a surprising reproach. Are lay people not members of the Church? Can they remain indifferent to the conflicts of the spiritual

society in which they live? If it is interest that creates competence, has one any right to exclude them from any questions except those they have not taken the trouble to study? They have as a matter of dogma been excluded from any share in the government of the Church and in the definition of dogmas, as a matter of diplomacy had their privilege in the election of bishops transferred to princes; but they have already created religious journalism and they have in this way, in our age of publicity and discussion, established for themselves a power of their own which is greater than any they have had refused or withdrawn. Abuses apart, what is regrettable about this development?[15]

Abuses or sharp practices are, of course, possible, indeed real enough: pressure groups, indiscretions invading personal integrity, the tendency to emphasise the superficial or the sensational, if not the downright scandalous. We understand, because we are involved ourselves, when a churchman suffers from the power of this base currency. All the media are implicated today. The solution does not consist in the imposition of censorship that limits freedom of speech or the expression of opinion. Our highest authorities have acknowledged their legitimacy and even their necessity [addresses by Pius XII and John XXIII to the press]. The problem is in the first place one of *information* and therefore also of *communication*. People have talked of a right to information. Distortion of opinion and of its expression may well reflect distortions at the level of information.

(C) WHAT CHRISTIANS DO

… [The 'sensus fidelium'] is also a subject on which a great deal has been written. The term covers two things that are related but do not coincide. On the one hand, there is the *sensus fidei*, which is a quality inherent in a *subject*, on whom the grace of faith, charity, the gifts of the Spirit confer *a faculty of perceiving the truth of the faith and of discerning anything opposed to it*. The *sensus fidelium*, on the other hand, is what can be grasped from outside, objectively, about *what the faithful, and especially layfolk, believe and profess*. It tends towards a consensus which can only be partial. Such a consensus, when it expresses itself, is akin to public opinion. It is clear that where Christanity is concerned the sense of the faith cannot be individualist: it is conditioned by the authenticity of a life in community. A Christian is not a Christian alone; he is assured of holding the truth only in the Church.

Möhler and Newman loved to cite Hippolytus' 'phronēma ekklesiastikon', Vincent of Lérins' 'ecclesiae intelligentiae auctoritas'. We consider that the Holy Spirit – the 'Holy One', says *Lumen Gentium* § 12, with reference to 1 John 2:20–27 – ensures the *sensus fidei* of the people of God in so far as it is possessed of a universal consensus along with its pastors and is indefectibly attached to the apostolic faith. We must not idealise the *sensus fidei* of individuals or of particular groups too much: the socio-psychological tests used by J.P. Deconchy disclose the influence of psychological and social conditioning. Fervent but directionless communities can deviate or slip into syncretism … .

We do, however, attach great value to what Christians *declare by their behaviour* when they risk their peace, or the pleasures and amenities of life, even life itself, in order to testify to the gospel and seek to realise society's needs, especially in situations of oppression and

---

15. Ollivier, E: *L'Eglise et L'etat au concile du Vatican*, 2nd edn, 1879, 446.

injustice. This is what gives 'theologies of liberation' their original epistomological status: the practice of a Christian and poor people fertilises thought. The blood of witnesses guarantees the seriousness involved. The Church of our time has once again become a Church of martyrs. This supreme witness is also a word. 'Who speaks in the Church?' Witnesses, martyrs. And the second line is constituted by those who speak for the cause, for example Justice and Peace Commissions at the Roman and national level. They have often spoken a Christian word in the Church and in the world ... .

[Congar turns then to the role of theologians in the Church. They are called to interpret the *sensus fidelium* which they do as members of the people of God]:

Research by very definition, implies that the theologian *cannot be content to respect and comment on what has been achieved and rounded out, to gloss and justify official language* ... Whereas the characteristic of theological work is the fact that it questions, it is the business of the pastoral authorities, of the body of bishops, to affirm, testify to and perpetuate the testimony of the apostles ... .

[Finally, Congar considers the ecumenical implications and the movement towards a common confession of the truth]:

It seems to me that the major ecumenical question for us today is precisely this question as to how much diversity is compatible with communion. *Truth is symphonic.* The conductor is the Spirit of truth. Who better to speak in the Church and to bring us into and keeping us in the truth?

5.6 YVES CONGAR: *RECEPTION AS AN ECCLESIOLOGICAL REALITY* – 1972

The same Congar has written an important article on the 'reception', an aspect of the *sensus fidelium*: *La 'Réception' comme réalité ecclésiologique* (in the *Revue des sciences philosophiques et théologiques*, 56 (1972), 369–403); he also wrote a shorter version, much of which is included below.[16] Against more narrow definitions, Congar believes that reception is much more than subordination and obedience. Furthermore, he argues that it involves *consent* and even, on occasion, judgement.

❀

Even if this is not a dangerous theme, it is one that is not often examined. This is strange, for it is of major importance from the viewpoint of ecumenism as from that of a wholly traditional and Catholic ecclesiology.

The very term 'reception' has been used in modern times by legal historians, mainly Germans, in regard to the part played by Roman law in the usage of ecclesiastical or civil society, as in Germany from the fifteenth century … . According to A. Grillmeier, reception would exist properly only in the case of the reception of specific synods by the universal Church or by a very large part of the Church, or by separate Churches: for example, if the Nestorians were to accept Ephesus, or the Monophysites Chalcedon. Anything else is reception in a wider, imprecise sense.[17]

This way of looking at reception seems too narrow. Of course there must always be a certain distance, a certain difference, between the party which gives and that which receives. But if one remains within the framework of the one Church, its nature or its firm requirement of communion prevents the difference from being total. It is true that the theme of reception may have an ecumenical interest: there is a concern for reception within the framework of the ecumenical Council of Churches, for example in regard to the re-establishment of communion between the pre-Chalcedonics and the Orthodox (or the Catholics): this is a sign that a new chapter is beginning in this regard. But history offers an enormous array of actual 'receptions', and theories of reception within the one Church. I want to explain the ecclesiological value of this fact. By 'reception' I understand (in the present article) the process by means of which a church (body) truly takes over as its own a resolution that it did not originate in regard to itself, and acknowledges the measure it promulgates as a rule applicable to its own life. Reception includes something more than what the Scholastics called 'obedience'. For the Scholastics it is the act by which a subordinate submits his will and conduct to the legitimate precepts of a superior, out of respect for the latter's authority.

---

16. 'Reception as an Ecclesiological Reality', in *Election and Consensus in the Church*, G. Alberigo and A. Weiler (eds), *Concilium*, 77 (1972), 43–68.
17. Grillmeier, A., 'Konzil und Rezeption. Methodische Bemerkungen zu einen Thema der ökumenischen Diskussion der Gegenwart', *Theologie u. Philosophie*, 45 (1970), 321–52.

Reception is not a mere realisation of the relation 'secundum sub et supra': it includes a degree of consent, and possibly of judgement, in which the life of a body is expressed which brings into play its own, original spiritual resources.

THE FACTS

That the concept of reception is still valid was shown adequately by Vatican II in its envisaging a collegial initiative emanating from the bishops, which could be a 'verus actus collegialis' only if the pope approved it 'vel libere recipiat' (*Lumen gentium*, 22 end). This text speaks of the reception of the privilege of the bishop of Rome that Vatican II so firmly reaffirmed and to which history bears adequate witness. It constitutes an authentic statement regarding reception since it is a matter of consent (by means of judgement) by one church body to a resolution put forward by others. Apart from this, law as at present knows no case of reception (as far as I am aware) other than the acceptance by the pope, and, after him, by the world episcopate, of new bishops of the Eastern rite elected to their patriarchate after a mere 'nihil obstat' from Rome, but neither named nor confirmed by the Holy See. The word 'reception' was not pronounced, but its essence inhered in the expression 'recognise in its communion', 'put its trust in and adhere to the free decisions of the patriarchs and their synods'.[18]

It is not in the present *jus conditum* that we can find anything substantial on reception. The actual life of the Church should prove more instructive. But it is history that we must interrogate for positive information.

(a) *The Councils.* The creed of Nicaea was 'received' *in toto* only after fifty-six years of contentions punctuated by synods, excommunications, exiles, and imperial interventions and violence. The synods of Tyr and Jerusalem, in 335, deposed Athanasius and rehabilitated Arius. Pope Julius himself would not seem always to have been of the opinion that the judgement of Nicaea was irrevocably established. The Council of Constantinople of 381 marked the end of these quarrels. And that very Council owes its designation as ecumenical not to its composition (which was not at all ecumenical: St Ambrose complained that Rome and the West were ignored and absent – Epist. 14:4–8; PL, 16:952–3) but solely to the reception of its creed by the Council of Chalcedon as the most proficient expression of the faith of Nicaea. In fact the so-called Chalcedonian creed was read after the Nicene creed, and the canons of 381 were taken as 'synodikon of the second Council'. But it was only in 519, and at first more by tacit acquiescence that Rome or rather Pope Hormisdas, in 'receiving' the profession of faith of Patriarch John, recognised Constantinople as second of the first four Councils. The history of the third Council was hardly such as to allow it to be considered as properly ecumenical. A decision was rushed through by Cyril of Alexandria before the arrival of the Syrian bishops four days later, and that of the legates eighteen days later; and there were two assemblies (without any contacts between them). It was only because of the agreement reached during the two subsequent years between Cyril and his group, and John of Antioch

---

18. Communication from the Cardinal president of the Central Commission for the Co-ordination of Post-conciliar work and Interpretation of decrees of the Council, 24 May 1966, and a letter from the Eastern Congregation to Patriarch Maximos IV, 22 June 1966.

and his supporters, that Ephesus was able to reach an elementary state of ecumenism. Newman often argued from this historic episode to the usage of those for whom the opposition of a large minority (during the First Vatican Council until the definition of 18 July 1870 inclusively) constituted a decisive barrier. The subsequent accession of those on the other side, that is their 'reception', was like a 'complement to the Council and integral part of it' … .

It is possible to study the history of all the Councils from the angle of their reception. The last that we had in common with the Orthodox East, the second Nicaean Council, of 787, itself proclaimed that for a Council to be considered ecumenical, it had to be received by the *praesules ecclesiarum*, and primarily by the pope. But this very Council had to wait a long time before it was accepted by the West: not only by the Frankish theologians of the Council of Frankfurt of 794, under the influence of a bad translation and rivalry towards another Empire, but by the papacy, maimed and under attack from the Byzantine Caesaro-papism that seduced into its realm of obedience Sicily, Calabria and Illyria. Not until the profession of faith sent by Leo IX to Peter of Antioch in 1053, was there any *express* reception of Nicaea II by the popes.

I should like to cite a few examples from the West in the second millennium. The Fourth Lateran Council (1215) was received in the West in such a way as permanently to affect the life of the Church: whether because its profession of faith *Firmiter*, reproduced at the head of the Decretals, became a fourth creed and a kind of syllabus of instruction for clergy and faithful, or because sixty of its texts and fifty-nine of its seventy canons entered into ecclesiastical law and then into the Codex of 1917. In this regard, the reception of a Council is identical with its effectiveness; this point has a certain value, as will become clear, in respect of a theological interpretation of reception. The case of the Council of Trent will serve to illustrate the same remark. In addition, the problem and the difficulty of its 'reception' by Protestants recurred incessantly in the correspondence between Leibnitz and Bossuet. This was already a case of the 'exogenous' reception looked for today in the ecumenical movement in order to bring about a consensus between separated ecclesiastical bodies.

The acceptance of the dogma [of Papal infallibility] of 18 July 1870 by the minority bishops who had left Rome the day before in order to avoid pronouncing a 'non placet' when the voting was clear, was also a case of reception, and all the more interesting a one inasmuch as many of them, faithful to their principles, grounded this acceptance on the fact that the dogma was 'received' by the whole Catholic Church. This was the argument of Mgr Maret. But it was not a convincing argument for Döllinger.

Within the framework of present christological research, which is concerned more with the man-Jesus of the synoptic gospels, there has been talk of the 're-reception' of Chalcedon. Chalcedon was accepted and not contested. But within a new context of christological vision, and of ecumenical inquiry, a new reading of its history and of its underlying intentions is necessary in order to 'receive' it once again. It is possible, analogously, to speak of a 're-reception' of Vatican I by Vatican II and, again, in a new context and by means of a renewed reading such as that which allowed the minority of Vatican I to be represented as the *avant-garde* of Vatican II … .

Many local councils or specific documents acquired a universal value because the Church acknowledged its faith in them, and did so by 'reception', by means of a process in which, above all in the West, reception by the see of Rome often played a decisive role … . In this way, individual Councils, whose actual representation was quite small, came almost, by reception, to rank with general Councils of the Church.

What is essentially important here is what constitutes the authority of Councils and what makes their decisions valid. Some first-class studies are available on this subject. The validity of the councils derives from their expression of the faith of the Apostles and the Fathers, the tradition of the Church (*vide* Athanasius, Cyril of Alexandria and Vincent). The Councils expressed the apostolicity and catholicity of the church inasmuch as they represented the totality of the Church and realised a consensus. Athanasius does not appeal to any other principles. After Nicaea (and always taking Nicaea as a model) there was a tendency to stress the assurance that Christ presided over, and the Holy Spirit was present at, Councils of the Church. But the essential thing was to detect in them the faith of the apostles transmitted from the apostolic era by the Fathers of the Church (*Paradosis*). It was certainly for this reason that a Council in ancient times began with a reading of the decrees of previous Councils: it was intended only as a new stage in the process of transmission, but it was also an act of reception. Conciliar theology seems now to be linked with that of apostolicity, of which it is an aspect. Just as the most decisive factor is not the formal succession (*nuda successio*), but the profound identity of the contents and of the faith; just as the two should go together, the most decisive element of the Council is neither the number of participants nor the juridical control of its procedure, but the content of its decisions, even though the two should go together.

If there is a truth universally acclaimed from early times to Vatican II, it is that faith and tradition are borne by the whole Church; that the universal Church is the sole proper subject, under the sovereignty of the Spirit who has been promised to the Church and who dwells in it: 'Ecclesia universalis non potest errare.' This is why the witness of several neighbouring bishops is required, and indeed that of the community of the faithful, in the case of an election and an ordination. This is why the greatest possible unanimity, agreement and consensus have always been a sign of the action of the Holy Spirit, and therefore a token of truth. A specific theology was able to monopolise the recognition of the ecumenicity of Councils and the infallibility only by identifying the pope with the Roman church and the Roman church with the universal Church (of which one would not deny the pope was the supreme pastor). It was not by chance that Nicholas I thought of the Roman Church as the 'epitome' of the Church, and Pius IX uttered that almost incredible statement: 'La tradizione sono Io!'

Liturgy. The extension of certain liturgical forms and unification occurred by means of 'receptions' that were in some cases enforced. I shall cite only the reception of the Roman liturgy in the empire of Charlemagne (*Codex Hadrianus* and the Council of Aix, 817); the reception by Rome (then, after and since Rome, by the Latin Church) of the Mainz pontifical in the tenth century, which was of considerable theological significance, and then its ordinal, lent support to the thesis that connected the form of Orders with the 'porrectio instrumentorum'.…

It is well known that the see of Rome, after Alexander II, then formally and *de jure* from Gregory IX (1234), claimed the sole right to canonise saints. Canonisation, which was more a liturgical fact than a juridical decision, had previously been a matter for local churches, and was generalised '*accedente totius Ecclesiae consensu et approbatione*', as Mabillon says.[19] In this way a decision of the local cult was extended by means of reception … .

In the same way it is possible to retrace the history of the adoption of liturgical feasts and their diffusion in the West, and, especially in Rome, of a number of Marian feasts celebrated in the East: the Purification, the Nativity, the Presentation, whereas the Immaculate Conception was received progressively from its base in England … . Just like canonisations, the saints' feasts spread by 'reception' before the papacy started to regulate the calendar of what is (improperly) called the 'universal Church'.

Law and discipline. The theologians did not wait for the legalists to use the notion of reception. Of course it was mainly the German legal historians who, in the nineteenth century, accredited the term and the concept, in regard to the 'reception' of Roman law in Germany from the fifteenth century onwards. But, before that, there was a form of 'reception' in the Church. This process has been studied age by age. Roman law became an auxiliary form of law, supplying maxims and directives where the canons offered none (Gratian, Lucius II, the decretal *Intelleximus*). As far as I am aware, there has been no adequate study of the reception or non-reception by the Roman Church of the canons accepted in the East. Hence the Roman Church received only the last thirty-five of the eighty-five so-called apostolic canons accepted in the East, and did not receive the canons of the Quinisext Synod or the Trullan Synod of 692 until they had been expurgated. For its part, the East sorted out the canons admitted by Rome, accepting some of them and rejecting others, and not always following exactly the same text; the same is true of the canons of the Council of Sardica.

I have already mentioned some cases of non-reception: the non-reception of Chalcedon is all the more significant inasmuch as it did not touch upon essentially profound aspects of christological belief. Later there was the non-reception of the *filioque* clause by the East, the non-reception of the union of Florence by the Orthodox faithful, more or less alarmed by enthusiasts. H. Dombois cites also the example of the extended non-reception of the bull *Execrabilis* of Pius II (1460), which forbade any appeal to the Council. It also happened that some doctrine or maxim received for a fairly long time might cease so to be accepted: for example, the pope's right to depose monarchs. In our own age, we have the case of the constitution *Veterum sapientia* of John XXIII, prescribing the use of Latin in the instruction of the clergy (1960), and cases of non-reception of the papal dogma of July 1870 by a number of Catholics, and of the teaching of *Humanae vitae* by a section of the Christian laity and even of Catholic theologians. Is this 'non-reception', or 'disobedience', or what? The facts are there.

[Congar continues his article, explaining some theories justifying reception and concludes with a theological interpretation and justification]:

'Reception' has suffered from a construction and presentation on the level of constitutional law, like any legal theory. It was also by putting it on the juridical level and by using a dissociative polemical method that Capellari tried to refute the theory, at the risk of ignoring the historical fact and theological depth of reception. This last derives from another level, as noted by P. Fransen, who qualifies it as 'organic' in contradiction not to 'juridical' but to purely 'jurisdictional'. It derives from a theology of communion, itself associated with a

---

19. *Acta* SS.O.S.B, *Praefatio ad saeculum decimum* (saec. V O.S.B.), VII, 1585, q. LVIII, sectio 6.

theology of local churches, a pneumatology and a theology of tradition and a sense of profound conciliarity of the Church. The notion of reception – but not its whole reality, since life is resistant to theories – is excluded (or even expressly rejected) when for all the foregoing there is substituted a wholly pyramidal conception of the Church as a mass totally determined by its summit, in which (quite apart from any consideration of a largely private spirituality) there is hardly any mention of the Holy Spirit other than as guarantor of an infallibility of hierarchical courts, and where the conciliar decrees themselves become papal decrees 'sacro approbante concilio'.

This ecclesiological process has been associated with another process that accords with it entirely: the transition from a primacy of truthful content; which it was the grace and the mission of the whole Church to protect, to the primacy of an authority. In the theology of tradition it would be put thus: a transition from the *traditio passiva* to the *traditio activa*, or from *traditum* to *tradens* the latter being identified with what, since the beginning of the eighteenth, has in fact been called the 'teaching Church'. I have pointed out that the authority of the 'Nicene creed' was attributed not to a 'power' of the hierarchical assembly, but to the conformity of its teaching with the faith received from the apostles. Essentially, in the doctrinal area, only the truth has authority. 'Hierarchical' ministers exercise no more than a service, a function and a mission (Cajetan, in a commentary on St Thomas, calls the Church 'ministra objecti'), it being understood that a mission includes the means necessary for its accomplishment: in this case, grace or charism. But this charism cannot, as such, be interpreted in terms of juridical 'power'. Such a 'power' certainly exists; it is the jurisdictional authority which, in the Church and on behalf of its members, adds to the authentic proposition of the faith an obligation which comprises 'dogma' and is handed on, in the course of history, by means of an 'anathema sit'. But the accession of faith, when doctrine is in question, concerns the content of truth. In scholastic terminology, one would say that it concerns the *quod* and not the *quo*. If an *authority* relative to the content of truth as such is attributed to the ministry, one argues upon the juridical level, and the only permissible connection is one of obedience. If the *content* of truth and of good is taken into account, the faithful and, better, the *ecclesia*, may be allowed a certain activity of discernment and 'reception'.

We may now try to define the theological (ecclesiological) status of 'reception'…, then its legal status, remembering that this legality is still clearly *theological* … .

The whole body of the Church, which is structured locally as individual churches, is enlivened by the Holy Spirit. The faithful and the churches are true subjects of action and free initiative. Of course there is no true pneumatology without christology: that is, without a normative reference to something given. The Spirit unceasingly renews that which is given, but he does not create anything which is substantially other. One of Sohm's errors is to have conceived a kind of pneumatocracy without given structures. But the faithful and the local churches are not inert and wholly passive in regard to the structures of belief, and ethical and cultic rules that history has necessarily defined since the original apostolic transmission. They have a faculty of discernment, of co-operation with the determination of their forms of life. Of course, in those matters which concern the unity of the Church, and therefore the unity of the faith, all must unite in a substantial unanimity, but they should come to that unity as living independent subjects. Naturally obedience is itself an activity of life and the Holy Spirit inspires it. But not everything is laid down in the tradition of the Church, and the dogmatic formulas themselves require a form of adherence which does not call merely upon volition, but upon intelligence and its conditioning factors, which are culture, knowledge language and so on. The history of the slow reception of Nicaea or of Chalcedon cannot be explained other than in this context.

Hence we can see that there are two means of arriving at unanimity: obedience, and reception or consent. The first is insisted upon if the Church is conceived as a society subject to a monarchical authority; the second comes into question when the universal Church is seen as a communion of churches. It is certain that this second conception was the one that prevailed effectively during the first thousand years of Christianity, whereas the other one dominated in the West between the eleventh century reformation and Vatican II. It is true that this rule of local churches in communion with one another was the only form possible before the Constantinian peace allowed an open organisation of ecumenical life within the framework of the Empire. I admit that another means of unanimity is possible: one by means of submission to a unique head of the Church viewed as a kind of unique and immense diocese. But, apart from the fact that the East and a part of the West never accepted this idea, and never experienced such a form of rule, we have to ask whether it accords with certain aspects of the very nature of the Church, whose authenticity is indefeasible and which Vatican II rediscovered. There are two conditions, supported by numerous witnesses, for this particular ecclesiology:

1 THE UNIVERSAL CHURCH CANNOT ERR IN FAITH

Consensus, or unanimity is an effect of the Holy Spirit and the sign of his presence. It is the Holy Spirit who brings about the unity of the Church in space and time; that is, according to the dual dimension of its catholicity and its apostolicity or tradition. It is in fact a matter of acknowledging and expressing the tradition of the Church, in the sense spoken of by Eusebius when (HE V, 28:6) citing a treatise against the heresy of Artemon. The unanimity which the Councils tried to attain to, and which should not be too idealised, intends this. It does not express a more or less perfect numerical sum of individual ways, but a totality such as that of the memory of the Church. This is the meaning of the formula 'ego consensi et subscripsi': I have entered in the consensus which has emerged and by virtue of which it is clear that the Church believes because the truth has been handed down to it in this way. *It is this* which constituted the authority of the Councils in the eyes of the early Fathers of the Church. In this respect, reception is no more than the extension or prolongation of the conciliar process: it is associated with the same essential 'conciliarity' of the Church. It may be opined (and this is the basis of the Orthodox position) that the ground of this vision is to be found in 'theology', in the sense that the Cappadocian Fathers think of theology: the mystery of the Holy Trinity … .

It is not reception which bestows their legitimacy upon a conciliar decision and an authentic decree: they obtain their legitimation and their obligatory value from the authorities who have supported them … . Even though reception creates neither legitimacy nor a legal force of obligation, one has had immediately to add that, in the soundest Christian tradition, those *ministers exercising authority never act alone*. This was true of the apostles: cf. Acts

15:2–23 and 16:4; 2 Tim. 1:6 and 1 Tim 4:14; 1 Cor. 5:4–5, where it is possible to discern an application of the communitarian discipline reported in Mt. 18:17–20 (see also Clement, Cor. 44:3). This was true of the bishops of the age of the martyrs, Ignatius of Antioch and Cyprian. The basis for this, well brought out by Möhler, is that a Christian always has need of a Christian brother: he has to be supported and confirmed by another, and, as much as possible, by a community. This is the basis of the 'fraternal correction' which is also a real aspect of the life of the Church. The principle enunciated in Dt. 19:15 on the necessity of two or three witnesses was taken up in the New Testament in a way that goes beyond the juridical or procedural framework, and assumes a general value as a rule of Christian behaviour.

If reception confers neither legitimacy nor an obligatory value, what does it do? R. Sohm says that it is an open process, and juridically very unsatisfactory:[20] this is very true. In addition, he attributes to it a purely declaratory value, 'the significance of attestation'. It attests that these decisions really arise from the Spirit which directs the Church, and that they are of value for the Church as such (and not primarily by virtue of their reception). I am not far from subscribing to this formula. Bossuet also says, speaking of the judgements made by the bishop of Rome: 'Since he is in effect at the head of the ecclesial communion, and since his definition intends nothing other than what he knows to be the feeling of all the churches, the subsequent consent only attests that everything has been done in due order and in accordance with truth'[21]... .

Reception is not constitutive of the juridical quality of a decision. It has no bearing on the formal aspect of the action, but on its content. It does not confer validity, but affirms, acknowledges and attests that this matter is for the good of the Church: because it concerns a decision (dogma, canons, ethical rules) that should ensure the good of the Church. This is why the reception of a Council is practically identical with its efficacy, as may be seen from Lateran IV, Trent, and even Nicaea, Chalcedon or Nicaea II. On the other hand, as Ph. Bacht remarks, non-reception does not mean that the decision given is a false one. It means that this decision does not call forth any living power and therefore does not contribute to edification:[22] for religious truth, and what is sometimes called the development of dogma, do not derive from a pure conceptuality of the mathematical or geometrical type; they derive from what tradition calls 'pietas fidei' or 'veritas secundum pietatem' (in reference to 1 Tim. 6:3; 3:16; Tit. 1:1; Rom. 1:18) or, in St Thomas, 'sacra doctrina', 'doctrina salutaris' ... .

[Congar concludes with some historical remarks about the difference between power and authority. And he explains]:

... [C]ertain qualified defenders of papal monarchy also introduce some interesting considerations. Thomas de Vio (Cajetan) asks what the Council may add to the pope, when he answers the Gallican Jacques Almain. The answer is: nothing, from the degree of authority, but something, and indeed a large thing, in regard to the richness and extension of the

---

20. *Da altkatholische Kirchenrecht und das Dekret Gratians* ... , Munich and Leipzig, 1918 (reprinted Darmstadt, 1967), 134.

21. *Dissertatio praevia* of 1696 to the Gallican clergy, n. 78.

22. H. Bacht: 'Vom Lehramt der Kirche und in der Kirche', *Catholica*, 25 (1971), 147–67 (pp. 157ff.: 'Das Problem der Rezeption im katholischen Verständnis').

doctrine, for its acceptance without opposition and thus by all.[23] Cajetan's predecessor, like him a Dominican, Juan de Torquemada, acknowledged that in a case of extreme doubt respecting a matter of faith, a Council had to be summoned. In answer to the objection that this would imply that a Council was of more account than a pope, Torquemada remarked that this was not so in the case of a greater power of jurisdiction and when the pope was incontestable (even though he was writing in 1457, he had experienced the situation that arose from the great Western schism); on the other hand, it was true of a greater authority of faculty of judgement: for a Council was held to be able to bring to its deliberations more reasoning power than a single man. Torquemada composed a reply to the demand of Charles VII of France, who wanted a third general Council to be held beginning in 1442. The bishop of Meaux, Pierre de Versailles, ambassador of Charles VII to the pope on this point (16 December 1441), put forward the following argument: there are two kinds of authority, that of the *power* that one has received, and that of the credence (or credibility) that one may enjoy. Although power is the same power in the case of all the pontiffs, the credence accorded to each of them differs: St Gregory and St Leo had more than others, and the general Council is superior in his respect. This is very like the distinction I have suggested between 'power' and 'authority'. The concept of 'credence' or 'credibility' is in favour today. It may certainly be used to characterise the support that reception gives to a decision that is legitimate in itself.

---

23. *Apologia de comparata auctoritate Papae et Concilii,* c. XI (1514): ed. V.M.I. Pollet, Rome, 1936, n. 636, 269.

5.7 HERMANN POTTMEYER: *RECEPTION AND SUBMISSION* –1991

According to Pottmeyer, for far too long, reception was considered in the Catholic Church as passive obedience instead of having, also, an active role. He developed his interpretation in the following article.[24] Amongst the issues raised are the limits of commanding assent to non-definitive teachings and the importance of the magisterium taking the credibility of its teaching into account, as opposed to merely basing its claim to obedience upon its own formal authority. Furthermore, 'Before the teaching office can teach the Church, it must have listened to the Church and learned its faith'. Reception is a more complex concept than many have previously believed and is better described as a social or ecclesial 'process', which can work both ways: from the universal to the local church and yet vice versa. The outcome of the process is a consensus which provides a criterion of truth.

❋

In most of the theological lexica you can search in vain for an entry called 'reception'. The same is true for theological handbooks even today. Only because of and since Vatican II has 'reception' become a topic of discussion, specifically in ecclesiology, in theological cognition theory, canon law, and in ecumenical theology. Nevertheless, this topic remains in the documents of the council and in contemporary theology, albeit in the shadow of another topic which receives more space and attention: the power and authority of the hierarchy, especially of the pope, to lead and to teach … .

Reception, as a characteristic mode of communication in a Church which thinks and acts as a *communio ecclesiarum* increasingly attracted the attention of ecclesiologists after Vatican II. What mattered was to draw the conclusions from the new orientation of the council toward an ecclesiology of the people of God and a *communio ecclesiarum*. In the early 1970's, Anton Grillmeier and Yves Congar – both early church experts – took up the extant results of research into the processes of reception in the early church. They placed this subject in ecclesiological discussion with the express intention to push forward the post-conciliar reform movement. The new attention to reception as a reality in the Church as well as to its ecclesiological rank, has, therefore, a concrete 'Sitz im Leben': to overcome the counterreformational-ultramontane understanding of the Church and its one-sided structure, communication system, and exercise of authority … .

According to Congar the early church's manner of reception is 'dangerous' for the ultramontane concept of the Church because reception includes an evaluation by the local churches or other recipients as to whether the matter in question fits in with their life and faith – that is, it requires personal judgement: 'Reception includes something more than what the Scholastics called "obedience". For the Scholastics it is the act by which a subordinate submits his will and conduct to the legitimate precepts of a superior, out of respect for the latter's

---

24. Hermann Pottmeyer, 'Reception and Submission', *Jurist*, 51 (1991), 269–92.

authority. Reception is not a mere realisation of the relation "secundum sub et supra": it includes a degree of consent, and possibly of judgement, in which the life of a body is expressed which brings into play its own, original spiritual resources.'[25]

This quote accentuates the difference between obedience and the early church's method of reception, and not without reason. The demand for obedience to the directives of superiors within the Church has become more and more insistent in modern times. Even the adoption and propagation of faith became increasingly determined and ruled by the hierarchical teaching office – especially that of the pope – which demanded obedience to the magisterium. As far as the adoption and propagation of faith is concerned, this meant a decisive change.

We can sketch the scene briefly as follows. Since the nineteenth century the pope has increasingly appeared as the principal deciding bearer of the Church's teaching office. At the same time, his magisterium was conceived of primarily as an emanation of jurisdiction, and exercised as legislation. The required adherence to binding teachings set down by the pope began to assume increasingly the forms of obedience to the orders of a superior. In more recent documents, 'religious *obsequium* of will and mind' was required even for those decisions which the teaching office cannot or will not present as finally binding. The question arises as to whether reception has begun to take on the form of obedience.

A second question, therefore, deals with the difference between reception and *obsequium*. Are these two ideas mutually exclusive, or can agreement out of obedient submission to the teaching office be conceived as a sort of reception, even though it differs from that kind of reception which Congar determined to have been typical of the early church?

1 THE ULTRAMONTANE 'REVOLUTION FROM ABOVE': REQUIRED OBEDIENCE INSTEAD OF RECEPTION BASED ON UNDERSTANDING

The time in which the obligation to obey the hierarchical teaching office was increasingly strongly emphasised begins with the Counter-Reformation. As the teaching office came forward as the *norma proxima* for revealed truth, obedience to the ordinary not-infallible magisterium of the pastors was increasingly demanded. In the nineteenth century the pope became emphasised as the primary representative of the teaching office. While the ordinary magisterium of the pope as a fixed concept is first mentioned in 1740 by Benedict XIV, the series of modern papal encyclicals begins with *Mirari vos* of Gregory XVI in 1832.

Besides Congar, Joseph A. Komonchak[26] has investigated the appearance of the demand for obedience to the teaching office of the pope. He finds this demand for the first time in the letter *Tuas libenter* from Pius IX to the archbishop of Munich-Freising in 1863.[27] In it the pope rejected the statements made by Ignaz von Döllinger at an academic congress in Munich

---

25. [Congar, Yves, 'Reception as an Ecclesiological Reality', in *Election and Consensus in the Church*, eds G. Alberigo and A. Weiler, *Concilium*, 77 (1972)], 45 [see previous readings].
26. Komonchak, Joseph A., 'Ordinary Papal Magisterium and Religious Assent', in *The Magisterium and Morality*, Charles E. Curran and Richard A. McCormick (eds), vol. 3 of Readings in Moral Theology, New York, Paulist, 1982, 67–90.
27. DS, 2879–880.

in 1863 concerning the independent role of modern theology, and demanded the submission of Catholic intellectuals to the decisions of the papal congregations and the ordinary magisterium of the Church. This initiated the conflict between the ordinary magisterium of the pope and theologians who were using new interpretative methods, especially the historical-critical method. This conflict reached its fateful climax in the so-called 'Modernism Crisis' at the beginning of this century.

Theologians demanded a relative degree of autonomy for Catholic scholarship in relation to the teaching office. The Holy Office's decree *Lamentabili* in 1907 condemned the emancipation of exegesis from the teaching office of the Church. The encyclical *Pascendi* of Pope Pius X followed in 1907 and thereafter the introduction of the 'Anti-Modernist Oath', which was still required until Vatican II. Disciplinary actions on this scale were unprecedented in the previous history of the Church.

Under Pius XII, a new wave of restrictions began for many theologians, especially for the advocates of the 'Nouvelle Théologie' in France. In his 1950 encyclical *Humani generis* the pope demanded assent to papal encyclicals with dogmatic content. The encyclical's closing sentence has become famous: 'And if the Supreme Pontiffs, in their official documents, deliberately pass judgement on a matter hitherto controverted, it is evident to all that, in accordance with the mind and intention of the same Pontiff, that question can no longer be considered a subject for free debate among theologians.'[28] Many of the theologians who were forbidden to teach during this time later became important advisers to Vatican II.

The term 'religious *obsequium* of will and intellect' toward the ordinary magisterium of the bishops (especially the pope) as it is stated in *Lumen gentium* 25 can be found for the first time in the original draft concerning the Church which the preparatory commission presented to the Second Vatican Council. The phrase just quoted from *Humani generis* was also cited in the corresponding paragraph. This phrase is missing in the revised draft and in the final version of the Constitution on the Church. The petitions of certain council members show their uneasiness that the freedom of theology could be limited and its progress hindered … .

'Religious *obsequium* of will and intellect' to the non-definitive magisterium of the pope and the College of bishops is demanded also by the revised Profession of Faith of 1989. The last section of *Lumen gentium* 25, which emphasises the flexibility of the pope's way of teaching and the consequent flexibility of response, is omitted by canon 752 and in the even shorter text of the Profession of Faith. This omission leaves both of them more rigid and less nuanced than either the conciliar text or even the 1967 Profession of Faith, which included the phrase 'according as they are proposed by (the ordinary magisterium)'.[29]

Even more rigid is the Oath of Fidelity required by the Apostolic See since 1989. It demands 'Christian obedience' for 'what the sacred pastors declare as authentic doctors and teachers of the faith' as well as what they 'establish as leaders of the Church'. Obedience is claimed without any distinction for teaching and for disciplinary directives. Derived from canon 212, the Oath drops the reference of this canon to a sense of Christian responsibility that bears critically upon its meaning. Canon 212 states that it is with a consciousness of their own responsibility that Christians are to obey their pastors; in the canon this is followed by

---

28. … *AAS*, 42 (1950), 568.
29. *Report of the Catholic Theological Society of America Committee on the Profession of Faith and the Oath of Fidelity*, Washington, CTSA, 1990, 87.

the rights of the faithful to make known their desires and opinions to the pastors and the other faithful.

Meanwhile the Roman Curia deems the problem of obedience of the theologians to the non-definitive magisterium to be so grave that the Congregation for the Doctrine of the Faith issued its 1990 'Instruction on the Ecclesial Vocation of the Theologian' dealing substantially with this question, especially in no. 17 and no. 23–31.

In all these documents it is striking that the relationship between the teaching office and the faithful is defined above all as a juridical one. It is less the contents of the pastoral teachings and more their formal authority for which obedient submission is demanded … .

The instruction shows more clearly than the other documents where the increasing call to obedience to the ordinary magisterium of the pope is leading. The reception of the encyclical *Humanae vitae* by the faithful, by moral theologians and – as many defenders of the encyclical proclaim – by several bishops' conferences has not occurred. Since, in this case, the reception by the local churches has not occurred, the urgency of obedience is invoked and enforced through disciplinary measures. The means employed for this purpose are reminiscent of the battle against Modernism at the beginning of the century. At that time exegesis and historical method stood in the centre of the struggle. Today the focus is on moral theology. The damage that this method of exercising authority does to church authority itself and to its very purpose is made clear not only by the crisis with Modernism, but today as well. We see the restoration of a type of magisterium and ecclesiology which we thought had been curtailed, though not completely eliminated, by Vatican II … .

The obvious parallels to the developments in the nineteenth century are based on an understanding of the Church that we designate as 'ultramontane' or 'preconciliar'. One characteristic of this ecclesiology was the subordination of the magisterium to the *potestas jurisdictionis*. This made the authoritative determination of doctrine increasingly the exclusive domain of the sovereign papal jurisdiction. Several long-term developments stand behind this trend: the reinterpretation of the *principalitas* of the Church of Rome into the *principatus* of the pope, the separation of *ordo* and *jurisdictio*, and the interpretation of *jurisdictio* less as a judicial and more as a legislative power. The right to decide was increasingly emphasised, while the preparation for and the process of deciding receded into the background. The consequence was the shift of legitimising criteria from the content to the formal authority of legal decisions.

This development corresponds to the ultramontane view of the Church. The ultramontane ecclesiology which was formed in the last century was universalist, centralist, and authoritarian: universalist because it understood 'Church' to be the entire Church, not the local church; centralist and authoritarian because it made a monopoly out of the jurisdictional primacy of the pope and viewed all other members of the Church, including the bishops, as subordinates of the pope. The *hierarchia jurisdictionis*, legal superordination and subordination, has become the primary structural principle of the Church in place of the *hierarchia ordinis*. The *communio* of the local churches and the College of Bishops receded into oblivion as one of the constituting structural elements of the Church. The long-standing, traditional participation of the bishops as witnesses and judges at the formulation of church teachings was no longer viewed as legally binding, but rather as – at most – a moral duty of the pope. In this conception of the Church, reception in its older sense no longer had any place in the life and growth of the Church, nor as a legally relevant expression of *communio*.

It seemed to be superseded by the absolute obligation of Church members to obey. Hans Dombois sees in this 'a revolution from above, the destruction of a traditional sense of community by the introduction of a dominating sovereignty'.[30]

The way theologians already in the nineteenth century occupied themselves with the problem of the one-sided jurisdictional interpretation of the teaching office shows the controversy to be whether the teaching office should be assigned to the *potestas jurisdictionis* or the *potestas ordinis* or whether it represents a legal power *sui generis*. The prevailing ultramontane view assigns the teaching office to jurisdiction. Authentic teaching proceeds, according to this view, by legislation; the teaching office is a *potestas in subditos* which can demand obedience.

2   THE DISTINCTION BETWEEN OBSEQUIUM AND OBOEDIENTIA

English commentaries on some recent Roman documents raise an issue which, I suspect, is not only a semantic one: the correct translation of the term *obsequium*. The *obsequium religiosum intellectus and voluntatis* which those documents require for the non-definitive teaching of the magisterium has been translated with 'deference' or 'respect' or 'acceptance', but mostly as 'submission'. While the German commentaries translate both *obsequium* and *oboedientia* as 'Gehorsam', the English translations mostly avoid using the term 'obedience' for *obsequium*. They try to make a difference between *obsequium* and *oboedientia*, between 'submission' and 'obedience'.

The reason seems to be that 'obedience' in contemporary English is normally used in connection with the execution of a command to perform some external action. Understood in this way, obedience is the correct response to the ruling power (*potestas regendi*) of the bishops and the pope, but not to their magisterium. The proper attitude toward an authoritative teacher is rather a docility, a teachability.

I agree totally on this point. The assent to a non-definitive teaching cannot simply be commanded. In this sense the increasing recognition of the distinction between the two Latin words represents a progress in the emphasis on the free and personal character of the assent to authoritative teaching. But the point is that the problem of the recent Roman documents cannot be solved by insisting on the difference of the terms *obsequium* and *oboedientia* because Rome itself does not make a difference in its use of these two terms. Rome sees the magisterium as a part of the juridical power, and it views the relationship between the authoritative teacher and the faithful as that of superior and subject.

I agree with Richard A. McCormick and Richard P. McBrien: 'The key element in this ecclesiology (that of the recent Roman documents) is the pyramidal structure of the church and, as a result, the heavily obediential character given to the teaching-learning process in the church … The teaching-learning process of the church is viewed within the dominance of the superior-subject relationship.'[31]

---

30. Dombois, Hans, *Das Recht der Gnade. Ökumenisches Kirchenrecht*, I, Witten, Luther-Verlag, 1961, 829.
31. McCormick, Richard, A. and McBrien, Richard P., 'Theology as a Public Responsibility', *America*, 165 (1991), 186.

A recent expression of this attitude is the new formulation of the Profession of Faith and the new Oath of Fidelity. Even though the former document uses *obsequium* and the latter *christiana oboedientia*, both texts employ these terms in the same sense, that is, to demand obedient submission to the teaching office.

The 'Draft of a Dogmatic Constitution on the Church' prepared by the Roman Curia for Vatican II says in no. 13 that the bishops 'have no power to command the laws that bind in conscience, and this not only in matters pertaining to doctrine and morals … .' This text refers to the 'First Draft of a Dogmatic Constitution of the Church of Christ' of Vatican I which begins by declaring that there are only 'two types of power in the Church, power of orders and power of jurisdiction',[32] subordinating the magisterium to the juridical power.

In the same draft, prepared by the Curia for Vatican II and truly representing the preconciliar ecclesiology, we find in no. 30 already the demand of the *obsequium religiosum intellectus et voluntatis* to the non-infallible teaching of the pope. The demand refers to the encyclical *Casti connubii* of Pius XI which says that the believers 'must necessarily give this obedience not only to the more solemn definition of the Church, but also, in the proper mode, to other Constitutions and Decrees in which some opinions are proscribed and condemned as dangerous or perverse'.[33]

In no. 31 the same draft states that the pope does not exercise his magisterium solely by himself but in part also by the sacred congregations and by other groups of experts. It continues teaching: 'To the decisions and declarations of such groups also, therefore, even though they are not infallible or irreformable, is owed not only a merely external submission but a religious and internal assent of the mind.'

The final chapter of this draft has the title 'Authority and Obedience in the Church'. It clearly defines the relationship between the hierarchy and the other members of the Church as that of superiors and subjects. No. 38 states: 'But when a legitimate authority has commanded something, those who are led by a Christian spirit, instead of opening the door to free criticism, should strive rather to submit their own judgement and carry out the command in ready obedience.'

No. 39 speaks about 'a certain supernatural sense of the faith on the part of the whole Christian people' as 'an indefectible and unique mark of the Catholic Church.' It continues: this supernatural sense of the faith 'comes from above and is nothing other than the agreement of faithful and pastors in matters of faith and morals, an agreement governed by the authoritative magisterium'. The agreement of the faithful is aroused by the Holy Spirit, who 'is also at work in the faithful so that they may obediently accept the doctrine presented' by the magisterium.

Certainly, it can be said that this draft was rejected by Vatican II. But, on the other hand, we find in no part of *Lumen gentium* such a continuity between the draft and the final text as in article 25 and in the paragraph on the *religiosum voluntatis et intellectus obsequium*.[34]

Perhaps in the 1990 CDF instruction can be found a very cautious differentiation between *obsequium* and *oboedientia*. It seems that the instruction does not rule out the possibility of legitimate interior non-assent to specific teachings of the ordinary, non-definitive

---

32. *Sacrorum Conciliorum Nova et Amplissima Collectio*, ed. Johannes Mansi et al., 51, Arnhem & Leipzig, 1926, 543.

33. Pius XI, encyclical, *Casti connubii*, 31 December 1930, *AAS*, 22, 1930, 580.

34. See *Constitutionis Dogmaticae Lumen Gentium Synopsis Historica*, 126.

magisterium. As to the external expression of disagreement it recommends on the one hand to 'suffer for truth' in silence, on the other hand – so Avery Dulles – it 'does not seem to me to forbid the airing of such (discreet and constructive) criticisms in scholarly journals, theological conferences, classroom situations and other appropriate forums. What the authorities do not forbid is, I take it, still permitted'.[35] The fact that it needs such a benevolent interpretation for disclosing this differentiation and perhaps further the authority of a Cardinal Ratzinger to make the differentiation possible proves the lasting powerful influence of the Curia's tradition.

This tradition is rooted in the ultramontane ecclesiology whose one-sided character Vatican II tried to overcome. This tradition makes no clear distinction between *obsequium* and *oboedientia*. Together with the draft the recent Roman documents represent this tradition. Therefore, without denying the right of the magisterium to demand to a certain extent obedience, it is all the more important to show that there are limits of commanding assent to non-definitive teachings.

3   THE REDISCOVERY OF *COMMUNIO* AND *RECEPTIO*

The ecclesiological change which the Second Vatican Council tried to bring about oriented itself on the biblical concept of the people of God and on the concept of *communio* as found in the early church. For the council fathers and theologians who wanted this change, it was a matter of overcoming the ultramontane view of the Church and its corresponding practice. They won over the vast majority of the council for this change. However, an influential minority succeeded in saving some ultramontane emphasis by appealing to the dogmas of Vatican I. From this situation arose the divided impression which the ecclesiological documents of Vatican II give.

This ecclesiological fence-straddling is visible not least of all in the matter of reception. In this case, the possibility referred to in *Lumen gentium* 22, whereby the pope can freely receive an initiative from the bishops, corresponds to the *communio* ecclesiology without difficulty. It agrees with the *communio* ecclesiology in that bishops and local churches appear here as active subjects. On the other hand, the primacy of papal jurisdiction is not restricted because it depends upon the pope's assent whether the bishops' initiative will take effect. The sovereignty of the pope is underscored by the emphatic addition of the word 'free'.

A statement in *Lumen gentium* 25 is similar. Although the word itself never appears, it doubtlessly deals with reception by the Church – more exactly, reception of dogmatic definitions of the college of bishops, or of the pope:

> The assent of the Church can never be lacking to such definitions on account of the same Holy Spirit's influence, through which Christ's whole flock is maintained in the unity of the faith and makes progress in it.[36]

Even though this statement can already be found in the records of Vatican I, the fact that it

---

35. Dulles, Avery, 'The Question of Dissent', *The Tablet*, 18 August 1990, 1033.
36. [ET] from *Vatican Council II – The Conciliar and Postconciliar Documents*, ed. Austin Flannery, New York, Costello, 1981, 380.

was written into *Lumen gentium* is one evidence of the importance which is ascribed to the reception of a dogma by the whole Church: it belongs to a *communio* ecclesiology. On the other hand, this statement does not disturb the ultramontane view of the Church because the process of reception is naturally assumed to occur. An independent judgement of the local churches is not contemplated. The question as to the meaning of reception being refused by the whole Church, however, has been constantly discussed by theologians throughout church history.

Indeed, no claim to authority, not even one so heightened as the dogma of infallibility declared by Vatican I, can annul the responsibility of the bishops and the local churches to examine the content of church decisions, nor the criteriological meaning of such reception. Joseph Ratzinger states, 'Conversely criticism of papal declarations will be possible and necessary to the degree that they do not correspond with Scripture and the Creed, that is, with the belief of the Church. Where there is neither unanimity within the Church nor clear testimony of the sources, then no binding decision is possible; if one is formally made, then its preconditions are lacking, and therefore the question of its legitimacy must be raised'.[37] Likewise Walter Kasper: 'The pope can only be infallible as far as the Church recognises him as the voice and the testimony of its own infallibility. If it withholds this recognition (which is not to be confused with the subsequent agreement to an *ex cathedra* declaration as a required condition for its juridical binding force which was rejected by Vatican I), then the pope would, in an extreme case, be heretical or schismatic: he would no longer be pope.'[38] ...

The renewed interest in the early church's process of reception must nevertheless confront an objection. Is not the great importance of reception in the early church a result of the historical situation of that time? In antiquity, widely dispersed congregations – the fruit of the first missionary efforts – gathered together into larger groupings, finally into patriarchal churches. The lack of communication among the local churches, persecution, political barriers, and cultural differences allowed the functioning world-wide church (even within the Roman Empire) to grow only very slowly. Only a small number of the churches were represented by their bishops in ecumenical councils. A common theology and a church-wide structure had hardly been formed. For such a Church which exhibited so many characteristics of provincialism, reception in that form was the only appropriate means of bringing about a consensus of faith, and assuring a common and unifying tradition.

In fact, a return to the early church is neither possible nor appropriate. The whole question has nothing to do with a restoration of a bygone era, but with a 're-reception' of the early church's basic ideas within the conditions of our own time. It was not just the cultural-social circumstances which gave rise to the Church as *communio ecclesiarum*, but the conviction of the presence of Christ and His Spirit within the various Christian communities. This original view of the Church as being structured from the local churches on up, whose mutual *communio* is based on a shared *communio* with Christ is taken up by Vatican II in *Lumen gentium* 26:

---

37. Ratzinger, Joseph, *Das neue Volk Gottes. Entwürfe zur Ekklesiologie*, Düsseldorf, Patmos, 1969, 144.
38. Kasper, Walter, 'Zur Diskussion um das Problem der Unfehlbarkeit', in *Fehlbar? Eine Bilanz*, Hans Küng (ed.), Zürich, Benzinger, 1973, 84.

> This Church of Christ is really present in all legitimately organised local groups of the
> faithful, which, in so far as they are united to their pastors, are also appropriately called
> churches in the New Testament. For these are in fact, in their own localities, the new
> people called by God, in the power of the Holy Spirit and as the result of full conviction
> (cf. 1 Thess. 1:5).[39]

After the presence of Christ in every church body has been pointed out the council continues:
'In these communities ... Christ is present through whose power and influence the One,
Holy, Catholic and Apostolic Church is constituted.' As to the relationship between the local
churches and the Church as a whole, *Lumen gentium* 23 says: 'It is in these and formed out of
them that the one and unique Catholic Church exists.'

Thus, as much as socio-historical circumstances may influence the processes of reception,
the theological significance of reception does not depend upon these. It is actually based more
on the theological understanding of the relationship between the Church universal and the
local churches. They are not related to each other as superior and inferior. Rather they enjoy
organic mutuality or *perichoresis* which expresses itself in reciprocal communication. The pope
is not the delegate of the local churches, nor are the local churches and their leaders mere
subjects of Rome. To allow reception of authoritative teachings as the old tradition
understood it instead of demanding the immediate execution along the lines of obedience
means taking seriously the presence of Christ and His Spirit in the local churches.

However the recent interest in the topic of reception is not based solely on the
rediscovery of a *communio* ecclesiology. It also has a specifically contemporary *Sitz im Leben*:
namely, the demand of people today for responsible self-determination. This includes the
right and moral duty to take personal responsibility for religious decisions. This is only
possible when such decisions are based on well-founded understanding and a personal
judgement of conscience. Any teaching office which bases its claim to obedience purely on its
own formal authority without establishing the credibility of its teaching does not take this
demand seriously.

Vatican II emphasised the importance of conscience and personal decision regarding
religious questions in *Dignitatis humanae* 3:

> For this reason everybody has the duty and consequently the right to seek the truth in
> religious matters so that, through the use of appropriate means, he may prudently form
> judgements of conscience which are sincere and true.
>
> The search for truth, however, must be carried out in a manner that is appropriate
> to the dignity of the human person and his social nature, namely, by free enquiry with
> the help of teaching and instruction, communication and dialogue. It is by these means
> that men share with each other the truth they have discovered, or think they have
> discovered, in such a way that they help one another in the search for truth. Moreover,
> it is by personal assent that men must adhere to the truth they have discovered. It is
> through his conscience that man sees and recognises the demands of the divine law.[40]

If this occupation with reception is to be more than theoretical, it must be considered with
regard to the Church and society today. Corresponding to the demand for responsible

---

39. Flannery, 381.
40. Flannery, 801.

participation of all believers in the church's life and search for truth is a manner of reception which, unlike a formally based obedience, can be realised only as a conscious and responsible adoption of tradition and of magisterial decisions.

4   THE THEOLOGICAL CONCEPT OF RECEPTION

… In the Bible faith is repeatedly identified as obedience. This obedience is offered to God, his Word and the gospel (Rom. 1:5, 10:16; 1 Pet. 2:8). This identification expresses the moment of *recipere* in faith, the acceptance, recognition and the complete dedication to God. Vatican II uses this kind of language in a remarkable text. It is noteworthy in the current context because the obedience of will and understanding occur in its original context. *Dei verbum* 5 says:

> The obedience of faith (Rom. 16:26; cf. Rom. 1:5; 2 Cor. 10:5–6) must be given to God as he reveals himself. By faith man freely commits his entire self to God, making 'the full submission of his intellect and will to God who reveals' and willingly assenting to the Revelation given by him. Before this faith can be exercised, man must have the grace of God to move and assist him; he must have the interior helps of the Holy Spirit, who moves the heart and converts it to God, who opens the eyes of the mind and 'makes it easy for all to accept and believe the truth'.[41]

This quotation from Vatican II, which itself quotes Vatican I, shows that obedience of will and understanding was originally attributed to the total devotion of the believer to God. Here, referring to God, the obedience of will and understanding has its original and full meaning. It is certainly the good news of the gospel that we are obliged to be obedient *only* to God, our Saviour. Since God reveals himself only through those he sends, obedience to God can also be expressed as obedience to his messengers without ceasing to be obedience to God (2 Cor. 5:10). Obedience to these messengers is coupled, however, to the condition that they also are obedient to God. Paul praises the Thessalonians because they 'received the word of God, which you heard from us' and 'accepted it not as the word of men, but as it actually is, the word of God' (1 Thess. 2:13). That is why the apostles call themselves not only messengers, but also witnesses. A witness recedes behind the person to whom he is testifying; he directs attention away from himself toward the person he wants to make known. Because he fully accomplished obedience and was a perfect witness, Jesus is called the 'true and faithful witness' (Rev. 3:14). All teaching and interpretation of the gospel should be a testimony which makes very present the word of God. Therefore, the authority of the teaching office is fundamentally the authority of a witness. *Dei verbum* 10 states exactly that:

> Yet this magisterium is not superior to the Word of God, but is its servant. It teaches only what has been handed on to it. At the divine command and with the help of the Holy Spirit, it listens to it devotedly, guards it with dedication and expounds it faithfully. All that it proposes for belief as being divinely revealed it draws from this single deposit of faith.[42]

---

41. Flannery, 752.
42. Flannery, 756.

This passage makes it clear that the teaching office, in order to be a witness of the word of God, must itself be a recipient. The teaching office receives the word of God as it is passed on by the faith and the tradition of the Church. Before the teaching office can teach the Church, it must have listened to the Church and learned its faith. Just as receiving the word of God is the foundational action of the Church and its faith, so also reception is the foundational act of the teaching office. However, just as reception by local churches and their members contains an element of perception, interpretation and judgement of their own, so also the determination of doctrine by the teaching office requires perception, interpretation and judgement. Receiving, transmitting, and teaching are not just the repetition of something already known, said, and acknowledged. If the contribution of the local church is worthy of respect when it credibly gives testimony to the word of God, then the same must be applied to the testimony of the teaching office and its official decisions.

The leading position of the teaching office vis-à-vis the rest of the Church becomes conspicuous when the interpretation of the word of God is debatable, and the debate threatens the unity of believers and the loyalty of the Church to the word of God. Based on the calling of the shepherds to feed the flock of Christ while preserving the word of God, their teaching authority is not just the authority of witnesses, but also of decision-makers. This distinguishes the pastors from other believers whose testimony likewise has authority, but who do not have to decide on doctrine for the local or universal Church. In case of such a debate, there can arise a conflict between the teaching authority and the party who disagrees with the teaching; the submission which is called for by the teaching office becomes a problem. The teaching office, for its part, can intensify the conflict by demanding obedient submission in such a way that it damages the conscience of the believer. This does not encourage reception in the sense of free assent.

The resolving of this conflict is possible only through dialogue. It is the responsibility of the teaching office to substantiate the content of its official decisions as a true testimony of the word of God and the tradition of the Church's faith. Only in this way can obedient submission to the teaching office have some real meaning and lead to obedience to and reception of God's word. In the final analysis, the teaching office can only demand obedience toward God and his word.

Reception can be defined theologically as the faithful acceptance by the Church and its members of God's word and the recognition of its truth based on discernment of its presence in the testimony of Holy Scripture, the tradition of the Church, and the teaching office.

5   RECEPTION BASED ON OBSEQUIUM OR ON UNDERSTANDING

Finally the question remains whether agreement out of *obsequium* to the magisterium can be conceived of as a sort of reception, even though it differs from that kind of reception which was typical in the early church. The question arises whether we translate *obsequium* as 'obedience' or as 'submission'. In any case the authoritative declaration of the magisterium contains a juridical element, the *potestas docendi*. Its bearers act not only as witnesses and teachers of faith, but also as pastors and superiors. Nevertheless the authoritative teaching of the magisterium cannot be understood simply as a command to perform some external action, and obedience to the magisterium cannot mean simply an action of external respect. The 1990 instruction of the CDF states: 'This kind of response cannot be simply exterior or disciplinary, but must be understood within the logic of faith and under the impulse of obedience to faith' (no. 23). The qualification of *obsequium* as *religiosum* underlines that the motivation of submission is rooted in the belief that pastors are commissioned by God and enjoy divine assistance in the exercise of their teaching office. But that means also that the magisterium itself can demand *obsequium* only within the logic of faith and on condition of its obedience to the faith.

Thus even if we understand *obsequium* as obedience, like the Roman Curia, the obedience to the non-definitive teaching of the magisterium is a very special one. Two elements are constitutive for the Christian concept of obedience: the legitimacy of the superior, and the moral character of the order. Christian obedience is not blindly offered, but rather requires the understanding that both elements are present. As to the moral character of an order of the *potestas docendi*, the truth of doctrine is the scope of the teaching office. Thus, it would be just as immoral to demand agreement on an untruth as to give such an agreement. As long as no personal judgement concerning the truth of the proposed teaching is possible, the presumption of its truth can be viewed as a moral attitude. This presumption depends on the reliance based on faith that the pastors do not lack divine assistance for the responsible execution of their teaching office. Whenever assent based on obedience and not because of a personal insight in truth is given to a non-definitive teaching, there is always a kind of presumption present. The presumption becomes morally questionable if there are reasonable doubts about its truth. Christian obedience, therefore, calls for an examination of the truth of such declarations to the extent that the teaching office is not willing to exclude the possibility of an error or other defect.

In any case, the assent of the faithful given out of obedience or submission is characterised *not* by a motivation based on a personal evaluation of the truth of a particular teaching, but on the formal authority of pastors and the presumption of truth based upon it. Since the assenting person accepts here a particular teaching as true, it would also stand to reason to speak of reception in connection with agreement based on obedient submission. Moreover, the examination of the truth which is demanded by any reception of truth is not ruled out because of the presumption of truth submits itself, if necessary, to an examination of its content. This is where the limits of obedience to teaching appear.

In contrast to reception based on obedience, the early church's manner of reception can be termed reception based on examination and understanding of truth. In this case; the receiving body tests and recognises first and foremost the content-based authority of the teaching – that is, its truth and the appropriateness of its definition or formulation. The receiving body compares the teaching with the standards that are valid for the whole Church, namely the word of God and its testimony in the Holy Scriptures and tradition. In this way, the body in question comes to its own conclusion. It naturally gives due regard to the formal authority which has issued the determination. The God-given responsibility of the pastors is part of the belief and tradition of the believing body. Still, their formal authority is not the deciding reason for the assent.

Further it is characteristic that, in contrast to contemporary calls for obedience which tend to be aimed at individuals, the body responsible for reception is the local church. Reception appears as a social process, or better, an ecclesial process. The local church realises itself as *communio fidelium* in reception, taking into consideration the *sensus fidei* of its members. For its part, the local church was never seen as an inferior instance within the *communio ecclesiarum*, so that no power relationship existed that required obedience to a dominant higher authority.

The difference between this kind of reception and obedience is also that reception based on examination can happen in both directions. Thus the whole Church can be the 'receiver' of a decision or initiative which comes from a local church. Church history furnishes sufficient examples of an ecumenical council accepting the decision of a regional synod or a local church. The Second Vatican Council calls the eventuality that a pope might approve an initiative from the bishops *vel libere recipiat*. Authority based on content as a reason for this kind of reception is especially clear in such a case, since there is certainly no relation of juridical subordination. This is conformed by historical evidence; it was not because of the councils' formal authority that their decisions during the first centuries were accepted and that some regional synods enjoyed greater esteem than several ecumenical councils. Moreover, the process of reception was often quite drawn-out, which is not alone attributable to the poor communication of past centuries, but more to the in-depth examination of the content of these decisions and the subsequent debate at all levels of the Church. The authority of a council came into full effect when its decisions were generally approved by this process of reception. The ratifying consensus of the local churches as a result of 'reception' was understood as a confirmation of the 'received' decision. The decision of the local church carried weight because an independent judgement was contained in it.

Therefore reception as the early church understood it is not just a descriptive category which might identify how a religious tradition or church decision was put into effect. It is much more a process, the result of which – the consensus of the local churches – has the meaning of a 'criterion of truth'. The criteriological meaning of reception becomes theologically justified if reception implies a well-founded judgement by the local churches in which their *sensus fidei*, guided by the Spirit, is believed to be effective. The fundamental basis of this understanding of reception is, therefore, a pneumatologically based *communio* ecclesiology. Congar has provided the historical and theological evidence for this.

6   CONCLUSION

… If we view reception not in terms of its end result but as a process of increasing understanding and agreement, then reception based on obedience to the teaching office is something like the beginning of a learning process which leads to reception based on understanding. Reception based on obedience has only a temporary, subsidiary function. Only when we understand that we truly encounter God's word in the testimony of the teaching office does reception achieve its purpose: a believing assent to the word and will of God.

A certain willingness to listen and to learn expresses itself in the obedience or submission to the teaching office. The 1990 instruction of the CDF, indeed, described the *religiosum intellectus et voluntatis obsequium* as 'the willingness to submit loyally to the teaching of the magisterium on matters per se not irreformable' (no. 24). This willingness gives room for the working of the Holy Spirit, 'who moves the heart and converts it to God, who opens the eyes of the mind and makes it easy for all to accept and believe the truth' (DV 5).

A non-definitive doctrinal decision of the pastors is, therefore, the completion of one phase of reception, but also the starting point for a new phase of reception of God's word 'through the contemplation and study of believers who ponder these things in their hearts' (cf. Lk. 2:19 and 51) and 'from the intimate sense of spiritual realities which they experience' (DV 8).

The determination of a relationship between reception based on obedience or submission and reception based on one's own perception of truth, which we have now made, follows from a change in perspective. Reception is not just viewed in terms of its result – a final agreement to and acceptance of a doctrinal decision. Rather, its essence is a process of diligent study, increasing insight, and maturing judgement which makes possible assent by the Church and its communities and members in the light of faith and under the guidance of the Holy Spirit.

Reception can be defined theologically as the faithful acceptance by the Church and its members of God's word and the recognition of its truth based on discernment of his presence in the testimony of Holy Scripture, the tradition of the Church, and the teaching office.

5.8 THOMAS P. RAUSCH: *RECEPTION PAST AND PRESENT* – 1986

Taking into account the context of an accelerating ecumenical movement after Vatican II, Rausch wrote the following inspirational article.[43] In it, he considers the processes by which one church may recognize the 'faith and ecclesial life' of another church as 'authentically Christian'. In the main, he explores the ecumenical implications of the various interpretations of the notion of 'reception' to such processes. A major difficulty is how theological consensus becomes *ecclesial* consensus. To explore such issues, Rausch looks at the history of the concept both in the early Christian centuries and in recent ecumenical history. He suggests the church must discern how the process of reception can be facilitated today and his article further includes practical suggestions to this end.

❀

The term 'reception' is generally used today in two distinct but related senses. The historical or 'classical' concept refers to the acceptance by local churches of particular ecclesiastical or conciliar decisions. A more recent, ecumenical usage of the concept refers to the acceptance by one church of a theological consensus arrived at with another church, and ultimately the recognition of the other church's faith and ecclesial life as authentically Christian.

In the last few years reception has become a crucial issue in the ecumenical context, for it emerges precisely at the point of the discrepancy between the progress made in the ecumenical dialogues and the apparent inability of the sponsoring churches to build and move forward on the basis of what the dialogues have accomplished. Since the Second Vatican Council, the Roman Catholic Church has been in official dialogue with other churches on both the international and the regional level. Among the more significant dialogues on the international level are those carried on by the Anglican-Roman Catholic Study Commission (ARCIC), the Joint Lutheran-Roman Catholic Study Commission, the Joint Commission of the Roman Catholic Church and the World Methodist Council, the Reformed-Roman Catholic Study Commission, and the Orthodox-Roman Catholic Theological Commission. In the United States the Catholic Church is involved in dialogues with Episcopalians, Lutherans, Southern Baptists, Methodists, the Presbyterian/Reformed Church, the Eastern Orthodox, the Oriental Orthodox, and the Polish National Catholic Church. Yet, so far, none of the statements produced by these dialogue commissions has been received by the sponsoring churches, with the exception of the Episcopal Church in the United States, which has begun the process of officially receiving the ARCIC Final Report. The one semiofficial response of the Roman Catholic Church, the 'Observations on the ARCIC Final Report' by the Congregation for the Doctrine of the Faith (CDF),[44] has generally been perceived as a negative one.

---

43. Rausch, Thomas P., SJ, 'Reception Past and Present', *Theological Studies*, 47 (1986), 497–508.
44. … [In] *Origins*, 11 (1982), 752–6.

The CDF's cool response to the Final Report occasioned considerable disappointment; it was interpreted by many as an unwillingness on the part of Rome to receive the considerable agreement arrived at through the ARCIC dialogue. Indeed, the CDF singled out what is considered to be the Final Report's understanding of reception as one of its objections, arguing that it was in conflict with the Catholic teaching on magisterial infallibility expressed at Vatican I in the constitution *Pastor aeternus* (DS 3074) and at Vatican II in *Lumen gentium* (no. 25). But it may be that the general frustration with the failure of the churches to officially receive the bilateral statements reflects the same tendency to place too much emphasis on what formal authority can accomplish by itself that one sees in the CDF's sharp juxtaposition of magisterial infallibility against reception. Perhaps too much has been expected of authority, as if reception were a purely juridical process. But it is much more. As Cardinal Willebrands has recently observed, the problem that arises in respect to the bilateral documents is 'how *theological* consensuses and convergences can become *ecclesial* consensuses and convergences'.[45]

The current ecumenical discussion of reception is very much concerned with this issue. In what follows I would like to address it by focusing on some of the past and present implications of reception. I will first consider the biblical roots of the concept; second, review the classical and ecumenical concepts; third, analyse reception as an ecclesiological reality; finally, offer some suggestions for facilitating the process of reception.

BIBLICAL ROOTS

Various authors point out that the process of reception is constitutive for the life of faith and for the Church itself. Behind the Latin words *receptio* and *recipere* lie in the New Testament Greek words *lambanein* ('to receive') and *dechesthai* ('to accept') and their derivatives. Paul reminds the Corinthians that they have 'received' the gospel he preached (1 Cor 15:1); similarly, he tells them that they have received the Holy Spirit (1 Cor 1:12; cf. 1 Thess 2:13; Col 2:6). In the parable of the seed the word is accepted (Mk 4:20); in Acts, Peter's preaching is accepted by those who are subsequently baptised (Acts 2:41). Those who accept Jesus and his messengers in doing so also accept God (*dechesthai*, Mt 10:40; *lambanein*, Jn 13:20). In Paul the idea of reception appears in the context of tradition, for he several times uses the Greek equivalents for the technical rabbinic terms for the process of handing on (*paradidonai*) and receiving (*paralambanein*) the tradition.

What resulted from the reception of the apostolic preaching by those who became the converts of the apostles and other early Christian missionaries was the Church itself. The same dynamic can be seen in the formation of the New Testament canon. Those Christian writings which were accepted by the early communities as expressions of the apostolic faith became, through this process of reception, part of the Church's canon of Sacred Scripture. Still later the receiving of liturgical practices, church laws, and customs of one church by others further illustrates the process of reception. Edward Kilmartin points, as examples, to the

---

45. Willebrands, Johannes Cardinal, 'The Ecumenical Dialogue and Its Reception', *Bulletin/Centro pro unione,* 27 (1985), 6.

fourth-century reception of the Spirit epiklesis in the East, to the acceptance of the Roman liturgy in Germany beginning in the sixth century, and to the reception of the Mainz Pontifical by Rome in the tenth.[46]

RECEPTION: CLASSICAL AND ECUMENICAL

Although reception as an ecclesiological reality has a broad application, the term in its classical sense is used restrictively to refer to the acceptance in the early Church of conciliar decrees and decisions, particularly those of the great ecumenical councils. Ulrich Kuhn points out that those writing in the last 20 years tend to speak of reception in the ancient Church in two main connections. First, in the pre-Constantinian period reception is primarily concerned with the process through which decisions of local or regional synods were made known to and accepted by other churches. Kuhn stresses that what underlies this practice is the recognition that a particular church is authentically church only if it lives in communion with other churches.[47]

Secondly, after Constantine, the focus is generally on the process through which those decisions made by the great 'ecumenical' councils were discussed, interpreted and received by a later council, though the process might also lead to a rejection. Kilmartin points, as a prime example, to the eventual reception of Nicaea I (325) after a long process involving considerable opposition.[48] Other examples include that of Leo II, who both confirmed the teaching of Constantinople III (681) and asked the Spanish bishops to support it with their own authority, which they did at the regional Council of Toledo XIV (684). On the other hand, the theologians of Charlemagne decided that the decisions of the Council of Nicaea II (787) on icons did not reflect the universal faith and authority of all the churches.[49]

The classical concept of reception must be understood as an ecclesiological reality which emerged in the life of the Church of the first millennium. It is most important to note that during this period the Church was understood as a communion of churches. It is this ecclesiology of communion as well as the practice which it grounded which have important implications for the church of today. Attempts to explain reception which look to the late-medieval or post-Tridentine Church are less helpful; for the excessively hierarchical concept of Church which developed tends to reduce reception to a purely juridical category, if indeed it does not so emphasise the role of ecclesiastical authority that the notion of reception is virtually rejected.

While the classical concept emerged in a Church which understood itself as a communion of churches, it was nonetheless a united Church. In the ecumenical context, however, a new element appears; for now what is involved is a process of reception between churches separated from one another by differences of history, doctrine, and structure. In the

---

46. Kilmartin, Edward, 'Reception in History: An Ecclesiological Phenomenon and Its Significance', *Journal of Ecumenical Studies*, 21 (1984), 41–3.
47. Ulrich Kuhn, 'Reception – An Imperative and an Opportunity', in *Ecumenical Perspectives on Baptism, Eucharist and Ministry*, Max Thurian (ed.), Geneva, *World Council of Churches*, 1983, 166.
48. Kilmartin, 'Reception in History', 40.
49. Ibid., 49.

absence of communion between the churches, the process of reception is complicated considerably; as Anton Houtepen observes, 'more theological consensus is needed to restore unity than to preserve unity'.[50]

From the time of its founding in 1948, the World Council of Churches [WCC] has been working to build consensus among the churches, receiving reports and statements and forwarding them to its member churches 'for their study and appropriate action'.[51] So the ecumenical process of reception has already been initiated.

As a formal, ecumenical concept, reception first began to emerge as a result of a meeting on the ancient councils, organised by the Faith and Order Commission at Oxford in 1965 and then at Bad Gastein, Austria, in 1966. Gradually both the concept and the term became part of the ecumenical vocabulary. Zizioulas mentioned an attempt to use the concept in a decisive way at the Faith and Order meeting at Louvain in 1972.[52] The WCC statement *One Baptism, One Eucharist and a Mutually Recognised Ministry* approved at Accra in 1974 did not speak specifically of reception, but it was 'submitted to the churches for consideration and comment'.[53] The WCC Assembly at Nairobi in 1975 specifically called the churches 'to receive, re-appropriate and confess together … the Christian truth and faith, delivered through the Apostles and handed down through the centuries'.[54] And when the WCC text *Baptism, Eucharist and Ministry (BEM)* was published and transmitted to the churches throughout the world in 1982, the Faith and Order Commission invited all the churches 'to prepare an official response … at the highest appropriate level of authority' as part of 'this process of reception'.[55]

Thus the ecumenical movement and, especially since the end of the Second Vatican Council, the appearance of the various bilateral dialogues, along with the official statements formulated by them, have made the issue of reception unavoidable … .

RECEPTION AS AN ECCLESIOLOGICAL REALITY

We have reviewed the classical and ecumenical concepts of reception. If both are understood in the context of the broader ecclesiological reality of reception of which each remains a part, a number of conclusions can be drawn.

Reception cannot be reduced to a juridical determination, either of authority or on the part of the faithful; it is a process involving the whole Church. In the ancient Church ecclesiastical decisions or teachings became normative for the later Church only when they were received by the communion of churches and ultimately by the faithful themselves. At the same time, reception does not constitute a decision as legitimate. Congar emphasises that

50. … 'Reception, Tradition, Communion,' in Thurian, *Ecumenical Perspectives*, 148.
51. See 'The Rules of the World Council of Churches', XIV, 6 (a) in *Breaking Barriers – Nairobi 1975*, David M. Paton (ed.), London, SPCK, 1976, 339. Cf. Houtepen [Anton: 'Reception, Tradition, Communion' in Thurian, *Ecumenical Perspectives*], 141.
52. Zizoulas, 'The Theological Problem of Recption', *Bulletin/Centro pro unione*, 26 (1984), 3.
53. *One Baptism, One Eucharist, and a Mutually Recognised Ministry*, Geneva, WCC, 1975.
54. *Breaking Barriers – Nairobi 1975*, Report of Section II, 66.
55. *Baptism, Eucharist, Ministry*, Geneva, WCC, 1982, x … .

reception 'does not confer validity, but affirms, acknowledges and attests that this matter is for the good of the Church'.[56]

Vatican II teaches that the whole Church is involved in grasping Christian truth:

The body of the faithful as a whole, anointed as they are by the Holy One (cf. 1 Jn 2:20, 27), cannot err in matters of belief. Thanks to a supernatural sense of the faith which characterises the people as a whole, it manifests the unerring quality when, 'from the bishops down to the last member of the laity', it shows universal agreement in matters of faith and morals (*Lumen gentium* no.12).

More recently, Cardinal Willebrands has stressed that reception cannot be understood 'as a purely technical or instrumental concept'. He argues that it involves the whole People of God and in this sense 'has certain aspects of a sociological process'. Thus it involves the research activities of theologians, 'the preserving fidelity and piety' of the faithful, and the binding decisions arrived at by the college of bishops.[57]

As a contemporary example of reception, Willebrands points to the reception of the ecumenical movement itself by Vatican II, a reception made possible by earlier developments in theology, in the Christian lives of the faithful, and in some 'often hesitant' statements of the magisterium. At the same time, not all initiatives on the part of the authority have been received by the faithful. John Long calls attention to the failure of church authorities in the 15th century to translate the agreements between the Eastern churches and the Latin West reached at the Council of Florence into terms intelligible to the clergy and faithful of both traditions, with the sad result that this attempt at reconciliation itself failed[58] ... . The question could also be raised as to whether or not *Humanae vitae*, Paul VI's encyclical on artificial contraception, has been genuinely received by the faithful, and thus, by implication, the question of the kind of authority the encyclical itself possesses.[59]

Reception also involves formal decisions on the part of those authorities who represent and serve the unity of the Church. In the classical model of reception the bishop symbolised the link between the local church and the universal Church by participating in conciliar gatherings. Sometimes it was the role of the bishops in council to initiate a process of reception through formal conciliar decisions. The creed proclaimed by the First Council of Nicaea is an obvious example. For a council itself, to be ecumenical, it must be received by the bishop of Rome. Sometimes the authority of the bishops served to give formal approval to a process of reception already underway, thus bringing the process to a juridical close. For example, the practice of private, frequent confession, brought to the European Continent by the Irish missionaries in the sixth and seventh centuries, was only gradually received there, though it finally became the official and universal practice when the Fourth Lateran Council

---

56. [Yves Congar, 'Reception as an Ecclesiological Reality', in *Election and Consensus in the Church*, Giuseppe Alberigo and Anton Weiler (eds), *Concilium*, 77, New York, Herder and Herder, 1972, 46–7. See reading 5.6 of this present chapter.]

57. Willebrands, 'The Ecumenical Dialogue', 5, 6.

58. Long, John, 'Reception: Ecumenical Dialogue at a Turning Point', *Ecumenical Trends*, 12 (1983) 19–20 ... .

59. See Komonchak, Joseph, '*Humane Vitae* and Its Reception: Ecclesiological Reflections', *Theological Studies*, 39 (1978) 221–57.

(1215) decreed that every Christian who committed a serious sin should confess it within a year.

Therefore church authorities have a role to play in the process of reception, but they do not carry out that role simply by making juridical decisions. Their role is to articulate what is the faith of the Church. Even the dogma of infallibility is essentially a statement about the Church, not about the pope, or pope and the bishops, apart from the church. The statement in *Pastor aeternus* at Vatican I that solemn definitions of the pope are 'irreformable of themselves (*ex sese*) and not from the consent of the Church',[60] means only that papal teachings are not dependent on subsequent approval by national hierarchies, as the Gallican view maintained. In saying that 'the Roman Pontiff ... is possessed of that infallibility with which the Divine Redeemer willed that the Church should be endowed', the Council was pointing to how the Church's infallibility comes to expression.[61] Vatican II clarified the teaching of Vatican I by including the college of bishops in the exercise of the Church's charism of infallibility, at the same time pointing out that to 'the resulting definitions the assent of the whole Church can never be wanting, on account of the activity of the same Holy Spirit, whereby the whole flock of Christ is preserved and progresses in unity of faith'.[62]

Reception cannot be reduced to the acceptance of doctrinal formulations; it involves the recognition and acceptance of a common faith. Forms of worship, life, and practice emerge out of a living tradition which bears the faith experience of a community. To accept a liturgical practice from another community is to acknowledge a shared faith which comes to expression through a ritual.

The same holds true for doctrinal formulations. When the representatives of churches in dialogue are able to arrive at a statement of consensus or agreement on those issues which have previously divided them, the completion of the dialogue process represents more than the mutual acceptance of a linguistic formula; it also implies the recognition of a common faith. That common faith is often expressed differently in the various Christian traditions, and no particular expression, no matter how true, completely captures the reality with which it is concerned. There will always be a diversity of expression. But when a consensus based on a common language is reached, the dialogue partners are beginning to discover each other in sharing the same faith.

The process of reception has already begun when two churches, in spite of their separate histories, commit themselves to the search for unity by entering into dialogue. Such a commitment implies not just a willingness to trust each other, but also the recognition of the dialogue partner as a community of Christians also living a Christian life. Furthermore, entering into dialogue commits each church to re-examine its own tradition and ecclesial life in the light of Scripture and the dialogue itself.

The norm for recognising a common faith is not agreement with one's own ecclesial position but agreement with the apostolic tradition. In his study Kilmartin singles out the work of Herman Josef Sieben as the best description of the relationship between reception and the authority of ecumenical councils, formulated as *consensio antiquitatis et universitatis*

---

60. DS, 3074.
61. Ibid.
62. *Lumen Gentium*, no. 25 ... .

grounded in the work of the Holy Spirit.[63] The *consensio universitatis* represented the 'horizontal consensus' of the whole Church which the council had to express and which had to be secured by reception. But the *consensio antiquitatis*, the 'vertical consensus' with the teaching of the Scripture and the apostolic tradition, had to be demonstrated by the council and tested by the whole Church. Of the two, Kilmartin argues, the vertical consensus, which includes the element of formal authority, has priority and 'is ultimately decisive because the truth of faith is, from its essence, a truth handed on'.[64] In other words, in receiving the teaching of a council an individual church was acknowledging that its own life of faith received from the apostolic tradition could be expressed by the conciliar decision.

J.M.R. Tillard also stresses the apostolic tradition as norm. He warns against making the term 'reception' so extensive that it loses any specific meaning. The correct approach in respect to any ecumenical accord must be found 'in subjecting it to the critical evaluation in the light of the apostolic tradition', for the essential requirement is not merely mutual understanding but rather 'a collective conversion to the claims of the apostolic faith *as such*'.[65] Tillard suggests several practical considerations for those willing to implement reception with the conversion it implies. First, they should beware of accepting only what is already included in their own tradition. Second, there must be a willingness to inquire if an ecclesial element present in another tradition and absent from one's own – even if one's own tradition dates from the earliest Christian centuries – is not a deficiency.[66] Finally, in the case of one tradition lacking something strongly present in another, the question must be asked: 'Does this lack arise from a denial of the point at issue, or from an alternative and valid interpretation which also has its roots in the great apostolic tradition?'[67]

RECEPTION TODAY

Agreed statements formulated by theologians are important steps on the road to a future communion between the sponsoring churches. But the statements by themselves will not be able to bring the churches together. The real breakthrough will only be realised when the people of God in different churches begin to discover for themselves that the consensus formulated reflects a common faith. When Christians from different traditions begin to experience each other's faith experience as their own, they will begin to experience communion. How can this process of reception today be facilitated?

1. On an educational level, the results of the dialogue must enter into the practical life of the churches. Liturgies should incorporate the consensus emerging on baptism and Eucharist. A particular tradition might have to reconsider the importance of the eucharistic epiklesis;

---

63. Kilmartin, 'Reception in History', 48–50; Sieben, Herman Josef, *Die Konzilsidee der alten Kirche*, Paderbohn, Schöningh, 1979, 511–16.
64. Kilmartin, 'Reception in History', 50 … .
65. Tillard, J.M.R.: '"Reception": A Time to Beware of False Steps', in *Ecumenical Trends*, 14 (1985), 145; Tillard's emphasis.
66. Ibid., 146–7.
67. Ibid., 148.

another might have to express more clearly the importance of personal belief in baptism. Catechisms should be updated to include the agreement reached through the dialogues. It will be interesting to see if the new Roman Catholic Catechism recommended by the 1985 extraordinary Synod of Bishops incorporates this ecumenical convergence.

2. The most effective way for Christians from different traditions to discover a common faith is through living and worshipping together. This is certainly the experience of those who have lived in ecumenical communities. The Third World Conference on Faith and Order (Lund, 1952) proposed as principle that the churches 'act together in all matters except those in which deep differences of conviction compel them to act separately'.[68] More recently; in responding to the Final Report, the Catholic bishops of England and Wales have made a similar affirmation:

> We wish to endorse, in particular, the spirit of the last sentence of the *Final Report*: 'We suggest that some difficulties will not be wholly resolved until a practical initiative has been taken and our two Churches have lived together more visibly in one *koinonia*.' It is widespread experience of many people in our countries that the work of ecumenism must be carried out at all levels and in all dimensions of Church life. Doctrinal discussions alone are not sufficient.[69]

Yet, too often the very thought of Christians from different traditions living and worshipping together is resisted; for it raises for many the issue of intercommunion, with its attendant difficulties and painfulness. A process of reception already underway has led to progress in this area; interim sharing of the Eucharist has been authorised for Episcopalians and some Lutherans on the basis of the dialogue between the episcopal Church in the United States and three Lutheran churches (the American Lutheran Church, the Association of Evangelical Lutheran Churches, and the Lutheran Church in America). Short of intercommunion – which presupposes an experience of koinonia – there are many areas in which local parishes can begin to co-operate by pooling their resources. Before talking about common worship, common schools, or common plants, neighbouring parishes might at least consider a joint vacation school or social-outreach programme.

A special case is presented by those Christians who have lived in ecumenical communities; their experience needs to be taken into consideration. If it is true that reception involves not just church authorities but the entire People of God, the question must be raised as to what it means when Christians from different traditions – Roman Catholics among them – are able to recognise the Lord's presence in one another's celebrations of the Eucharist, even though their church leaders have yet to acknowledge this. Is it not simply a fact that today many Christians would not raise questions about the 'validity' of Eucharistic celebrations in other churches unless the traditional difficulties were pointed out to them? Local church authorities should consider and weigh carefully the experience of their people, particularly those who have lived in ecumenical communities, not as an instance of the collapse of discipline but as part of the process of reception.

---

68. *The Third World Conference on Faith and Order, August 15-28, 1951*, Oliver Tomkins (ed.), London, SCM, 1953, 16.
69. *One in Christ*, 21 (1985), 179–80.

3. Local churches should themselves enter into the process of reception. An important precedent was set for the Roman Catholic Church, when, thanks to the Secretariat for Promoting of Christian Unity, the process of responding to *BEM* and the Final Report was broadened beyond the Church's central administration in Rome so that national episcopal conferences and ultimately local churches could also take part. The local Catholic churches throughout the world (or English-speaking churches in the case of the Final Report) for the first time are able to become involved in the process of reception. As of June 1986 in the United States, out of some 180 dioceses and archdioceses, only 21 had submitted reactions to *BEM* and eight to the Final Report. Certainly not an overwhelming response.

Often the objection is raised that the resources are lacking; the local church does not have the experts, theologians, seminaries, or institutes needed to formulate a response to an ecumenical text such as *BEM* or the Final Report. But that is to leave ecumenism in the hands of the specialists and runs the risk of reducing reception to the acceptance of doctrinal formulations. Local churches need to develop their own ways of responding, using the resources and structures available. A first step might be to conduct a series of hearings, listening to those involved in ecumenical encounters at university campus-ministry centres, retreat houses, ecumenical communities, the various renewal movements, and other activities in which Christians from different churches are engaged. The current hearings being conducted by the Catholic Church in the United States on the issue of women in the Church could serve as a model. Ecumenical groups might reflect together on a statement during a particular liturgical season such as Lent or Advent or at a weekend retreat. The local ecumenical commission could prepare a written response incorporating the experience of the people in the local church as well as theological reflection on the document itself.

4. Finally, churches at the national or regional level should begin to respond to ecumenical initiatives in a way that goes beyond offering theological reactions to the dialogue statements. One hopeful sign for such a step forward appears at the end of the National Conference of Catholic Bishops' [NCCB] evaluation of the Final Report in what appears to be a recommendation for a joint synod of Roman Catholic and Anglican bishops. The NCCB evaluation concludes: 'Looking ahead to the future, we hope that ARCIC II will be asked to prepare its conclusions for a session of the Synod of Bishops with Anglican input and *representation*.'[70]

It is unfortunate that today more energy seems to go into the preservation of confessional or doctrinal identity than into building on the ecumenical progress that has already been achieved. The ecumenical dialogues have displayed substantial areas of agreement. They need to be received, but this demands more than a juridical decision on the part of church authorities. If the concept of reception originally presumed an ecclesiology of communion, then it is essential today that local and regional churches themselves become involved in the reception process.

---

70. 'Evaluation of the Final Report', *Ecumenical Trends*, 14 (1985), 23 [Rausch's emphasis].

5.9 LADISLAS ORSY: *PARTICIPATION AND THE NATURE OF THE CHURCH* – 1988

We include this article[71] for the obvious reason that the *sensus fidelium* is bound up with the broader theme of participation in the life of the church, not least of all where this life touches doctrine. At the same time we relate *reception* to both the topics of *synodality* and *collegiality*. For Orsy, the notion of *participation* in all aspects of the life of the church is an integral part of our ecclesial heritage and should not be confused with any notion of introducing political models of democracy into the church. Yet this jewel of our rich ecclesial heritage was somehow 'lost' along the way in the historical life of the church. Orsy attempts to explore why this might be so. He views participation as a *seminal*, as opposed to a mature concept, and suggests this is cause for great hope. He illustrates how participation runs throughout the key documents of Vatican II and then argues that it is also a yearning evident throughout the whole church from the grass-roots up. He goes on to set out the *theological* case for *increased* participation today. Orsy believes there are strong cultural reasons to support his argument.

❈

The purpose of these reflections is to see whether or not the new use of universal participation in the life of the Church is in harmony with the very nature of the Church; that is, whether or not this quest for participation is a manifestation of our authentic tradition.

There is a fact which cannot be contested: a strong and universal sense of participation pervades the whole Church. But before such a movement can be accepted and be given a full scope, we must know whether it springs from the authentic sources of life, or it represents some dark forces of destruction.

As it is, the responses and reactions of the community at large are ambivalent: they range from strong approval to firm resistance. Such conflicting attitudes often lead to serious tensions in the social body of the Church.

Given this situation, the need for the study and clarification of the issue is obvious. Admittedly, a short article cannot accomplish the task. Yet, even an article, short as it must be, can indicate the direction that future investigation must take. Our purpose, therefore, is: first, to reflect on the meaning of participation, then to see how far participation belongs to, and is an expression of, the very nature of the Church, and finally, if so warranted, to indicate how it can be given its full scope in the life and work of the Church.

HOW TO UNDERSTAND THE CONCEPT OF PARTICIPATION

We do not begin by a precise definition. Rather, we lay down a claim that *participation* cannot

71. Orsy, Ladislas: 'Participation and the Nature of the Church', *Priests and People*, 2 (1988), 356–62.

be so defined because it is a *seminal concept*. But what is a seminal concept? – you may well ask. Let me explain by contrasting two types of concepts.

On the one hand, there are concepts which are developed to the point that their meaning can be expressed with a definition which has a precise content and is nearly complete. Many legal concepts are such: for instance jurisdiction, delegation, ownership, contract, and so forth.

On the other hand, there are concepts which signify an intuition which has a well identified object but as yet the process of discovery has not gone so far as to provide a detailed knowledge of its content. Many theological concepts are such: the New Testament is full with them. The specific promises of Jesus to Peter and the other apostles indicate a direction toward some hierarchical structures but they do not define such structures with any precision or completeness.

At the Second Vatican Council we find both types of concepts. On the one side in the *Constitution on the Sacred Liturgy* there are well chiselled definitions of sacraments; on the other side in the *Dogmatic Constitution on the Church* there are intuitive insights about communion, collegiality and *participation* which are far from well defined. They are seminal concepts or seminal locutions.

Once such intuitive insights have been injected by the Council into the life of the Church, it is the turn of the people (all included, even the Fathers who went home) to pick up them and develop them further. The Council perceived that such insights expressed with authenticity diverse aspects of the life of the Christian community, but it did not (it could not) go so far as to explicate them. *That* was left to all those who heard and received the proclamation and continued to ponder them in their mind and heart.

To mistake a seminal concept for a matured one is bound to lead to incorrect results. A rigid definition imposed on it in the name of, or under the pretext of, a scientific method is likely to strangle it; it impedes its development. There have been, and there are, such attempts (well meant, no doubt) even among the theologians of great repute, commentators of the Second Vatican Council. One party keeps defining collegiality in such a way that it can happen only once in a few centuries when an ecumenical council is in session; another party keeps defining it so that it happens every time when two or three get together in the name of the Lord. Once the lines are drawn, it is easy for each side to cling to its own precise formula and enter into a righteous battle – which can only be futile and fruitless. The root of the trouble is that neither of the warring parties may understand the peculiar nature of a seminal concept, or if they do, they have no patience to work and wait for its slow development. They may be forgetting that living beings cannot be handled as inanimate objects.

The correct methodological solution is to retreat from precise definitions, admit the existence of seminal concepts, and then work together for their slow maturation.

Such maturation happens in two ways – at least when we are dealing with a seminal concept which refers to the practical life of the Church. It happens through lived experience, and through a reflective process.

It was through experience that the early Church developed many of the seminal concepts found in the earliest of our written documents: the writings of the New Testament. The sacramental structure, apart from baptism and the Eucharist, was mostly hinted at in seminal events and words: such as Jesus' actions and sayings concerning the forgiveness of sins, the sanctity of marriage, the sending of the disciples, and so forth. They inspired the early Church to develop sacred signs and symbols which spoke of the sanctifying actions of the Spirit in the community.

But it was through a conceptual and reflective process that the articulation of the specific sacraments eventually developed. Critical reflections made possible the precise identification of the seven signs – no more and no less.

In the developing understanding of participation both processes must play their part. There are developments which can be known through experience only; there are developments which need strong theoretical foundations.

To accept that *participation* is a seminal concept is foundational for its understanding. It is vital also for the designing of a strategy for putting participation into practice. In introducing it we cannot follow a blueprint; we must follow an inspiration. It is like entering into the creative work of an artist: the final picture becomes known when it is there.

Whatever more we may say about participation later, it is already clear that we all must participate in the process of developing the understanding of this concept!

THE ASSUMPTIONS ON WHICH OUR REFLECTIONS ARE BUILT

No speaker can start from scratch: we all build on some assumptions. It is, therefore, fair that before we delve more deeply into the issue of participation, I should give an account of my own assumptions. They determine to an extent what I am going to say.

1   The Church is an historical reality; it is embedded in the history of the human family. Now, history means changes. Yet, we believe that in the Church there is a permanent core which endures in the midst of all changes. In it the Word of God is preserved, in it the sources of grace are ever fresh. Beyond that permanent core, however, many structures and policies can and at times must change. The distinction between what is constant (by the strength of the Holy Spirit) and what is variable (by divine help and human ingenuity) is of the greatest importance. To disregard it may lead either to an attempt to destroy a divine gift, or to the strangling of a needed development. Clearly, while the seminal concept of participation is being put into practice, this distinction must be kept in mind.

2   Today our Church is undergoing a very deep transformation; not in the permanent core, but nearly everywhere else. It is a rapidly developing social body. It follows that participation can be understood correctly only in relation to an evolving and changing community; not in relation to a somewhat ossified static body.

3   There is turbulence in the life of the Church today; not unlike a turbulence which arises when two rapid currents rushing down from the mountains meet on the plain. There is an ideological current which originated in the immediate post-Reformation period and has been nourished ever since until recently, and there is another one which represents trends originating in the early centuries, but somewhat forgotten later and now revived by the Second Vatican Council's instruction to go back to our earliest traditions. Participation belongs firmly to the older current.

4   No matter how thorough our investigations may be, no matter how close to the truth we may come, we must be aware that the *full truth* is likely to elude us. We shall be able

only to approximate to it. This should make us humble, but it should make us also suspicious of any claim that others may advance saying that they know the final answer. Undoubtedly, concerning certain articles of faith, the Church has come into permanent possession of the truth, but no one has been granted in all things the final revelation of the full truth. John quotes the Lord: 'When the Spirit of truth comes, he will guide you into all truth' (16:13). This 'being guided into all truth' is still going on.

WHAT IS THE SOURCE OF THIS NEW SENSE OF UNIVERSAL PARTICIPATION?

Why the question? Because we have to decide whether or not this sense of participation is authentic. For this we have to determine its sources.

After all, it could be a mere aberration inspired by secular politics, unsuitable for the Church. We never cease to hear about the power of the people; so it could be an attempt to apply an otherwise sound political principle to the Church – which is not a political body but God's mysterious gift to mankind.

But it could be also a manifestation of the very nature of the Church, which is an *ecclesia*, 'an assembly duly summoned', a *gathering* of the believers. In other terms, the Church is an organic body, and if so participation can be nothing else than the members of the body coming alive and fulfilling their functions.

Indeed the immediate prompting of this new sense of participation comes from an eminently theological source: from the Second Vatican Council.

The *Dogmatic Constitution on the Church* in its Second Chapter describes the Church as the one and undivided people of God; all belong to it by equal right. From such a solemn proclamation the need for participation follows logically; and the desire for it in the same people comes quite naturally.

The Third Chapter on the hierarchy makes it clear that the supreme power in the Church is a shared power; it is with a college in which all bishops participate, with the bishop of Rome presiding over them.

The Fourth Chapter on the laity asserts clearly that the laity has the right to participate in the apostolic work of the Church: 'The lay apostolate, however, is a participation in the saving mission of the Church itself. Through their baptism and confirmation, all are commissioned to that apostolate by the Lord himself' (§ 33).

Further, the *Declaration on Religious Freedom* is a great charter on the dignity of the human person. This dignity cannot be effectively honoured unless an opportunity is given to the faithful (human persons!) to contribute effectively to the life of the Church.

Now that we have made it clear that the primary source for this new sense of participation is theological, it is fair to add that some inspiration toward it has come also from modern social and political developments.

The doctrine of the Reformers about the unique authority of the conscience eventually led to a greater appreciation of the value of human persons, which in its turn helped the creation of various types of political democracy, setting a pattern for participation in the civic life of the community.

Moreover, there has been great progress in universal education, which produced a better informed citizenry with a new habit of critical thinking. Clearly, the faithful did not wish to leave behind such advances in their relationship to the Church. They realised quickly that they have much to contribute to its life and work.

Thus, we can conclude that the primary source of this new sense of participation is theological; not excluding however other sources of human development.

THE MANY FACETS OF PARTICIPATION

Participation has many facets; it can operate throughout the Church on different levels.

The laity wish to participate in the life of the parish by being members of the parish council – provided the council is not mere formality but takes significant decisions concerning the life of the parish. After all, if they have the mandate to proclaim the Good News, they must have the mandate to have some initiatives as well about apostolic activities. They remember Paul's description of the many gifts in a community: wisdom, knowledge, faith, ability to heal, power to work miracles, prophecy, discernment of spirits, tongues and interpretation of tongues. They wonder what a variety of gifts would emerge in their community if the opportunity were there.

The diocesan clergy wish to participate more intensely in the pastoral work of the bishops, in the formulating of policies and in the making of decisions. They remember the times when the bishop and his *presbyterium* together shepherded the people with one mind and one heart. Besides, how could the bishop be the principle of unity in the diocese if he does not have a strong and practical bond with his own clergy?

The bishops wish to have a larger share in the solicitude for all the churches. The Second Vatican Council reminded them that such a solicitude is part of their office. Moreover, they too remember the various forms of synodal government in the early centuries. If the apostolic college is the prototype of the episcopal college, the successor of Peter is certainly the leader, but not without the successors of the other apostles around him, following him, supporting him, occasionally even correcting him (as Paul did it to Peter) – all being at the same time united in the proclamation of the message.

Women want to have a greater share in the overall life of the Church. They are reminding us of the evangelical gifts granted to women: they were given the strength to stand by the cross and they were chosen to carry the good news of resurrection to the apostles.

Magisters in sacred theology desire to co-operate more closely with the hierarchy in the process of reflecting on the word of God, recalling how much the achievement of the Second Vatican Council was due to the service of theologians. They know also that some of the greatest Doctors of the Church were not part of the hierarchy but humble teachers in schools of theology.

The list could go on. Young persons want to share their enthusiasm and their creative talents with their elders. Old people want to help with their accumulated wisdom and experience. Without exaggeration it could be said that many of the faithful are willing and ready to accept greater responsibility in building the body of Christ that is the Church.

It is conceivable that the Spirit of God is moving them no less than he moved the members of the Church of Corinth to utter wisdom, to display knowledge, to proclaim the faith, or to speak in tongues. Is this new sense of participation a manifestation of the same Spirit who creates and sustains the Church in all ages?

If Rabbi Gamaliel were here, he would certainly counsel us caution about any condemnation. If this new sense of participation does not come from God it will evaporate anyway, if it does, no human power will be able to resist it.

RICH AND UNUSED SOURCES OF ENERGY

It could be argued that much of this inspiration to participate in the life of the Church springs and flows from rich and unused sources of energy. Energy in God's assembly (that the Church is) means a gift from God granted to individuals or to groups for the 'edification', that is, for the building up of the community of the believers. Throughout the history of the Church, a variety of gifts has indeed been given to lay persons, to presbyters, to bishops, prompting them to enrich the community – as the members of the Corinthian assembly did.

The nature of energy, of any energy, however, is such that if it is not channelled for good use it can become restless, and even turn into a destructive force. As a matter of fact, we have a great deal of restlessness in the Church. Thus, the question comes quite logically: is this restlessness caused by unused and dissipating energies which we could put to better use by judicious participation?

PARTICIPATION IS COMMUNION

Much of the opposition to participation probably comes from a misconception that identifies it with the model of political democracy where votes are counted and the winner gets all. Nothing is further from truth.

To use a simple image: participation means that the whole body is alive and active; the members 'have the same care for one another' – as Paul urged the Corinthians (cf. 1 Cor. 12). This 'care' means to reach a common judgement about how the good of the whole can be best served, and to come to a common decision as to what to do about it. To accept this process is not to exclude the specific role of the head, neither is it to exclude the indispensable play of the limbs. The progress toward being of one mind and of one heart requires a radically different process from the one used in political democracies; it is process which was well used in the Church of the early centuries but which is much less known or practised today. An example can illustrate our lack of perception: when a diocesan pastoral council insists that the bishop must not disregard a proposition voted in by a majority, or, when the bishop stresses he has the right to reject anything approved by the council, each is thinking on the model of a political process. The Christian truth is that neither side has understood the ways and means of communion.

Of course, we all can get tired of long discussions – the practical drawback from the practice of participation – but we have to remember that we have little experience in these matters. It will take some time for all of us to handle participation expeditiously.

At this point the question may come into the mind: if participation is so much part of our ecclesiastical heritage, why have we lost it? What happened?

HISTORICAL DEVELOPMENTS WHICH REDUCED PARTICIPATION

My aim is not to write the history of a long and complex process but to single out two historical trends which undoubtedly contributed to the loss of the sense and the practice of participation.

The shift in emphasis from the sacrament of baptism to that of orders. The early Christian communities saw baptism as the greatest among the sacraments: they accorded the highest honours to the newly baptised. External symbols spoke of their dignity: they were dressed in white robes, they were granted a special place in the gatherings of the community. Prayer for them dominated – and still dominates – the Easter liturgy. But later the balance shifted. Baptism became commonplace, and orders emerged as conferring the highest dignity. Baptism was taken for granted, after all no major theological debates developed around it. The sacrament of order in its various forms became the centre of attention and debates. The symbolism began to focus on the person who had orders: in titles, in dress, in life style, and so forth.

Now, symbols used by a community are also teachers of that community. The daily message that went out spoke highly of the dignity of the ordained; it said little of the dignity of the baptised. The result was that gradually a conception developed that the Church principally consisted of the clergy; all the others had a merely passive role to play.

The process of centralisation which developed after the Reformation. In order to preserve its unity in doctrine and discipline, from the sixteenth century onwards, the Church developed a new style of life, away from the great intellectual debates of the Middle Ages, away from the plurality of customs. More and more power became vested in the newly created offices of the Holy See. Whenever there was a doubt about a point of doctrine, they alone had the right to clarify it. Whenever there was a case of dispute about the rights and wrongs, they alone were the judges. Furthermore, this new trend received re-enforcement from a new definition of law, construed in the schools.

Law was not conceived any more as an expression of reason bringing order into the life of the community (in harmony with the Aristotelian and Thomistic tradition), but the manifestation of the will of the legislator (according to a subtle nominalistic trend among Christian philosophers). If there was any doubt, recourse to reason was out of place, the legislator had to be consulted. Thus he became the supreme arbiter of all laws. Moreover, a tendency developed to handle doctrinal problems in a similar way. If there was any doubt, research in the sources was not needed, there was a competent authority to resolve it. A new habit was built up in the whole Church: to turn to a Roman office with appropriate jurisdiction for the resolution of a theological issue. One can see that in such an environment, there was little possibility for participation on any level.

THEOLOGICAL REASONS FOR THE INCREASED PRACTICE OF PARTICIPATION

1   *To be baptised into the Christian communion is to be baptised into participation.* We usually conceive baptism as an individual act: the person becomes an adoptive child of God. But that is a one-sided description. The newly baptised becomes a member of a body. Like any member it cannot exist outside of the body, but the body cannot exist without the members either. Every new member brings new balance into the body with its own qualities which are irreplaceable – they do not exist anywhere else. Hence, without participation the body is not whole; the body does not have its integrity.

2   *When a person is confirmed he or she receives the Holy Spirit not only for the sake of personal sanctification but for the building of the Church, which undoubtedly means some kind of participation in the life and work of the community.* The theology behind this statement is that the Holy Spirit was poured out on the disciples as the final act of creation of the Church. In the sacrament of confirmation, when a person receives the Holy Spirit, the Church is re-created by the divine strengthening of that member. Clearly, such incorporation postulates also participation.

3   *To celebrate the Eucharist is to participate in the living and active body of Christ;* it is not simply an individual devotional act. Someone received into the body of Christ cannot be a stranger to the sacred activities of the body. It is interesting how strongly Paul insists that at the table of the Lord there are no differences: 'We were all baptised into one body – Jews and Greek, slaves and free – and all were made to drink of one Spirit' (1 Cor 12:13). This oneness at the table would be ineffective if it did not overflow into oneness in action, which can hardly exist without participation.

4   *The ordination of a bishop was traditionally understood as the reception of a person into a college.* The instances to show this mentality are many. From earliest times the ordination of a new bishop had to be done by all the bishops of the province, or at least by three of them. In Gratian's *Decretum* (about 1140) the rule is stated that the election of a candidate for a vacant see should be done by the bishops of the province in which that see is located.

In a more general way, Christian history is full of instances of participation at so many levels. One cannot do more here than simply quote some telling facts, enough to show that we are not advocating some strange novelty: in one way or another lay persons participated in the celebration of most ecumenical councils, either by convoking them, or by being part of them with full deliberative vote; over long periods and in many places the laity had a voice in the election of bishops; in the early centuries the bishops governed their dioceses in full union with the clergy; in various regions patriarchs and metropolitans consistently practised a synodal form of government, in fact the institution of the college of cardinals grew out of such a custom; and finally the emergence of ecumenical councils is nothing else than the full development of synodal structures at the highest level. (The Second Vatican Council made it clear that the episcopal college can operate with full power even without calling a council into session – meaning they can participate *even in ordinary circumstances* in the full supreme and universal power to govern.)

RECENT CULTURAL DEVELOPMENTS FACILITATING PARTICIPATION

The rising of the level of education among the laity. Right from the fourth century (when for the first time the Church became a public corporation) until modern times, intellectual education was not the lot of the common people. The clergy fared better, especially the higher clergy. (This is not to say, of course, that all the clergy were always well educated.) Yet, by and large, they were the learned ones; the common people needed to be taught. Such a situation postulated its own style of ecclesiastical government: benevolent, ready to instruct, unwilling to listen to the ignorant. This situation began to change at a dramatic rate in the second half of the nineteenth century, and has kept changing ever since. By now, in some countries at least, the standard of education has reached a level never known before. Clearly, there is a need for a new style of government where those who now exercise power (which is not denied) over those who are intellectually no less competent and as a matter of fact may not be less learned either. Intense participation may be a part of this new style.

In several countries, including the United States, the Church enjoys an unprecedented freedom. It is the first time since its foundation that the Church in some parts of the world suffers no oppression, is not tangled with the secular powers and owes nothing to anybody by way of some worldly alliance.

Historically, in the first three centuries the Church suffered an ongoing oppression and periodical persecutions. From the fourth century it entered into an alliance with the state (various states), which still continues in several countries. This participation of the secular power in the life and the work of the Church genuinely impeded the participation of the faithful; in several countries civil authorities had extensive powers in the nomination of bishops, in the administration of church property, in educational matters. With the doctrine of the separation of Church and State, a radically different situation has emerged. The Church is perfectly free – it does not receive any support from the secular power. The faithful can now be invited to take a larger share in the life of their community … .

By expanding participation, our modern Church is entering into a new era. It has to build up a 'new habit of mind' – an expression that was dear to Paul VI. It has to construe new policies. This means that it must abandon centuries old (from four to eight centuries old) modes of thinking and ways of acting … .

QUESTIONS FOR DISCUSSION

1   What is the relationship between the life of pastoral councils and priestly councils and the bishops' conferences? Rarely, it seems, what lives 'from below' is received 'above', notwithstanding the fact that we claim the Spirit is everywhere at work.

2   To what extent does the church listen to the experience of renewal in religious orders and new movements? Often the members of these creative groups read the 'signs of the times' much earlier than other elements of the 'institutional' church, thanks to their attentiveness to what takes shape in the community of the faithful.

3   How might we discern and develop new ways for receiving the creativity of other churches in the Roman Catholic church?

4   How far are councils and bishops' conferences taking into account the lives of those in the wider community, beyond the confines of the formal ecclesia? Indeed, do we not believe that the Spirit is also at work in such places?

5   Too often the reflection on the *sensus fidelium* is limited to the male part of the believing community. In many parts of the church the voices of women are not taken into account, bishops and the majority of teaching theologians being male. Why might this be so and how can it be overcome?

6   The dialogue between the sciences and faith has become a crucial one. Seldom do church leaders enter into a frank dialogue with believing scientists. In a period of historical acceleration this leads often to a 'schizophrenic' situation, whereby the church fails to answer pressing questions. What possible solutions are there to this predicament?

7   Why do you think are there so many differing interpretations of the *sensus fidelium* and reception in the church?

8   In terms both of church governance and in a practical sense, at every ecclesial level from the grass roots up, how can greater participation be encouraged throughout the whole church?

9   How can the church move further away from purely 'juridical' interpretations of fundamental concepts to a level of understanding which is more life-giving and community oriented?

10 What models of participation, consultation and reception might best help in fulfilling the aspirations inherent to each of the above questions?

FURTHER READING

DISCUSSION AND DEBATE

ARCIC II, *The Gift of Authority – Authority in the Church III*, London, CTS, 1999.

Burkhard, John, 'Sensus Fidei – Theological Reflection Since Vatican II', *The Heythrop Journal*, 34 (1993).

Butler, B.C., 'Infallible – Authenticum: Assensus, Obsequium. Christian Teaching Authority and the Christian's Response', *Doctrine and Life*, 31 (1981).

Costigan, Richard F., 'The Consensus of the Church – Differing Classic Views', *Theological Studies*, 51 (1990).

Dobbin, Edmund J., 'Sensus Fidelium reconsidered', *New Theology Review*, 2 (1989).

Dulles, Avery, 'Sensus Fidelium', *America*, 1 November 1986.

Glaser, John W., 'Authority, Connatural Knowledge and the Spontaneous Judgment of the Faithful', *Theological Studies*, 29 (1968).

Grillmeier, Alois, 'The reception of the Church Councils', in P. McShane (ed.), *Foundations of Theology*, Papers from the International Lonergan Congress, Dublin, 1971.

Komonchak, Joseph, 'Humanae Vitae and its reception', *Theological Studies*, 39 (1978).

König, Cardinal Franz, 'My vision for the Church of the future', *Tablet* (27 March 1999).

Orsy, Ladislas, 'Magisterium – Assent and Dissent', *Theological Studies*, 48 (1987).

Ruggieri, Giuseppe, 'The Rediscovery of the Church as an Evangelical Brotherhood', in *Where Does the Church Stand?*, Giuseppe Alberigo and Gustavo Gutierrez (eds), *Concilium*, (1981/6).

Rusch, W.G., *Reception. An Ecumenical Opportunity*, Geneva, Lutheran World Federation, 1988.

Sartori, Luigi, 'What is the Criterion for the Sensus Fidelium?', in *Who has the Say in the Church*, J. Moltmann and H. Küng (eds), *Concilium*, 148/8 (1981).

Scanlon, Michael J., 'Catholicism and Living Tradition – The Church as a Community of Reception', *Empowering Authority: The Charism of Episcopacy and Primacy in the Church Today*, Patrick J. Howell and Gary Chamberlain (eds), Kansas City, Sheed and Ward, 1990.

Scheffczyk, Leo, 'Sensus Fidelium – Witness on the Part of the Community', *Communio*, 15 (1988).

Thompson, William M., 'Sensus Fidelium and Infallibility', *American Ecclesiastical Review*, 167 (1973).

Tillard, Jean M.R., 'Sensus Fidelium', *One in Christ*, 11 (1975).

Tillard, Jean M.R., 'Reception–Communion', *One in Christ*, 28 (1992).

Tillard, Jean M.R., 'Tradition, Reception', in *The Quadrilog: Essays in Honor of George H. Tavard*, ed. Kenneth Hagan, Collegeville, Liturgical Press, 1994.

Van Iersel, Bas, 'Who according to the New Testament has the Say in the Church?', in *Who has the Say in the Church*, J. Moltmann and H. Küng (eds), *Concilium*, 148/8 (1981).

Vorgrimmler, Herbert, 'From Sensus Fidei to Sensus Fidelium', in *The Teaching Authority of Believers*, Johann Baptist Metz and Edward Schillebeeckx (eds), *Concilium* (1985/4).

Wolfinger, F., 'Theological Reception and Ecumenism', *Theology Digest*, 27 (1979).

Part 6:

The Role of the Theologian – Saints and Scholars

Gerard Mannion

In a broader sense, as many recent 'professional' or 'academic' theologians have been keen to emphasise, amongst the practitioners of theology are included all those human beings grasping after meaning, purpose and fulfilment in relation to the transcendent whom Christians call God. The issues prevalent in this chapter begin, however, with those involving the 'professional' theologians, though, as will become evident, official church teaching in relation to theologians has much wider-reaching implications. Throughout the history of the church, many church leaders have also been gifted and highly competent theologians, but the reverse has not always equally been the case. Specialist theologians have helped advise bishops, councils and popes down through the Christian centuries. At various times they have either set the ecclesiastical agenda or been charged with merely expounding or interpreting the teachings of powerful church figures. There have always been lay people amongst the Roman Catholic theologians but, certainly by the Middle Ages and in connection with ecclesiastical domination of educational establishments, as well as the rapid expansion of many religious orders and their influence upon schools of theology, it did come to pass that it was the norm for professional or academic theologians also to be ordained clergy or members of religious orders. With the Enlightenment and the dawn of modernity came an accompanying expansion of university education, the rise of the natural sciences and an explosion in new methods and schools of thought in both theology and philosophy. All of these posed serious challenges to the authority of the Roman Catholic church in general, and to its understanding of the nature, role and form of theology in particular.

The enlightenment had challenged dogmatism in all its forms (though, ironically, new forms of dogmatic philosophy and science would subsequently replace old forms of dogmatic theology and metaphysics). Many theologians and philosophers, particularly those of Protestant persuasions (or at least background) began to try and utilize the best aspects of these new and exciting intellectual developments in attempting to shape a theology and hence Christianity more at ease with and relevant to the emerging modern world. The major paradigm shifts brought about by Descartes' 'turn to the subject' along with Kant's revolution in epistemology and metaphysics meant that theology and philosophy could do no other than to embark upon a radical self-examination and transformation. Not least of all, critical thinking and scientific method were applied to the study of the Bible and hence biblical criticism became a thriving and increasingly expanding industry, from gradual developments in the eighteenth century onwards.

However, some Roman Catholic theologians and philosophers[1] also sought to embrace new schools of thought in order to renew their methodologies and to express the fundamentals of the Catholic faith to a new and challenging era. They sought a method to address the people of those times and in a manner to which they could more readily relate, accordingly seeking to focus upon concerns more pertinent to the day. Yet the Roman Catholic church, by the second half of the nineteenth century and the pontificate of Pius IX (pope from 1846–78), embraced dogmatism anew. This was seen in the continuation of the centralisation upon Rome begun under Gregory XVI (pope from 1831–46), the rise of ultramontanism, and the rejection of 'modernity' with its many new and seemingly revolutionary demands and principles.

The mistrust of novelty and a fear of the old orders being swept away provoked a very conservative reaction upon the parts of the central church authorities against a perceived uniform enemy in the form of 'liberalism'. Many looked to Rome to see which new theories, ideas and schools of thought could be 'safely' examined. 'Orthodoxy' was gradually being defined in stricter terms and in terms dictated by the central authorities in Rome. Additions to the *Index of Forbidden Books* and the *Syllabus Errorum* (1864) illustrated how the 'official' church wished to control what Roman Catholics could and should read, the currents of thought the church authorities believed to be erroneous and dangerous, and which tenets of modern intellectual and political life were incompatible with adherence to the Catholic faith. The First Vatican Council (1869–70) and the pronouncement of its understanding of Papal Infallibility further diminished, in the eyes of many, freedom of theological and philosophical enquiry in the church. These conservative developments had strong support throughout much of the Catholic world.

Hence many innovative and progressive Roman Catholic scholars were forced to adopt a more cautious tone in their studies or to face having their works placed on the *Index* (hence to become prohibited reading matter for most Roman Catholics) and being subsequently ostracised. For example, one of the most relatively progressive thinkers to suffer such a fate was Antonio Rosmini-Serbati (1797–1855) who (belatedly) received a qualified rehabilitation by the CDF in July, 2001. In Germany, suspicions surrounding the many innovative works of the 'Catholic Tübingen School' often resulted in the appointment of their authors to higher positions being blocked by various figures of church authority.

Nonetheless, interesting and open developments in Roman Catholic theology continued until two major factors combined to stamp a particular character upon 'official' and officially sanctioned Roman Catholic Theology. The first was the endorsement of Thomas Aquinas's thought as an official theological system of the Roman Catholic church by Leo XIII in *Aeterni Patris* (1879 – this was to eventually do a great disservice to Aquinas's reputation amongst generations of Protestant theologians, many of whom did not engage with his thought in a serious fashion, as a result). The second, and more decisive in terms of its effect upon Roman Catholic theology in the twentieth century was the so-called 'Modernist' crisis thanks to

---

1. For it is Roman Catholic theologians who have most often stressed how blurred the distinctions between these two disciplines are.

which, by the end of the first decade of that century, theology would be 'policed' in the church in a heavy-handed fashion for decades to come.

The reinvigoration of the procedures of church censorship meant that *Nihil Obstat* ('nothing stands in the way') and the *Imprimatur* ('it may be printed') became the hallmark of a work's 'orthodoxy'. This is not to say that innovative theology and philosophy, which took account of the latest intellectual and political developments and which might challenge official church teaching, ceased to be pursued by Catholic scholars. It is simply that, particularly amongst those ordained, only the more brave of their number would *publish* their work (e.g. many of Pierre Teilhard de Chardin's works were written in the 1920s and 1930s, but not published until after his death in 1955 – the Vatican having actually prohibited him from publishing anything outside the realm of science).

By the 1940s and 1950s, although the official church was making some encouraging noises about biblical scholarship, it was equally steadfast in its opposition to many developments in Catholic theology and philosophy, and leading thinkers again came under much suspicion, scrutiny and censure.

However, for many, the theological tide seemed to be turning beyond such control. Many scholars of the *Nouvelle Theologie* ('new theology'), so suspect in the 1940s, and other scholars (including Karl Rahner), under suspicion in the 1950s, were to become the church's most influential voices, not least of all in the effect their works and advice had upon the lead up to, discussions throughout and formation of documents resulting from Vatican II. For any, the council meant a new dawn for theology and philosophy in the Catholic church, with later church documents and the setting up of such ventures as the Theological Commission by Paul VI in 1969 further encouraging such hopes of a new theological 'spring'. So, too, did the emergence of many new theologies in response to world events (in particular the Second World War, third world poverty, global racism, discrimination and oppression) and Vatican II itself (e.g. political theology and the theologies of liberation).

Yet many opposed to how Vatican II was being interpreted and implemented throughout the church began to make their voices heard. The controversy over *Humanae Vitae* and the open 'rebellion' against the official magisterium which ensued, led to a hardening of attitudes amongst the 'conservative-minded' in positions of power in the church. Further retrogressive steps against theological dissent were to follow.

In 1972, those (most of whom could safely be defined as ecclesial 'conservatives') that wished to see Vatican II implemented in a very different fashion, set up the journal *Communio* (particularly to counter the viewpoints regularly expressed in the post-council journal, *Concilium*, established in 1965). Their number would increasingly have the ear of Paul VI and his advisers. Documents such as *Mysterium Ecclesiae* (1973, in particular reaction to Hans Küng's book, *Infallible*, of 1970) were released which again sought to set definite limits to theological and philosophical enquiry in the church. Investigations were instigated once more against leading and progressive theologians and whole schools of theology, most notably the theology of liberation (which would be investigated throughout the 1970s and 1980s), but also theologians who advocated further reforms in the church and new formulations and interpretations of key doctrines. The election of John Paul II in 1978 and his appointment of the once-progressive Joseph Ratzinger as Prefect of the Congregation for the Doctrine of Faith in 1981, further marked a definite decline, in the view of many, in the hopeful and embracing dialogue between the church and the world which Vatican II had initiated.

Documents were increasingly released by the official church, most often at the behest of the CDF, which once again sought to assert the clear and absolute authority of the magisterium, papacy and institutional church, itself, in matters of faith and morals (even, on many occasions, in matters beyond these parameters). The lines of orthodoxy were being drawn more rigidly once again and theologians were expected to give their faithful assent and obedient service to the church's teaching. Many scholars believed the very definition of the magisterium and/or of its remit were being rewritten here. Documents came out which sought to define what was legitimate and permissible enquiry for scholars and what was not. Much debate surrounded the theological interpretation of the so-called 'non-definitive' magisterium.

Dissent was not tolerated and many scholars found themselves called to account before the church authorities, following often secretive investigations of their works by curial officials. Harsh penalties, even excommunication awaited those who would not, or whose consciences *could* not allow them to retract what they had said or written which was unacceptable to the 'official church'. In 1989, a 'Profession of Faith' was released to which all lecturers and teachers in Catholic educational institutions were expected to sign up. John Paul II issued a lengthy document on the nature and role of a Catholic University (*Ex Corde Ecclesiae*, 1990). Document after document, notification after notification and investigation after investigation were issued concerning aspects of particular theologies, theological or philosophical opinion and individual scholars. Things became particularly difficult for those scholars who were ordained or religious, for the church's sanctions against them could be all the more effective. Amongst the key issues which came to preoccupy the institutional church's concerns were the theology of liberation (again), religious pluralism, the very notion of dissent to the magisterium, advocating or even discussing the ordination of women, and challenging church teaching on issues such as the objective existence of hell, papal infallibility, the interpretation of the incarnation, the hierarchical element of the church, the priority of the universal over the local church and, of course, sexual ethics.

To name but a few of those scholars who fell foul of such developments and suffered, to varying degrees as a consequence, we mention Karl Rahner, Hans Küng, Edward Schillebeeckx, Leonardo Boff, Tissa Balasuriya, Aloysius Pieris, Paul Collins, Lavinia Byrne, Jacques Dupuis, Roger Haight and countless others. Although the procedures of investigation and discipline were modified in the 1997 *Ratio Agendi*, this did not result in any noticeable let up in the number of investigations, nor in the inhuman manner and severity of much of the treatment received by such individuals.

Our extracts deal with issues related to those considered above and many other questions. Perhaps one question most of all draws them together: whence – ultimately – do theology and the theologian derive their authority? This is a central issue facing Roman Catholic theology today. Does theology have authority only when it is totally or broadly in step with official church teaching and/or when it has the approval of the magisterium, as many church documents appear to argue? And, following from this question, what of differing interpretations concerning what *constitutes* the magisterium or its competence/remit itself? Is there such a thing as 'loyal dissent' or 'creative fidelity'?

Saints *and* scholars: many theologians have aspired towards both holiness and fine professionalism, expertise and competence in their field. It is all the more sad, then, that amongst the number of those investigated and disciplined by the institutional church authorities are those who could be deemed to be such 'saints' *and* scholars: those devoted to a life of holiness and service to the church and theology alike. As Edward Schillebeeckx once said, the harshest treatment seems to be reserved for those who give the *most* to the church.

To be sure, some theologians have used their work to damage the church community or attack the very notion of the church itself. Others, and increasingly in the so-called 'developed' Euro-American world, merely see their membership of the theological community as a career and stepping stone to further personal advancement and comfort. One does not have to be a saint to be a theologian, but surely theologians who lay claim to the title of '*Christian* theologian', must aspire towards the life of holiness which Christianity is all about if their work is to have any authority. Hence there are both pastoral and political (i.e. pertaining to the *polis*, the community) duties and responsibilities for all Christian theologians. All too often in the postmodern world this is forgotten, ignored and crushed under the weight of the blinding arrogance and privilege of bourgeois theology in that so-called 'developed world'. The plank must be removed from one's own eye before one may see clearly enough to point out the splinter in the eye of another.

Indeed, if theology is, with any credibility, justification and, most of all *moral* authority to challenge a world or a church which does not always live up to its potential, principles or duties, then theologians who call themselves Christian must, as the gospel teaches us so definitively, put their theology into *practice*. Theology which has no practical outcome is not really theology at all. That practical outcome may take a multitude of forms. Amongst them, of course, must sometimes be the challenging of church authorities when theologians think they must. Their craft could not teach them otherwise.[2]

---

2. In addition to the texts included below, see, also, *Dei Verbum*, especially nos 7–10, 23–4. Some extracts can be found in Chapter 7 of the present volume.

6.1 PASCENDI DOMINICI GREGIS – 1907

'Catholic Modernism' is the name which describes the attitude of those who, towards the end of the nineteenth and beginning of the twentieth centuries, sought to embrace intellectual, scientific and political developments in the modern world, believing them to be compatible with faithful adherence to Roman Catholic Christianity. Pius X's encyclical 'On the Doctrine of the Modernists' is the singlemost document which marked a severe clampdown by the central Roman Catholic authorities on intellectual, in particular theological, enquiry and elements of 'liberalism' within the church. It followed the earlier *Lamentabili* (1907), a decree which condemned many viewpoints associated with modernism. Of course no such 'modernist movement' existed, in any concrete sense. Modernism could only be described as a movement in a *dynamic*, rather than a *collective* sense. In other words, 'movement' is only accurate in describing *what* was happening, namely the attitude of certain individuals towards their contemporary world led to a motivation towards action concerning greater reconciliation between that world and the Roman Catholic faith. The first 43 sections of this encyclical (penned by the ultra-conservative Joseph Lemius) actually brought together a whole range of opinions and viewpoints culled from a disparate array of thinkers and writings deemed to be suspect by the church. But this was the era when attacking 'straw men' was in vogue: one induced support for one's own position by exaggerating or even inventing an exact antithesis of that viewpoint, which thus provided an excellent backdrop and sounding board against which to present the reasonableness of one's own standpoint. In the main, the document attacks grossly caricaturized elements of the writings of Alfred Loisy (1857–1940) and the protestant theologian Auguste Sabatier (1839–1901), and champions an 'integralist' view of Catholic doctrine, i.e., the church's teaching constitutes a logical and harmonious whole which must be assented to by all the faithful without deviation. It portrays modernism as agnosticism and immanentism (seeing the origins of religious truth in humanity's needs). It further criticized elements of biblical scholarship and apologetics linked with the 'movement'. Our extract[3] sets out the chilling disciplinary procedures set in place by the encyclical to root out all aspects of modernism in the church. All suspect persons were henceforth banned from positions of authority and teaching in the church. Its provisions were to be policed by 'committees of vigilance' in every diocese. It was followed, in 1910, by an anti-modernist oath (in the letter *Sacrorum Antistitum*), designed to elicit unswerving clerical allegiance to the magisterium, and not rescinded until 1967. Loisy was excommunicated in 1908 and, although the fervour of the anti-modernist witch-hunts subsided somewhat with the death of Pius X, theologians would be forced to work under the constant, excessive and suspicious scrutiny for a further 50 years. Some believe the more negative elements of this 'policing of theological enquiry' have been increasingly revived since the early 1970s.

❋

I THE STUDY OF SCHOLASTIC PHILOSOPHY

In the first place, with regard to studies, We will and ordain that scholastic philosophy be made the basis of the sacred sciences. It goes without saying that *if anything is met with among*

---

3. *ET* from *The Holy Father – Archives of the Holy See*, www.vatican.va/holy_father/pius_x/encyclicals/.

the scholastic doctors which may be regarded as an excess of subtlety, or which is altogether destitute of probability, We have no desire whatever to propose it for the imitation of present generations (Leo XIII. Enc. *Aeterni Patris*). And let it be clearly understood above all things that the scholastic philosophy We prescribe is that which the Angelic Doctor [Thomas Aquinas] has bequeathed to us, and We, therefore, declare that all the ordinances of Our Predecessor on this subject continue fully in force, and, as far as may be necessary, We do decree anew, and confirm, and ordain that they be by all strictly observed. In seminaries where they may have been neglected let the Bishops impose them and require their observance, and let this apply also to the Superiors of religious institutions. Further let Professors remember that they cannot set St. Thomas aside, especially in metaphysical questions, without grave detriment [45].

On this philosophical foundation the theological edifice is to be solidly raised. Promote the study of theology, Venerable Brethren, by all means in your power, so that your clerics on leaving the seminaries may admire and love it, and always find their delight in it … . We deem worthy of praise those who with full respect for tradition, the Holy Fathers, and the ecclesiastical magisterium, undertake, with well-balanced judgment and guided by Catholic principles (which is not always the case), seek to illustrate positive theology by throwing the light of true history upon it. Certainly more attention must be paid to positive theology than in the past, but this must be done without detriment to scholastic theology, and those are to be disapproved as of Modernist tendencies who exalt positive theology in such a way as to seem to despise the scholastic … [46].

II   PRACTICAL APPLICATION

All these prescriptions and those of Our Predecessor are to be borne in mind whenever there is question of choosing directors and professors for seminaries and Catholic Universities. Anybody who in any way is found to be imbued with Modernism is to be excluded without compunction from these offices, and those who already occupy them are to be withdrawn. The same policy is to be adopted towards those who favour Modernism either by extolling the Modernists or excusing their culpable conduct, by criticising scholasticism, the Holy Father, or by refusing obedience to ecclesiastical authority in any of its depositaries; and towards those who show a love of novelty in history, archaeology, biblical exegesis, and finally towards those who neglect the sacred sciences or appear to prefer to them the profane. In all this question of studies, Venerable Brethren, you cannot be too watchful or too constant, but most of all in the choice of professors, for as a rule the students are modelled after the pattern of their masters. Strong in the consciousness of your duty, act always prudently but vigorously [48].

Equal diligence and severity are to be used in examining and selecting candidates for Holy Orders. Far, far from the clergy be the love of novelty! God hates the proud and the obstinate. For the future the doctorate of theology and canon law must never be conferred on anybody who has not made the regular course of scholastic philosophy; if conferred it shall be held as null and void. The rules laid down in 1896 by the Sacred Congregation of Bishops and Regulars for the clerics, both secular and regular, of Italy concerning the frequenting of the Universities, We now decree to be extended to all nations. Clerics and priests inscribed in a Catholic Institute or University must not in the future follow in civil Universities those courses for which there are chairs in the Catholic Institutes to which they belong. If this has been permitted anywhere in the past, We ordain that it be not allowed for the future. Let the Bishops who form the Governing Board of such Catholic Institutes or Universities watch with all care that these Our commands be constantly observed [49].

III EPISCOPAL VIGILANCE OVER PUBLICATIONS

It is also the duty of the bishops to prevent writings infected with Modernism or favourable to it from being read when they have been published, and to hinder their publication when they have not. No book or paper or periodical of this kind must ever be permitted to seminarists or university students. The injury to them would be equal to that caused by immoral reading – nay, it would be greater for such writings poison Christian life at its very fount. The same decision is to be taken concerning the writings of some Catholics, who, though not badly disposed themselves but ill-instructed in theological studies and imbued with modern philosophy, strive to make this harmonize with the faith, and, as they say, to turn it to the account of the faith. The name and reputation of these authors cause them to be read without suspicion, and they are, therefore, all the more dangerous in preparing the way for Modernism [50].

   To give you some more general directions, Venerable Brethren, in a matter of such moment, We bid you do everything in your power to drive out of your dioceses, even by solemn interdict, any pernicious books that may be in circulation there. The Holy See neglects no means to put down writings of this kind, but the number of them has now grown to such an extent that it is impossible to censure them all. Hence it happens that the medicine sometimes arrives too late, for the disease has taken root during the delay. We will, therefore, that the Bishops, putting aside all fear and the prudence of the flesh, despising the outcries of the wicked, gently by all means but constantly, do each his own share of this work, remembering the injunctions of Leo XIII, in the Apostolic Constitution *Officiorum: Let the Ordinaries, acting in this also as Delegates of the Apostolic See, exert themselves to prescribe and to put out of reach of the faithful injurious books or other writings printed or circulated in their dioceses.* In this passage the Bishops, it is true, receive a right, but they have also a duty imposed on them. Let no Bishop think that he fulfils this duty by denouncing to us one or two books, while a great many others of the same kind are being published and circulated. Nor are you to be deterred by the fact that a book has obtained the *Imprimatur* elsewhere, both because this may be merely simulated, and because it may have been granted through carelessness or easiness or excessive confidence in the author as may sometimes happen in religious Orders. Besides, just as the same food does not agree equally with everybody, it may happen that a book harmless in one may, on account of the different circumstances, be hurtful in another. Should a Bishop, therefore, after having taken the advice of prudent persons, deem it right to condemn any of such books in his diocese, We not only give him ample faculty to do so but We impose it upon him as a duty to do so. Of course, it is Our wish that in such action proper regard be used, and sometimes it will suffice to restrict the prohibition to the clergy; but even in such cases it will be obligatory on Catholic booksellers not to put on sale books condemned by the Bishop. And while We are on this subject of booksellers, We wish the Bishops to see to it that they do not, through desire for gain, put on sale unsound books. It is certain that in the catalogues of some of them the books of the Modernists are not unfrequently announced with no small praise. If they refuse obedience let the Bishops have no hesitation in depriving them of the title of Catholic booksellers; so too, and with more reason, if they have the title of Episcopal booksellers, and if they have that of Pontifical, let them be denounced to the Apostolic See … [51].

IV CENSORSHIP

But it is not enough to hinder the reading and the sale of bad books – it is also necessary to prevent them from being printed. Hence let the Bishops use the utmost severity in granting permission to print. Under the rules of the Constitution *Officiorum*, many publications require the authorisation of the Ordinary, and in some dioceses it has been made the custom to have a suitable number of official censors for the examination of writings. We have the highest praise for this institution, and We not only exhort, but We order that it be extended to all dioceses. In all episcopal Curias, therefore, let censors be appointed for the revision of works intended for publication, and let the censors be chosen from both ranks of the clergy – secular and regular – men of age, knowledge and prudence who will know how to follow the golden mean in their judgments. It shall be their office to examine everything which requires permission for publication according to Articles XLI and XLII of the above-mentioned Constitution. The Censor shall give his verdict in writing. If it be favourable, the Bishop will give the permission for publication by the word *Imprimatur*, which must always be preceded by the *Nihil obstat* and the name of the Censor. In the Curia of Rome official censors shall be appointed just as elsewhere, and the appointment of them shall appertain to the Master of the Sacred Palaces, after they have been proposed to the Cardinal Vicar and accepted by the Sovereign Pontiff. It will also be the office of the Master of the Sacred Palaces to select the censor for each writing. Permission for publication will be granted by him as well as by the Cardinal Vicar or his Vicegerent, and this permission, as above prescribed, must always be preceded by the *Nihil obstat* and the name of the Censor. Only on very rare and exceptional occasions, and on the prudent decision of the bishop, shall it be possible to omit mention of the Censor. The name of the Censor shall never be made known to the authors until he shall have given a favourable decision, so that he may not have to suffer annoyance either while he is engaged in the examination of a writing or in case he should deny his approval. Censors shall never be chosen from the religious orders until the opinion of the Provincial, or in Rome of the General, has been privately obtained, and the Provincial or the General must give a conscientious account of the character, knowledge and orthodoxy of the candidate. We admonish religious superiors of their solemn duty never to allow anything to be published by any of their subjects without permission from themselves and from the Ordinary. Finally We affirm and declare that the title of Censor has no value and can never be adduced to give credit to the private opinions of the person who holds it [52].

PRIESTS AS EDITORS

Having said this much in general, We now ordain in particular a more careful observance of Article XLII of the above-mentioned Constitution *Officiorum.* It is *forbidden to secular priests, without the previous consent of the Ordinary, to undertake the direction of papers or periodicals.* This permission shall be withdrawn from any priest who makes a wrong use of it after having been admonished. With regard to priests who are *correspondents* or *collaborators* of periodicals, as it happens not unfrequently that they write matter infected with Modernism for their papers or periodicals, let the Bishops see to it that this is not permitted to happen, and, should they fail in this duty, let the Bishops make due provision with authority delegated by the Supreme Pontiff. Let there be, as far as this is possible, a special Censor for newspapers and periodicals written by Catholics. It shall be his office to read in due time each number after it has been published, and if he find anything dangerous in it let him order that it be corrected. The Bishop shall have the same right even when the Censor has seen nothing objectionable in a publication [53].

V   CONGRESSES

We have already mentioned congresses and public gatherings as among the means used by the Modernists to propagate and defend their opinions. In the future Bishops shall not permit Congresses of priests except on very rare occasions. When they do permit them it shall only be on condition that matters appertaining to the Bishops or the Apostolic See be not treated in them, and that no motions or postulates be allowed that would imply a usurpation of sacred authority, and that no mention be made in them of Modernism, presbyterianism, or laicism … [54].

VI   DIOCESAN WATCH COMMITTEES

But of what avail, Venerable Brethren, will be all Our commands and prescriptions if they be not dutifully and firmly carried out? … We decree, therefore, that in every diocese a … 'Council of Vigilance', be instituted without delay. The priests called to form part in it shall be chosen somewhat after the manner above prescribed for the Censors, and they shall meet every two months on an appointed day under the presidency of the Bishop. They shall be bound to secrecy as to their deliberations and decisions, and their function shall be as follows: They shall watch most carefully for every trace and sign of Modernism both in publications and in teaching, and, to preserve from it the clergy and the young, they shall take all prudent, prompt and efficacious measures. Let them combat novelties of words remembering the admonitions of Leo XIII. (Instruct. S.C. NN. EE. EE., 27 Jan., 1902): *It is impossible to approve in Catholic publications of a style inspired by unsound novelty which seems to deride the piety of the faithful and dwells on the introduction of a new order of Christian life, on new directions of the Church, on new aspirations of the modern soul, on a new vocation of the clergy, on a new Christian civilisation.* Language of this kind is not to be tolerated either in books or from chairs of learning. The Councils must not neglect the books treating of the pious traditions of different places or of sacred relics ... . Finally, We entrust to the Councils of Vigilance the duty of overlooking assiduously and diligently social institutions as well as writings on social questions so that they may harbour no trace of Modernism, but obey the prescriptions of the Roman Pontiffs [55].

VII   TRIENNIAL RETURNS

Lest what We have laid down thus far should fall into oblivion, We will and ordain that the Bishops of all dioceses, a year after the publication of these letters and every three years thenceforward, furnish the Holy See with a diligent and sworn report on all the prescriptions contained in them, and on the doctrines that find currency among the clergy, and especially in the seminaries and other Catholic institutions, and We impose the like obligation on the Generals of Religious Orders with regard to those under them ... [56].

6.2 *HUMANI GENERIS* – 1950

Released by Pius XII, this text, '*Of the Human Race*'[4] addressed innovations in theology, philosophy and science. Most notably it opposed academic, pastoral and ecclesial dispositions associated with the French *Nouvelle Théologie* 'movement', which sought to reintegrate certain aspects of biblical, patristic and medieval thought into Roman Catholic theology, in order to supplement the dominant neo-scholastic method prevalent since the latter stages of the nineteenth century. The encyclical also condemns theories such as evolutionary theory in science and existentialism in philosophy. In particular, the document condemns all 'dogmatic relativism' (i.e., historically relativising church dogma) and states that once a pope has issued his definitive judgement on contentious issues in theology through his encyclicals, the matter is no longer open for debate. Vatican II would later modify this interpretation of the papal teaching authority.

❀

If anyone examines the state of affairs outside the Christian fold, he will easily discover the principle trends that not a few learned men are following. Some imprudently and indiscreetly hold that evolution, which has not been fully proved even in the domain of natural sciences, explains the origin of all things, and audaciously support the monistic and pantheistic opinion that the world is in continual evolution … [5].

Such fictitious tenets of evolution which repudiate all that is absolute, firm and immutable, have paved the way for the new erroneous philosophy which, rivaling idealism, immanentism and pragmatism, has assumed the name of existentialism, since it concerns itself only with existence of individual things and neglects all consideration of their immutable essences [6].

There is also a certain historicism, which attributing value only to the events of man's life, overthrows the foundation of all truth and absolute law, both on the level of philosophical speculations and especially to Christian dogmas [7].

In all this confusion of opinion it is some consolation to Us to see former adherents of rationalism today frequently desiring to return to the fountain of divinely communicated truth, and to acknowledge and profess the word of God as contained in Sacred Scripture as the foundation of religious teaching. But at the same time it is a matter of regret that not a few of these, the more firmly they accept the word of God, so much the more do they diminish the value of human reason, and the more they exalt the authority of God the Revealer, the more severely do they spurn the teaching office of the Church, which has been instituted by Christ, Our Lord, to preserve and interpret divine revelation. This attitude is not only plainly at variance with Holy Scripture, but is shown to be false by experience also. For often those who disagree with the true Church complain openly of their disagreement in matters of dogma and thus unwillingly bear witness to the necessity of a living Teaching Authority [8].

---

4. *ET* from *The Holy Father – Archives of the Holy See*, www.vatican.va/holy_father/piux_xii/encyclicals/.

Now Catholic theologians and philosophers, whose grave duty it is to defend natural and supernatural truth and instill it in the hearts of men, cannot afford to ignore or neglect these more or less erroneous opinions. Rather they must come to understand these same theories well, both because diseases are not properly treated unless they are rightly diagnosed, and because sometimes even in these false theories a certain amount of truth is contained, and, finally, because these theories provoke more subtle discussion and evaluation of philosophical and theological truths [9].

If philosophers and theologians strive only to derive such profit from the careful examination of these doctrines, there would be no reason for any intervention by the Teaching Authority of the Church. However, although We know that Catholic teachers generally avoid these errors, it is apparent, however, that some today, as in apostolic times, desirous of novelty, and fearing to be considered ignorant of recent scientific findings, try to withdraw themselves from the sacred Teaching Authority and are accordingly in danger of gradually departing from revealed truth and of drawing others along with them into error [10].

Another danger is perceived which is all the more serious because it is more concealed beneath the mask of virtue. There are many who, deploring disagreement among men and intellectual confusion, through an imprudent zeal for souls, are urged by a great and ardent desire to do away with the barrier that divides good and honest men; these advocate an 'eirenism' according to which, by setting aside the questions which divide men, they aim not only at joining forces to repel the attacks of atheism, but also at reconciling things opposed to one another in the field of dogma. And as in former times some questioned whether the traditional apologetics of the Church did not constitute an obstacle rather than a help to the winning of souls for Christ, so today some are presumptive enough to question seriously whether theology and theological methods, such as with the approval of ecclesiastical authority are found in our schools, should not only be perfected, but also completely reformed, in order to promote the more efficacious propagation of the kingdom of Christ everywhere throughout the world among men of every culture and religious opinion [11].

Now if these only aimed at adapting ecclesiastical teaching and methods to modern conditions and requirements, through the introduction of some new explanations, there would be scarcely any reason for alarm. But some through enthusiasm for an imprudent 'eirenism' seem to consider as an obstacle to the restoration of fraternal union, things founded on the laws and principles given by Christ and likewise on institutions founded by Him, or which are the defense and support of the integrity of the faith, and the removal of which would bring about the union of all, but only to their destruction … . [12].

In theology some want to reduce to a minimum the meaning of dogmas; and to free dogma itself from terminology long established in the Church and from philosophical concepts held by Catholic teachers, to bring about a return in the explanation of Catholic doctrine to the way of speaking used in Holy Scripture and by the Fathers of the Church. They cherish the hope that when dogma is stripped of the elements which they hold to be extrinsic to divine revelation, it will compare advantageously with the dogmatic opinions of those who are separated from the unity of the Church and that in this way they will gradually arrive at a mutual assimilation of Catholic dogma with the tenets of the dissidents [14].

Moreover, they assert that when Catholic doctrine has been reduced to this condition, a way will be found to satisfy modern needs, that will permit of dogma being expressed also by the concepts of modern philosophy, whether of immanentism or idealism or existentialism or any other system. Some more audacious affirm that this can and must be done, because they hold that the mysteries of faith are never expressed by truly adequate concepts but only by approximate and ever changeable notions, in which the truth is to some extent expressed, but is necessarily distorted. Wherefore they do not consider it absurd, but altogether necessary, that theology should substitute new concepts in place of the old ones in keeping with the various philosophies which in the course of time it uses as its instruments, so that it should give human expression to divine truths in various ways which are even somewhat opposed, but still equivalent, as they say. They add that the history of dogmas consists in the reporting of the various forms in which revealed truth has been clothed, forms that have succeeded one another in accordance with the different teachings and opinions that have arisen over the course of the centuries [15].

It is evident from what We have already said, that such tentatives not only lead to what they call dogmatic relativism, but that they actually contain it. The contempt of doctrine commonly taught and of the terms in which it is expressed strongly favor it. Everyone is aware that the terminology employed in the schools and even that used by the Teaching Authority of the Church itself is capable of being perfected and polished; and we know also that the Church itself has not always used the same terms in the same way. It is also manifest that the Church cannot be bound to every system of philosophy that has existed for a short space of time. Nevertheless, the things that have been composed through common effort by Catholic teachers over the course of the centuries to bring about some understanding of dogma are certainly not based on any such weak foundation. These things are based on principles and notions deduced from a true knowledge of created things. In the process of deducing, this knowledge, like a star, gave enlightenment to the human mind through the Church. Hence it is not astonishing that some of these notions have not only been used by the Oecumenical Councils, but even sanctioned by them, so that it is wrong to depart from them [16].

Hence to neglect, or to reject, or to devalue so many and such great resources which have been conceived, expressed and perfected so often by the age-old work of men endowed with no common talent and holiness, working under the vigilant supervision of the holy magisterium and with the light and leadership of the Holy Ghost in order to state the truths of the faith ever more accurately, to do this so that these things may be replaced by conjectural notions and by some formless and unstable tenets of a new philosophy, tenets which, like the flowers of the field, are in existence today and die tomorrow; this is supreme imprudence and something that would make dogma itself a reed shaken by the wind. The contempt for terms and notions habitually used by scholastic theologians leads of itself to the weakening of what they call speculative theology, a discipline which these men consider devoid of true certitude because it is based on theological reasoning [17].

Unfortunately these advocates of novelty easily pass from despising scholastic theology to the neglect of and even contempt for the Teaching Authority of the Church itself, which gives such authoritative approval to scholastic theology. This Teaching Authority is represented by them as a hindrance to progress and an obstacle in the way of science. Some non-Catholics consider it as an unjust restraint preventing some more qualified theologians from reforming their subject. And although this sacred Office of Teacher in matters of faith and morals must be the proximate and universal criterion of truth for all theologians, since to it has been entrusted by Christ Our Lord the whole deposit of faith – Sacred Scripture and divine Tradition – to be preserved, guarded and interpreted, still the duty that is incumbent on the faithful to flee also those errors which more or less approach heresy, and accordingly 'to keep also the constitutions and decrees by which such evil opinions are proscribed and forbidden by the Holy See',[5] is sometimes as little known as if it did not exist. What is expounded in the Encyclical Letters of the Roman Pontiffs concerning the nature and constitution of the Church, is deliberately and habitually neglected by some with the idea of giving force to a certain vague notion which they profess to have found in the ancient Fathers, especially the Greeks. The Popes, they assert, do not wish to pass judgment on what is a matter of dispute among theologians, so recourse must be had to the early sources, and the recent constitutions and decrees of the Teaching Church must be explained from the writings of the ancients [18].

Although these things seem well said, still they are not free from error. It is true that Popes generally leave theologians free in those matters which are disputed in various ways by men of very high authority in this field; but history teaches that many matters that formerly were open to discussion, no longer now admit of discussion [19].

Nor must it be thought that what is expounded in Encyclical Letters does not of itself demand consent, since in writing such Letters the Popes do not exercise the supreme power of their Teaching Authority. For these matters are taught with the ordinary teaching authority, of which it is true to say: 'He who heareth you, heareth me';[6] and generally what is expounded and inculcated in Encyclical Letters already for other reasons appertains to Catholic doctrine. But if the Supreme Pontiffs in their official documents purposely pass judgment on a matter up to that time under dispute, it is obvious that that matter, according to the mind and will of the Pontiffs, cannot be any longer considered a question open to discussion among theologians [20].

It is also true that theologians must always return to the sources of divine revelation: for it belongs to them to point out how the doctrine of the living Teaching Authority is to be found either explicitly or implicitly in the Scriptures and in Tradition. Besides, each source of divinely revealed doctrine contains so many rich treasures of truth, that they can really never be exhausted. Hence it is that theology through the study of its sacred sources remains ever fresh; on the other hand, speculation which neglects a deeper search into the deposit of faith, proves sterile, as we know from experience. But for this reason even positive theology cannot be on a par with merely historical science. For, together with the sources of positive theology God has given to His Church a living Teaching Authority to elucidate and explain what is contained in the deposit of faith only obscurely and implicitly. This deposit of faith our Divine Redeemer has given for authentic interpretation not to each of the faithful, not even to theologians, but only to the Teaching Authority of the Church. But if the Church does exercise this function of teaching, as she often has through the centuries, either in the ordinary or in the extraordinary way, it is clear how false is a procedure which would attempt to explain what is clear by means of what is obscure. Indeed, the very opposite procedure must be used. Hence Our Predecessor of immortal memory, Pius IX, teaching that the most noble office of theology is to show how a doctrine defined by the Church is contained in the sources of

---

5. *CIC.*, can 1324; cfr. Conc. Vat., D.B., 1820, Cont. *De Fide cath.*, cap. 4, *De Fide et ratione*, post canones.
6. Luke, 10:16.

revelation, added these words, and with very good reason: 'in that sense in which it has been defined by the Church' ... [21].

It is well known how highly the Church regards human reason, for it falls to reason to demonstrate with certainty the existence of God, personal and one; to prove beyond doubt from divine signs the very foundations of the Christian faith; to express properly the law which the Creator has imprinted in the hearts of men; and finally to attain to some notion, indeed a very fruitful notion, of mysteries. But reason can perform these functions safely and well only when properly trained, that is, when imbued with that sound philosophy which has long been, as it were, a patrimony handed down by earlier Christian ages, and which moreover possesses an authority of an even higher order, since the Teaching Authority of the Church, in the light of divine revelation itself, has weighed its fundamental tenets, which have been elaborated and defined little by little by men of great genius. For this philosophy, acknowledged and accepted by the Church, safeguards the genuine validity of human knowledge, the unshakable metaphysical principles of sufficient reason, causality, and finality, and finally the mind's ability to attain certain and unchangeable truth [29].

Of course this philosophy deals with much that neither directly nor indirectly touches faith or morals, and which consequently the Church leaves to the free discussion of experts. But this does not hold for many other things, especially those principles and fundamental tenets to which We have just referred. However, even in these fundamental questions, we may clothe our philosophy in a more convenient and richer dress, make it more vigorous with a more effective terminology, divest it of certain scholastic aids found less useful, prudently enrich it with the fruits of progress of the human mind. But never may we overthrow it, or contaminate it with false principles, or regard it as a great, but obsolete, relic. For truth and its philosophic expression cannot change from day to day, least of all where there is question of self-evident principles of the human mind or of those propositions which are supported by the wisdom of the ages and by divine revelation. Whatever new truth the sincere human mind is able to find, certainly cannot be opposed to truth already acquired, since God, the highest Truth, has created and guides the human intellect, not that it may daily oppose new truths to rightly established ones, but rather that, having eliminated errors which may have crept in, it may build truth upon truth in the same order and structure that exist in reality, the source of truth. Let no Christian therefore, whether philosopher or theologian, embrace eagerly and lightly whatever novelty happens to be thought up from day to day, but rather let him weigh it with painstaking care and a balanced judgment, lest he lose or corrupt the truth he already has, with grave danger and damage to his faith [30].

If one considers all this well, he will easily see why the Church demands that future priests be instructed in philosophy 'according to the method, doctrine, and principles of the Angelic Doctor',[7] since, as we well know from the experience of centuries, the method of Aquinas is singularly preeminent both of teaching students and for bringing truth to light; his doctrine is in harmony with Divine Revelation, and is most effective both for safeguarding the foundation of the faith and for reaping, safely and usefully, the fruits of sound progress ... [31].

---

7. *CIC*, can. 1366, 2.

It remains for Us now to speak about those questions which, although they pertain to the positive sciences, are nevertheless more or less connected with the truths of the Christian faith. In fact, not a few insistently demand that the Catholic religion take these sciences into account as much as possible. This certainly would be praiseworthy in the case of clearly proved facts; but caution must be used when there is rather question of hypotheses, having some sort of scientific foundation, in which the doctrine contained in Sacred Scripture or in Tradition is involved. If such conjectural opinions are directly or indirectly opposed to the doctrine revealed by God, then the demand that they be recognized can in no way be admitted [35].

For these reasons the Teaching Authority of the Church does not forbid that, in conformity with the present state of human sciences and sacred theology, research and discussions, on the part of men experienced in both fields, take place with regard to the doctrine of evolution, in as far as it inquires into the origin of the human body as coming from pre-existent and living matter – for the Catholic faith obliges us to hold that souls are immediately created by God. However, this must be done in such a way that the reasons for both opinions, that is, those favorable and those unfavorable to evolution, be weighed and judged with the necessary seriousness, moderation and measure, and provided that all are prepared to submit to the judgment of the Church, to whom Christ has given the mission of interpreting authentically the Sacred Scriptures and of defending the dogmas of faith [36] ... .

Let the teachers in ecclesiastical institutions be aware that they cannot with tranquil conscience exercise the office of teaching entrusted to them, unless in the instruction of their students they religiously accept and exactly observe the norms which We have ordained. That due reverend and submission which in their unceasing labour they must profess toward the Teaching Authority of the Church, let them instill also into the minds and hearts of their students [42].

Let them strive with every force and effort to further the progress of the sciences which they teach; but let them also be careful not to transgress the limits which We have established for the protection of the truth of Catholic faith and doctrine. With regard to new questions, which modern culture and progress have brought to the foreground, let them engage in most careful research, but with the necessary prudence and caution; finally, let them not think, indulging in a false 'eirenism', that the dissident and the erring can happily be brought back to the bosom of the Church, if the whole truth found in the Church is not sincerely taught to all without corruption or diminution ... [43].

6.3 *DONUM VERITATIS – INSTRUCTION ON THE ECCLESIAL VOCATION OF THE THEOLOGIAN – 1990*

Beginning by contextualizing theology in the inherent human quest for truth, in particular for answers to the fundamental questions concerning human existence, the instruction,[8] as a whole, sets forth the Congregation for the Doctrine of the Faith's current understanding of the nature and task of theology as faith's quest for understanding, informed by reason and the word of God. The instruction strongly reasserts that the magisterium is the supreme authority in all matters pertaining to these quests, that is to matters relating to faith and morals. It defines what is deemed to be appropriate interaction between theologians and various cultures. It sets forth guidelines concerning the relation of theology and theologians to the ('official') magisterium, including defining when it may be appropriate for theologians to raise questions about elements of the magisterium's teaching and when they cannot. In particular, our extract focuses upon the faithful assent the magisterium demands of theologians and the CDF's understanding of what constitutes a 'legitimate concern' and what constitutes erroneous and therefore forbidden *dissent* on the part of theologians. The church is *not* a democracy, according to the instruction, and those theologians who apply the tenets of philosophical liberalism and political movements for greater democracy within the church are in error.

❈

CHAPTER II   THE VOCATION OF THE THEOLOGIAN

… Since the object of theology is the Truth which is the living God and His plan for salvation revealed in Jesus Christ, the theologian is called to deepen his own life of faith and continuously unite his scientific research with prayer. In this way, he will become more open to the 'supernatural sense of faith' upon which he depends, and it will appear to him as a sure rule for guiding his reflections and helping him assess the correctness of his conclusions … [8].

Even though it transcends human reason, revealed truth is in profound harmony with it. It presumes that reason by its nature is ordered to the truth in such a way that, illumined by faith, it can penetrate to the meaning of Revelation. Despite the assertions of many philosophical currents, but in conformity with a correct way of thinking which finds confirmation in Scripture, human reason's ability to attain truth must be recognised as well as its metaphysical capacity to come to a knowledge of God from creation.[9] Theology's proper task is to understand the meaning of revelation and this, therefore, requires the utilisation of philosophical concepts which provide 'a solid and correct understanding of man, the world,

---

8. *ET* from *Archives of the Holy See*, www.vatican.va/ roman_curia/congregations/cfaith/index.htm.
9. Cf. Vatican Council. I, Dogmatic Constitution *De fide catholica, De revelatione*, can. l: DS 3026.

and God'[10] and can be employed in a reflection upon revealed doctrine. The historical disciplines are likewise necessary for the theologian's investigations. This is due chiefly to the historical character of revelation itself which has been communicated to us in 'salvation history'. Finally, a consultation of the 'human sciences' is also necessary to understand better the revealed truth about man and the moral norms for his conduct, setting these in relation to the sound findings of such sciences. It is the theologian's task in this perspective to draw from the surrounding culture those elements which will allow him better to illumine one or other aspect of the mysteries of faith. This is certainly an arduous task that has its risks, but it is legitimate in itself and should be encouraged. Here it is important to emphasise that when theology employs the elements and conceptual tools of philosophy or other disciplines, discernment is needed. The ultimate normative principle for such discernment is revealed doctrine which itself must furnish the criteria for the evaluation of these elements and conceptual tools and not *vice versa* [10].

Never forgetting that he is also a member of the People of God, the theologian must foster respect for them and be committed to offering them a teaching which in no way does harm to the doctrine of the faith. The freedom proper to theological research is exercised within the Church's faith. Thus while the theologian might often feel the urge to be daring in his work, this will not bear fruit or 'edify' unless it is accompanied by that patience which permits maturation to occur. New proposals advanced for understanding the faith 'are but an offering made to the whole Church. Many corrections and broadening of perspectives within the context of fraternal dialogue may be needed before the moment comes when the whole Church can accept them'. Consequently, 'this very disinterested service to the community of the faithful', which theology is, 'entails in essence an objective discussion, a fraternal dialogue, an openness and willingness to modify one's own opinions'.[11] [11].

Freedom of research, which the academic community rightly holds most precious, means an openness to accepting the truth that emerges at the end of an investigation in which no element has intruded that is foreign to the methodology corresponding to the object under study. In theology this freedom of inquiry is the hallmark of a rational discipline whose object is given by Revelation, handed on and interpreted in the Church under the authority of the Magisterium, and received by faith. These givens have the force of principles. To eliminate them would mean to cease doing theology. In order to set forth precisely the ways in which the theologian relates to the Church's teaching authority, it is appropriate now to reflect upon the role of the Magisterium in the Church [12].

'God graciously arranged that the things he had once revealed for the salvation of all peoples should remain in their entirety, throughout the ages, and be transmitted to all generations'.[12] He bestowed upon His Church, through the gift of the Holy Spirit, a participation in His own infallibility. Thanks to the 'supernatural sense of Faith', the People of God enjoys this privilege under the guidance of the Church's living Magisterium, which is the sole authentic interpreter of the Word of God, written or handed down, by virtue of the authority which it exercises in the name of Christ … [13].

---

10. Decree *Optatam totius*, n. 15.
11. John Paul II, 'Discorso ai teologi ad Altötting', 18 November 1980: *AAS*, 73 (1981) 104; cf. also Paul VI, 'Discorso ai membri della Commissione Teologica Internazionale', 11 October 1972: *AAS*, 64 (1972), 682–3; John Paul II, 'Discorso ai membri della Commissione Teologica Internazionale', 26 October 1979: *AAS*, 71 (1979), 1428–33.
12. Dogmatic Constitution, *Dei verbum*, n. 7.

The pastoral task of the Magisterium is one of vigilance. It seeks to ensure that the People of God remain in the truth which sets free. It is therefore a complex and diversified reality. The theologian, to be faithful to his role of service to the truth, must take into account the proper mission of the Magisterium and collaborate with it. How should this collaboration be understood? How is it put into practice and what are the obstacles it may face? These questions should now be examined more closely [20].

CHAPTER IV   THE MAGISTERIUM AND THEOLOGY

A   COLLABORATIVE RELATIONS

The living Magisterium of the Church and theology, while having different gifts and functions, ultimately have the same goal: preserving the People of God in the truth which sets free and thereby making them 'a light to the nations'. This service to the ecclesial community brings the theologian and the Magisterium into a reciprocal relationship. The latter authentically teaches the doctrine of the Apostles. And, benefiting from the work of theologians, it refutes objections to and distortions of the faith and promotes, with the authority received from Jesus Christ, new and deeper comprehension, clarification, and application of revealed doctrine. Theology, for its part, gains, by way of reflection, an ever deeper understanding of the Word of God found in the Scripture and handed on faithfully by the Church's living Tradition under the guidance of the Magisterium. Theology strives to clarify the teaching of Revelation with regard to reason and gives it finally an organic and systematic form [21].

Collaboration between the theologian and the Magisterium occurs in a special way when the theologian receives the canonical mission or the mandate to teach. In a certain sense, such collaboration becomes a participation in the work of the Magisterium, linked, as it then is, by a juridic bond. The theologian's code of conduct, which obviously has its origin in the service of the Word of God, is here reinforced by the commitment the theologian assumes in accepting his office, making the profession of faith, and taking the oath of fidelity.[13] From this moment on, the theologian is officially charged with the task of presenting and illustrating the doctrine of the faith in its integrity and with full accuracy [22].

When the Magisterium of the Church makes an infallible pronouncement and solemnly declares that a teaching is found in Revelation, the assent called for is that of theological faith. This kind of adherence is to be given even to the teaching of the ordinary and universal Magisterium when it proposes for belief a teaching of faith as divinely revealed. When the Magisterium proposes 'in a definitive way' truths concerning faith and morals, which, even if not divinely revealed, are nevertheless strictly and intimately connected with Revelation, these must be firmly accepted and held.

When the Magisterium, not intending to act 'definitively', teaches a doctrine to aid a better understanding of Revelation and make explicit its contents, or to recall how some teaching is in conformity with the truths of faith, or finally to guard against ideas that are incompatible with these truths, the response called for is that of the religious submission of

---

13. Cf. Code of Canon Law, can. 833; *Professio fidei et Iusiurandum fidelitatis. AAS*, 81 (1989), 104f.

will and intellect.[14] This kind of response cannot be simply exterior or disciplinary but must be understood within the logic of faith and under the impulse of obedience to the faith [23].

Finally, in order to serve the People of God as well as possible, in particular, by warning them of dangerous opinions which could lead to error, the Magisterium can intervene in questions under discussion which involve, in addition to solid principles, certain contingent and conjectural elements. It often only becomes possible with the passage of time to distinguish between what is necessary and what is contingent. The willingness to submit loyally to the teaching of the Magisterium on matters *per se* not irreformable must be the rule. It can happen, however, that a theologian may, according to the case, raise questions regarding the timeliness, the form, or even the contents of magisterial interventions. Here the theologian will need, first of all, to assess accurately the authoritativeness of the interventions which becomes clear from the nature of the documents, the insistence with which a teaching is repeated, and the very way in which it is expressed.

When it comes to the question of interventions in the prudential order, it could happen that some Magisterial documents might not be free from all deficiencies. Bishops and their advisors have not always taken into immediate consideration every aspect or the entire complexity of a question. But it would be contrary to the truth, if, proceeding from some particular cases, one were to conclude that the Church's Magisterium can be habitually mistaken in its prudential judgements, or that it does not enjoy divine assistance in the integral exercise of its mission. In fact, the theologian, who cannot pursue his discipline well without a certain competence in history, is aware of the filtering which occurs with the passage of time. This is not to be understood in the sense of a relativisation of the tenets of the faith. The theologian knows that some judgements of the Magisterium could be justified at the time in which they were made, because while the pronouncements contained true assertions and others which were not sure, both types are inextricably connected. Only time has permitted discernment and, after deeper study, the attainment of true doctrinal progress [24].

Even when collaboration takes place under the best conditions, the possibility cannot be excluded that tensions may arise between the theologian and the Magisterium. The meaning attributed to such tensions and the spirit with which they are faced are not matters of indifference. If tensions do not spring from hostile and contrary feelings, they can become a dynamic factor, a stimulus to both the Magisterium and theologians to fulfill their respective roles while practising dialogue [25].

In the dialogue, a two-fold rule should prevail. When there is a question of the communion of faith, the principle of the 'unity of truth' (*unitas veritatis*) applies. When it is a question of differences which do not jeopardise this communion, the 'unity of charity' (*unitas caritatis*) should be safeguarded [26].

Even if the doctrine of the faith is not in question, the theologian will not present his own opinions or divergent hypotheses as though they were non-arguable conclusions. Respect for the truth as well as for the People of God requires this discretion (cf. *Rom* 14:1–15; 1 *Cor* 8; 10:23–33). For the same reasons, the theologian will refrain from giving untimely public expression to them [27].

---

14. Cf. *Lumen Gentium*, n. 25; Code of Canon Law, can. 752.

The preceding considerations have a particular application to the case of the theologian who might have serious difficulties, for reasons which appear to him well-founded, in accepting a non-irreformable magisterial teaching.

Such a disagreement could not be justified if it were based solely upon the fact that the validity of the given teaching is not evident or upon the opinion that the opposite position would be the more probable. Nor, furthermore, would the judgement of the subjective conscience of the theologian justify it because conscience does not constitute an autonomous and exclusive authority for deciding the truth of a doctrine [28].

In any case there should never be a diminishment of that fundamental openness loyally to accept the teaching of the Magisterium as is fitting for every believer by reason of the obedience of faith. The theologian will strive then to understand this teaching in its contents, arguments, and purposes. This will mean an intense and patient reflection on his part and a readiness, if need be, to revise his own opinions and examine the objections which his colleagues might offer him [29].

If, despite a loyal effort on the theologian's part, the difficulties persist, the theologian has the duty to make known to the Magisterial authorities the problems raised by the teaching in itself, in the arguments proposed to justify it, or even in the manner in which it is presented. He should do this in an evangelical spirit and with a profound desire to resolve the difficulties. His objections could then contribute to real progress and provide a stimulus to the Magisterium to propose the teaching of the Church in greater depth and with a clearer presentation of the arguments. In cases like these, the theologian should avoid turning to the 'mass media', but have recourse to the responsible authority, for it is not by seeking to exert the pressure of public opinion that one contributes to the clarification of doctrinal issues and renders service to the truth [30].

It can also happen that at the conclusion of a serious study, undertaken with the desire to heed the Magisterium's teaching without hesitation, the theologian's difficulty remains because the arguments to the contrary seem more persuasive to him. Faced with a proposition to which he feels he cannot give his intellectual assent, the theologian nevertheless has the duty to remain open to a deeper examination of the question. For a loyal spirit, animated by love for the Church, such a situation can certainly prove a difficult trial. It can be a call to suffer for the truth, in silence and prayer, but with the certainty, that if the truth really is at stake, it will ultimately prevail [31].

B   THE PROBLEM OF DISSENT

The Magisterium has drawn attention several times to the serious harm done to the community of the Church by attitudes of general opposition to Church teaching which even come to expression in organised groups. In his apostolic exhortation *Paterna cum benevolentia*, Paul VI offered a diagnosis of this problem which is still apropos.[15] In particular, he addresses here that public opposition to the Magisterium of the Church also called 'dissent', which must be distinguished from the situation of personal difficulties treated above. The phenomenon of dissent can have diverse forms. Its remote and proximate causes are multiple.

---

15. Cf. Paul VI, Apost. Exhort. *Paterna cum benevolentia*, 8 December 1974: *AAS*, 67 (1975), 5–23. Cf. also Congregation for the Doctrine of the Faith, *Mysterium Ecclesiae*: *AAS*, 65 (1973), 396–408.

The ideology of philosophical liberalism, which permeates the thinking of our age, must be counted among the factors which may exercise their remote or indirect influence. Here arises the tendency to regard a judgement as having all the more validity to the extent that it proceeds from the individual relying upon his own powers. In such a way freedom of thought comes to oppose the authority of tradition which is considered a cause of servitude. A teaching handed on and generally received is *a priori* suspect and its truth contested. Ultimately, freedom of judgement understood in this way is more important than the truth itself. We are dealing then here with something quite different from the legitimate demand for freedom in the sense of absence of constraint as a necessary condition for the loyal inquiry into truth. In virtue of this exigency, the Church has always held that 'nobody is to be forced to embrace the faith against his will'.[16] The weight of public opinion when manipulated and its pressure to conform also have their influence. Often models of society promoted by the 'mass media' tend to assume a normative value. The view is particularly promoted that the Church should only express her judgement on those issues which public opinion considers important and then only by way of agreeing with it. The Magisterium, for example, could intervene in economic or social questions but ought to leave matters of conjugal and family morality to individual judgement. Finally, the plurality of cultures and languages, in itself a benefit, can indirectly bring on misunderstandings which occasion disagreements.

In this context, the theologian needs to make a critical, well-considered discernment, as well as have a true mastery of the issues, if he wants to fulfil his ecclesial mission and not lose, by conforming himself to this present world (cf. *Rom* 12:2; *Eph* 4:23), the independence of judgement which should be that of the disciples of Christ [32].

Dissent has different aspects. In its most radical form, it aims at changing the Church following a model of protest which takes its inspiration from political society. More frequently, it is asserted that the theologian is not bound to adhere to any Magisterial teaching unless it is infallible. Thus a kind of theological positivism is adopted, according to which, doctrines proposed without exercise of the charism of infallibility are said to have no obligatory character about them, leaving the individual completely at liberty to adhere to them or not. The theologian would accordingly be totally free to raise doubts or reject the non-infallible teaching of the Magisterium particularly in the case of specific moral norms. With such critical opposition, he would even be making a contribution to the development of doctrine [33].

Dissent is generally defended by various arguments, two of which are more basic in character. The first lies in the order of hermeneutics. The documents of the Magisterium, it is said, reflect nothing more than a debatable theology. The second takes theological pluralism sometimes to the point of a relativism which calls the integrity of the faith into question. Here the interventions of the Magisterium would have their origin in one theology among many theologies, while no particular theology, however, could presume to claim universal normative status. In opposition to and in competition with the authentic magisterium, there thus arises a kind of 'parallel magisterium' of theologians.

Certainly, it is one of the theologian's tasks to give a correct interpretation to the texts of the Magisterium and to this end he employs various hermeneutical rules. Among these is the

---

16. Vatican II *Declaration on Religious Liberty Dignitatis humanae*, n. 10.

principle which affirms that Magisterial teaching, by virtue of divine assistance, has a validity beyond its argumentation, which may derive at times from a particular theology. As far as theological pluralism is concerned, this is only legitimate to the extent that the unity of the faith in its objective meaning is not jeopardised. Essential bonds link the distinct levels of unity of faith, unity-plurality of expressions of the faith, and plurality of theologies. The ultimate reason for plurality is found in the unfathomable mystery of Christ who transcends every objective systematisation. This cannot mean that it is possible to accept conclusions contrary to that mystery and it certainly does not put into question the truth of those assertions by which the Magisterium has declared itself. As to the 'parallel magisterium', it can cause great spiritual harm by opposing itself to the Magisterium of the Pastors. Indeed, when dissent succeeds in extending its influence to the point of shaping a common opinion, it tends to become the rule of conduct. This cannot but seriously trouble the People of God and lead to contempt for true authority [34].

Dissent sometimes also appeals to a kind of sociological argumentation which holds that the opinion of a large number of Christians would be a direct and adequate expression of the 'supernatural sense of the faith'. Actually, the opinions of the faithful cannot be purely and simply identified with the 'sensus fidei'.[17] The sense of the faith is a property of theological faith; and, as God's gift which enables one to adhere personally to the Truth, it cannot err. This personal faith is also the faith of the Church since God has given guardianship of the Word to the Church. Consequently, what the believer believes is what the Church believes. The 'sensus fidei' implies then by its nature a profound agreement of spirit and heart with the Church, 'sentire cum Ecclesia'. Although theological faith as such then cannot err, the believer can still have erroneous opinions since all his thoughts do not spring from faith. Not all the ideas which circulate among the People of God are compatible with the faith. This is all the more so given that people can be swayed by a public opinion influenced by modern communications media. Not without reason did the Second Vatican Council emphasise the indissoluble bond between the 'sensus fidei' and the guidance of God's People by the magisterium of the Pastors. These two realities cannot be separated. Magisterial interventions serve to guarantee the Church's unity in the truth of the Lord. They aid her to 'abide in the truth' in face of the arbitrary character of changeable opinions and are an expression of obedience to the Word of God. Even when it might seem that they limit the freedom of theologians, these actions, by their fidelity to the faith which has been handed on, establish a deeper freedom which can only come from unity in truth [35].

The freedom of the act of faith cannot justify a right to dissent. In fact this freedom does not indicate at all freedom with regard to the truth but signifies the free self-determination of the person in conformity with his moral obligation to accept the truth. The act of faith is a voluntary act because man, saved by Christ the Redeemer and called by Him to be an adopted son (cf. *Rom* 8:15; *Gal* 4:5; *Eph* 1:5; *Jn* 1:12), cannot adhere to God unless, 'drawn by the Father' (*Jn* 6:44), he offers God the rational homage of his faith (cf. *Rom* 12:1). As the Declaration *Dignitatis humanae* recalls,[18] no human authority may overstep the limits of its competence and claim the right to interfere with this choice by exerting pressure or constraint.

---

17. Cf. John Paul. II, Apost. Exhort. *Familiaris consortio*, n. 5: *AAS*, 74 (1982), 85–6.
18. *Dignitatis humanae*, nn. 9–10.

Respect for religious liberty is the foundation of respect for all the rights of man. One cannot then appeal to these rights of man in order to oppose the interventions of the Magisterium. Such behaviour fails to recognise the nature and mission of the Church which has received from the Lord the task to proclaim the truth of salvation to all men. She fulfils this task by walking in Christ's footsteps, knowing that 'truth can impose itself on the mind only by virtue of its own truth, which wins over the mind with both gentleness and power'[19] [36].

By virtue of the divine mandate given to it in the Church, the Magisterium has the mission to set forth the Gospel's teaching, guard its integrity, and thereby protect the Faith of the People of God. In order to fulfil this duty, it can at times be led to take serious measures as, for example, when it withdraws from a theologian, who departs from the doctrine of the faith, the canonical mission or the teaching mandate it had given him, or declares that some writings do not conform to this doctrine. When it acts in such ways, the Magisterium seeks to be faithful to its mission of defending the right of the People of God to receive the message of the Church in its purity and integrity and not be disturbed by a particular dangerous opinion. The judgement expressed by the Magisterium in such circumstances is the result of a thorough investigation conducted according to established procedures which afford the interested party the opportunity to clear up possible misunderstandings of his thought. This judgement, however, does not concern the person of the theologian but the intellectual positions which he has publicly espoused. The fact that these procedures can be improved does not mean that they are contrary to justice and right. To speak in this instance of a violation of human rights is out of place for it indicates a failure to recognise the proper hierarchy of these rights as well as the nature of the ecclesial community and her common good. Moreover, the theologian who is not disposed to think with the Church ('sentire cum Ecclesia') contradicts the commitment he freely and knowingly accepted to teach in the name of the Church[20] [37].

Finally, argumentation appealing to the obligation to follow one's own conscience cannot legitimate dissent. This is true, first of all, because conscience illumines the practical judgement about a decision to make, while here we are concerned with the truth of a doctrinal pronouncement. This is furthermore the case because while the theologian, like every believer, must follow his conscience, he is also obliged to form it. Conscience is not an independent and infallible faculty. It is an act of moral judgement regarding a responsible choice. A right conscience is one duly illumined by faith and by the objective moral law and it presupposes, as well, the uprightness of the will in the pursuit of the true good. The right conscience of the Catholic theologian presumes not only faith in the Word of God whose riches he must explore, but also love for the Church from whom he receives his mission, and respect for her divinely assisted Magisterium. Setting up a supreme magisterium of conscience in opposition to the magisterium of the Church means adopting a principle of free examination incompatible with the economy of Revelation and its transmission in the Church and thus also with a correct understanding of theology and the role of the theologian. The propositions of faith are not the product of mere individual research and free criticism of the Word of God but constitute an ecclesial heritage. If there occurs a separation from the Bishops who watch

---

19. Ibid. n. 1.
20. Cf. John Paul II, Apost. Const. *Sapientia Christiana*, 15 April 1979, n. 27, 1: *AAS*, 71 (1979), 483; Code of Canon Law, can. 812.

over and keep the apostolic tradition alive, it is the bond with Christ which is irreparably compromised [38].

The Church, which has her origin in the unity of the Father, Son, and Holy Spirit, is a mystery of communion. In accordance with the will of her founder, she is organised around a hierarchy established for the service of the Gospel and the People of God who live by it. After the pattern of the members of the first community, all the baptised with their own proper charisms are to strive with sincere hearts for a harmonious unity in doctrine, life, and worship (cf. *Acts* 2:42). This is a rule which flows from the very being of the Church. For this reason, standards of conduct, appropriate to civil society or the workings of a democracy, cannot be purely and simply applied to the Church. Even less can relationships within the Church be inspired by the mentality of the world around it (ct. *Rom* 12:2). Polling public opinion to determine the proper thing to think or do, opposing the Magisterium by exerting the pressure of public opinion, making the excuse of a 'consensus' among theologians, maintaining that the theologian is the prophetical spokesman of a 'base' or autonomous community which would be the source of all truth, all this indicates a grave loss of the sense of truth and of the sense of the Church [39].

The Church 'is like a sacrament, a sign and instrument, that is, of communion with God and of unity among all men'.[21] Consequently, to pursue concord and communion is to enhance the force of her witness and credibility. To succumb to the temptation of dissent, on the other hand, is to allow the 'leaven of infidelity to the Holy Spirit' to start to work.

To be sure, theology and the Magisterium are of diverse natures and missions and cannot be confused. Nonetheless they fulfil two vital roles in the Church which must interpenetrate and enrich each other for the service of the People of God. It is the duty of the Pastors by virtue of the authority they have received from Christ Himself to guard this unity and to see that the tensions arising from life do not degenerate into divisions. Their authority, which transcends particular positions and oppositions, must unite all in the integrity of the Gospel which is the 'word of reconciliation' (cf. 2 *Cor* 5:18–20).

As for theologians, by virtue of their own proper charisms, they have the responsibility of participating in the building up of Christ's Body in unity and truth. Their contribution is needed more than ever, for evangelisation on a world scale requires the efforts of the whole People of God. If it happens that they encounter difficulties due to the character of their research, they should seek their solution in trustful dialogue with the Pastors, in the spirit of truth and charity which is that of the communion of the Church ... [40].

---

21. *Lumen Gentium*, n. 1.

6.4 JOHN PAUL II: *MAGISTERIUM EXERCISES AUTHORITY IN CHRIST'S NAME* – 1995

Addressing the members of the CDF, the Pope here[22] reinforces the message of recent Curial documents concerning the authority and remit of the magisterium, particularly vis-à-vis the Catholic theologians. In the light of reactions to *Donum Veritatis*, he reinforces particular aspects of that document. Theology, he argues, is not a private enterprise and should never be divorced from the wider context of the life and vitality of the church. The power and authority of the magisterium are the power and authority of Christian truth. Theologians guilty of 'dissent' seem to set themselves up as a 'counter-magisterium', but theology only has freedom in so far as it serves the truth of the Catholic faith – it has no freedom with regards to what constitutes that 'truth'. Thus the remit of the magisterium, in safeguarding this truth, extends beyond those teachings which are deemed to be infallible i.e., the Pope particularly addresses the problem of the obedience of theologians to the non-definitive magisterium. He argues that the 'authentic' conception of authority in the church must be recovered.

❈

… The continual dialogue with Pastors and theologians throughout the world enables you to be attentive to the demands of understanding and reflecting more deeply on the doctrine of the faith, which theology interprets, and at the same time, it informs you of the useful efforts being made to foster and strengthen the unity of the faith and the Magisterium's guiding role in understanding the truth and in building up ecclesial communion in charity.

The unity of the faith, for the sake of which the Magisterium has authority and ultimate deliberative power in interpreting the Word of God written and handed down, is a primary value, which, if respected, does not involve the stifling of theological research, but provides it with a stable foundation. Theology, in its task of making explicit the intelligible content of the faith, expresses the intrinsic orientation of human intelligence to the truth and the believer's irrepressible need rationally to explore the revealed mystery.

To achieve this end, theology can never be reduced to the 'private' reflection of a theologian or group of theologians. The Church is the theologian's vital environment, and in order to remain faithful to its identity, theology cannot fail to participate deeply in the fabric of the Church's life, doctrine, holiness and prayer [2].

MAGISTERIUM IS A SERVICE TO THE TRUTH

This is the context in which the conviction that theology needs the living and clarifying word of the Magisterium becomes fully understandable and perfectly consistent with the logic of

---

22. Address to the CDF, 24 November 1995, ET: *L'Osservatore Romano* (English edn), 29 November 1995, 3 (see, also, http://www.ewtn.com/faith/teachings/papad1.htm).

the Christian faith. The meaning of the Church's Magisterium must be considered in relation to the truth of Christian doctrine. This is what your Congregation has carefully explained and spelled out in the Instruction *Donum veritatis* on the ecclesial vocation of the theologian.

The fact that the dogmatic development which culminated in the solemn definition of the First Vatican Council has stressed the Magisterium's charism of infallibility and clarified the conditions of its exercise must not lead to the Magisterium's being considered only from this standpoint. Its power and its authority are actually the power and authority of Christian truth, to which it bears witness. The Magisterium, whose authority is exercised in the name of Jesus Christ (cf. *Dei Verbum*, n. 10), is an organ of service to the truth and is responsible for seeing that the truth does not cease to be faithfully handed on throughout human history [3].

... In this regard, it is certainly necessary to distinguish the attitude of theologians who, in a spirit of cooperation and ecclesial communion, present their difficulties and questions, and thus positively contribute to the maturing of reflection on the deposit of faith, from the public stance of opposition to the Magisterium, which is described as 'dissent'; the latter tends to set up a kind of counter-magisterium, presenting believers with alternative positions and forms of behavior. The plurality of cultures and of theological approaches and systems themselves has its legitimacy only if the unity of the faith is presupposed in its objective meaning. The very freedom proper to theological research is never freedom with regard to the truth, but is justified and realized when the individual complies with the moral obligation of obeying the truth presented by Revelation and accepted in faith [4].

At the same time, as you have rightly considered in your assembly, it is necessary today to foster a climate of positive reception and acceptance of the Magisterium's documents, calling attention to their style and language, so as to harmonize the solidity and clarity of the doctrine with the pastoral concern to use forms of communication and means of expression that are incisive and effective for the consciousness of contemporary man.

It is not possible, however, to overlook one of the decisive aspects that lies at the base of the malaise and uneasiness in certain parts of the ecclesiastical world: it is a question of the way authority is conceived. In the case of the Magisterium, authority is not exercised only when the charism of infallibility is involved; its exercise has a wider field, which is required by the appropriate defense of the revealed deposit.

For a community based essentially on shared adherence to the Word of God and on the resulting certainty of living in the truth, authority for determining the content to be believed and professed is something that cannot be renounced. That this authority includes various degrees of teaching has been clearly stated in two recent documents of the Congregation for the Doctrine of the Faith: the *Professio Fidei* and the Instruction *Donum veritatis*. This hierarchy of degrees should not be considered an impediment but a stimulus to theology [5].

AUTHENTIC CONCEPT OF AUTHORITY MUST BE RECOVERED

However, this does not entitle one to hold that the pronouncements and doctrinal decisions of the Magisterium call for irrevocable assent only when it states them in a solemn judgment or definitive act, and that, consequently, in all other cases one need only consider the arguments or reasons employed … .

It therefore seems urgently necessary to recover the authentic concept of authority, not only from the formal juridical standpoint, but more profoundly, as a means of guaranteeing, safeguarding and guiding the Christian community in fidelity to and continuity with Tradition, to make it possible for believers to be in contact with the preaching of the Apostles and with the source of the Christian reality itself … [6].

6.5 HANS URS VON BALTHASAR: *THE PLACE OF THEOLOGY* – 1960

Our extract[23] was originally published prior to Vatican II. In it Balthasar crafts a picture of theology as bearing witness to the incarnation through the continued inspiration of the spirit. No theology is to remain mere theory, for its purpose is to bear witness to the life of faith in the divine word made flesh in Christ. Theology serves to bring forth greater adoration and holiness in the face of the incarnation. As such, it stands apart from other sciences, though it must avail itself of the 'laws of human thought' in order to shape and explicate its witness. In relation to the church 'theology … is a function, a corrective, a preliminary to the official teaching'. Theology must always (1) 'be governed according to revelation' yet: (2) always remember that it serves a *contemporary*, not a timeless preaching and teaching of the word, without being the slave of current trends and whims. The theologian must be driven by a spirit of adoration and obedience, yet nonetheless realize that he or she also has a creative duty and responsibility towards the formulation of doctrine. Finally, (3) The theologian must always be wary of ignoring historical context – the spirit's guidance takes different forms at different times. The concept of tradition involves freedom, responsibility and even (Christian) audacity. Above all, it is the passion of the theologian who seeks to bring Christians closer to the mystery of the God incarnate in Christ which shows the true 'glory' of theology. Despite being the 'court theologian' of many involved in the conservative reaction against certain post-Vatican II developments, Balthasar here stresses the importance of freedom in the church to the very notion of tradition. Indeed, many of his words are equally addressed to church leaders and authorities. He believes no leader can justify their authority by complacently relying on appeal to their office alone.

❈

I. The Word that is God became man, without ceasing to be God. The Word that is infinite becomes finite, without ceasing to be finite. The Word that is God took a body of flesh, in order to be man. And because he is Word, and, as Word, took flesh, he took on, at the same time, a body consisting of syllable, scripture, ideas, images, verbal utterance and preaching, since otherwise men would not have understood either that the Word really was made *flesh*, or that the divine Person who was made flesh was really the *Word* … .

In the holiness of the communion of saints the world should come to learn what the holiness (that is, the divineness) of the incarnate Word on earth was. Without this holiness of the Word we live by, the holiness of the Word we worship would lack full incarnational truth. The Word in the world has the power to turn speculative truth into actual living, the exercise of authority into holiness of life, theology into Christian practice, reflection into irrefutable witness of life to the point of martyrdom. This is what its credentials consist in, but they derive ultimately from men's utter surrender to it and adoration in faith, hope and love to the indwelling Word.

---

23. From *The Word Made Flesh*, vol. I of Explorations in Theology, San Francisco, Ignatius Press, 1989, 149–60.

Whatever external graces and 'signs' the Church has been endowed with by her Founder are not ends in themselves, but means to the above-mentioned end and incentives to its attainment. The infused holiness of the Church as 'institution' is simply the source and starting point of the interior and practical holiness of the Christian, which is what her Founder intended thereby. Her given unity, made visible in the hierarchy, is simply the basis for that living, perfect unity of love which inwardly sustains and builds up the body of Christ. The totality (catholicity) of the truth and love implanted in her by her Founder must be continuously unfolded in fullness of life by the workings of the Holy Spirit; apostolicity, the exterior uninterrupted succession in time, is simply the guarantee and starting point for all generations of Christians, of an ever-fresh and immediate relation to the apostles and, through them, to Christ, an incentive to seek this ever anew and to renew the apostolic witness by their own holiness to life. To call these 'means' is not to say that, once the end is reached, they can be discarded. They are part of the structure of the Church in the world and, so long as she retains her present form, so long must they endure. But when this structure passes away, the means also pass away; already they have within themselves an element directing them to what is quite other, and alone an end in itself: adoration and holiness, in other words, love of God and one's neighbor.

This applies to the whole official side of the Church. Thus it applies equally to theology, insofar as it is something other than direct adoration of the divine Word in the finite word, other than the act of direct obedience to the Word in the Christian life. To that extent therefore, lying between these two interdependent poles of the Christian's intercourse with the Word of God, there is intercalated something which might be called theorizing about the Word of God – a form of contemplation which is neither an act of worship nor conjoined with action wherein the truth is embodied. Like all the modes in which the Church sets forth her teaching, theology can only be oriented toward these two poles, and so toward the purity and fullness of the Church's teaching, with which it partially coincides. For, while being a special form of the Church's teaching (the theologian, too, has an official role), theology is, at the same time, a function, a corrective, a preliminary to the official teaching. Together with this latter and the sacraments, theology is a means, an active agency for pouring the infinite riches of diving truth into the finite vessels in which revelation is given to us, so that the believer may be made capable of encountering this infinity in adoration and active obedience. Revealed truth, since it is both divine truth and the truth we live by, is so constituted that the amount of truth in theology (as it prepares the way to worship and a life of obedience) must be measured in terms of worship and practical obedience. For Christ is no theory, not even insofar as he is the truth (not the truth as human knowledge is true). The flame of worship and obedience must burn through the dispassionateness of speculation, as it always does through the entire Word of God: the Word that was Christ, and that gave itself to be consumed in this same fire; the word that once again is Christ and is called 'scripture', the letter aglow with the Spirit and fire, scorching those who approach it without first taking off their shoes.

Now, in the very fact of God's existence in the flesh, there must be a level on which the word of God (since it is a truly human word) meets with other human words. This is the level of disputation, of argument. This level is laid open to being controverted, to arguments for and against, to the cavils and quibbles of the scribes, to the groping incomprehension of the disciples, to the doubtings of the fearful, who 'see men as trees' (Mk 8:24). God's word here always speaks with the same infinite superiority that characterized it in the Old Testament, but always in the same human situation. It lets itself enter into human contact and man's concerns. It lays itself open to contradiction, to argumentation, to syllogistic and theological deduction. Coming out into the open, it denudes itself. In this consists the abasement of the Word, for the very beginning, that so stirred Hamann that he made it the center of his theology: the condescension not only of the Lord to the Status of servant, but of the sovereign Spirit to the servitude of the letter, and this in the very act of creation, culminating in his embodiment in the Church. Yet it must always be borne in mind that this concession to human understanding is only made for the purpose of leading it away from its own natural level to that of faith and to a corresponding decision. Furthermore (and this is very clear in John), all theological dispute with the Word is a stage on the way either to the act of faith or of disbelief ... . Not for a single moment can theology forget its roots, from which all its nourishment is drawn: adoration, in which we see, in faith, the heavens opened; and obedience in living, which frees us to understand the truth.

II. ... [M]any conclusions follow regarding the structure of theology. In the first place, a general truth: that in theology all that has to do with the finite aspect of the Word (with concepts, images, the letter) must be considered solely a means to reaching the infinity incarnated therein. There is urgent need of a thorough investigation into the formal logic of the mode of speech and thought of the Word of God. This would of necessity bring out how the formal laws of human speech and thought are in no way superseded, but rather carried up to a higher plane, since all the laws applying to what is finite become functions of a truth infinite in every 'part' or manifestation, and not susceptible of being parcelled into finite dictums and laws. Such an investigation would bear many points of resemblance to that of Bultmann, and yet would be very different. It would not approach the Word of God through any philosophic, existential presuppositions, but would be developed from the basic fact of the incarnation (accepted in faith). It cannot be said that, through the incarnation, or even through the resurrection, human 'flesh' (human nature with all its laws of finite being and thought) has been 'relativized'. That would be, once again, a category of this world, finite and wholly inadequate for this absolutely unique, unparalleled event. This is why modernism, thought often near the mark, was basically off-target.

Neither history nor evolution nor philosophy has the Word for its province, but faith alone, which requires that theology be presented in such a way as to foster a more profound spirit of adoration, a more exact obedience in practice. The theologian, therefore, is required to apply the laws of human thinking in such a way as to bring out clearly the law of faith. The laws of thought are primarily concerned with drawing limits, defining, even if this is done so as subsequently to interrelate more precisely the fields thus delimited. So long as the various contents of truth are themselves finite, there is nothing to object to in this process of defining and contrasting. The case is otherwise when the laws of faith come into action, for then the truth comprised within the drawn limits is the same (not only generically, but substantially and personally) as the truth outside them. The drawing of the boundary does not involve falsehood (for it is all part of the movement of the Word's incarnation), provided that one is always aware of the presence, within the boundary, of the unbounded, the presence in the concept of what is beyond concept, in the definition of the presence of the divine object of faith. And this applies even more to the subsequent operations in which this first delimited sphere (of infinite content) is brought into relation with others (also of infinite content).

In other words, every concept in theology must be catholic, universal, which means it must present the whole truth, either by drawing it into itself or by opening itself out thereto, discarding its own boundaries, dying in order to rise again into the truth which is of heaven. This is a work of faith, not of a Hegelian dialect of knowledge; it is the work of a knowledge that is itself a faith which seeks, and then finds according to the measure of adoration, obedience and grace. A Catholic concept is by no means the same as a Platonist or Aristotelian one, for the simple reason that God's Word in human form (flesh or scripture) is not just any kind of work. The 'inclusiveness' or 'openness' that is the essence of Catholic logic does not authorize us to allow everything to drift away into a kind of vague infinity, as furthering devotion. On the contrary, it is the most stringent requirement in thinking there could be. It demands that our thinking should be continuously and deliberately subject to the Word of God not only in its content, but also in its form, in the very act of thought, which must, perforce, bear the mark of Catholic logic. Theology is the expression of the verdict passed by the divine word over the human. This is, in fact, the form taken, from the beginning, by the entire word of scripture; and it is impossible for theology to evade this form.

From this general characteristic follows the detail of theology, its material.

1. This material, in its whole range, its basic structure, its essential features, must be governed according to revelation, and this in the way in which it actually was given in history – or, more precisely, as it happened historically within the human race and is described in scripture. This means, in the first place, that theology has to understand and interpret the divine content in this history and not leave it to one side while drawing from it an unhistorical, supratemporal (and thus not truly eternal) 'moral of history'. The incarnation is no mere 'figure' of a truth, but truth itself. It means further, that theology has to consider this history (for even the didactic parts of the Old and New Testaments are a function of the history) in its essential course, and not simply in certain episodes or concepts chosen at will. Scripture is not a quarry out of which theology can hew individual sentences to suit its purpose. It is the witness of a total event, a unity in itself; and it is as a totality that it is the object of theology.

The proportions of the structure of theology must be governed by those of revelation, that is to say, not of scripture as a book, but of the event described in scripture. The Holy Spirit is always sovereign in this sphere; he breathes where he will, leads into all truth in the way he chooses, and throws his light on the meaning of the Word in the sources of revelation according to his will. Therefore we must always read scripture in the light of the Spirit (the Spirit of the Church and of Catholicism). This does not imply that the theologian is entitled to settle down comfortably in some corner, to specialize there, without further concern with the totality of revelation. There is, of course, bound to be specialization, owing to the limitations of science. But the difference between theology and other sciences is that in the former the object is not a finite one, corresponding to the limitations of our powers. And there is another, even more important difference: whereas in other sciences progress consists in increasing differentiation and refinement of the subject matter, here the work leads further and further in the direction of the infinity that pertains to the object, which has presented itself to us in a finite form adapted to our understanding. A man can write on theology without being obliged to deal with the whole of it; but he must always preserve the totality, the catholicity of truth in every detail of his thought.

However important mariology may be in these times, one cannot escape the impression that it affords a welcome excuse for theologians to avoid subjects which, if the proportions of revelation are to be preserved, demand greater attention, but also more courage and expository skill. The doctrines of the Trinity, of the incarnation, of the redemption, of the resurrection, of predestination and eschatology bristle with problems that all too often we prefer to bypass. Such an attitude is inexcusable. The thought of previous generations (even if it has resulted in conciliar definitions) is never a pillow for future thought to rest on. Definitions are not so much an end as a beginning. Nothing that is the fruit of hard struggle is ever lost to the Church, but this does not mean that the theologian is spared further work. Whatever is merely put in storage, handed down without any fresh efforts being made on one's own part (and *ab ovo*, the very source of revelation) putrifies, like the manna did. And the longer the living tradition has been broken through purely mechanical repetition, the more difficult it may become to renew it.

2. The whole span of revelation, which provides the basic dimension of theology, broadens as theology becomes the regulative principle not of a timeless, but of a contemporary preaching and teaching of the word. This does not, of course, mean that theology must adopt a servile and timorous attitude towards current fashions of thought, so as to 'keep abreast of the times' (for example, by becoming existentialist or by demythologizing), or that it should provide an apologetic palatable to modern man, but that, in obedience to its own inmost law, it should attend to the light which the Holy Ghost sheds here and now on revealed truth. The Spirit who breathes where he will is not the mild, diffused timeless beacon of the Enlightenment always present in the same fashion. Rather he is the Spirit of missions and special functions within the mystical body, the Spirit who, in fulfilling the Old Testament, continues its historical course, in which ever new, unforeseeable tasks sent by God erupt. It would indeed be all too simple (and a complete justification of Buber's penetrating objections) if the Christian could ignore the tremendous and inescapable unrest created in us by a revelation at once contemporaneous and leading into the future, and could live on in the past, that forever is sinking further into the past. Yet who, if not the theologian, is the watchman on the tower ready to proclaim the hour not of world history, but of Christian history, reading for us today the signs in the meridian light of eternal revelation?

There are, of course, many signs by which to read and interpret and to discern the spirits. There are, first of all, the different kinds of sanctity and of missions conferred on a given epoch, which may in turn call attention to the modes of sanctity of earlier times and in the light of the present and its needs, make them more comprehensible. Those who truly adore and are truly obedient are those in whom the present truth of the Word is most clearly embodied. Their life is doctrine put into practice; and if they have a special mission in life, it throws an especially actual and God-intended light on doctrine. It is a light of the Spirit, illuminating the light of the Son. There is no question of persons involved, still less any question of psychology or biography, but rather one of the intrinsic content of mission, insofar as it is the voice, the word and the light of God for the times.

The same light will not be withheld from the theologian himself, provided that, in his work, he draws on the spirit of adoration and obedience. It is the self-same light that unfailingly guides the teaching authority (and thereby points the way for the individual theologian), on condition that, also for the official leaders of the Church and community, it is a light sought for in prayer and suffering, and not simply borrowed, something taken out of storage. Here we come up against profound and terrible mysteries concerning the Church: the 'angels of the churches' are under the most severe judgment of the Lord of the Church, for this Lord does not tolerate any complacent dependence on office alone, any decline in initial fervour and love, but demands the utmost zeal of watchman and shepherd. The theologian who lets himself be guided by authority and must have an especially strong sense of his own responsibility towards the teaching authority, for, if he is exercised thoroughly in obedience to the Spirit, his own suggestions, emendations, his general view or new insight may have an important part to play in the formulation of doctrine and its promulgation.

3. The third and most difficult question can now be approached, that of the relation between revelation today (1 and 2) and tradition yesterday, a relation resulting in tradition today. Its difficulty stems from the fact that, since tradition must always remain a living principle, the theology of all past ages has to be incorporated as a living thing, it being remembered that the guidance of the Spirit yesterday is not identical with that of today; in fact, insofar as it was guidance for a particular situation in the past, it cannot be applicable to the present.

This does not mean we must look with suspicion at the formulations, the systems and worldviews of the theology of the past. Suspicion is an unprofitable attitude and the reverse of inclusive. What it does mean, what it requires, is that the theology of today must have such a certainty and fullness-derived from the eternal fullness of revelation, of the Spirit given at this time, and of the fullness of the tradition received – as to embrace the riches of past theology as a living thing, and to endow it with fresh vitality. But if the theologian of today is to preserve a living contact with the tradition of yesterday, he has the grave responsibility of conjoining his reverence for the abiding words of the Father, the Scholastics, the spiritual writers with an undimmed view of the temporal element from which none are exempt.

Nothing brings so much harm in its train as the failure to appreciate a historical context. It is bound adversely to affect the theology of the present. It is an ostrich-like proceeding – with this difference, that the ostrich, in hiding its head in the sand, counts on not being seen at all, whereas the theologian, hiding in the sands of timelessness, hopes despite his disregard of history, to be taken account of by history. What is required is neither an enthusiastic revival of something or other (for example, the 'Fathers'), nor pure historical research, but rather that kind of Christian humanism that goes to the sources to find what is living and truly original (and not to a school of thought long since dried up), in a spirit of joy and freedom able to weigh the true value of things. This is the spirit from which we may hope for a tradition that is truly contemporary.

Like all good things in the world, the capacity to hand down requires a full measure of freedom, responsibility and Christian audacity. We can see this very clearly in the way in which St. Paul handed down what was delivered to him. Anyone without that capacity who wants to form a link in the chain of tradition, and hands down the goods of theology more or less like a workman passing bricks from hand to hand so that they are least likely to be damaged, is profoundly misled – simply because thoughts are not bricks; and, besides, since the first Easter morning, the fight between Spirit and stone, the stone which held the body captive, has not slackened.

These three lines of reflection serve, simply, to mark out a space, and to incite theology to build on it. Having seen it, one finds it difficult to understand why so few theologians have attempted the task; and even those few have applied themselves to only a section of the edifice, and left the main part alone. It is useless to look to theological commissions; their business is to point out what is defective. We need individuals who devote their lives to the glory of theology, that fierce fire burning in the dark night of adoration and obedience, whose abysses it illuminates.

6.6 HANS KÜNG: *WHO IS A CATHOLIC THEOLOGIAN?* – 1980

This[24] is a sometimes impassioned defence of 'catholicity' and a dynamic sense of the church (Catholic in time and space, i.e., across centuries of history and diversity, and in fellowship with Christians the world over). This, Küng asserts, is what it truly is to be a Catholic and a Catholic theologian in particular. Against 'Roman imperialism' (perceived Vatican intransigence), the true criterion of catholicity is Jesus Christ, himself. Thus the Catholic theologian must be evangelically oriented, just as Protestant (evangelical) theologians should be 'oriented in a Catholic way.' For Küng, catholicity is both a gift and a task.

❈

In accordance with the original meaning of the word and with ancient tradition, anyone can describe himself as a Catholic theologian if he is aware of being obliged in his theology to the 'Catholic' – that is, to the '*whole*', the 'universal, comprehensive, total' – Church. This catholicity has two dimensions: temporal and spatial.

First, *catholicity in time*. A theologian is Catholic if he is aware of being united with the whole Church – that is, with the Church of all times. He will therefore not describe from the outset certain centuries as 'un-Christian' or 'unevangelical'. He is sure that in every century there was a community of believers who listened to the gospel of Jesus Christ and tried in one way or other, so far as it is possible for human beings in their frailty and fallibility, to live according to his example.

Protestant radicalism on the other hand (not to be confused with evangelical radicality) is always in danger of wanting unhistorically to begin at zero and so to pass from Jesus to Paul, from Paul to Augustine, and then in a great leap to pass over the Middle Ages to Luther and Calvin, and from that point to leap across one's own 'orthodox' tradition to the more recent church fathers or, better, heads of schools.

The *Catholic* theologian, by contrast, will always start out from the fact that there was never a time when the gospel was left without witness and he will try to learn from the Church of the past. While insisting on the necessity of critical scrutiny, he will never overlook the boundary posts and danger signals which the Church in former times, in its concern and struggle for the one true faith, often at times of great distress and danger, set up in the form of creeds and definitions to distinguish between good and bad interpretations of the message. He will never neglect the positive and negative experiences of his fathers and brothers in theology, those teachers who are his older and more experienced fellow students in the school of sacred Scripture. It is precisely in this critical scrutiny that the Catholic theologian is interested in the *continuity* which is preserved through all disruptions.

---

24. From the postscript to the English Edition of *The Church – Maintained in Truth*, London, SCM, 1980, 80–87.

Second, *catholicity in space*. A theologian is Catholic if he is aware of being united with the Church of all nations and continents. He must therefore not orient himself only to the church of this country or to a national church and will not isolate himself from the Church as a whole. He is sure that in all nations and on all continents there is a community of believers who in the last resort want nothing other than their own church, a community which is driven no less than the local church by the gospel and which itself has something to say for this local church and its theology.

Protestant particularism on the other hand (not to be confused with evangelical congregational attachment) will always be inclined to orient itself to the locally restricted church, its faith, and its life, and to be content with a theological (occasionally intellectual, highly cultivated) provincialism.

The Catholic theologian will always start out from the fact that the gospel has not left itself without witness to any nation, any class or race, and he will try to learn from other churches. However deeply rooted he may be in a particular local church, he will not tie his theology to a particular nation, culture, race, class, form of society, ideology or school. Precisely in his specific loyalty, the Catholic theologian is interested in the universality of the Christian faith embracing all groups.

It is in this twofold sense then that I want to be and remain a Catholic theologian and to defend the truth of the Catholic faith in Catholic depth and breadth. And there is no doubt that a number of those who describe themselves as Protestant or evangelical can be and are in fact catholic in this sense, particularly in Tübingen. There ought to be joy at this, even on the part of the institutional Church.

THE CRITERION OF WHAT IS CATHOLIC

Does this affirmation of what is Catholic in time and space, depth and breadth, mean that you have to accept more or less everything that has been officially taught, ordered, and observed in the course of twenty centuries? Is it such a total identification that is meant by the Vatican Congregation for the Doctrine of the Faith and the German Bishop Conference when they speak of the 'complete', 'full', 'uncurtailed' truth of the Catholic faith?

Surely what is meant cannot be such a totalitarian conception of truth. For, even on the part of the institutional Church, it is now scarcely disputed that momentous and even theologically 'justified' errors have occurred in the history of Catholic teaching and practice and have been corrected (most tacitly) up to a point even by the Popes. This list is immense and includes the excommunication of the Ecumenical Patriarch of Constantinople and of the Greek Church, prohibition of vernacular liturgy, condemnation of Galileo and the modern scientific world-view, condemnation of Chinese and Indian forms of divine worship and names of God, the maintenance of the medieval secular power of the Pope up to the First Vatican Council with the aid of all the secular and spiritual means of excommunication, condemnation of human rights and particularly freedom of conscience and religion, and discrimination against the Jewish people; finally, in the present century, the numerous condemnations of modern historical-critical exegesis (with reference to the authenticity of the books of the Bible, source criticism, historicity, and literary genres) and condemnations in the dogmatic field, especially in connection with 'modernism' (the theory of evolution, understanding of development of dogma); and, in very present times, Pius XII's cleaning-up measures (likewise dogmatically justified) leading to the dismissal of the most outstanding theologians of the pre-conciliar period such as M.D. Chenu, Yves Congar, Henri de Lubac, Pierre Teilhard de Chardin, who almost all became conciliar theologians under John XXIII.

Is it not obvious that a distinction must be made, precisely for the sake of what is truly Catholic? Not everything that has been officially taught and practised in the Catholic Church is Catholic. Is it not true that catholicity would harden into 'Catholicism' if that which has 'become the Catholic reality' (the words are those of Joseph Cardinal Ratzinger of Munich) is simply accepted instead of being submitted to a criterion? And for the Catholic Christian too this criterion can be nothing but the Christian message, the *gospel* in its ultimate concrete form, *Jesus Christ himself*, who for the Church and – despite all assertions to the contrary – also for me is the Son and Word of God. He is and remains the norm in the light of which every ecclesiastical authority – and this is not disputed – must be judged: the norm by which the theologian must be tested and in the light of which he must continually justify himself in the spirit of self-criticism and true humility.

All this means that to be 'Catholic' does not imply – for the sake of a supposed 'fullness', 'integrity', 'completeness', 'uncurtailedness' – a false humility obediently accepting *everything*, putting up with *everything*. That would be a fatal pooling of contradictions, a confusion of true and false.

Certainly Protestantism has often been reproached for accepting too little, for making a one-sided selection from the whole. But on the other hand, it is often impossible to avoid reproaching Catholicism for accepting too much: a syncretistic accumulation of heterogeneous, distorted, and occasionally sub-Christian, pagan elements. Which is worse: a sin by defect or a sin by excess?

In any case then Catholicity must be critically understood – critically, according to the gospel. Together with the Catholic 'and' there must be considered the repeatedly necessary protest of the 'alone', without which the 'and' can never be meaningful. Reforms – in practice and teaching – must remain possible. For the theologian, this means nothing other than the fact that the Catholic theologian in a genuine sense must be evangelically oriented and conversely that the evangelical theologian in a genuine sense must be oriented in a Catholic way. Admittedly, this makes the theological demarcations objectively and conceptually more complicated than they might seem to be in the light of official doctrinal documents which are often terribly simple and display little catholic depth and breadth. Why then do I remain a Catholic? Precisely because as such I can assert an 'evangelical catholicity' concentrated and organized in the light of the gospel, which is nothing but genuine ecumenicity. Being Catholic, then, means being ecumenical in the fullest sense.

But what of the Roman factor?

'Roman Catholic' is a late and misleading neologism. Once again, I have nothing against Rome. I mean that precisely because I wanted to be a Catholic theologian, I could not tie my Catholic faith and Catholic theology simply to the ingrown Roman absolutist claims from the Middle Ages and later times. Certainly, there must be development in doctrine and practice, but only an *evolutio secundum evangelium*, or 'a development in accordance with the gospel'. An *evolutio praeter evangelium*, or 'a development apart from the gospel', may be tolerated. But an *evolutio contra evangelium,* 'a development contrary to the gospel', must be resisted. Applied to the papacy, this means that I have always acknowledged and defended the pastoral primacy of the Bishops of Rome linked to Peter and the great Roman tradition as an element in Catholic tradition that is supported by the gospel. But Roman legalism, centralism, and triumphalism for teaching, morality, and church discipline, dominant especially from the 11th century onward, but prepared long before then, are supported neither by the ancient Catholic tradition nor – still less – by the gospel itself; they were also disavowed by the Second Vatican Council. On the contrary, these things were mainly responsible for the Schism with the East and with the Reformation churches. They represent the 'Catholicism' about which the present controversy is being carried on in the name of the catholicity of the Catholic Church.

Are there some of our cardinals and bishops who do not want to see that in individual points of theory and practice their thinking is more Roman than Catholic? Perhaps my Protestant colleagues, Walter von Löwenich, an authority on both Luther and modern Catholicism, has rightly seen this in the infallibility debate when he writes: 'The essential question in the Küng case is not appropriately stated as "Is Küng still a Catholic?" It should be, "Will Catholicism struggle out of its dogmatic constriction into genuine catholicity?"'

Catholicity then is gift and task, indicative and imperative, origin and future. It is within this tension that I want to continue the pursuit of theology and as decisively as hitherto to make the message of Jesus Christ intelligible to people of the present time, while being ready to learn and to be corrected whenever it is a question of discussion between equal partners in a fraternal spirit. I must insist, against all the repeated assertions to the contrary by the German bishops, that I have never refused such a discussion even in regard to the Roman authorities, and that I have frequently had this kind of discussion both with representatives of the German Bishops Conference and with the local bishop. But, for the sake of protecting human and Christian rights and for the sake of the freedom of theological science, I have had to resist throughout all the years an interrogation of an Inquisition according all rights to itself and practically none to the accused person. That much I owe to those also who have suffered – and, as it seems, will suffer in the future – under these inhumane and un-Christian measures.

Catholic Church, yes! Roman Inquisition, no!

I know that I am not alone in this controversy about true catholicity. I shall fight against any acquiescence together with the many people who have hitherto supported me. We must continue to work together for a truly Catholic Church that is bound by the Gospel. For this, it is worthwhile to remain a Catholic.

6.7 FRANCIS A. SULLIVAN: *THE MAGISTERIUM AND THE ROLE OF THEOLOGIANS IN THE CHURCH* – 1983

The work[25] from which our extract is taken has been a highly influential text in relation to debates concerning such issues. Our extract is from Chapter 8 in which Sullivan provides an extended commentary on the International Theological Commission's (ITC's) document: *Theses on the Relationship between the Ecclesiastical Magisterium and Theology* (1975). Here, Sullivan believes the ITC to be an organization over-influenced by the *Congregation for the Doctrine of the Faith*, both in membership and outlook. Hence the theses reflect this fact. Nonetheless, by focusing upon the positive suggestions of a number of leading theologians in relation to the document, Sullivan works towards further suggestions concerning what steps may contribute towards providing a framework for truly collaborative and harmonious relations between Roman Catholic theologians and the institutional church, (here represented by the CDF) and, in particular, on matters of faith and morals. After drawing upon several studies to affirm the document's contention that the relation between the magisterium and theologians has been most varied throughout history, Sullivan makes a strong and thoughtful case for the freedom of theological enquiry, wedded to a faithful concern for the church. Dialogue and mutual learning should govern relations between the magisterium and Roman Catholic theologians.

❀

THE AREAS OF DIFFERENCE BETWEEN THE MAGISTERIUM AND THEOLOGIANS

> *Thesis 5. We must first speak of the difference between the functions which are proper to the magisterium and to theologians.*
> *1. The function of the magisterium is authoritatively to maintain the catholic integrity and unity of the Church's faith and practice. From this there follow specific functions which, at first sight, seem rather negative in character, but which are actually a positive service on behalf of the Church's life. These include 'the function of authoritatively interpreting the Word of God, both in Scripture and in Tradition' (DV10); the censuring of opinions which endanger the faith and morals of the Church, and the setting forth of truths which are especially relevant to the current situation. Although it does not seem appropriate for the magisterium to propose theological syntheses, still, in view of its concern for unity, it has to consider particular truths in the light of the whole, since the integration of particular truths into the whole is an important factor in truth itself.*

---

25. From *Magisterium – Teaching Authority in the Roman Catholic Church*, Dublin, Gill & Macmillan, 1983, 190–218. The theses from the International Theological Commission's document are quoted in italics.

2. The theologians' function can be described as one of mediating – in both directions – between the magisterium and the people of God. For 'theology has a two-fold relation, both with the Church's magisterium, and with the whole Christian community. In the first place it holds a sort of midway position between the faith of the Church and its magisterium'.[26] On the one hand, 'in each major socio-cultural region, theology, guided by the tradition of the universal Church, brings fresh scrutiny to bear upon the deeds and words revealed by God, recorded in the Scriptures and explained by the Fathers of the Church and by the magisterium. (Ad gentes, 22) Moreover, 'recent research and discoveries in the sciences, in history and in philosophy raise new questions which also require fresh investigation by theologians' (GS62). In this way, theology 'is to provide the help which the magisterium needs in order to fulfill its mission as light and norm for the Church'.[27] On the other hand, by their work of interpretation, teaching, and translation into contemporary thought-forms, theologians integrate the doctrine admonitions of the magisterium into a broader synthesis, and help the people of God to understand them better. In this way, they provide 'effective help so that the truth which the magisterium authoritatively proclaims, may be spread abroad, explained, confirmed and defended'.[28]

[Sullivan further elucidates theses 6–8, before offering the following incisive analysis.]

FREEDOM AND RESPONSIBILITY OF THEOLOGIANS

Since pertinent passages of the documents of Vatican II are quoted so often in these theses, it is a bit surprising that no reference was made here [i.e. in theses 8] to the statement of *Gaudium et spes* on the freedom to be accorded to all, whether clerics or lay people, who cultivate the sacred sciences.

> It is hoped that many laymen will receive an appropriate formation in the sacred sciences, and that some will develop and deepen these studies by their own labors. In order that such persons may fulfill their proper functions, let it be recognized that all the faithful, clerical and lay, possess a lawful freedom of inquiry and of thought, and the freedom to express their minds humbly and courageously about those matters in which they enjoy competence. (*GS*, 62)

If a theologian is going to pursue his vocation with genuine freedom, he has to be able to do research, to publish the fruits of his research, and to teach, with no limits set to his freedom other than the two mentioned in the thesis: namely, the truth, and his personal and social responsibility.

The problem is: how does one establish, in the concrete, the limits set by the truth, and the limits set by a sense of responsibility?

First: the limits set by the truth. Obviously, for the theologian, it is a question of the revealed truth, and for a Catholic, of revealed truth as this is handed on and understood in

---

26. Paul VI to the International Congress on the Theology of Vatican II, *AAS*, 58 (1966), 892.
27. Ibid.
28. Paul VI [to the International Congress on the Theology of Vatican II], 891.

the Catholic Church. The *sensus Ecclesiae* is a norm of truth for the theologian who does his work 'in a living communion with the faith of the Church'. This *sensus Ecclesiae* is found most authoritatively in the doctrine that has been infallibly taught by the Church's magisterium, 'whether by solemn judgment or by its ordinary and universal magisterium' (DS, 3011).

Now, as Pope John XXIII pointed out in his opening address to the Fathers of Vatican II, the truth of the doctrine of the Church is one thing; the form in which it has been expressed is another.[29] So 'being bound to the truth' does not mean being bound to the formulas in which the formulas in which that truth has been expressed in the past, even in solemn dogmatic definitions. A new formulation, or new conceptualisation, is possible, provided it does justice to the truth of the dogma.

Of course the question will arise whether a new formulation really does justice to the truth of the dogma. A theologian may well believe that his interpretation is within the limits set by the truth of the dogma; others may dispute this. This is the kind of issue that calls for the critical function which theologians are to exercise with regard to one another. It may even call for the critical function which the magisterium exercises with regard to the work of theologians, when it judges an opinion incompatible with the truth of the faith. How such a critical function should be exercised is the subject of theses 10–12. The present thesis points out that it should be exercised in a way that avoids giving the impression of being arbitrary or excessive.

Perhaps the more troublesome question concerning the limits of truth within which a Catholic theologian has to work is raised by the assertion of Pope Pius XII that for a Catholic theologian, 'the sacred magisterium ought to be the proximate and universal norm of truth in matters of faith and morals' (*Humani generis*, DS, 3884). The schema of the Constitution on the Church prepared for Vatican II by the preparatory commission, adding a reference to this place in *Humani generis*, stated that theologians must always look upon the ecclesiastical magisterium as the 'proximate norm of truth'.[30] Although no such statement was retained in any document of the Second Vatican Council, Pope Paul VI, on several occasions, returned to Pius XI's description of the magisterium as the 'proximate and universal norm of truth' for the Catholic theologian.[31]

Now if by the magisterium here one meant the infallible teaching of the magisterium, I could understand describing this as 'the proximate norm of truth' with regard to those elements of Christian faith which have actually been infallibly taught. On the other hand, the statement as it stands would seem to mean that even the non-infallible or ordinary magisterium is to be accepted by Catholic theologians as a 'proximate and universal norm of truth in matters of faith and morals'. It is my guess that this is one of the statements that Yves Congar had in mind when he wrote that some of the claims made by the magisterium in modern times 'seem excessive and unreal'.[32] At any rate, this is what he says in reference to this claim, when speaking of the new approach taken by Vatican II.

> With regard to the magisterium, the Council re-established the traditional relationship of subordination of pastoral authority to what is given, to the object, in short the primacy

29. Pope John XXIII, Opening address at the Second Vatican Council, 11 October 1962, *AAS*, 54 (1962), 792.
30. Schema Constitutionis De Ecclesia, cap. VII, n. 32; *Acta Synodalia*, I/4, 52.
31. Paul VI, 'Libentissimo sane', 1 Oct. 1966, *AAS*, 58 (1966), 891; 'Siamo particolarmente lieti', 11 July 1966, *AAS*, 58 (1966), 653; 'Praesentia vestra', 24 September 1967, *AAS*, 59 (1967), 962.
32. 'Bref historiane des formes du "Magistère" et ses rélations avec les decteurs', pp. 99–112.

of the *quod* over the *quo*. It did this both by insisting that the magisterium is bound to the Word of God and is at its service (LG 25, 4; DV 10, 2), and by not taking up the statement which the preparatory schema of 1962 had borrowed from *Humani generis*, namely, the idea that the magisterium is the 'proximate norm of truth'.[33]

It is obvious that the ITC did not take up this idea either, in the theses we are considering. It did say, in the first part of the present thesis, that 'respect for the magisterium is one of the specific elements of the science of theology'. But it also assigned to theologians a critical role with regard to the magisterium. I do not see what criteria would be available on which to base any criticism of magisterial statements, if one were to accept the magisterium itself as the proximate and universal norm of truth … .

THE CRITICAL ROLE OF THEOLOGIANS WITH REGARD TO THE MAGISTERIUM

[Thesis number *Five*] sees this critical role entailed in the theologian's task of interpreting statements of the magisterium, putting them into a wider context, and applying to them the science of hermeneutics.

We can distinguish between the critical work theologians do with regard to defined dogmas, and the critical approach theologians may take toward the ordinary, non-infallible teaching of the magisterium.

Juan Alfaro describes the interpretation of dogmas which it is the theologian's task to undertake, as 'critical, methodical and systematic'. He observes that dogmas always arise out of a prior theology, whose concepts and language the dogmas make their own. Inevitably this theology will involve limitations, and the kind of historical conditioning which no human thinking can escape. It will involve presuppositions which may not have been recognised at the time, but which exercised a hidden influence on the way the dogma was formulated.[34]

The result, as Rahner expresses it, is that every dogmatic formula will represent a kind of 'amalgam' of a faith-content and a theological conceptualisation.[35] Thus it is possible, and can become necessary, for the theologian to exercise his critical role with regard to those elements in the 'amalgam' which do not really belong to the essential faith-content of the dogma, and which may now render the dogma less intelligible or even less credible to the modern mind. An example would be the association of the dogma of original sin with the assumption that the Genesis story of the creation and fall of man is to be taken as straightforward history.

Joseph Ratzinger has also spoken of the grounds on which even radical criticism of papal doctrinal statements could be based.

> Criticism of papal pronouncements will be possible and even necessary, to the degree that they lack support in Scripture and the Creed, that is, in the faith of the whole

---

33. Ibid., 110–11 [see chapter 2 of present volume] (my translation). Another English version in 'A Brief History' (see note 17 above), p. 326.
34. J. Alfaro, 'Theology and the Magisterium', in *Problems and Perspectives of Fundamental Theology*, R. Latourelle and G. O'Collins (eds), New York, Ramsay, 1982, p. 351.
35. K. Rahner, 'Lehramt und Theologie', *Schriften*, 13, 83–4.

Church. When neither the consensus of the whole Church is had, nor clear evidence from the sources is available, a definitive decision is not possible. Were one formally to take place, while conditions for such an act were lacking, the question would have to be raised concerning its legitimacy.[36]

The question of the limits of the freedom of Catholic theologians to exercise a critical function with regard to the ordinary, non-infallible teaching of the papal magisterium has been a matter of intense discussion since the publication of the encyclical *Humanae vitae* in 1968.[37] In the previous chapter I have spoken about the possibility of legitimate internal dissent from such teaching. What must be raised now is the further question about the limits of the freedom of Catholic theologians publicly to express their dissent from such teaching, if they are convinced that some statement of this magisterium is erroneous.

It will be recalled that according to the encyclical *Humani generis* of Pius XII, when a pope, in an encyclical, expresses his judgment on an issue that was previously controverted, this can no longer be seen as a question for free discussion by theologians (D-S 3885). The schema on the Church presented to Vatican II in 1962 by the preparatory commission followed Pius XII on this point,[38] but there is no such statement in any of the documents that were approved by the Council. There is, however, the statement of *Gaudium et spes* quoted above, to the effect that all the faithful, clerical or lay, are free to express their minds humbly and courageously about those matters in which they enjoy competence (GS 62).

While the documents of Vatican II make no mention of the possibility of legitimate dissent from ordinary papal teaching, the Council can be said to have expressed its own dissent from previous papal teaching on several important questions, such as religious liberty, and the identification of the Mystical Body of Christ with the Roman Catholic church. Theologians who had been censured or silenced for their dissent on these issues during the pontificate of Pius XII came to be among the most highly respected *periti* of Vatican II. The Council could hardly have arrived at a number of its innovative decisions if it had not been for the preparatory work done by the theologians who had taken a critical stance towards what had been the official teaching of the Holy See.

One important aspect of the kind of teaching that is found in papal encyclicals, which justifies a critical approach by theologians, is the extent to which such teaching goes beyond the pastoral exposition and defence of the doctrine of the faith, and takes on the character of strictly theological discourse. As Yves Congar puts it:[39]

---

36. Joseph Ratzinger, *Das Neue Volk Gottes*, Düsseldorf, 1969, 144.
37. To mention just a few contributions: C.E. Curran and R.E. Hunt, *Dissent In and For the Church*, New York, 1969; C.E. Curran (ed.), *Contraception: Authority and Dissent*, New York, 1969, especially the article in this by J. Komonchak, 'Ordinary Papal Magisterium and Religious Assent', 101–26; J.F. Kippley, 'Continued Dissent: Is it Responsible?', *Theological Studies*, 32 (1971), 48–65; K. Rahner, 'On the Encyclical "Humanae vitae"', *Theological Investigations*, 11, 263–87; idem, 'The Dispute concerning the Church's Teaching Office', *Theoogical Investigations*,, 14, 86–97; R.M. Gula, 'The Right to Private and Public Dissent from Specific Pronouncements of the Ordinary Magisterium', *Eglise et Theologie*, 9 (1978), 319–43; H. Küng and J. Moltmann (eds), *The Right to Dissent, Concilium*, 158 (8/1982).
38. *Acta Synodalia*, I/4, 50.
39. 'Bref Historique', 110.

In their encyclicals (the series begins with *Mirari vos* of Gregory XVI, 1832) modern Popes have *done theology*. And a specific kind of theology, the kind practiced in the Roman schools, whose personnel were recruited and kept under surveillance along a very definite line.

Archbishop Coffy has also noted the problem that arises from the fact that when the magisterium 'does theology' in its authoritative pronouncements, it inevitably makes theological options.

> The situation gains in complexity as one accepts theological pluralism – and how can one do otherwise when faced by facts? To accept pluralism is to accept that the faith can legitimately express itself in different theologies ... This explains the reaction of theologians when faced with certain interventions of the magisterium. They have the impression that the magisterium imposes on them its particular theology. What they ask is that it make explicit its theological options and abstain from presenting them as the only possible way of expressing the faith.[40]

It is my impression that the criticism of the ordinary magisterium that has been most consistently voiced by Catholic theologians in recent decades is along the lines suggested here by Congar and Coffy: namely that on certain issues the official teaching of the Holy See (encyclicals, declarations of the CDF) seems to them to reflect, in too narrow a way, theological options which are not seen as representing the most widely respected theological opinion available in the Church today. If I am not mistaken, it was with the intention of providing a remedy for this situation that the Episcopal Synod of 1967 recommended the setting up of the International Theological Commission. The question is how effectively this body is being consulted in the preparation of the doctrinal statements that are issued by the Holy See. In any case, I do not see how one can deny to a theologian the right to express his criticism of what he perceives to be a strictly theological option, even when it is incorporated into a document of the ordinary magisterium.

At the same time, of course, such criticism must be of the positive, not the destructive kind, and in choosing the manner and medium of its expression, the theologian has to observe the moral principle of personal and social responsibility. What concretely does this involve?

With regard to the manner of expressing criticism or dissent, it seems obvious that it must not only be in accord with the canons of professional courtesy, but must also show the religious respect which is due to the bearers of pastoral authority in the Church.

It is not so easy to determine what the principle of personal and social responsibility requires with regard to the medium in which a theologian may express his criticism of official teaching. The question was fairly easy to decide when theologians could share their views with their professional colleagues through the medium of scholarly journals, with little likelihood that their ideas would reach the wider public. However, the 'information explosion' of modern times, and the tendency of popular journals to publicise any opinion that is critical of positions taken by those in authority, drastically increases the probability that what is

---

40. Robert Coffy, 'The Magisterium and Theology', in *Readings in Moral Theology No. 3, The Magisterium and Morality*, C. Curran and R. McCormick (eds), New York, Ramsay, 1982 p. 212.

carefully and moderately put forward in a scholarly article may subsequently be broadcast to the general public in a crude or tendentious way.

Pope John Paul II, in his address to the faculty and students of the Catholic University in Washington, D.C. (7 October 1979), said that theologians must take into account 'the right of the faithful not to be troubled by theories and hypotheses that they are not expert in judging or that are easily simplified or manipulated by the public opinion for ends that are alien to the truth'.[41] The question, then, is: does the possibility that the critical opinion which a theologian has published in a scholarly journal might be picked up and manipulated by the mass-media for ends alien to the truth, mean that theologians may never publish opinions which, if so manipulated, could 'trouble the faithful'?

The supposition of this question is that the kind of publicity which could trouble the faithful is an effect that is foreseen as possible, but is not intended. It would be another question if theologians deliberately sought to stir up public opinion against the teaching of the magisterium: this is mentioned in thesis 11 among tactics that would be harmful to a spirit of dialogue.

In the hypothesis that the kind of publicity that could trouble the faithful is an effect which the theologian does not intend, then the 'moral principle of personal and social responsibility' would require that he weigh the value which he intends to promote by publishing his criticism against the value which he foresees might be damaged by the unwanted publicity that might be given to his criticism. It seems to me that this would be a case of a conflict of values, neither of which can be simply given an absolute priority over the other. I do not see how one could maintain that the protection of the faithful from being troubled by the criticism of official teaching is a value that would always and necessarily have to be preferred to the value involved in the exercise by theologians of their critical function with regard to the magisterium. Nor do I see how they could exercise their critical function effectively if they could not share their views with their colleagues in serious theological publications. Such communication is the very lifeblood of scholarly work. To stifle it would be to deprive the Church of a vital factor in its striving for the truth … .

> *Thesis 12. Before instituting any formal process about a question of doctrine, the competent authority should exhaust all the ordinary possibilities of reaching agreement through dialogue in order to clarify a questionable opinion (for example, by discussing the matter in person or by correspondence in which questions are asked and replies given). If no genuine agreement can be reached by such dialogical methods, the magisterium should employ a broad and flexible range of measures, beginning with various kinds of warnings, 'verbal sanctions' etc. In the most serious kind of case, when all the methods of dialogue have been used to no avail, the magisterium, after consulting theologians of various schools, has no choice but to act in defence of the endangered truth and the faith of the believing people.*
>
> *According to the time-honored rules, the fact of 'heresy' can be definitively established only if the theologian accused of this has been clearly guilty of 'obstinacy', that is, if he has closed himself off from any discussion aimed at elucidating an opinion that seems contrary to the faith – and in effect, refuses to engage in dialogue. The fact of heresy can be determined only*

---

41. *AAS*, 71 (1979), 1264.

when all the rules concerning the interpretation of dogmatic statements and all theological qualifications have been applied to the case. In this way, even when a grave decision cannot be avoided, the genuine spirit of dialogical procedure can still be maintained.

This final thesis deals with the critical function which the magisterium exercises in regard to theologians when serious questions are raised about the orthodoxy of their teaching or their published writings. According to K. Lehmann, the thesis does not intend to discuss specific questions about the juridical procedure to be followed in such cases. What it proposes is that the method of dialogue be used at every stage: both prior to and during any formal process that is undertaken.

The principles of subsidiarity and decentralisation would seem to require that such dialogue begin at the diocesan level, and, if necessary, continue at the level of an episcopal conference, before a case is referred to Rome. If it is referred to Rome, the case will be handled by the Sacred Congregation for the Doctrine of the Faith, according to the rules of procedure approved by Pope Paul VI and promulgated on 15 January 1974.[42] It was not the intention of the ITC to express a judgment on these rules, or to suggest changes in them, but rather to suggest that the spirit and method of dialogue should characterise the procedure at every step.

It is well known that various aspects of the procedure of the CDF has been criticised in Catholic publications, especially in connection with the 'colloquium' to which Edward Schillebeeckx was summoned by the CDF in December 1979.[43] Given this criticism, one could suggest that the CDF, which surely approved this thesis of the ITC, review its procedure precisely with a view to making sure that there can be no legitimate complaint about a failure to respect a genuine spirit of dialogue at any point from the acceptance of a case by the CDF to a final deliberation and judgment by its board of cardinals.

One final word. A genuine spirit of dialogue calls for both sides to be willing to learn as well as to teach. In an allocution given just about six years prior to the opening of the Second Vatican Council, Pope Pius XII denounced the 'evident error' of thinking that theologians could be '*magistri Magisterii*'.[44] But was not the success of Vatican II due in large measure to the recognition by the magisterium – in the persons of the assembled bishops – of their need to learn as well as to teach? The four years of Vatican II are often spoken of, with nostalgia, as the golden age of collaboration between theologians and the magisterium. Anyone who lived in Rome during those years, as I did, saw abundant evidence that many bishops were willing to be taught by theologians, obviously careless of the accusation that they might be committing the error of accepting theologians as '*magistri Magisterii*'.

If a teacher must keep on learning in order to teach well, he has to accept his need to be taught. This applies both to the *magisterium cathedrae pastoralis* and to the *magisterium cathedrae magistralis*. Fruitful dialogue is impossible when either claims a monopoly on the role of the teacher, and refuses to be taught by the other.

---

42. *ASS*, 63 (1974), 234–6. J. Hamer, Secretary of the CDF, has explained this procedure in 'In the service of the Magisterium: The Evolution of a Congregation', *The Jurist*, 37 (1977), 340–57.

43. Bas van Iersel, 'Le colloque Schillenbeeckx vu par un témoin', Études 353 (1980), 255066; also some remarks of Y. Congar in his article 'Les théologiens dans l'Église aujourd'hui', *Les Quatre Fleuves*, 12 (1980), 22–7.

44. Allocution 'Di gran cuore', 14 September 1956, *AAS*, 48 (1956), 709.

6.8 MARC REUVER: *EMERGING THEOLOGIES –*
FAITH THROUGH RESISTANCE – 1993

Our next extract[45] demonstrates that, particularly in the third world where an estimated 80 per cent of the world's population now live, there are very different theological priorities and methods in comparison to the so-called 'developed'/industrialized world of Europe and North America. Reuver agrees with those critics who see such 'western' theology as 'imperialistic, capitalistic and authoritarian'. Our extract outlines how the struggles of various peoples against poverty, oppression, repression and discrimination have influenced theology. In particular, *resistance* to such dehumanizing forces has helped shape the theologies in many regions and influenced the shape and self-identity of the church in such parts. What emerges is that such theology carries the true authority of the people for it seeks to address and be informed by their struggles and to represent their resistance, hopes and triumphs against the oppressive forces which they face. People come to a greater understanding of God through their *experiences* of God's liberating power. Such theology is firmly wedded to history in its making. In particular, Reuver explores liberation theology in its Latin American context with an overriding emphasis upon *praxis* and upon love, peace and justice over oppression and death. Next he turns to Africa's 'Prophetic Theology', seeking to relate their theology to the pressing events in the here and now. Finally, he turns to Asia's 'Contemplative Commitment' articulated in a 'Spirituality of Action'. Reuver believes that the so-called 'developed' world can learn much from these new ways of doing theology which derive their authority from the struggles of the downtrodden. All of the theological methods outlined have come under close scrutiny by the institutional church bodies in Rome. Reuver is critical of Vatican attempts to 'reign in' such theologies, as such actions thereby question the very authority of the people's experiences of struggle. Christianity, it emerges, should challenge *all* forms of oppressive power and authority.

❁

The people's struggle for liberation and emancipation certainly is one of the major characteristics of our present time. This phenomenon is the result of a growing awareness of the people that manipulation and oppression undermine their human dignity. Instead of being at the mercy of the powerful they want to assume full responsibility for their own life and destiny. The desire to rediscover their own cultural and religious identity is an important element in this process.

This process comes up against power mechanisms eager to maintain the *status quo*. The emergence of the people is felt by the dominating élite as a real threat.

The present essay focuses on the religious and theological elements of the people's struggle. Through resistance to oppression, dictatorships, racism and sexism the people create new theologies.

---

45. In *The Ecumenical Movement Tomorrow*, Marc Reuver, Friedrich Solms and Gerrit Huizer (eds), Kampen, Kok Publishing, 1993, 263–80.

COMMON CHARACTERISTICS

The emerging theologies have different names: liberation theologies, third world theologies, emancipation theologies, feminist theology, prophetic theologies, living theologies or contextual theologies. The most significant and unifying aspect of all these theologies is the people's resistance to oppression ... . Sacred Scriptures and traditional sources have become important sources of inspiration and strength in the struggle. Both the Christian faith and traditional religious convictions and cultures fortify the people who assert their rights. A new sense of equality and dignity, an ardent desire for freedom and a centuries-old memory of oppression and humiliation constitute the link of the people's resistance movements across nations and continents ... .

The new theologies are born of suffering, humiliation and death. They are signs of rebellion and protest against personal and structural sins, against various forms of evil and inhuman domination. The starting point of the emerging theologies is the experience of faith and the awareness and description of the socio-economic and cultural reality understood in an analytical and intuitive way, together with the struggle for change and transformation. The story of Jesus of Nazareth and the traditional religious heritage are re-read and assessed anew in the light of the present suffering and the struggle for change.

People encounter God in the struggle for life. The new, emerging theologies are not concerned with the neatness of a theological system, but with the people who discover the presence of God in the history of struggles of the poor and the oppressed. It is the role of the theologians to interpret and systematize the people's discovery of God's presence.

The theological core of these new emerging theologies is the conviction or the belief that God is a liberating God. He reveals himself as a liberating God in the voices of the poor.[46] The conviction that God can be encountered in the resistance of the poor is based both on actual experience and on insight in the Bible and the Tradition.

The inhuman situation and the suffering and struggle of the people for liberation is the starting point of theological reflection. Theologians discover signs of God in his role as liberator of the poor and oppressed. They read the Bible in the light of God's concern with the human family and its history. The Sacred Scriptures appear as a collective work with many stories illustrating God's liberating activities. The same liberating God reveals himself presently in the oppressed people of our time.[47] In this context the stories in which God's liberating action is most evident are the story of the Exodus out of Egypt, the critical voice of the prophets against society and its leaders, the conflicts of Jesus with the leaders of the Jewish people, his death on the Cross and his Resurrection. Christology plays a fundamental role in the new emerging theologies, since it associates Jesus of Nazareth with the actual life of the people who now experience God's liberating action in history.

The new theologies begin with the conviction that the Christian faith is directly connected with the way people make history. The reading of the historical Jesus should be placed in a context of the present oppression and resistance.[48] The Jesus of the Gospel, in the context of his commitment to the liberation of the poor and the oppressed, has a message for

46. G. Gutiérrez, *The Power of the Poor in History*, Selected Writings, Orbis Books, New York, 1983, 208–9.
47. Ibid.
48. J. Sobrino, *Christology at the Crossroads*, London, SCM, 1978, 9–13.

those actually engaged in the history of the human family, especially of those who are in need of liberation. This theological concept of Jesus Christ enables theologians to see the resistance against suffering and oppression as the action of God's grace and the spirit of liberation, as the spirit of Jesus Christ and of God whom he called his Father, or the Spirit who lives among Christians and people of other faiths. The church must obey this Spirit, because it does not exist for itself, but for the proclamation of God's Kingdom and the liberation of the people.[49] ...

THE NEW EMERGING THEOLOGIES AND THE CHURCHES

Gustavo Gutiérrez [argues that], in continents like Latin America, Africa and Asia the challenge [for the churches] does not come from indifferent people who are affected by the secularization process, or from non-believers. In the third world countries the challenge comes in the opinion of many from a non-person, i.e., from the person who is not recognized as a human being by the dominant social order: the poor, the exploited, the one who is systematically and legally despoiled of his human nature, the one who hardly feels human. The non-person questions not so much our religious world, as our economic, social, political and cultural world. Therefore, all transformation is concentrated on a de-humanized society. The question is not so much how to speak of God in an indifferent and non-believing world, but how to proclaim the Father, the Son and the Spirit in an inhuman world. How to tell the non-person that she or he is a child of God, of a God who is a liberating God.[50]

What Gutiérrez is saying here is that the origin and development of the Christian doctrine of faith is conditioned, limited and strongly coloured by the socio-economic, historical, cultural and political context. The new emerging theologies have accused the western theology of being imperialistic, capitalistic and authoritarian. In principle they are right. In the West also the dominant theology is contextual, but this context differs from the one experienced in third world countries.

For centuries the Christian doctrine of faith has been proposed as unique, uniform and universal. Considering the main sources of the Christian faith, the Old and New Covenants, it becomes obvious that these writings were conditional and coloured by the way of thinking and culture of the Jewish people and of the particular context of the Mediterranean people. A second source, the interpretation produced by the Fathers of the post-apostolic centuries and the formulation of the profession of faith as the result of the first Ecumenical Councils does not escape a very specific context. A further source includes the first theological treatises and official statements by popes, bishops and local synods and councils. Then appeared the first prayer books and the disciplinary rules of various regions. All these sources were systematized, rationalized and promoted to become an abstract, academic science in the universities from the 12th century onwards. The great majority of all these sources – differently judged by Roman Catholics, Orthodox and Protestants – originated and developed in the Western context with its own political and cultural history.

---

49. Eric Borgman, *Sporen van de Bevrijdende God*, Kok, Kampen, 1990, 27–31.
50. G. Gutiérrez, *Bevrijdingsbewegingen en Theologie*, in *Concilium*, 10 (1974), 122–33.

For many centuries as well the Church was considered as the exclusive instrument of salvation of humanity. It was seen as actualizing the redemptive act of Jesus Christ through the sacraments, the liturgy, through the study of the Bible and the right interpretation of the Tradition. The pope, the bishops and the hierarchical structures constituted the organizational instrument for the understanding of the Church, its proper functioning and its missionary task. This Church was essentially clerical; the voice of the laity was hardly heard.

Tradition, official dogmas and doctrinal declarations, a fixation on juridical-canonical codes of moral doctrine and liturgy offered the official and obligatory directives for the faith of the believers. The world and the issues of society had a mere relative value: they were to be converted through the mediation of the Church.

This Church model became the official religion of the empire in the 4th century, under Emperor Constantine. Consequently, the Church became an instrument for legitimizing the expansion of the empire, and later for the colonization of the peoples.

In 1989 a document was published, entitled 'The Road to Damascus, Kairos and Conversion', signed by Christians from seven different nations: the Philippines, South Korea, Namibia, South Africa, El Salvador, Nicaragua and Guatemala. The signatories wrote: 'European nations that colonised our countries pride themselves on being Christian. Conquest and evangelisation, colonisation and the building of churches advanced together. The cross blessed the sword which was responsible for the shedding of our people's blood. The sword imposed the faith and protected the churches, sharing power and wealth with them. As a result of discovery and conquest millions of people have been killed; indigenous populations have been eliminated; entire civilisations and cultures have been destroyed. Millions have been enslaved, uprooted from their native land, deculturised, and deprived of their wealth and resources. Women and children have been victims of additional and distinct oppression. Natural resources have been exploited and abused to the extent that they cannot be replenished. One of the most serious and lasting legacies of European colonialism is racism. In South Africa it has been institutionalised and legalised in the form of the notorious system of apartheid.[51]

Under the influence of Protestantism and the ecumenical movement the Roman Catholic Church slowly opened up to society, social participation and integral development of the human family. The Second Vatican Council legitimized this openness. It confirmed that although the Roman Catholic Church possesses in its fullness the truth given to the human family, elements of truth can also be found in other Christian churches. The most revolutionary affirmation of the Council was that the Church of Christ is first and foremost the People of God. The mystery of salvation is to be found in the inter-action of Christ with his people (*Constitution of the Church*). Only thereafter the Council deals with the hierarchical structures of the Church, the role and the authority of the pope and the bishops.[52]

---

51. *Kairos, Three Prophetic Challenges to the Church*, ed. Robert McAfee Brown, Grand Rapids, Eerdmans, 1990, *The Road to Damascus, Kairos and Conversion*, 115–16.

52. *Dogmatic Constitution on the Church* (*Lumen Gentium*), in *The Documents of Vatican II*, ed. Walter M. Abbot, SJ, Chicago, Associated Press, 1966, 14–86.

In this context the Latin American theologian Leonardo Boff speaks of a new way of being church. The tens of thousands of basic ecclesial communities whose members are the poor and the oppressed form the People of God, the Church of Jesus Christ … .[53]

Boff thinks that the Gospel is the challenging chart of the basic ecclesial communities. The Gospel is heard, shared and believed within the community; in its light the members reflect on the problem of life. The Gospel and faith in the Word of God become the great doorway into the actual social and political problems. Surprisingly this popular exegesis comes very close to the exegesis of the Fathers of the Church. 'It is an exegesis that goes beyond the words and captures the living, spiritual meaning of the text.'[54]

This is a new way of being church, Boff says. The church is not only an institution with its sacred scriptures, canon law, liturgical norms, or orthodox and moral imperatives. The church is also an event. The church is where the community meets. In many places the basic ecclesial communities threaten the established social order. The communities are repressed, persecuted and have their saints and martyrs … .

LATIN AMERICAN LIBERATION THEOLOGY

Among the new emerging theologies the Latin American liberation theology is the most elaborated and systematized one. This theology 'from the underside of history' has gone through several phases:

1) The preparatory phase (1962–1968), from the beginning of the Second Vatican Council until the acceptance of its doctrine and teachings by the Second Conference of the Latin American bishops in Medellin.

2) The formative phase (1968–1975), from the Medellin Conference to the conference in 1975 in Detroit on the 'Theology in the Americas'. At this conference contacts were made with representatives of black theology and feminist theology and one began to speak of 'liberation theologies'.

3) The systematizing phase, from 1975 onwards. Liberation theologians started to reflect on the methods of the liberation theology and to rethink the main themes, particularly christology and ecclesiology. With the formation of the Ecumenical Association of Third World Theologians, EATWOT (1976) liberation theologies found a place in the broader context of third world theologies.[55]

The first authors, Gustavo Gutiérrez, Hugo Assmann and Leonardo Boff, emphasized the fact that liberation theology is not just another theology, but a different way of doing theology. Gutiérrez gives the following definition: 'Theology in this context will be a critical reflection both from within and upon the historical praxis, in confrontation with the word of the Lord as lived and experienced in faith.'[56] Experience of faith is a first act, theological reflection a second act. The experience of faith is contextualized. It is militant and a praxis that aims at transforming the relationships of oppression and domination. 'The theology of

53. L. Boff, *Church, Charism and Power, Liberation Theology and the Institutional Church*, London, SCM Press, 1985, 126.

54. Ibid., 127.

55. R. Gibellini, *The Liberation Theology Debate*, London, SCM Press, 1987, 1–5.

56. G. Gutiérrez, *The Power of the Poor in History*, 60.

liberation means a critical reflection on the human praxis of Christians in the light of the praxis of Jesus and the demands of the faith.'[57]

The theology of liberation tries to articulate a reading of reality beginning from the poor and with a concern for the liberation of the poor. To do this the theologian uses human and social sciences, engages in theological reflection and calls for practical actions which help the life of the oppressed. The theologian, therefore, has a political and ethical option for the poor in the light of the Gospel. This option is determined by the socio-political context.

He has to interpret Scriptures and other sources of the Christian tradition not in the abstract, but on the basis of a specific political and social situation. In order to understand the socio-political context concepts were taken from social and political sciences.

Christology is central in liberation theology. The theologian has to discover the story of Jesus in its total historical depth. He has to rediscover the historical Jesus in his praxis, that is to say, Jesus in his transforming reality towards the Kingdom of God. Christians have the mandate to follow Jesus in their specific context. Like the historical Jesus, Christians should not only announce the Kingdom of God, but make it present in their concrete situation. In this way the story of Jesus is continued in the discipleship of Christians.

A second characteristic is the ecclesiology of the liberation theology ... .[58] 'If the church wishes to be faithful to the God of Jesus Christ, it must become aware of itself from underneath, from among the poor of this world, the exploited classes, despised ethnic groups and marginalized cultures. To be born, to be reborn, as church from below, from among them, today means to die, in a concrete history of oppression. In this ecclesiological approach, which takes up one of the central themes of the Bible, Christ is seen as the Poor One identified with the oppressed and plundered of the world. Here new paths open wide, for this is what is called the underside of history.'[59]

A third important issue is spirituality. Discipleship of Jesus is seen as a collective way to holiness. Spirituality is an individual feature, but more so a community feature... . 'The issue of spirituality is nothing else but conformity with the revelation of God in the concrete history' ... .[60]

On 3 September 1984 the Vatican Congregation for the Doctrine of the Faith issued an 'Instruction on certain aspects of the theology of liberation'. This document argues against the danger of reducing the Gospel and the Kingdom of God merely to earthly realities. It strongly denounces the so-called scientific approach to the historic development of society as formulated by Marxist analysis. 'A disastrous confusion is created between the poor of the Scriptures and the proletariat of Marx.' Furthermore, the so-called Church of the Poor becomes a Church of a class which can easily become a challenge to 'the sacramental and institutional Church which was willed by the Lord himself'.[61]

Almost two years later, on 5 April 1986, the same Vatican Congregation published an 'Instruction on Christian freedom and liberation'. This document intends to offer a correct

57. L. Boff, *Eine kreatieve Recepzion des II Vatikanums aus der Sicht des Armen: Theologie der Befreiung, Orientierung*, 46 (1979), 640.
58. [See, also, readings nos 1.7 and 1.10 in this present volume.]
59. G. Gutiérrez, *The Power of the Poor in History*, 211.
60. J. Sobrino, *Liberación con Espiritu, Appuntes para una nueva Espiritualidad*, Sal Terrae, Santander 1985, 32.
61. *Osservatore Romano*, 3 Settembre 1984.

view of the relationship between faith and praxis. Liberation theology proposes the primacy of praxis, but according to the document praxis must be interpreted in the light of the truth which precedes praxis. The document agrees with liberation theologians who state that liberation is a problem of the entire human family. The consequences of sin and evil in the form of misery and oppression affect above all the poor. The preferential option for the poor – although not exclusive – is based upon the life and teaching of Jesus Christ. The Vatican document recognizes the legitimacy of a 'theological reflection developed from a particular experience' which derives from a 'commitment to the complete liberation of the human person'.[62] The second Vatican Instruction certainly does not approve liberation theology, but it takes up issues, concepts and themes emphasized by liberation theologians. A few days after its publication Pope John Paul II wrote in a letter to the Brazilian Bishops' Conference that insofar as liberation theology conforms to the teaching of the Gospel, the living tradition and the magisterium of the Church, it is 'not only opportune but useful and necessary'.[63]

LIBERATION THEOLOGY IN SOUTH AFRICA

The South African liberation theology or anti-apartheid theology came into being between 1960 and 1970. The black consciousness movement became increasingly convinced that within South African society no process towards a growing multi-racial coexistence would come about. Consequently, it became a resistance movement against the socio-economic, cultural and political oppression of the black people by the white minority. Church and theology played an important role from the outset. Church and pulpit were considered as the most effective means to propagate the ideas of liberation and emancipation.

God and religion are at the centre of the struggle between the black people and the whites. The dominating white minority bases its apartheid, that is, racial discrimination, on the Scriptures. The oppressed black population appeals to the very same Scriptures in support of their liberation.

The black liberation theologian underlines the fact that the identity of the black population is equal to that of the white. All human beings are created in the image of God. For the Creator there is no difference between white and black. The black theologian criticizes the white oppressors who invoke the Bible in support of racism. He asserts that in the struggle against discrimination and oppression Jesus Christ is present. He is on the side of those who suffer and struggle for liberation.

Steve Biko emphasized the role of Christianity, churches and religion in the South African society. Christianity, he says, is responsible for the colonization and the submission of the blacks. Christian religion was associated with the culture of the whites. This process still continues; the blacks are accused of all existing evils, but there is no mention of a relationship between these evils and poverty, unemployment and lack of education which characterize the

---

62. *Osservatore Romano*, 5 Aprile 1986.
63. *Osservatore Romano*, 13 Aprile 1986.

life of the black population.[64] In the eyes of Biko, Christianity of the whites covers up oppression.

The black liberation theologian wants to show, in the words of Desmond Tutu, 'that the Christian Bible and the Gospel of Jesus Christ are subversive in regard to all evil, oppression and exploitation, and that God stays at the side of the oppressed and the humiliated, that he is the liberating God of the Exodus, who liberates his people from all forms of captivity'.[65]

In opposition to the white theologians who defend the political ideology with arguments taken from the Scriptures, the black theologian does not associate his political viewpoint with a specific ideology, but he sees his resistance as a consequence of his obedience to God, in response to the Gospel of Jesus Christ. Consequently, the conflict of apartheid is above all a theological problem, and only in a second instance does it become a political question.

From this conviction and in this context South African theologians, both black and white, elaborated in 1985 'The Kairos Document, A Challenge to the Church'. This document is a Christian, biblical and theological commentary on the political crisis in South Africa. It is a serious attempt to reflect on the present situation in the country. It also is a critique of the current theological models that determine the attitude of the leading white churches. It is an attempt to offer biblical and theological alternatives, in order to design a model for a different future.[66]

The Church in South Africa is divided, the document states. Three theologies can be identified which represent the different theological stances in relation to the present situation. First of all there is the 'State theology' as the theological justification for the *status quo* with its apartheid, racism, capitalism and totalitarianism. State theology abuses theological concepts and biblical texts for its own political interests. The document illustrates this by referring to concrete examples. The text of the letter to the Romans (13:1–7) is used to provide the State with an absolute and divine authority which demands blind obedience of all citizens. A second example is the idea of law and order to determine and control what can be allowed to the people, what is just or unjust. Precisely this concept has produced the unjust and discriminatory laws of apartheid, and has institutionalised oppression. A further example is the use of the word communism to brand as a communist anyone who rejects State theology.

There also is a 'Church theology' which represents the theological stance of leaders of liberal English-speaking churches. This theology is critical of apartheid, but its criticism is superficial and rather counter-productive, since it uses a few general Christian concepts to be applied to the South African situation. It does not provide a real socio-political analysis, guided as it is by the conviction that social and political matters are not the concern of the Church.

The Kairos Document opts for a 'Prophetic theology'. This differs from academic theology which deals with all biblical themes in a systematic way and formulates general Christian principles and doctrines. Prophetic theology concentrates on those aspects of the

---

64. S. Biko, *I write what I like*, in *The Church [as] seen by a Young Layman*, A selection of his writings, ed. A. Stubbs, London, SCM Press, 1978, 56–7.
65. Desmond Tutu, *Hope and Sufferings. Sermons and Speeches*, ed. J. Webster, London, Collins, 1984, 155.
66. *Kairos, Three Prophetic Challenges to the Church, A Theological Comment on the Political Crisis in South Africa*, 15–65.

Word of God that have an immediate bearing upon the critical situation in which the people live. It does not pretend to be comprehensive; it speaks to the particular circumstances of a particular time and place. It reads the signs of the times and it calls to action. It takes a firm stand and deals with the good and evil, justice and injustice, God and the devil. It denounces sin, announces salvation and emphasizes hope.

Analysing suffering and oppression in the Bible and reading the signs of the times, the document concludes … 'To say that the Church must now take sides unequivocally and consistently with the poor and the oppressed is to overlook the fact that the majority of Christians in South Africa have already done so. By far the greater part of the Church is poor and oppressed. Of course, it cannot be taken for granted that all who are oppressed have take up their cause and are struggling for their liberation. Nor can it be assumed that all oppressed Christians are fully aware of the fact that their cause is God's cause. Nevertheless it remains true that the Church is already on the side of the oppressed because that is where the majority of its members are to be found. This fact needs to be appropriated and confirmed by the Church as a whole'.

CONTEXTUAL AFRICAN THEOLOGIES

'Among the Third World continents, Africa appears essentially as a land of domination and exploitation, quartered, torn apart, divided, atomized, trampled underfoot. It is the continent where frequently the people have no dignity, no rights and hope.' These gloomy remarks open the African Report to the General Assembly of the Ecumenical Association of Third World Theologians, held in December 1986 in Oaxtepec.[67]

The Report attempts to provide a general framework in which the African liberation theologies originate and develop; it firstly refers to the political challenges. Africa appears as a puzzle made up to fifty-five countries, thousands of ethnic groups and dialects, and arbitrary boundaries inherited from the colonization period. The continent now lives neo-colonialism which through technical assistance and forms of cooperation and the present debt system has made the African people dependent on industrialized power forces. There exists, furthermore, a permanent State crisis which leaves African countries and their peoples in a political void. The militarization of African States aggravates the dependence. Poverty and misery are created artificially by the pauperization of the great majority, and the brutal enrichment of a few.

Not only material misery is the dominant feature; cultural and social underdevelopments have led to anthropological pauperization. It is precisely in the field of culture that the colonization process has had most devastating effect. In the colonial system the most effective means to dominate the African population was to destroy their culture. The greatest tragedy of Africa resides in the permanence of this state of annihilation following independence. More than 25 years after the colonial times, most African countries have recovered neither their language, history and art or their rich spiritual heritage.

---

67. *Third World Theologies, Commonalities & Divergencies*, ed. K.C. Abraham, New York, Orbis Books, 1983; A document based on the Seventh International Conference of the Ecumenical Association of Third World Theologies, 197–8, *African Report*, 28–56.

Ethnologists agree in stating that traditional Africa is primarily religious … . At present traditional religions are re-awakening. The people welcomes these, because they speak their own language and propose answers to their fundamental questions about life. This re-awakening is not aggressive, but discrete and conciliatory. They adapt themselves to the religion received from the missionaries. The result is a kind of syncretism, a reduction and translation of the Bible and the Christian liturgy into African categories and rites.[68]

New theologies in Africa emerge within this context. African theologies are contextual. They have the same elements of liberation and resistance as in other continents. However, it is not so much from material exploitation and oppression that the African theologies help the people to liberate themselves. African theologies are born among the people, and the people want to live in conformity with their own culture and religion. Consequently, the African theologies aim at anthropological liberation.

The main question is how to cope with the Christian heritage the Africans received from the missionaries. Hence, the African reading of the Bible is a problem for the people and the theologians. 'Bible and Black Africa' was the theme of a congress held in 1972 in Jerusalem. A second congress took place in 1987 in Cairo. The African theologians discovered that the Bible, the Word of God as transmitted by Western missionaries must undergo a liberation process. The concepts of race, chosen people, and covenant, can be extrapolated, twisted and manipulated to the advantage of oppressors. This indeed has happened to justify racism, domination and oppression. An African reading must re-assess the biblical terms, demythologise and free them, and restore them to their original function and meaning in a language the people understand. 'Such a task demands a re-reading not only of the revealed Word of God, but also of the whole of Western civilisation and its venture to dominate the world, a venture more menacing than ever before because it is entering a cosmic and apocalyptic phase.'[69]

The various elements of the traditional African religions form another problem. For the Negro-African the whole creation is defined as a life-death conflict. The world in which we live is a real battlefield. Each creature is an agent either of life or of death. Hence the importance of traditional medicine, rites and cults. Law and justice are an expression of the forces of life organized against the forces of death. Ethical laws, power, authority, common welfare and even States and governments derive their value and power from this view on life. The meaningfulness of the human life consists in the fact that human beings are bound to achieve the victory of life over death. Religious praxis in traditional Africa is centred on the life of the human person, his health or illness, survival, fertility, family and offspring.

Ancestor veneration is another common element. It is an issue of consanguinity and family life, which comprises both living and the dead. These traditional concepts cannot be interpreted by the Western concepts of the natural and the supernatural order. For the Africans it is a question of the one and the other, of one's own people and other people, of kinsman and stranger. The difference between the Christian faith and indigenous religions has frequently been interpreted as an opposition between monotheism and paganism. However, according to African theologians this opposition is not insurmountable at all.

---

68. E. Mvenge, *African Liberation Theology*, in *Concilium*, 5 (1988), 20–34.
69. Ibid., 17–19.

The anthropological and cosmological dimensions have a strong affinity for the African. Humankind and the whole creation are in solidarity in the life–death conflict and in the final victory of life over death.

Many churches of Western origin are reluctant to promote inculturation in Africa. They mistrust the independent African churches, but also the new emerging theologies. They fear an ambiguous syncretism which undermines the orthodoxy as propagated and practised in the West.

The African Catholic theologian Englebert Mvenge speaks about the African liberation theologies as theologies emerging from the people. They express the experience, the faith and the hope of the living Christian community. They mobilize the people against neo-colonialism. Furthermore, the new theologies take the form of inculturation or africanization of christianity to the point that they become a constituent of the spiritual and cultural inheritance of Africa. They are, furthermore characterized by a strong ecumenical dimension, transcending all denominational barriers and church walls[70] …. . Africans in different parts of the continent are becoming ever more aware that not only cultural and religious liberation are needed, but that economic and political emancipation and independence are equally important.

CONTEXTUAL ASIAN THEOLOGIES

The great variety of socio-economic, demographic and political realities is a dominant characteristic of the Asian continent in which live 58 per cent of the world's population.

Despite this great variety there is a number of common issues. The continuing reality of poverty and misery in which masses of people live alongside the luxury and opulence of a small elite is a dominant feature. A second issue is the control of the economies of Asian countries by industrialized powers such as the USA, Western Europe and Japan. Thirdly, the systematic exclusion of the masses from any meaningful participation in the decision-making processes of society and political structures of the nations. The general trend is for the rise of the omnipotent State which exercises centralised and authoritarian power to the advantage of social, economic and political elites. Growing militarization is another issue. Military values, ideology and patterns have a dominating influence on domestic and foreign affairs of States. All these issues add new ingredients to the traditional sources of social conflict, the suppression of minorities, the tension between religious groups and the rivalry between ethnic and tribal loyalties within the countries.

There is a growing consciousness of women movements, ethnic and cultural movements which question the injustice and inequity of present society. There are organized movements and groups of ethnic and cultural minorities, of students and teachers who work for a people-oriented education, movements against foreign domination, in favour of human rights and political freedom and against militarization. These new movements of popular struggle and people's resistance create great tension and unrest in many Asian countries.

---

70. Ibid., 35–41.

Christians in Asia form a small minority. The organized world religions, Hinduism, Buddhism, Islam and religious–philosophical systems such as Confucianism and Shamanism have marked a long, centuries-old tradition of spirituality.

Against this background, Asian theologies become contextual and have their roots in the concrete resistance against the dominating and oppressing systems. But the Asian approach is different from the attitudes in other continents. The Asian way is that of a 'contemplative commitment'. It is a response to God and a source to understand reality. It is an act of contemplation and union with God that leads to commitment.

'This is an approach towards a spirituality of action, that is holistic, unitive and mystical. This spirituality takes place prior to the elaboration of theological concepts. It seeks God in the other, in the situation and in creation. This is an influence of the meditational and contemplative traditions of Asian religions, Hinduism and Buddhism, including Zen, the mystical tradition of Islam and the general Oriental temperament that seeks interiority and harmony.'[71]

The people's movements have had during the last two decades a decisive influence on the Asian Christian community. Many Christians have joined groups and movements of students, youth, workers, peasants, fishermen, women, tribals, outcasts, different oppressed groups and intellectuals who struggle for a more just society. They work with persons and groups of similar orientation, although they differ in belief and religious conviction.

Poverty and exploitation demand concentration on the poor, who represent 97 per cent of the total population. Asian Christians are oriented towards the poor and committed to raise their living conditions, and to fight for their liberation. This commitment is one of the dominant characteristics of Asian liberation theologies.

In *India* the cultural and theological resistance finds new forms in the solidarity with the Dalit Movement. The Dalits form 15 per cent of the Indian population. They are viewed as the outcasts in the caste hierarchy. The Dalits are becoming aware that historically they are the indigenous people of India. Over the centuries they lost their territory and were enslaved by the ruling classes and made a people without rights. Christians are taking an active part in the process of the Dalits regaining their identity, their own culture and religious heritage. The spirituality of the Cross helps them to support the Dalits in their struggle.

The struggle of the more committed groups in *South Korea* has been against the repressive regimes backed by the USA military presence. From this resistance originated the powerful theological concepts of 'the suffering, dominated people', the 'minjung' whom God has promised liberation. Minjung theology links socio-political analysis, re-reading of the Bible and liberation practice against the injust and oppressed situation.[72]

Other Christian groups are actively engaged in pressing for the Korean people's future. The division into North Korea and South Korea is seen as an artificial political and economic decision to the advantage of the powerful, but which creates great suffering among the people.[73]

The living reality of commitment to the struggle against injustice together with members of other religions greatly favour interreligious dialogue and collaboration. At the same time

---

71. *Third World Theologies*, Tissa Balasuriya, *Divergencies: An Asian Perspective*, 113–14.

72. *Minjung Theology*, ed. Kim Yong Bock, Singapore, Christian Conference of Churches, 1981.

73. *Background Information of the World Council of Churches' Commission of the Churches on International Affairs*, no. 1, Geneva, WCC, 1990.

this collaboration has theological implications. Several Christian positions which are taken for granted in other parts of the world are questioned. The crucial issue is the exclusive role of the Bible as the only source of God's revelation. Questions on the person of Jesus Christ as only mediator and redeemer, salvation, original sin, justification and grace, and the mission of the Church also cause difficulties.[74]

In several countries of Asia meetings and conferences take place where these problems are discussed. Asian theology is trying to seek clarity on the dogmas which have been defined in the course of history. In the Asian context of religious and philosophical pluralism, there is 'a trend towards a dedogmatisation of theology insofar as some dogmas are based on assumptions that can be questioned or lead to consequences that are disastrous for many sections of humanity'.[75]

As happens in many other circumstances, here, too, people take the lead. They find in liturgies, oral traditions, hymns, poems and stories of Buddhist and Hindu origin inspiration and strength in their struggle against oppression. They have a dynamic understanding of interreligious prayer and worship unthought of in traditional theologies … .

This kind of theology and theological praxis in Asia provoke fierce and indignant reactions from Christian church authorities. They speak about syncretism and paganization of Christianity. At the Canberra Assembly of the World Council of Churches in February 1991 the Korean woman theologian Chung Hyun Kyung spoke about the way to discern the Holy Spirit in our time. Her presentation was preceded and followed by dance and an invocation of the spirits of those who have gone before us, especially those who have suffered injustice. For her, these spirits are the presence of the Holy Spirit. The spirits of the ancestors are the icons of the Holy Spirit who became tangible and visible in us.

Reacting to the protests her performance caused at the Assembly the Roman Catholic theologian from Sri Lanka, Tissa Balasuriya, writes that 'everything truly humanizing and ennobling in any religion or ideology is also ultimately from the Holy Spirit and must be respected as such'. He strongly feels that theological positions must be liberated from elements which cannot be from God. Christian theology elaborated in relative isolation in medieval Europe can be harmful in a pluralistic context of different religions and social systems. 'Traditional theology, I believe, has more or less imprisoned the Holy Spirit within the power of the ecclesiastical authorities.'[76]

CONCLUSION

In this essay on contextual theologies I purposely concentrated on a few of these theologies which emerged among third world people. In the year 2000, 80 per cent of the world's population will live in developing countries. By the end of the century, the overwhelming majority of the earth will live in the third world. The third world is not just a numerical reality; it also is a human, religious and cultural reality of primary importance.

---

74. Bruno Chenu, *Théologies Chrétiennes des Tiers Mondes*, Paris, Centurion, 1987, 170–7.
75. *Third World Theologies*, Tissa Balasuriya, *Divergencies: An Asian Perspective*, 117.
76. Tissa Balasuriya, *Liberation of the Holy Spirit, Ecumenical Review*, 43 (1991), 200-205.

Christianity was brought to the third world in the colonial context. Christianity can have a future only if it allows space to the people of the third world for finding their own identity. This is closely connected with the decolonization process. If we take the third world as Christianity's new horizon, we should also take into account the fundamental contradiction experienced by its people; the contradiction between the masses struggling for survival and the financial, technological, political and ideological power centres situated in the developed countries, which spread poverty, misery and death among the poor masses of the South.

The emerging theologies in the third world mark, according to the German theologian Johann Baptist Metz, the transition from a Western Church with a more or less unitary culture, and in this sense poly-centric, in which moreover the Western legacy is not destined to be repressed, but to be provoked and challenged anew.[77]

The new theologies emerging from the third world represent indeed a challenge for European and Western theology. They will also play a decisive role in the orientation of the ecumenical movement tomorrow.

The Canberra Assembly of the World Council of Churches (February 1991) already discussed the importance of a dialogue between contextual theologies and Western classical theologies. The Assembly placed this dialogue in the context of mission and indigenization or inculturation. However, it is not so much the inculturation of the Gospel message, but the contextualization of the message which is at stake. The debate on the ecumenical movement is no longer about the legitimacy of contextualization, Konrad Raiser states. 'The burning issue today is: How to communicate between differently contextualized theologies and spiritualities? How to deal with the new diversity that is beginning to emerge?' Raiser suggests that a first prerequisite is the acknowledgement that the message of salvation continuously needs to become incarnate in the life situation of particular people and communities. Contextualization of the Christian message is subject to a continuous transformation. All transformation is oriented towards the eschatological horizon of God's reign. Meanwhile, the ecumenical communication between the contextual confessions is more safeguarded by 'a flexible rule of faith' than by a body of 'doctrinal confessions'.[78]

The contextual theologies are a different way of doing theology. The phenomenon induces the Vatican to do its utmost – through special Synods and Bishops' Assemblies – to defend the universal Western theologies and to undo the new discoveries of the contextual theologies. The task of the ecumenical movement tomorrow seems to consist in finding a way where both the classical theologies and the emerging contextual theologies are recognized as authentic interpretations of the Word of God. In this manner a sincere and open dialogue and communication will shed new light on the good news of salvation Jesus Christ has brought to the human family and the entire creation. What is really at stake is the encounter between the Gospel and cultures. No prefixed rule or method is regulating this encounter. The Ecumenical Movement should trust the Spirit to guide this encounter.

---

77. J.B. Metz. *Thesen zum theologischen Ort der Befreiungstheologie*, 147–57, in *Die Theologie der Befreiun, Hoffnung oder Gefahr für die Kirche*, ed. J.B. Metz, Düsseldorf, Patmos, 1986.
78. Konrad Raiser, *Beyond Tradition and Context, In Search of an Ecumenical Framework of Hermeneutics*, *International Review of Mission*, 319/320, July/October 1991, 347–54.

6.9 ROGER HAIGHT: *THE CHURCH AS LOCUS OF THEOLOGY* – 1994

Our extract from John Paul II's address (no. IV), spoke of the church 'as the theologian's vital environment'. Our next extract[79] agrees with such a principle, but develops its implications in a much broader context. Working upon the assumption that theology 'includes reflection on the basis, goals and intrinsic ministerial operations of the church' and the reciprocal provision by the church of the 'living version of the faith out of which the theologian works', Haight examines how the interrelationship between theology and the church has been transformed as a result of developments in knowledge, ecumenism, interreligious dialogue and the movements for human liberation. His analysis leads him to argue that we cannot confine theology to patently ecclesial matters alone, nor can one church alone authorize and dictate the shape and form of theology in our ecumenical age. Furthermore, theology has much to learn and gain from its dialogue with other faiths, establishing new horizons for its sources and norms. Finally, theology should never be a purely individualistic discipline in its chief areas of concern: it must always bear in mind the fundamental social and public dimensions of human existence. Essentially, Haight is seeking to answer the question: 'what constitutes authoritative theology today?' in a manner that seeks to move theology beyond all narrow, sectarian, absolutist and universalising stances: 'theology transcends the church'. There is a new reality for the church to take account of, and this naturally means a new reality for authority, structures and theology throughout the Christian church.

❀

The church is the home of theological reflection. The importance of theology for the church lies in the fact that theology includes reflection on the basis, goals and intrinsic ministerial operations of the church. Every organization needs ongoing critical review of its grounding vision and mission. And reciprocally, the church is important for theology as the institution dedicated to preserving and nurturing the faith in the light of which theologians speak. The church provides the living version of the faith out of which the theologian works.

This article attempts to give an account of these mutual relationships … . Four developments have had a direct influence on the place of theology in the church today: the knowledge explosion, the ecumenical movement, inter-religious dialogue, and the rise of liberation movements … .

THE IDEA OF PLACE

One spontaneously speaks of the church as the locus or place for the unfolding of theological reflection. One does theology in the church. However, because the metaphor of 'place' is a physical and spatial image, it connotes clear boundaries. And some analyses of the distinct nature of theology as a discipline have strengthened the idea that the range of the object of

---

79. In *Why Theology?*, eds Geffré, Claude and Jeanrond, Werner, *Concilium* (1994/6), 13–22.

theology is limited. As a first thesis I want to stress that while theology is at home in the church, its subject matter is not limited to ecclesial matters.

One of many historical developments that have encouraged a limiting conception of the church as the place of theology is the explosion of knowledge in the modern period. In archaic societies it is sometimes difficult to distinguish the boundaries between religion, social arrangement and economic life. By contrast, modern developed societies have become more complex. Within the congeries of relationships that make up contemporary life people distinguish between ways of knowing, kinds of knowledge and kinds of reality that are known. Along with an increasing number of differentiations in knowledge one also finds a tendency toward compartmentalization of separate spheres of knowledge. Theology pertains to religion; Christian theology is what is done in and for the church; theology becomes more and more sectarian. At an extreme, theology becomes incomprehensible to any one who is not an educated church member.

The localization and compartmentalization of theology is a temptation for many today. Some theologians have become seduced by the very systems of modernity and post modernity which they attack. That is, they try to escape them by isolating the church from culture and conceiving of theology as a purely confessional and fideist discipline. Other people compartmentalize reality psychologically. They say, for example, that a particular course of action is a business decision but not an ethical decision or an ethical decision but with no religious import. These divisions between spheres of reality are forms of blindness, or at least myopia. Formal differentiations of methods and kinds of knowledge are essential for clear, critical thinking, but they do not define separable spheres of reality. As in archaic societies the reality of human life is one, and its various facets are organically inter-related. One cannot carve out a space for theology that is unrelated to the whole sphere of human life including all of its actual physical, secular, cultural and religious dimensions.

This first thesis is against one form of Christian sectarianism. The church is the place of theology, but the church cannot and does not limit or confine theology to merely ecclesial matters. In the Roman Catholic Church, Vatican II's decree *Gaudium et spes* overcame all such sectarianism by proposing the church as an open community defined by its mission to the world. All reality is the subject-matter of theology and therefore provides data for it. Theology seeks to understand all reality through the light of Christian symbols. Besides God, the whole of the *humanum* and the *mundum* define the range and scope of theology.

THE IDEA OF CHURCH

A second development in the conception of theology in the church has been occasioned or caused by the ecumenical movement. The seeds of the ecumenical movement were sown with the nineteenth-century consciousness of historicity and it emerged formally in the twentieth century. The Roman Catholic Church at first resisted ecumenism as a sign of religious indifferentism, but with Vatican II it has committed itself to participation in the quest for Christian unity. From the earliest witness to church life in the New Testament and the Apostolic Fathers, the unity of the church has been a dominant value and theme in the church's self-understanding.

At present one could probably divide all Christian theologians into two camps: those evangelicals who reject the ecumenical movement and those who have internalized the premises upon which it rests. Conservative evangelical theologians look with suspicion on what, from the point of view of fundamentalism and naïve ideas of biblical inerrancy, appears to be liberal unfaithfulness to scriptural revelation. But from the perspective of the various mainline churches of the world the church itself must be conceived universally as the one great church which is in fact institutionally divided. Seen historically in its genesis and development, and against the background of other religions, the church appears as one but fragmented. The task of ecumenism, therefore, is to give historical form to already existing reality. Within the ecumenical movement, theology that is done in the church is done ecumenically; it is a function of the great church. Theology that is purely confessional, that is, the theology of a particular church over against the great church, would be anti-ecumenical in so far as it did not take into account the existence and data of the whole church. Such a theology would not promote unity but would work against it.

The relation between ecumenical theology and that of particular churches is dialectical. The primary referent of 'the Christian church' is recognized to be the great church, the whole historical movement of Christianity. Historical consciousness and the ecumenical movement forbid *a priori* definitions of the church that exclude particular churches without making a detailed historical and doctrinal case for it. But at the same time no church theologian or ecclesiologist is a member of the church at large. Theology is done by particular theologians within a particular church. It is inevitable, then, that the historical context of the theologian provides the matrix for his or her theology. But theologians should be aware of this and consciously frame their theology in the broader perspective. Their reasoning must take other churches into account. In various degrees present-day theologians have been able to transcend the narrow confines of their own churches without being unfaithful to them; they have read and been influenced by other theologians and churches and adopted an ecumenical perspective. More and more today Christian theology is becoming an ecumenical discipline in fact without particular theologians surrendering their confessional alliances and identities.

But if these reflections on the ecumenical character of theology are accurate, then the role of the authority of any particular church relative to the theologian and his or her theology will have changed. And by extension, the role of the authority of individual churches shifts with respect to the discipline of theology itself. In an ecumenically conscious theology the witness and data of the magisterium of the particular theologian by definition ceases to be the sole point of reference for authoritative statements. Again, by extension to the discipline, ecumenical theology must consider a variety of authoritative witnesses from many churches. It must also employ various comparative and dialectical procedures to frame a more general statement of the issue than will be reflected in the particular view of only one church. Theology that is ecumenically conscious is led by a logic other than reliance on the magisterium of a single church and is forced to consult the authorities of all churches in a reverent and critical manner.

The authority structures of different churches vary in many respects. But as far as the Roman Catholic Church is concerned, its commitment to the ecumenical movement at Vatican II alters the role of the magisterium when it is directed towards theology and changes the role of theology as well. Perhaps a loose historical analogy will help to indicate the nature of the shift. Theology in the Roman Catholic Church after Vatican II's endorsement of ecumenism is roughly analogous to theology during the Western Schism (1378–1417). Catholic theologians then existed within the sphere of one of the two popes or three popes. Theoretically they were bound by the magisterium and papal authority of their particular pope. Yet most of those theologians, especially those in the university centres, knew they had a higher loyalty to the *congregatio fidelium* which was one in Christ. Here theology rose above 'local' or 'sectarian' or 'confessional' authority, was critical of it and of the situation itself, and in this transcending role helped form the atmosphere or situational climate in which a resolution was effected.

It should not be thought that the role or importance of the magisterium of any particular church is minimized by these considerations. Only exaggerated claims of the authority within any particular communion is affected. Particular structures of authority in different communions are essential for preserving the distinctive spirit of these traditions in a pluralistic church. A magisterium is absolutely necessary to define the beliefs of a particular tradition, to establish boundaries of this or that communion, to organize and regulate and thus preserve the identity of it and the people in it. What the internalization of the ecumenical imperative by the churches has done, then, is to moderate the absolutistic or universalistic claims of certain structures of authority in particular churches.

Let me summarize this point in the form of a thesis. It is directed against another form of sectarianism. The church is the place for theology. But the church at the end of the twentieth century as a result of the ecumenical movement is recognized to be the whole or total church, despite its disunity and divisions. This means, negatively, that the church in the sense of a particular communion cannot by itself be a final or exclusive limit or constraint or criterion or norm for Christian theology today. Rather, positively, the many magisteria of various churches are witnesses to Christian truth and sources for data for Christian theology.

THE IDEA OF THEOLOGY

It is not my intention at this point to propose an integral concept of the sources, nature and method of theology in the church. Rather, I want simply to indicate one way in which the discipline of theology has been altered during the course of the twentieth century by interreligious encounter.

People who have received a university education ordinarily acquire an historical consciousness. This awareness of the historically conditioned character of all human reality, of its particularity in time and place, is mediated by critical study. However, an historical consciousness can also be mediated more generally by the experience of pluralism across cultures in every domain of life, especially the most fundamental, such as family, the sphere of national and cultural values, and religion. To the extent that various forms of communication today allow people to share in a global consciousness, in the same measure they recognize that religious pluralism is simply a fact or a given. Consciousness of it is becoming more accentuated as groups migrate and carry their religions with them. More and more religious pluralism is directly visible as religions share space in cities around the world.

As the fact of religious pluralism becomes accepted, and then taken for granted, attitudes towards other religions also change. Given the transcendent mystery of God, should one not expect different religions that correlate closely with different cultures? And given the Christian conception of a God of boundless love, should one not expect God to engage all people, and thus interact with different people on their own terms? The attitudes of Christians towards other religions have changed profoundly in recent times; they view other religions more positively. And Christian theology has reflected these attitudes by a variety of explanations of how God's salvific grace is at work in them.

The development entails a new posture of the church *vis-à-vis* other religions and consequently a new dimension for theological reflection within the church. In very broad terms one can define the new stance of the church in terms of the categories of witness and dialogue. The mission of the church in one respect remains the same: it is a mission of evangelization or giving witness to its faith in God mediated by Jesus Christ. Its intent is to be a sign of this faith and to establish and nurture a local church to continue the mission of Jesus. But at the same time the notion of dialogue has come to inform and qualify the method and immediate goals of the witness. Dialogue means entering into a respectful and attentive exchange with people, their cultures and their religions. The metaphor of a dialogue or conversation supplies the rules for how the church should encounter the people of other religions at all levels. In other words, a phenomenology of an authentic dialogue reveals the characteristics that should qualify the unfolding of the church's mission.

What does the encounter with and consciousness of other religions and the consequent dialogical character of the church's mission imply for the nature of theology today? How do the characteristics of dialogue come to bear on theology? Much could be said here, but two points go some distance towards the essence of the matter.

First, the interiorization of historicity encourages a certain humility or modesty in the Christian witness to ultimate truth. This is not a modesty that stems from uncertainty and doubt: Christians know what they have experienced of God through Jesus Christ. But Christian experience of God is also characterized by mystery and unknowing. And Jesus is a particular, historically conditioned mediation of God. The Christian today should share a sense of the limitations and culturally conditioned character of the Christian tradition. The Christian should also be open to more and fuller dimensions of an encounter with the same God that is revealed in Jesus but also mediated through other religions.

Secondly, and correspondingly, in a situation that can be characterized as dialogical in nature, as opposed to being initially polemical, Christian theology is attentive to the voice of dialogue partners. Christian theology is open to learning. The experience of non-Christians becomes in some sense data for Christian theology. The consequences of this have been clearly described by theologians who have engaged in inter-religious dialogues: the understanding of their own faith has been changed. The dialogue, the passing over and entering into the world of the other religion, to whatever extent this is possible, and the return, transform Christian self-understanding.

This third thesis can be stated succinctly; it too is against yet another form of Christian sectarianism. The church is the place for theology, but the encounter of the church in this century with other religions has transformed the church's understanding of its mission. Theology in such a church is also transformed. On the one hand, in a dialogical situation its affirmations become more modest, less all-knowing, simpler, and more open to deepening and renewal. On the other hand, theology learns from non-Christian experience. The sources and data for Christian theology are thus further expanded beyond the Christian sphere to the worlds of religious experience in which it is in dialogue.

THE FOCUS OF THEOLOGY

Finally, there is another shift in theology within the church which has occurred over the past two centuries but which has been accented in the last three decades. This shift moves from a focus on human existence individually conceived to human existence both personally and socially conceived. The media of this development most recently have been the problems addressed by liberation theology, political theology, feminist theology and those particular theologies that attend to specific forms of corporate human suffering and oppression.

Modern theology is often characterized as shifting its point of departure and focus from the positive, objective data of Christian tradition and authority to religious experience. Modern theology has turned to the subject, to religious anthropology, to experience of transcendence as the basis for theological affirmation. But the social consequences of the industrial revolution which spawned the social gospel, and the increasingly global, social, political and economic problems of the twentieth century which have generated various liberation theologies qualify how the turn of the human subject is to be understood. An individualistic understanding of the human is simply inadequate: its abstraction leaves behind the real situation of the individual. The fundamental character of the shift mediated by socially conscious theologies, therefore, is anthropological. Human existence cannot be understood outside a social-historical context. The individually unique and spiritual person, when he or she is really understood existentially and concretely, is seen to be a social individual.

This new social focus of Christian theology has several consequences for theology in the church today. Of the many, two seem to be most important.

First, theology today must explicitly address the seeming meaninglessness of human history for so many human beings. The message of hope for an external fulfilled life with God certainly does address the question of human history with the conviction that history has an ultimate aim or goal. But it is not the end of history or human life that is so problematic for so many people today. The problem is time or history itself. Evil has taken on a qualitatively new historical dimension. The increase of world population plus the advances in modern technology have resulted in shocking and scandalizing levels of mass human suffering. One must show how God's end for history bends back and influences the unfolding of history itself. The problem is serious: human experience rebels at the senselessness of the human condition that human beings have created and there does not seem to be any conceivable way to redress the suffering. Human beings have to get on with their own lives; they have to build defences against too much exposure to massive human suffering; they have to get used to it. This necessary cynicism, as it were, has begun to operate as an alternative to Christian faith. Theology must address this deep layer of unfaith in believers and unbelievers alike. The intelligibility of the church's theology is at stake here because increasingly people can find no coherent intelligibility in history itself.

Secondly, the church's theology must address the question of human freedom on both its social and individual levels. This issue is intimately connected with the problem of the meaningfulness of history, but it also converges closely on the issue of Christian life and spirituality. There is a growing sense that human freedom is a power of creativity, the ability to plan and accomplish new things, distinctive and original things. The theology of creation, providence, grace and salvation as well as the role of the church and its ministry must be brought into correlation with this new human experience. The relevance of the church is at stake here. Increasing numbers of people find traditional church teaching on the Christian life irrelevant to actual life in the world today.

In sum, this thesis is against individualism in theology. Every theology that does not address the social and public character of human life in history is inadequate today.

CONCLUSION

The church is the natural place for Christian theology. Theology construes the world, human existence and God through the symbols of scripture and tradition which are preserved in the community called church. I can summarize how this task is to be carried out in a way distinctive to our time on the basis of four historical developments which have significantly influenced both the church and the discipline of theology, that is, the complexification and explosion of knowledge, historical consciousness and the ecumenical movement, the encounter with world religions and interreligious dialogue, and the population explosion and its attendant massive social suffering.

In responding to these historical developments we have discovered the following things: first, that theology in the church is not limited by the boundaries of the church. From the standpoint of the church, theology transcends the church. It deals with the whole sphere of reality itself from within the purview of the symbols of Christian revelation. Second, the church itself which is the natural home of theology cannot be restricted to any confessional communion today. The premises and values underlying the ecumenical movement, which reach back to the essence of apostolic faith, break open the necessary and legitimate role of authority within any particular Christian tradition. To be ecumenical, Christian theology must both attend and transcend the specific authorities and magisteria of particular churches. The great church, in its long history and especially in its united future, is theology's primary context. Third, this Christian church co-exists with other religions in a new common human history. This new context imposes what might be called a dialogical situation. Christian theology in this situation will attend to the faiths of other peoples and, being influenced by them, reformulate its self-understanding accordingly. Fourth, and in common with other religions, human beings must address the elements of our common existence which are senseless, murderous and scandalous. God's revelation to human beings in this world is for human existence in this world. To be credible and relevant, theology must address the actual lives of human beings in this world by formulating its meaning in social-historical terms as well as interpersonal and transcendent terms.

6.10 LINDA HOGAN: *A THEOLOGY FOR THE FUTURE* – 1995

Many in positions of ecclesial authority within the 'institutional' church and scholars of like theological mind are viewed by their critics as being too 'universalizing' in their outlook. In turn, such critics are perceived as being overtly relativistic in their own dispositions and writings. Naturally, both theological poles affect respective claims to authority. In addressing such themes in a feminist context, Linda Hogan[80] examines the feminist theory which seeks to build upon the emphasis on praxis in liberation and political theology. On the one hand our extract stresses the importance and authority of *women's experience* for theology. On the other (and more controversially), it challenges universalizing tendencies both from a patriarchal and even a feminist perspective. Hogan proposes a 'pragmatic priority' *via media* between a universalist theology and absolute relativism. This can serve as an important contribution to understanding the task of the theologian in the church today: i.e., it is not simply the theologian's job to disseminate a universal theology from 'above', nor to replace the latter with a formally similar alternative from 'below', but to be aware of the relative and contextual aspects of our theologizing and to seek an ethical justification (and hence authorization) for one position over another. Thus Hogan rejects absolutising tendencies in all theology, whether patriarchal or feminist. Hers is a further attempt to elucidate what constitutes authoritative theology – in this case for women today. The authority of women's experience is considered vis-à-vis the claims to authority of other theological methdologies.

❁

… I have been anxious to insist on the radical newness of feminist theology. Its alternative vision is based primarily on how it chooses its starting points and how it proceeds methodologically. Thus, feminist theology has essentially effected a revolution in theological scholarship – in both content and method … .

[L]iberation and political theology have provided the methodological framework for feminist theologians. The integration of the Marxian category of revolutionary praxis has enabled theologians to understand their resources differently. The inclusion of praxis as the starting point and norm of evaluation for theological scholarship has radically altered both methodology and epistemology.

This choice of a praxis-based methodology is not simply a whim, but is dependent on the motivation of communities of women, in the case of feminist theology, or *communidades de base* in the case of liberation theology. In the analysis of how research ought to proceed, liberation and political theologians adopted, with modification, Marxian methodology and epistemology, in particular the famous eleventh thesis which insists that 'the philosophers have only interpreted the world in various ways; the point is, to change it'.[81] Philosophy would then be the theoretical arm of revolutionary praxis. Liberation and feminist theologians envisage a similar role for theology.

---

80. In *From Women's Experience to Feminist Theology*, Sheffield, Sheffield Academic Press, 1995, 163–77.
81. K. Marx, in L.D. Easton and R.H. Guddat (eds), *Writings of the Young Marx on Philosophy and Society*, New York, Doubleday, 1967, 400.

Adoption of this perspective has altered the epistemological presuppositions of feminist theology. Theological knowledge is gained from a commitment to the examination of women's experiences of oppression and to envisioning a liberative alternative. It is praxical as opposed to theoretical … .

The appropriation of the methodology and the epistemology of Marxism and of critical theory, with its emphasis on praxis and the dialectical relationship with theory, is the backdrop against which feminist theological have justified their employment of the category of women's experience and activity as source and content of feminist theology.

However, theology based on women's experience and praxis must be subject to the same critique as traditional theories. We have discovered in our examination of the category of women's experience that theorists need to acknowledge the perspectival character of the truth claims. Since all scholarship bears the biases and concerns of its source we cannot claim a universal normativity for feminist theory or theology … .

The problems that plague the works of feminist theologians are not unique to this discipline, but arise wherever scholars attempt to take seriously the historical and social character of human experience. Postmodern relativism, arising from the abandonment of any pretensions to universality or to objectivity in relation to knowledge, and which provides feminist theology with important tools with which to critique patriarchy, raises profound questions for feminist theory itself.

Feminist theologians must face squarely the challenge of rigorously applying the insights of historicism to our own appeals to women's experience and praxis. Indeed, it has been my contention throughout that a thorough understanding of the categories of women's experience and praxis will necessarily lead to a recognition of the difficulties that emerge if we apply the rigours of critique to our epistemological and methodological assumptions.

I would suggest therefore that our examination of the use of the categories of women's experience and praxis raises two fundamental points for feminists, which may enable us to do our theology with greater methodological precision in the future. First, feminist theologians must place a 'hermeneutic of difference' at the core of theologizing; secondly, we must acknowledge the fact that universalism is not an appropriate attitude for feminist theology to adopt.

I am aware of my tendency in this conclusion, and indeed throughout the entire work, to equate universalism with imperialism in theorizing. Although many may take issue with this I believe that an impulse towards sameness and uniformity has been central to universalizing tendencies in much of patriarchal scholarship. It is only when we begin to envisage a universalism based on difference and not on its obliteration that the spectre of imperialism will recede; hence my emphasis on the pejorative connotation of the term.

A HERMENEUTIC OF DIFFERENCE

… A theology based on women's experience and praxis must of necessity acknowledge and learn to value difference. However, an evaluation of most feminist theory of the last three decades would conclude that much theorizing has tended towards imperialism. Women of colour have alerted the feminist community to its racist and classist potential and practice.

The works of Barbara Smith, bell hooks and Alice Walker, among others, have taught white feminists that we have repeated the central crime of patriarchy in failing to acknowledge the particularity of our own experience. White women's experience and praxis has be 'honoured' with the badge of normativity, while women of colour have been further marginalized, in the name of justice. Such a whitewashing of experience has not gone unchallenged. Womanists have demanded that white feminists own this history of oppression … .

A feminist theology must be constantly vigilant lest it fall into the amorphous mass that Ntozake Shange identifies. As women, individually and in community, begin to articulate their priorities and values, theorists need to resist the desire to propose some form of universal normativity.

As women attempt to formulate theologies, the notion of difference must be centrally located. The articulation of symbols, hermeneutical principles, values and so on must be grounded in the complexities and contradictions of women's concrete experience and praxis. The absence of a cohesive and universal perspective in feminist theology based on an understanding of women's experience and praxis, which is sensitive to racial, class and sexual differences among women, must recognize women's 'different primary emergencies'.[82]

If we appreciate, in our theology, that women have 'different primary emergencies', be they racial, sexual or class-based, we will be more modest in our claims for our theology. The life experience, commitments and priorities of those who articulate theology are inextricably bound to theology itself. As life experiences change, as alternative voices are allowed to be heard in the theological realm, our theory too must change and develop.

Difference, then, must emerge in feminist theology as a key hermeneutic principle. To employ a hermeneutic of difference is to celebrate and truly value diversity, and ultimately to be challenged in one's own vision.

But to employ a hermeneutic of difference is not simply to value difference but to consider it to be central to the process of interpretation. It means employing difference as an analytic category and allowing it to inform both our interpretation and indeed its underlying philosophy. In our attempts to speak of women's experience or women's praxis, particularly in our search to describe a common experience or praxis, we cannot begin from the assumption of sameness. Indeed if there is a commonality to be described it should rightfully originate from those on the margins. Any minimizing of differences must legitimately come from women who have previously been excluded from defining the category of women's experience. In the final instance, employing a hermeneutic of difference may revolutionize our theological endeavour … .

A NORMATIVE FEMINIST VISION?

Feminist theologians across the spectrum seem to make claims regarding the normative status of a feminist theological position, in ways that a true appreciation of radical historicity and diversity of their primary resources may render problematic. Indeed we have seen from our

---

82. M. Quintales, quoted in E. Culpepper's 'New Tools for the Theology: Writings by Women of Color', *Journal of Feminist Studies in Religion*, 4 (1988), 45.

consideration of the categories of women's experience and praxis in the early chapters of this book that one should be reluctant to make any such claims, apart from a recognition of the utterly social and historical character of feminist theology's resources, and the difficulties in employing a language of certitude that this implies. Yet theologians appear to claim a normative status for their work that may be methodologically impossible.

Sheila Greeve Davaney[83] is indeed critical of feminist theologians, both reformist and revolutionary, who, she claims, imply that there is a correspondence between their feminist vision and divine reality and will. In her critique of Schüssler Fiorenza, Ruether and Mary Daly she claims that each theologian implies that feminist analysis provides us with a vision that has an ontological normativity, which those of patriarchy do not. It is her contention that such theoretical assumptions cannot be made, in the light of both the diversity of women's experience and praxis and the methodological issues that originate in the social and historical character of these categories.

Davaney is adamant that if feminists take seriously the nihilistic implications of this historical consciousness, we can no longer claim some privileged access to understanding reality. Since we recognize that all knowledge bears the biases and interest of the knower, how can feminists or indeed any other group claim validity for their unique perspective? Feminist theory must therefore abandon any belief that it critiques from a location of special insight. She suggests that feminist theology provides an alternative vision which is no more accurate than that of patriarchy. The diversity revealed by the categories of women's experience and praxis, together with the recognition of the perspectival character of theological knowledge, must, according to Davaney, lead us to abandon all claims to certitude and all appeals to an ontological grounding for feminist theology.

The problems that this presents for feminist theology are indeed deep-rooted. While one would acknowledge the importance of appreciating the historicity of experience and praxis, and the diversity of perspectives that feminist theology encompasses, to embrace this form of relativism seems impossible for an engaged theology. Undoubtedly the resources that feminist theology has chosen to use for its methodological framework and norms for evaluation give rise to these difficulties … .

It must be admitted also that our examination of the works of feminist theologians of all persuasions has highlighted these difficulties. Most theologians appear to be unwilling to work out the ambiguities in their respective positions. It is precisely because most feminist theologians have failed to address this issue that Davaney has engaged in such a thoroughgoing critique. Her position is indeed persuasive and demands that feminist theologians begin to address explicitly the issues surrounding the nihilistic and relativistic directions towards which their primary theological resources appear to be pointing.

Although I would be reluctant to accept unreservedly Davaney's position, I do believe that feminist theologians need to address this basic challenge. As has already been mentioned,

---

83. In this conclusion I use two articles by Davaney, both of which address the methodological issues described: 'Problems with Feminist Theory: Historicity and the Search for Sure Foundations', in P. Cooey, S. Farmer and M. Ross (eds), *Embodied Love: Sensuality and Relationship as Feminist Values*, San Francisco, Harper & Row, 1987, 79–95, and 'The Limits of the Appeal to Women's Experience', in C. Atkinson, C. Buchanan and M. Miles (eds), *Shaping New Vision: Gender and Values in American Culture*, Ann Arbor, University of Michigan Research Press, 1987, 31–49.

the logical conclusion to the employment of women's experience and praxis as one's primary resources ought to be relativism. However, in an effort to avoid a relativism that would lead one to fail to distinguish between the experience and praxis of oppressors and those of their victims, we must consider 'the limits of the appeal to women's experience'.[84]

This radical relativism implied by the use of the categories of women's experience and praxis may be limited by the appeal to pragmatic, ethical foundations rather than to ontological ones, by placing the experiences of communities rather than individuals at the centre of feminist theology, and finally by truly appreciating the embodied nature of all our knowledge.

PRAGMATISM

If we identify women, and indeed the category of women's experience, not in terms of biological essentialism but by women's position within (or, as is more likely, outside) a network of relations we may avoid claiming ontological priority for women's experiences. We may indeed come close to the view of standpoint epistemology, which would recognize that those in oppressed groups may be in a position to have a more complete vision than their oppressors. This is not because of any *a priori* access to truth (as against, for example, Mary Daly's contention that women-identified women are at the centre of all true interpretations[85]), but because of women's particular location in history.

Arising from women's experiences of oppression and because of the collective articulation of and commitment to justice and to right relationships, feminist theological thinking may claim a pragmatic, but not an ontological priority. In location the significance of the feminist theological vision in the type of commitments that it inspires, and not in any abstract claim to correspondence with divine (or other) reality, one does not abandon oneself to relativism.

Although I do not agree completely with Davaney's position I recognize the importance of her proposal that feminist theology give up appeals to ontological reality for validation and appeal instead to pragmatism. By grounding validation in the life-experience, values and commitments that such a vision inspires, feminist theology would be taking seriously the epistemology that flows from the use of the categories of women's experience and praxis. The feminist vision is valid, because women (and feminist men), attentive to the voices of marginalized groups, have collected, analysed and critiqued in 'communities of resistance and solidarity'. Because of the values it inspires feminist theology may claim an ethical priority. Feminists may not claim a universal enduring significance for their vision; however, we may, and indeed we do maintain that the commitments central to the feminist vision are foundational for our age.

The feminist vision may be considered to be more adequate than the patriarchal one because it is committed to providing a more complete description of reality. It seeks to do this by being attentive to the embedded nature of all experience and attempts to celebrate rather

---

84. This phrase forms the title of the excellent article by Davaney.
85. M. Daly, *Pure Lust*, London, Womens Press, 1984, 163ff.

than to obliterate difference. Indeed, when we accept that there is a variety of standpoints among feminists – for example lesbian or womanist – we must move from grounding validity for the feminist vision in ontology, and move towards an appreciation of the contextual nature of all truths.

Grounded in a reluctance to move towards a normative theory for feminists, this tendency towards relativism need not imply an inability to choose among competing values. Liz Stanley, for example, in opposition to radical relativism, defines the relativism appropriate for feminists as the belief that 'judgments of truth are always and necessarily made relative to the particular framework of the knower (while its perceived opposite, "foundationalism", is an insistence that "the truth" rather than a number of truths, exist independently of the knower)'.[86] Such a relativism, she suggests, recognizes the significance of the subjective in the categories of women's experience and praxis while accounting for resistance to a patriarchal telling of reality. Although this may be helpful to some extent in formulating an epistemology that is responsive the debates concerning the nature of the relationship between power and knowledge, I suspect that employing such terminology may lead to further confusion.

THE CENTRALITY OF COMMUNITY

Without denying the importance of each individual's experience and praxis, feminist theology need not attach equal importance to each individual's subjective, unfocused and unanalysed experience. Beverly Harrison, citing Michelle Russell, alerts us to the dangers of 'taking our own particular form of victimization, isolated from a collective context, and making that our morality'.[87] An emphasis on community and on the realization that interconnection and relationality are the keys to creative and mutually enriching discourse is therefore vital.

An emphasis on the communitarian and collective nature of all women's experience and praxis ought to be central to feminist theology. Such a perspective enables us to avoid the dangers of either universalism or unrestrained relativism. The community out of which a woman articulates her experience is reflected in the stances adopted by that individual. Thus women's experience and praxis is never unmediated, unadulterated by the collective within which and out of which we theologize. All our theology bears the limitations and indeed the strengths of the community from which it emerges.

Thus one of the elements that distinguishes the position of feminist theology from 'mere subjectivism' is the presence of community. Undeniably great diversity and indeed much disagreement is evident in the priorities of feminists of all persuasions. An enlightened theology must neither disregard the often substantial differences of priorities and commitments, nor abandon the desire for a certain cohesion among the seemingly inevitable conflicting experiences.

Such a community must be rooted at its most fundamental level in the ambiguity, complexity and difficulties of diverse human nature … . In avoiding neither the particular nor the embodied character of our theology we are challenged to communicate and to make

---

86. L. Stanley and S. Wise, 'Method, Methodology and Epistemology in Feminist Research Processes', in L. Stanley (ed.), *Feminist Praxis: Research, Theory and Epistemology in Feminist Sociology*, London, Routledge, 1990, 41.
87. B. Harrison, *Making the Connections: Essays in Feminist Social Ethics*, Boston, Beacon Press 1985, 240.

certain commitments. The community endeavouring to engage in feminist theology is required to be a community of enquiry, debate, dialogue. Undoubtedly the conditions essential to the promotion of such a community are much debated.

The later works of Jürgen Habermas,[88] together with those of Michel Foucault,[89] provide important discussion of such matters. Access to reality or to truth is not the preserve of majorities, not the property of those sufficiently strong to impose their definitions and values on others with less wealth, less political power, less education. The creation of conditions in which creative, mutually empowering discourse can occur is the first step in the theological process. We must recognize and critique the power element implicit in most patriarchal theory. To divest such knowledge of its power is impossible. One is therefore obliged, in the service of dialogue, to acknowledge and if necessary compensate for the interest factor in all our knowing and discourse.

The language of universals tends to be that of the dominant classes, the privileged. Feminist theology must eschew all impulses to claim a universalist position, since in so doing it would essentially deny the possibility of discourse and the value of diversity. Indeed many feminist theologians have begun to explore the importance of such an alternative vision. Sharon Welch in her *Communities of Resistance and Solidarity*[90] asserts the primacy of the particular and suggests that the possibility for our critique of racism, imperialism or sexism lies not in a universal, abstract sense of justice, devoid of any concrete sense, but in our engagement in actual situations of resistance and solidarity. Our ability to evaluate is sourced in praxis and concrete experience, not in allegiance to abstract, benign universals.

Without dispute one must recognize the tensions that exist between an understanding of the relational and perspectival character of the theology I am suggesting, and the extreme relativism so feared by many commentators. Feminist theology must guard against such a potential danger with a very clear understanding of the accountability of individuals and communities. Feminist theologians are alert to the possibility that in their praxis and theorizing they are unaware of their perpetuation of yet unrecognized instances of subjugation. Instability is therefore a vital component in the feminist theological arena. With the deepening of our realizations of the significance of our differences, and with the emergence of new voices, a realism which is nonetheless responsive to the contextual character of our experience is essential in order to promote further dialogue. In the words of Mary Daly: '"together" does not mean in lockstep or simultaneously, but each according to her own lifetime. The moving presence of each Self calls forth the living presence of other journeying/enspiriting selves.'[91]

88. J. Habermas, *Knowledge and Human Interests*, London, Heinemann, 1973; *Legitimation Crisis,* Boston, Beacon Press, 1973.

89. M. Foucault, *The Archaeology of Knowledge*, New York, Harper & Row, 1976; *Power/Knowledge: Selected Interviews and Other Writings*, New York, Pantheon Books, 1980.

90. S. Welch, *Communities of Resistance and Solidarity: A Feminist Theology of Liberation*, Maryknoll, NY, Orbis Books, 1985.

91. M. Daly. *Gyn/Ecology*, Boston, Beacon Press, 366.

CONCLUSION

EMBODIED THINKING

In dealing with the potentially radical implications of the centrality of the categories of women's experience and praxis we should also be attentive to the feminist understanding of embodied thinking. Indeed, an appreciation of embodied thinking, as articulated by Carol Christ,[92] will enable us to reconcile the relativism towards which employment of the categories of women's experience and praxis seems to be pointing with our unshakeable commitment to feminist vision.

Christ, in opposition to Davaney, does not see the embrace of thoroughgoing relativism to be a necessary consequence of our employment of women's experience and praxis. Instead she argues that feminists must acknowledge the ambiguity of our conditional acceptance of the postmodern framework alluded to by Davaney, but not embrace it absolutely. Inhabiting this ambiguity rather than unequivocally accepting relativism is the course of action proposed by Christ.

If we use women's experience and praxis as our primary resources, and if we are attentive to Davaney's insistence that we acknowledge their radical historicity and their perspectival character, then of necessity we must recognize the limited nature of our truth claims. Yet we need not infuse patriarchal perspectives with a similar authority or validity. Our experience and praxis would not allow us this.

The function of feminist theology is not to provide a universally normative vision with unique access to the 'way things are'. Feminist theology must understand itself to be rooted in women's particular experience and praxis. 'We can affirm the relativity of all universal truth claims, because we know that all truth claims are rooted in time and space, in experience and body.'[93]

All knowledge in some way reflects the interests of the knower. Because of the embodied, experiential character of all knowledge we should not be hesitant to accept that our truth claims are in some senses relative. Yet although we can affirm this embodied character we need not abandon our belief in the value of the feminist theological enterprise. The values promoted by feminist theology will continue to function as the basis for our theory and praxis. They will however have an ethical rather than an ontological reference, since there is no experience that is not perspectival.

The programme for feminist theology, then, ought not to be an embrace of the relativistic and nihilistic impulses that are potentially present in our resources, although an awareness of the ambiguity is essential. Feminist theology ought instead, according to Christ, to become more embodied, 'by acknowledging and affirming the conditions of time and space, which limit our perspectives as well as giving them their distinctive perspectival power'.[94]

---

92. C. Christ, 'Embodied Thinking: Reflections on Feminist Theological Method', *Journal of Feminist Studies in Religion*, 5.1 (1989), 7–15.
93. Ibid., 14.
94. Ibid., 15.

I would therefore suggest that an appreciation of embodied thinking, regard for the centrality of community in feminist theory and praxis, appeals to the pragmatic rather than the ontological, together with the recognition of women's unique position in patriarchal society, will enable feminist theologians to eschew the extreme relativism proposed by Davaney, while accepting the ambiguities involved in using as one's primary resources women's experience and praxis.

... I have been exploring the meaning and the employment of the categories of praxis and women's experience in feminist theology. From our examination two major methodological issues have been raised. It is absolutely vital, in my opinion, that feminist theologians place a hermeneutic of difference at the core of their theory. So too is it essential that they be attentive to the ambiguity confusing experience and praxis as resources and yet claiming validity for the feminist agenda. In so doing feminist theologians will achieve greater methodological integrity. Certainly the works of the feminist theologians that I have considered do contain these elements. It is my suggestion however that feminist theologians become more attuned to the methodological implications of their primary resources.

Feminist theology then will be modest in its claims. A theology that flows from the complex nature of its primary resources demands this. Because of the contextually bound nature of all knowledge and commitments, feminist theology in its entirety may envisage itself to be akin to Schüssler Fiorenza's notion of prototype.[95] Indeed, when theologians are truly aware of their work as prototypical rather than archetypical they will have begun to integrate the epistemological consequences of the fractured nature of their primary resources.

How then will this affect the shape of feminist theology in the future? I believe that a hermeneutic of difference and an awareness of the ambiguities arising from the limits of the appeals to women's experience may result in a theology that is conceptually unstable. As women and feminist men embark on theological journeys it may be helpful to consider Sandra Harding's suggestion that we embrace conceptual instability in our analytic categories.[96] This is neither to choose anarchy nor to adopt nihilism. It is, however, to adopt a risk-filled and thoroughly honest stance in relation to the universalizing potential in our theology. Conceptual instability would renounce all attempts to regulate and define women's experience and praxis in the service of universalist position. Without denying our common bonds and commitments, our interconnectedness, it is essential that feminist theology integrate the methodological implications of using as its primary resources women's experience and praxis ... .

---

95. This suggestion is forwarded by R. Chopp in her enlightening article 'Feminism's Theological Pragmatics: A Social Naturalism of Women's Experience', *Journal of Religion* 67.1 (1987), 239–56 and can be referenced in Schüssler Fiorenza, *In Memory of Her*, NY, Crossroad, 1983, 33ff., and *Bread Not Stone*, Boston, Beacon Press, 1984, 14.
96. In 'Instability of the Analytical Categories of Feminist Theory' in *Signs: Journal of Women in Culture and Society*, 11.4 (1985), pp. 545–64.

QUESTIONS FOR DISCUSSION

1   Amongst the crucial questions our chapter raises is 'what *constitutes* the role of the theologian in the Roman Catholic church today'?

2   Is the theologian simply to serve the church, bowing to all official pronouncements and teachings, even when the expertise, learning and conscience of the individual suggest otherwise?

3   Are there set limits to what the magisterium has a right and is competent to pronounce upon?

4   Can a theologian be faithful to the church and yet show dissent to official teaching and actions at the same time? On what grounds could theologians justify such dissent?

5   What of questions of contextuality – differing circumstances, geographical, economic and cultural settings? What of the voices of those who are marginalized and oppressed – who speaks for them, particularly when they may feel the institutional church has historically sided with their oppressors and/or participated in their marginalization and oppression?

6   Should the church's teaching *always* be obeyed?

7   What does it mean to speak of the *development* of doctrine and what is the role of theologians in this process?

8   How should the 'Official' institutional church deal with theologians it deems to be in error?

9   Peter Hebblethwaite wrote a study entitled *The New Inquistion*[97] – does this phrase accurately describe the current state of relations between the 'Official' institutional church and theologians it perceives to be outspoken?

10 In relation to the above questions, should they be answered differently in relation to the *definitive* magisterium and the *non-definitive* magisterium?

11 What *sort* of theology do popes 'do'?

---

97. London, Fount, 1980.

FURTHER READING

CHURCH DOCUMENTS

Divino Afflante Spiritu, 1943 (On the Promotion of Biblical Studies).
Dei Verbum, 1965.
Paul VI: *Address to the International Congress on the Theology of Vatican II*, *AAS*, 58, 1966, 890f.
Mysterium Ecclesiae, 1973.
Instruction on Certain Aspects of the Theology of Liberation, 1984.
Instruction on Christian Freedom and Liberation, 1986.
Profession of Faith & *Oath of Fidelity*, *AAS*, 81, 1989, 104–16.
Ex Corde Ecclesiae, 15 August 1990 (Apostolic Constitution on Catholic Universities).
Ratio Agendi (Regulations for Doctrinal Examination), 1997.
Ad Tuendam Fidem, in *Osservatore Romano*, 1 July 1998.

DISCUSSION AND DEBATE

Alfaro, Juan, 'Theology and the Magisterium', in R. Latourelle (ed.), *Problems and Perspectives of Fundamental Theology*, New York, Paulist Press, 1980, 340–56.
Anderson, P.M., *Worldviews and Warrants – Plurality and Authority in Theology*, Lanham MD, University Press of America, 1987.
Chung Hyun Kyung, 'The Future of Asian Women's Theology', in *The Ecumenical Movement Tomorrow – Suggestions for Improvements and Alternatives*, Marc Reuver, Friedhelm Solms and Gerrit Huizer (eds), Kampen, Kok, 1993.
Congar, Yves, 'Magisterium, Theologians, the Faithful and the Faith', *Doctrine and Life*, 31 1981, 548–64.
Cox, Harvey, *The Silencing of Leonardo Boff*, London, Collins Flame, 1988.
Curran, Charles E. and McCormick, Richard A., *Natural Law and Theology*, vol. 7 of Readings in Moral Theology, New York, Paulist, 1988.
Curran, Charles, E. and McCormick, Richard A., *Dissent in the Church*, vol. 6 of Readings in Moral Theology, New York, Paulist, 1991.
Daly, Gabriel, 'The Dissent of Theology – The Modernist Crisis', in *The Right to Dissent*, Hans Küng and Jürgen Moltmann (eds), *Concilium*, 158 (1982).
Dulles, Avery, 'The Theologian and the Magisterium', in *Proceedings of the Catholic Theological Society of America*, 31 (1976), 235–46.
Gibellini, Rosino, *The Liberation Theology Debate*, London, SCM, 1987.
Häring, Bernard, *A Theology of Protest*, New York, Farrar, Strauss and Giroux, 1970.

Häring, Hermann, 'The Rights and Limits of Dissent', in *The Right to Dissent*, Hans Küng and Jürgen Moltmann (eds), *Concilium*, 158 (1982).

Hebblethwaite, Peter, *The New Inquisition*, London, Fount, 1980.

Hogan, Linda, *Confronting the Truth – Conscience in the Catholic Tradition*, London, DLT, 2001.

Küng, Hans, 'Why I Remain a Catholic', Postscript to the English edition of *The Church – Maintained in Truth*, London, SCM, 1980.

Lacugna, Catherine Mowry, *Freeing Theology – the Essentials of Theology in Feminist Perspective*, San Francisco, Harper, 1993.

Lash, Nicholas, 'Criticism or Construction? The Task of the Theologian', in *Theology on the Way to Emmaus*, London, SCM, 1986.

McBrien, Richard P., 'Muzzling the Theologians', in *The Tablet*, 253, 20 March 1999.

McCormick, Richard A., 'Theologians and the Magisterium', in *Corrective Vision: Explorations in Moral Theology*, New York, Sheed and Ward, 1994.

Provost, James, 'The Catholic Church and Dissent', in *The Right to Dissent*, Hans Küng and Jürgen Moltman (eds), *Concilium*, 158 (1982).

Rahner, Karl, 'The Second Vatican Council's Challenge to Theology', 'The Historicity of Theology' and 'Theology and the Church's Teaching Authority after the Council', in *Writings of 1965–7*, vol. 9 of *Theological Investigations*, London, DLT, 1972.

Rahner, Karl, 'Pluralism in Theology and the Unity of the Council', 'Reflecting on Methodology in Theology' and 'The Future of Theology', in *Confrontations I*, vol. 2 of *Theological Investigations*, London, DLT, 1974.

Rahner, Karl, 'The Congregation of the Faith and the Commission of Theologians', in *Ecclesiology, Questions in the Church, The Church and the World*, vol. 14 of *Theological Investigations*, London, DLT, 1976.

Rahner, Karl, 'Mysterium Ecclesiae', in *Jesus, Man and the Church*, vol. 17 of *Theological Investigations*, London, DLT, 1981.

Rahner, Karl, 'Magisterium and Theology' and 'Yesterday's History of Dogma and Theology for Tomorrow', in *God and Revelation*, vol. 18 of *Theological Investigations*, London, DLT, 1984.

Ratzinger, Joseph, *The Nature and Mission of Theology*, San Francisco, Ignatius Press, 1993.

Russel, Letty M., *Household of Freedom – Authority in Feminist Theology*, London, Westminster Press, 1987.

Schoonenberg, Piet, 'The Theologian's Calling, Freedom, and Constraint', in *Authority in the Church*, ed. Piet F. Fransen, Leuven, Peeters (eds), University Press, 1983.

Segundo, Juan Luis, *Theology and the Church – A Response to Cardinal Ratzinger and a Warning to the Whole Church*, London, Geoffrey Chapman, 1985.

Sullivan, Francis, *Creative Fidelity – Weighing and Interpreting Documents of the Church*, New York, Paulist Press, 1996.

Part 7

Doctrine and Development – The Dynamics of Tradition and Truth

Kenneth Wilson

The truth on which the Gospel is firmly based is personal: the church is the community of faith which enjoys the truth of the Gospel and freely proclaims it. Being personal, the gospel cannot be reduced to sentences and functions. Word and practice will, in a sense, embody the truth but the truth as personal is known by the church to be Jesus Christ, the revelation of God. Scripture and tradition, indwelt by the Holy Spirit are the lively embodiment of God's revelation of God's self. They inform each other. Scripture is the written Word of God: tradition that lively conversation of all the faithful beginning with the apostles. Tradition witnesses to God's revelation, the truth of the Scriptures, celebrates a lively sense of God's presence, and develops the understanding, faithfulness and charity of all the people of God.

Culture gives a society identity, a common feeling of well-being and a sense of purpose. A culture links a society to the past by story and practice, and anticipates the future in word and action. Whilst the Church is not a society like any other, it has a culture which comes from being bound into the Body of Christ, whose focus is God, whose life is the Spirit, and whose conversation, study and practice is intended to sharpen awareness of the world-transforming truth of the Gospel for the sake of the charitable energy of grace.

Protestants at the Reformation denied the wholeness of scripture and tradition. They, confusing Tradition with what they saw as 'mere' traditions and believing the latter to be no more than bad habits, claimed that the focus of the Christian should exclusively be upon the Scriptures in order to be nourished by the Spirit of Christ and led to God. The implausibility of this is apparent when one considers any culture, particularly any culture that depends particularly upon a book for its self-understanding. Books come into existence as the result of life-experience, depend upon faithful, intelligent interpretation for their continued influence, and require the committed attention of a whole community, if their truth is both to be practised and developed. Hence the church, as the people of God, is not an optional extra but the form in which the Gospel is presented in the world.

But the world is not static. Lively conversation will tend to stimulate innovation; growth in knowledge will challenge conventional understanding and contribute to new perspectives on human nature; 'common' understandings over time become 'complex' pluralities. The question is how we should read the signs of the times so as to discern the hand of the Spirit and retain a continuity of understanding that presents a faithful witness to the faith once given to our fathers. That there is room for conflict in such a process is plainly obvious.

7.1 *DEI VERBUM* – 1965

The Second Vatican Council approved *Dei Verbum* (The Word of God),[1] the Dogmatic Constitution on divine revelation, on 18 November 1965. Significantly it gives equal emphasis to both scripture and tradition while, at the same time, confirming the primacy of scripture. It does so by noting that scripture is the word of God, and tradition is the means whereby the word of God is transmitted 'in its full purity' and so passed on to each generation. The church depends upon both, given as they are by the Spirit, if the church is to continue to enjoy and grow in the Spirit of Christ.

John XXIII intervened to allow the influence of progressive theologians to supplement the originally conservative draft version. The final document asserts that the task of interpreting the word authentically falls to the teaching office of the church alone, which derives its authority from Christ. However, the document also endorses biblical scholarship and the engagement of Catholic scholars in a diligent study of scripture, albeit 'under the watchful care' of the magisterium.

❈

CHAPTER I   REVELATION ITSELF

… In His goodness and wisdom God chose to reveal Himself and to make known to us the hidden purpose of His will (see Eph. 1:9) by which through Christ, the Word made flesh, man might in the Holy Spirit have access to the Father and come to share in the divine nature (see Eph. 2:18; 2 Peter 1:4). Through this revelation, therefore, the invisible God (see Col. 1;15, 1 Tim. 1:17) out of the abundance of His love speaks to men as friends (see Ex. 33:11; John 15:14–15) and lives among them (see Bar. 3:38), so that He may invite and take them into fellowship with Himself. This plan of revelation is realized by deeds and words having an inner unity: the deeds wrought by God in the history of salvation manifest and confirm the teaching and realities signified by the words, while the words proclaim the deeds and clarify the mystery contained in them. By this revelation then, the deepest truth about God and the salvation of man shines out for our sake in Christ, who is both the mediator and the fullness of all revelation … [2].[2]

God, who through the Word creates all things (see John 1:3) and keeps them in existence, gives men an enduring witness to Himself in created realities (see Rom. 1:19–20). Planning to make known the way of heavenly salvation, He went further and from the start manifested Himself to our first parents. Then after their fall His promise of redemption aroused in them the hope of being saved (see Gen. 3:15) and from that time on He

---

1. *ET* from *Documents of Vatican Council II: Archives of the Holy See,* www.vatican.va/archive/hist_councils/ii_vatican_council/index.htm.
2. Cf. Matt. 11:27; John 1:14 and 17; 14:6; 2 Cor 3:16 and 4:6; Eph. 1, 3–14.

ceaselessly kept the human race in His care, to give eternal life to those who perseveringly do good in search of salvation (see Rom. 2:6–7). Then, at the time He had appointed He called Abraham in order to make of him a great nation (see Gen. 12:2). Through the patriarchs, and after them through Moses and the prophets, He taught this people to acknowledge Himself the one living and true God, provident father and just judge, and to wait for the Savior promised by Him, and in this manner prepared the way for the Gospel down through the centuries [3].

Then, after speaking in many and varied ways through the prophets, 'now at last in these days God has spoken to us in His Son' (Heb. 1:1–2). For He sent His Son, the eternal Word, who enlightens all men, so that He might dwell among men and tell them of the innermost being of God (see John 1:1–18). Jesus Christ, therefore, the Word made flesh, was sent as 'a man to men'.[3] He 'speaks the words of God' (John 3;34), and completes the work of salvation which His Father gave Him to do (see John 5:36; 17:4). To see Jesus is to see His Father (John 14:9). For this reason Jesus perfected revelation by fulfilling it through his whole work of making Himself present and manifesting Himself: through His words and deeds, His signs and wonders, but especially through His death and glorious resurrection from the dead and final sending of the Spirit of truth. Moreover He confirmed with divine testimony what revelation proclaimed, that God is with us to free us from the darkness of sin and death, and to raise us up to life eternal.

The Christian dispensation, therefore, as the new and definitive covenant, will never pass away and we now await no further new public revelation before the glorious manifestation of our Lord Jesus Christ (see 1 Tim. 6:14 and Tit. 2:13) [4].

'The obedience of faith' (Rom. 13:26; see 1: 5; 2 Cor 10: 5–6) 'is to be given to God who reveals, an obedience by which man commits his whole self freely to God, offering the full submission of intellect and will to God who reveals,'[4] and freely assenting to the truth revealed by Him. To make this act of faith, the grace of God and the interior help of the Holy Spirit must precede and assist, moving the heart and turning it to God, opening the eyes of the mind and giving 'joy and ease to everyone in assenting to the truth and believing it.'[5]

To bring about an ever deeper understanding of revelation the same Holy Spirit constantly brings faith to completion by His gifts [5].

Through divine revelation, God chose to show forth and communicate Himself and the eternal decisions of His will regarding the salvation of men. That is to say, He chose to share with them those divine treasures which totally transcend the understanding of the human mind.[6] As a sacred synod has affirmed, God, the beginning and end of all things, can be known with certainty from created reality by the light of human reason (see Rom. 1:20); but teaches that it is through His revelation that those religious truths which are by their nature accessible to human reason can be known by all men with ease, with solid certitude and with no trace of error, even in this present state of the human race [6].[7]

---

3. Epistle to Diognetus, c. VII, 4: F.X. Funk, Apostolic Fathers, I, 403.
4. First Vatican Council, Dogmatic Constitution on the Catholic Faith, Chap. 3, 'On Faith': D1789 (3008).
5. Second Council of Orange, Canon 7, D180 (377); First Vatican Council, Chap. 3: D1791 (3010).
6. First Vatican Council, Chap. 2, 'On Revelation': D1786 (3005).
7. Ibid., D1785 and 1786 (3004 and 3005). Chapter 2. Article 7.

CHAPTER II   HANDING ON DIVINE REVELATION

In His gracious goodness, God has seen to it that what He had revealed for the salvation of all nations would abide perpetually in its full integrity and be handed on to all generations. Therefore Christ the Lord in whom the full revelation of the supreme God is brought to completion (see Cor. 1:20; 3:13; 4:6), commissioned the Apostles to preach to all men that Gospel which is the source of all saving truth and moral teaching,[8] and to impart to them heavenly gifts. This Gospel had been promised in former times through the prophets, and Christ Himself had fulfilled it and promulgated it with His lips. This commission was faithfully fulfilled by the Apostles who, by their oral preaching, by example, and by observances handed on what they had received from the lips of Christ, from living with Him, and from what He did, or what they had learned through the prompting of the Holy Spirit. The commission was fulfilled, too, by those Apostles and apostolic men who under the inspiration of the same Holy Spirit committed the message of salvation to writing.[9] But in order to keep the Gospel forever whole and alive within the Church, the Apostles left bishops as their successors, 'handing over' to them 'the authority to teach in their own place'.[10] This sacred tradition, therefore, and Sacred Scripture of both the Old and New Testaments are like a mirror in which the pilgrim Church on earth looks at God, from whom she has received everything, until she is brought finally to see Him as He is, face to face (see 1 John 3:2) [7].

And so the apostolic preaching, which is expressed in a special way in the inspired books, was to be preserved by an unending succession of preachers until the end of time. Therefore the Apostles, handing on what they themselves had received, warn the faithful to hold fast to the traditions which they have learned either by word of mouth or by letter (see 2 Thess. 2:15), and to fight in defense of the faith handed on once and for all (see Jude 1:3).[11] Now what was handed on by the Apostles includes everything which contributes toward the holiness of life and increase in faith of the peoples of God; and so the Church, in her teaching, life and worship, perpetuates and hands on to all generations all that she herself is, all that she believes.

This tradition which comes from the Apostles develops in the Church with the help of the Holy Spirit.[12] For there is a growth in the understanding of the realities and the words which have been handed down. This happens through the contemplation and study made by believers, who treasure these things in their hearts (see Luke, 2:19, 51) through a penetrating understanding of the spiritual realities which they experience, and through the preaching of those who have received through episcopal succession the sure gift of truth. For as the centuries succeed one another, the Church constantly moves forward toward the fullness of divine truth until the words of God reach their complete fulfillment in her.

The words of the holy fathers witness to the presence of this living tradition, whose wealth is poured into the practice and life of the believing and praying Church. Through the

---

8. Cf. Matt 28:19–20, and Mark 16:15; Council of Trent, session IV, Decree on Scriptural Canons: D783 (1501).
9. Cf. Council of Trent, loc. cit.; First Vatican Council, session III, Dogmatic Constitution on the Catholic Faith, Chap. 2, 'On Revelation': D1787 (3005).
10. St. Irenaeus, 'Against Heretics', III, 3, 1, *PG*, 7, 848; W. Harvey, edn., Cambridge, 1857, New edn. London, Gregg Press, 1965, 2, 9.
11. Cf. Second Council of Nicea: D303 (602); Fourth Council of Constance, session X, Canon 1: D336 (650–52).
12. Cf. First Vatican Council, Chap. 4, 'On Faith and Reason': D1800 (3020).

same tradition the Church's full canon of the sacred books is known, and the sacred writings themselves are more profoundly understood and unceasingly made active in her; and thus God, who spoke of old, uninterruptedly converses with the bride of His beloved Son; and the Holy Spirit, through whom the living voice of the Gospel resounds in the Church, and through her, in the world, leads unto all truth those who believe and makes the word of Christ dwell abundantly in them (see Col. 3:16) [8].

Hence there exists a close connection and communication between sacred tradition and Sacred Scripture. For both of them, flowing from the same divine wellspring, in a certain way merge into a unity and tend toward the same end. For Sacred Scripture is the word of God inasmuch as it is consigned to writing under the inspiration of the divine Spirit, while sacred tradition takes the word of God entrusted by Christ the Lord and the Holy Spirit to the Apostles, and hands it on to their successors in its full purity, so that led by the light of the Spirit of truth, they may in proclaiming it preserve this word of God faithfully, explain it, and make it more widely known. Consequently it is not from Sacred Scripture alone that the Church draws her certainty about everything which has been revealed. Therefore both sacred tradition and Sacred Scripture are to be accepted and venerated with the same sense of loyalty and reverence [9].[13] Sacred tradition and Sacred Scripture form one sacred deposit of the word of God, committed to the Church. Holding fast to this deposit the entire holy people united with their shepherds remain always steadfast in the teaching of the Apostles, in the common life, in the breaking of the bread and in prayers (see Acts 2:42, Greek text), so that holding to, practicing and professing the heritage of the faith, it becomes on the part of the bishops and faithful a single common effort.[14] But the task of authentically interpreting the word of God, whether written or handed on,[15] has been entrusted exclusively to the living teaching office of the Church,[16] whose authority is exercised in the name of Jesus Christ. This teaching office is not above the word of God, but serves it, teaching only what has been handed on, listening to it devoutly, guarding it scrupulously and explaining it faithfully in accord with a divine commission and with the help of the Holy Spirit, it draws from this one deposit of faith everything which it presents for belief as divinely revealed.

It is clear, therefore, that sacred tradition, Sacred Scripture and the teaching authority of the Church, in accord with God's most wise design, are so linked and joined together that one cannot stand without the others, and that all together and each in its own way under the action of the one Holy Spirit contribute effectively to the salvation of souls [10].

CHAPTER III   SACRED SCRIPTURE, ITS INSPIRATION AND DIVINE INSPIRATION

Those divinely revealed realities which are contained and presented in Sacred Scripture have been committed to writing under the inspiration of the Holy Spirit. For holy mother Church,

---

13. Cf. Council of Trent: D783 (1501).
14. Cf. Pius XII, ... *Munificentissimus Deus*, 1 November 1950: *AAS*, 42 (1950), 756; Collected Writings of St Cyprian, Letter 66, 8: Hartel, III, B, 733: 'The Church [is] people united with the priest and the pastor together with his flock.'
15. Cf. First Vatican Council, Chap. 3 'On Faith': D1792 (3011).
16. Cf. Pius XII, ... *Humani Generis*, 12 August 1950, *AAS*, 42 (1950), 568–69: D2314 (3886).

relying on the belief of the Apostles (see John 20:31; 2 Tim. 3:16; 2 Peter 1:19–20, 3:15–16), holds that the books of both the Old and New Testaments in their entirety, with all their parts, are sacred and canonical because written under the inspiration of the Holy Spirit, they have God as their author and have been handed on as such to the Church herself.[17]

In composing the sacred books, God chose men and while employed by Him[18] they made use of their powers and abilities, so that with Him acting in them and through them,[19] they, as true authors, consigned to writing everything and only those things which He wanted.[20]

Therefore, since everything asserted by the inspired authors or sacred writers must be held to be asserted by the Holy Spirit, it follows that the books of Scripture must be acknowledged as teaching solidly, faithfully and without error that truth which God wanted put into sacred writings[21] for the sake of salvation. Therefore 'all Scripture is divinely inspired and has its use for teaching the truth and refuting error, for reformation of manners and discipline in right living, so that the man who belongs to God may be efficient and equipped for good work of every kind' (2 Tim. 3:16–17, Greek text) [11].

However, since God speaks in Sacred Scripture through men in human fashion,[22] the interpreter of Sacred Scripture, in order to see clearly what God wanted to communicate to us, should carefully investigate what meaning the sacred writers really intended, and what God wanted to manifest by means of their words.

To search out the intention of the sacred writers, attention should be given, among other things, to 'literary forms'. For truth is set forth and expressed differently in texts which are variously historical, prophetic, poetic, or of other forms of discourse. The interpreter must investigate what meaning the sacred writer intended to express and actually expressed in particular circumstances by using contemporary literary forms in accordance with the situation of his own time and culture.[23]

For the correct understanding of what the sacred author wanted to assert, due attention must be paid to the customary and characteristic styles of feeling, speaking and narrating which prevailed at the time of the sacred writer, and to the patterns men normally employed at that period in their everyday dealings with one another.[24]

But, since Holy Scripture must be read and interpreted in the sacred spirit in which it was written,[25] no less serious attention must be given to the content and unity of the whole of Scripture if the meaning of the sacred texts is to be correctly worked out. The living

---

17. Cf. First Vatican Council, Chap. 2: D1787 (3006); Biblical Commission, Decree of 18 June 1915: D2180 (3629): *EB*, 420; Holy Office, Epistle of December 22 1923: *EB*, 499.

18. Cf. Pius XII, *Divino Afflante Spiritu*, 30 September 1943: *AAS* 35 (1943), p. 314; *EB*, 556.

19. 'In' and 'for' man: cf. Hebrews 1, and 4, 7; ('in'): 2 Samuel 23:2; Matthew 1:22 and various places; ('for'): First Vatican Council, Schema on Catholic Doctrine, note 9: Coll. Lac. VII, 522.

20. Leo XIII, … *Providentissimus Deus*, 18 November 1893: D1952 (3293); *EB*, 125.

21. Cf. St. Augustine, 'Gen. ad Litt.' 2, 9, 20: *PL*, 34, 270–71; Epistle 82, 3: *PL*, 33, 277: *CSEL*, 34, 2, 354. St Thomas, 'On Truth', Q. 12, A. 2, C. Council of Trent, session IV, Scriptural Canons: D783 (1501). Leo XIII, *Providentissimus Deus*, *EB*, 121, 124, 126–7. Pius XII, … *Divino Afflante Spiritu*: *EB*, 539.

22. St. Augustine, 'City of God', XVII, 6, 2: PL 41, 537: CSEL. XL, 2, 228.

23. St Augustine, 'On Christian Doctrine' III, 18, 26; *PL*, 34, 75–6.

24. Pius XII, Denziger 2294 (3829–3830); *EB*, 557–62.

25. Cf. Benedict XV, … *Spiritus Paraclitus*, 15 September 1920: *EB*, 469. St Jerome, 'In Galatians', 5, 19–20: *PL*, 26, 417 A.

tradition of the whole Church must be taken into account along with the harmony which exists between elements of the faith. It is the task of exegetes to work according to these rules toward a better understanding and explanation of the meaning of Sacred Scripture, so that through preparatory study the judgment of the Church may mature. For all of what has been said about the way of interpreting Scripture is subject finally to the judgment of the Church, which carries out the divine commission and ministry of guarding and interpreting the word of God [12].[26]

In Sacred Scripture, therefore, while the truth and holiness of God always remains intact, the marvelous 'condescension' of eternal wisdom is clearly shown, 'that we may learn the gentle kindness of God, which words cannot express, and how far He has gone in adapting His language with thoughtful concern for our weak human nature'.[27] For the words of God, expressed in human language, have been made like human discourse, just as the word of the eternal Father, when He took to Himself the flesh of human weakness, was in every way made like men [13].

---

26. Cf. First Vatican Council, Dogmatic Constitution on the Catholic Faith, Chap. 2, '*On Revelation*': Denziger 1788 (3007).
27. Ibid.

7.2 ALFRED LOISY: *THE GOSPEL AND THE CHURCH* – 1902

But is it true? The question of the truth of the Bible is asked in many ways. Did the events of salvation really happen? Is the evangelists' account of the life and teaching of Jesus true? Did Jesus really feed 5000 people? Did Jesus rise from the dead on the third day? Did Jesus found a Church? The questions are far from easy to understand, let alone answer. Indeed, as frequently asked they are as likely to be misleading, as they are to be helpful. One response has been to 'reduce' the gospel to a simple nostrum, 'Trust God', or 'Sola Scriptura'.

Loisy[28] achieved notoriety for his views on scripture, but he was clear that without the tradition, which included scripture, scripture would be unintelligible. Moreover, the wholeness of scripture and tradition as received in the life of the church demanded, he believed, the response of the whole church in every time and place, if the freedom of life which was God's gift in the gospel was to be enjoyed and communicated. The Gospel was dependent upon the person of Jesus and lived in the life of the church, it was not reducible to textual quotation, historical arguments or philosophical proofs.

❀

To build a general theory of Christianity on a small number of texts of moderate authority, neglecting the mass of incontestable texts of clear significance, would be to sin against the most elementary principles of criticism. Following such a method, a more or less specious doctrinal synthesis might be offered to the public, but not the essence of Christianity according to the gospel. Herr Harnack has not avoided this danger, for his definition of the essence of Christianity is not based on the totality of authentic texts, but rests, when analysed, on a very small number of texts, practically indeed on two passages – 'No man knoweth the Son, but the Father: neither knoweth any man the Father, save the Son',[29] and 'The kingdom of God is within you',[30] both of them passages that might well have been influenced, if not produced, by the theology of the early times. This critical prepossession might thus have exposed the author to the misfortune, supreme for a Protestant theologian, of having founded the essence of Christianity upon data supplied by Christian tradition. No great harm would be done from the point of view of history, if it were not that these texts are isolated by having preference given to them over the others. It must be admitted that it is often difficult to distinguish between the personal religion of Jesus and the way in which his disciples have understood it, between the thought of the Master and the interpretations of apostolic tradition. If Christ had Himself drawn up a statement of His doctrine, and a summary of His prophecy, a detailed treatise on His work, His mission, His hopes, the historian would submit it to a most attentive examination, and would determine the essence of the gospel, according

---

28. Loisy, Alfred, *The Gospel and the Church*, ET, Christopher Home, London, Isbister and Co., 1903, 11–14; 165–8; 170–1; 177–9.
29. Matthew 11:27.
30. Luke 17:21.

to irrefutable testimony. But no such treatise has ever existed, and nothing can take its place. In the Gospels there remains but an echo, necessarily weakened and a little confused, of the words of Jesus, the general impression He produced upon hearers well disposed towards Him, with some of the more striking of His sentences, as they were understood and interpreted; and finally there remains the movement which He initiated.

Whatever we think, theologically, of tradition, whether we trust it or regard it with suspicion, we know Christ only by the tradition, across the tradition, and in the tradition of the primitive Christians. This is as much as to say that Christ is inseparable from His work, and that the attempt to define the essence of Christianity according to the pure gospel of Jesus, apart from tradition, cannot succeed, for the mere idea of the gospel without tradition is in flagrant contradiction with the facts submitted to criticism. This state of affairs, being natural in the highest degree, has nothing in it disconcerting for the historian: for the essence of Christianity must be in the work of Jesus, or nowhere, and would be vainly sought in scattered fragments of his discourse. If a faith, a hope, a feeling, an impulse of will, dominates the gospel and is perpetuated in the Church of the earliest times, there will be the essence of Christianity, subject to such reservations as must be made on the literal authenticity of certain words, and on such more or less notable modifications that the thought of Jesus must of necessity have endured in transmission from generation to generation … .[31]

Thus to reproach the Catholic Church for the development of her constitution is to reproach her for having chosen to live, and that, moreover, when her life was indispensable for the preservation of the gospel itself. There is nowhere in her history any gap in continuity, or the absolute creation of a new system: every step is a deduction from the preceding, so that we can proceed from the actual constitution of the Papacy to the Evangelical Society around Jesus, different as they are from one another, without meeting any violent revolution to change the government of the Christian community. At the same time every advance is explained by a necessity of fact accompanied by logical necessities, so that the historian cannot say that the total extent of the movement is outside the gospel. The fact is, it proceeds from it and continues it.

Many objections, very grave from the point of view of a certain theology, have little significance for the historian. It is certain, for instance, that Jesus did not systematize beforehand the constitution of the Church as that of a government established on earth and destined to endure for a long series of centuries. But a conception far more foreign still to His thoughts and to His authentic teaching is that of an invisible society formed for ever of those who have in their hearts faith in the goodness of God. We have seen that the gospel of Jesus already contained a rudiment of social organization, and that the kingdom also was announced as a society. Jesus foretold the kingdom, and it was the Church that came; she came, enlarging the form of the gospel, which it was impossible to preserve as it was, as soon as the Passion closed the ministry of Jesus. There is no institution on the earth or in history whose status and value may not be questioned if the principle is established that nothing may exist except in its original form. Such a principle is contrary to the law of life, which is movement and a continual effort of adaptation to conditions always now and perpetually changing. Christianity has not escaped this law, and cannot be reproached for submission to it. It could not do otherwise than it has done.

---

31. Cf. E. Caird, 'Christianity and the Historical Christ', *The New World*, 6, 21 (March 1897), 7, 8.

The preservation of its primitive state was impossible, its restoration is equally out of the question, because the conditions under which the gospel was produced have disappeared for ever. History shows the evolution of the elements that composed it. These elements have undergone, as they could not fail to undergo, many transformations: but they are always recognizable, and it is easy to see in the Catholic Church, what stands today for the idea of the heavenly kingdom, for the idea of the Messiah, the maker of the kingdom, and the idea of the apostolate, or the preaching of the kingdom, that is to say, the three essential elements of the living gospel, which have become what they were forced to become in order to endure at all. The theory of a purely inner kingdom suppresses them and makes an abstraction of the real gospel. The tradition of the Church keeps them, interpreting them and adapting them to the varying condition of humanity.

It would be absurd to desire that Christ should have determined beforehand the interpretations and adaptations that time would exact, since they had no reason to exist before the hour which rendered them necessary. It was neither possible nor useful for Jesus to reveal to His disciples the future of the Church. The thought that the Saviour left to them was that they must continue to wish, to prepare, to await and to realize the kingdom of God. The view of the kingdom has been enlarged and modified, the conception of its definite advent fills a smaller place, but the object of the gospel remains the object of the Church … .

The Church, to-day, resembles the community of the first disciples neither more nor less than a grown man resembles the child he was at first. The identity of the Church or of the man is not determined by permanent immobility of external forms, but by continuity of existence and consciousness of life through the perpetual transformations which are life's condition and manifestation. Setting aside all theological subtleties, the Catholic Church, as a society founded on the gospel, is identical with the first circle of the disciples of Jesus if she feels herself to be, and is, in the same relations with Jesus as the disciples were, if there is a general correspondence between her actual state and the primitive state, if the actual organism is only the primitive organism developed and decided, and if the elements of the Church today are the primitive elements, grown and fortified, adapted to the ever-increasing functions they have to fulfil.

It is the very duration of Christianity which has caused this evolution. If the end of the world had arrived in the years that followed the publication of the Apocalypse, the ecclesiastical development would not have taken place, and the Church even would hardly have existed. But the world did not perish: the Church retained a reason for existence and retains it still. Her history is that of the gospel in the world … .

The power of adaptation recognized in the Roman Church is its best title to the admiration of the impartial observer. It does not follow that the Church alters either the Gospel or tradition, but that she knows how to understand the needs of the time. It cannot be too often repeated that the gospel was not an absolute, abstract doctrine, directly applicable at all times and to all men by its essential virtue. It was a living faith, linked everywhere to the time and the circumstances that witnessed its birth. In order to preserve this faith in the world, a work of adaptation has been, and will be, perpetually necessary. Though the Catholic Church has adapted, and still adapts, the faith, though she adapts herself continually to the needs of new ages, that is no proof that she forgets the gospel or despises her own tradition, but that she wishes to display the value of both, and has confidence that they are flexible and capable of further perfection.

The 'reasons of superior order',[32] which, according to Herr Harnack, caused orthodoxy to be corrected, ancient dogmas to be interpreted, new dogmas to be produced, new practices and devotions to be authorized, are not to be sought in the caprices or calculations of an arbitrary or egoistic despotism. Whatever may have been the external circumstances surrounding any particular fact, all this development proceeds from the innermost life of the Church, and the decisions of authority only sanction, so to speak, or consecrate, the movement that arises from general thought and piety. If it does not please the Catholic Church to bury herself, immovably, in the contemplation of traditional formulas, if she scrutinizes and explains them, it is because she employs activity and intelligence in the faith. If she modifies her discipline and modes of action, it is because she wishes to act, seeing that she lives. As the Church she has a collective life which, notwithstanding partial failures, is the universal life of the gospel. She is not content to make only Christians, she tends to create a Christian world state. It is easy enough to understand that individualist theologians have no sense of this collective and continuous life of the gospel in the Church, and do not always see it even when they look at it. Its reality is none the less definite, and its variety does not prove that the 'essence of Christianity' is, as it were, hidden and stifled there under an accumulation of foreign material, but that this essence dwells in it perpetually in action, under the forms that display its abundant fruitfulness.

---

32. Adolf Harnack, *What is Christianity?*, Trans. J.B. Saunders, London, Williams and Norgate, 1901, 155.

7.3 W.L. KNOX: *THE AUTHORITY OF THE CHURCH* – 1926[33]

The authority of scripture is a contentious matter. W.L. Knox stated that, notwithstanding 'the scientific development of the [nineteenth] century has rendered untenable the whole conception of the Bible as a verbally inspired book, to which we can appeal with absolute certainty for infallible guidance in all matters of faith and conduct',[34] 'At the same time all Christians would agree that in some sense the Bible possesses a paramount authority in matters of belief and conduct.'[35] He pointed to the 'divine assistance' in the writing of scripture, but also identified the process by which the religious experience of the writers, prophets, teachers and apostles was informed by the perceptions and knowledge of the time when they wrote. It would necessarily be the case if they were to be understood. This process is true, too, of the life and teaching of Jesus himself, and of the way in which the apostles, St Paul, and the other New Testament writers remembered, responded to and developed it during the apostolic period. 'In other words we see the mind of the Church, as reflected by the writers of these works, developing under the influence of Christian experience.'[36] In effect, Knox suggests, it is the profound conversation of the Catholic Church that holds together all Christian truth and stimulates the development of doctrine. But how, then, is the authority of the Church best understood? Like many Anglicans, Orthodox etc., Knox understands 'Catholic' in a wider sense than simply referring to the *Roman* Catholic church.

❈

THE FORMULATION OF CHRISTIAN DOCTRINE

It is clear ... that the general Christian consciousness is by itself a vague and fluctuating mass of individual opinions, approximating in each case to the truth, yet perhaps in no case fully grasping the whole truth with no admixture of error. Even in the most rigidly orthodox body of Christians different individuals will base their religious life more definitely on some elements of the whole Christian system than on others. A Christian who could grasp not only in theory but in the practice of his life the whole system of Christian teaching in all its fullness and with no admixture of error would obviously be a perfect saint and a perfect theologian; he would indeed see the truth as it is present to the mind of God and correspond with it perfectly: for moral failure inevitably carries with it failure to apprehend the truth. The whole sum of the Christian experience of the Church at any given moment must be an inarticulate mass of opinion comprehending in general the whole body of divine truth as revealed in Jesus; its only way of articulating itself will be its power to express approval of some particular statement of the faith as put forward by an individual theologian, unless the Church is to have

---

33. Ibid., 107–13.
34. Wilfred L. Knox, *The Authority of the Church*, in E.G. Selwyn (ed.), *Essays Catholic and Critical*, London, SPCK, 1926, 98. Our extract comes from pp. 107–13.
35. Ibid., 101.
36. Ibid., 104.

some means for expressing its corporate voice. Hence it was natural that with the ending of the ages of persecution the Church should find some means of articulating her teaching and putting into a coherent form the sense in which she interpreted in the light of Christian experience the original deposit of faith which she had received from her Lord.

We are not here concerned with the history of the Councils which decided the great Christological controversies, nor yet with the process by which the decisive influence in all matters of doctrine passed, at the cost of the Great Schism between the East and West, into the hands of the Papacy. The important matter for our present purpose is to consider the claims which are made on behalf of the various definitions of Christian doctrine by bodies claiming to voice the authority of the Holy Ghost speaking through the Church, and the sense in which these claims can be regarded as justified.

It has in many if not in all cases been claimed that the various doctrinal pronouncements of Councils and Popes are simply the affirmation of what the Church has always believed. In the strict sense that cannot be maintained; for it is easy to find cases in which theologians of the most unquestioned orthodoxy put forward doctrines which were subsequently condemned, or rejected doctrines which were subsequently affirmed as parts of the Catholic faith. Hence it is now generally admitted that such pronouncements are to be regarded as affirmations in an explicit form of some truth which was from the outset implied in the original deposit of the Christian revelation, though hitherto not explicitly realised. This claim is in itself a perfectly reasonable one. For the Christian revelation begins with the life of Jesus, presenting itself as a challenge first to the Jewish nation and then through His Apostles to the whole world, not with the formulation of a dogmatic system. It was only when Christian thought began to speculate on the whole subject of the relations of God to man and man to God implied in that revelation that the need was felt for some body of authoritative teaching which would serve both to delimit the Christian faith from other religions and to rule out lines of speculation which were seen, or instinctively felt, to be fatal to the presuppositions on which the religious experience of the Christian body rested. It should be borne in mind that the great majority of authoritative statements of doctrine have been of the latter kind, and that they usually aimed rather at excluding some particular doctrinal tendency, which was seen to be fatal to the Christian life, than at promulgating a truth not hitherto generally held.

In this sense it seems impossible to deny that the Church ought to possess some means for formulating her teaching, which will enable her to adjust that teaching to the developments of human thought, while eliminating doctrines which would, if generally accepted, prove fatal to the preservation and propagation of the life of union which God through the person of our Lord, which it is her duty to convey to mankind. It might indeed be argued that even without such means for formulating her teaching the Church did in the first three centuries eliminate several strains of false teaching, which would appear on the surface to be more fatal to the specifically religious experience than any which have threatened her in later ages. It must however be remembered that unless the Church has some means of defining her teaching in the face of error there is always a grave danger that the simple may make shipwreck concerning the faith. This might not be a very serious matter, if we were merely concerned with intellectual error as to some point of theology; the danger is that large numbers of the faithful may fall into conceptions of the nature of God which are fatal to the attainment by them of the specifically Christian character and the specifically Christian religious experience. Even though in the long run the truth should, by the action of the Holy Spirit on the whole Christian body, succeed in overcoming error, the Church is bound to exercise the authority given to her by our Lord in order to preserve her children from this danger. If this account of the reasons which underlie the formulation of the teaching of the Church be accepted, certain conclusions will follow. The organ through which the Church pronounces must be in a position to judge correctly what the Christian religious experience really is. This involves not merely intellectual capacity to understand the meaning of any doctrine and its relation to the rest of the Christian system, but also that insight into the Christian character which is only derived from a genuine attempt to live the Christian life. The same applies to all theological thought: Christian theology no less than other sciences has suffered profoundly from the disputes of theologians and authorities who, often unconsciously, confused the attainment of truth with the gratification of the natural human desire to achieve victory in controversy or the natural human reluctance to admit error.

It is however more important for our present purpose to observe that if the authority of the Church is to decide whether a particular doctrine is compatible with the religious experience of the whole Christian body, it must be able to ascertain what the religious experience of the whole body really is. In other words it must be able to appeal not merely to the religious consciousness of a few individuals, however eminent they may be in respect of sanctity and learning. So far as is possible, it must be able to appeal to the whole body of the faithful in all places and all generations. It must inquire whether any particular form of teaching is compatible with that experience of union with God through our Lord which all generations and nations of Christians believe themselves to have enjoyed; whether it is implied in it or whether it definitely destroys it. The extent to which any pronouncement can claim to be authoritative will depend on the extent to which it can really appeal to a wide consensus of Christian experience. Naturally it will not be content merely with counting numbers; it is also necessary to consider how far the consensus of the faithful on any given matter represents the free assent of men who were able to judge, or on the other hand merely represents the enforced consent of those who either through ignorance or even through political pressure were more or less compelled to accept the faith as it was given to them.

THE CLAIMS OF CATHOLIC AUTHORITY

It is from this point of view that the claims of the Catholic tradition are most impressive. For it cannot be denied that the Catholic tradition of faith and devotion manifests continuous development reaching back to the origins of Christianity. In spite of wide divergences in its external presentation of religion, it can show a fundamental unity of religious experience throughout all ages and all nations of the world, reaching back to the times when the Church had to propagate her teaching in the face of the bitter persecution of the State. Although in later times the Catholic Church has lost her visible unity, yet the general system of Catholic life and worship has shown its power to survive and even to revive from apparent death. The exercise of the authority of the Church has indeed been impaired by the divisions of the Church; but the general unity of the trend of Catholic development in spite of these divisions is an impressive testimony to the foundations laid in the period of her unity.

None the less it is necessary to inquire exactly what measure of assent may be claimed for those definitions of doctrine which have the authority of the undivided Church, and how we may recognise those pronouncements which really have the highest kind of authority. It is usually held that any definition of doctrine promulgated by a Council which can really claim to speak in the name of the whole Church, as a doctrine to be accepted by all Christians, is to be regarded as the voice of the Holy Ghost speaking through the Church, and is therefore infallible. The same claim is made by those who accept the modern position for pronouncements made by the Pope, in his character of supreme Pastor of the whole Church, on matters of faith and morals … . It is however convenient to consider first the whole conception of authority as residing in the nature of the organ which claims to speak with final authority. From this point of view it is in the first instance only possible to defend the claim that any organ can claim infallibility by means of the distinction generally drawn between doctrinal definitions which all Christians are bound to believe and disciplinary regulations intended to govern the details of ecclesiastical procedure and the popular exposition of the Christian faith. In itself the distinction is a sound one; for it is reasonable that the Church should have the right to exercise some control over such matters as the conduct of Christian worship and also the teaching of the Christian faith. For instance, it may be desirable to control the extent to which new teaching, which at first sight seems difficult to reconcile with existing beliefs, should be expounded to entirely ignorant audiences. A further implication arises from the fact that it is by no means always clear whether a particular organ has a right to speak, it is at any given moment speaking in the name of the whole Church. For instance, there are numerous cases in which bodies professing themselves to be general Councils have promulgated decisions which have since been seen as untenable. It is usually said that these bodies were not in fact general Councils at all. The same difficulty applies under modern Roman theories to papal pronouncements, for it is difficult to say with precision which pronouncements on the part of the Papacy are promulgated with the supreme authority of the Holy See and which are only uttered with the lesser authority of disciplinary pronouncements. Hence it has happened in the past that the decisions of Councils which claimed to be general Councils have been reversed by Popes or later Councils, and that papal decisions have been tacitly abandoned. Thus in fact the mere nature of the authority which utters the decision, whether Pope or Council, is itself of no value as a test of infallibility.

If in fact we inquire what decisions made by authorities claiming to speak for the whole Church are generally regarded as infallible, we shall find that they are those which have won the assent of the whole Christian body, or, as in the case of the more modern Roman pronouncements, of a part of that body which claims to be the whole. It has been urged above that the function of the authority in the Church is to formulate and render explicit, where need arises, truths implied in the spiritual experience of the Christian consciousness, and it is therefore not unnatural to suspect that the measure of truth, which any such pronouncement can claim, is to be tested by the extent to which after its promulgation it commends itself to the authority which it claims to represent. In point of fact it is manifest that this is what has actually taken place. Pronouncements which have in fact commended themselves to the general Christian consciousess have gained universal acceptance and have come to be regarded as expressing the voice of the whole Church. Those which have been found in practice to be inadequate, or have been shown to be untenable by the advance of human knowledge, have been relegated to the rank of temporary and disciplinary pronouncements, or else the body which promulgated them has been held not to have spoken in the name of the whole Church, sometimes at the cost of a considerable straining of the facts of history.

It seems however more reasonable to recognise the facts rather than strain them in order to suit a preconceived idea of what the authority of the Church should be. From this point of view it would appear that just as the inherent authority of a particular pronouncement depends on the extent to which it really represents a wide consensus of Christian experience, so the proof of that authority will lie in the extent to which it commends itself by its power to survive as a living element in the consciousness of the whole Christian body. Its claim to validity will depend very largely on the extent to which that body is free to accept it or not, and also on the extent to which it is competent to judge of the matter. It will be observed that this does not imply that the truth of a pronouncement is derived from its subsequent acceptance by the faithful. Obviously truth is an inherent quality, due to the fact that the Holy Ghost has enabled the authority which speaks in the name of the Church to interpret aright the truth revealed by our Lord and realised in the devotional experience of the Church, and to formulate that truth correctly. But the test of any individual pronouncement, by which it can be judged whether it possesses the inherent quality of truth or not, will be its power to survive and exercise a living influence on the general consciousness of Christendom over a wide area of space and time.

THE CERTAINTY OF THE CATHOLIC TRADITION

At this point the obvious objection will be raised that on the theory outlined above the Christian will at any given moment be unable to know precisely what he is bound to believe. He will never know whether a particular doctrine, which has for centuries enjoyed a wide veneration, but has in later days come to be assailed, is really as true as it seems to be. The objection is often raised in controversy with the Roman Catholic side and has a specious sound. In reality its apparent force is due to the fact that it rests on a confusion of thought. For it confuses the act of faith by which the individual submits his mind and conscience to the authority of Jesus in the Catholic Church with the quite different act of acceptance of the whole system of truth as the Church teaches at any given moment. The first of these two acts is necessarily an act of private judgment pure and simple. The individual can only accept the faith on the ground of his own purely personal conviction that it is true, although that conviction may be very largely determined by the fact that the faith is accepted by others, and by the impressive spectacle of the faith of the Catholic Church. The second act is a surrender of the private judgment by which the individual, having decided that the Catholic faith as a whole is true, proceeds to accept from the Church the detailed filling-in of the main outlines which he has already accepted.

Now on the theory put forward in this essay the position of the individual is no worse than it is on the most ultramontane theory of ecclesiastical authority. For the determining factor in his acceptance of the Catholic system will be, as it must always be, the belief that it is the truest, and ultimately the only true, account of the relations of God to man. This act of faith, rendered possible by a gift of divine grace, can never rest on anything but the personal judgment that the Catholic system as a whole is true. As regards the structure of Christian doctrine he will find, precisely as he does at present, a large body of doctrine and of ethical teaching which is set before him with very varying degrees of authority. Some elements in the system will present themselves to him with a vast amount of testimony to their proved efficacy as means for enabling the believer to attain to the genuine religious experience of Christianity, in other words to realize communion with God through the Person of Jesus, dating back to the most venerable ages of the history of the Church. Some, on the other hand, will present themselves as no more than minor regulations, judged desirable by the Church as aids to his private devotion. Between these two extremes there will lie a certain amount of teaching which presents itself to him with varying degrees of authority. This he will accept as true on the authority of the Church; and unless he be a competent theologian he has no need to trouble himself about it. He will know that it has behind it the guarantee that it has proved fruitful as an aid to the developments of the Christian life; and even if he is unable to find in some parts of it any assistance for his personal devotion, he will be content to recognise their value for others. If, on the other hand, he be a theologian, he will still respect the various elements in the Catholic system as a whole merely on the strength of the fact that they form part of so venerable a structure. Further, he will recognise that every part, in so far as it has in practice served to foster the spiritual life of the Church, contains an element of truth which all theological inquiry must account for. The greater the extent to which it has served that purpose, the greater will be the respect he will accord it. At the same time he will regard the Catholic faith as an organic whole, the truth of which is guaranteed more by its intrinsic value as proved by past experience than by the oracular infallibility of certain isolated definitions. He will indeed reverence such definitions, and he will reverence them the more in proportion to the extent and the quality of the assent they can claim. But he will recognise that their claim to be regarded as absolutely and finally true is not a matter of absolute certainty or of primary importance. It may be that the progress of human knowledge will lead to a better formulation of the most venerable articles of the faith; but it will always preserve those elements in them which are the true cause of their power to preserve and promote the devotional life of the Catholic Church. It will be observed that in acting thus he will be acting precisely as the investigator does in any branch of science, who recognises that any new advance he may make must include all the elements of permanent truth discovered by his predecessors in the same field, even though it may show that their discoveries had not the absolute truth originally supposed … .

… [T]he Christian should have sufficient confidence in the inherent strength of the Catholic system to view with equanimity the exploration of every possible avenue of inquiry. If a particular line of thought is really, as it seems to him at the moment, fatal to the whole content of Christian devotion, it will certainly come to nought. If his fears are unfounded, it can only lead to a fresh apprehension of the truth and the enrichment of Christian devotion.

7.4 KARL RAHNER: *CONSIDERATIONS ON THE DEVELOPMENT OF DOGMA* – 1957

The nature of tradition and its relationship with revelation is a controversial matter, especially when it comes to thinking through exactly how arguments might be used to justify a particular 'new' dogma which is not obviously present, for example, in scripture. Such doctrines might be those of transubstantiation, or the Bodily Assumption of the Blessed Virgin Mary. How do we justify them? What analogies can we draw on to help us? Rahner has a view which, while giving due significance to logic, points to the character of an affectionate relationship as potentially more illuminating. Both excerpts were written prior to the Second Vatican Council and represent influences on the Council's fruitful development of ecclesial understanding as 'communion'. The first[37] is from a lecture given in Innsbruck, on 3 October 1957, at a congress of German professors of dogmatic theology. The second is an extract from a paper that Rahner wrote in 1961.

❊

If we are to address ourselves to the problem of the development of dogma, the difficulty and importance of the question will be clear at once to all of us who are engaged with dogmatic theology. Our vocation is to treat of the dogmas of the Church. We have not merely to propound and explain them, to bring them within the range of the understanding of modern man; we have also the task of showing, as well as we can, that these dogmas of the Church are contained in the original revelation. For the Church and its magisterium recognize that they are not the mediators of a revelation which is now being granted for the first time. They do not look upon their office as prophetic, but as one that has only to guard, transmit and explain the divine revelation which came in Jesus Christ at a given point of past history. Thus the function of the Church and the magisterium differs in quality from the process of the original revelation, though the task of the Church is not to be conceived as merely that of repeating the original revelation, and presenting it as something *once* uttered long ago. The Church presents revelation as something that takes place 'now' as it is uttered by the living voice and offers itself to be appropriated this day in the hearing of believers. Thus the Church and the magisterium distinguish their function – by differentiation, not separation – from the process of revelation itself, and see their function as that of teaching men authoritatively in each age. It is true that the very fact of the Church and the magisterium, once it has been recognized by faith, is the immediate guarantee of a legitimate connexion between the original revelation and the pronouncements of the magisterium. But this does not render superfluous the efforts of theologians who are trying to demonstrate such a connexion. First of all, this connexion, according to the doctrine of Scripture and the Church is not absolutely transcendent with regard to history. It is found, at least to some extent, on the plane of the historical transmission

---

37. Rahner Karl, 'Considerations on the Development of Dogma', in *Theological Investigations*, vol 4, London, DLT, 1966, 3–7, 24–7.

of the original message and hence is still accessible to the historian, even though a comprehensive view of it, like that of all supernatural salvific acts of God, may be reserved for the believer alone. We could undoubtedly say: the connexion between the later dogmas of the Church and the original revelation is, on principle, a necessary subject in any comprehensive fundamental theology; but since it is concerned with the individual mysteries of faith, it must also be investigated by the dogmatic theologian and its study will be his contribution, so to speak, to fundamental theology. Secondly, this task has a special significance within theology. If the theologian must explain the doctrine of the Church as such and try to make it accessible to his contemporaries, so that they can assimilate it conceptually and existentially, one of his ways of explaining the dogmas of the Church will be to show how they derive from the original revelation. For the meaning, implications and limitations of the derivative dogma can only be clearly seen when one constantly returns to its source, especially as the official magisterium of the Church always makes such an effort when propounding its doctrines, at least by having recourse to Scripture. But if one of the tasks of the theologians is to demonstrate analytically and synthetically the relations between Church dogma and the original revelation, then he has a further task which he cannot avoid. It is to reflect on the *formal* structure of such connexions in general; he must consider the development of dogma as a whole, and not merely the question of the derivation of any individual dogma from its original utterance.

We are likewise well aware of the difficulty of the task thus described. The question was indeed never totally absent from Church history. Theology was never completely without the theme of the legitimate mode of tradition, nor did systematic reflexion in scientific form on the nature of theology and the connexions between the articles of faith and the individual truths of faith ever die out altogether, especially when apologetics on behalf of Church dogma against the *sola Scriptura* doctrine of Protestantism made this question more urgent in itself. But in the form in which we have to take up the question today, it is still very recent and hence to a great extent lacks clarification. In its present form and urgency it can only have existed since the 19th century. For it is only since the rise of modern historical science and of historicism that we can measure really clearly the difference and the distance between the forms adapted by the history of the spirit in general and the history of religious assertions in particular. The heresies of liberal Protestantism and modernism on the one hand, with their denial of the identity throughout the ages of Church dogma; the insufficiency of much current apologetics on behalf of this identity, on the other hand, conceding only a minor change in verbal formulas – both show how difficult and how little mastered the question still is. If one is honest one will hardly say that '*Humani Generis*' did more than accomplish one task, a primary one indeed, of the magisterium, namely to warn negatively against a historicist relativization of Church dogma. A really positive and progressive doctrine on the positive legitimacy of such development and its positive modes and possibilities, will undoubtedly be sought in vain in '*Humani Generis*'. The question is all the more difficult today, because we have experienced a remarkable change of fronts in recent years. In the 19th century, Protestant liberal theology reproached the Catholic Church with an unreal and fatal petrifaction of ancient dogma. Now neo-Protestant orthodoxy, with a renovated doctrine of *sola Scriptura*, charges the Catholic magisterium with an arbitrary search for novelty, which creates new dogmas without any foundation in Scripture. Hence while we formerly had to defend our maintenance of ancient Christian dogma, in fact and on principle, and our right to understand it today as it has been understood for fifteen hundred years, now on the contrary we have to uphold positively the right of dogma to undergo development. The question is therefore controverted on two sides: namely how authentic identity on the one hand and really genuine development on the other can be reconciled. The problem is undoubtedly very difficult, because it ultimately reaches down to the obscure depths of a general ontology of being and becoming, of the persistence of identity in change – and also comprises the general metaphysics of knowledge and mind, which frames the same questions in searching for truth, with regard to its identity and real historical involvement. On all these questions therefore we must confine ourselves to a few remarks, rather loosely put together, which are only meant as a basis of discussion.

For apologetics, and for the understanding of the history and development of dogma in the Church it is of supreme importance to reflect on the fact that such a development can be already observed within the New Testament. As Catholic theology is normally studied, we are accustomed, apart from a very few particular problems (perhaps especially in Christology and – naturally – in fundamental theology), to accept unquestioningly the Scriptures, especially the New Testament, as an absolutely homogeneous and undifferentiated quantity, a sort of Summa of revealed statements all laid down at once, like a code of law or a catechism composed in one piece under the same enterprise. We have of course to some extent an indisputable right to this method, which then goes on to prove individual dogmatic assertions of Church doctrine by means of *dicta probantia* chosen more or less at random from the Scriptures. Scripture, the inspired word of God, is for us as a whole and in all its parts an unquestionable authority; we see each of its assertions as dogma and not merely theology, and take each of its assertions as a legitimate starting-point for our own theology. True as this may be, and correct as may be therefore the method in question in its positive bearings, it is none the less a one-sided view of Scripture and gives a one-sided method in our dogmatic work. Modern exegesis has taught us that we can no longer reasonably overlook the fact that within what we call one Sacred Scripture, and within the New as well as the Old Testament, the assertions undergo a history and a development. No doubt the contents of Scripture are all dogma, *quoad nos*, and not just debatable theology. But it is equally certain that we must affirm that much of this scriptural dogma, which has for us the quality of inerrant assertions of revelation, is itself derivative theology with regard to a more primordial utterance of revelation. We must not naively imagine that because of inspiration (which for that reason is not to be confused with new revelation), each sentence of Scripture as such stems from a new original revelation, tributary only to an act of divine revelation which takes place here and now. Not every single sentence of Scripture was heard as it were on its own by a sort of direct telephone connexion to heaven. We may leave aside the difficult question, too little debated from fear of modernist ideas, of how an original revelation of God to the first recipients is to be conceived. But it is imperative to say that not every sentence in Scripture is this type of original revelation. Many assertions, guaranteed as inerrant at once by the Church of apostolic times and by the inspiration of Scripture, are theology derived *from* the original revelation. Since this is so, and since this derivative theology within the Scriptures still makes the just claim on us to be accepted as obligatory doctrine of faith, while it is itself a stage of development with regard to its own origin, there is therefore in Scripture itself a real development of dogma, and not merely of theology. Thus the development of dogma within Scripture is the authenticated exemplary instance for the development of dogma in general, an example which is in itself obligatory for all who view Scripture as a whole as authentic testimony of faith. St Paul's doctrine, for instance, of the sacrificial character of the cross of Christ, of Christ as the second Adam, of original sin, many sayings about eschatology etc., much of the Johannine theology etc., are theological developments from a very few simple assertions of Jesus about the mystery of his person, and from the experience of his resurrection. One could be tempted therefore, simply because such assertions are the obligatory norm of faith for us, to regard them as having fallen straight from heaven, even as they stand. One could be tempted therefore to spare oneself the labour of reaching an exact understanding of them by referring them back to the original source of revelation distinct from them. But in the long run one would risk either of misunderstanding them or of accepting them as a Summa of positively ordained truths of faith without any real internal connexions, and thus endangering their credibility to those who are without, Since however for the most part we are still unable to manipulate this multi-dimensional disposition of the truths of faith in our theology, these facts can scarcely yet be the exemplary instance which we can use to study the laws of the development of dogma … .

[The development of dogma, Rahner argues is not a single process since we are talking of the unfolding of the final divine revelation. Moreover, 'It is a closure, which in the last resort causes revelation to be closed, because this revelation is the dis-closure and openness for the absolute and unsurpassable self-communication of God to the created spirit. Revelation in Jesus Christ is not just the finite sum of finite single sentences, though the subject of these may be infinite. It implies the real, eschatological self-communication of God by incarnation, and by grace as glory already begun, to the created spirit'.[38] The development of dogma is not therefore simply a syllogistic process; it is a process which involves the development of all the elements which go to build up a dogma, or Dogma. There are four essential ingredients: (a) the grace of God which informs and delights the created spirit of man; (b) the magisterium as the vehicle which celebrates and teaches the faith; (c) the range of language and concept which makes the word of God arguable and intelligible. Further there is (d) tradition.]

TRADITION

As the fourth element of a truth of faith and hence of dogmatic development we must expressly underline the process of 'being handed on'. A divinely revealed utterance is essentially something that takes place when person speaks to person, since divine revelation, being strictly supernatural, is essentially the self-disclosure of God. From the very start therefore, and by their very nature, revealed truths are truths which are spoken to someone. This handing on of revealed truths is therefore also valid for the dogma of the Church. This element of being handed on, constitutive in the *traditio*, which is the handing on of truth and reality together, brings with it basically at once the development of dogma. For such a *traditio* takes place at a given moment of space and time, is necessarily historical, and absorbs the recipient and his historical uniqueness, which is also a property of his knowledge, into the process of *traditio* itself. In other words, anything said to anybody, if it is really to

---

38. Loc. cit., 9.

communicate, also of necessity implies that what is said undergoes a history in the utterance; it is not a mere repetition of the same thing. This is not of course to maintain that the assertion does not remain the same, in the sense of an evolutionist theory of dogmatic development contrary to the doctrine of the first Vatican Council. But if we start from this consideration we can make it clear – just as from the *a posteriori* of Scripture – that every kerygma, by the very fact of its being proclaimed, undergoes development, and therefore, since it must remain revealed kerygma which calls for faith, gives rise not merely to theology in history but to dogma in history and hence to dogmatic development.

One might then ask oneself what direction must necessarily be taken by this development, which is already contained in the initial stage of the dogma. Such a question could only be answered by taking into account the other elements which we discover in dogma. We have said above (a), that the Spirit, grace and the light of faith are one of the essential elements of dogma and therefore of its development. If one could enquire, more closely than is possible here, into the way in which this element affects the whole grasp of dogma, we should have to deduce that the light of faith, brought by the Spirit and ultimately identical with him, is the *a priori* within which the individual objects of revelation are grasped. This is comparable to natural knowledge, where being in general is the *a priori* horizon in relation to which the spirit in its transcendence grasps each object and first makes it truly intelligible. From this we are to expect *a priori* a two-fold movement within the development of dogma. The infinite breadth and intensity of the supernatural *a priori* must necessarily lead to a constantly increasing articulateness in the *unfolding* of the objects comprised within its horizon. In the confrontation and synthesis between the formal *a priori* and the *a posteriori* object of faith, the object is necessarily displayed ever more fully in its virtualities. For each *a posteriori* object of faith is grasped *as* a moment of the movement of the spirit towards the one self-communication of God, which is not merely grasped in the act of faith as a statement *about* a future thing, but actually takes place in that act. But since each fruit of truth is in this way a moment of this movement towards the unifying self-communication of God, which is absolutely unified and utterly intensive, the assertion can only function when it is open to more than it contains, to the whole, in fact. But it is only open – unless it is to fulfil this demand by the mere extinction of itself in the mystic darkness of the silent mystery in general – if it unfolds itself in a greater fullness of assertions, through which it is referred ever more fully to revelation as a whole.

The theology of the increasingly lucid *analogia fidei* is therefore not just the result of an ingenious formal logic which constantly produces new combinations, constantly finds new cross-references and connexions and deduces consequences from them. The theology in question is rather legitimated by the connexion that exists between the comprehension of an individual truth of faith and the enveloping *a priori* (given in its own reality in grace) of its comprehension in true faith. This divine *a priori* of faith inaugurates the unfolding of the ancient *depositum fidei* from its virtualities. Thus the dynamism of dogmatic development aims at an ever fuller expression of the individual dogma. It is expansive. But we must likewise expect, by virtue of the same origin, a dynamism that runs counter to this. For the formal *a priori* of faith, in contrast to the natural transcendence of the spirit and its *a priori* relationship, is not a formal abstract *a priori*, founded on the potentiality of the developing spirit and its openness; it is not merely an *a priori* of possibility. It is in fact the real intensive fullness of what is meant in each individual object of faith, and that not merely in notion or idea, but in the reality itself, which is none other than the triune God in his real self-communication.

In the act of faith therefore, in the utterance and the hearing of revelation, a synthesis takes place between this *a priori* and each individual object of faith. But then such a synthesis must also launch the dynamism in the direction of a constantly progressive concentration of the variety of the contents of revelation upon this *a priori* unity which is intended in all this variety. Dogmatic development must also contain a dynamism of compression and simplification, tending towards the blessed darkness of the one mystery of God. It is not at all as if dogmatic development must always move in the direction of multiplying individual assertions. Just as important, indeed, strictly speaking still more important, is the development in the line of simplification, towards an ever clearer view of what is really intended, towards the single mystery, an intensification of the experience of faith of what is infinitely simple and in a very essential sense obvious. The more clearly the ultimate themes are disentangled from the variety of the assertions of faith, the more clearly they are grasped through the acceptance of individual assertions, the more 'dogmatic development' do we have. In practice, the former of these dynamisms will be sustained more by popular piety than by the magisterium, which is responsible to it on justifiable pastoral grounds. The latter contrary, dynamism, will be sustained in practice primarily, though not solely, by the esoteric studies of theology itself. Theology at present however, in our non-authoritative opinion, should not be confined to the service, however justifiable, of popular piety, which strives inevitably and justifiably after the greatest possible diversity, and necessarily explains to itself the fullness of divine reality by a constantly increasing number of particulars. Theology today might well take up more intensively the other charge that falls to it, and in practice, to it alone: the reduction of the multiplicity of faith's assertions to their ultimate structures, in the intelligence of which under certain circumstances the all-embracing and overwhelming mystery of God is more powerfully present for us today than where the spirit only enlarges upon the variety of the individual assertions and further distinctions among them. To use a comparison and meet the facts at the same time one might say: there is a theology of the commonplace in the supernatural by which one tries to find God in a constant multiplication of newer and more distinct particulars. But there is also a theology of the 'mystical' or the silent mystery, in which as in mysticism proper, the particulars are lost to sight as though at night, so that the one totality may become more powerful. One might well think that the second, which demands of theology just as much precision and discernment as the first, is too little practised today. It exists however in the form of a need, mostly not quite conscious of itself, even in the theology of de-mythization.

7.5 KARL RAHNER: *THE DEVELOPMENT OF DOGMA* – 1961

Rahner suggests that the starting point of a dogmatic explication is not *always* a *proposition* in the proper sense.[39]

❁

In the first place it cannot be doubted that there exists in the natural world a kind of knowledge, which, while it is itself not articulated in 'propositions', is the starting-point of an intellectual process which develops into propositions. Let us suppose that a young man has the genuine and vital experience of a great love, an experience which transforms his whole being. This love may have *presuppositions* (of a metaphysical, psychological and physiological kind) which are simply unknown to him. His love *itself* is his 'experience'; he is conscious of it, lives through it with the entire fullness and depth of a real love. He 'knows' much more about it than he can 'state'. The clumsy stammerings of his love-letters are paltry and miserable compared to this knowledge. It may even be possible that the attempt to tell himself and others what he experiences and 'knows' may lead to quite false statements. If he were to come across a 'metaphysics' of love, he might perhaps understand absolutely nothing of what was said there about love and even his love, although he might know much more about it than the dried-up metaphysician who has written the book. If he is intelligent, and has at his disposal an adequately differentiated stock of ideas, he could perhaps make the attempt, slowly and gropingly, approaching the subject in a thousand different ways, to state what he knows about his love, what he is already aware of in the consciousness of simply possessing the reality (more simply but more fully aware), so as finally to 'know' (in reflexive propositions). In such a case it is not (merely) a matter of the logical development and inference of new propositions from earlier ones, but of the formulation for the first time of propositions about a knowledge already possessed, in an infinite search which only approaches its goal asymptotically. This process too is an explication. Here too there is a connexion *in re* between an earlier knowledge and later explicit propositions. But the starting-point and the procedure are not those of the logical explication of propositions, which we first took as the model for the development of dogma.

This case, which we are going to make use of in the field of dogma as a natural analogue for an explication other than that of the logical explication of propositions, must however be examined from a different angle. The lover knows of his love: this knowledge of himself forms an essential element in the very love itself. The knowledge is infinitely richer, simpler and denser than any body of propositions about the love could be. Yet this love never lacks a

---

39. Karl Rahner, 'The Development of Dogma', in *Theological Investigations*, vol.1, London, DLT, 1961 (2nd edn, 1965), 63–5.

certain measure of reflexive articulateness: the lover confesses his love at least to himself, 'states' at least to himself something about his love. And so it is not a matter of indifference to the love itself whether or not the lover continues to reflect upon it; this self-reflexion is not the subsequent description of a reality which remains in no way altered by the description. In this progressive self-achievement, in which love comprehends itself more and more, in which it goes on to state something 'about' itself and comprehends its own nature more clearly, the love itself becomes ordered; it has an increasing understanding of what must properly be the foundation of its own activity, mirrors its own nature with increasing clarity, approaches its own goal, with an increasingly clear awareness, what it always has been. Reflexion upon oneself (when it is accurate) in propositions (i.e. in *pensees* which the lover produces about his love) is thus a part of the progressive realization of love itself; it is not just a parallel phenomenon, without importance for the thing itself. The progress of love is a living growth out of the original (the originally conscious) love *and* out of just what that love has itself become through a reflexive experience of itself. It lives at every moment from its original source *and* from that reflexive experience which has immediately preceded any given moment. Original, non-propositional, unreflexive yet conscious possession of a reality on the one hand, and relexive (propositional), articulated consciousness of this original consciousness on the other – these are not competing opposites but reciprocally interacting factors of a single experience necessarily unfolding in historical succession. Root and shoot are not the same thing; but each lives by *the other*. Reflexive consciousness always has its roots in a prior conscious entering into possession of the reality itself. But just this original consciousness possesses itself later in a new way, such that its life is now the accomplishment of that personal act of reflexive apprehension by which it has enriched itself. Reflexive consciousness would inevitably wither if its life were not rooted in the simpler basic consciousness, or if it were to reproduce this in every particular. The simple basic consciousness would become blind if, because it is richer and fuller, it refused to allow itself to grow out into a reflexive consciousness involving 'pensees' and 'propositions'.

The question now arises whether in the development of dogma there is to be found an interrelationship of types of explication, (analogically) similar to that which has just been indicated by way of example in the natural order. We believe it is possible to reply in the affirmative.

7.6 YVES CONGAR: *TRADITION AND TRADITIONS* – 1966

It is all too easy to confuse tradition with traditions. It is not that one is 'valid' and the other not, but that without tradition there can be no valid traditions. Thus Congar begins his 'historical and theological essay',[40] with an exposition of the essential meaning and its communication; he links the 'handing over' of the gospel, the word of God, 'the word made flesh' to the world, which 'handing over' is the one continuing present handing over celebrated today in word and action and the conversation of all Christian people. It is not surprising that Congar should also be the theologian who offers profound insights into the role, obligation and opportunities of the laity. After all, it transpires that without the laity, – which might be said in one sense to include all the faithful, there would be no conversation, and neither creation nor redemption.

❀

Tradition comes from the Latin *traditio*, the noun of the verb *tradere*, to transmit, to deliver. It was a term of ratification in Roman law: for example, the legal transfer of a shop or house was accompanied by the act of handing over its keys, *tradition clavium*; the sale of a piece of land was accompanied by the act of handing over a clod of earth. *Tradere, traditio* meant to hand over an object, with the intention, on the one hand, of parting with it, and, on the other, of acquiring it. *Tradere* implied giving over and surrendering something to someone; passing an object from the possession of the donor to the receiver … .

Taken in its basic, exact, and completely general sense, tradition or transmission is the very principle of the whole economy of salvation. Tradition, in this sense, encloses and dominates it completely, from its very beginning, which is none other than God; God as the word is understood in the New Testament, referring to the Father, the absolute Origin, the uncreated Principle, the primordial source, not only of all things visible and invisible, but of the very divinity of the Son and the Spirit, by procession. God (the Father) then gives his Son to the world, he *delivers* him to the world. Here, the New Testament uses our verb 'to deliver' to show that the Father did not spare his Son, but gave him up for us (Rom. 8:31–32), to show that the Son 'gave himself up for us' (Gal. 2:20; Eph. 5:2, 25), and finally that he delivered or bestowed his Spirit on John and on Mary, at the foot of the Cross, representing the Church (John 19:30).[41]

---

40. *ET*, Congar, Yves, *Tradition and Traditions – an Historical and Theological Essay*, London, Burns & Oates, 1966, 14–17, 29–36 From the French, *La Tradition et les Traditions*, Paris, Fayard.
41. All the exegetes link John 19:30 with 20:22 (the 'Johannine Pentecost'); cf. 19:34.

Thus the economy[42] begins by a *divine* transmission or tradition; it is continued in and by the men chosen and sent out by God for that purpose. The sending of Christ and of the Spirit is the foundation of the Church, bringing her into existence as an extension of themselves: 'I came upon an errand from my Father, and now I am sending you out in my turn'[43] ... .

Usually, when it is a question of handing over a material object, the donor loses possession of it and can no longer enjoy it. But this is no longer true when it is a question of spiritual riches – when a teacher transmits a doctrine he commits it into the keeping of another, to be enjoyed by him, without losing any of it himself. This is very true of Christianity.

Firstly because it is above all a doctrine; what God transmits in his Son, what Christ delivers to his apostles, and the apostles to the Churches, is in the first place the Gospel, the divine and saving doctrine which is the object of our faith. *Tradere*, in Latin, often means 'to teach'. Secondly, because Christianity is essentially a fellowship ... .

Tradition is the sharing of a treasure which itself remains unchanging: it represents a victory over time and its transience, over space and the separation caused by distance.

The reality which it communicates is primarily a doctrine, but not exclusively so. Indeed, if 'tradition' is taken in its basic, strict sense, signifying transmission, or delivery, it includes the *whole* communication, excluding nothing. If, then, we consider the *content* of what is offered, tradition comprises equally the holy Scriptures and, besides these, not only doctrines but things: the sacraments, ecclesiastical institutions, the powers of the ministry, customs and liturgical rites, in fact, all the Christian realities themselves ... .

One last characteristic of tradition as a living transmission is that, in this way, Christianity is possessed wholly, and regarded as a totality, defying perfect comprehension and formulation; it also escapes external justification, of a historical and critical nature. This particular point has been enlarged upon by Maurice Blondel, in three articles, the third of which remains, after sixty years, one of the finest descriptions of traditions that exist. This is how they came to be written.

In rapid succession books by Albert Houtin and Alfred Loisy had appeared. In 1903 the exegetical problem was placed before Catholic opinion as a choice between the traditional dogmatic pronouncements and textual criticism of the Scriptures which employed, not only the same philological methods, but the same critical criteria and tests of authenticity as those currently used in any historical field.

Maurice Blondel, a lay philosopher whose charity made him particularly attuned to the Catholic spirit, entered the discussion by writing a series of three articles, the third of which, in particular, provided a decisive contribution, not only to the difficult problem raised, but to the notion of tradition.[44] For Blondel showed that, while it depends on the historical attestation, the Christian faith is not bound by it. Christianity has another source at its disposal, that of the ever present *experience of reality*, to which the documents testify in their fashion. This experience itself is not shared by a few isolated individuals, but by a whole people, that is, the Church; and taken as a coherent whole it is an authentic means of

---

42. In ecclesiastical terminology 'economy' is the name for the series of acts planned by God for the salvation of mankind. The Latin word is *dispensatio*.

43. John 20:21; 17:18; cf. 1 John 1–3; John 10:14–15; 17:26; Luke 22:29, 31–3; cf. Romans 1:1–6; 1 Corinthians: 3.23; 11:3.

44. 'Histoire et Dogme: les lacunes de l'exégèse moderne', *La Quizaine*, 56 (January and February 1904), 145–67, 349–73, 433–58.

reference. The transition from the material aspect of the historical evidence to the definitions of faith, which is contested by the purely rational critics in the name of historicity, is actually affected by a living synthesis in which all the forces of the Christian spirit play their part: speculation, ethics, history ... and this is Tradition.

Blondel then went on to define this tradition: 'it is not merely as oral substitute for the written teaching: it retains its *raison d'etre* even in matters where Scripture has spoken'; it is the progressive understanding of the riches possessed objectively from the beginning of Christianity, held and enjoyed in a truly Christian spirit, and transformed by reflection from 'something lived implicitly into something known explicitly':

> Tradition brings to the surface of consciousness elements previously imprisoned in the depths of the faith and of its practice, rather than expressed, expounded and reasoned. So this conservative and protective force is also instructive and progressive. Looking lovingly towards the past, where its treasure is enshrined, tradition advances towards the future, where its victory and glory lie. Even in its discoveries it has the humble feeling of faithfully regaining what it possesses already. It has no need of innovation since it possesses its God and its all: but its constant task is to provide us with fresh teaching, because it transforms something lived implicitly into something known explicitly. Whoever lives and thinks in a Christian fashion is in fact working for tradition, whether it is the saint perpetuating the presence of Jesus among us, the scholar returning to the pure sources of Revelation, or the philosopher engaged in opening the way to the future and ensuring the continual production of the Spirit of renewal. And this activity, shared by the different members, contributes to the health of the body, under the direction of its head, who, united to a conscience receiving divine assistance, alone orders and encourages its progress.

Blondel considered that a living fidelity would be more likely to keep the totality of the deposit intact right from the beginning than would a conscious and explicit record: 'Action has the privilege of being clear and complete, even when it is implicit, while reflection, with its analytic character, only becomes a science after lengthy and hesitant consideration: and that is why it seems essential to me to relate dogmatic knowledge, which is never perfect, to the Christian life, which does not need an explicit science in order to reach perfection.' There is nothing pragmatic about that; it is merely a recognition of the privileged position held by the Christian reality and the living fidelity enshrining it, and of its superiority over ideological assertions, fully analysed and elaborated.

This value of totality has a further implication: it is not a matter of a particular environment, but of a *catholic* one; it is not a question of adapting ourselves to a particular spirituality, to the values characteristic of one of the religious communities of authorized Catholicism – precisely because it is catholic. It is a question of adapting ourselves to what our fathers held and what was held from generation to generation since the time of the apostles.[45] It is a question of becoming the beneficiaries of the apostles' heritage, or of the Gospel, as the Council of Trent called it, handed down and communicated to us. St. Irenaeus, the glorious

---

45. St Gregory of Nyssa, *Contra Eumnomium*, c, 4: 'The truth of our teaching is more than sufficiently attested by tradition, that is, the truth that has reached us from the apostles, having been handed down, like a heritage' (G. 45, 653). Other texts in *EH*, 105, n. 4: *ET*, I, section A, nn. 15–24.

bishop-martyr of Lyons, wrote in approximately A.D. 180: 'The Church, implanted throughout the universe and reaching the ends of the earth, has received from the apostles and their disciples this faith in one God, the Father Almighty ... .'[46] 'Having received this message and this faith, the Church, implanted as we have said throughout the earth, keeps it most carefully, as though she formed a single household ... for though languages on the earth vary, yet the virtue (*dunamis*) of tradition is unique.'[47]

The faith – we could even say the Christian life – is something interior and personal; it is definitely not an individualistic principle of life, but a corporate and communal one, something we receive and in which we are incorporated and take part. We must believe and live like *those* who have believed and lived before us, since the apostles and Jesus Christ. The true religious relationship implies believing and living with our fellow men, for them and by them.

There is one action by which this communication is effected decisively, and which reveals itself as the chief vehicle for tradition; this is baptism, where the faith is transmitted in its entirety: knowledge, principle of life and salvation, catechetics, sacrament and 'mystery' in the sense of knowledge and in the sense of a saving act of God operating under sacred signs and apprehended by faith. The Fathers considered it an essential stage in the operation of 'tradition'; St Gregory of Nyssa calls it *prote paradosis*, the first tradition or handing on.[48]

In the fourth century this aspect of transmitting the faith by baptism was expressed in a rite resulting from the liturgical organization of the catechumenate, whose origins go back to the fourth century. On a fixed day during the baptismal initiation, which lasted during the whole of Lent, the bishop *delivered* the text of the baptismal creed to the catechumen, explaining it phrase by phrase, and the catechumen had to 'return' it to him eight days later, reciting it by heart. This was the double ceremony of the *traditio* and the *redditio symboli*, to which St Ambrose and St Augustine testify in the West, and the *Catecheses* of St Cyril of Jerusalem (348) and *Pilgrimage of Etheria* bear witness in the East.

With a richness that defies analysis the patristic writings and ancient liturgies express a continuity – a profound unity even – between the faith received in the heart, nurtured progressively in the Church's maternal womb, professed at baptism, where we commit ourselves and are consecrated, by the ratification of the material rite of baptism, and the faith confessed before all and expressed as praise in the service of God, 'It is necessary to be baptized according to what we have received by tradition (by transmission: *os parelabomen*), and to believe as we have been baptized, and thus to give praise as we believe'.[49] As a believer took the necessary steps to enter into the community of the Church, going from height to height in the Christian life, the Lord's command constituting the Apostolate and the Church was simultaneously fulfilled: 'You, therefore, must go out, making disciples of all nations and baptizing them in the name of the Father, and of the Son, and of the Holy Ghost ... He who believes and is baptized will be saved' (Matt. 28:19; Mark 16: 16a). The apostolic faith was passed on, which is the very substance of tradition; it was passed on as an objective reality, equally by verbal teaching, everyday discipline, instructive example, the entry into a

---

46. AH, I, 10, 1 (P 7, 549).
47. Ibid., 2 (G. 7, 552).
48. *Epistula* 24 (G. 46, 1088D).
49. St Basil, *Epistula* 125, 3 (G. 52, 549 B).

community and acceptance of its rules and behaviour, and finally by the material reception and efficacy of the sacrament. It is really and truly a communication of the whole Christian faith, and that is the profound meaning of Tradition, in the chief sense which we are here considering.

The process continued after baptism, throughout the Christian life – life in the Church – its elements maintained by the continuing action of the principles which gave it birth. The Christian, born of the Spirit and of water administered with a verbal formula (John 3:5; Eph. 5:26; Titus 3:5), was not subsequently left alone with the text of Scriptures, which, it may be noted in passing, had also been 'delivered' to him;[50] nor did his formation in the Church consist solely of catechetics and verbal instruction. The Church, the fellowship of the faithful of Jesus Christ, has the same structure as the material churches where the community gathers, a structure which might be described as 'bipolar'. She has a single centre, Jesus Christ, who loves her as his own flesh (Eph. 5:29) and feeds her with himself, the true Bread of Life, in two ways and under two forms: by the Bread of the Word, given from the pulpit, and by the Bread of the Sacrament, given from the altar.[51]

Although different, these two ways blend and converge, and are meant by the Lord to be used in conjunction to obtain the *fullness* of life. When Ignatius the martyr-bishop of Antioch wrote the following in approximately A.D. 107, he was making no distinction between the sacrament and its spiritual fruit: 'Faith which is the Lord's flesh and *agape* which is the blood of Jesus Christ.'[52] All the early baptismal theology does the same. There is no sacrament without words, and the celebration of the liturgy itself is very instructive: it is the present announcement of the mysteries it commemorates, the fruits of which it bestows. It is the most concentrated and efficacious element of this propagation of Christianity which immediately concerns us. The liturgical celebration is the chief influence in shaping the Christian spirit, formed, as we have seen, by Tradition. It is unsurpassed for its arrangement of the biblical texts in a way that reveals their consonance, which points in turn to the fullness of the salvation which they contain, by leading them to the centre of the complete Revelation … .

The fruit or the result and what might be called the sum total of Tradition, in the objective sense which we have just explained, is what the Fathers and the Councils have often termed the *Catholic spirit* or the *mind of the Church*. This idea can be interpreted in two ways, corresponding to an objective or subjective sense.

In the objective sense it is the unanimous belief common to the whole Church, considered not only from the aspect of present-day Catholicity, but from that of its continuity, and identity even, throughout the ages; it is the practice of the faith common to the faithful today, to the preceding generations from whom they inherited it, and, through them, to the apostles and first Christians themselves. It is the heritage of the Catholic Communion, a heritage that is truly 'catholic' and total, which greatly surpasses the past that is recorded, and even more the part that we have understood and are capable of explaining.

---

50. There existed a delivering of the Gospels, *traditio Evangeliorum*, for which the Gelasian Sacramentary (seventh century) gives a rite; the salient features of each of the four Gospels were briefly explained and the opening words of each were read. In Naples there existed a delivering of the Psalms, *tradition Psalmorum*.

51. See the author's study, 'Les deux formes du Pain de vie dans l'Evangile et la Tradition', in *Sacerdoce et laicat*, Paris, 1962, 123–59.

52. *Ad Tralles*, VIII, 1.

For, on the one hand, united with the totality, we hold all that it contains, and on the other, owing to its transmission, what we hold is not merely a theoretic statement, or even a profession of faith, but the *reality that is Christianity itself.* We received it with our baptism, the beginning of our initiation, and subsequently throughout our life in the Church, in the highest degree in the celebration of the Eucharist, by which Christ *delivers* himself to us; this reality is entrusted to our fidelity, with the injunction to keep and transmit it faithfully, without adding to it anything alien, taking anything away or changing its meaning.

In the subjective sense the *Catholic spirit* is a certain instinct, an intimate feeling or disposition, which springs from the awareness the Church has of her own identity and of what would threaten to change her identity, in the event of danger.

7.7 JOHANN BAPTIST METZ: *TRADITION AND MEMORY* – 1980

The understanding of tradition presumes it to be prospective as well as retrospective, both active and inspirational. As Johannes Metz[53] discusses the matter, memory is where reason and history are held together to produce the dynamic of hope. The 'intelligibility' of Christianity is expressed in narrative, in the story that God tells in Christ, is told of Christ in the Church, is proclaimed by the Church in the world, and lived by Christians in the world. Rahner pointed out, indeed, that the focus of tradition, of the conversation that was a part of the Christian becoming was essentially eschatological. The revelation of God, while complete and entire, looks to future fulfilment. Above all it challenges any tendency to accept present experience as inevitable. Doctrine is dynamic in the Christian memory; it offers both confirmation of what has been received and an anticipation of all that it may mean 'in the end' for the Church and the world.

❀

[Memory] should above all, in the sense of a dangerous memory, be thought of as the expression of eschatological hope, elaborated in its social and historical mediation.

In this context, then, memory has a fundamental theological importance as what may be termed anamnetic solidarity or solidarity in memory with the dead and the conquered which breaks the grip of history as a history of triumph and conquest interpreted dialectically or as evolution.

Going beyond its local application, memory can have a very decisive ecclesiological importance in defining the Church as the public vehicle transmitting a dangerous memory in the systems of social life.

As the excursus that follows will show, memory is also of importance in our dynamic understanding of dogmatic faith. With its help, dogmas can be seen as formulae of dangerous memory.

In this approach to a fundamental theology, too, memory, as the memory of suffering, is the basic concept in a theological theory of history and society as such[54] and at the same time the basic concept of a theology in the 'age of criticism'.[55]

In this connection, memory is of fundamental importance in our theological understanding of man as a subject. It can therefore be called memory as a category of the salvation of identity.

---

53. From Metz, Johann Baptist, *Faith in History and Society*, ET, David Smith, London, Burns & Oates, 1980, 184–5; 189–97. German original, pub. 1977.
54. See my contribution to Metz, Moltmann and Oelmüller, *Kirche in Prozess der Aufklärung*, Mainz and Munich, Harper & Row, 1970; ET *Religion and Political Society*, New York, 1974.
55. See my contribution, 'La théologie a l'âge de la critique', *Le Service théologique dans l'église*, Mélanges Congar, Paris, 1974, 134–48.

Finally, memory is also of central importance in any theory of history and society as a category of resistance to the passage of time (interpreted as evolution) and, in this sense, as the organon of an apocalyptical consciousness … .

MEMORY IN THE SPHERE OF HERMENEUTICS AND CRITICISM

Memory, as the systematic expression of the relationship between reason and history, can be found above all in two post-Hegelian philosophical movements. Although Hegel's thought has had a different effect on each of these tendencies, both are to a greater or lesser degree explicitly influenced by it and both have come to function, in their different ways, as criticisms of historical reason.

(a) The first is the movement of hermeneutical philosophy. This is directed against historicism and its destruction of the relationship between life and history and its abstract tendency to contrast history as memory and history as science. As a result of this historical contrast, the science of history is not in a position to become, in its extension, memory, nor does the historical memory possess the factual and logical pre-conditions at its disposal to enable it to realize itself.[56] The purely historical relationship with the past not only presupposes that the past is past; it also works actively to strengthen the fact that what has been is not present. History has replaced tradition, in other words, it occupies the place that should be occupied by tradition.[57]

The contemporary hermeneutical tendency in philosophy, then, developed as a reaction against a world dominated by science and deprived of memory and tradition, the theoretical basis of which is to be found in historicism. Its immediate predecessor was the so-called philosophy of life, one of the leading exponents of which was Wilhelm Dilthey. Dilthey's reflections about the structure of the historical world based upon the 'cultural sciences' were an extension of Droysen's view that memory functioned as a condition governing the possibility of historical investigation and that history could not be objectivized to an unlimited degree. Because he tried to base the concept of memory on the category of experience, Dilthey was, however, unable to free it from the suspicion of historical psychologism.

Neitzsche's criticism of the contrast between life and history also forms part of this general philosophical tendency. This criticism resulted in a plea against memory and for forgetfulness as the factor that made life possible. He added memory as a fitting in and interlocking process[58] to the isolated historical consciousness, to which he accredited 'a degree of sleeplessness, rumination and historical sense, in which what is living is harmed'.[59] Since he overlooked the critical function of the memory of suffering in the same way as he underestimated the calming effect or 'submissiveness' of forgetfulness, he rejected as 'masochistic' the formula that was offered to him in the statement: 'only what does not cease to hurt remains in the memory' as a means of understanding the continuity of history in the sense of a 'remembered history of suffering'.[60]

---

56. A. Heuss, *Verlust der Geschichte*, Gottingen, 1959, 68.
57. G. Kruger, 'Die Bedeutung der tradition fur die philosophische Forschung', *Studiun Generale*, 4 (1951), 322ff.
58. Nietzsche, F., *Werke in Drei Bänden*, K. Schlecta (ed.), 3rd edition, Munich, Carl Hangers, 1965, III, 829.
59. Ibid, 1965, I, 213.
60. Ibid, 1965, II, 802.

Bergson's idea of memory also belongs to this philosophy of life. He made a clear distinction between memory as the dynamic basis of the unity and continuity of the spiritual life of the person, and perception. His ideas were in turn developed at the level of social history and social psychology by Halbwachs.[61] Finally, Scheler's attempt to free memory from psychological conceptions and to understand it as the foundation of a free, critical relationship with regard to the 'historical determination' that is active in a pre-rational and natural way in the person's experience also forms part of this philosophical movement.[62]

It is also clear from the fact that many of these varieties of the philosophy of life function as encoded philosophies of history, life appearing in them as the subject and sphere of meaning of history as a whole, in the same way as nature appears in several forms of the natural philosophy as the subject of the historical processes of becoming, that these philosophies of life are very close to the hermeneutical problem of memory. In various ways, memory is always central to these philosophical processes. In the case of Schelling, for example, 'all philosophy consists of a process of remembering the state in which we were at one with nature'.[63] In the case of Bloch, on the one hand (and in some of the less frequently discussed representatives of the Frankfurt school),[64] memory accompanies all utopian philosophies of history and functions as a 'mole in the ground', pointing to a universal 'resurrection of fallen nature' and 'going forward as a movement back into the ground'.[65]

I am also bound to point in this context to the impulses that are active in this understanding of memory in the criticism of historical reason that is current in contemporary hermeneutical philosophy. These impulses have been developed above all with the problem of being in mind, a question that has been discussed at length in existential and ontological hermeneutics. Heidegger, for example, regarded remembering as 'the foundation of metaphysics in so far as it is the fundamental ontological act of the metaphysics of being'. Since, however, 'authentic memory ... always has to interiorize what is remembered, that is, re-encounter it more and more in its inner possibility',[66] the idea of being must also go forward, remembering, to meet what memory preserves in the word 'being' as something that is still outstanding and belongs to the future. History mediated in the memory thus remains 'fate'. This also applies to the way in which memory presents history as a making present of the past. As Picht has said, 'we experience the present effect of the past and are quite upset. History takes place by our being upset. It is experienced, but we are for the most part not aware of this experience. The presence of the past is therefore different from memory. It is memory in the mode of forgetfulness.'[67]

(b) The second of the two philosophical movements which can be contrasted with this first movement of the philosophy of life and existential and ontological hermeneutics, in which memory plays a leading part, is connected with the critical use of memory in those philosophies that attempt to continue the process that began in the Enlightenment to emphasize the practical aspect of reason. They do not, however, want to neglect the

61. M. Halbwachs, *Das Gedächtnis und seine sozialen Bedingungen*, Berlin and Neuweid, 1966.
62. See 'Reue und Wiedergeburt', *Gesammelte Werke* , Max Scheler, Bern, Francke, 1954, I, 35.
63. *Werke*, K.F.A. Schelling (ed.), 4, 77.
64. See M. Theunissed, *Gesellschaft und Geschichte*, Stuttgart, Knommen-Holzboeg, 1976.
65. E. Bloch, 'Subjekt – Objekt', *Gesamtausgabe*, 8, Suhrkamp Verlag Frankfurt/M., 1977, 476, 474.
66. *Kant und das Problem der Metaphysik*, Frankfurt, V. Klosterman, 2, 1951, 211.
67. G. Picht, *Wahrheit – Vernunft – Verantwortung*, Stuttgart, Klett, 288.

relationship between reason and history, between criticism and tradition and so on in favour of an abstract form of reason that is divorced from history or abandon it as erroneous, as wrongly ideological or as a threat to praxis. What we have here are above all forms of a practical and critical philosophy of history and society that have been inspired by Kant's philosophy of practical reason and the Marxist and psychoanalytical criticism of ideology.

These forms of philosophy can be seen – especially in the context of the introduction and use of memory – as debates with historical criticism and the criticism of ideology. (Historical criticism has proved and still proves its value as a criticism of ideology in its criticism of authorities, institution and unenlightened traditions.) Confronted with the directness of this criticism, these philosophers also investigate its interests and motives and raise the question (that has been asked since the time of Kant) of the so-called criticism of criticism, which in turn questions the abstract will to criticism and exposes it as an ideology that unquestioningly accepts a gradual progression in the forward movement of the critical consciousness. In this process, the criticism of criticism is not regarded as a formal metacriticism – in the sense of analytical systems or theories – which continues to discuss this problem and delegate it to a purely theoretical level (with a tendentious *regressus in infinitum*), but as a problem of theory and praxis in the context of practical reason that is, in its realization, always situated within certain social and historical relationships of foundation and reference. In this sense, history – as a structure of tradition that normalizes action – is always immanent in reason which becomes practical in its liberating task of criticism. This view of the irreplaceable relationship between reason and history, which is close to the hermeneutical standpoint, was not subsequently imputed to the Enlightenment. However well-founded, justified and necessary the criticism of traditions and their authorities that began during the Enlightenment was, this process that took place in the Enlightenment compelled man to recognize that memory was not simply an object, but an inner aspect of all critical consciousness which was seeking self-enlightenment. In this sense, critical enlightenment realizes itself in opposition to the tendency to denounce as superstition everything in the consciousness that is directed towards memory and tradition and that does not obey the calculation of scientific and technical reason, leaving it to private choice and individual lack of obligation or exposing it to the suspicion of a subjectivity without theory. This understanding of critical enlightenment is confirmed in the contemporary Enlightenment theories that are not primarily indebted to the tradition of the hermeneutical philosophy of history, in other words, in the relevant theories of the Frankfurt school, then, is similar to what is found in other positions in the tradition of practical philosophy,[68] a critical use of memory in the constitutive problem of practical reason.

This is already apparent in Walter Benjamin's theses on the philosophy of history. For Benjamin, memory, and especially the memory of the history of suffering in the world, is the medium of a realization of reason and freedom that is critically opposed to an unreflected and banal idea of a non-dialectical progress of reason.[69] Herbert Marcuse has suggested, within the referential framework of psychoanalysis, that critical measures are provided by the rediscovery of the past, that the restoration of the capacity to remember goes hand in hand with the

---

68. See, for example, W. Oelmüller, *Die unbefriedigte Aufklärung*, Frankfurt, Passelcq, 1969.
69. *Zur Kritik der Gewalt und andere Aufsätze*, Frankfurt, Suhrkamp 1965, 78–94.

restoration of the knowing content of the imagination and that in this way the *recherché du temps perdu* becomes a vehicle of liberation.[70] This insight is suggested as a fundamental postulate, that the restoration of memory to its rightful place as a means of liberation is one of the noblest tasks of philosophy.[71] Marcuse has elsewhere expressed this idea in terms of the theory of history and society, claiming that our memory of the past can give rise to dangerous insights and that established society seems to fear the subversive contents of memory. Remembering, Marcuse believes, is a way of relieving oneself from the given facts, a way of mediation that can momentarily at least break through the omnipresent power of the given facts. Memory recalls past fears and past hope and, in the personal events that arise again and again in the individual memory, the fears and longings of mankind are perpetuated. This, Marcuse suggests, is an example of the general in the particular.[72]

Theodor Adorno stressed the intention in the theory of knowledge and insisted that 'the tradition of knowledge is itself immanent as the mediating aspect of its objects. Knowledge changes the form of these objects as soon as it makes *tabula rasa* with them by virtue of objectivization. In itself, it shares, in its form that has become independent with regard to the content, tradition as an unconscious memory. No question could be asked in which knowledge of the past was not preserved and did not obtrude'.[73] If rational knowledge critically repudiates the directly normative compulsion of remembered contents, how can it then preserve memory in a changed form and eventually not let it sink down – as a vague and unconscious memory – to the level of an epiphenomenona of reason divorced from history? Adorno answered this question by referring to an aporia: 'Tradition is confronted by an insoluble contradiction. No tradition is present to be called upon. If all tradition is extinguished, however, the advance to inhumanity will begin.'[74]

Habermas has attempted to develop a practical philosophy of history and, in the interest of emancipation, to interpret the history of man and to orientate action in the present. He too has stressed the importance of memory in this process: 'The experience of reflection ... recalls the thresholds of emancipation in the generic history of man.'[75] The continued elaboration of the problem of memory in the concepts of reconstruction and self-reflection in fact conceals the connection that is revealed in memory between communicative action and historical frames of reference. It would seem that the interests of knowledge (emancipation and coming of age) are naturalized to such a degree as linguistic structures that are remote from history that the process of memory has ceased to take place in them.

The critical treatment of memory has therefore clearly run into some of the unsolved problems of hermeneutics. At the point where both intersect, certain characteristics of memory as a philosophical concept can be formulated in a manner that also expresses a number of previously unregarded aspects of the various philosophies of memory.

---

70. H. Marcuse, *Triebstruktur und Gesellschaft*, Frankfurt, Suhrkamp, 1968, 24f.
71. Ibid., 228.
72. *One-dimensional Man*, London, Sphere, 1968.
73. *Negative Dialectics*, London, RKP, 1973.
74. T.W. Adorno, 'Thesen über Tradition', *Ohne Leitbild*, Frankfurt, Suhrkamp, 1967, 34f.
75. J. Habermas, *Erkenntnis und Interesse* , Frankfurt, Suhrkamp, 1968, 31.

MEMORY AS THE MEDIUM BY WHICH REASON BECOMES PRACTICAL AS FREEDOM: CHARACTERIZATION AND CONSEQUENCES

In my outline of the extent of the problem of the concept of memory, I indicated that the process could be regarded as the means by which reason could become practical as freedom. In what follows, I shall deal with memory basically as the memory of freedom that, as a memory of suffering, acts as an orientation for action that is related to freedom, under the heading (a). I shall then discuss how its narrative structure (b) leads it to criticize historical technology that is dissociated from memory and to encounter the traditions of *anamnesis* and the Christian *memoria* (c).

(a) The form of memory that is immanent in critical reason is the memory of freedom. It is from this form of memory that reason acquires the interest that guides the process by which it becomes practical. The memory of freedom is a definite memory. In contrast to a vague use of freedom indiscriminately and on the basis of contradictory presuppositions, the definite memory of freedom is related to the traditions in which the interest in freedom arose. These traditions are, in the narrative characteristics, that is, as the narrated history of freedom, not the object, but the presupposition of any critical reconstruction of history by argumentative reason.

In its practical intention, the memory of freedom is primarily a *memoria passionis*, memory of suffering. As such, it mediates a praxis of freedom in a form that resists being identified, either openly or in secret, with a praxis that is expressed as a progressive control of nature. In its practical intention, a philosophy of history that is orientated towards the memory of suffering is therefore prevented from explaining history as the history of freedom simply in the categories of a history of domination, even if this domination is that by the introduction of a concept of the whole (of history) that is indispensable in any practical philosophy of history and by avoiding a concept of totality (of the praxis of control and domination) in that concept of the whole of history.

Respect for the suffering that has accumulated in history makes reason perceptive in a way which – in the abstract contrast between authority and knowledge within which the problem of the autonomy of reason is usually discussed and to which our understanding of emancipation as the *a priori* interest of reason is apparently fixed – cannot be expressed. In this perception, history – as the remembered history of suffering – has the form of a dangerous tradition. This dangerous tradition cannot be done away with or rendered harmless either in a purely submissive attitude towards the past – as it is in many approaches to hermeneutical theories of reason – or in an attitude towards the past that is based purely on the criticism of ideology, as it is in many approaches to critical theories of reason. It is, in any case, mediated in a practical way. It takes place in dangerous stories in which the interest in freedom is introduced, identified and presented in narrative form.

(b) This memory has an essentially narrative structure. It functions as a criticism of a concept of memory that is derived from an idea of the abstract identity of the consciousness that has determined all teaching about the memory since Kant's concept of the transcendental synthesis of apperception. Husserl's phenomenology has been particularly influential in this context.[76] Wittgenstein's *Philosophical Investigations*[77] and Schapp's later phenomenological studies[78] were directed against this memory. Schapp taught that a consciousness that was 'involved in stories' formed the basis of the abstract unity of the phenomenological subject and that this consciousness was made explicit in narrative form and pointed to a cognitive primacy of narrated memory in the connection between the historical nature of consciousness and what Lubbe called a 'consciousness in stories'.[79]

(c) This cognitive primacy of narrated memory has a number of consequences. I shall discuss the most important of them here. Because of this primacy, philosophy is obliged to make a link between narrative and argument. In addition to Danto's analytical theory of narrative,[80] for example, there is also a need for a hermeneutical and critical theory in which the relationship between philosophy and, on the one hand, literature, and, on the other, the antihistory of suffering that is narrated in it could be developed. The practical reason of philosophy cannot be expressed in the technology of the control of nature, in which science is made practical by application. The cognitive primacy of narrated memory would seem rather to point in the direction of a criticism of those forms of historical reason that become a technology turning backwards, after the magisterium of history has been dethroned, after what has been called the *historia magistra vitae*[81] has been ruled out as the basis of argument and after the art of narrative has been forgotten in the science of history.[82] That particular process is distinguished by a cybernetic use of memory.[83] It is also increasingly orientated towards a history that has been classified rationally and purposefully in a data bank and a computer memory that cannot forget and therefore cannot remember. There is a clear tendency in this process towards a total objectivization of history and man living in history – the stigma of the post-historical. As opposed to an abstract criticism, however, the cognitive primacy of narrated memory compels philosophy, which cannot be persuaded by universal criticism to abandon the question of truth or to reduce reflection, to consider carefully one of Nietzsche's hypotheses. According to Nietzsche, the, 'we who know today, we who are godless and opposed to metaphysics, take *our* fire from the blaze that was set alight by a faith that is centuries old, the Christian faith that was also the faith of Plato – faith that God is the truth and that the truth is divine'.[84] This cognitive primacy of narrated memory and therefore of a 'consciousness that is involved in stories' is therefore valid in contrast with the abstract unity of the consciousness and the various forms of doubt and criticism which are without presuppositions and which arise in that abstract unity. What is more, it also means the

76. See Husserl's fundamental work, 'Vorlesungen zur Phänomenologie des inneren Zeitbewusstein', also 'Cartesianische Meditationen', *Husserliana*, 1, The Hague, Den Waag, 1950/1989.

77. Oxford, Blackwell, 1958.

78. In *Geschichten verstrickt*, Hamburg, 1953; ibid., *Philosophie der Geschichten,* Leer, 1959; for Schapp, W. Frankfurt, see J. Habermas, *Logik der Sozialwissenschaften*, Nittorie Klostermann, Tübingen, 1967 and H. Lubbe, '"Sprachspiele" und "Geschichten". Neopositivismus und Phänomenologie im Spätstadium', *Bewusstsein in Geschichten*, Freiburg, 1972.

79. See note above, for the book of this name.

80. *Analytical Philosophy of History*, Cambridge, 1965 also in 'Narration and Knowledge', New York, Columbia University Press, 1985.

81. See R. Koselleck, *Natur und Geschichte. Festchrift für K. Löwith*, Stuttgart, Hain, 1967.

82. See H. Weinrich, *Literatur für Leser*, Stuttgart, 1972.

83. See K.W. Deutsch, *Politische Kybernetik*, Freiburg, 1967.

84. Edition Schlechta II, 208.

theological use of memory is not relegated in advance to a social zone which is inaccessible. Theology may at the same time also regard memory or its social counterpart, tradition, as the mediation between God's absolute revelation and the recipient of that revelation.[85] It is not purely by chance that Christian faith is categorically described as the *memoria passionis, mortis et resurrectionis Jesu Christi* and that attempts are made ... to justify that faith in the narrative and argumentative form of a liberating memory as a definitive form of hope.

---

85. See J. Pieper, *Überlieferung*, Munich, 1970; G. Scholem, 'Offenbarung und Tradition als religiöse Kategorien im Judentum', *Über einige Grundbegriffe dea Judentums*, Frankfurt, 1970, 90–120.

7.8 PAUL AVIS: *CONSENSUS AND CRITICISM* – 1986

Anglican and Orthodox theologians when faced with the issue of papal authority have pointed to the importance of the notions of reception and *sensus fidelium*. Complementing our discussions in Chapter 5, Avis[86] offers a perspective which relates these concepts to doctrinal development and the ecumenical context. They have, for example, figured prominently in the conversations between the Anglican and Roman Catholic churches. In particular, Avis, questions whether, the doctrine of reception can bear the weight that is placed upon it. Indeed, it appears that consensus is not always a guarantee of divine truth. It is important to be sure that the evangelical desire to recover the unity of all the faithful is securely based on good theology.

❄

Having said that reception by the faithful does not endow a definition with authority, for it must possess this in itself by virtue of its truth, the ARCIC report[87] goes on to enunciate the principle of *reception*. 'The assent of the faithful is the ultimate indication that the Church's authoritative decision in a matter of faith has been truly preserved from error by the Holy Spirit. The Holy Spirit who maintains the Church in the truth will bring its members to receive the definition as true and to assimilate it if what has been declared genuinely expounds the revelation' (p. 92:25).

Obviously, the confidence of the report in this matter presupposes a certain indefectibility of the Church and of the nature of truth. The document follows the line adopted by the Second Vatican Council which, while wary of the doctrine of reception, did stress the infallible instinct of the faithful, inspired by the Holy Spirit, which leads them to embrace the truths enunciated by the magisterium. The Constitution on the Church declares: 'The body of the faithful as a whole, anointed as they are by the Holy One ... cannot err in matters of belief.' Citing Augustine, the Constitution goes on to claim that, 'thanks to a supernatural sense of the faith which characterizes the People as a whole, it manifests this unerring quality when, "from the bishops down to the last member of the laity", it shows universal agreement in matters of faith and morals' [no. 12]. When the magisterium – the bishops together with the Pope – formally utters its mind, the assent of the Church will surely be forthcoming through the work of the Holy Spirit, 'whereby the whole flock of Christ is preserved and progresses in unity and faith' [no. 25].

The Declaration *Mysterium Ecclesiae* issued in 1973 by the Sacred Congregation for the Doctrine of the Faith with the backing of Pope Paul VI in order to combat subversive theologians, especially Hans Küng, speaks in the same vein of 'the unhesitating assent of the People of God concerning matters of faith and morals'. Although our obedience is ultimately

---

86. Avis, Paul, *Ecumenical Theology and the Elusiveness of Doctrine*, London, SPCK, 1986, 66–75.
87. *The Final Report of the Anglican-Roman Catholic International Commission*, London, CTS/SPCK, 1982.

to God himself, our 'conversion to God through faith' is itself 'a form of obedience' and shows itself in submission to the revelation that is mediated to us through the infallible teaching of the Church's pastors. Our conversion to God therefore takes the form of adhering to him 'in the integral doctrine of the Catholic faith' [ch. 4].

Karl Rahner has produced a critique of *Mysterium Ecclesiae* which will serve as a convenient stepping-stone to his thought on the question of consensus and reception. He raises several pertinent questions concerning the further statement of the declaration that there is 'a certain shared infallibility', restricted to matters of faith and morals, 'which is present when the whole people of God unhesitatingly holds a point of doctrine pertaining to these matters'.

The question Rahner raises about the notion of 'shared' infallibility and what precisely is meant by this – what delimitation of roles between magisterium and the faithful does it imply? – is one for purely internal consumption within the Roman Catholic Church. But Rahner also asks whether the criterion of a conviction being 'unhesitatingly held' is adequate, considering that many convictions unhesitatingly held throughout the Church from time to time have later been abandoned and would now be regarded as mistaken. He goes on to question whether the notion of 'the whole people of God' is an 'empirically comprehensible entity'. Only if it can be claimed convincingly that it is empirically cashable does it have relevance for determining the character of Christian faith (XVII, p. 143).[88]

Rahner's view of consensus and the process of reception has not always been so cautious. In the early 1960s he was expressing somewhat sanguine views about the possibilities of a consensus of faith. Writing after the promulgation of the dogma of the Assumption of Mary but before *Humanae Vitae* with its condemnation of modern methods of birth control, Rahner felt able to claim that a papal definition had never been given where the object of the definition was not already believed by the Church as a truth of faith. He envisages in an idealistic way the process whereby the Church comes to know its own mind: 'The church as a whole considers a thought which grows out of the whole content of its faith: it ripens, it merges ever more fully with the whole, while the church lives it and perfects it. And so the church of a certain day, if we may say so, finds itself simply there, believing in this special manner' (IV, pp. 31f). The Church will therefore receive the definitions of authority because it already tacitly believes them. The paper definition that follows simply ratifies what is already fact. A truth 'has impressed itself slowly and without flourish of trumpets on the believing consciousness of the church.'

Rahner's persuasive version of the role of the Pope in this process would, so it appears, receive the endorsement of the Anglican-Roman Catholic Commission. For Rahner, 'the Pope is the point at which the collective consciousness of the whole church attains effective self-awareness' as a focus of authority for its individual members. In his latest published writings Rahner reiterates this view, describing the Pope as 'the authentic spokesman of the church's sense of faith', whose infallibility stems from 'his appeal to the infallible sense of faith of the church as a whole' (XX, pp. 137f). Along the same lines, the *Final Report* reached agreement on the role of the pope as the one who can articulate the mind of the Church after

---

88. [Where Avis cites Karl Rahner, the Roman numerals refer to relevant volume of Rahner's *Theological Investigations*, London, Burns & Oates, various dates.]

full consultation, and do so in a way that is divinely preserved from error. Significantly, precisely the same idea is presented in Jean Tillard's recent book *The Bishop of Rome* (Tillard is, of course, a member of the Commission), where the 'infallible judgement of the Pope "articulates and brings to full expression the instinctively right" … judgements of the people of God'. However, Tillard's comments that this is an example of 'the phenomenon of corporate identity … at work' may be taken with a pinch of salt! (p. 177).

The thrust of Rahner's argument is obviously slightly different from that of the report. He is seeking to curb the propensity of the magisterium to multiply authoritative definitions, by limiting its role to that of articulating what has already emerged in the collective mind of the Church. The report, on the other hand, is attempting to find a place for papal authority in a united church in a form that safeguards the appeal to reason and the duty of private judgement that are vital to the Anglican tradition. There is, therefore, a difference of emphasis that ought not to be overlooked between progressive Catholic ecclesiologists such as Rahner, who call for a wide-ranging process of consultation within the Church *before* any definition is uttered, on the one hand, and Anglican ecumenical proposals that bend over backwards in the attempt to reach agreement by postulating a process of evaluation in the Church at large *subsequent* to the definition, on the other.

It is also significant that, while the report is happy to rest a great deal on the concept of consensus, Rahner himself has moved – as the later volumes of the *Theological Investigations* testify – to a much less sanguine view of the possibility of widespread agreement in the Church. This is due largely to his growing sombre awareness of the intractable problems of pluralism, and partly to the shock administered to progressive Catholic theology in its post-Vatican II euphoria by the papal encyclical *Humanae Vitae* of 1968, which conspicuously did *not* reflect the mind of the Church.

ARCIC's emphasis on reception by the faithful to validate (in the elusive sense of this concept employed in the *Final Report*) the decisions of the magisterium is also vulnerable from another angle. It involves a circular argument. The report is confident that the Holy Spirit 'who maintains the church in the truth' will guide the faithful to accept such a decision if it 'genuinely expounds the revelation' (pp. 92–95). This reflects closely the view presented by Peter Chirico:

> The only way the church can be sure that a pope or council has spoken infallibly is by finding the meaning proclaimed actually present in the consciousness of the faithful. Only when the vast numbers of the faithful discover that the meaning of a proclamation resonates with the meaning of the faith within them … can the church be assured that its authorities have spoken infallibly.[89]

In other words, whatever can be said to be both taught by the magisterium and accepted by the faithful is *ipso facto* revealed as being divine truth. Or, to put it another way, we can know that the magisterium has been preserved from error by the Holy Spirit (as ARCIC puts it) when we see that its decisions are received by the faithful, because we are here presupposing that the faithful themselves will be preserved from error by the same Spirit.

---

89. Peter Chirico, *Treatise on Infallibility*, Sheed and Ward, London, 1976, 241.

One reply to this would be to point to historical examples of both magisterium and faithful agreeing on some fundamental tenet that one side later repudiated. Hans Küng has done this in the case of birth control in his celebrated diatribe *Infallible?* Who can deny, he asks, that such a consensus has existed for centuries, that artificial methods of birth control have been consistently condemned in recent times by numerous Episcopal conferences and individual bishops giving judgement? Küng points out that the conservative minority on the papal commission – the commission whose recommendations were, notoriously, rejected by Pope Paul VI in *Humanae Vitae* – was able to point out that 'history provides the fullest evidence … that the answer of the church has always and everywhere been the same, from the beginning up to the present decade'. 'One can find', it continues, 'no period of history, no document of the church, no theological school, scarcely one Catholic theologian, who ever denied that contraception was always seriously evil.' The conservatives were able therefore to conclude that the Church's teaching on contraception was 'absolutely constant' (p. 54). The universal consent – classically expressed in the canon of St Vincent of Lerins, *semper, ubique, et ab omnibus*, 'always, everywhere and by all' – on the question of birth control has broken down in our lifetime, not because the magisterium has changed its mind, but because the faithful – who after all were the ones who had put it into practice – found the traditional view impossible.

This process is now being repeated in the matter of the ordination of women to the priesthood. In October 1976 the Sacred Congregation for the Doctrine of the Faith published with the approval of Pope Paul VI a 'Declaration on the Question of the Admission of Women to the Ministerial Priesthood'. It would be superfluous to say on which side of the argument the declaration came down! But it began by referring to the 'unbroken tradition throughout the history of the church, universal in the East and in the West', which indisputably and invariably excluded women from the priesthood. This was an unquestioned axiom of the Church which had never before required the intervention of the magisterium to defend it. (The Sacred Congregation for the Doctrine of the Faith's *Obervations* on the *Final Report* invoke the constant tradition alleged by this *Declaration* of 1976 as a barrier to union with a communion that ordains women.)

In criticizing the declaration, Karl Rahner makes the point that tradition is not a *carte blanche* that can be invoked to give an imprimatur to anything that has been taken for granted and remained unquestioned for centuries. Not all tradition is necessarily a vehicle of divine revelation which would be absolutely and definitively binding on the Church. There is obviously, he says, 'a purely human' tradition in the Church which offers no guarantee of truth even if it has long gone unchallenged (XX, pp. 35ff).

The criterion of consensus is not by itself a sufficient guarantee of divine truth. To appeal to a consensus which is by definition historically and empirically verifiable is to give hostages to fortune. But since awkward facts seem to have a minimal deterrent effect on the manufacture of dogma, a more conclusive reply to the ARCIC report's assertions about the *consensus fidei* would be simply to point out that it is (not viciously, but perhaps trivially) circular and therefore inconclusive.

Once we give up the view that consensus in the Church is – under certain ascertainable circumstances – a firm guarantee of the truth, we can go on to recognize the fact that consensus as such is a purely *natural* concept. It is not a good in itself. It is capable of being informed with truth or blinded by error and ignorance.

Translated into political terms, consensus is mandatory in a democracy under the rule of law. This is the grain of truth in the idea of 'consensus politics': in a democracy, government rules by consent. But it does not follow that the right political prescription for a nation's ills is to be found in the 'middle ground', any more than theological truth is to be found by seeking a *via media*. It is simply an acknowledgement of the fact that you have to carry people with you. On the other hand, there is no need to assume that a consensus is inherently suspect – as though the minority is always right. This is an assumption, moreover, that is as often as not tinged with disdain *de haut en bas* (whether based on class or intellectual superiority) for the ignorant masses in their Gadarene descent into prejudice and superstition.

A consensus, like any other ideological construct, is not purely the product of the object to which it ostensibly refers, but is conditioned by all sorts of extraneous influences – social, cultural, political and economic. Thus a consensus in the Church concerning some question of doctrine or ethics will incorporate not only the response of the faithful to God's revelations of his love in Jesus Christ, but also distortions of this revelation as it is communicated to us through the human and impersonal channels of history, as well as constraints upon our response by factors which are more appropriately studied by the social sciences than by theology. This is why, as Charles Davis and Nicholas Lash have argued, ideological criticism must be taken to the heart of the Christian theological enterprise, so that both the prevailing consensus among the faithful and the specific teachings of the magisterium may become subject to its discipline and so purged of any unworthy elements that serve to pervert the truth of God.

It is salutary to remind ourselves that consensus is not good in itself but morally neutral, becoming a good only when it is consensus in the truth. It is then transformed from mere consensus into the theological concept of *catholicity*. Whether a consensus in the Church on any given issue is equivalent to catholicity can only be known with any degree of assurance by appeal to objective sources of verification: historical, exegetical, ethical, philosophical.

Both Orthodox and Reformation theology can be cited in support of this view. Orthodox theology regards the Church's instinct for the truth (*sensus ecclesiae*) as the seat of a practical infallibility that preserves the whole people of God in the truth. This *sensus ecclesiae* must be allowed to exercise a monitoring function on any consensus that may emerge in the Church. John Meyendorff has shown how this works in the case of Augustinianism – which Orthodoxy rejects. In the western tradition, he writes, Augustine 'has been isolated from the entire tradition of the church and considered as the unique source of theological knowledge'. Thus, Meyendorff asserts, 'a new synthesis and a new consensus took place' that was not compatible with the received Greek patristic theology. The Orthodox reject this synthesis, he concludes, not because of its novelty – since, as Meyendorff significantly admits, 'new theologies, new formulations of doctrine' are unavoidable – but because it is found wanting when brought to the bar of independent assessment in the light of the gospel as we find it in Scripture and the Fathers (pp. 137, 148). Thus, in the Orthodox understanding, as Meyendorff presents it, mere consensus is no guarantee of truth, but needs to be evaluated by the theological criteria based on Scripture and patristic theology.

For the Reformers and the Anglican divines who followed them, catholicity is defined in relation to truth, not in relation to consent as such (nor, as they polemically asserted, to the universal jurisdiction of the papacy). Inward possession of truth was prized above outwards imposition of unity. The Reformers warned against the real possibility of consensus in error. As John Jewel pointed out, 'There was the greatest consent that might be amongst them that worshipped the golden calf and among them who with one voice jointly cried against our Saviour Jesus Christ, "Crucify him!"' And as Sandys quaintly remarked, 'Adam and Eve and the serpent were all of one mind'! For all the Reformers – and here the English divines quoted are merely representative – consensus is only equivalent to catholicity when it is founded on truth. As Bradford put it, 'Unity must be in verity'.

The ARCIC report seems to envisage a teaching authority with sufficient flexibility to respond immediately to any pressing issues that may arise within the Church. It will gird up its loins to tackle the matter without delay. Its considered judgement (the report takes for granted that it will be able to reach one) will then be submitted to a streamlined process of consultation and reception by the Church at large.

This scenario bears little relation to reality. It is highly implausible that the magisterium would have the ability to come to grips with the sort of urgent pastoral problems that the report seems to have in mind. It is unlikely that its eventual response would have the decisiveness required to settle the issue. However, supposing for a moment that the hierarchy did manage to achieve a swift and decisive response, the momentum would immediately be lost in the inevitable and slow process of reception by the faithful. There is no way in which a common mind can emerge in the Church with the rapidity that is needed to deal with pressing issues.

In his 'Dream of the Church', Karl Rahner has described the range of consultation that would be required if a judgement of the magisterium were to qualify as a true reflection of the mind of the Church. Such a process of consultation could not take place behind closed doors, 'in smoke-filled rooms', where concessions were extracted and bargaining counters traded. Of course Rahner does not say this in so many words; he is much more diplomatic. What he calls for is explicit, transparent, straightforward, sincere and public dialogue. There would have to be discussions with theologians, consultation of the world-wide episcopate, and conversation with the leaders of churches that had entered into union schemes with Rome while retaining their essential independence. Rahner optimistically concludes: 'With such procedures even non-Catholic Christians would no longer need to fear an arbitrary manipulation of the papal teaching authority opposed to the Spirit of Jesus and of the Church' (XX, p. 138).

That may be so, but the question that needs to be asked is, would the result be worth having? Would not the area of eventual agreement be so restricted as to amount to a statement of the obvious?

This leads us to observe that the statements of the magisterium, dependent as they are on the consensus of the whole Church, will be necessarily conservative. In other words, they will be platitudes. This is not to say that the Church has no teaching office – it must offer the gospel to the world and enunciate the primary truths of Christianity. Nor is it to disparage the notion of the mind of the Church – provided we do not attempt to put it to uses for which it is not adapted. Neither is it to dismiss the Church, on account of its conservative character, as irrelevant to the needs and questions of the modern world. Religion, bound up as it is with tradition and a community, is essentially conservative by nature; it is concerned with abiding truths and realities that will never pass away; and that is precisely where its relevance to a bewildered and fretful world lies. But the argument certainly does effectively undermine the hope expressed by the ARCIC report that the teaching office of the Church will be enabled 'to show how the Christian truth applies to contemporary issues' (p. 93:27). This task will best be performed by individuals and small study groups offering their own conscientious and informed opinion.

7.9 AVERY DULLES: *CATHOLICITY AT LENGTH: TRADITION AND DEVELOPMENT* – 1985

The abiding continuity of the Church throughout the centuries is a vital understanding of Christian faith. Avery Dulles[90] sees this, above all, as an essentially historical matter – the church really participates in the redeeming grace of Christ. This is not a claim for perfection, but a way of defining the nature of the church between Pentecost and the Parousia. The spirit-empowered church is not a society from time to time gathered in faith to fulfil God's call to holiness, but a divinely instituted eschatological community. Certainly, as at present involved in human history, the church is imperfect but as the eschatological society it shares in the life of God, Father, Son and Holy Spirit.

✻

Unlike the ancient Israel and John the Baptist, the Church cannot be content to point forward to something not yet given; it must guard and dispense what has been irrevocably given in the definitive sending of the Son and the Holy Spirit. In the perspectives of an incarnational theology the Barthian image of grace as a tangent touching a circle is misleading. The gift of God has truly entered the world and is at work transforming it …

Once this is granted, further questions arise about the relationships between the various eras of Church history. Should the history of the Church be seen as a decline from the original purity, as unbroken progress towards a future fullness, or as a simple perpetuation of the original endowment? All three of these positions have been proposed and defended, but how are they to be assessed by the standard of catholicity?

The Church historian, Ferdinand Christian Bauer, writing towards the middle of the nineteenth century, complained that up to his own day Protestants had tended to regard the history of the Church as a progressive falling away from the gospel.[91] The sixteenth-century Reformers, he explained, aimed to weed out the accumulated errors and restore the original purity. For them the privileged moment of Church history was the first, the time of foundation. Although some Protestants, like Bauer himself, reject this schematization, Bauer undoubtedly hit upon a characteristic and recurrent trend. Down to our own time, many Protestants hold that true Christianity can be found only in the apostolic Church and the apostolic writings of the New Testament. These alone for them, are the criterion by which all else is to be judged.

The sixteenth-century Reformers were not themselves critical of the dogmas of the early centuries, because they were convinced that the councils had defined only what was already the teaching of Scripture. But as Protestantism went on, there was an increasing disposition to invoke the Bible alone and to use it critically against the Fathers and the early councils. A

---

90. Dulles, Avery, *The Catholicity of the Church*, Oxford, Clarendon Press, 1985, 93–103.
91. Peter C. Hodgson (ed.), *Ferdinand Christian Bauer on the Writing of Church History*, New York, Oxford University Press, 1968, 4–16, 79–81, 115.

distinguished biblical theologian, Oscar Cullmann, comes close to this position. He regards apostolic tradition as divinely authoritative, but looks on ecclesiastical tradition, beginning with the second century, as highly untrustworthy. Generally speaking, Cullmann accepts the New Testament as a pure deposit of the original apostolic tradition.[92]

The logic of this primitivist approach can be applied against the New Testament itself. Some nineteenth-century liberal theologians, including Adolf Harnack, took the teaching of Jesus as the supreme norm for judging even the theology of John and Paul. Early in the twentieth century it became common to characterize the Christianity of the subapostolic period (roughly from AD 95 to 150) as being – in a pejorative sense – 'early Catholic'. Contemporary exegetes such as Ernst Kasemann and Willi Marxsen have taken a further step. Finding traces of early Catholicism in the New Testament itself, they compare the relatively late writings of Luke and the Pastoral Letters unfavourably with what they regard as the original gospel, as found, for example, in the authentic epistles of Paul. Behind this analysis we can detect the tendency to equate development with decline. What was first given is taken as normative. What comes later, it is assumed, will inevitably be a deviation, infected by human sinfulness.

This schematization is, of course, contested by scholars of a Catholic orientation – and not only by members of the Roman Catholic Church. A few contemporary Lutherans such as John Elliott and Robert Wilken have questioned the premises of their colleagues' reasoning. Wilken, for instance, protests:

> We cannot discover what Christianity 'is' by an exegesis of biblical texts or by uncovering the earliest strata of the Christian tradition. The Christian movement can be understood only in light of its historical development, i.e., what it *became* within the course of its history. The New Testament has a *future* as well as a past. What *becomes* of a historical phenomenon is as much a statement of what it is as what it was at the beginning.[93]

From a Roman Catholic perspective, Johann Sebastian Drey, early in the nineteenth century, pointed out a serious weakness in the Protestant appeal to Scripture alone. Christianity, he objected, cannot be reduced to an occurrence in the remote past as attested by contemporary witnesses. Protestants themselves have recognized the impossibility of deciding the questions of a later age without supplementing the Bible. Deprived of any authoritative tradition, they have been constrained to rely on subjective human efforts to breathe life into the dead records. Their arbitrary constructions cannot claim the authority of God's word. The actual and lived Christianity of Protestants is thus a product of human subjectivity.[94]

Anglicans and Orthodox, as well as Roman Catholics, have generally rejected the Protestant position, in so far as this is purely biblicist, and have insisted that the Bible cannot be the rule of faith except when conjoined with a continuous Church tradition. In this perspective, which is fundamentally Catholic, the very sections of the New Testament which the liberals tend to discount as too far removed from the events can be seen as providing

---

92. Oscar Cullmann, 'The Tradition', in his *The Early Church*, Philadelphia, Westminster, 1956, 59–99.

93. Robert L. Wilken, *The Myth of Christian Beginnings*, Garden City, NY, Doubleday, 1971, 155–6.

94. Johannes Sebastian Drey, 'Vom Geist und Wesen des Katholizismus', *Tubinger Theologische Quartalschrift*, 1 (1819), 8–23, esp. 20–23.

privileged interpretations, for, as Newman pointed out, events of great importance require a considerable span of time in order to be rightly comprehended.[95] On the same principle, the traditionalists argue that the assimilative process was not complete even with the last books of the New Testament. Only when Christianity became a historical religion through some distance from the apostles, and a universal religion through some dispersion from its Palestinian matrix, could certain important questions arise and be addressed. The New Testament, therefore, gives only the early stages of a continuing process whereby the revelation of Christ perpetuates itself in the Church.

The Orthodox differ on one important point from the Roman Catholics, and on this the Orthodox were, at least in the nineteenth century, joined by many Anglicans. They hold that Christianity must meet the test of antiquity, and that doctrines not attested by the consensus of the Fathers must be set aside as unfounded. John Henry Newman for a time accepted this position, and attempted to defend it in his *The Via Media of the Anglican Church*. But he soon became dissatisfied with his own arguments, which he then answered in his *Essay on the Development of Christian Doctrine*. The consensus of the Fathers, he concluded, gave only feeble support to certain basic beliefs of the Church of England, such as the Trinity, original sin, and the real presence. On the other hand, the Fathers were relatively concurrent in professing the universal authority of the successors of Peter, which the Anglicans rejected. Thus to Newman it began to appear that the principle of development, if it applied to the early centuries, must apply to subsequent centuries as well. The truth or falsehood of a doctrine could not be established by the date when it came to be believed, but by other criteria which Newman attempted to spell out in his famous *Essay* and in several other works.

In contrast to those theories which exalt the past at the expense of the present, there are others, equally opposed to authentic catholicity, which canonize the present or the future. As an example of this distortion one may cite the work of Alfred Loisy. Influenced in part by Newman's developmental theories, he wrote a mordant book-length response to Harnack's *What is Christianity?*[96] Ridiculing Harnack's effort to find a stable essence of Christianity in the message of the historical Jesus, he maintained on the contrary that the Church, as a living organism, was destined to develop far beyond all that Jesus had foreseen and all that the apostles had believed. In Loisy's theology, Christianity was portrayed as a movement that took its departure, and even its inspiration, from Jesus and the apostles, but was governed by them as its norm. Loisy was a brilliant writer. He argued his case with an extraordinary command of the biblical and historical materials, and inserted a number of cautionary remarks to forestall exaggerations. But the Roman authorities understood him as advocating an extreme historical relativism that would make the demands of the passing situation in effect the norm of faith. They accordingly condemned Loisy's doctrine and labelled it Modernism. The label has stuck.

Whatever judgement is to be passed on Loisy and his associates, we must, I think, grant that Catholic Christianity is committed to a fundamental continuity. It holds that the Holy Spirit, having inspired the apostolic Scriptures, continues to be with the Church at every stage of her development preventing her from betraying the apostolic heritage. Hence it must be possible to trace a direct line from past to present. Tradition is not infinitely fluid.

---

95. Cf. John Henry Newman, *An Essay on the Development of Christian Doctrine*, Garden City, NY, Doubleday Image, 1960, Introduction, sec. 21, 53.

96. Alfred Loisy, *The Gospel and the Church*, London, Isbister & Co., 1903; Philadelphia, Fortress, 1976.

Catholicism accordingly opposes both the archaism of Harnack and the Modernism of Loisy. For much the same reasons, Catholic Christianity has always resisted futurist movements that sought to play off both the past and the present against a coming golden age that was thought to be at hand. At various times sects have arisen proclaiming that the period of institutional Christianity was coming to an end and was about to be superseded by an age of the Spirit in which every individual would be guided by the inner leading of grace without need of external authority. These movements, from Montanism, through Joachim of Flora, to some more recent apocalyptic sects, have regularly led to bizarre exaggerations and have quite properly been repudiated as diverging from Catholic Christianity.

The position I have been advocating is not limited to Roman Catholics. It is defended, for example, in the report, *Catholicity*, submitted to the Archbishop of Canterbury in 1947 by a committee under the chairmanship of the future archbishop, Arthur Michael Ramsey. This report declares: 'Protestantism has not really come to terms with the reality of history as the scene of the continuous presence of Divine life that flows from the Incarnation.'[97] This sentence, however, raises the question how such continuity can be asserted notwithstanding the vicissitudes the Church has undergone in its two-thousand year history.

(5) It must be admitted, I think, that Catholic theology has not always found it easy to come to terms with the realities of history. F.C. Bauer, who objected to the Protestant tendency to look on history as a continual defection, could not do justice to the phenomenon of change. In effect, he argued, Catholics remove the Church from the realm of history.[98] These charges were not wholly unfounded. Just as in early modern times Catholics tended to confuse universality with uniformity, so they tended to equate continuity with immutability. The great Counter-Reformation historian, Caesar Baronius, composed his twelve volume *Annales ecclesiastici* to demonstrate that in the Catholic fold the divinely given constitution of the Church 'was preserved inviolate, was guarded scrupulously, and was never broken or interrupted but perpetually maintained'.[99] Shortly afterwards, Bossuet was to write an apologetic work in which he argued that, while the doctrines and systems of the Protestants continually change, the Catholic Church, unalterably attached to the institution of Christ, is so stable 'that not the least variation since the origin of Christianity can be discovered in her'.[100]

With the expanded historical consciousness of later centuries, this extreme conservatism became untenable. At the very time when Bauer was complaining about Catholic immobilism, theologians such as Möhler and Newman, without questioning the continuity, were excogitating theories of development. They appealed not only to the analogy of organic growth, whereby plants and animals develop from a tiny seed, but also to the analogy of consciousness. Just as a new idea, after taking root in the mind, gradually achieves its own proper formulation, so likewise, they argued, the Christian idea, though fully given at the beginning, takes time to find its appropriate expression in doctrines and institutions. Unlike some other Catholic theologians, Möhler and Newman did not require that the development

---

97. *Catholicity: A Study in the Conflict of Christian Traditions in the West*, Westminster, Dacre Press, 1947.
98. P.C. Hodgson (ed.), *Bauer on Church History*, Oxford, OUP, 1968, 13–14, 33, 115, and *passim*.
99. Quoted by Bauer, ibid., 108, from Preface to Baronius's *Annales ecclesiastici*.
100. Jacques-Benigne Bossuet, *The History of the Variations of the Protestant Churches*, 2 vols, Dublin, R. Coyne, 1829, vol. 2, 388.

of doctrine be homogeneous, in the sense that the later formulations could only explicate what was logically implicit in earlier formulations.

At Vatican II the views of Möhler and Newman, mediated by Blondel, Geiselmann, Congar, and others, seem to have prevailed. The Constitution of Divine Revelation opts for a dynamic, progressive theory of tradition. Inhering in the collective consciousness of the Church, tradition is said to develop constantly through the active assistance of the Holy Spirit, so that as a result 'the Church constantly moves forward toward the fullness of divine truth until the words of God reach complete fulfilment in her' (DV 8).

It must be admitted, I think, that Catholic authors until the middle of the present century have tended to speak as though the Church moved ahead without reference to its changing environment, but with Vatican Council II we begin to get a certain recognition that this is not the case. As a principle motive for calling the council, Pope John XXIII spoke of the need to bring the Church abreast of the times where required.[101] The Declaration on Religious Freedom was self-confessedly written as a response to the newly developing consciousness of the dignity of the human person (DH 1). The Pastoral Constitution on the Church in the Modern World, after commenting upon the Church's obligation to read and respond to the signs of the times, observed: 'In this way, revealed truth can always be more deeply penetrated, better understood, and set forth to greater advantage' (GS 44). The council makes it clear that the structures of the Church, although fundamentally given by Christ, must continually be adjusted to the times (ibid.).

These recent teachings add a further nuance to the Catholic insistence on continuity. Continuity is not best served by an endless repetition of the same rites and formulas, but periodically requires new doctrinal assertions, liturgical symbols, and pastoral structures to transmit the 'fullness' of Christ effectively to new generations. The faith, constantly present in a global way in the consciousness of the total Church, has to be articulated in forms appropriate to the place and time. Changes in the cultural climate thus introduce a certain discontinuity in the self-understanding and self-expression of the Church. A number of contemporary authors – Anglican, Lutheran, and Roman Catholic – speak in this connection of alterations in perspective. 'Historical perspective', writes Gabriel Daly, 'is rapidly becoming a normal characteristic of contemporary Roman Catholic theology.'[102]

It could easily seem that the Church's catholicity in time is impaired by the inevitability of change. Does not the Church, in accepting historical consciousness, renounce the continuity in which she has traditionally gloried? To answer this question, we need only recall the constant refrain of this study, that catholicity is not homogeneous but heterogeneous unity; it is unity in difference. Catholicity in time, therefore, includes an element of discontinuity. Just as the Church's geographical catholicity requires a variety of cultural forms, so her temporal catholicity calls for responsiveness to the times and seasons. 'The present form of the apostolic mission', writes Wolfhart Pannenberg, 'had the task of bringing to new expression in each age the catholic fullness of the church.'[103]

---

101. John XXIII, Opening Speech to the Council (11 October 1962), in Walter M. Abbott (ed.), *Documents of Vatican II*, New York, American Press, 1966, 710–19, esp. 712.
102. Gabriel Daly, *Transcendence and Immanence*, Oxford, Clarendon Press, 1980, 227.
103. Pannenberg, *The Church*, Philadelphia, Westminster, 1983, 68.

Carrying this thought a stage further, we may perhaps surmise that each major era of Christian history has a special task or vocation. By living out the integral Christian reality in its own way, it makes a distinct contribution to the ongoing tradition. The task of the apostolic age was to formulate the basic Christian message and to lay the foundations of the Church once and for all. The Church of succeeding generations can build on no other foundation than that which has been laid (cf. 1 Cor. 3: 11; Eph. 2: 20). One would, however, look in vain to the apostolic period and its Scriptures for detailed prescriptions by which to answer the problems of a later age. Fundamentalist Protestantism, with its rallying cry of 'Scripture alone', fails to make this important distinction.

The task of the patristic period was to establish the classic patterns of doctrine, church organization, and liturgical worship. In its own characteristic style – a style not ours – that age gave definitive answers to a number of central and recurring questions, such as the unity of the godhead, the trinity of divine persons, and the full divinity and humanity of the incarnate Word. No subsequent age will be required to do again what the Fathers accomplished. But in building on the work of the Fathers we are not obliged to repeat mechanically what they did and said. Their venerated formulations have to be reinterpreted through modern patterns of thought, probed with the help of contemporary investigative techniques, and restated in terms intelligible to present-day believers.

The work of subsequent centuries lacks the same foundational importance for the Church. We are not related in the same way to the mediaeval churchman and theologians, for example, as we are to the apostles and the Fathers. Standing further from the sources, these later figures could not so significantly shape the future of the Church, but they could explicate certain logical implications of what had already been defined. By their creative efforts, moreover, the mediaeval monks, academicians, and prelates illustrated the possibilities of adapting the Christian faith, as previously set forth, to the needs and possibilities of a very different culture. What the churchmen and theologians of the Middle Ages and early modern times did for their own day, we must do for ours, profiting as much as possible from their accomplishments.

QUESTIONS FOR DISCUSSION

Another way of referring to the development of doctrine would be 'the vitality of doctrine'. Properly understood the statement of doctrine at a given time is like a section of living tissue; what we learn is not insignificant, but since we are dealing with dynamic material we can be almost certain that there is more to know. There may be aspects of what we know which are virtually the same wherever the section is cut, but even when that is so the changing context of the whole will provoke us to make new judgements about the relationship of what we thought we knew to what we now believe we know.

We could also talk of a conversation with our Lord, who reveals himself in the gospel. Wherever we cut into it there will be things which we understand, things which we fail to understand and things which puzzle us. The important thing is to engage in the conversation, and that we are invited to do.

However, having realized the dynamic nature of our understanding of faith, we have then to come to terms with the ways in which the context gives new perspectives and insights to our faith. Our 'new' world does of course have much in common with our former worlds, but the ways in which it is different are so striking and so fundamental as to awaken the possibility of new and adventurous theological thinking. The question is what we mean by 'new' when, on the analogy of the section of living tissue or of conversation, what is new can only grow out of what is already implicit and pressing in the 'old'.

1 What constitute the foundations of dogma?
2 What are the links between doctrine and scripture?
3 How is 'tradition' related to revelation?
4 How should the church decide what constitutes a part of the 'tradition' of Catholic doctrine?
5 What does it mean when a later church teaching seemingly contradicts an earlier church teaching? What does this say about the 'Catholic system'?
6 How is a living gospel best sustained and proclaimed by the church?
7 How can we explain and interpret older teachings for a new age in a faithful manner?
8 How should the magisterium avail itself of positive historical developments?
9 Is historical relativism detrimental to Christian doctrine?
10 What is the difference between 'tradition' and 'traditions'?
11 In relation to doctrine, what do we mean by 'Catholicity'?

FURTHER READING

CHURCH DOCUMENTS

Fidei Depositum, 11 October 1992.

DISCUSSION AND DEBATE

Alszeghy, Z., 'The "Sensus Fidei" and the Development of Dogma', in vol. 1 of R. Latourelle (ed.), *Vatican II – Assessment and Perspectives,* New York, Paulist, 1988.

Anglican-Roman Catholic International Commission (ARCIC), *The Final Report*, London, CTS/SPCK, 1982.

Chadwick, Owen, *From Bossuet to Newman*, 2nd edn, Cambridge, Cambridge University Press, 1987.

Congar, Yves, *Tradition and the Life of the Church*, London, Burns & Oates, 1968.

Dulles, Avery, *The Survival of Dogma – Faith, Authority and Dogma in a Changing World*, New York, Crossroad, 1971.

Dulles, Avery, *The Resilient Church: The Necessity and Limits of Adaptation*, Garden City, NY, 1977.

Fransen, Piet, 'Criticism of Some Basic Theological Notions in Matters of Church Authority', in *Authority in the Church*, Piet F. Fransen (ed.), Leuven, Peeters University Press, 1983.

Hines, Mary, *The Transformation of Dogma*, New York, Paulist, 1989.

Lash, Nicholas, *Newman on Development – the Search for an Explanation in History*, London, Sheed & Ward, 1979.

Lash, Nicholas, *Change in Focus – a Study in Doctrinal Change and Continuity*, London, Sheed & Ward, 1981.

Mackey, John P., *Tradition and Change in the Church*, Dayton, OH, Pflaum Press, 1968.

Newman, J.H., *An Essay on the Development of Christian Doctrine*, Notre Dame, University of Notre Dame Press, 1989.

Nichols, A., *From Newman to Congar: the Idea of Doctrinal Development from the Victorians to Vatican II*, Edinburgh, Clark, 1990.

Pelikan, Jaroslav, *Historical Theology – Continuity and Change in Christian Doctrine*, London, Hutchinson, 1971.

Rahner, Karl, 'What is Heresy?', in *Later Writings*, vol. 5 of *Theological Investigations*, London, Burns & Oates, 1966.

Rahner, Karl, 'A Small Fragment on the Collective Finding of Truth', in *Concerning Vatican II*, vol. 6 of *Theological Investigations*, London, Burns & Oates, 1969.

Rahner, Karl, 'Heresies in the Church Today?' in *Confrontations II*, vol. 12 of *Theological Investigations*, London, Burns & Oates, 1974.

Rahner, Karl, 'Basic Observations on the Subject of Changeable and Unchangeable Factors in the Church' in *Ecclesiology, Questions in the Church, the Church and the World*, vol. 14 of *Theological Investigations*, London, Burns & Oates, 1976.

Rahner, Karl, *Concern for the Church*, vol. 20 of *Theological Investigations*, London, DLT, 1981.

Ratzinger, Joseph, *Church, Ecumenism and Politics*, Slough, St Paul's, 1987.

Segundo, Juan Luis, *Theology and the Church – a Response to Cardinal Ratzinger and a Warning to the Whole Church*, London, Geoffrey Chapman, 1985.

Segundo, Juan Luis, *The Liberation of Dogma – Faith, Revelation, and Dogmatic Teaching Authority*, New York, Orbis, 1992.

Ward, Keith, 'The Church as a Teaching Community', chap. 6 of *Religion and Community*, Oxford, Oxford University Press, 2000.

Wiles, Maurice, *The Making of Christian Doctrine – a Study in the Principle of Early Doctrinal Development*, Cambridge, Cambridge University Press, 1967.

Wiles, Maurice, *The Remaking of Christian Doctrine*, London, Xpress Reprints, 1994.

Yarnold, Edward and Chadwick, Henry, *Truth and Authority*, London, CTS/SPCK, 1977.

Part 8:

Reform and Renewal in the Church

Richard R. Gaillardetz

In the last four centuries of Roman Catholicism, questions of church reform and renewal have been tainted by Catholic–Protestant polemics. Luther's vigorous assertion that the church was an *ecclesia semper reformanda* led to Catholic counter-assertions regarding the church as a *societas perfecta* possessing an indefectible holiness. This Catholic viewpoint seemed to preclude any consideration of church reform beyond the reform of its individual members. In 1950 Yves Congar published his controversial study on the possibility of reform in the church, *Vrai et fausse réforme dans l'Église*, and in spite of the fact that the Vatican intervened to prevent future translations of this work, the book's central theme became an important topic at Vatican II. Pope John XXIII placed the topic at the forefront of conciliar reflection when he explicitly called for an *aggiornamento*, bringing the church 'up to date', in his address at the opening of the council. A fresh consideration of the topic was made possible by the fundamental shifts in Catholic ecclesiology reflected in the conciliar documents. First, a heightened appreciation for the eschatological dimension of the church as a pilgrim people made it easier to suggest that if the church does not 'achieve its perfection until the glory of heaven' (*LG*, no. 48) then substantive ecclesial reform must be possible. Second, the recovery of the pneumatological foundations of the church furthered this development by granting ecclesial change as potentially the work of the Spirit and not necessarily a departure from immutable ecclesial structures established by the will of Christ. Third, in 1964 Pope Paul VI issued his first encyclical, *Ecclesiam suam*, in which he encouraged the value of respectful dialogue both within the church and between the church and the world.[1] This important concept found its way into the council's Pastoral Constitution on the Church in the Modern World, *Gaudium et Spes*.

Since Vatican II, while all have admitted that the council envisioned the need for church reform, commentators have differed significantly regarding the nature and scope of reform appropriate for today's church. This diversity of viewpoints, from the primacy of interior reform stressed by Cardinal Ratzinger, to the much more radical critiques of the church's exercise of power by Boff and Ruether, suggests the vitality of the debate since the council.

---

1. This important document is included in chapter one of the present volume. In relation to renewal and reform see, especially, nos 10–11, 44–7, 70; 85–7, 113–17.

8.1 *LUMEN GENTIUM* – 1964

In its Dogmatic Constitution on the Church,[2] the Second Vatican Council stressed the dignity and equality of all the baptized and the rights and obligations of the baptized to active participation in the life of the church. This would provide the basis for the recognition of legitimate dialogue within the church. At the same time, by recovering a sense of both the pneumatological and eschatological dimensions of the church, the council was able to offer a theological basis for the ongoing need for ecclesial reform and renewal.

While Christ, holy, innocent and undefiled knew nothing of sin, but came to expiate only the sins of the people, the Church, embracing in its bosom sinners, at the same time holy and always in need of being purified, always follows the way of penance and renewal. The Church, 'like a stranger in a foreign land, presses forward amid the persecutions of the world and the consolations of God'[3] announcing the cross and death of the Lord until He comes. By the power of the risen Lord it is given strength that it might, in patience and in love, overcome its sorrows and its challenges, both within itself and from without, and that it might reveal to the world, faithfully though darkly, the mystery of its Lord until, in the end, it will be manifested in full light ... [8].

Moving forward through trial and tribulation, the Church is strengthened by the power of God's grace, which was promised to her by the Lord, so that in the weakness of the flesh she may not waver from perfect fidelity, but remain a bride worthy of her Lord, and moved by the Holy Spirit may never cease to renew herself, until through the Cross she arrives at the light which knows no setting ... [9] ... .

It is not only through the sacraments and the ministries of the Church that the Holy Spirit sanctifies and leads the people of God and enriches it with virtues, but, 'allotting his gifts to everyone according as He wills',[4] He distributes special graces among the faithful of every rank. By these gifts He makes them fit and ready to undertake the various tasks and offices which contribute toward the renewal and building up of the Church ... [12] ... .

The laity have the right, as do all Christians, to receive in abundance from their spiritual shepherds the spiritual goods of the Church, especially the assistance of the word of God and of the sacraments. They should openly reveal to them their needs and desires with that freedom and confidence which is fitting for children of God and brothers in Christ. [37] ... .

The Church, to which we are all called in Christ Jesus, and in which we acquire sanctity through the grace of God, will attain its full perfection only in the glory of heaven, when there

---

2. *ET, Documents of Second Vatican Council, Archives of the Holy See*, see: www.vatican.va/archive/histcouncils/ii_vatican_council/index.htm.

3. S. Augustinus, Civ. Dei, XVIII, 51, 2: *PL*, 41, 614.

4. 1 Corinthians 12: 11.

will come the time of the restoration of all things. At that time the human race as well as the entire world, which is intimately related to man and attains to its end through him, will be perfectly reestablished in Christ [48].

8.2 *UNITATIS REDINTEGRATIO – 1964*

In the council's Decree on Ecumenism[5] it enjoins Christians to recall that the restoration of unity involves the participation of the whole church. Roman Catholics, in particular, are reminded that their first obligation is to the renewal of their own 'Catholic household'.

❀

Catholics, in their ecumenical work, must assuredly be concerned for their separated brethren, praying for them, keeping them informed about the Church, making the first approaches toward them. But their primary duty is to make a careful and honest appraisal of whatever needs to be done or renewed in the Catholic household itself, in order that its life may bear witness more clearly and faithfully to the teachings and institutions which have come to it from Christ through the Apostles … [4] … .

Every renewal of the Church is essentially grounded in an increase of fidelity to her own calling. Undoubtedly this is the basis of the movement toward unity. Christ summons the Church to continual reformation as she sojourns here on earth. The Church is always in need of this, in so far as she is an institution of men here on earth. Thus if, in various times and circumstances, there have been deficiencies in moral conduct or in church discipline, or even in the way that church teaching has been formulated – to be carefully distinguished from the deposit of faith itself – these can and should be set right at the opportune moment [6].

---

5. *ET, Documents of Second Vatican Council, Archives of the Holy See,* www.vatican.va/archive/histcouncils/ii_vatican _council/index.htm.

8.3 *GAUDIUM ET SPES* – 1965

With the promulgation of *Gaudium et Spes*[6] in the final session of Vatican II, a new genre of conciliar document was created, a *pastoral* constitution. This document addressed the church's relationship to the modern world. Moving beyond the siege mentality of so many pre-conciliar approaches, this document sought an authentic and respectful dialogue with the world.

❋

By virtue of her mission to shed on the whole world the radiance of the Gospel message, and to unify under one Spirit all men of whatever nation, race or culture, the Church stands forth as a sign of that brotherhood which allows honest dialogue and gives it vigor. Such a mission requires in the first place that we foster within the Church herself mutual esteem, reverence and harmony, through the full recognition of lawful diversity. Thus all those who compose the one People of God, both pastors and the general faithful, can engage in dialogue with ever abounding fruitfulness. For the bonds which unite the faithful are mightier than anything dividing them. Hence, let there be unity in what is necessary; freedom in what is unsettled, and charity in any case [92].

---

6. *ET, Documents of Second Vatican Council, Archives of the Holy See*, www.vatican.va/archive/histcouncils/ii_vatican_council/index.htm.

8.4 HANS KÜNG: *THE PERMANENT NECESSITY OF RENEWAL IN THE CHURCH* – 1961

The following excerpt[7] is taken from an early work of Küng written before the council had begun entitled, *The Council and Reunion*. In this volume Küng offered his hopes for what the council might accomplish. In the chapter excerpted here he makes a theological and historical argument for the permanent necessity of reform in the church.

❋

In ordinary daily life we are always hearing the Church being spoken of in two different ways. The 'idealist', clerical or lay, whether preaching, giving instruction, or in ordinary conversation, sees the Church as the Church of God; pure, spotless, blameless, holy, concerned only with the salvation of men and the glory of God. The 'realist', the man in the street or the bar or reading his newspaper, sees the Church as a Church of men; all too human, both in head and members; a harsh, intolerant machine, opposed to freedom and greedy for power, immersed in the finance and politics of this world, full of every kind of failing. Who is right? Both are, in different ways – and both are wrong. Right, in so far as the church in a sense *is* what each of them sees (though 'is' has to be understood analogically); wrong in so far as they see the Church *only* thus, exclusively and onesidedly. Both idealist and realist are fundamentally uninterested in a renewal of the Church. The idealist, seeing only the light side of the church, thinks it unnecessary; the realist, limited to the dark side, thinks it impossible. Only those who, genuinely caring about the Church whose members they are, dare to see the darkness and still believe in the light can be open and ready for a renewal of the Church such as the Pope expects from the council … .

Renewal and reform of the Church are permanently necessary because the Church consists, first, of human beings, and, secondly, of sinful human beings.

THE CHURCH IS MADE OF HUMAN BEINGS

The world is never what it ought to be. Where there are men there is always failure, and where there is failure, there is need for improvement. What is deformed must be reformed. Hence, in the secular sphere, reform, and the constant introduction of new reforms, are simply taken for granted, not only by the crusading fanatic, but equally by the man on the street, who spontaneously raises his voice in opposition to any bad state of affairs and demands that it be put right.

---

7. Küng, Hans, 'The Permanent Necessity of Renewal in the Church', in *The Council and Reunion*, 14–52, London and New York, Sheed & Ward, 1961.

This is so in the world. But the Church is, precisely, *not* the world, understanding 'the world' at this stage simply in its ordinary, human, visible sense. In the ultimate ground of her being, the life of the Holy Spirit of Jesus Christ, the Church is actually invisible, or, we might also say, visible only to the believer. She lives wholly by the grace of God, she is God's spiritual temple, the mysterious reality of the body of Jesus Christ. The power which gives her form and structure is his Holy Spirit. It is he, the invisible, who founds the Church each day anew, who awakens and animates and enlightens her, makes her active and effective. It is he who causes her to lead her spiritual life as the community of grace and faith and love. What is there here for human beings to reform?

The Church is not the world, the Church is not of this world, but *the Church is in this world*. Precisely as the *people* of God, precisely as the *body* of Christ, the Church, for all her invisibility, is at the same time visible in the human beings and the organization which form her; she can be perceived historically, psychologically, sociologically. The Church is an institution set up by God through Christ which, as a community of believers always animated, moved and formed afresh by the Holy Spirit, is forever coming into being anew in the activity of her members. She has the character of both personal event and of institutional existence. By analogy with the God-Man, whose body she is, the church is both visible and invisible; visible in the preaching of the word, for which Christ set up the apostolic office, in the celebration of the sacraments, in the confession of faith and the practice of love. From the very time of her foundation the Church was a definite, delimited, organized community, with men in charge of her, with rules, rites and customs; and so today she remains visible in her individual members, in her preaching of the word, in her administration of the sacraments and in her law. As the Church of God made of men and for men, as a divine-*human* mystery, she is set in the dimensions of space and time; she is an earthly, historical fact, whose divine institutions and constitutions work themselves out on the human side in various intellectual, ritual, social, legal and aesthetic forms. Being in time, the Church can never be perfected on earth. Time never stands still, and so the Church cannot but keep marching forward. In every age she is faced with the difficult task of presenting herself anew. God's Church, made of men, is in the world and in its history.

But this also means that the world and its history are in the Church. The most widely differing mentalities and cultures, languages and backgrounds, questions and answers have contributed to shaping the two-thousand-year-old face of the Church. Often, in setting their imprint upon her, they have brought a development and enrichment of the Church, but often too it has been a deformation and constriction ... .

True, in what she is essentially – that is, in what she has from Christ – The Church is indestructible. But the particular historical form which God's Church takes in the world and its history can only ever be a realization of one among all the possible forms of the Church in different ages; along with gain, this means that there is always loss or at least the danger of loss ... .

We have to realize the immense difficulty of the Church's task in her journey down the ages if we are to avoid judging her harshly, self-righteously, and as though looking down from some superior plane. The Church, made as she is of men, *in* the world and yet not *of* the world, has no easy task in steering her course between Scylla and Charybdis, between surrender to the world on the left and hostility to the world on the right. It may be a help, and a help to those inside the Church who are often too little aware of her tremendous difficulties, if we give a brief outline here of certain types of danger to which the Church is subject, certain wrong developments and wrong attitudes which are possible within her.

On the left lies the threat of *surrender to the world*. The Church has to be *in* the world and *for* the world; but the very fact that she exists *for* the world has often, for the sake of the world's salvation, to take the form of being *against* the world. Her norm can never be the 'elements' of the world and the law of the world, but only Jesus Christ. But the Church, being of men, is forever under the temptation to make herself at home in the world, to regard her worldly successes as the coming of the Kingdom of God, to be intent only on making herself secure and powerful and free from opposition and persecution; to involve herself with some particular economic or social system, with some form of government or pattern of society or of thought, with a nation or a class or a particular line in politics: with some one fixed mental picture of the world or of humanity. It is very easy for her to develop fixed forms and find herself almost inextricably entangled in them, to conquer the world and be thereby conquered by the world. From being bound to the world she then becomes conformed to it, adopting a worldly spirit and making use of means, methods and institutions which are alien to the gospel … .

To the left, then, the Church, becoming subject to the world, is in danger of becoming worldly; but to the right, becoming hostile to the world, she is in danger of becoming 'churchy'. The Church has to be in the world and for the world but not of the world; for Christ's own sake she has to remain, ultimately, alien to it, forever swimming against the stream. Yet she must not live for herself alone, leaving the world to be the world; she has to be the leaven in the world, intent upon the coming of the Kingdom of God. But the Church, being made of men, is forever under the temptation to make herself at home within her own walls: to become the goal instead of only the way, to regard her organization as an end in itself, and so to make the attainment of the true goal harder instead of more possible and easier. The Church, pursuing her difficult journey, is here beset by a multitude of extremely concrete dangers, and if we are to judge her situation rightly it is absolutely necessary to see perfectly clearly how it is precisely what is best that can be misused (remembering that *abusus non tollit usum*). The danger of becoming 'churchy' can take innumerable forms. It is there when piety gives way to external Church practices; the care of souls to ecclesiastical administration; the Pope and the bishops to bureaucracy; the missions to religious propaganda; the apostolate to a struggle for social position and spheres of influence; charismatic gifts to unimaginative, routine administration; spiritual leadership to petty paternalism; preaching to dry rationalism or false rhetoric; the Sermon on the Mount to spiritual juridicalism: ecclesiastical discipline to the legalism of the Talmud; the sacraments to commercialized rites; the liturgy to empty ceremonies; zeal for the Lord to 'getting results'; spiritual growth to Church statistics; ancient tradition to established custom; the word of God to current ideas; the Gospel to a theological system, orthodoxy in doctrine to denunciation; unity to uniformity; faith in the Church to faith in a machine: in a word, when letter replaces spirit. Of course none of this *need* happen; but it *can* happen. There is always the danger that the spirit may become fossilized in permanent 'ecclesiastical' forms, customs, regulations; that the Body of Christ may become formalized and bureaucratic. A Church thus turned in upon herself would become, in her relations with the world, a polemically defensive ghetto-Church; clinging rigidly to forms whose value is all in the past, she would be unable to even hear the demand for new ones, and would hold aloof from the world in proud self-sufficiency. Such a Church would mirror only herself, praising herself instead of the Lord; her arrogant sense of superiority over against the world would be only the reverse side of a sense of inferiority. The root attitude in such a Church would be fear: fear of progress in the world and in history, fear of anything that had not already been tried, of the unaccustomed, the out-of-the-ordinary; fear of necessary changes, of risks, uncertainties, experiments, adventures … .

THE CHURCH IS MADE OF SINNERS

… All holiness during this earthly pilgrimage is precarious. The Church is the *communio sanctorum,* but, alas, the *communio peccatorum* too; the Epistles, and the Apocalypse even more, testify that this was so even in her glorious beginnings. She is the Church of poor sinners, who can and must pray every day afresh, 'Forgive us our trespasses' … . In all ages – against the Gnostics, Novatians, Donatists and Montanists of the early centuries, against the Cathar movement in the Middle Ages, against the sectarians of the present day – the Church has in fact rejected the appeal to any supposed 'Church of the pure'. She knows that the Church is not a pure Platonic Idea, that here on earth there is no ideal Church. Hence the necessity of always looking at the Church from above *and* from below, both as founded by God through Jesus Christ in the Holy Spirit *and* as the assembly of the faithful giving their consent to that divine decree, who are ceaselessly engaged in making their community a reality from below upwards, and in building it outwards into the world … .

But this does not present us with two Churches: from above, the real, pure Church of God, and from below, the impure Church of men. There is *one* Church with two distinct aspects which, while distinct, must both be simultaneously given their full value. We should be failing to give full value to the view from above if we saw the church only in terms of her members and so as ultimately only a human, indeed excessively human, social structure. We should be failing to give full value to the view from below if we saw her only in terms of her head, and so, ultimately, as already and without qualification an immaculate mystery of God in the Spirit.

We can indeed call the Church, even on earth, a Church 'not having spot or wrinkle', 'holy and without blemish' (Eph. 5.27); we are then speaking of the glory with which, by God's grace, she is endowed from above, in her innermost depths, even in this world: the 'pledge' of holiness. But the daily experience of the Church in the concrete will never allow us to forget that the Church 'not having spot or wrinkle' is on this earth a *hidden* reality, not seen but, in the teeth of all her human wretchedness, believed. Her glory shines only for the believer: 'Credosanctam ecclesiam.' Only at the end of time (as we are assured not merely by modern exegetes but by the Fathers of the Church) will the Church with spot or wrinkle be an actual, total, manifest reality … .

Here, though Christ and the Church are one, lies the difference between the Church and her Lord. Like him, the Church on earth is in a state of humiliation; as in him, so in her, the divine has united itself with the human, indeed with the flesh; like him she can be, and like him she *has* been, tempted. But (this is the decisive difference) Christ alone, who became like unto men in all else, is 'without sin' (Heb. 4.15). It is the misery of the Church, her chief suffering, that she can, in her members, yield to temptation ... .

A fully *adequate* concept of the Church will, then, include both sides of her: she is God's Church in her members. It includes at once what the Church receives from above, from God's sanctifying grace through Christ in the Spirit, and what the very same Church receives and absorbs below through her sinful members. The Church, adequately understood, is at one and the same time the holy Church, the holy bride, of Jesus Christ, and the Church of sinners. Whatever the individual Christian does, he does not do it only to his own personal profit or loss. Rather, he does it as a member of the Church fully responsible for the Church, for good or ill. And so, because sinners are the real members of the Church, and their sins remain in her through her members, the Body of Christ itself is burdened and stained with them; the sins of men are the wounds of the Church.

Can we then call the Church of the sinners a 'sinful Church'? Many theologians hesitate here, and not without reason. It is an expression that can be misunderstood; as though the grace of God, the Holy Spirit in the Church, were not pure and perfect, as though her divine constitution, coming from above, were not truly holy, but in itself corrupt; as though the Church were not set apart from the world as belonging to the Lord, with the risen Christ and his Spirit active in her ('church' being from the Greek *kyriake*, 'belonging to the Lord'); as though the Church were not the new People of God, willing and ready, but the unfaithful Synagogue, unwilling and unworthy, herself resisting God's choice of her.

We must not understand the expression 'the sinful Church' in any such way as this. All that is good and holy, all that is of God, cannot but remain what it is; the Church of God cannot but remain God's Church. As coming from God, the Church is and remains holy. Her holiness is from Christ; she is holy not through the spirit of her sinful members but through Christ's Holy Spirit, not through their words and actions, but through Christ's doctrine and sacraments. But it is precisely in seeing this that we must be careful not to ignore or explain away the frightful reality of sin in the Church, whose members, inseparable from herself, are sinners. Obviously it is not that the holiness and the sinfulness are two equally valid aspects of the one Church. The holiness is the light of the Church, the sinfulness her shadow; the holiness reveals her nature, the sinfulness obscures it. Sin does not arise from the nature of the Church but breaks into her from outside, through the power of the Evil Spirit at work in men. Sin does not belong to the nature of the Church but must be reckoned as part of the unnatural condition in which she is during her earthly pilgrimage. To put it in the way in which it is usually put sin in the Church is that *failure* in holiness caused by the power of the Evil Spirit through men as members of the Church. Sin in the Church, as part of the Church (as indeed elsewhere), can only be seen as a dark, incomprehensible, ultimately meaningless paradox. But as such it must be taken seriously. 'Deus, qui ecclesiam tuam purificas' – 'O God, who dost purify *thy Church*', we pray on the first Sunday in Lent. And on the fifteenth Sunday after Pentecost: 'Let thy continual pity purify and defend thy Church; and because she cannot continue in safety without thee, direct her always by thy gracious help.'

The idea of the holy Church, distinct from her often unholy members, mentally hypostatized into a sort of a pure substance, is a dangerous abstraction. All too many good Christians are put off today by an idealizing type of speech and sermon about the faultless Church without reference to the concrete reality. But all too many will, on the other hand, excuse themselves from taking part in the life of the concrete reality of the holy Church on the ground that they accept the Church 'in herself' (which is the abstract, 'pure' Church again, perhaps 'as she used to be') but not the Church 'as she is'. As though it were not the Christian's task to love the Church just *as she is*, in and in spite of the sinfulness of her members.

If we merely say, 'Of course there are sinners in the Church, but this fact has nothing to do with the Church herself', then we are presupposing a highly questionable idealist notion of the Church, theologically speaking. The Church is then an idea, an ideal, something that is eventually to be, something to which appeal can be made from the concrete reality, something which is, as it were, only to be attained slowly, asymptotically, approximately. Of course one can always love such a thing as that, always give it one's allegiance; it is something invulnerable, untouched by the wretchedness of daily life. But it is not what is meant by the theological concept of the Church. According to this the Church is something real; the only Church there is, and in which we believe, is simply and always the visibly and hierarchically organized totality of the baptized, united in the external profession of faith and in obedience to the Roman Pope. And of this Church we cannot simply say that she has nothing to do with the sins of her members. Of course she does not approve of their sins; of course there are people in her (and perhaps many such) who are in some true sense, which does not enter into this discussion, to be described as saints. But if she is something real, and if her members are sinners and, as sinners, remain her members, then she herself is sinful … .

When we are concerned with the reform and renewal of the Church it would be particularly dangerous to see the evil in her as being only on the surface; it grows 'not from', but 'in her womb'. In so far as the body of the Church is divine and *human*, the human and all *too* human elements, actual sin and evil, can insinuate themselves into her; though without ever being able to overmaster her. This applies to ecclesiastical institutions and ordinances as well. Wherever men build their own institutions and ordinances onto the Church's divine ones, there sin can enter in and extend its domain; the holier the thing itself is, the greater the sin … .

Yet the 'gates of hell', however we are to understand them, cannot prevail against the holy Church of God because her ultimate stability is not in herself but in Jesus Christ and the protection of his Holy Spirit. Essentially, she remains the true, the holy, the Church who cannot, unlike the Synagogue, fall away from grace and truth. Her innermost being – Jesus Christ himself, his Spirit and his grace – can never turn sinful; her innermost being, her head, her life-principle and hence her Gospel and her sacraments are holy. Out of regard for this fact it is better, after all, not to call holy Church a 'sinful Church', but in general, to avoid misunderstanding, to prefer the expression, 'the Church of sinners'. But both expressions can be misunderstood, the one as too superficial, the other as too radical. Basically, they correct one another. 'The Church of sinners' stresses that the sin is not in the head or the Spirit, not in any divine institution or ordinance; the 'sinful Church', that the sin in the Church really does affect, oppress, wound and deform the Church herself … .

RENEWAL OF THE CHURCH IS ALWAYS NECESSARY

If we put together everything that we have said, or might have said, about the Church as made of men and of sinful men, everything that has happened in the Church's worldly and sinful history – the human, the all-too-human, the lethargy, the refusals, the mediocrity, the ill-will, the innocently-mistaken deviations and the actually sinful perversions – then only one thing remains to be done: *metanoia*, conversion of thought and deed. In so far as the Church is not only a divine institution but also a sociological human structure, in so far as God's holy Church is a Church of men and of sinful men, she, with everything that she is and has, is subject to that word of the Lord which reads 'Do penance and be converted'. In so far as the Church is deformed, she has to be reformed: *ecclesia reformanda*.

And in so far as the Church, because of her human frailty and sinfulness, always needs to be better; in so far as she can never sit back and bask in the warmth of her own self-satisfaction but must always be pressing on with all the earnest zeal of the penitent – this renewal of the Church is never something finished and done with but is always a permanent duty: and this precisely because she is, and is to remain, the *holy* Church. In so far as the Church is constantly, repeatedly deformed, she has to be constantly, repeatedly reformed: *ecclesia semper reformanda*.

But reform is necessary not only because of deformation. Fundamentally, it is not just a negative matter of house-cleaning and repairs, but a vast positive task of constructive building. It is not only because there are mistaken developments and mistaken attitudes in the Church that she has this task. Even if there were none (there always will be) the Church would still have the great task of renewal. For the mustard-seed must grow. The Church, as we said at the beginning of this chapter, is in the stream of time: she has to keep adopting new forms, new embodiments. She has to keep giving herself a new form, a new shape in history; she is never simply finished and complete. She must go into all the world and preach the good news to every creature (Mark 16.15); to all nations, to all cultures, to all ages, until Christ comes again. Such is her incomparably happy mission. Hence she is forever faced afresh with the task of renewing herself. Hence, again, this renewal is not just about something which she stringently *must* do, but which she joyously *may* do; a joyful service to the Kingdom of God, looking towards him who will make *all* things new, a new heaven and a new earth. The Pope's summons to renew the Church is, most solemnly and truly, a joyful summons.

8.5 YVES CONGAR: *RENEWAL OF THE SPIRIT AND REFORM OF THE INSTITUTION* – 1972

In the following essay[8] Congar insists that church reform must go beyond moral reform to include structural or institutional reform. He carefully distinguishes between those ecclesial institutions which are divinely willed and the historical form of those institutions which are subject to reform.

❇

'Institution' is not a very precise term and is open to a number of definitions. It is derived from the Latin *instituere, statuere, stare*, and from the Greek *istêmi*, meaning to establish or erect. It usually designates a certain structure of a relatively permanent nature which is the product of a superior will (not simply of nature) and answers an aim or a need, and in which individuals find a model for their behaviour and an inclination of their group role. The apostolate, the Church and the sacraments are institutions proceeding from a divine institutional will, but their historical forms – that is, their structures – were the work of human interventions.

The religious orders, the demarcation of dioceses, and the organization of ministries and offices, schools or hospitals, are ecclesial institutions. Revelation is a divine institution, but dogmatic formulas – and still more preaching, the teaching of the ordinary magisterium, dogmatic theologies and theologies proper – are its human ecclesiastical expressions.

Every society features tensions between its acquired forms, its institutions and structures, and the free movement of the spirit, since the spirit never ceases to create, and the constant advance into the unknown future of history calls for a no less constant questioning of acquired forms. This is equally true for the society which is the Church. In this case there are specific reasons in view of the fact that the Church, while being historical and man-made, is not a purely human society. This is apparent in two main ways: (1) the Church possesses a truth which it does not freely bestow upon itself, but which comes to it from God: either at its origin, in the models which it has in the Old Testament, the incarnation of the suffering servant, the *ecclesia primitiva* (a constant point of reference, even though it has been idolized in all reforms), or at its ending. It does not know this end in the way in which one would be aware of a definite project, but it exists, God calls the Church to it, and it must tend towards it.

God is not only behind the Church, at its beginning; he is also before it: he calls it to prepare and to anticipate his reign. The feeling of the never bridged distance between the historical Church and its truth, that of its Alpha and that of its Omega, is the major source of

8. Congar, Yves. 'Renewal of the Spirit and Reform of the Institution', in *Ongoing Reform of the Church*, Alois Müller and Norbert Greinacher (eds), *Concilium*, vol. 73, 39–49, New York, Herder and Herder, 1972.

all reform movements. It grounds the consciousness of historicity, and therefore that of relativity and of the forms in which the institution is realized. There is no ecclesiology which does not have to assume as a statutory fact the irreducible duality of that which exists in fact and that which ought to exist. All descendants of Abraham are not true sons of Abraham (Rom. 9: 7), the people can be a non-people (Hos. 1: 9); several appear to be within who are in fact without (St. Augustine).

(2) The Church has as its inward principle of unity and life the person of the Holy Spirit (whether by means of the category of appropriation or in some other way, this affirmation must hold). Yet it is true that the Spirit has no autonomy in relation to Christ in the work that he does (cf. Jn. 16: 13–15); but it is also true that in the realization of his work, he is grace, and therefore liberty – the Event. The event cannot be set against, or reduced to, the institution. Yet that was certainly the tendency of the dominant ecclesiology during the anti-Protestant centuries, the times of set affirmation of authority (the nineteenth century), whatever the actual life of the Church (which this ecclesiology interpreted so inadequately) may have been. I could cite many witnesses for the reduction of the Holy Spirit to the role of guarantor of the hierarchical, sacramental or magisterial institution. Yet the Spirit, according to Hans Urs von Balthasar's profound definition, is the 'Unknown beyond the Word'.[9] The Church does not proceed from the unique mission of the word, which has established in this world, at least in substantial terms, a definite form of faith, sacraments and ministry. It also proceeds from a second mission: that of the Spirit, which continually bears forward into the unknown future of history the work done once for all by Christ, and which on that account never ceases to stimulate and inspire men, while constantly bringing new life to the Church (St Irenaeus).

Since St. Paul (Rom. 12: 2; Eph. 4: 23), there has always been an advocacy in the Church of a renewal of life by means of a transformation of the spirit. The theme of 'reform' is so fundamental to, and coextensive with, the life of the Church that the '*Textus emendatus*' of the *Lex Ecclesiae Fundamentalis* (1971) has acknowledged it (can. 2, art. 4); initially, it was treated by the Fathers and by the liturgy as a Christian anthropological theme. It was a question essentially of the reshaping of man in the likeness of God that sin made him lose. *Intus reformari* is the work in us of the saving incarnation. That is a chapter of 'spirituality': that is, of life according to the Spirit, whose truth is always up to date. It is the preaching of *metanoia* and Shrovetide. To take self-reform seriously according to the standards of the Gospel and the *sequela Christi* can lead one far. Francis of Assisi did no more than this.

Yet this is not enough.

First of all, we must remember that the unconditional defenders of authority (when it was not the authority of the *status quo*) freely developed a theme which went like this: reform yourselves and all will go well; then the most urgent problems are resolved. This may also be seen as one form of a widespread tendency among Catholics (at least until their recent awakening to the meaning of the political dimensions of things, and of the conditions for any real efficacy): a tendency to see only the moral aspect of problems – or rather that part of their moral aspect deriving from intentions and purity of intention. Yet history already had some significant lessons to offer. Some strong and pure reformist currents failed to be more effective

---

9. von Balthasar, Hans Urs, 'Der Unbekannte jenseits des Wortes', in *Interpretation der Welt*, Würzburg, 1966, 638–45.

because they stayed too much in a spiritual and private realm: the movement of the 'Friends of God' in the second half of the fourteenth century, and, however powerful it was, that of the *Devotio moderna* and the Brothers of Life in Common in the latter part of the same century. A spiritual renewal, limited in the first case, and more widespread in the second, had no effective impact on institutions, from the viewpoint of reform that was really required.

Institutions have their own weight, density and permanence. Even those of the Church depend on society as a whole. This is well known to those Christians in politically committed movements who expect a radical change in the structures of the Church to come from a social revolution. It is impossible to ignore the influence of political ideas and the social context as a whole on the conception of authority and the actual conduct of life in the Church. It was not without reason that St. Leo formulated his theology of papal power in terms of *principatus*. It is obvious that the absolutist and centralistic ideas which characterized monarchical power in the sixteenth, and then in the nineteenth century (with the haunting memory, then, of an ever-looming revolution and of an authority that *had* to be affirmed), were reflected in the ecclesiology of those times.

It is true that purely spiritual attitudes also have an impact on social structures: St Francis, in rejecting oaths and recourse to arms, challenged the social structures of his own time. The Pilgrim Fathers and other emigrants for conscience' sake helped to determine the spirit of the United States. This shows that the spiritual element does take effect. It is necessary; yet it is not sufficient. There is in fact a density proper to impersonal and collective structures which has to be reached: otherwise the most generous reformist intentions would exhaust themselves in a never-ending effort that the opposing structures, keeping their place, would condemn to remain only half-effective.

History also provides us with significant examples of reforms which were *both* spiritual and structural. Examples are: the reform of the eleventh century (the 'Gregorian' reform), that of the mendicant orders in the thirteenth century, that bought about by the Council of Trent, and that of Vatican II.

It is not my task here to retrace the complex history of the reform in the eleventh century. Several aspects of it are nevertheless worthy of discussion. It began before the pontificate of Gregory VII, but it was Gregory who was its most decisive agent. Fliche has shown[10] (the criticisms of his book seem to me to allow this general schema to remain) that it is possible to isolate two reformist projects in the eleventh century: the first, which he calls 'Italian' because it was promoted by Atto of Vercelli and Peter Damian, looked for a moral reform, through preaching and example, of the abuses from which the Church suffered: simony and nicolaitanism (clerical unchastity). The 'Lorraine project' (Wason of Liège, Ratherius of Verona, and – above all – Humbert of Silva Candida) was more radical. Without ignoring the moral aspect, it attacked the cause. The root of all the evils was lay investiture, by which the lay powers disposed of ecclesiastical offices and treated them in a secular fashion. When he became Gregory VII, Hildebrand adopted these views. The usual effectiveness of his action results from his inspiration of a radical programme of reform of the structures and legal status of ecclesial life, by means of a simple, fervent and intransigent mysticism of the sovereignty of God, of which papal authority was the reflection and instrument. Gregory VII's

---

10. Fliche, Augustin, *La réforme grégorienne* – I. La formation des idées grégoriennes – II. Grégoire VII, Louvain, 1924–25.

power depended wholly upon his spiritual conviction. The effectiveness of his reforms was linked to various economic and political expressions of this conviction: the reform of the law relating to ecclesiastical property; support for a semi-political resistance movement against the married clergy – like the Milan *Pataria*; the financial independence of the clergy which gave rise, for example, to such a canon as the following: '*ut omnis christianus procuret ad missarum sollemnia aliquid Deo offere*' (cf. Schreiber); and the elevation and expansion of the *vita apostolica*; and so forth.

The reform introduced by St Francis and St Dominic was, originally, purely spiritual: in the case of Francis, being a conversion to the practice of the Gospel '*sine glossa*', poverty was the condition for an evangelical attitude of absolute dependence with regard to God the Father and of absolute brotherhood with God's creatures; in the case of Dominic, the reform was the consistent practice of an apostolic charity vowed to the doctrinal service of mankind, with mendicant poverty and an organization of fraternal communities for prayer and study. These two designs were fairly diverse at the start and came to approximate one another; they had considerably revolutionary consequences in regard to the structure of both society as a whole and of ecclesial service. They broke with the territorial and all but fixed nature of the structures produced by the feudal system; they supported the communal movement of solidarity of citizens freed from subjection to church or feudal lords. They proved so adaptable to a process of urbanization that medievalists have suggested that the 'town' of the Middle Ages should be defined in terms of the establishment of a mendicant house; they endowed the Word with a sort of dynamic independence, and opened the way for new missionary initiatives, detached from any context of conquest or crusade. Finally, the condition of poverty enjoined upon the mendicants allowed Jean de Paris (1302) to distinguish the Church from induced hierocratic pretensions when he made his distinction between Christ as God, who possesses the kingdom of the world, and Christ in his humanity, who has chosen poverty. If Jean de Paris was able to approximate to the principles posited by Thomas Aquinas in favour of an appropriate distinction between the spiritual and temporal realms, it was the system inaugurated by St Dominic which freed them both from the temporal burdens of the feudal Church.

John XXIII more than once described the aim of the Second Vatican Council as, optimally, both a renewal of the pastoral structures of the Church (the emphasis was often put, at first, on the revision of canon law), and a renewal – an increase – of faith and Christian life. He also often stated the spiritual conditions necessary on the way towards such a process. In connecting the spiritual renewal of Christians with the canonical and pastoral reform assigned as the goal of the Council, John XXIII returned to the ancient tradition for which a reform was primarily a spiritual re-formation of the Christian individual.

How have things gone? The council would seem to have done remarkably well in realizing its programme. God granted his Church a great access of grace on the eve of a deep-reaching, world-wide and rapid process of cultural transformation. It is very difficult to speak of the post-conciliar period proper. It presents aspects of rupture and crisis that the Council did not seem to promise. This is partly the result of the fact that a too long period of narrowness and ossification had stifled initiative: once the valves were opened, the flood was all the heavier because it had the forces of all the currents of the age behind it. Perhaps another reason is that the Vatican II reform was a reform made from above – a fairly unusual phenomenon – which was not prepared from below. Regional synods followed rather than preceded the council, whereas Vatican I, far less innovatory, was preceded by several local councils, which were for their own part scarcely innovatory at all. History shows that a reform requires the commitment of all the forces of the Church. This is one of the main reasons why, historically, reforms and councils have so often been linked with one another.

THE SITUATION TODAY

The crisis is of such a nature and the questions posed are so radical and so universal that one is permitted to ask whether an *aggiornamento* is enough and whether something more is not required. The question arises to the extent that the institutions of the Church are part of a cultural world which will no longer enjoy the same place in the new cultural world born of the hegemony of technology, mass media, the human sciences, and characterized by a universal secularization. We are faced by questions that are much more radical than those of the past – both from without and from within. The questions which the other Christian communions set us already put many institutions in question, but all that is now a thing of the past. The other Christian communions – those of the West at least – are now in question just as we are … .

Theologically, a reformist programme derives from the ideal imposed on the Church, either in regard to its origins, or in regard to what it is called to become throughout history in the direction of eschatology. In both cases, in fact, one can and ought to criticize its present historical *forms* in order to make them conform more (and therefore reform them) to what is required by a more demanding form of faithfulness.

In the first case, those who must speak are primarily the exegetes, historians and sociologists of knowledge. Their disciplines are powerful instruments of purification and renewal, always provided one's will and spirit are open enough to a *metanoia* to allow of any reaching of conclusions. The second case – the progress in time towards eschatology – concerns the vast realm of pastoral, missionary, liturgical and scientifico-apostolic adaptation to the requirements of the age. Our epoch of rapid change and cultural transformation (philosophical ferments and sociological conditions different from those which the Church has accustomed itself to until now) calls for a revision of 'traditional' forms which goes beyond the level of adaptation or *aggiornamento*, and which would be instead a new creation. It is no longer sufficient to maintain, by adapting it, what has already been; it is necessary to reconstruct it.

This kind of reconstruction cannot occur effectively except on the basis of a very determined revision of the historical character of institutions, forms and structures, and of a very genuine spiritual potential. It is a question of *transmitting*, in new forms, the same faith, the same Eucharist and the same prayer, the same ministry that the Church received and by which it has been constituted from the start. Christianity, in fact, is an 'instituted' religion, in the sense in which Wach uses this expression in opposition to 'natural' religion. It is essentially transmission – 'tradition'. One can recreate only the forms of what one has already received. In order to make the *paradosis* – the transmission – effective and authentic, this or that form in which the transmission occurred in the past, but which would nowadays be an obstacle to its reality, must eventually be revised and renewed. This is why every reform requires not only an analysis of the situation and its demands, but basic resources of a very pure kind in the form of a knowledge of the indefeasible content of the Christian realities which are to be handed on.

It often happens nowadays that sociological or psychological inquiries or a socio-political analysis takes pride of place, or that two treatments are conducted on different levels without contact with one another. One example of this in regard to the celibacy of the priesthood is a treatment that develops only mystical considerations, whether they be profound or not, and a treatment offering the results of an inquiry or a psycho-sociological analysis, potentially of real value. On the one side, there is a total historicity, and on the other an a-historical position which inhibits perhaps legitimate or even necessary reforms in the name of unduly sacralized models, or of a legalism which absolutizes the rules acquired in the past. Catholics are led, even in social and political matters, to believe that there are ideal, given models, whereas social forms are to be created in variable contexts.

We must have neither a pure spirituality nor a pure sociological analysis. What is required is a union of the spirit and an effort to renew the structures.

The spirit can never wholly free itself from the structures. Today the spirit would create its own spontaneous structures – informal in the sense of not being predetermined by authority, by the directors of the group-Church, by some 'total pastoral'. I believe that the phenomenon of 'basic groups', now considerable, is a vehicle of great positive values. It is at this level, to a great extent, that the tissues of a living Chritianity will be reformed. It is here, probably, that new forms will be found for the transmission of Christian reality. But the last word is not a specific anti-institutionalism nor the ideal of a Christianity diluted like mere yeast into the dough of the age. I could not subscribe without reservations to an assertion of the following kind: 'The ideal would be a Church without any specific location ... .'[11] Declarations of this kind are made by men who enjoy all the benefits of a solidly based Church that has allowed them their education in faith and prayer. What would things be like for the second generation that took such a proposition as its starting-point? What would become of evangelization if there were no institution to bear it, feed it, and promote it? A reform should ensure that institutions serve the evangelical and messianic work of Jesus; it should not dissolve them into the mist. The spirit, in its biblical sense, is not opposed to the 'body', but to the 'earthly' and 'immobile'. Jesus compares it to the wind, which one cannot see even though it is shifting something (Jn. 3. 8.).

---

11. Besret, B., *Clefs pour une Eglise nouvelle*, Paris, 1971, 214.

8.6 JOHN W. O'MALLEY: *REFORM, HISTORICAL CONSCIOUSNESS AND VATICAN II'S AGGIORNAMENTO* – 1971

In this small excerpt[12] from a much larger essay, O'Malley contends that our conceptions of church reform, the *aggiornamento* called for by Pope John XXIII, and, in substance, the Second Vatican Council itself, depend on our philosophical presuppositions regarding the nature of history. O'Malley sketches out five conceptions of history and the way each both relates the past to the present and understands the possibility of change and reform. He then argues for the appropriation of a contemporary historical consciousness necessary to grasp adequately the nature of authentic church reform today.

❈

The turbulence into which Vatican II threw the Catholic Church was due not only to the abruptness with which its reform was thrust upon us. It was due as well to the fact that in our consciousness no paradigms of reform were operative which were appropriate to the reality we began to experience. Despite the incalculably great impact the idea of reform has had on the thought and practice of the Western church, theological reflection upon it has been minimal and its history has never been fully written. The practical repercussions of this situation have not been happy. An almost despairing confusion has hallmarked Catholicism since Vatican II's *aggiornamento* got under way … . We failed to grasp the profound shift from previous Catholic thinking on reform which was implied by Vatican II's decision to take 'accommodation to the times' as the fundamental axiom of its reform… .

This brings us to the heart of the problem of Vatican II and, indeed, of any Christian reform. How are we to know what from the past can be changed? How is the present to deal with the past, and what legitimate hold does the past have on the present? What is historical authenticity, and what bearing does it have on the present? …

AGGIORNAMENTO AND HISTORICAL CONSCIOUSNESS

The documents of Vatican II make it perfectly clear that a number of different styles of historical consciousness were operative in the Council, styles not always easily reconcilable with one another. Moreover, the Council failed to take adequate account of what is most characteristic of contemporary historical thinking, such as the emphasis on discontinuity with the past and the subjectivism resulting from an awareness of the historical conditioning of the historian himself. Thus the relationship of past to present was never resolved. In fact, it was

---

12. O'Malley, John W., 'Reform, Historical Consciousness, and Vatican II's *Aggiornamento*', *Theological Studies*, 32 (1971), 573–601.

never even raised in a manner to satisfy contemporary thinking on the nature of history. Yet, in this question of the idea of reform, the relationship of past to present is crucial. In the absence of a consistent understanding of it, the Council's fundamental injunction to remain faithful to the authentic past while adjusting to contemporary needs was transformed from a practical norm for reform into an explosive problematic.

At any rate, the basic problem raised by *aggiornamento* will be better understood if we now try to see it as part of a larger pattern. We shall try to describe various styles of reform as they relate to various styles of historical thought or philosophies of history which were operative in the councils and, finally, try to suggest the style of reform thinking which is required by our contemporary historical consciousness.

The first style of historical thinking we encounter wants to see the Church as immune to process or to change in doctrine and discipline. The Church moves through history unaffected by history. This style of thinking is sometimes described as 'classicism'. R.G. Collingwood described it even more aptly as 'substantialism' and saw it as the chief defect of Greco-Roman historiography.[13] What it is intent upon is celebrating the voyage through history of some enduring substance which is really untouched by history. Rome, for instance, was such a substance for Livy. In conciliar terms, the unchanging substance of the Church is clearly distinguished from the contingencies which affect at least some of its members. This style does not admit that change exists except in the form of certain external challenges to the existence of the substance. These challenges could conceivably destroy the substance, but they cannot intrinsically modify or change it … .

In the early Christian era substantialistic historical thinking itself underwent a significant change when it confronted the idea of a providential guidance of the course of events. Eusebius' *Praeparatio evangelica* would be an example of this style. Although the idea of a providence guiding history tolerated and perhaps even suggested the idea of development and stages or periods in a master plan, it had a large dose of substantialism in it as it was actually practiced, especially as substantialistic thinking related to the enduring character of Christian dogma, moral teaching, and the structure of ecclesial government.

What was characteristic of this providentialism in the Middle Ages was that it made God the principal agent in history. Man proposed but God disposed. Thus what happened in the past was endowed with a superhuman and even sacred quality. If the earlier substantialistic historical thinking was incapable of recognizing change, providential thinking made legitimate change the work of God alone. Any change introduced by man was sacrilegious. True reform, therefore, consisted in removing threats to the sacred. Men were to be changed by religion, not religion by men. Whatever human element was recognized in the past tended to be identified with what was strictly accidental. It was an appendage, an external dressing, which could be modified or adjusted in the case of *urgens necessitas vel evidens utilitas*. What was permissible was 'emendation', to use the word of Constantinople I and John XXIII. This emendation could take the form of modification of something already in existence, or even the introduction of something new, e.g., a new regulation or penalty, especially if thereby an old custom or discipline, would be reinforced. But the sacred patrimony was to be kept untouched. Metaphysical thinking now combined with metahistorical thinking.

---

13. Collingwood, R.G., *The Idea of History* (New York, 1956) 42–5.

Sacred metahistory could easily incorporate into itself the Roman idea, notably revived in the Renaissance, that history was nothing else than philosophy teaching by example, especially moral example. History in this view has an ethical, edifying or exhortatory purpose. The record of the past was viewed as a storehouse of *exempla* from which one drew prescriptive patterns of action which were directly transferable to the present situation. If the lives of illustrious orators and statesmen were example to be imitated, how much more worthy of imitation were the examples of the saints and especially the Saint of saints! The behavioral patterns of the sacred past were under the special guidance of providence and therefore provided models of behavior that were beyond criticism.

What is common to all three styles of historical thinking we have been describing is their minimal awareness of change, especially of change in the sense of the 'new'. This does not mean that change had not taken place. It simply means that men did not have the perspectives to recognize it as having taken place. The result was that the past was seen, not on its own terms, but exclusively according to the realities of the present. That is why medieval Englishmen, Frenchmen, and Germans thought they were Romans. No change, therefore, was desirable or necessary in the present, for none had taken place in the past.

There was another style of antique thinking which did recognize change, but it was change in the form of decline from an earlier and better state or condition. This style is generally described as 'primitivism'. The idea of such a decline or fall was expressed in the story of Adam and Eve as well as in Hesiod's myth of the golden age. Conciliar documents suggest an earlier period of Christianity as the golden age, which by its presumed purity stands as a norm, model, and ideal for all that follows. Reform is effected by a return to it. Despite what we may think at first glance, primitivism, as it is known, can be reconciled with the other forms of historical thinking we have described. The decline can be restricted to just one aspect of reality, such as morals, or it can be applied to 'men' as distinct from the divine society to which they belong. As applied to Christianity in the later Middle Ages, it was precisely these adaptations which at times primitivism underwent.

The style of reform which is appropriate to primitivism is 'rejuvenation', 'revival', 'rebirth', and even 'reform' itself. This style of historical thinking recognizes change for the worse, a decline from an earlier and presumably normative state or condition. It was in the context of a secularized application of this style that the idea of a 'renaissance' of arts and literature was born in Italy in the fourteenth and fifteenth centuries. Reform consists, therefore, in breathing new life into what has wilted, in healing what is sick, in reconstructing what has disappeared. The pattern of history, if it is not to be utterly pessimistic, is cyclic or repetitive, and it looks to the past for its substance and norms.

What distinguishes decline-history from the others we have seen is that it takes account of change. It realizes that the present is different from the past. Thus it has a sense of distance from the past and a perspective on it. The late Erwin Panofsky noted how the sense of historical perspective influenced painting and sculpture during the Renaissance: medieval artists who worked from literary sources dressed ancient gods or heroes in medieval costumes, whereas the Renaissance recognized that such a procedure was not 'historically true'. Between the times of the Romans and the present there was an intervening something, a 'middle age', which was different. To recover the Roman past, Renaissance men realized they had to leap over what had intervened. In other words, what was gradually dawning was a sense of discontinuity in history.

The first Protestants exploited this discovery of discontinuity to the disadvantage of their Catholic counterparts. The Catholics were often willing to acknowledge a discontinuity in the standard of moral behavior in the church, but not in its enduring substance. Both parties, in any case, looked backwards to the early Church as to a period of special purity in doctrine and morals. What especially distinguished Catholics from Protestants was their belief that the intervening tradition was continuous, homogeneous, undeviating, and therefore just as 'venerable' as the early Church itself.

The Enlightenment threw history's goal into the future and gave nineteenth-century historiography its orientation towards 'progress'. The philosophers and historians of this period accepted the idea of change, of discernable and coherent pattern, and of golden age. They transformed these ideas by secularizing them and by turning them around to make them forward-looking. In searching for models to explain progress, they easily turned in the nineteenth century to ideas of evolution and organic growth. They were thus able to explain both change and continuity. The present was still found in the past. The present was the best explanation of the past, for it showed where the past was naturally tending all the time.

The most distinguished and sophisticated Catholic work of the nineteenth century which shows the influence of this style of thinking was Newman's *Essay on the Development of Christian Doctrine*. Present reality is the term towards which earlier reality naturally tended. According to at least one critic of Newman, entelechy is the key to his system: 'a thing's true nature is best revealed in its later history and final state: in becoming a butterfly the chrysalis becomes itself.'[14] Authentic change is never by way of reversal, but only by way of further development of the already existing. Doctrinal reform is by way of growth or accretion, never by way of rejection of what has gone before. In the early years of the present century such thinking had a natural affinity for the conception of the Church as the Mystical Body of Christ, which was then gaining prominence and which continued to dominate Catholic thinking on the nature of the Church until the very eve of Vatican II.

In summary, we can say that we have seen a number of styles of historical thought which have conditioned the idea of reform as we have known it in the past. These styles all appear or are suggested in the documents of Vatican II. What all these 'philosophies of history' have in common is that they are all traditional or conservative as regards the past. We can list, for instance, five reform procedures which such styles of thinking allow: (1) reform by excision or suppression (keep what you have by removing threats to it); (2) reform by addition or accretion (keep what you have untouched, but add new things alongside it); (3) reform by revival (keep what you have by breathing new life into it); (4) reform by accommodation (keep what you have by making adjustments for differences in times and places); (5) Reform by development (keep what you have, but let it expand and mature to its final perfection). What is notably absent from this listing, of course, is reform by transformation or even by revolution, for both of these imply at least a partial rejection of the past in the hope of creating something new. In practice, Vatican II's *aggiornamento* has been just such a transformational

---

14. Anthony A. Stephenson, SJ, 'Cardinal Newman and the Development of Doctrine', *Journal of Ecumenical Studies*, 3 (1966), 467.

or revolutionary reform. But much of our present confusion concerning it is due to the fact that we have not as yet explicitly related this transformational or revolutionary practice into an adequate contemporary philosophy of history.

CONTEMPORARY HISTORICAL CONSCIOUSNESS

The possibility of the 'new' has been opened up by modern historical consciousness. This is the style of historical thinking which has its remote origins in the Renaissance discovery of discontinuity, but whose implications are being worked out only in our own day. Its immediate academic history, therefore, stretches from von Ranke or Dilthey to the present. Hence it is associated with the elusive problematic known as historicism, even though it is by no means identified with it. There has, of course, been considerable disagreement even among historians about the implications of modern historical method and historical consciousness. Today, however, perhaps enough convergence of views has taken place to allow us to speak of some of them compositely as a 'contemporary philosophy of history'. Since some understanding of this philosophy is essential to our topic, I shall attempt a brief description of what seems to me characteristic of it.

Contemporary philosophy of history is based upon one fundamental presupposition: history as a *human* phenomenon. By history is meant both past reality as it actually happened and the reconstruction or understanding of that reality as it takes place in the historian's mind and imagination. Contemporary philosophy of history labors to explore the implications of this fundamental presupposition.

What are some of these implications? First, the scope of the historian's inquiry, insofar as he is a historian, is the past *as human*, i.e., the past as it resulted from human passions, decisions, and actions. This means that for the historian the past is radically contingent and particular. Just as each person is different from every other, so is each event, each culture. In this sense history can never repeat itself, for the same contingent concatenation of human factors can never be reassembled. Each word, document, event is historically and culturally conditioned, radically individualized, and understandable as history only insofar as it is unique and the result of man's more or less free action and decision.

The result of this approach to the past is that it is desacralized. Events are seen as the result of human and contingent causes, not as the result of divine interventions. If you will, the past is 'deprovidentialized', as every effort is made to explain it as the result of human and earthly factors. God may have hardened Pharaoh's heart, but the historian is interested only in the contingent social, economic, and psychological factors which were at work on Pharaoh. These factors, as the results of human passion and decision, inject discontinuity into history; for man is capable of reversing himself, of changing direction, and thus of being discontinuous with himself.

The historian, accordingly, becomes deeply aware of the discontinuity in the past, and he is forced to remove from his consideration any over-arching divine plan. Indeed, historicism was born out of disillusionment with attempts to discover and expose such plans either in their sacral or secularized forms. The past is human. This means it is to be understood in terms of man, who is free and contingent and who has not masterminded a coherent pattern for the history of his race. Biological models for man's course through time are just as inappropriate as elaborate metaphysical ones. They imply that whatever is new in the present is simply the natural unfolding of the potential of the past. They make inadequate allowance for human freedom. In philosophy of history as well as ecclesiology, we must bring our theory into agreement with our anthropology. Evolutionary progress is an inappropriate postulate; for it hypostasizes history apart from man, who is capable of reversing himself.

What modern historical method enables us to understand more clearly than we ever understood before, therefore, is that every person, event, and document of the past is the product of very specific and unrepeatable contingencies. These persons, events, and documents are thus contained within very definite historical limits. By refusing to consider them as products of providence or as inevitable links in a preordained chain of historical progress, decline, or development, we deprive them of all absolute character. We relativize them ... .

The historian's realization that he is different from previous generations is simply a further ramification of his realization of man's radical historicity. What the contemporary historian is very much aware of is that he himself is *in* history and cannot step outside of it as he searches for the past. He himself is culturally conditioned. He does not bring pure intellect to his research. He brings a mind filled with questions, methods, prejudices, and personal quirks which are the result of his own personal, cultural, and psychological history. History in the sense of man's understanding of his past is thus further relativized – relativized by the contingency of the historian's own understanding... .

HISTORICAL CONSCIOUSNESS AND REFORM

What remains to be done is to examine what 'contemporary historical consciousness', i.e., the realization of man's radical historicity, means for the problem of reform. In the first place, if we are to think rationally about reform, we must 'demythologize' our style of historical thinking. Our consciousness must be purified of 'substantialism', 'primitivism', etc. When I say we should purify our understanding, I do not mean we should jettison the truth which these forms of historical thinking tried to express but could do so only in an unhistorical way. For instance, what is common to all these earlier approaches to history is their emphasis on historical continuity. The fact is that there *is* a strong continuity in history, whether we are speaking of history as past human reality itself or as historians' understanding of the past reality. As regards the latter, there are at least three sources for continuity: (1) continuity of the documentary evidence, e.g., the primary documents of any Christian reform, The Word of God as contained in the canonical Scriptures, are now textually verified and major textual changes seem most unlikely; the hard core of data in these documents acts upon the scholar and thereby imposes limits upon 'interpretation,' i.e., upon discontinuity; (2) continuity deriving from the fact that the basic operations of the human mind do not radically change from culture to culture; (3) continuity of 'tradition,' i.e., the historians are produced by an earlier generation of historians and hence are culturally linked to them; this is the other side of the fact that the historian himself cannot step outside of history. What is to be corrected in Catholic reform though, therefore, is the exclusiveness of its emphasis on continuity. With such an exaggerated emphasis as we have had until now, we have been inhibited from undertaking a really critical review of the past so that a new break for the future could logically be opened up.

A critical review of the past implies at least the possibility of rejecting the past, i.e., of acknowledging that there were certain realities *quae minus accurate servata fuerint*. It seems to me that such an acknowledgment is permissible if we correctly make use of contemporary philosophy of history. In the first place, this philosophy denies entelechy as a reliable principle of interpretation. An institution or an idea could have developed otherwise, for it is the product of human and contingent causes. To reply that providence ordained such a development simply removes the institution or idea from the area of human examination and hence silences both the historian and the theologian. If some given historical reality *could* have developed otherwise, and if we are still human agents operating in *human* history, we are free to change and even to reverse the direction of that reality if we so choose. What I am talking about, of course, is revolution, a term which historians use to describe certain phenomena which have occurred in the Church but which ecclesiastical documents never employ except in a pejorative sense.

In the second place, the contemporary historian realizes that data is subject to many 'interpretations'. That is, different scholars and different ages will have different questions encased in different presuppositions to address to the data … . Such an approach to authenticity needs to be tempered by at least two considerations. First, although we hope for an ever more accurate understanding of the past as we labor for it in research and discussion, we realize we shall never fully appropriate any past reality in its totality and on its own terms. No insight will perfectly exhaust the data's intelligibility, most especially if the 'data' is God's self-communication in revelation. Any authenticity, therefore, is at least somewhat partial and incomplete. Unlike Trent, we realize that our authenticity will not be *omni ex parte perfecta*. Secondly, we realize that our authenticity is not perfectly distinct from relevancy. The only meaningful questions we can ask the past are ones which are somehow relevant to our own needs and interests, and these needs and interests vary with different individuals, generations, and cultures. As Michel de Certeau observed a few years ago, 'En changeant, nous changeons le passé'.[15]

We are thus brought to the final implication that contemporary philosophy of history has for reform. It teaches us that we must create the future. In other words, it forces upon us the realization that, in the case of Christian reform, understanding of the past, howsoever authentic it might be, is not enough. Reform is also a practical matter. It requires not only understanding but also a translation of understanding into reality through our powers of imagination and creativity.

Imagination and creativity must enter every reform if it is not to be utterly irrelevant and dreary beyond human endurance. As a matter of fact, creativity has been at the heart of every successful reform and renaissance, even when men sincerely believed that they were doing nothing else than transposing the past into the present. Creativity, which is radically opposed to slavish imitation, implies both utilization of the past and rejection of the past. The outcome of creativity, in any case, is something *new*.

---

15. 'L'Epreuve du temps', *Christus*, 13 (July 1966), 314.

We have seen that we have to allow for a considerable difference of emphasis in our 'authentic' insights into the past. Even greater variety will surface when it comes to the question of translating insight into action, i.e., of producing that creative transformation which is genuine reform. At this juncture what is required is decision. What is required is to choose one or other practical course of action, after respective merits have been reviewed. What is not required is further reflection provoked by the misapprehension that, because a variety of options is offered as 'authentic', '*the* true mind' has not as yet been discovered.

The *aggiornamento* of Vatican II was our starting point. What I have tried to show is that, in the context of the philosophies of history upon which it seems to have rested, it is an inadequate expression of what is required today and, indeed, of what is actually happening today. We are not experiencing a 'reform' as that term is traditionally understood as a correction, or revival, or development, or even updating. We are experiencing a transformation, even a revolution.

As we are all keenly aware, such a transformation or revolution raises immense practical and theoretical questions. This article certainly did not intend to satisfy these questions except by helping to clarify one aspect of the relationship of the past to present and future. What we tried to do was to put the question of Christian reform into the context of various philosophies of history which have conditioned it in the past, and then to suggest how the problematic changes if reform is put into the context of contemporary philosophy of history. Such philosophy helps us to interpret more accurately what is happening. At least it should disabuse us of the illusion that the past will tell us what to do and that we do not have to be as decisive and creative as our Christian predecessors were. In fact, we should be even more decisive and creative. To a degree inconceivable to previous generations of Catholics, we realize that such a decision and creativity, with its heavy responsibilities, is required. We have this new understanding of what we are, beings of radical historicity. This new understanding of ourselves imposes upon us a new way of thinking and acting about 'reform'.

8.7 AVERY DULLES: 'IUS DIVINUM' AS AN ECUMENICAL PROBLEM – 1977

This essay[16] was originally published in *Theological Studies* and then was included in his collection of essays entitled, *A Church to Believe In* (1982). In an earlier section of the essay not included here, Dulles surveys contemporary theological treatments of the question whether there are church structures that exist by divine will and therefore are permanent features of the church. This is followed by the material included below in which Dulles proposes four different categories of church structures defined in terms of their particular relationship to the divine will.

❊

With reference to the problem of permanence and mutuality, the Church appears to be confronted with a dilemma. To the extent that it becomes tied to the specific circumstances of its own origins, its adaptability and consequently its mission are likely to suffer. There is always the danger that in new situations the inherited structures may become dysfunctional. But if, on the other hand, there are no limits to change, the Church runs the risk of sacrificing its identity. It could cease to be the same institution as that which existed in apostolic times and lose its formal continuity with the original community … .

The answer, I believe, is to be sought by reflection on the fundamental nature of the Church. By very definition the Church is, under Christ, the universal sacrament of salvation or, in other words, the sacrament of Christ in the world. In order to be a sacrament, the Church must be an efficacious sign – one in which the reality signified is manifestly present and operative. The Church, in other words, must be a lasting incarnation in the world of God's redemptive love for all humankind as originally signified and concretized in Jesus Christ … .

What is unchangeable about the Church, therefore, would seem to be best described in relational rather than essential terms. The Church is constituted on the one hand by its relationship to Jesus Christ, and on the other hand by its relationship to those whom it mediates that presence of Christ. These two relationships cannot be in conflict with each other, for unless the Church were itself related to Christ it could not mediate his presence to others; nor could it mediate his presence without really being related to the people of each time and place.

In Jesus Christ, 'the same yesterday and today and forever' (Heb 13:8), the Church has a stable reference point. In particular, it recalls and mystically relives by sacramental re-enactment the paschal event from which it takes its rise. Only by recapturing in its contemporary life the mysteries of Jesus' death and resurrection does the Church bring its own members into a saving relationship with God.

---

16. Dulles, Avery, '*Ius Divinum* as an Ecumenical Problem', *Theological Studies*, 38 (December 1977), 681–708.

This relatedness to Christ does not prevent the Church from adapting its forms of life and speech to the people of various ages and cultures. The Church in a given time and place consists of a specific group of people who have to actuate for themselves the Christ-relatedness of which we have been speaking. The abiding structures of the Church, therefore, must undergo ceaseless modification, not in order to weaken or dissolve its bonds with Christ, but precisely in order to keep them intact. An analogy may clarify this point. A growing child has to relate itself to his or her parents in constantly new ways, not in order to destroy the relationship the child formally had, but rather in order to keep that relationship alive. So, too, the Church has to adapt itself as may be necessary to maintain a living relationship to its Lord.

In the light of these general principles, we may consider ecclesial structures under four general headings, each of which is related in different ways to the concept of *ius divinum*[17] ... . The four classes may be conceived as concentric circles or spheres.

Neo-Lutheran theology has turned the spotlight on the innermost circle – that of the fundamental mission of the Church as attested by the dominical sayings preserved for us in the New Testament. Whether or not these sayings are authentic words of Jesus, Edmund Schlink's conclusions, in what they positively affirm, may be accepted, for the later Church would not be an efficacious sign of God's redemptive act in Christ unless it had the four elements on which Schlink insists.[18]

First, an apostolic ministry appears to be required in order that Christian proclamation and pastoral care may be extended to peoples of various times and places. Thanks to this apostolic ministry, the Church is assured of always possessing an authority which in some sort represents Christ its Lord. According to the representative theory I have outlined, it is important that the pastoral leaders be seen as endowed with the authority of him who said 'He who hears you hears me' (Lk 10:16). Yet this identity must not be too materialistically understood, as though Christ were somehow reincarnated in his ministers, or as though their relationship to him were independent of their solidarity with the ongoing community of Christian faith.

Second, one may affirm as divinely instituted and essential the rite of baptism by which individuals are initiated into the community of those whose lives are placed in subjection to Christ the Lord. It seems to be demanded in the nature of the case that such an entry into the community of believers be sealed with a visible sign, in order that through the sign itself deeper relationships may be fostered among all those who belong to the community.

Third, the community of believers must have at the center of its worship the meal which the New Testament sees as invested with sacramental significance both as the anamnesis of what Jesus did at the Last Supper and as a sign and anticipation of the eschatological banquet. Without the Eucharist the community would be deprived of its most powerful liturgical link to the paschal event on which its existence is founded and to the heavenly consummation toward which it tends.

Finally, the Church must continually reappropriate its fundamental nature as a community in which God's forgiveness is shown forth and mediated. The sacramental

17. [Literally, the will or law of God. When Dulles refers to the *Ius Divinum* he means 'divine law' in distinction from natural law or positive ecclesiastical law.]
18. Schlink, Edmund, 'Zur Unterscheidung von Ius Divinum und Ius humanum', in Max Seckler (ed.), *Begegnung, Festschrift für H. Fries*, Graz, Styria, 1972, 235–50.

enactment of that 'binding and loosing' which Jesus entrusted to the apostolic ministry would seem to be a necessary feature of any community that claims to mediate God's merciful pardon.

These four basic structural elements, representing Christ's irrevocable gift to his Church, correspond in a general way to what the Catholic tradition has recognized as the sacraments of ordination, baptism, Eucharist, and penance. Whether the term 'sacrament' is used in each of these four cases is not of crucial import, for the category of 'sacrament' is not itself a foundational element but is a product of ecclesiological reflection. Yet the category does seem meaningful and valid. Not only Catholics, Orthodox, and Anglicans but many Lutherans have been willing to recognize these four rites as deserving to be called 'sacraments', for they are viewed in the New Testament as divinely instituted and may be thought to involve a promise of grace.

No sharp line can be drawn between this innermost circle of sacramental structures which the New Testament ascribes to the founding action of Jesus himself and the second circle to which we now turn. There are certain institutional features which first clearly appeared as distinct entities sometime subsequent to the apostolic age but which, once they did appear, were able to be traced to a biblical basis and, moreover, they were found to be expressive of the very nature of the Church. Structures of this category seem to be best explained not by the static theory of tradition characteristic of Neo-Scholasticism but by the developmental theory I have ascribed to [Karl] Rahner and [Carl] Peter. These developments, inasmuch as they may not be reversed by the free, discretionary action of church authorities, may be called *iure divino* in a somewhat more extended sense than structures that pertain to our first category … .

The majority of Christian traditions accept the creeds of the early Church and the canon of Scripture drawn up in the early centuries, even though these norms are themselves postapostolic; for the Church in later ages finds that these doctrinal norms enable it to express and maintain the apostolic faith. So likewise we may suppose that certain sacramental and ministerial structures which cannot themselves be surely traced back to the apostolic generation may nonetheless be essential to the Church in later ages. Among these structures we may plausibly reckon the three sacraments not listed in our first category: confirmation, marriage, and the anointing of the sick. These rites are not without a biblical basis, and when they did become universally practiced they were seen as expressing aspects of the Church's abiding nature. Confirmation effectively symbolizes the special assistance of the Holy Spirit promised to, and conferred upon, those who enter the community of faith. Christian marriage transforms nuptial relationships in the light of the union between Christ and his Church, thus making the Christian family what Vatican II does not hesitate to call a 'domestic church'. The anointing of the sick perpetuates in a visible and sacramental way the healing that belongs so prominently to the ministry of Jesus and the apostles.

It is along these lines that some recent scholarship has attempted a justification of the papacy as divinely instituted. It may plausibly be argued that the papal office, as an embodiment of the Petrine ministry, even though it cannot be historically traced to the first few generations, has won for itself an enduring place in the Church. True, there are doubts and differences of opinion as to the exact shape that the papacy may be called to assume for the Church of the future, but this uncertainty does not negate the judgement that an office concerned with the ministry of worldwide unity will and should remain. The same, I believe, may be held regarding the episcopacy as a ministry of supervision over more particular ministries to congregations. But to discuss in detail exactly what features of any given sacrament or ministry are essential and enduring would be to exceed the scope of the present chapter, which is concerned only to clarify the notion of *ius divinum*. In agreement with Karl Rahner and Carl Peter, I believe that the notion is applicable to this second circle.

Can there be temporary, reversible developments truly willed by Christ and inspired by the Holy Spirit? This possibility, envisaged by Johannes Neumann and Edward Schillebeeckx, cannot, in my judgement, be ignored. As I have already argued, the maintenance of a living relationship to Christ may actually demand adaptations to a given period of history or given to a geographical or cultural situation. Such adaptations are not arbitrary. In admitting them, the Church is not acting on its own initiative but is exercising obedience to its Lord ... .

On the positive side, we may think that in our time God's will for his Church – and hence, also, the appropriate realization of the Church's essence in history – demands a less juridical and more consensual form of leadership than has prevailed in recent centuries. Just as in the civil arena the participation of every individual in the life of the state is increasingly recognized as a right founded in natural law, so in the ecclesiastical arena the current demand for greater participation and dialogue seems to be a uniquely fitting institutionalization for our time of what the Church is by nature and by God's intention, namely, an interpersonal communion established by means of the grace of the Holy Spirit. The Vatican II principles of collegiality and conciliarity may be taken as responses to this demand. In addition the vital insertion of Christian faith into the cultures of various peoples, combined with the avoidance of cultural imperialism, seems to call for a greater degree of cultural and regional pluralism than has prevailed since the centralization and the Counterreformation. In this context we may theologically situate the discussion of regional and local autonomy which surfaced at the 1974 World Synod of Bishops.

On the negative side, it may be necessary to ask whether certain historical forms previously regarded as irreversible ought not to be subject to critical scrutiny. Because of the inevitable restrictions imposed upon us by our own cultural ambience, we can all too easily confuse divinely willed but reversible developments with those that are irreversible. In the past, theologians have often tended to overextend the sphere of the essential. Jean Gerson, for instance, has been summarized as holding: 'The Church is so integrally and perfectly constituted in its essential hierarchy, that is, papacy, cardinalate, patriarchate, archiepiscopacy, episcopacy and priesthood, that if it lost one of these hierarchical orders it would cease to be the Church that Christ established.'[19] To our contemporaries it seems clear that cardinalate, patriarchate, and archiepiscopacy are not divinely mandated grades of the hierarchical ministry, even for a given historical era, and yet many theologians are convinced that papacy, episcopacy, and presbyterate are permanently essential. In view of the past confusions concerning divinely instituted ministries, we have to ask ourselves continually whether we have drawn the line at the right point. Ecumenical dialogue with other Christian communities raises this question in a particularly poignant way, for non-Roman Catholic communities are asking the Catholic Church to recognize that their historic structures could continue to exist

---

19. L.B. Pascoe, *Jean Gerson: Principles of Church Reform*, Leiden: Brill, 1973, 28.

in a reunited church. And the Catholic Church is asking other churches to accept its own essential structures, both sacramental and hierarchical.

Do we have any criteria for distinguishing between the second and third spheres just described? In the last analysis the decision must rest on an act of discernment that cannot be justified by demonstrative proofs. But there are indications. When, for instance, a given ecclesiastical structure seems to be an impediment to the Church's mission as embodied in the divine mandates of our first sphere, or when it conflicts with the transcendental precepts that hold good for any society, we may have reason to think that this particular structure can and should be radically changed or suppressed. For it is difficult to see how God could will for his Church something that is a countersign or is counterproductive.

Applying these criteria, one might ask, for example, whether the papacy must be regarded as a permanent feature of the Church. With most Catholics, I would answer in the affirmative, on the ground that it remains important in every age for the Church to possess an efficacious sign of its worldwide unity and to perpetuate what has been called the 'Petrine' ministry ... .

Beyond these three spheres of divinely required structures lies an outer realm of discretionary matters, corresponding approximately to what Scholasticism calls *ius mere ecclesiasticum* and what Lutheranism has traditionally regarded as 'adiaphora' (matters of indifference). In the more modern terminology, Michael A. Fahey refers to 'operational' and 'ad hoc' structures.[20] The Church has the obligation to make certain provisional dispositions that are neither contrary to God's will nor expressly required by it. In many cases one cannot say that either of two alternative regulations is more consonant with the Church's nature and mission, but a decision has to be made – somewhat as civil authorities have to regulate, more or less arbitrarily, whether cars are to drive on the right or the left hand side of the street. In these cases it is unhelpful to speak of divine law except possibly in a merely permissive sense.

On the basis of these four classes of structure we may now proceed to draw some conclusions about divine positive law. With regard to the continued usage of the term itself, we must acknowledge, with Lindbeck, certain real disadvantages. *Ius divinum* terminology tends to make too sharp a separation between divine and human activity, to absolutize what is historically conditioned, and thus to lend support to ideological distortions, as did the political theory of the 'divine right of kings'. And yet the term does have the value of calling attention to the fact that the Church stands under its divine Master, that there is a point at which the Church itself must say 'I can do no other, so help me God. Here I stand'.

The traditional category of divine law, in my judgment, is applicable with varying degrees of appropriateness to each of the first three of the four types of structure discussed above. The first type offers the least difficulty, for here we find verified not only God's will but also divine institution (by Jesus Christ as attested by the Scriptures), apostolic origin, and permanence.

For our second class, *ius divinum* terminology is less appropriate but still meaningful. The term expresses the divinely willed and irreversible character of certain structures, even though they came into being since apostolic times. Yet the terminology is questionable, since we have no assurance of immediate and specific institution by Christ or even by the apostles. Without this element the traditional category of *ius divinum* is weakened.

---

20. Fahey, Michael, 'Continuity in the church amid Structural Changes', *Theological Studies* 35 (1974), 427.

For our third class, which includes structures willed by God for his Church in a certain passing phase of its existence and in a certain historical situation, *ius divinum* terminology still has the merit of bringing out that in establishing or maintaining these structures the Church has a sense of not acting arbitrarily but under a divine imperative. It would not be proper to speak in such instances of merely ecclesiastical law or even adiaphora. But the *ius divinum* terminology is only marginally applicable, because both apostolic origin and irreversibility are lacking.

For many of our contemporaries, it may seem presumptuous to categorize ecclesiastical structures by reference to God's will and misleading to depict God in the likeness of a human lawgiver. Such persons may find it more helpful to define the structures in question by their relationship to the Church itself. The innermost circle would then be seen to include what is necessary *ad esse ecclesiae*, 'for the very being of the Church' – to borrow a term from the discussions concerning episcopacy within the Anglican communion. The second circle corresponds to what may, in the same terminology, be called *ad plene esse ecclesiae*, for without these features the Church would lack something that pertains to its integral and developed existence. The Church would indeed exist, but only in rudimentary or mutilated form. Our third circle would correspond to what is, for a certain time or situation, *ad bene esse ecclesiae*. If these structures were lacking, the Church would be present and integral, but not in a healthy condition. The fourth circle includes structures that do not belong to the Church's *esse*.

This alternate set of terms, while laboring under certain disadvantages such as the danger of contributing to an exorbitant ecclesiocentrism, has the merit of bringing out into the open some of the distinctions we have found it necessary to build into the notion of *ius divinum*. Doubtless, still other vocabularies can be proposed. Whatever terminology is employed, it will be necessary to differentiate, as we have done, between the biblical and the nonbiblical, the apostolic and the postapostolic, the reversible and the irreversible.

8.8 LEONARDO BOFF: *THE POWER OF THE INSTITUTIONAL CHURCH – CAN IT BE CONVERTED? – 1981*

In our selection,[21] Boff's theological starting point is Jesus' preaching of the kingdom of God. For Boff the kingdom of God refers to God's intentions for the transformation of the world. The world, in turn 'is the arena for the historical realization of the Kingdom' (10). The church is 'that part of the world that, in the strength of the Spirit, has accepted the Kingdom made explicit in the person of Jesus Christ' (2). Consequently, all church structures and relations in the church are subject to the core values found in Jesus' preaching of the kingdom of God. In this selection, Boff analyses the institutional church and its exercise of power throughout history and finds it wanting. Church reform must be nothing less than a re-creation of the church according to the values of the gospel.

❁

FRUSTRATED BUT LIVING HOPES

Is the Church as institution able to be a liberator among the poor and oppressed? Is conversion possible given the spirituality of the sacredness of power held only by pastors and bishops? Is it possible to trust the stated preferential option for the poor, to hope that the Church may break its historical pact with temporal rulers and be converted to gospel poverty, in solidarity with those who are denied their rights, converted to prophetic courage, fearless in the face of persecution, torture, and death, and so follow the Suffering Servant, Jesus Christ?

Committed by faith in this Church, we will attempt to analyze the reasons behind these hopes, frustrated as they may be. Through this analysis we hope to nourish faith in the strength of the Spirit that is capable of awakening the dormant heart of the institutional Church, encouraging the living presence and the dangerous yet powerful memory of the life, death, and resurrection of Jesus Christ.

When we speak of the Church as institution, we do not mean the community of believers who give witness in the world to the presence of the risen Christ. We refer to the organization of this community with its hierarchy, sacred powers, dogmas, rites, canons, and traditions. By means of its institutional organization the community responds to the needs for stability, for identity, the spreading of the Gospel, internal assistance, government, and so on. No community can exist without some institutionalization that lends it unity, coherency, and identity. The institution does not exist for itself but is in service to the community of faith. As such, it evolves, following the same path as the historical transformation of the community itself that faces crises and discovers institutional responses to them. What we call ongoing or

---

21. *ET*, Boff, Leonardo, 'The Power of the Institutional Church: Can it be Converted?', in *Church, Charism and Power – Liberation Theology and the Institutional Church*, New York, Crossroad, 1985, 47–64.

permanent conversion belongs to this historical process of fidelity and service to the community and the Lord. This presupposes an interior attitude of detachment and poverty that allows the institution to abandon its search for glory in order to better serve the community and the Lord present within it. It is only by means of this ongoing conversion that the community with its institutions will be of salvific service to the world. Otherwise it will become an empty ghetto, thereby betraying its vocation of universality.

The Church as an institution is characterized by endurance, stability, and by the rules of the game followed by its members. It runs the risk of losing the beat of history, of stagnating, of forgetting its primary function of service, of fostering passivity, monotony, mechanization, and alienation. It begins to understand itself ideologically, as the epiphany of the promises it safeguards. It imposes itself on the community it is meant to serve. Truth is substituted by internal certainty and factions are created by cutting these movements that will not be constrained by the institution. Every institution runs these risks and has the tendency to become autocratic, that is, to become a system of power and repression over creativity and criticism. Institution means power. And, as Lord Acton rightly observed 'Power tends to corrupt and absolute power corrupts absolutely'.[22]

The institution of the Church has suffered from this; power became a powerful temptation for domination and a substitution for God and Jesus Christ. This institutional sclerosis has kept the Church from responding properly to the challenges of the modern world. It has become conservative and has created a deep chasm between the Church-People of God and the Church-hierarchy in terms of ecclesial praxis, between the Church that thinks, speaks, and yet does not act and that Church which does not dare to think, cannot speak, and yet acts. This breach in practice is so serious that the proclamations of the Second Vatican Council on the place of the laity in the Church as People of God are only now reaching the level of general theological discussion … .

There is a great difference between the Church of the first three centuries and the later Church which rose to power. The primitive Church was prophetic; it joyfully suffered torture and courageously gave its life through martyrdom. It did not care about survival because it believed in the Lord's promise that guaranteed it would not fail. Success or failure, survival or extinction, was not a problem for the church; it was a problem for God. The bishops were at the forefront, convincing their brothers and sisters to die for the Lord. The later Church was opportunistic; that it would not fail was a question of prudence and compromise that allowed it to survive in the midst of totalitarian regimes, at the expense of gospel demands. The bishop in this later Church does not freely walk in witness to his death; rather, he pushes others, walking behind his flock and often assisting in the death of its prophets, fearful and reticent, calling for fidelity not to Christ but to the institutional Church … .

Such practices of power in the Church, generating ecclesial marginality, tenuous and lifeless communication between its members, as well as religious and evangelical underdevelopment, result in the image of a Church almost neurotically preoccupied with itself and, as such, lacking a real interest in the major problems facing humanity.

But the Church *does* speak out and makes calls to conversion and eventually recognizes its historical errors. Vatican II explicitly stated the need for ongoing conversion in the notion

---

22. [Letter to Bishop Mandell Creighton, 3 April 1887, in Louise Creighton, *Life and Letters of Mandell Creighton*, 1904, vol. 1, Chap. 13.]

of *Ecclesia semper reformanda* (Church always in need of reform). Unfortunately, conversion is interpreted in such a way that allows the power structure to remain as it is. An intimate and private meaning is given to conversion: the members of the Church must be converted, that is, live a morally holy life and achieve a purity of intentions. This does not touch upon the institution with its structures of ongoing iniquity, discrimination, lack of full participation, and so on. Institutions have a life of their own, independent of the good or ill intentions of individuals within them. If conversion does not reach the institution of the Church, if it does not call into question the way in which power is exercised, if it does not reach the wider society, then we cannot speak of gospel conversion. We end up with extremely good-willed individuals with pure intentions but who are faithful, loyal, and uncritical toward the institution, who through this institution cause serious damage to people and to the Church. Pascal noted that evil is not so perfectly achieved as when it is done with good will and purity of heart … .

THE GOAL OF REFORM: THE NEED TO RECREATE

In order to reform an institution it is necessary to be clear about one's understanding of the institution. The Church as an institution of power would be summed up as follows:

1. As much as it may irritate those in positions of ecclesiastical power, we must repeat that the institutional Church has not passed the test of power. We might have hoped that it would have bought forth a new manner of exercising power according to the call of the Gospel. However, the Church's exercise of power followed the patterns of pagan power in terms of domination, centralization, marginalization, triumphalism, human *hybris* beneath a sacred mantle. Sociologically, Christianity was not sufficiently negative or critical … . It is not enough to say that one must judge history with the criteria of the time. Why, in treating the history of the church, should not the criteria of the Gospel have greater value?

2. With the conversion of Constantine, Christianity had no other alternative than to assume a historical role in terms of sacred and political power. Inheriting the empire, it had the opportunity to become truly ecumenical and universal. This it did. Christianity is not against power in itself but its diabolical forms which generally show themselves as domination and control of the masses. It lost the opportunity to incarnate a new way of relating through power as pure service for the good of all persons.

3. Despite having continued the pagan form of power, Christianity marked first the West and then the entire world. The history of the world can never be told without mentioning the presence of Christianity. Yet there can be no illusions as to the quality of Christianity present in western culture: it was superficial and contained profoundly anti-Christian elements. Atheism as a cultural phenomenon came from Christianity; the western world gave rise to the great totalitarian ideologies of Nazism, capitalism, Marxism, colonialism, and slavery, with all their offshoots such as oppression, unjust wars, and colonial rule.

4. Everything seems to indicate that the Church's experience with power is approaching its inevitable end. There are two basic reasons for this: first, Christianity is becoming more and more a dispensable ideology for modern secular, pragmatic, and industrial society. It can

no longer serve to legitimate affluent social power structures. Second, Christian consciousness is itself aware of the trouble with ecclesiastical institutions … .

Those in the hierarchy who do not understand this *kairos* are not learning the lesson of the signs of the times and so stop working toward the future of the Church. Even with all the good will and pure intentions that we do not deny they have, they are drowning in the attempt to renew a type of Church's presence that is neither evangelical nor responsive to the call of the historical moment. The Church finds itself faced with a new society and with new opportunities for presence. With a view to the present and toward the future, there is no time to sing the praises of the past; the institution has already celebrated them.

5. Faced with a new situation, the Church, in the words of Karl Rahner, 'must march valiantly toward the new and not yet experienced, to the outer limits, there where Christian doctrine and conscience can travel no further. In the practical life of the Church today, the only fitting theology is a daring theology … . What is certain in this day and age is not the past but the future'.[23] Who may dare if not Christians, for they know they are led by the Spirit from truth to truth? As long as it is supported by its past and itself, the Church runs the risk of unfaithfulness to the call of the Lord, present in the world as the risen Christ.

6. To recognize the past history of the Church with its exercise of power is not to reject the institution of the Church. The institution is a concrete reality that makes explicit the Christian mysteries and preaches Jesus Christ as liberator, in spite of all internal contradictions. Every Christian must accept this past without running away from it, yet at the same time preventing its continuation in the present and future. To accept the past is not to justify it. We must courageously accept it because it is *our* past as much as we are members of the People of God of which the hierarchical institution is a part. Nor does the past allow us to sit back; rather, it calls us to be co-responsible for the future of the Christian faith in the world. The cause of Christ and the People of God is too important to leave to the hierarchy. 'The institution is not an evil. We might attribute it to St Paul's words about law: necessary but alone it is insufficient good and may even become an occasion for sin for anyone who seeks refuge in it.'[24]

Only a true gospel love, which is critical and free, can accept the Church with its limitations and errors, because only through loving it are we converted, thus revealing the fascinating beauty of the Church, the bride of Christ and mother to all peoples.

A RETURN TO THE SOURCES: THE GOSPEL MEANING OF AUTHORITY

Everything points to the following conclusion: The goal is one of reform, the need to create a model for the institutional Church because the model of power has given all it has to give. The attitude of the institution must be one of conversion with everything that term implies: poverty, rejection of false security, acceptance of the inability to control the future, the challenge of faith, trust, and surrender to the Spirit who was given to the Church not to develop an already received and guaranteed deposit of faith but to guarantee fidelity to its

---

23. *Handbuch der Pastoraltheologie*, II/1, 275–6.
24. Liégé, P.A., 'A Igreja diante de seu pecado', in *A Igreja do futuro*, Petrópolis, 1973, 121.

essential element, Jesus Christ, in every confrontation between faith and the world (cf. Matt 10:20; John 15:26; 16:8).

The sources of faith need to be reexamined, no longer with the eyes of those with power but with the eyes of all who have abandoned the perspective of power. In the past, ecclesiastical power read and re-read the New Testament (almost only the epistles) for the first signs of thinking in terms of power, orthodoxy, tradition, preservation more than creation, moralizing more than prophetic proclamation. The cause of Christ, of the historical Jesus who was poor, weak, powerless, critical of the social and religious status quo of his time, was enshrined and spiritualized by the institution and so divested of its critical power.

For a Church that seeks a new presence in the world and wants to avoid the structures and pitfalls of yesteryear, a very pure rereading of the central message of Jesus Christ, of the gospel understanding of the structures of power and the importance of the Spirit in the Church, is essential. This will be done below in a general way because I have already developed this more thoroughly elsewhere.

JESUS' FUNDAMENTAL PROJECT OF LIBERATION AND FREEDOM

Jesus did not preach the Church but rather the Kingdom of God that included the liberation of the poor, comfort for those who cry, justice, peace, forgiveness, and love. He did not proclaim an established order; he did not call others to be rulers but to be submissive, humble, and loyal. He liberates for freedom and love that allow one to be submissive yet free, critical, and loyal without being servile, that call those in power to be servants and brothers free from the appetite for greater power. Fraternity, open communication with everyone, solidarity with all people, with the little ones, the least of the earth, sinners and even enemies, goodness, undiscriminating love, unlimited forgiveness are the great ideals put forth by Jesus. He does not introduce or bless privileges that give rise to classes and divisions between persons. The *exousia*, that is, the sovereignty, that appears in his attitudes and words is not power in the terms of human power. It is the power of love. If he proclaims that he 'was given all power in heaven and on earth' (Matt. 28:18) and passes this power on to the apostles, we must understand the nature of that power. It is the power of God.

What is the power of God? It is the power of the Father of our Lord Jesus Christ who showed him to be the Father of infinite goodness, revealing an astounding power of the infinite capacity to support and be patient with human persons, the power to love the 'ingrates and evil ones' (Luke 6:35). Power is the power to love. The power of love is different in nature from the power of domination; it is fragile, vulnerable, conquering through its weakness and its capacity for giving and forgiveness. Jesus always demonstrated this *exousia* in his life. He renounced power as domination; he preferred to die in weakness rather than use his power to subjugate people to accept his message. In this way he de-divinized power: he no longer made it proof of his transcendence, rejecting requests for proof of miraculous power (Mark 15:32). It is in weakness that the love of God and the God of love are revealed (1 Cor 1:25; 2 Cor 13:4; Phil 2:7).

CRITICISM OF ALL DOMINATING POWER

It is from the fundamental project of Jesus and the new way of relating that underlies his message that the criticisms he levies against the power structures in his world are to be understood. 'You know how those who rule the nations exercise tyranny over them and they practice violence against them. This is not to be among you: on the contrary, if one of you wishes to be great, he must be your servant; and he who desires to be first among you must serve all; because the Son of Man did not come to be served but to serve and to give his life for the redemption of many' (Mark 10:42–44; Luke 22:25–27). These words were provoked by the disputes about power and privilege among the disciples … .

The one who represents Christ and his *exousia* must be a servant just as Jesus was. Without this, one is no different from a pagan tyrant. Matthew is equally against any power/domination within the community: 'You shall not be called masters because there is only one Master and all of you are brothers. Nor must you call anyone on earth "father" because you have one Father who is in heaven. Do not call yourself doctors because only one is your Doctor, Christ' (32:8–11). It is strange to see that the Church institution has developed into exactly that which Christ did not want it to be: from the will for power, hierarchies of teachers, doctors, fathers, fathers of fathers, and servants of servants have all arisen.

The apostles are the bearers of the *paradosis*, the essence of Christ's message and salvific events; this fact gives them special authority; but that authority is not the basis for any privilege, any domination over others' freedom. They must be the servants of the servants. *Exousia* leads to *diakonia*. To live power as service and as servant is the greatest challenge facing the institutional Church. There are tensions and temptations but no ideology contrary to the Gospel can justify what has happened throughout the history of the Church when members of the hierarchy took on titles, honors, secular and sacred powers, often to satisfy primal instincts for possession and self-aggrandizement.

The *exousia* of the apostles, yesterday and today, is not only a diaconal authority of preaching and transmitting the message but also of building up and defending the community. Paul is conscious of the 'authority that the Lord gave to me to build and not to destroy' (2 Cor 13:10). He is not afraid to conflict with the community and in order to defend it (not punish it) he feels the need to cut off certain members from it (1 Cor 5: 3–5). But he never forgets the diaconal sense of authority: 'We do not want to dominate your faith but to contribute to your joy' (2 Cor 1:24; 13:10).

These considerations are extremely important for the functions of unity and government in the ecclesial community. The one in these positions, in relation with the universal Church and in continuity with its history, has legitimate authority. This authority, however, is empty if it is not supported by the example of the humble, poor, weak, and servant Jesus. This authority must be exercised diaconally, like Jesus, full of respect between brothers and sisters and not between lords and subordinates … .

ECCLESIOGENESIS: THE NEW CHURCH BORN OF THE OLD

Meditating on the Gospels and with a theological reading of the signs of the times, a significant portion of the Church as institution has understood the current challenges for Christian faith and responsibly tries to respond to them. We are seeing the rising of a new Church, born in the heart of the old Church, in the form of *comunidades de base*, communities on the peripheries of our cities, a Church of the poor, comprised of poor people, in the form of bishops, priests, and religious entering into the life of the marginalized, centers of evangelization headed by lay people, and so on. It is a Church that has definitely renounced the centralization of power; unity resides in the idea of Church as the People of God, a pilgrim Church, open to the historical march of peoples, a Church that shares in all the risks and enjoys the small victories with a very deep sense of following Jesus Christ, identified with the poor, the rejected, the disinherited of the earth. This Church is being built day by day, open to new ministries answering the needs of the community and responding to all human life and not just culture, a Church involved in the working world and living out the meaning and joy of the resurrection in the heart of the secular world.

Today we are witnessing a true ecclesiogenesis precisely where the institutional structure shows the most visible signs of disrepair. The Gospel is no longer tied to a classic and consecrated presentation that was inherited from an institutionally glorious past but rather it is being lived as a movement, creating structures that are more in tune with the present. This new way of being Church understands that it does not exist for itself; it is to be sign of Christ for the world and a place where the Spirit is explicitly active. A sign does not exist for itself but for others. The Church as a sign is *from* Christ *for* the world. It never judges itself to be complete but always returns to what it should be, that is, the sacrament of Christ and of the Spirit. The Church thus bubbles with an inner, creative, and self-critical dynamic, with a heart that is sensitive to the presence of the risen Christ and his grace in the world, even before its proclamation of the gospel.

This new Church, as in all renewal movements, first appears on the periphery. Given the power structure at the center, the periphery is the only place where true creativity and freedom is possible. Faith is born and made present through personal witness; it is not being watched over by the institution. Thus, there is the opportunity for a pure and evangelical authenticity not found within the institution with its bureaucratic preoccupations and its time and energy spent to justify, defend, preserve, and expand its structures.

It is to be expected that the old Church will distrust the new Church on the periphery with its gospel freedoms. It will call it a parallel Church, with its own magisterium, disobedient and disloyal to the center! The new Church will have to be careful to develop intelligent strategies and tactics; it must not be drawn into the center's game of condemnation and suspicion. It will have to be evangelical and understand that the institution can do nothing else but make use of a language that safeguards its own power, that the institution fears any withdrawal from its dictates, viewing such as disloyalty. The new Church will have to remain faithful to its path. It will have to be loyally disobedient. It will have to seek a profound loyalty to the demands of the Gospel; it will also have to listen to the old Church's questioning of the truth of its interpretation of the Gospels. Critically reflecting upon these questions and convinced of its path, it must have the courage to be disobedient to the demands of the center, without anger or complaint, in deep adherence to the desire to be faithful to the Lord, the gospels, and the Spirit – the same desire that is presumed to motivate the institutional Church. This is the root of basic communion. Gospel purity awakens the institution to the Spirit that cannot be channeled along the lines of human interests. For the new Church, its openness to communion with everyone and its attempts at avoiding even the slightest possibility of a break that could destroy unity and charity – though this may lead to isolation, persecution, and condemnation by the institution – is the guarantee of its Christian authenticity inspired by the Gospel.

The future of the institutional Church lies in this small seed that is the new Church growing in the fields of the poor and powerless. It will be an alternative for the incarnation of new ecclesial institutions whose power will be pure service. The papacy, the episcopacy, and the presbyterate will not lose their evangelical ideals of strengthening the brothers and sisters in faith, of being the principal of unity and reconciliation in the community, of being religious leaders able to interpret the meaning of events and desires of all people, especially those of the poor, according to the light of the mystery of Christ... .

SARA HAS CONCEIVED

Can the Church be converted to a more vibrant witness of the Gospel in our world today? It can, because it is happening. But it must renounce a certain type of power. By virtue of its vocation, the Church exists for a future Kingdom and so must proclaim its own provisory character. Its true identity is not in a past that it often vainly tries to restore but in a future that is still to be revealed. If change and human development prepares for and anticipates the Kingdom, as the Council teaches (*Gaudium et Spes*, 34, 39), how much more must change in the Church also prepare and anticipate the new heaven and the new earth! The 'peace of order', stagnation in fixed models, obstinate repetition of past statements compromise the true dimension of openness to the future and eschatological hope proper to Christian faith and instead causes us to forget our condition as pilgrims and strangers on our way to the dynamic rest of God. The Church will be a sign of liberation and will enter into the struggle with all peoples only insofar as it is converted and becomes more and more an incarnation of the Gospel.

Perhaps the institutional Church, with the experience and prudence of all older people, will smile upon hearing these reflections – like old Sara. Putting ourselves in Abraham's place, we hear God's question: 'Why has Sara smiled? Is anything impossible for God?' (Gen 18:14). Smile, Sara, because once sterile you have become fertile, you have become a new creation! Sara has already conceived. There, in Sara's womb, the signs of new life are already beginning to appear: a new Church is being born, in the dark recesses of humanity.

8.9 ROSEMARY RADFORD RUETHER: *THE ECCLESIOLOGY OF WOMEN-CHURCH: MINISTRY AND COMMUNITY – 1985*

Our extract[25] comes from a volume in which Ruether offers a historically and theologically informed vision of the church as a community of liberation and suggests the need for women to form liturgical communities removed from 'male-dominated spaces' in order to develop a critical feminist culture. This separation from men must be viewed not as an end in itself but as a necessary stage that can serve as the critical foundation for a new community of women and men freed from the oppressive power of patriarchy

Constructing a church liberated from patriarchy will require the dismantling of clericalism. To do this we need to understand the utter incompatibility of clericalism with a liberation understanding of ministry. Clericalism is the separation of ministry from mutual interaction with community and its transformation into hierarchically ordered castes of clergy and laity. The clergy monopolize teaching, sacramental action, and administration and turning the community into passive dependents who are to receive these services from the clergy but cannot participate in shaping and defining themselves. An understanding of ministry as originating from the community and continually based in it is suppressed in favor of ministry as 'the ordained' who possess a heteronomous power beyond the capacity of the community.

In the official clerical mythology, an ordained priesthood is declared to have been established by Christ (as representative of God), who founded a hierarchy to pass down this divine power in a line of succession. Bishops dispense divine power to priests, and priests, in turn, dispense forgiveness, truth, and divine life to the laity, if the laity submits to the rules laid down by the hierarchy. In this way the entire teaching and sacramental life of the Church is turned into a power tool of the clergy over the people.

This clerical use of the powers of service is not only found in religious organizations such as the Church. We find the same deformation in other service professions such as medicine, psychology, teaching, and social work. In each case clients are made to feel a need that they are incapable of servicing through their own abilities or with the help of friends and peers. Indeed, the possibility of acquiring the knowledge, skills, and implements to do so is removed from access and made available only to those who are going to be the credentialed professionals. Having identified or created a need, people are turned into clients who must depend on a professional to service this need. In the process of receiving help from the

25. Ruether, Rosemary Radford, 'The Ecclesiology of Women-Church: Ministry and Community', in *Women-Church – Theology and Practice of Feminist Liturgical Communities*, 75–95, San Francisco, Harper & Row, 1985.

professional, clients are progressively disempowered, made more and more dependent on the professional, and made to feel incapable of taking care of this need themselves.

Clericalism is built upon patriarchalism. The basic symbol and mode of the cleric's relationship to a lay person is that of an all-knowing father over a helpless child. The image of the patriarchal husband over the dependent wife is also used to image the relationship of clergy to laity, even though this image, drawn from Ephesians 5 in the New Testament (where it images the relationship of Christ to the Church) is not actually applied in the New Testament to the relationship of ministry to laity, because this hierarchy had not yet emerged in the Church.

What we see in all forms of paternalism and clericalism is the relationship of a dependent adult to a dominant adult being assimilated into that of a child to a male parent. Because the power exercised by the father is presumed to be benevolent and wise, it is psychologically and culturally difficult to criticize it. Deep resonances of childhood guilt are evoked to keep such a relationship in place. The dependent person is made to feel both ungrateful and ostracized for rejecting parental authority. Thus it is difficult to articulate the inappropriateness of such father-child relationships between adults and to name their function as disempowerment.

The symbolism of Christ as husband and Church as wife, applied to clerical-lay relationships, is an example of such an assimilation of adult relationships into father-child relationships. The 'wife' in this relationship is not a peer or partner of her husband, but she is the dependent wife-child of classical patriarchy. The image of laity as sheep and clergy as shepherds, an image drawn from ancient kingship imagery is also used to suggest a relationship of a herd of senseless animals to an all-wise guide. The identification of women with the dependent child-wife or sheep who are to be directed by the paternal clergy, functions as a powerful psychological bar to the ordination of women. The image of Christ as father-husband, Church as child-wife, applied literally to maleness and femaleness in the Church, has emerged as a key argument against the ordination of women in Anglican, Roman Catholic, and Eastern Orthodox polemic in recent years. It is unlikely that women will be able to function in more than token ways in the ordained ministry, even in those denominations who have chosen to do so, as long as this patriarchal-clerical model of ministry is maintained.

The disempowerment of the people by clericalism takes place in sacramental life, teaching, and in church administration. In sacramental life, all the symbols of the life of the community, as a life grounded in the divine and experienced together, are alienated from the people and made into magic tools possessed by the clergy through an ordination that comes from 'above' … .

The disempowerment of the people educationally is a second essential element in clericalism. The clergy monopolize theological education, removing it to a place inaccessible to the people. Theological education is also developed in a language unknown to the people. This may be either a foreign language, such as Latin, which traditionally the laity and even nuns were not taught, or else, in modern times, a learned jargon that most people cannot understand. Theology is turned into a specialized culture available only to the professional. The people are thus made to feel helpless and dependent on the clergy to interpret the Scriptures and to analyze theological ideas and symbols. Yet the laity are also told that the essence of faith is simple and easy and based on a docile acceptance of the rules of life given them by the clergy. So there is no need for them to think for themselves, but only to do as they are told … .

Fundamentalism also has become highly authoritarian. It is based on the notion that literal belief in a series of magical events and the repression of critical consciousness derived from history and science are the proofs of salvation. Metaphorical and paradigmatic ways of interpreting scripture, which had been well understood before the Reformation, are repressed in favor of a pseudoscientific literalism that interprets events such as the virgin birth as biological 'facts'.

Roman Catholic basic Christian communities, fed by the rediscovery of prophetic tradition in liberation theology, have recovered today an understanding of populist Bible reading. Even though Roman Catholicism has been, until recently, suspicious of popular Bible reading, the new encouragement of biblical literacy in the Second Vatican Council allowed popular groups to discover Bible reading as a subversive activity, which had made the Bible a tool of liberation of the people from clerical and ruling class oppression in medieval times.

Clericalism in church administration is the third area of hierarchical control over the people. The most hierarchical churches, such as Roman Catholicism, give the laity no effective role in administration at all. The laity neither ordain nor call their pastors nor their bishops. They are not elected to church councils on a diocesan, national, or international level. They do not participate in decisions governing the life of the church, either organizationally, doctrinally, or financially. The Second Vatican Council tried to change this stratified pattern of church government for a more collegial relationship of pope with national episcopacies, bishops with priests, and priests with laity. But these changes were quickly resisted by the Curia in Rome, which had never really welcomed Vatican II ... .

The most closely guarded secret in modern Roman Catholicism is the late development of this pattern of hierarchical government and its nondominical origins. Vatican power depends on promulgating the belief that the Roman hierarchical form of church government was literally founded by Christ and has been in place, virtually unchanged, from the beginnings of the church, although no one with even the most cursory understanding of church history could possibly believe this ... .

Women-Church, as a community of redemption from patriarchy, must take responsibility for a more radical reappropriation of ministry from clericalism. It must understand ministry as the articulation of the community whereby the community symbolizes its common life, communicates it to one another, and engages in mutual empowerment ... .

All the functions of church – the repentance by which we enter it, the Eucharist by which we commune with it, and the ministry by which we mutually empower it – are simply expressions of entering and developing a true human community of mutual love. The greatest possible distortion of church is to identify it with an ecclesiastical superstructure that distorts our true nature and has been created by competitive and oppressive hierarchicalism. The whole concept of ministry as an ordained caste, possessing powers ontologically above nature and beyond the reach of the people, must be rejected. Instead, ministry must be understood as the means by which the community itself symbolizes its common life to itself and articulates different aspects of its need to empower and express that common life.

If we understand clericalism as the expropriation of ministry, sacramental life, and theological education from the people, then women-church – and indeed all base Christian communities – are engaged in a revolutionary act of reappropriating to the people what has been falsely expropriated from us. We are reclaiming sacramental life as the symbol of our own entry into and mutual empowerment within the redemptive life, the authentic human life or original blessing upon which we stand naturally when freed from alienating powers. Theological education and teaching are our own reflections on the meaning of reclaiming our authentic life from distortion. Ministry is the active praxis of our authentic life and the building of alternative bases of expression from which to challenge the systems of evil.

We should then think of our baptism as the process of *metanoia* or turning around by which we see through the ideologies of alienated life and get in touch with the original blessing, which is the true ground of our being. This turning around may be experienced as such a gradual process that one has no sense of when it began, or it may be experienced as such a decisive breakthrough that one can date the day and the hour when new perception dawned. But the argument among Christians as to whether it is a decisive event or a gradual and ongoing process is a false one. It is both event and process. As long as the powers and principalities of alienated life are still in place in the world, it must necessarily be an ongoing and unended process.

Because true human life is communal, and not one of isolated individuals, this *metanoia* is appropriately expressed by entering into a community that affirms authentic life as the principle of our common humanity together. Needless to say, many people today, who have some intimations of this process of conversion, are searching for a community that represents the communal dimension of this life. But they are unable to find such a community, except perhaps in supportive affinity groups. Many lack even this community base and thus hover on the edge of thinking themselves unacceptable or mad.

Most institutional churches not only fail to become communities that nurture liberated being, but they in fact disallow it. They instead represent the sacralization of inauthentic, oppressive systems of power. Thus for many people, the process of conversion, becomes also the process of leaving the church. This makes it all but impossible for many people who have left the church in the process of claiming their authentic humanity to recognize their process as conversion. Indeed, without a community that affirms redemptive life and names it as authentic humanity in communion with God/ess, such conversion remains truncated, lacking in a positive sense of newness of life.

The dismantling of clerical concepts of ministry and church organization might suggest an anarchism that rejects all leadership. Groups that reject patriarchal models of leadership often go through a pathological phase in which any talent or expertise is rejected and those who have such talents are sabotaged for exercising leadership. Confusion reigns in which nothing gets done because people cannot agree on delegating tasks. But once this phase is worked through, it becomes evident that dismantling clericalism does not do away with authentic leadership based on function and skills. This means that the community itself decides what expressions of liturgy, learning, and service it wishes to engage in as expressions of its growth in community life. It then becomes fairly easy to delegate various tasks to people who have the readiness to undertake these tasks.

A ministry of function, rather than of clerical caste, can allow the true plurality of the ministerial needs of the community to be defined and met. It can also draw on many people in the community who have a variety of skills or gifts and thus activate their gifts as ministries. Full community life needs a variety of enablers. Lumping all ministry into one ordained caste means that many of the community's needs go unmet, since no one person possesses all these skills and gifts. A congregation needs at a minimum: (a) liturgical creators: poets, artists, and choreographers who can bring forth in creative expression the community's symbolic life; (b) teachers who know the history of religious ideologies and their relationships to various social systems and can help the community critically reflect upon and reconstruct its inherited symbols; (c) administrators who are skilled at organizing and developing the material resources of the community; (d) community organizers who can critically analyze the different structures of social oppression and organize community power to make social change; (e) spiritual counselors who have deep wisdom in the inner life and its relationship to life with others in community, and who can be guides in this journey.

Every community that is engaged in a full community life should be engaged to some extent in each of these areas of liturgy, education, and theological reflection, organizing its own material and human resources, committing itself to some social praxis, and deepening its inner life. Communities need to find among their own members, or call into themselves, persons who have particular skills in these various areas. Such persons are designated as enablers or ministers in these various areas, but not in order to do these things for others, who will then simply passively consume their services. Rather, the function of the ministers is to be the helpers and teachers who equip the community itself to engage in these various activities.

One might say that the more the poets, artists, and choreographers liturgize, the more the teachers teach, the more the administrators plan, the more the community organizers generate effective action, and the more the spiritual directors deepen the inner journey, the more the whole community should feel empowered in these various capacities. Although no one need feel competent in all these areas, everyone should feel that they are learning to participate in these various spheres. Increasing numbers of the community members should be able to take leadership in one or more areas of the community's life. Thus it becomes more and more possible to rotate many roles, since many people feel somewhat competent in one or another area and are able to grow through exercising leadership in that area … .

The most important reason for designating one person to play a leadership role regularly for a certain period of time would be to symbolize the unity of the community. This may be an important reason to join leadership in liturgical and pastoral functions. But it should be understood that liturgical presidency does not mean that this person possesses a power to create redemptive life and mediate it to others, but rather that she or he sums up the redemptive life of the community in its symbolic unity. To closely associate several other members of the community on a rotating basis with this person, not only in distributing, but also in blessing the symbols of sacramental life, may be one way both to unify and to communalize this act … .

This summary of different aspects of community life – study, liturgy, social praxis … does not mean that every group that wishes to identify as engaged in liberation from patriarchy need put all these aspects together in one community. Those who wish to underline the dialectical relationship between women-church as an autonomous community and the historical church institution may choose to limit their participation in women-church to a study group or a worship group that accompanies their participation in another worship assembly. Such persons would also connect themselves with a local church or other structures of a particular historical institution and try to feed the ideas generated in the women-church study or worship group into gatherings of the historical church.

Other persons may focus on some particular social praxis, such as work in a battered women's shelter or a drop-in center for homeless women. This social ministry would then become central to their critical analysis of patriarchy and work for change. Some people working on projects might also join a feminist study group that is not made up of the same people as the social ministry, but that serves as a forum for reflection on this and other struggles for change. Some may also attend a feminist liturgy and/or a more traditional liturgy. In other words, instead of unifying all these activities in one community, richness may be found in experiencing them in a series of different communities, each of which links up with different, but perhaps overlapping, networks of people in a particular region who are working for social transformation.

... [W]hen speaking of different aspects of community, one speaks in an ideal way of church as one community where all these various aspects would flow from one coherent vision. But this demands a high level of intentionality that is both difficult and dangerous, although it can be rewarding as well. It is dangerous because the more a group brings together many aspects of its life into one system, the more tendencies it has toward close-minded sectarianism and the misuse of power. So communities should engage in careful reflection on each new step toward communalization to be sure that personal initiative and autonomy is safeguarded.

In actuality, in the present transitional and fragmented situation, most will probably choose a variety of communities. For some people it may actually seem better not to put all their eggs in one basket, but to express different aspects of their communal life and transformational vision through different groups, thus interacting with a diversity of networks that reach out in various directions ... .

8.10 JOSEPH RATZINGER: *A COMPANY IN CONSTANT RENEWAL* – 1990

The following selection[26] originated as an address Cardinal Ratzinger gave at the annual 'Meeting of Friendship among the Peoples', held in Rimini in 1990 and sponsored by *Communione e Liberazione*. In this address he attempts to explain why the church is so often discredited in the modern world. He decries futile approaches to church reform and then describes what he believes is the 'essence of true reform'.

DISSATISFACTION WITH THE CHURCH

It requires no great imagination to realize that the 'company' about which I am going to speak here means the Church. The word Church was probably avoided in the title because it immediately provokes defensive reactions in the vast majority of people today. We have already heard, they say to themselves, all too much about the Church, and more often than not what we have heard has not been encouraging. The word Church and the reality it stands for have been discredited. It seems that even constant reform can hardly do much to change this situation. Or is it just that so far no one has discovered the kind of reform that could make of the Church a company worth belonging to?

But let us pause for a moment to ask a question: Why does the Church incur such a dislike of so many men, even of believers, even of those who yesterday could be reckoned among the most faithful and who, despite their pain, probably still are today? The reasons are diverse, even contrary, depending on one's standpoint. Some are unhappy because the Church has conformed too much to the standards of the world; others are angry that she is still very far from doing so. Most people have trouble with the Church because she is an institution like many others, which as such restricts my freedom... .

Because the Church is not as our dreams picture her to be, a desperate attempt is undertaken to bring her into conformity with our wishes: to make her a place for every freedom, a space where we can move freed of our limits, an experiment in utopia, which, after all, must exist somewhere. Just as our aim in politics is to introduce at long last a better world, we think that we must establish – perhaps as a first step toward the political goal – a better Church: a Church full of humanity, pervaded by a spirit of brotherhood and large-minded creativity, a place of reconciliation of all and for all.

---

26. Ratzinger, Joseph, 'A Company in Constant Renewal', in *Called to Communion – Understanding the Church Today*, 133–56, San Francisco, Ignatius, 1996.

FUTILE REFORM

But how is this to happen? How can such reform succeed? Well, the response is, we are just beginning. This is often said with the naïve arrogance of the self-appointed enlightener who is convinced that previous generations did not get it right, or else were too fearful and unilluminated; we, on the other hand, supposedly now have the courage for the task and for the understanding to go with it. However much reactionaries and 'fundamentalists' may resist this noble project, it must begin in earnest.

For the first step, at least, there is a thoroughly obvious recipe. The Church is not a democracy. She has not yet – so it seems – integrated into her constitution that basic patrimony of rights and freedoms elaborated by the Enlightenment that has since then been acknowledged as the basic rule for the political organization of communities. It thus appears as the most normal thing in the world to make up for lost time, which means first establishing once and for all this basic patrimony of structures of freedom. We must move – it is maintained – from the paternalistic Church to the community Church; no one must any longer remain a passive receiver of the gift of Christian existence. Rather, all should be active agents of it. The Church must no longer be fitted over us from above like a ready-made garment; no, we 'make' the church ourselves, and do so in constantly new ways. It thus finally becomes 'our' Church, for which we are actively responsible. The passive yields to the active. The Church arises out of discussion, compromise and resolution. Debate brings out what can still be asked of people today, what can still be considered by common consent as faith or as ethical norms. New short formulas of faith are composed … .

But questions immediately arise concerning this work of reform, which in place of all hierarchical tutelage will at long last introduce democratic self-determination into the Church. Who actually has the right to make decisions? What is the basis of the decision-making process? …

But there is a general question that is more relevant to our problem. Everything that men make can also be undone again by others. Everything that has its origin in human likes can be disliked by others. Everything that one majority decides upon can be revoked by another majority. A church based on human resolutions becomes a merely human church. It is reduced to the level of the makeable, of the obvious, of opinion. Opinion replaces faith. And in fact, in the self-made formulas of faith of which I am acquainted, the meaning of the words 'I believe' never signifies anything beyond 'we opine'. Ultimately, the self-made church savors of the 'self', which always has a bitter taste to the other self and just as soon reveals its petty insignificance. A self-made church is reduced to the empirical domain and thus, precisely as a dream, comes to nothing.

THE ESSENCE OF TRUE REFORM

The maker is the opposite of the wonderer (*ammiratore*). He narrows the scope of reason and thus loses sight of the mystery. The more men themselves decide and do in the Church, the more cramped it becomes for us all. What is great and liberating about the church is not something self-made but the gift that is given to us all. This gift is not the product of our own will and intervention but precedes us and comes to meet us as the incomprehensible reality that is 'greater than our heart' (cf. 1 Jn 3:20). The reform that is needed at all times does not consist in constantly remodelling 'our' Church according to our taste, or in inventing her ourselves, but in ceaselessly clearing away our subsidiary constructions to let in the pure light that comes from above and that is also the dawning of pure freedom … .

Saint Bonaventure, explains the path by which man truly becomes himself with the help of the likeness of the sculptor. The sculptor, says the great Franciscan theologian, does not *make* anything, rather his work is '*ablatio*' – the removal of what is not really part of the sculpture. In this way, that is, by means of *ablatio*, the *nobilis forma* – the noble form – takes shape. In the same way, continues Bonaventure, man, in order that God's image may shine radiantly in him, must first and foremost receive the purification whereby the divine Sculptor frees him from that dross that conceals the authentic figure of his being, making him appear to be nothing more than a stone block, whereas the divine form dwells in him.

Rightly understood, this image contains the proto-typical model of Church reform. The Church will constantly have need of human constructions to help her speak and act in the era in which she finds herself. Ecclesiastical institutions and juridical organizations are not intrinsically evil; on the contrary, to a certain degree they are necessary and indispensable. But they become obsolete; they risk setting themselves up as the essence of the Church and thus prevent us from seeing through to what is truly essential. This is why they must always be dismantled again, like scaffolding that has outlived its necessity. Reform is ever-renewed *ablatio* – removal, whose purpose is to allow the *nobilis forma*, the countenance of the bride, and with it the bridegroom himself, the living Lord, to appear. Such *ablatio*, such 'negative theology', is a path to something wholly positive. This path alone allows the divine to penetrate and brings about '*congregatio*', which as both gathering and purification is that pure communion we all long for, where 'I' is no longer pitted against 'I' and self against self. Rather, the self-giving and self-abandonment that characterize love become the reciprocal reception of all that is good and pure. Thus, the word of the kindly father who reminds the jealous older son what the content of all freedom and the realization of utopia consist of becomes true for every man: 'All that is mine is yours' (Lk 15:31; cf. Jn 17:10).

True reform, then, is *ablatio* (removal), which as such becomes *congregatio* (gathering). Let us attempt to formulate this fundamental idea somewhat more concretely. In our initial approach we had said that we were contrasting the wonderer (*ammiratore*) to the maker and were deciding for the former. But what is the meaning of this contrast? The maker values his own activity above all. He thereby restricts his horizon to the realm of things that he can grasp and that can become the object of his making. Strictly speaking, he sees only objects. He has absolutely no capacity to perceive what is greater than he is, since such a reality would set a limit to his activity. He squeezes the world into the empirical realm; man is amputated. Man builds himself his own prison, against which he then noisily protests. True wonder, on the other hand, is a No to this confinement in empirical, this-worldly reality. It prepares man for the act of faith, which opens him to the horizon of the eternal and infinite. And only the unlimited is large enough for our nature and in accord with the call of our essential being. When this horizon disappears, every remaining freedom becomes too small, and all the liberations that may then be offered are a vapid substitute that never equals what has been lost. The primary, the fundamental *ablatio* that is needed for the Church is the act of faith itself, which breaks the barriers of finitude and thus creates the open space that reaches into the unlimited. Faith leads us into the 'broad places', as the Psalms put it (for example, Ps 31 [30]:9) ... .

The fundamental liberation that the Church can give us is to permit us to stand in the horizon of the eternal and to break out of the limits of our knowledge and capabilities. In every age, therefore, faith itself in its full magnitude and breadth is the essential reform that we need; it is in the light of faith that we must test the value of self-constructed organizations in the Church. This implies that the Church must be on the bridge of faith and must not – especially in her life as an inner-worldly association – become an end in herself. Nowadays the opinion surfaces occasionally even in ecclesiastical circles that a man is more Christian the more he is involved in Church activities. We have a kind of ecclesiastical occupational therapy; a committee, or at any rate some sort of activity in the Church, is sought for everyone. People – according to this way of thinking – must constantly be busy about the Church, or doing something to or in her. But a mirror that reflects itself is no longer a mirror; a window that no longer lets us see the wide open spaces outside, but gets in the way of the view, has lost its reason for being.

There can be people who are engaged uninterruptedly in the activities of Church associations and yet are not Christians. There can be people who simply live by word and sacrament alone and practice the love born of faith without ever having attended Church groups, without ever having concerned themselves with the novelties of ecclesiastical politics, without ever having taken part in synods and voted in them – and yet are true Christians. We need, not a more human, but a more divine Church; then she will also become truly human. And for this reason everything man-made in the Church must recognize its own purely ancillary character and leave the foreground to what truly matters.

The freedom that we rightly expect from and in the Church is not achieved by introducing the principle of majority. This freedom does not rest on the fact that as many as possible prevail against as few as possible. Its basis is rather that no one may impose his own will on the others, since all know themselves to be bound to the word and will of the One who is our Lord and our freedom.

In the Church the atmosphere becomes cramped and stifling when her officebearers forget that the sacrament is, not an allocation of power, but dispossession of myself for the sake of the one in whose 'persona' I am to speak and act. But when the ever-greater self-dispossession matches ever-greater responsibility, no one is the servant of another; there the Lord rules, and there it proves true that: 'The Lord is the Spirit. But where the Spirit of the Lord is, there is freedom' (2 Cor 3:17). The more administrative machinery we construct, be it the most modern, the less place there is for the Lord, and the less freedom there is.

It is my opinion that we ought to begin an unsparing examination of conscience on this point at all levels in the Church. On every level this would have real consequences and would be bound to bring about an *ablatio* that would allow the true inherent form to reemerge and could restore to us in a wholly new way the feeling of freedom and of being at home.

MORALITY, FORGIVENESS AND EXPIATION – THE PERSONAL CENTER OF REFORM

Before we proceed further, let us look back for a moment on our considerations up to this point. We have spoken of a double 'removal' (*ablatio*) – of a double act of liberation, which is a double act of purification and renewal. The first point of discussion was faith, which breaches the wall of finitude and opens up an unobstructed view into the broad spaces of eternity – not only the view, but also the way. For faith is not just cognition but action; it is not only a cleft in the wall but the saving hand that leads us forth out of the cave. We had drawn the conclusion that this implies for institutions: the essential basis of Church order constantly needs to be developed and applied concretely so that the Church's life can unfold in a particular period; but what we create for this purpose must never take the place of what is at the heart of the matter. For the Church, unlike an inner-worldly association, does not exist in order to keep us busy and to support *herself* but in order to break free into eternal life in all of us.

We must now make a further step and transpose the whole of this from the general and objective to the personal. For here, too, there is need of liberating 'removal'. Indeed, it is hardly the case that we always and immediately see in the other the 'noble form', the image of God that is inscribed in him. What first meets the eye is only the image of Adam, the image of man, who, though not totally corrupt, is nonetheless fallen. We see the crust of dust and filth that has overlaid the image. Thus, we all stand in need of the true sculptor who removes what distorts the image; we are in need of forgiveness, which is the heart of all true reform … .

When we read the New Testament attentively, we discover that there is nothing magical about forgiveness. But neither is it a fictitious forgetting, a refusal to accept the truth, but an entirely real process of change carried out by the sculptor. The removal of guilt truly *gets rid* of something; the proof that forgiveness has come in us is that penance springs up from us. Forgiveness is in this sense an active-passive event: the creative word of power that God speaks to us produces the pain of conversion and thus becomes an active self-transformation. Forgiveness and penance, grace and personal conversion are not contradictions but two sides of one and the same event. This fusion of activity and passivity expresses the essential form of human existence, for all of our creativity begins with our having been created, with our participation in God's creative activity.

Here we have reached a very central point: I believe that the core of the spiritual crisis of our time has its basis in the obscuration of the grace of forgiveness … . Morality retains its seriousness only where there is forgiveness – real forgiveness ensured by authority; otherwise it lapses back into the pure empty conditional. But true forgiveness exists only when the 'price', the 'equivalent value', is paid, when guilt is atoned by suffering, when there is expiation. The circular link between morality, forgiveness and expiation cannot be forced apart at any point; when one element is missing, everything else is ruined. Whether or not man can find redemption depends on the undivided existence of this circle. In the Torah, the five books of Moses, these three elements are knotted together inseparably, and it is therefore impossible to follow the Enlightenment in excising from this core of Old Testament canon an externally valid moral law, while consigning the rest to past history. This moralistic manner of giving the Old Testament relevance for today is bound to fail; it was already the pith of the heresy of Pelagius, who has more followers today than appears at first glance.

Jesus, on the other hand, fulfilled the *whole* law, not a portion of it, and thus renewed it from the ground up: he himself, who suffered the whole tale of guilt, is at once expiation and forgiveness and is therefore the only reliable and perennially valid basis of our morality. It is impossible to detach morality from Christology, because it is impossible to separate it from expiation and forgiveness.

In Christ, the whole law is fulfilled, and morality has thereby become a more concrete claim on us that it is now more possible to satisfy. From the core of faith, then, the way of renewal opens again and again for the individual, for the Church as a whole and for humanity ... .

QUESTIONS FOR DISCUSSION

1   Does the church today require *reform* or *reconstruction*?
2   How should the church go about renewing itself in the present age?
3   Who should dictate the form and type of reforms and new initiatives in the church?
4   How might Roman Catholics best discern the will of God and hence allow the work of the Spirit in bringing about renewal and reformation of the church?
5   Do you believe that the church is *always* in need of reform?
6   What areas and aspects of the Roman Catholic church today are most urgently in need of reform (if any)?
7   What other answers can be given to John O'Malley's questions: 'How are we to know what from the past can be changed? How is the present to deal with the past, and what legitimate hold does the past have on the present?'
8   Would another Council be the best way to reform the church for today and tomorrow? If so, who should participate and what preparatory procedures should proceed it?
9   How is dialogue best facilitated throughout the church and between the church and others beyond its confines?
10 What part should 'grass-roots' groups such as base communities and woman-church groups play in renewing and reforming the church?

FURTHER READING

DISCUSSION AND DEBATE

Basset, William W., 'Canon Law and Reform – An Agenda for a New Beginning', in *Toward Vatican III – The Work that Needs to Be Done*, David Tracy, Hans Küng and Johan Baptist Metz (eds), Dublin, Gill & Macmillan, 1978.

Bianchi, E. and Reuther, R.R., *A Democratic Catholic Church*, New York, Crossroads, 1992.

Collins, P., *Papal Power – Proposals for Change in the Earth's Third Millennium*, London, Fount, 1997.

The Cologne Declaration, 1989.

Drane, James F., *Authority and Institution – a Study in Church Crisis*, Milwaukee, Bruce, 1969.

Dulles, Avery, *The Reshaping of Catholicism*, London, Harper & Row, 1988.

Egan, Joseph F., *Restoration and Renewal*, Kansas, Sheed & Ward, 1995.

Fries, Heinrich, *Suffering from the Church – Renewal or Restoration?*, Collegeville, Liturgical Press, 1995.

Greeley, Andrew and Durkin, Mary, *How to Save the Catholic Church*, New York, Viking Press, 1984.

Hegy, Pierre M. (ed.), *The Church in the Nineties – Its Legacy, Its Future*, Collegeville, Liturgical Press, 1993.

Küng, Hans, *The Church – Maintained in Truth*, London, SCM, 1980.

Küng, Hans, *Reforming the Church Today – Keeping Hope Alive*, New York, Crossroad, 1990.

Laurentin, Rene, 'Vatican III – Elsewhere or Something Else? – What Does the Church Need?', in *Toward Vatican III – the Work that Needs to Be Done*, eds David Tracy, Hans Küng and Johan Baptist Metz, Dublin, Gill & Macmillan, 1978.

Rahner, Karl, 'Dialogue in the Church', in vol. 10 of *Theological Investigations*, 1973.

Rahner, Karl, 'Perspectives for the Future of the Church' in *Confrontations II*, vol. 12 of *Theological Investigations*, London, Burns & Oates, 1974.

Rahner, Karl, 'Concern for the Church', vol. 20 of *Theological Investigations*, London, DLT, 1981.

Ratzinger, Joseph, *The Ratzinger Report*, San Francisco, Ignatius, 1985.

Rausch, Thomas P., *Authority and Leadership in the Church – Past Directions and Future Possibilities*, Wilmington, M. Glazier, 1989.

Rosmini-Serbati, Antonio, *The Five Wounds of the Church*, Leominster, Fowler-Wright, 1987.

Siebel, Wigand, 'The Exercise of Power in Today's Church', in *Power in the Church*, James Provost and Knut Walf (eds), *Concilium*, 197 (1988).

Timms, Noel (ed.), *Diocesan Dispositions and Parish Voices in the Roman Catholic Church*, Chelmsford, Matthew James, 2001.

BIOGRAPHIES

Giuseppe Alberigo (b. 1926) was Professor of Church History at the university of Bologna (Italy). He is secretary of the Institute of Religious Sciences and editor of the quarterly *Cristianesimo nella Storia*. As editor of the *Conciliorum Oecumenicorum Decreta* he is a noted authority in this area. His many works include *La Réception de Vatican II* (Cerf, Paris, 1985, with J.-P. Jossua).

Paul Avis is an Anglican priest, sub-Dean of Exeter Cathedral, and General Secretary of the Council of Christian Unity. He is an Honorary Research Fellow in the Department of theology in the University of Exeter and Director of the Centre for the Study of the Christian Church. His many writings include *Faith in the Fires of Criticism* (London, DLT, 1995); *Divine Revelation* (ed.) (Grand Rapids, Eerdmans, 1997); *The Anglican Understanding of the Church* (London, SPCK, 2000) and *The Christian Church – an Introduction to the Major Traditions* (ed.) (London, SPCK, 2002). He also co-edits the *International Journal for the Study of the Christian Church*.

Hans Urs von Balthasar (1905–88), was born in Switzerland. He joined the Jesuits in 1929 but reluctantly parted company with them, in 1950, to devote himself to the experimental 'secular' order he had founded – the 'Community of St John'. During this time he was suspect in many church circles. Amongst his major influences were the *Nouvelle Théologie* movement, literature (his doctoral dissertation was on eschatology in modern German literature), the mystical disposition of the physician Adrienne von Speyr, Karl Barth (on whose theology he wrote a definitive textbook, in 1951) and the church itself. He believed that grace was ever present to humanity and he constructed an eclectic and deeply contemplative theology. Clashes with his fellow theologians, most notably Hans Küng and Karl Rahner, along with Pope John Paul II's personal endorsement of his theology, led to Balthasar being labelled a conservative. Although he helped to found the more conservative journal, *Communio*, in 1972, his life and work are more complex than the label 'conservative' can do justice to. However, much of his work can be seen as a reaction to a perceived 'liberal-radical' accommodation of the church and faith to secular culture following Vatican II. Amongst a multitude of publications, his most noteworthy are the multi-volume trilogy: theological logic, *Theologik*, his theological dramatics, *Theodramatik*, and a theological aesthetics, *The Glory of the Lord* (*Herrlichkeit*), all published between 1961 and 1987.

Leonardo Boff (b. 1938) has been one of the leading advocates for a theology of liberation in the Catholic church. Formerly a Franciscan priest, Boff studied theology in Western Europe. He would go on to teach theology in Brazil where he sought to develop an ecclesiology and Christology within a liberationist perspective. Because of controversies instigated by his 1981 book, *Church, Charism and Power*, Boff was investigated by the Congregation for the Doctrine of the Faith was ordered to submit to a year of 'obedient silence'. Finally, frustrated by the Vatican's continued attack on his views, he left the Franciscan order. He is currently working in Brazil as an advocate for the poor and a critic of the horrific consequences of economic globalization for the poor and the environment. His many works include *Jesus Christ Liberator* (New York, Orbis, 1979); *Liberation Theology – from Dialogue to Confrontation* (with his brother, Clodovis, San Francisco, Harper & Row, 1986); *Trinity & Society* (Tunbridge Wells, Burns & Oates, 1988); *Faith on the Edge – Religion and Marginalised Existence*, (San Francisco, Harper & Row, 1989) and *Good News to the Poor – a New Evangelisation* (Tunbridge Wells, Burns & Oates, 1992).

John P. Boyle is a diocesan priest and Professor Emeritus of Religion at the University of Iowa. A noted moral theologian, he has published *The Sterilization Controversy – a New Crisis for the Catholic Hospital* (New York, Paulist, 1995 and *Church Teaching Authority – Historical and Theological Studies* (Notre Dame, University of Notre Dame Press, 1995). Boyle is a past president of the Catholic Theological Society of America.

Giovanni Colombo, Cardinal (1902–1992) was the Titular Bishop of Vittoriana, and the President of the Theological Faculty of Milan. Msgr Colombo, as he then was, had been a member of the preparatory Theological Commission of Vatican II and the sub-commission *De Ecclesia*. He was the theological adviser to Cardinal Montini of Milan (later Paul VI). Together with G. Philips, theological adviser to Cardinal Suenens and Professor at Louvain, Colombo worked on the draft of *De episcopis* which led to *De Ecclesia*. Colombo was a most active supporter of Bishop (later Cardinal) Suenens in the preliminary processes leading up to the Council, and was prominent in Council debates. He was favourably disposed towards the views of Congar on the laity.

George-Yves Congar (1904–95) entered the Dominican Order in 1925 and was, in many ways, the founder of modern Catholic ecumenism. Often associated with the nouvelle théologie movement, Congar made immense contributions to the flourishing of Catholic ecclesiological studies in the decades prior to Vatican II. He studied at Le Saulchoir (Belgium) where he was encouraged by M.-D. Chenu, to study J.A. Möhler, the nineteenth-century German ecclesiologist, and to write a thesis on the unity of the Church. Congar's approach to ecumenism was forged through contact with the other traditions of Christianity, some of it stimulated by a period as a prisoner of war in Colditz where the hostility of non-Catholics to the Catholic church sharpened his desire to bring about change. Suspicion of 'false ecumenism' led to his suspension from teaching in 1954, and periods in Jerusalem and Cambridge before moving to Strasbourg. The election of Pope John XXIII in 1958 changed the situation. Congar became theological consultor to the preliminary commission of Vatican II and influential on the text of such documents as *Dei Verbum, Lumen Gentium, Gaudium et Spes* and *Unitatis Redintegratio*. His theology focused on a return to the source of the gospel as a means of getting behind subsequent divisions. Unity could thereby be recovered, true catholicity enjoyed, the wholeness of lay participation realized, and the mission of the church prosper. Indeed, he was arguably the singlemost influential *peritus* at the council. He was made a cardinal in 1994, in recognition of his outstanding contributions to the church, having previously been a founder member of the Pontifical Theological Commission and a participant in the Catholic-Lutheran Commission of dialogue. His many writings include *Divided Christendom* (London, Geoffrey Bles, 1939), *Tradition and Traditions* (London,

Burns & Oates, 1966), *I Believe in the Holy Spirit* (3 vols, London, Geoffrey Chapman, 1983), *True and False Reform in the Church* (Paris, Du Cerf, 1968) and *Lay People in the Church*, (London, Bloomsbury, 1957).

Avery Dulles (b. 1918) is currently the Laurence J. McGinley Professor of Religion and Society at Fordham University. On 21 February 2001 Dulles was created cardinal by Pope John Paul II. He is one of the American Catholic Church's most respected and prolific theologians. He is a past member of the International Theological Commission and past president of the Catholic Theological Society of America. Dulles has been an active participant in numerous national and international ecumenical dialogues and was the 1970 recipient of the Cardinal Spellman Award for theology. Some of his major works include *Models of the Church* (Dublin, Gill & Macmillan, 1988), *Models of Revelation* (Dublin, Gill & Macmillan, 1992), *The Craft of Theology* (Dublin, Gill & Macmillan, 1982) and *The Assurance of Things Hoped For* (New York, Oxford University Press, 1994).

Christian Duquoc OP (b. 1926) became Professor of Dogmatic Theology in the Theology Faculty in Lyon, France, after having studied in Le Saulchoir (France), Fribourg (Switzerland) and at the Ecole Biblique in Jerusalem. He is a member of the editorial board of *Lumière et Vie*. Among his many publications are *Christologie* (2 vols, Paris, Du Cerf, 1972) and *Provisional Churches – an Essay in Ecumenical Ecclesiology* (London, SCM, 1986).

Elisabeth Schüssler Fiorenza (b. 1938) is currently Krister Stendahl Professor of New Testament Studies at Harvard Divinity School. She specialises in biblical interpretation and feminist theology and feminist studies in religion. She has taught at the University of Notre Dame, Episcopal Divinity School, Union Theological Seminary, the Humboldt University in Berlin and the universities of Tübingen and Heidelberg. Her main areas of particular interest include issues in hermeneutics, epistemology, equality, democracy and the politics of interpretation. A co-founder of the *Journal of Feminist Studies in Religion*, her many publications include *In Memory of Her* (London, SCM, 1983), *But She Said* (Boston, Beacon, 1992), *Discipleship of Equals* (London, SCM, 1994), *The Power of Naming* (ed.) (London, SCM, 1996) and *Rhetoric and Ethic* (Minneapolis, Fortress, 1999).

Patrick Granfield, OSB, is a Benedictine theologian and Professor of Theology at the Catholic University of America. He is a past president of the Catholic Theological Society of America, the 1989 recipient of the John Courtney Murray Award and a leading American ecclesiologist and expert on the papacy. His principal theological works include *Ecclesial Cybernetics* (New York, Macmillan, 1973), *The Papacy in Transition* (New York, Doubleday, 1980) and *The Limits of the Papacy* (New York, Crossroad, 1997).

Roger Haight, SJ (b. 1936) is Professor of Systematic Theology at the Western Jesuit School of Theology, Cambridge, Massachusetts, in the USA. His books include *The Experience and Language of Grace* (New York, Paulist, 1979), *Dynamics of Theology* (New York, Paulist, 1990), *An Alternative Vision – an Interpretation of Liberation Theology* (New York, Paulist, 1985) and *Jesus – Symbol of God* (New York, Orbis, 1999).

Linda Hogan (b. 1964) studied theology at Maynooth and Trinity College, Dublin in the Republic of Ireland, completing her doctorate under the supervision of Enda McDonagh. She has taught at Chester, the University of Leeds and, currently, at the Irish School of Ecumenics. Her main work focuses upon issues in ethics and feminist theology and, in particular, epistemological issues in relation to the latter. Her publications include *From Women's Experience to Feminist Theology* (Sheffield, Sheffield Academic Press, 1995), *Human Rights* (Dublin, Trócaire/Veritas, 2000) and *Confronting the Truth – Conscience in the Catholic Tradition* (New York, Paulist, 2000/London, DLT, 2001).

Peter Huizing, SJ, (1911–95) was, after studies in Amsterdam, Louvain and Rome, Professor of Canon Law at the University of Nijmegen and at the Gregorian University in Rome. He was a consultor of the pontifical commission for the revision of the Code of Canon Law. He has published several books and many articles in *Periodica, Concilium, The Jurist, Gregorianum*, etc.

John Paul II, Karol Wojtyla (b. 1920), became, in 1978, both the first Slav and non-Italian pope for four centuries. He adopted the title 'Universal Pastor of the Church', declined to have a coronation ceremony and pledged to see Vatican II through to its full implementation. His encyclicals bear the hallmarks of his background – under the totalitarian regimes of the Nazis then the communists, he developed a philosophical and theological outlook that has been described as a Christian humanism or personalism. His calls for a new economic way between capitalism and Marxist communism would prove to be pre-emptive of later developments in world politics, at least in terms of political ideology, if not practice. A relentless traveller, his social progressiveness and earlier philosophical dynamism became matched in intensity by a theological conservatism. He has vociferously upheld church opposition to many things such as artificial birth control, priestly celibacy and the ordination of women.

Under John Paul II, the church has become still more centralized in authority and governance, with dissent little tolerated and outspoken theologians, philosophers and church people often harshly rebuked. During his pontificate, the 'official' church has condemned many progressive movements (e.g., liberation theology, 'We Are Church') for aspects of their calls for ecclesial and societal reform. Yet conservative and right-wing movements (e.g., Opus Dei, 'Communion and Liberation', Focolare) have been actively encouraged and positively facilitated. Many have struggled to unravel the paradoxes that embrace a radical commitment to social justice, combined with a most authoritarian rule of the church from Rome. This pope regarded the downfall of the old 'pseudo-communist' Eastern European states as a major triumph for the church, yet, elsewhere, he has forbidden priests to engage actively in politics. He vociferously defends human rights and yet some of his curial departments have been accused of flagrant breaches of the rights of church members accused of dissent and error. In the early years of his reign, ecumenism flourished, but in more recent times, it has stalled, despite the pope inviting dialogue on the future nature of the papacy and his primacy. Statements on numerous topics, such as theological enquiry, inter-faith questions, and lay ministry have similarly become more and more conservative in outlook. Yet, with a fervent energy, he prepared the church for a new millennium calling all to renewal and forgiveness. He apologized for many of the past failings and wrongs of those in the church.

Critics point to a 'betrayal' of Vatican II, others wonder how much John Paul is a 'prisoner' of the Vatican and curial system. He was a great pastor and churchman in Poland

and initially transferred this personal devotion to the faithful onto the world stage. But, in recent years, many Catholics have become increasingly ambivalent towards this long serving pontiff.

Ludwig Kaufmann, SJ (1918–91) was a Swiss publisher who studied in Italy, England, Germany and France. For many years he was the editor of the bi-monthly *Orientierung* (Zürich). He has written books on the Holy Land, on Pope John XXIII and on Charles de Foucauld. He was one of the best-informed reporters of the Second Vatican Council and of many Roman Synods.

Wilfred Laurence Knox (1886–1950). The son of an evangelical bishop of Manchester, he was educated at Rugby, Trinity and Oxford. He served at the Trinity Mission, Stratford, took a vow of poverty and was ordained in 1915. Influenced by socialism, he joined a group of unmarried Anglican priests who had founded the Oratory of the Good Shepherd in Cambridge, in 1920. Its first profession of full members was in 1919. Focused upon prayer, study and the spiritual life it was very influential in the Anglo-Catholic tradition. Aside from a brief service at Hoxton (1922–24), he remained at their oratory until his death, serving as Superior from 1941. He was a member of the Cambridge New Testament Seminar, and author of several books in that field. He was made a Canon of Ely Cathedral (though scarcely audible!) and served on the Church of England's doctrine commission (expressing decidedly liberal opinions concerning birth control). The Second World War brought him a crisis of faith.

In 1926, a group of distinguished Anglo-Catholics scholars published an influential collection entitled *Essays Catholic and Critical* (London, SPCK). In it the contributors attempted to reconcile contemporary scholarship and traditional faith. Knox contributed the article on authority. Amongst his other works is (along with Alec Vidler) *The Development of Modern Catholicism* (London, Philip Allan, 1933).

Hans Küng, born in Switzerland (in 1928), was ordained a priest in 1954. Following doctoral research in Paris (1957), he spent two years working in a large parish in Lucerne. In 1960, he took up a chair in Theology at Tübingen, Germany, becoming Professor of Dogmatic and Ecumenical Theology, there, in 1963. A special adviser (peritus) at the Second Vatican Council, his ecclesiological works soon began to attract the investigative attention of the Vatican's *Congregation for the Doctrine of the Faith* (*CDF*). In particular, his books, *The Church* (1967, ET, London, Search, 1968)) and *Infallible? An Inquiry* (1971, ET, rev. edn, London, SCM, 1994), aroused questions concerning his 'orthodoxy'. Over the years, he has continued to teach and conduct research on a variety of subjects, from Christian faith and life to dialogue with world religions; from the philosophical question of God's existence, to the possibility of a 'global ethic'. Nonetheless, ecclesiology and church reform have never been far from his mind. His uneasy relations with the Vatican came to a head when he published a short text, *The Church – Maintained in Truth*, in 1979 (ET, London, SCM, 1980). In it he extolled the virtues of a teaching authority of the church which could admit it was fallible and live and learn by its failings. The CDF issued a declaration on 18 December that same year, stating that the book proved Küng had 'departed from the integral truth of the Catholic Faith' and went on to assert that Küng could no longer be considered a Catholic Theologian, nor function as one in his teaching. Much controversy followed and many theologians rallied to

Küng's defence. Suffice to say, Küng has tried to remain faithful to his principles and has continued to speak out against what he considers to be the Curial authorities' betrayal of the hope of Vatican II in the decades since that council.

Karl Lehmann (b. 1936) is the bishop of Mainz, Germany. A former Professor of Theology at the universities of Mainz and Freiburg and author of many publications, he is the several times re-elected chairman of the German bishops' conference. He was often faced with the protests of people demanding more say in church affairs. In agreement with the vote of the famous German national synod (1972–75), he attempted to combine the drive for greater ecclesial participation with the tradition of a hierarchical church. Likewise, he strived to keep his faithful together and in communion with the whole Church. This led to a qualified acceptance of a certain process of democratization within the Church.

Alfred Loisy (1857–1940), was ordained priest in 1879. After a short period as a country curé and further periods of study encouraged by Louis Duchesne, he was appointed Professor of Sacred Scripture at the Institut Catholique at Paris, in 1890. His views caused serious anxiety and he was dismissed in 1893. He was stimulated (and provoked), on reading Adolf Harnack's *What is Christianity* (1900), to reflect upon the nature of the Catholic church, publishing the results of his work in *The Gospel and the Church* in 1902 (ET, London, Isbister, 1903). The response was hostile and confused, though despite local condemnation (for example from the Archbishop of Paris) the Papacy did not take any action. However, on the succession of Pius X, the volume was placed on the Index in 1904. Loisy resigned his priestly responsibilities in 1906. After the condemnation of Modernism by Pius X in the decree *Lamentabili* and the encyclical *Pascendi* in 1907, Loisy sought other work and became Professor of the History of Religions at the College de France, a post he held until 1930. He continued to write extensively on Christian origins though none of his subsequent publications had the dynamic impact of *The Gospel and the Church*.

John L. McKenzie, SJ (1910–91), was born in Indiana, USA, and became a Jesuit in 1928, leaving the Society after disagreeing with its attitude to those members who were pacifist and opposed to the Vietnam War. He was a leading biblical scholar whose major achievement was an ability to discuss sensitive issues and stimulate scholarship when Church authority was not sympathetic. He published an influential *Dictionary of the Bible* (Milwaukee, Bruce, 1965). He taught at Loyola, Notre Dame and De Paul whence he retired in 1979. He was a President of the Catholic Biblical Association and the Society of Biblical Literature.

Alvaro Quiroz Magaña, SJ (b. 1942) is a native of Guadalajara, Mexico and currently Professor of Ecclesiology at the Theological Institute in Mexico City. After studying theology and philosophy in Mexico, he gained his doctorate from the University of Barcelona. He is the author of many publications, including his contribution to the monumental study, *Mysterium Liberationis*, eds. Ignacio Ellacuria and Jon Sobrino (New York, Orbis, 1993).

Johann Baptist Metz (b. 1928) is a foremost political theologian, and actually credited with coining the term 'political theology', itself. He was Professor of Catholic Theology and Director of the Institute of Fundamental Theology in the University of Münster between 1963 and 1993. He also held a position in the Centre for Interdisciplinary Study at the University of Bielefeld. His thinking has been much influenced by (though also critical of) the thoughts of Karl Rahner with whom he wrote *Courage to Pray* (London, Burns & Oates, 1980). Other collaborative works include *Religion and Political Society* (with J. Moltmann, London, SCM, 1995) and *Towards Vatican III* (with D. Tracy and H. Küng, Dublin, Gill & Macmillan, 1978). His other major studies include: *The Church in the World*, (New York, Paulist, 1965) and *Faith in History and Society* (London, Burns & Oates, 1980).

Charles M. Murphy, teaches at St John's Seminary, Brighton, Massachusetts. He is the author of *At Home on Earth – Foundations for a Catholic Ethic of the Environment* (New York, Crossroad, 1989) and *Wallace Stevens – a Spiritual Poet in a Secular Age* (New York, Paulist, 1997).

John Henry Newman (1801–90). As an Anglican, Newman was a noted scholar, particularly at home in the world of the Fathers of the Church, as well as in church history. Before the end of 1841 he began to turn his thoughts to the problem of the development of doctrine. On 9 October 1845 he was received in the Roman Catholic church. Much of his later writing has been deemed to be prophetic in its insightfulness with regard to the direction the church should take in the modern world. His many sermons are pearls and his style of prose majestic. A standard work on Newman has been written by Ian Ker, *John Henry Newman – a Biography*, (Oxford, 1988). There are numerous editions of his works, including the famous *Essay on the Development of Christian Doctrine* (1845), *Apologia Pro Vita Sua* (1869) and *An Essay in Aid of a Grammar of Assent* (1870).

John W. O'Malley SJ (b. 1927) is a Professor of Church History at the Weston Jesuit School of Theology. A noted church historian, O'Malley's publications include *Trent and All That – Renaming Catholicism in the Early Modern Era* (Cambridge, MA, Harvard University Press, 2000), *The First Jesuits* (Cambridge, MA, Harvard University Press, 1993) *Catholicism in Early Modern History* (St. Louis, Center for Reformation Research, 1988) and *Tradition and Transition – Historical Perspectives on Vatican II* (Wilmington, Michael Glazier, 1989).

Ladislas Orsy was born in Hungary (in 1921). He is a theologian and trained canon lawyer who has written prolifically on the ecclesiological consequences of the teaching of the Second Vatican Council. He holds a degree in canon law from the Gregorian University in Rome, a degree in civil law from Oxford University and he pursued advanced theological studies at Louvain University. He is the 1999 recipient of the John Courtney Murray Award and is currently on the Law School faculty of Georgetown University. The author of many books and articles, some of Orsy's more significant works include: *Open to the Spirit – Religious Life after Vatican II* (London, G. Chapman, 1968) and *The Church – Learning and Teaching* (Wilmington, Glazier, 1987). He is a regular contributor to the weekly, *America*.

Paul VI, Giovanni Battista Montini (b. 1897), was pope from 1963 to 1978. He had a famed passion for books and disliked much of the pomp that surrounded his office – selling the papal tiara and giving the proceeds to the poor. Whilst Archbishop of Milan, his social views and policies earned him the nickname of 'the Workers' Archbishop'. His many travels, including to the Holy Land (1965) and Fatima (1967) earned him a further popular title, that of 'the Pilgrim Pope'. He embraced ecumenism, and engaged in important discussions and gestures aimed at promoting greater unity. He was strong on issues of social justice and came to advocate greater ecclesial participation by the laity. He had helped in the preparation for

Vatican II and was to see it through to its close, himself. However, many would later say that he did not do enough to see the council's decisions through to their full *implementation*.

Viewed as a forward-looking moderate on many issues, he could also lean towards or succumb to the influence of the conservative wing of the church on other issues and this is particularly evident in some of his encyclicals. He ignited a period of fierce controversy and discord throughout the church when he released *Humane Vitae* (1968), which upheld the ban on all forms of artificial contraception. This was despite the majority of the pontifical commission on the subject recommending that, in certain cases, such contraception should be permitted. He established many new consultative bodies in the church to deal with issues such as ecumenism, inter-faith dialogue, theology, justice and peace and also the Synod of Bishops. In truth, he faced opposition from all sides of the church and the later years of his papacy lacked much of the fervour of his earlier ones.

Pius IX, Giovanni Mastai-Ferretti (b. 1792), was pope from 1846 to 1878 – longer than any other pope in history. Initially open to new ideas, the political events which swept Europe during the early years of his pontificate meant that his outlook swiftly became very reactionary and of conservative inclination. Under him, power and authority in the church would become centralized upon Rome to a degree which increased in inverse proportion to the decline of the Papacy's temporal power (not least of all with the loss of the Papal States and the unification of Italy). His was the first papacy around which a 'personality cult' developed, his image being honoured in many Italian homes. He greatly encouraged personal piety and devotion, notably to the Sacred Heart and Mary. In 1854, the church promulgated the dogma of the Immaculate Conception of Mary. In terms of modern thought and politics, Pius and his advisers ensured that the church virtually turned its back upon all things 'liberal' in terms of innovative schools of thought, political ideologies and even such notions as the freedom of the press and democracy itself.

This outlook was transferred into ecclesial policy in his encyclical, *Quanta Cura* and its attendant 'Syllabus of Errors' (1864), which listed certain propositions, views and schools of thought deemed to be incompatible with faithful adherence to the Catholic faith. The number of texts placed upon the 'Index of Forbidden Books', greatly increased. The First Vatican Council (1869–70) sealed the character of his papacy – along with church authority and governance for many decades to come. Its constitution, *Pastor Aeternus* (1870), enshrined the doctrine of papal infallibility in relation to those occasions when the pope, himself, speaks definitively and *ex cathedra* on matters of faith and morals. This marked the definitive triumph of the 'ultramontane' ('over the mountains', i.e., always looking towards Rome) faction in the church. Many split from the church as a result; others were severely admonished for outspoken opposition. Many secular powers actively began to oppose and obstruct the church and its members in their territories. Yet the church flourished in other respects under Pius. The creation of many new dioceses, its consolidation in the so-called 'new world' and positive developments in spirituality bear witness to this. For many, the centralization gave the church and grass-roots faithful a strong and guiding focal point in uncertain times. For others, the church had adapted an outlook which cut it off from many of the most fundamental cultural and political developments in the world for decades to come. He was beatified in 2000.

Pius X, Giuseppe Melchiorre Sarto (b. 1835), was pope from 1903 to 1914, his motto being 'to restore all things in Christ'. His pontificate was marked by a firm refusal to engage in ecclesial, theological or political compromise. He acted against socialist and left-wing developments and approved of groups such as the right-wing 'Action Française'. He reorganized the Roman Curia, set in motion the revision of Canon Law and introduced measures aimed at improving the moral and spiritual comport of the clergy. Pius also encouraged lay movements (later to be known as 'Catholic Action', when they were under the control of the hierarchy). He was also noted for encouraging greater piety and devotion, such as the frequent reception of the Eucharist, along with many liturgical reforms. Remembered chiefly as the arch-conservative who presided over the stern backlash against all forms of 'modernism' in the church, he was also known for his personal holiness. He was canonized in 1954.

Pius XII, Eugenio Maria Giuseppe Giovanni Pacelli, (b. 1876) was pope from 1939 to 1958. An accomplished linguist and diplomat, he was Vatican secretary of state when elected to the see of Rome. He led the church through the extremely challenging years of the Second World War, constantly calling for peace and helping to initiate and support much relief work (especially through the Pontifical Aid Commission). He allowed the Vatican to be used as a refuge when Hitler occupied Rome, particularly for Jewish people. Nonetheless, there continues to be much debate surrounding the *level* of his *active* involvement and *outspokenness* in opposing the Nazi persecution of the Jewish people. He further centralized ecclesial authority upon Rome and instituted the dogma of the Assumption of the Blessed Virgin Mary in 1950. He opposed certain innovations in theology, philosophy and science, though allowed a greater degree of freedom in biblical studies than had hitherto been permitted. He allowed that the church should recognize the ecumenical movement, though was wary of the process. He created many new dioceses and installed indigenous bishops in Asia and Africa. His increasingly tight grip upon the reigns of power in the church led to a decline in his stature within the church, although many non-catholics held him in high esteem.

Hermann J. Pottmeyer (b. 1934) is Professor Emeritus of Fundamental Theology at the Ruhr-Universität, Bochum. He is currently a member of the International Theological Commission and an internationally respected expert in Catholic ecclesiology. In 1991 he received the Johannes Quasten Award from the Catholic University of America and was given an honorary doctorate of theology by the Pontifical Theological Academy in Krakow, Poland in 1998. Among his many published books and articles is his seminal study of Vatican I, *Unfehlbarkeit und Souveränität* (Mainz, Grünewald, 1975).

Archbishop John R. Quinn (b. 1929) now retired, served as the archbishop of San Francisco and was past president of the National Conference of Catholic Bishops. His 1996 lecture at Campion Hall, Oxford, inspired great debate throughout the church. It was later published in *The Reform of the Papacy – the Costly Call to Christian Unity* (New York, Crossroad, 1999).

Karl Rahner (1904–84) joined the Jesuit Order in 1922. Brought up on a typical seminary version of traditional Catholic theology (which he dubbed 'school theology'), Rahner was anxious to change direction. Academic theology was not studied for its own sake, but for the service which it could render to the life of the faithful and the Church's mission. His prodigious output bears testimony to his vast erudition and pastoral sensitivity. It includes 23 volumes (in English translation) of essays published under the title *Theological Investigations* (London, DLT, 1961–92), four editions of the *Enchiridion Symbolorum*, the editing (with Adolf Darlap) of *Sacramentum Mundi* (6 vols, London, Burns & Oates, 1967-69), the influential *Concise Theological Dictionary* (Freiburg, Herder, 1965) and he was a founding father of the international theological journal *Concilium*.

One of the most distinguished Catholic theologians of the twentieth century, Rahner established what was tantamount to a new theological foundation for Catholic theology by developing Thomism's conversation with the thought of such modern philosophical figures as Kant and Heidegger. A faithful Jesuit inspired by Ignatius Loyola's exhortation to 'find God in all things', Rahner developed a rich theology of the universality of grace and the church as itself a sacramental sign of that grace. Rahner was a very influential *peritus* at Vatican II, leaving his mark on the council's treatment of the church and its relationship to the world, a theology of revelation and the universality of God's saving offer.

He fell out of favour with the Curial authorities because of his commitment to theological renewal, especially because of the apparent attitude to tradition and the development of doctrine in an unpublished paper which he wrote consequent upon the publication by Pius XII in 1950 of the Dogma of the Immaculate Conception. The pontificate of John XXIII changed the scene when he became private adviser to Cardinal König of Vienna on Council documents in the period leading up to the Council. Very soon after the Council began, Rahner became one of the official periti. In this position he substantially influenced *Lumen Gentium*, *Dei Verbum* and *Gaudium et Spes*, amongst others. He was professor in Munich from 1964, succeeding to Münster in 1967, retiring to write and lecture in 1971.

Joseph Ratzinger (b. 1927), as a gifted young theologian, taught at universities in Bonn, Münster, Tübingen and Regensburg from 1959 to 1977. Many of his most important ecclesiological insights during this period are found in his major work, *Das neue Volk Gottes – Entwürfe zur Ekklesiologie*, published in 1969 (Dusseldorf). He was a *peritus* to Cardinal Joseph Frings of Cologne during the final three sessions of Vatican II and was himself made archbishop of Munich in 1977. In 1981 Pope John Paul II appointed him as the prefect for the CDF. During his tenure as prefect Ratzinger has continued to publish and speak extensively on theological issues concerning the church. He chairs the Pontifical Biblical Commission and the International Theological Commission. His many other works include *The Ratzinger Report* (San Francisco, Ignatius, 1985), *Church, Ecumenism and Politics* (Slough, St Paul's, 1988) and *Called to Communion – Understanding the Church Today* (San Francisco: Ignatius Press, 1996).

Thomas P. Rausch, SJ (b. 1941) is the T. Marie Chiltern Professor of Catholic Theology at Loyola Marymount University, Los Angeles, and has specialized in the area of ecumenism. From 1983 to 1984 he was appointed by the Secretariat for Christian Unity as Catholic Tutor to the Ecumenical Institute at the World Council of Churches study centre at Bossey, Switzerland. He was rector of the Jesuit community at Loyola Marymount from 1988 to 1994. He was appointed to the US Catholic/Southern Baptist Conversation in 1994 and was one of the signatories of the Richard John Neuhaus/Charles Colson Evangelicals and Catholics Together 1997 document, 'The Gift of Salvation'. He is a member of the Theological Commission and the Ecumenical Commission of the Archdiocese of Los Angeles, and is also a member of the Editorial Commission for *The Tidings*. He serves as co-chair of the Los Angeles Catholic-Evangelical Committee. Among his many publications are *The Roots of the Catholic Tradition* (Wilmington, Michael Glazier, 1986), *Authority and Leadership in the Church: Past Directions and Future Possibilities* (Wilmington, Michael Glazier, 1989), *Radical Christian Communities* (Collegeville, Liturgical Press, 1990) and *Catholicism at the Dawn of the Third Millennium* (Collegeville, Liturgical Press, 1996).

Marc Reuver was born in Holland, in 1926, and studied philosophy, theology and church history. Previously, he served as the Director of the Centre IDOC (the International Documentation Centre in Rome) and later as theological consultant to the World Council of Churches on Roman Catholic affairs. His many books and articles have included studies of human rights and peace issues; church–state relations and ecumenical issues. His recent books include *Requiem for Constantine* (Kampen, Kok, 1996), *Faith and Law – Juridical Perspectives for the Ecumenical Movement*, (Geneva, WCC Publications, 2000) and the forthcoming *Letters on Christian Spirituality*.

Herwi Rikhof (b. 1948) is Professor of Systematic Theology at the Catholic University of Utrecht. Following studies in Utrecht and Oxford, he became a university lecturer in dogmatics at the Theological Faculty of the Catholic University in Nijmegen (The Netherlands). He is the President of the Dutch ecumenical organization of dogmatic theologians – *Christian Articles of Faith* (XART) – and the President of the Thomas Institut, dedicated to the study of Aquinas. He has published widely on the interpretation of Vatican II, and is the author of *The Concept of Church* (London, Sheed & Ward, 1981) and *Over God spreken. Een tekst van Thomas van Aquino uit de Summa Theologiae (I, Q. 13)* (Delft, Meinema, 1988).

Rosemary Radford Ruether (b. 1936) is the Georgia Harkness Professor of Applied Theology at Garrett Theological Seminary and is a member of the Graduate Faculty of Northwestern University in Evanston, Illinois. Originally trained in the field of patristics, Ruether has become one of the most prolific advocates of feminist theology. She has authored or edited 32 books and numerous articles and has received 11 honorary doctorates in recognition of her significant contributions to feminist thought. She writes a regular column for both the *National Catholic Reporter* and *Sojourners* and is a board member of Catholics for a Free Choice. Amongst her many publications are *Sexism and God-Talk* (London, SCM, 1983), *To Change the World – Christology and Cultural Criticism*, (London, SCM, 1991) and *Christianity and Ecology* (Cambridge, MA, Harvard University Press, 2000).

Rudolf Schnackenburg (b. 1914) is one of Europe's most outstanding scripture scholars and was Professor of New Testament Studies at the University of Würzburg, Germany. He is the editor of the famous series Herders theologischer Kommentar zum Neuen Testament and (with H. Fries) of the series Questiones Disputatae. Among his many publications we mention his *Die sittliche Botschaft des Neuen Testaments* (2 vols, Freiburg im Breisgau, Herder, 1986).

Léon-Jozef Suenens, Cardinal (1904–96), the poorest boy in the class of his Brussels school, he entered the major seminary of Malines and was sent by Cardinal Mercier for studies in Rome. Influenced by both Dom L. Beaudouin, OSB, of Chevetogne and by the China missionary Vincent Lebbe, he developed a feeling for ecumenism and a great sensitivity for the universal Church. After having been vice-rector of the University of Louvain, he became archbishop of Malines-Brussels (1961–79). Pope John XXIII appointed him as one of the four moderators of the Second Vatican Council. Later, he was considered to be a major patron of the Catholic Charismatic Movement. Deeply committed to the participation of the laity in the life of the Church, he established the 'interdiocesan pastoral council' in Flanders. His *Coresponsibility in the Church* (New York, Herder & Herder, 1968), was translated into many languages.

Francis A. Sullivan, SJ (b. 1922) is an internationally respected theologian and a member of the Jesuit Order. In a lifetime of theological enquiry his writing has focused on the generosity and inclusiveness of catholic theology, working in every way to be true to the gospel, aware of the tradition and accurate in exposition. His writing, always eirenic and orthodox, includes work on the charismatic gifts, the magisterium, and ecclesiology. He was for many years a member of the faculty of theology of the Gregorian University in Rome. His many writings include *Magisterium* (Dublin, Gill & Macmillan, 1983), *The Church We Believe In* (Dublin, Gill & Macmillan, 1988), *Salvation Outside the Church? – Tracing the History of the Catholic Response* (London, Chapman, 1992) and *Creative Fidelity* (Dublin, Gill & Macmillan, 1996).

Christoph Theobald, SJ was born in Cologne (in 1946) and became a Jesuit in the Province of France in 1978. He is Professor of Fundamental and Dogmatic Theology in the Theological Faculty of the Centre Sevres, Paris and editor of *Recherches de Science Religieuse*, to which he contributes a bulletin on systematic theology (God – Trinity). His publications include works on the history of modern theology and systematic theology, including *Maurice Blondel und das Problem der Modernität* (Frankfurt am Main, Knecht, 1988) and *Penser la foi: recherches en théologie aujourd'hui – mélanges offerts à Joseph Moingt* (Paris, Du Cerf, 1993).

Jean-Marie Roger Tillard (1927–2000) was a French Dominican who as a young theologian served as a *peritus* at the final two sessions of the Second Vatican Council. After the council he would later serve as vice-president of the Faith and Order Commission of the World Council of Churches, consultor to the Vatican's Secretariat for Christian Unity, and as a member of several ecumenical commissions. At the time of his death in the autumn of 2000 he was considered one of today's most distinguished Catholic ecclesiologists. Some of his most influential works include *The Bishop of Rome* (London, SPCK, 1983), *The Church of Churches* (Collegeville, Liturgical Press, 1992) and *L'église locale – ecclésiologie de communion et catholicité* (Paris, Cerf, 1995).

Wilhelm de Vries, SJ, (1904–97) was born in Saarbrücken, Germany. He studied in Rome and Beyrouth and was a professor at the Oriental Pontifical Institute in Rome. His important study, *Rom und die Patriarchate des Ostens* (Freiburg, K. Alber), appeared in 1963. He was appointed a cardinal by Pope John-Paul II. Amongst his other works are *Kirche und Staat in der Sowjetunion* (München, Verlag Anton Pustet, 1959) and *Orthodoxie und Katholizismus – Gegensatz oder Erganzung?* (Freiburg, Herder, 1965).

INDEX OF NAMES